AFRICAN HISTORICAL DICTIONARIES
Edited by Jon Woronoff

1. *Cameroon,* by Victor T. Le Vine and Roger P. Nye. 1974. *Out of print. See No. 48.*
2. *The Congo,* 2nd ed., by Virginia Thompson and Richard Adloff. 1984. *Out of print. See No. 69.*
3. *Swaziland,* by John J. Grotpeter. 1975.
4. *The Gambia,* 2nd ed., by Harry A. Gailey. 1987.
5. *Botswana,* by Richard P. Stevens. 1975. *Out of print. See No. 70.*
6. *Somalia,* by Margaret F. Castagno. 1975.
7. *Benin (Dahomey),* 2nd ed., by Samuel Decalo. 1987. *Out of print. See No. 61.*
8. *Burundi,* by Warren Weinstein. 1976. *Out of print. See No. 73.*
9. *Togo,* 3rd ed., by Samuel Decalo. 1996.
10. *Lesotho,* by Gordon Haliburton. 1977.
11. *Mali,* 3rd ed., by Pascal James Imperato. 1996.
12. *Sierra Leone,* by Cyril Patrick Foray. 1977.
13. *Chad,* 3rd ed., by Samuel Decalo. 1997.
14. *Upper Volta,* by Daniel Miles McFarland. 1978.
15. *Tanzania,* by Laura S. Kurtz. 1978.
16. *Guinea,* 3rd ed., by Thomas O'Toole with Ibrahima Bah-Lalya. 1995.
17. *Sudan,* by John Voll. 1978. *Out of print. See No. 53.*
18. *Rhodesia/Zimbabwe,* by R. Kent Rasmussen. 1979. *Out of print. See No. 46.*
19. *Zambia,* 2nd ed., by John J. Grotpeter, Brian V. Siegel, and James R. Pletcher. 1998.
20. *Niger,* 3rd ed., by Samuel Decalo. 1997.
21. *Equatorial Guinea,* 3rd ed., by Max Liniger-Goumaz. 2000.
22. *Guinea-Bissau,* 3rd ed., by Richard Lobban and Peter Mendy. 1997.
23. *Senegal,* by Lucie G. Colvin. 1981. *Out of print. See No. 65.*
24. *Morocco,* by William Spencer. 1980. *Out of print. See No. 71.*
25. *Malawi,* by Cynthia A. Crosby. 1980. *Out of print. See No. 84.*
26. *Angola,* by Phyllis Martin. 1980. *Out of print. See No. 52.*
27. *The Central African Republic,* by Pierre Kalck. 1980. *Out of print. See No. 51.*
28. *Algeria,* by Alf Andrew Heggoy. 1981. *Out of print. See No. 66.*
29. *Kenya,* by Bethwell A. Ogot. 1981. *Out of print. See No. 77.*
30. *Gabon,* by David E. Gardinier. 1981. *Out of print. See No. 58.*
31. *Mauritania,* by Alfred G. Gerteiny. 1981. *Out of print. See No. 68.*

32. *Ethiopia,* by Chris Prouty and Eugene Rosenfeld. 1981. *Out of print. See No. 56.*

23. *Libya,* 3rd ed., by Ronald Bruce St John. 1998.

34. *Mauritius,* by Lindsay Riviere. 1982. *Out of print. See No. 49.*

35. *Western Sahara,* by Tony Hodges. 1982. *Out of print. See No. 55.*

36. *Egypt,* by Joan Wucher King. 1984. *Out of print. See No. 67.*

37. *South Africa,* by Christopher Saunders. 1983. *Out of print. See No. 78.*

38. *Liberia,* by D. Elwood Dunn and Svend E. Holsoe. 1985. *Out of print. See No. 83.*

39. *Ghana,* by Daniel Miles McFarland. 1985. *Out of print. See No. 78.*

40. *Nigeria,* 2nd ed., by Anthony Oyewole and John Lucas. 2000.

41. *Côte d'Ivoire (The Ivory Coast),* 2nd ed., by Robert J. Mundt. 1995.

42. *Cape Verde,* 2nd ed., by Richard Lobban and Marilyn Halter. 1988. *Out of print. See No. 62.*

43. *Zaire,* by F. Scott Bobb. 1988. *Out of print. See No. 76.*

44. *Botswana,* 2nd ed., by Fred Morton, Andrew Murray, and Jeff Ramsay. 1989. *Out of print. See No. 70.*

45. *Tunisia,* 2nd ed., by Kenneth J. Perkins. 1997.

46. *Zimbabwe,* 3rd ed., by Steven C. Rubert and R. Kent Rasmussen. 1998.

47. *Mozambique,* by Mario Azevedo. 1991.

48. *Cameroon,* 2nd ed., by Mark W. DeLancey and H. Mbella Mokeba. 1990.

49. *Mauritius,* 2nd ed., by Sydney Selvon. 1991.

50. *Madagascar,* by Maureen Covell. 1995.

51. *The Central African Republic,* 2nd ed., by Pierre Kalck; translated by Thomas O'Toole. 1992.

52. *Angola,* 2nd ed., by Susan H. Broadhead. 1992.

53. *Sudan,* 2nd ed., by Carolyn Fluehr-Lobban, Richard A. Lobban, Jr., and John Obert Voll. 1992.

54. *Malawi,* 2nd ed., by Cynthia A. Crosby. 1993. *Out of print. See No. 84.*

55. *Western Sahara,* 2nd ed., by Anthony Pazzanita and Tony Hodges. 1994.

56. *Ethiopia and Eritrea,* 2nd ed., by Chris Prouty and Eugene Rosenfeld. 1994.

57. *Namibia,* by John J. Grotpeter. 1994.

58. *Gabon,* 2nd ed., by David E. Gardinier. 1994.

59. *Comoro Islands,* by Martin Ottenheimer and Harriet Ottenheimer. 1994.

60. *Rwanda,* by Learthen Dorsey. 1994.

61. *Benin,* 3rd ed., by Samuel Decalo. 1995.

62. *Republic of Cape Verde,* 3rd ed., by Richard Lobban and Marlene Lopes. 1995.
63. *Ghana,* 2nd ed., by David Owusu-Ansah and Daniel Miles McFarland. 1995.
64. *Uganda,* by M. Louise Pirouet. 1995.
65. *Senegal,* 2nd ed., by Andrew F. Clark and Lucie Colvin Phillips. 1994.
66. *Algeria,* 2nd ed., by Phillip Chiviges Naylor and Alf Andrew Heggoy. 1994.
67. *Egypt,* 2nd ed., by Arthur Goldschmidt, Jr. 1994.
68. *Mauritania,* 2nd ed., by Anthony G. Pazzanita. 1996.
69. *Congo,* 3rd ed., by Samuel Decalo, Virginia Thompson, and Richard Adloff. 1996.
70. *Botswana,* 3rd ed., by Jeff Ramsay, Barry Morton, and Fred Morton. 1996.
71. *Morocco,* 2nd ed., by Thomas K. Park. 1996.
72. *Tanzania,* 2nd ed., by Thomas P. Ofcansky and Rodger Yeager. 1997.
73. *Burundi,* 2nd ed., by Ellen K. Eggers. 1997.
74. *Burkina Faso,* 2nd ed., by Daniel Miles McFarland and Lawrence Rupley. 1998.
75. *Eritrea,* by Tom Killion. 1998.
76. *Democratic Republic of the Congo (Zaire),* by F. Scott Bobb. 1999. (Revised edition of *Historical Dictionary of Zaire,* No. 43)
77. *Kenya,* 2nd ed., by Robert M. Maxon and Thomas P. Ofcansky. 2000.
78. *South Africa,* 2nd ed., by Christopher Saunders and Nicholas Southey. 2000.
79. *The Gambia,* 3rd ed., by Arnold Hughes and Harry A. Gailey. 2000.
80. *Swaziland,* 2nd ed., by Alan R. Booth. 2000.
81. *Republic of Cameroon,* 3rd ed., by Mark W. DeLancey and Mark Dike DeLancey. 2000.
82. *Djibouti,* by Daoud A. Alwan and Yohanis Mibrathu. 2000.
83. *Liberia,* 2nd ed., by D. Elwood Dunn, Amos J. Beyan, and Carl Patrick Burrowes. 2001.
84. *Malawi,* 3rd ed., by Owen J. M. Kalinga and Cynthia A. Crosby. 2001.

Historical Dictionary of Malawi

Third Edition

Owen J. M. Kalinga
Cynthia A. Crosby

African Historical Dictionaries, No. 84

The Scarecrow Press, Inc.
Lanham, Maryland, and London
2001

SCARECROW PRESS, INC.

Published in the United States of America
by Scarecrow Press, Inc.
4720 Boston Way, Lanham, Maryland 20706
www.scarecrowpress.com

4 Pleydell Gardens, Folkestone
Kent CT20 2DN, England

British Library Cataloguing-in-Publication Information Available

Library of Congress Cataloging-in-Publication Data

Kalinga, Owen J. M.
    Historical dictionary of Malawi / Owen J. M. Kalinga, Cynthia A. Crosby.—3rd ed.
    p. cm.—(African historical dictionaries ; no. 84)
    Rev. ed. of: Historical dictionary of Malawi / Cynthia A. Crosby. 2nd ed. 1993.
    Includes bibliographical references (p.).
    ISBN 0-8108-3481-2 (alk. paper)
    1. Malawi—History—Dictionaries. I. Crosby, C. A. II. Crosby, C. A. Historical
dictionary of Malawi. III. Title. IV. Series.
DT3169 .C76 2001
968.97'003—dc21   2001020060

♾™ The paper used in this publication meets the minimum requirements of
American National Standard for Information Sciences—Permanence of
Paper for Printed Library Materials, ANSI/NISO Z39.48-1992.
Manufactured in the United States of America.

To the people of Malawi in their pursuit of
chitukuko, *ufulu,* and *umodzi*

Contents

Editor's Foreword   *Jon Woronoff*   xi

Acknowledgments   xiii

Acronyms and Abbreviations   xv

Maps   xx

Chronology   xxiii

Introduction   xxxi

THE DICTIONARY   1

Bibliography   417

About the Authors   487

Editor's Foreword

Malawi is one of Africa's smaller countries, both in area and in population. Thus one would hardly expect it to go against most of the historical currents. Yet that is what it did for about two decades, basically because this is what was decided by its Life President, Dr. Hastings Kamuzu Banda. Malawi remained staunchly capitalist when socialism was fashionable, maintained close relations with the West instead of seeking nonalignment, and most notably kept on good terms with its enemies in the struggle for liberation, Portugal and South Africa. It followed historical currents in establishing a one-party state and personal rule, which under the aging Banda became increasingly intolerant. Now that Banda is gone, Malawi is more like its neighbors, partly because they too have tilted westward and embraced capitalism but also because it is giving democracy another chance. This "new" Malawi is far more promising than the "old," although it will have to work hard to keep democracy on track and encourage economic and social development.

With so much change it is obviously time for a new *Historical Dictionary of Malawi*. This third edition is very different from its predecessors in terms of the valuable information it includes about the "new" Malawi while retaining considerable material on the "old" independence, colonial, and precolonial periods. It includes an expanded introduction and chronology and many especially useful dictionary entries on the recent period, describing new leaders, new political parties, and policies. Others provide the broader background, dealing with geographical features, ethnic and religious groups, agricultural crops and manufacturing, educational institutions and women, and so on. The bibliography, also updated and expanded, offers a good overview of the literature on all periods of Malawi history.

This third edition of the *Historical Dictionary of Malawi* was updated and written by Owen J. Kalinga. He was born and educated in Malawi and Great Britain and taught for well over a decade in the University of Malawi's Department of History, of which he became associate professor and head. Dr. Kalinga's teaching career also took him to Canada, Nigeria,

Lesotho, and South Africa, and finally to his present position as professor of history at North Carolina State University. Along with numerous articles on the Lake Malawi region, he has written a book on the Ngonde Kingdom and is completing another on cooperative societies in colonial Malawi. This all contributed to a very useful volume on a country that is still not well understood abroad. However, the foundations of the current book can be traced to the author of the first and second editions. Written at a time when Malawi was even less known and harder to research, Cynthia Crosby's work serves as a solid base on which the new edition expands. Dr. Crosby has long been interested in the country, researching various aspects of its colonial past and more recently the status of women. She, along with others, welcomes this new edition.

Jon Woronoff
Series Editor

Acknowledgments

This third edition has greatly benefited from the help of many people and institutions. Thanks go to the always friendly and ever efficient staff of the Inter-Library Loan Department at North Carolina State University for never failing to secure documents required for the preparation of this dictionary. Contacts at the National Archives of Malawi, Zomba, also rendered useful assistance. Special gratitude is due to Margaret Kalinga for commenting on the work as it progressed and for painstakingly proofreading the final draft of the manuscript. Four other Kalingas—Chawupi, Irene, Nganiwe, and Godfrey—helped at various stages. I also wish to express gratitude to Dr. John Drake of Marine, Earth and Atmospheric Sciences at North Carolina State University for modifying the map to include more ethnic groups. Last, though not least, thanks to the staff in the History Office at NCSU for solving numerous administrative problems associated with work on the dictionary.

Acronyms and Abbreviations

ABC	American Baptist Church
ACS	African Cooperative Society
ADB	African Development Bank
ADD	Agricultural Development Division
ADF	African Development Fund
ADMARC	Agricultural Development and Marketing Corporation
AID	U.S. Agency for International Development
AIDS	Acquired Immune Deficiency Syndrome
AFORD	Alliance for Democracy
ALC	African Lakes Company (Corporation)
AME	African Methodist Episcopal Church
AP&MB	Agricultural and Production and Marketing Board
BCA	British Central Africa
BCAC	British Central Africa Company
BCGA	British Cotton Growers Association
BEA	British & East Africa
BIM	Baptist Industrial Mission of Scotland
BSAC	British South Africa Company
CAA	Central African Airways
CABS	Central African Broadcasting Service
CAFA	Confederation of African Football Associations
CAP	Central African Planter
CAR	Central African Railway Company
CAT	*Central African Times*
CATCO	Central African Transport Company
CBM	Commercial Bank of Malawi
CCAM	Chitukuko Cha Amai M'Malawi
CCAP	Church of Central Africa Presbyterian
CDC	Colonial Development Corporation
CHAMA	Christian Hospitals Association of Malawi
CID	Criminal Investigation Division

CIDA	Canadian International Development Agency
CLC	Civil Liberties Commission
CNU	Congress for National Unity
CO	Colonial Office
COMESA	Common Market for Eastern and Southern Africa
CRI	Crisis Response Initiative
CSC	Christian Service Committee
CSDP	Christian Social Democratic Party
CSR	Congress for the Second Republic
DANIDA	Danish International Development Agency
DC	District Commissioner
DEC	Distance Education Center
DRC	Dutch Reformed Church
DWASCO	Dwanga Sugar Corporation
EEC	European Economic Community
EHP	Essential Health Package
ESAF	Enhanced Structural Adjustment Facility
ESCOM	Electricity Supply Commission of Malawi
EU	European Union
EXCO	Executive Council
FAM	Football Association of Malawi
FAO	Food and Agriculture Organization
FBC	Federal Broadcasting Corporation
FIFA	Federation of International Football Associations
FMB	Farmers Marketing Board
FO	Foreign Office
HAM	Herbalist Association of Malawi
HHI	Henry Henderson Institute
IBRD	International Bank for Reconstruction and Development (World Bank)
ICFTU	International Confederation of Trade Unions
IDA	International Development Association (World Bank)
IFC	International Finance Corporation (World Bank)
ILO	International Labour Organization
IMF	International Monetary Fund
INDEBANK	Investment and Development Bank
ITC	Imperial Tobacco Company
JAH	*Journal of African History*
JICA	Japanese International Cooperation Agency
K	Kwacha

KAR	King's African Rifles
KCMG	Knight Commander, Order of St. Michael and St. George
£ (L)	Pounds sterling
LBSC	London & Blantyre Supply Company
LEGCO	Legislative Council
LEPRA	Leprosy Relief Association
LESOMA	Socialist League of Malawi
LMS	London Missionary Society
LRC	Legal Resources Centre
MA	Malawi Army
MACOH	Malawi Council for the Handicapped
MACRA	Malawi Communications Regulatory Authority
MAFREMO	Malawi Freedom Movement
MANEB	Malawi National Examinations Board
MBC	Malawi Broadcasting Corporation
MCC	Malawi Correspondence College
MCP	Malawi Congress Party
MCTU	Malawi Congress of Trade Unions
MDC	Malawi Development Corporation
MDP	Malawi Democratic Party
MDU	Malawi Democratic Union
METB	Malawi Examination and Testing Board
MIDCOR	Mining Investment and Development Corporation
MIM	Malawi Institute of Management
Mk	Malawi kwacha
MNDP	Malawi National Democratic Party
MP	Member of Parliament
MR	Malawi Railways
MRA	Malawi Revenue Authority
MYP	Malawi Young Pioneers
NA	Native Authority
NAC	Nyasaland African Congress
NB	National Bank
NCC	National Consultative Council
NCU	Congress for National Unity
NDC	National Development Corporation
NFRA	National Food Reserve Agency
NGO	Nongovernmental Organization
NIM	Nyasaland Industrial Mission
NLS	National Library Service

NNNA	North Nyasa Native Association
NRDP	National Rural Development Program
NSO	National Statistical Office
NTA	Nyasaland Tea Association
OAU	Organization of African Unity
OBE	Order of the British Empire
ODA	Overseas Development Administration
PAC	Public Affairs Committee
PCD	Presidential Committee on Dialogue
PDP	Pan-African Democratic Party
PHAM	Private Hospitals Association of Malawi
PIM	Providence Industrial Mission
PMF	Police Mobile Force
PTA	Preferential Trade Area
QC	Queen's Counsel
RDP	Rural Development Program
RENAMO	Resistencia Nacional Mocambicana
RNLB	Rhodesia Native Labour Bureau
SADC	Southern Africa Development Community
SADCC	Southern Africa Development Coordination Conference
SARAM	Settlers and Residents Association of Malawi
SATUCC	Southern Africa Trade Union Coordinating Council
SDA	Seventh-Day Adventist
SDB	Seventh Day Baptist
SEDOM	Small Enterprise Development Organization of Malawi
SEIA	Sabbath Evangelizing and Industrial Mission
SGR	Strategic Grain Reserve
SHR	Shire Highlands Railway Company
SRAS	Southern Rhodesia Air Services
SWAPO	Southwest People's Party Organization
TAMA	Tobacco Association of Malawi
TANU	Tanzanian African National Union
TEBA	Temporary Employment Bureau
TUC	Trades Union Congress
UCMD	United Committee for Multiparty Democracy
UDF	United Democratic Front
UDI	Unilateral Declaration of Independence
UDM	United Democratic Movement
UFMD	United Front for Multi-Party Democracy
UFP	United Federal Party

UMCA	Universities' Mission to Central Africa
UNHCR	United Nations High Commissioner for Refugees
UNIP	United National Independent Party
UP	United Party
VC	Victoria Cross
WENELA	Witwatersrand Native Labour Association
ZIM	Zambezi Industrial Mission

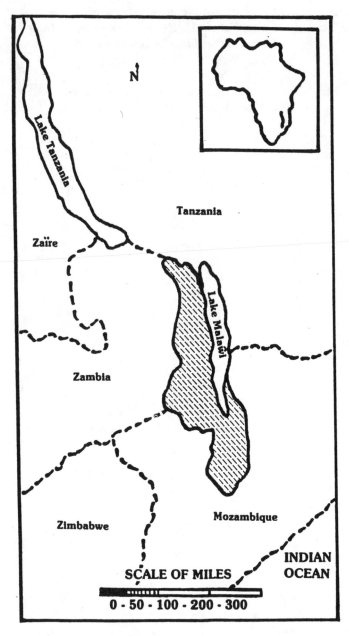

Malawi and Surrounding Countries. Highlighted Area is Malawi.

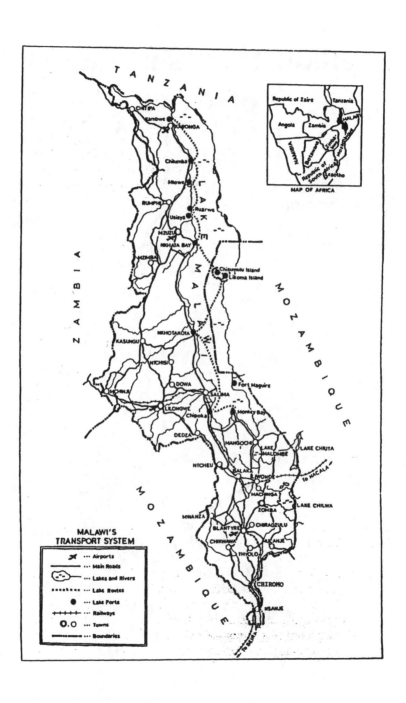

MALAWI'S
TRANSPORT SYSTEM

✈	··· Airports
	··· Main Roads
	··· Lakes and Rivers
	··· Lake Routes
●	··· Lake Ports
+++++	··· Railways
O, ●	··· Towns
	··· Boundaries

MAP OF AFRICA

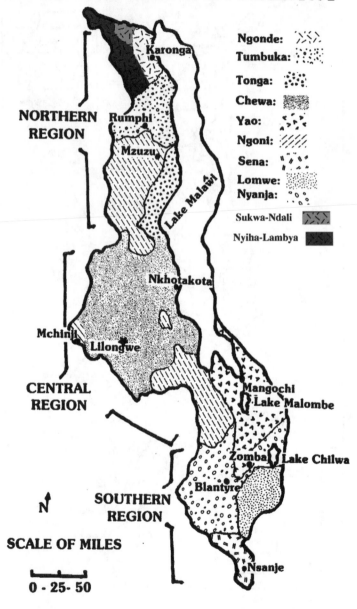

ETHNIC GROUPS IN MALAŴI

Ngonde:
Tumbuka:
Tonga:
Chewa:
Yao:
Ngoni:
Sena:
Lomwe:
Nyanja:

Sukwa-Ndali
Nyiha-Lambya

Karonga

NORTHERN
REGION

Rumphi

Mzuzu

Lake Malaŵi

Nkhotakota

Mchinji

Lilongwe

CENTRAL
REGION

Mangochi
Lake Malombe

Zomba Lake Chilwa

Blantyre

SOUTHERN
REGION

N

SCALE OF MILES

0 - 25- 50

Nsanje

Chronology

100,000–50,000 B.C. Early Stone Age.

50,000–8000 B.C. Middle Stone Age.

8000–1700 B.C. Later Stone Age (rock paintings).

A.D. 200–1000 Iron Age (Nkope and Mwabulambu pottery).

1000–1400 Iron Age (Kapeni ware).

1400–1800s Iron Age–Modern Age (Mawudzu and Nkudzi ware).

c. **1200–1450** Maravi clans migrate from Shaba province to Malawi.

Late 1400s Tumbuka peoples move to northern Malawi; Ngonde peoples migrate from Tanzania.

1530 Portuguese settle Tete.

1560 Portuguese send Resident to Mwenemutapa's empire.

1600s Maravi empire (confederacy) at zenith.

1616 Gaspar Boccaro (Portuguese) travels through Maravi empire.

1660 Jesuit priest Manual Barretto records his observations of the Maravi confederacy.

c. **1660–***c.* **1730** More migrations from Zambia and Tanzania (Phoka, Nkhamanga, Henga).

c. **1730** Portuguese influence declines as Arab trade expands in east coast Yao trade caravans at Kilwa.

c. **1750** The coming of Balowoka.

1820s Ngoni leave South African homeland and trek north.

1835 Maseko and Jere Ngoni enter Malawi.

1840s Swahili Arab Jumbe establishes a trade center at Nkhotakota.

c. **1848** Zwangendaba (of Jere Ngoni) dies.

c. **1850** Yao migrate to Malawi.

1857–1891 Reign of Inkosi M'Mbelwa (Jere Ngoni).

1858–1863 Dr. David Livingstone makes his four journeys to Malawi as part of the Zambezi expedition.

1861 Universities' Mission to Central Africa (UMCA) mission at Magomero begins but fails shortly thereafter.

1867 Maseko Ngoni returns to Malawi from Tanzania (Songea).

1873 Dr. Livingstone dies at Chitambo in Zambia (May).

1874–1880 Tonga-Tumbuka revolts against Ngoni rule.

1875 Livingstonia mission station opens at Cape Maclear.

1876 Blantyre Mission established.

1878 John and Frederick Moir begin to manage the African Lakes Company (ALC).

1881 Bandawe becomes the headquarters of the Livingstonia Mission; construction of Stevenson Road begins.

c. **1884** Swahili-Arab Mlozi establishes trade center at Karonga.

1885 UMCA reestablished at Likoma Island.

1887–1889 Swahili War.

1889 Dutch Reformed Church starts mission at Mvera; White Fathers (Missionaries of Africa) arrive at Mponda.

1890 H. H. Johnston takes over administration of British South Africa Company (BSAC) sphere of influence north of Zambezi (including Malawi).

1891 British protectorate declared over region of Malawi; Harry Johnston becomes commissioner of British Central Africa Protectorate (1891–1897); Anglo-Portuguese Treaty determines southern boundary of Malawi; White Fathers leave Mponda for northern Zambia.

1892 Joseph Booth forms the Zimbabwe Industrial Mission (ZIM); Harry Johnston establishes protectorate bureaucracy (postal, medical, and security services, financial units, courts).

1894 Blantyre Mission under Rev. D. C. Scott ordains seven African deacons; Dr. Robert Laws moves the Livingstonia Mission headquarters to Khondowe, where he also founds the Overtoun Institution.

1895 The British Central Africa (BCA) Chamber of Agriculture and Commerce formed; Last Jumbe deported to Zanzibar; Yao chiefs (Kawinga, Makandanji, Makanjira, Matapwiri, Zarafi) defeated by the British; Mwase Kasungu defeated by British and commits suicide rather than be taken prisoner; Mlozi is captured and executed (December).

c. **1896** Dr. H. Kamuzu Banda is born near Kasungu; Inkosi Chitanthumba Gomani I refuses to submit to British authority; soldiers capture and kill him.

1898 British Central Africa Rifles under Col. William Manning defeat Mpezeni.

1900 John Chilembwe begins his mission station, the Providence Industrial Mission (PIM).

1901 Montfort missionaries arrive; Malawian soldiers see service against the Ashanti in the Gold Coast.

1902 Foreign Office (FO) permits railway (Shire Highlands Railway) construction between Blantyre and Chiromo; White Fathers return to the Lake Malawi area.

1904 FO relinquishes control of British Central Africa to the Colonial Office.

1907 BCA Protectorate changes name to Nyasaland Protectorate; the commissioner becomes governor; Executive and Legislative Councils established with an all-European membership.

1908 Blantyre-Nsanje rail line opens.

1907–1910 Sir Alfred Sharpe becomes governor.

1910–1913 William Manning replaces Sharpe as governor.

1912 First African association formed (North Nyasa Native Association).

1914   The Livingstonia Mission ordains its first African ministers: Jonathan Chirwa, Yesaya Z. Mwase, and Hezekeya M. Twea.

1914–1918   World War I: A quarter million Malawians serve as porters or soldiers.

1915   George Smith becomes governor; John Chilembwe uprising (January 23–February 4).

1916   Report of Commission of Inquiry on the Chilembwe uprising.

1923   Devonshire Memorandum.

1924   Rev. Hanock Phiri founds the African Methodist Episcopal (AME) Church in Malawi; Charles Bowring becomes governor.

1929   Hilton-Young Report.

1930   Passfield Memorandum.

1933   Mchape witch cleansing movement sweeps Malawi.

1935   Lower Zambezi Bridge opens. Malawi railway connects Salima with Beira; the Lacey Report on migrant labor is released.

1937   Banda receives his medical degree from Meharry Medical College, Nashville, Tennessee, and moves to Scotland.

1939   The Bledisloe Commission Report is released.

1939–1945   World War II: Malawi soldiers distinguish themselves in Ethiopian and Burma campaigns.

1941   Detachment of the Malawi contingent of the King's African Rifles (KAR) distinguish themselves at the siege of Moyale on the Kenya-Ethiopia border (July).

1944   Nyasaland African Congress (NAC) organized with Levi Mumba as president.

1944–1945   African Provincial Councils formed.

1946   Society of Malawi (Nyasaland Society) founded.

1949   First Malawians appointed to the Legislative Council (LEGCO); first Asians appointed to LEGCO.

1952   Nyasaland Asian Convention is founded.

1953 Federation of Rhodesia and Nyasaland is established; Thyolo riots and disturbances elsewhere in the colony; Inkosi Zintonga Philip Gomani of Ntcheu is arrested Inkosi Z. Philip Gomani dies on May 12 and is succeeded by his son, Willard Gomani; Dr. Banda leaves the U.K. to live in Kumasi, Gold Coast.

1955 NAC demands right to secede from the Federation.

1956 First Africans elected to LEGCO; Sir Geoffrey Colby retires as governor and is replaced by Sir Robert Armitage.

1957 The NAC requests Dr. Banda to return home.

1958 Dr. Banda returns home to Malawi on July 6 and assumes headship of the NAC; League of Malawi Women and League of Malawi Youth are formed.

1959 NAC nonviolent campaign against Federation begins. March 3: state of emergency declared; "Operation Sunrise"; Banda and many NAC officials and members arrested; first Malawians on Executive Council; Devlin Commission of Inquiry and Report; Malawi Congress Party (MCP) formed; *Malawi News* established; Lazalo Mkhosi Jere, Inkosi Ya Makosi M'Mbelwa II, dies and is succeeded by Maxon Jere.

1960 Monckton Commission of Inquiry and Report; Harold Macmillan visits Nyasaland (February); Southworth Commission of Inquiry; Banda and many nationalists released.

1961 Sir Glyn Jones succeeds Sir Robert Armitage as governor. First general elections in Malawi; the Malawi Congress Party wins overwhelmingly.

1962 Marlborough House Conference formalizes self-government for Malawi; British government announces Nyasaland will withdraw from the Federation of Rhodesia and Nyasaland.

1963 The Organization of African Unity (OAU) formed; Dr. Banda sworn in as prime minister; LEGCO renamed Legislative Assembly; Executive Council replaced by a cabinet system; the Federation is dissolved.

1964 Reserve Bank of Malawi established; Skinner Report on civil service (May); Malawi becomes independent of British rule; Malawi joins OAU; Cabinet Crisis in September; major government reorganization.

1965 Chipembere rebellion (February); University of Malawi opens (September).

1966 New constitution adopted; Sir Glyn Jones retires to England; Malawi becomes a republic within the British Commonwealth; Dr. Kamuzu Banda becomes president; first hydroelectric station opens at Nkula Falls; Blantyre granted city status; Forfeiture Act permits seizure of property belonging to "subversives."

1967 Malawi establishes diplomatic relations with South Africa, which grants Malawi a loan to build a new capital in Lilongwe; Yatuta Chisiza leads a group to overthrow the government; he and some in his party are killed by the Malawi army.

1968–1969 The Chilobwe murders.

1969 The University of Malawi graduates its first baccalaureate students.

1970 Malawi changes its fiscal year to April 1–March 31.

1971 Banda declared Life President of Malawi; cabinet members appointed by president are de facto MPs; Malawi adopts decimal system of currency and introduces the kwacha, abandoning British pounds/shillings; Banda makes state visit to South Africa.

1973 European representation in parliament ceases.

1974 Party constitution equates MCP with government of Malawi.

1975 Henry Masauko Chipembere dies in the United States.

1977 Albert Muwalo-Nqumayo is convicted of sedition and sentenced to death; co-conspirator Focus Gwede is sentenced to life imprisonment.

1978 Asian businesses required to operate in designated urban areas; general elections held in June.

1979 Malawi's economy deteriorates after 15 years of prosperity.

1980 Malawi becomes a founding member of the Southern Africa Development Co-ordination Conference (SADCC).

1981 Functional literacy program starts; the International Monetary Fund (IMF) structural adjustment of Malawi economy is initiated; Orton, Vera, and Fumbani Chirwa kidnapped from Chipata, Zambia; Malawi becomes a founding member of the Preferential Trade Area (PTA).

1982 Malawi establishes diplomatic relations with North Korea.

1983 Kamuzu International Airport inaugurated in Lilongwe; three cabinet ministers and one MP are murdered in Mwanza District in May; general elections held in June; Attati Mpakati of the Socialist League of Malawi (LESOMA) is assassinated in Harare, Zimbabwe; National Traditional Court sentences Orton and Vera Chirwa to death.

1985 Malawi establishes diplomatic relations with Romania, Albania, and Tanzania.

1986 Malawi establishes diplomatic relations with Finland; meeting in Blantyre attended by Presidents Banda, Kenneth Kaunda, Samora Machel, and Robert Mugabe to discuss the activities of the Mozambique Resistance Movement in Mozambique.

1987 General elections held.

1989 Malawi celebrates 25th year of independence; Gomile Kuntumanji dies in prison and has a hero's burial in his home area.

1991 General elections; external aid to Malawi greatly reduced because of abuse of human rights; national economy begins to be adversely affected; political parties in exile form the United Front for Multi-Party Democracy (UFMD) in Lusaka.

1992 Increased demand for political reform; Catholic bishops' pastoral letter read in all Catholic churches (March); Chakufwa Chihana openly challenges government to initiate reform; Chakufwa is arrested, tried, and imprisoned; riots in Blantyre; protesters shot by police; Public Affairs Committee (PAC), Presidential Committee on Dialogue (PCD), National Consultative Council (PCC) established; two opposition political parties formed: the Alliance for Democracy (AFORD) and the United Democratic Front (UDF); national referendum on political change is announced; Orton Chirwa dies in prison and has a nationally attended funeral in Nkata Bay District; *Malawi Financial Post* becomes the first independent newspaper; Machipisa Munthali released as a political prisoner after 27 years; Civil Liberties Commission (CLC) founded to monitor human rights.

1993 National referendum takes place and political reform wins overwhelmingly; general elections promised for May 1994; political exiles allowed to return to the country; election campaigns begin; President Banda falls ill and is taken to the Garden Clinic, Johannesburg, South Africa; he returns to Malawi after some weeks and campaigns; Law Society of Malawi founds the Legal Resources Center (LRC), headed by Vera Chirwa; Operation Bwezani (November).

1994 General elections take place (June); Banda and the MCP are defeated; Bakili Muluzi becomes state president and UDF forms government, which later in the year includes members of AFORD; Chakufwa Chihana becomes one of the two vice presidents; Mtegha Commission looks into the Mwanza murders of 1983; Malawi hosts PTA summit; PTA is replaced by the Common Market for Eastern and Southern Africa (COMESA).

1995 Government arraigns Dr. Banda, Cecilia Kadzamira, and John Tembo on charges of complicity in the Mwanza murders of 1983; first major civil service strike; Malawi Stock Exchange opens.

1997 Malawi hosts Southern Africa Development Community (SADC) summit in Blantyre; Dr. Bingu wa Mutharika forms the United Party (UP); November 25, Dr. Banda dies at the Garden City Clinic in Johannesburg; December 3, national funeral for Dr. Banda at the Heroes' Acre in Lilongwe.

1998 Government and Banda family dispute the former president's will; riots in various towns to protest the rising cost of living (October); Malawi Congress Party (MCP) and Alliance for Democracy (AFORD) decide to campaign in the next general elections as an alliance.

1999 General elections held in June; Muluzi and the United Democratic Front (UDF) returned to power; MCP and AFORD challenge election results; MDP and Congress for National Unity (CNU) also question results; postelection violence against Muslims in parts of northern Malawi; local government elections are postponed until 2000.

2000 A major dispute in the leadership of Malawi Congress Party practically splits the party into two factions; Malawi Congress Party (MCP), Alliance for Democracy (AFORD), and Malawi Democratic Party (MDP) lose lawsuit challenging the 1999 presidential elections; report of the Public Accounts Committee of the Malawi Parliament detailing evidence of major fraud in government departments (October); cabinet ministers are implicated; British High Commission in Malawi and International Monetary Fund threaten to withhold aid owing to evidence of corruption in government; cabinet is reshuffled; President Muluzi drops three senior ministers: Cassim Chilumpha (Education), Peter Chupa (Labour), and Brown Mpinganjira (Public Works); local government elections take place in November; low turnout; United Democratic Front wins overwhelmingly.

Introduction

Scottish people call Malawi "Livingstone's country" partly because Dr. David Livingstone drew British attention to the existence of the area and partly because, after his death in neighboring Zambia in 1873, Scottish Presbyterian missions set up operations there, establishing a major influence that continues to be felt today. Malawians themselves prefer to call their country "the warm heart of Africa," reflecting the friendliness of its inhabitants. Formerly a colony of Great Britain known as Nyasaland, Malawi assumed its present name on July 6, 1964, when it became a sovereign nation-state; two years later it was transformed into a republic within the British Commonwealth.

LAND AND PEOPLE

Landlocked, Malawi borders on Tanzania to the northeast, Mozambique to the southeast, south, and southwest, and Zambia to the west. Some 560 miles long from north to south and ranging from 5 to 150 miles wide, it is blessed with fairly fertile soils, adequate rainfall (25 to 35 inches) in most seasons, and temperatures that range between 57 degrees Fahrenheit (14 degrees centigrade) in the cold-dry season (May to August) and 84 degrees Fahrenheit (29 degrees centigrade) in the warm-dry season (September to April). One of the most scenic countries in Africa, Malawi has a landscape that is dominated by 360-mile-long Lake Malawi, which forms part of the southern section of the Great Rift Valley and drains into the Indian Ocean through its outlet, the Shire River, itself a major tributary of the Zambezi River, which flows into the ocean. There are four smaller lakes—Phalombe, Chiuta, and Chilwa in the south and Kazuni in the north. The actual landmass comprises 36,325 square miles and consists largely of plateaus, highlands, and a few mountains; among the most notable of these are Nyika and Viphya plateaus in the north, Dedza-Kirk mountain range in the center, and in the south, the Shire Highlands with its two prominent massifs, Zomba (6,841 feet) and Mulanje (9,849 feet).

A large percentage of the 10 million Malawi people live along the various lakeshores, the Shire valley, and near the rivers in the plateau and highland regions, which are part of the Lake Malawi drainage system. There is also a major concentration of population in the fertile Shire Highlands and in the urban centers, principally Blantyre, Zomba, Lilongwe, and Mzuzu. The prevailing economic hardships in Malawi have accelerated migration from rural to urban areas, which are having to deal with unprecedented problems, including a shortage of housing, jobs, and health facilities. This is exacerbated by the spread of the AIDS virus, a factor that will affect the projected 0.03 percent annual growth in the population and will adversely affect the development of much needed human resources.

Largely because Malawi has always been the poorest country in Southern Africa, many of its peoples have migrated to the mines and commercial farms in the region. In fact, from the beginning of the 19th century, Malawi became one of the major catchment areas of the labor recruiting agencies from South Africa and Southern Rhodesia (Zimbabwe). There the "Nyasas," the people from Nyasaland, generally established themselves as reliable and hardworking. The money that the labor migrants remitted home formed an important aspect of foreign exchange earnings for the country.

About 75 percent of Malawians are Christians and 20 percent are Muslims; the rest practice traditional religions. There are also some few Hindus, mainly among the Asian trading community. English is the official language of communication in schools, bureaucracy, and parliament; however, the majority of Malawians speak ciChewa, also known as ciNyanja. Other notable languages are ciYao, ciLomwe, and ciSena in the Southern Region, and ciTumbuka, ciTonga, KyanGonde, ciLambya/Nyiha, and Sukwa/Ndali in the Northern Region.

Most peoples practice mixed agriculture, that is, they grow food and cash crops and they raise animals, mainly cattle and goats. Those near lakes and rivers also catch fish, some of which they dry and sell upcountry. The main food crops are maize, cassava, rice, and beans, the leading cash crops being tobacco, tea, cotton, sugar, and peanuts, all which are exported mostly to Malawi's principal trading partners—South Africa, the European Union, and the United States. In the 1970s and 1980s, Malawi consistently produced surplus food; nevertheless, the country has been riddled by poverty-related problems such as recurring malnutrition and child mortality. This is largely attributable to the fact that the policy of the first postcolonial government favored the estate sector represented by politicians and expatriate interests. There has been little foreign investment in this Southern African country. However, except for the 1992–1994 period, Malawi has regularly received development aid and has mostly invested it in the improvement of education, transportation and communications, health, and agricultural programs.

Until 1994 Malawi was dominated by Dr. Hastings Kamuzu Banda and his Malawi Congress Party (MCP), the organization that led the fight for decolonization. Known for his anticommunist views and his stance against corruption in the public service, Banda made Malawi a favorite of the Western powers, receiving European, Canadian, Japanese, and American aid. The World Bank and the International Monetary Fund (IMF) also viewed Banda's Malawi as a model state where their prescriptions could work. Banda's gross abuses of human rights were overlooked until the Soviet bloc broke up, when the very Western powers that had supported him insisted that henceforth aid would be contingent on political reform. That forced Banda to accept multiparty politics and to call for democratic general elections in June 1994, the first in 30 years. He and the MCP lost to Bakili Muluzi and the United Democratic Front (UDF), which was returned to power in 1999. Muluzi inherited an unhealthy economy, and with a per capita gross domestic product of US$689, Malawi continues to be one of the poorest countries in the world.

EARLY HISTORY

The early occupation of Malawi by Stone Age peoples was a function of environment, that is, they chose sites that provided a favorable supply of game and water. Most of the Early Stone Age sites may be found along the lakeshore and in the river valleys. Later Stone Age humans were more adaptable and more venturesome, often occupying the upland regions of Malawi. The artifacts of the Late Stone Age, which presently is estimated to have begun 10,000 years ago, consist of very specialized microliths and comparatively sophisticated rock paintings.

From the second to the third century A.D., Malawi was extensively occupied by ironworking agriculturalists. These cultivators, who coexisted with the men and women of the Late Stone Age, introduced the earliest pottery known to date, called Nkope ware. In their permanent settlements at Nkope Bay, these people produced many bowls with decorated rims. Their diet, probably consisting of fish, turtles, wild game, cereals, and vegetables, was cooked and served in these bowls. Archaeologists have discerned a later type of pottery, called Kapeni, which was produced sometime between the 10th and the 13th centuries A.D. The Kapeni pot makers apparently had contact with the Nkope ware makers. The Kapeni potters also were influential when the Maravi peoples migrated into the area: a pedestal-based bowl has been found to be common to both Kapeni and Mawudzu potters. Mawudzu pottery (dated 15th–17th centuries A.D.) was produced throughout the period of Maravi dominance.

The Maravi, or Phiri, migrated into the Lake Malawi area probably during the drought period of 1400–1409. Linguistic evidence and oral tradition suggest that they originated from Luba country in the modern Democratic Republic of the Congo; tradition also says that the migrating party was led by Chinkhole Phiri and his mother, Nyangu. Successors to Chinkhole were known by the title Kalonga, and they settled at Mathimba, near the southwestern shores of the lake. In all likelihood, the formation and rise of the Kalonga state was a slow process, developing as the invaders interacted with the existing pre-Chewa inhabitants, including the Mbewe and Banda. Ruling from about 1480 to the early 18th century, the Kalonga dynasty had many effective rulers, one of whom was Chidzonzi (1505–1530). He is credited with integrating Maravi leaders by using annual religious ceremonies such as the Mlira cult and by assigning various headmen with specific responsibilities within the state. While recognizing the pre-Chewa religious shrines such as the one at Msinja and using them to gain and maintain the support of the autochthones, the Phiri, as Kalongas, promoted their own so as to consolidate their authority over the region.

In the 16th and 17th centuries, the Maravi extended their political influence into adjacent areas; as some members of the Phiri group chose to become independent of the Kalonga, new kingdoms were established. One such separatist group, led by Kaphwiti and his nephew Lundu, developed its own polities in the Lower Shire Valley and western Shire Highlands. By the mid-17th century the Lundu bureaucracy was well established near present-day Chiromo, and it continued to expand east into the Makua-Lolo area in Mozambique.

The westward Maravi expansion was led by Undi, who, with his followers, occupied the area north of Tete along the Kapoche River. Migration from the main Kalonga kingdom also occurred north into other Chewa localities and into the Tumbuka- and Tonga-speaking areas: Mwase, Chulu, and Kaluluma in Kasungu and its periphery, Kanyenda in Nkota Kota, and Kabunduli in Nkhata Bay. By the 17th century, the Kalonga was based at Manthimba at the southern end of the lake; his subordinates were the southern and western and northern strongholds in the Maravi confederacy. Often dynastic differences would dissolve as economic concerns, especially the ivory trade with the Portuguese at Tete, united them. After reaching its zenith in the 17th century, the empire declined. Maravi kings who traded in ivory, iron, and slaves with the Portuguese and the Arabs grew increasingly independent of the Kalonga. The sheer distances involved in administering the empire also favored the decentralization of the Kalonga confederacy. By the early 1800s, it had virtually collapsed.

The area immediately north of the Maravi sphere was inhabited by Tumbuka-speaking peoples who practiced mixed agriculture. Their political system was decentralized in the sense that it was clan based. Groups migrating into the area tended to adopt the language and organization of the autochthones, and among the immigrants were the Phoka and the Nkhamanga. As a result of this integration and cultural layering, linguistic differences are found between Tumbuka speakers in Rumphi-Chitipa-Karonga Districts and Nkhata Bay-Mzimba Districts.

However, all this changed in the second half of the 18th century, when the arrival of new immigrants altered the cultural mix of northern Malawi—the Balowoka, or those who "crossed over" Lake Malawi from Tanzania. Mlowoka Gondwe, leader of this small group of traders, sought alliances of friendship that in the end enabled him to expand the incipient ivory trade and promote long-distance trade. Aligning himself with local leaders and marrying into the most powerful clan, the Luhanga, Mlowoka soon established economic control over the Henga-Nkhamanga-Phoka areas. He secured his economic position by placing his compatriots along the ivory trade route that extended from eastern Zambia to Lake Malawi. Oral tradition suggests that Mlowoka's sphere remained economic and did not develop into a political hegemony.

However, at Mlowoka's death in the early 19th century, his son usurped the succession line from the Luhangas, and from this point is dated the beginning of the Chikulamayembe line. The new authority followed Luhanga administrative patterns and allowed the local judicial system to continue. The Chikulamayembes established no bureaucracy and no army in the area; in fact, their subordinate rulers were given a significant measure of autonomy. Although economically powerful, the dynasty exercised political leadership only in Nkhamanga, just east of modern Rumphi *boma*.

Further north, in present-day Karonga and Chitipa Districts, the political structure in the pre-1400 period was clan based. There was no form of centralized leadership; instead, in the Karonga lakeshore, authority was religious and exercised through a snake cult. Even when the Simbowe established themselves at Mbade hill in the 15th century, attaining the respect of the indigenous peoples and assuming political control of the area, the clans retained some independence. The Simbowe seem to have been selling ivory to an east coast network (15–17th centuries) when the Portuguese were in command of the coast. Their successors, the Kyungu, originated from Ukinga in southwestern Tanzania, and around 1600 successfully plotted the death of the Simbowe leader, wresting power from the trader family. The Kyungu ruled the Ngonde until Nyasaland became a British colony.

At about the time the Kyungu were forging the Ngonde kingdom, two polities emerged in Ulambya and Misuku in present-day Chitipa, specifically in the areas of the Lambya/Nyiha and Sukwa, respectively. The region between Ulambya and the Nyika plateau was inhabited by Nyiha-speaking peoples, but no central authority emerged until the 18th century when the Kaonga and Kayira, both from modern Tanzania, founded Ntalire and Wenya.

NINETEENTH-CENTURY INCURSIONS

In the 19th century the inhabitants of the Lake Malawi region witnessed the arrival of the Yao, Ngoni, and Swahili-Arabs, all of whom were prepared to take power from existing authorities by violence where they met resistance. The Yao moved from their nuclear area in northern Mozambique when they were attacked by the Makua-Lomwe (Lolo) peoples, their neighbors to the east. Furthermore, a severe famine aggravated Yao life and caused them to flee to southern Malawi. The Yao were established long-distance traders, having bartered with the east coast since the early 1700s. At Mozambique and Kilwa, the Yao had traded with the Portuguese, Indians, Arabs, and French; ivory was the desired item of exchange, followed by others such as beeswax and tobacco, all of which were exchanged mainly for cloth. In fact the Yao were the principal middlemen in the commercial region that stretched from the Mozambican coast in the east to the Bisa country east of Luangwa valley in modern Zambia. Their involvement in the slave trade was a much later development and remained subsidiary to their ivory commerce.

Small groups of Yao traders conducted their business in the villages of southern Malawi before midcentury, but after 1860 they arrived in the region in greater numbers. As conflicts between the different Yao groups increased and the Ngoni exerted pressure on peoples of northern Mozambique, more Yao fled south to the southern Malawi lakeshore and Shire Highlands, homeland of the Nyanja/Mang'anja, who lived in small villages each led by a chief. By the late 1860s, most of the area east of the Shire River had fallen under Yao authority. Many of the Yao were involved in the ivory trade, some were more interested in the slave trade, and still others actively participated in both forms of commerce. Among the latter were Makanjira, Mponda, Kawinga, Matapwiri, all heads of powerful chiefdoms, who dominated the commerce of the east coast and the interior. Through their association with the Swahili-Arabs many, but not all, Yao embraced Islam. When European Christian missionaries arrived in Malawi in the 19th century, Yao chiefs permitted mission stations to be built in their areas. The missionaries hoped to lure the Yao into their sphere of influence, but Commissioner H. H. Johnston (1890s), intent on "pacifying" the Yao, ended their opposition to the European intrusion and curbed Yao commercial activities, including the slave trade. In 1896, after five years of war, Johnston broke the Yao dominance of commerce in that area.

The Ngoni had preceded the Yao into Malawi by several decades. In about 1819 two groups of Ngoni fled the powerful Zulu king, Shaka, and migrated north, crossing the Zambezi River in the 1830s. One group, the Jere Ngoni, was led by Zwangendaba and his successor M'Mbelwa; the second group, the Maseko Ngoni, was headed by Mputa and later by Chikusi and Chidyawonga. Both the Jere and Maseko Ngoni were highly organized politically and militarily, and both plundered and captured peoples during their northern trek.

The Maseko Ngoni first entered the Dedza District of Malawi in the 1830s and then proceeded south to the Shire Valley and east of Lake Malawi to Songea, Tanzania. After Mputa's death, his brother Chidyawonga returned to southern Malawi (1860s) and settled in Chewa country. The Ngoni adopted the Chewa language, while the Chewa imitated many Ngoni customs and Chewa men joined Ngoni military regiments. Chikusi, son of Mputa, succeeded as chief when his uncle Chidyawonga died. The Maseko were undecided over whether Chikusi or Chifisi (Chidyawonga's son) should reign. As a result, two lines of succession were established. Today Chikusi's successor is Gomani III and Chifisi's descendant chieftain is Kachindamoto II.

Zwangendaba led his Jere Ngoni into what is today Lilongwe district, raiding and terrifying the local inhabitants. Upon hearing rumors of cattle herds to the north, Zwangendaba directed his followers to an area south of Lake Tanzania. After his death (c. 1848) there was a dispute over succession; subsequently, some Ngoni moved north and others migrated east. But the main body traveled south and settled in Malawi, in the area between the Henga valley and southern Viphya. In 1857 Mhlahlo M'Mbelwa became *inkosi* (paramount chief) of the Jere Ngoni. Under his rule (1857–1891) both Tonga and Tumbuka peoples were subjugated.

The Chikulamayembe were unable to resist the superior military organization of the Ngoni. Some accommodation did occur, however, as Tumbuka headmen and Tumbuka religion were permitted to continue. With further assimilation, the Tumbuka and Ngoni intermarried and the Ngoni, like so many other groups before them, also adopted the local language. Although neither the Tonga nor the Tumbuka relished being integrated into the Ngoni state, their attempts at revolt (1874–1880) were not successful. Only the imposition of British rule restricted the activities of the Ngoni. However, even with the establishment of the British protectorate in 1891, the country of the northern Ngoni was not annexed and they did not pay taxes to the new colonial government. In 1904 the Ngoni agreed to accept British rule, in part because of the ameliorating effects of Scottish missions on Ngoni life. Today's descendants of the sons of Zwangendaba hold chiefly offices in the name of M'mbelwa, Mabulabo, Mperembe, Mtwalo, Mzukuzuku, Chinde, and Mzikubola.

The third group that moved into Malawi in the 19th century was the Swahili-Arabs. Swahili traders arrived in northern Malawi just prior to the coming of the Ngoni. In the 1840s the Jumbe, Salim bin Abdallah, brought an impressive number of guns and ammunition when he and his retinue made Nkhotakota an east-west commercial center. Both the Chewa and the Tonga sought alliances with these well-armed representatives of the sultan of Zanzibar to fend off the Ngoni. When European missionaries arrived in the 1870s, they abhorred, but tolerated, the Jumbe's trade in slaves. The British took more direct action in 1894 when they deposed the last Jumbe and sent him to Zanzibar. In the early 1880 another Swahili-Arab trader, Mlozi bin Kazbadema, established himself at Karonga, which he used as a base for his ivory business. Karonga had also just become the major station for the African Lakes Company (ALC). Conflict between them was inevitable, especially after the Ngonde complained of Swahili-Arab harassment and appealed to the ALC and the British for assistance. In 1889 Harry Hamilton Johnston, the British consul general, attempted to negotiate an end to the conflict, but the terms of the treaty were largely ignored. Finally, in 1895, with 400 troops as reinforcements, Johnston destroyed Mlozi's stockade; Mlozi was captured, tried, and executed.

Europeans were another group to enter and settle in Malawi in the 19th century. Although the Portuguese were the first Europeans to visit Malawi (in about 1616), and even though the Universities' Mission to Central Africa (UMCA) had briefly operated in the Shire Highlands in the 1860s, it was only after the death of Dr. David Livingstone in 1873 at Chitambo, Zambia, that many of them turned their attention to the Lake Malawi region. First to arrive were Scottish Presbyterian missionaries who established centers in the south and north of Malawi. The Dutch Reformed Church, Anglicans (UMCA), Catholics, Baptists, and others followed. By the early 1890s there was also a significant number of Europeans who were in the area to farm and conduct other business.

FROM PROTECTORATE TO NATION

Although traders, planters, and missionaries were in the region of Malawi, it was not until 1891 that a protectorate was declared by the British. Called British Central Africa, the protectorate was administered by Harry Johnston, who was appointed commissioner and consul general. Certainly the British did not rush to add this overseas possession to their empire but felt increasingly obliged to protect the missionaries, traders, and early settlers from other European powers (i.e., the Germans and Portuguese) who were game players in the "scramble for Africa."

Harry Johnston spent the next five years establishing British authority in the area. He led several military expeditions against slavers and local chieftains in order to assert British paramountcy. In addition to administering these territories, Johnston also exercised authority over lands chartered by the British South Africa Company. The Scottish missionaries, operating in the Shire Highlands following the death of David Livingstone, and the trader-planter communities had exercised their own "administrative powers" for many years but were now subordinate to British rule and Commissioner Johnston. Prior to 1895, when the British Treasury assumed full financial responsibility for British Central Africa, Johnston had little money. Nevertheless, during his brief tenure, he ended the slave trade and set up the administrative infrastructure for governing the protectorate. He gathered together an effective staff: Alfred Sharpe, John Nicoll, C. A. Edwards, and William Manning, as well as a small number of civil servants who were responsible for taxes, public works, customs, and postal services.

Johnston left the territory in 1897, and his deputy, Alfred Sharpe, succeeded him. During the administrative reign of the colorful Sharpe, the name of the protectorate was changed to Nyasaland. The Order in Council of 1907 also changed the commissionership to a governorship and created an Executive Council of three senior officials (European) and a Legislative Council (LEGCO) consisting of nominated nongovernment members (European planters, traders, and missionaries). This would remain the constitutional basis for the central government of Nyasaland until the end of World War II, with changes occurring in numbers or composition, most notably the addition of one Indian and two African representatives to LEGCO in 1949. Until then, governors seeking African opinion had to rely on their district commissioners, missionaries, one of whom, a member of LEGCO, was to represent African interests, or the native associations.

The first welfare/native association, North Nyasa Native Association (NNNA), was established in 1912 and was followed in 1914 by the West Nyasa Native Association (WNNA); others emerged in succeeding decades. As political organizations reacting to the laws of the new colonial administration, the associations held formal meetings with minutes, rules, and elections. Consisting mostly of Western-educated members, these Malawians sought to make recommendations to the British authorities, who invariably found their suggestions inappropriate. In 1930 the associations began working with and through district councils. There was one issue in the 1930s that drew the associations together: the proposed union with Rhodesia. A decade later the associations merged, creating the Nyasaland African Congress (NAC). At its first conference (1944) Levi Mumba was elected president. Dr. Hastings Kamuzu Banda would become one of its most steadfast supporters and its main financial underwriter. In 1959 the NAC became the Malawi Congress Party (MCP).

Membership in the associations began to wane when the independent churches seemed to become more effectual. Usually the leaders of the associations were also active in the independent churches. Early independence initiatives by Malawians included the formation, before World War I, of churches separate from the Scottish mission at Livingstonia, such as Charles Domingo's Seventh Day Baptist and Elliott Kamwana's Watchtower. Malawians understandably resented the Europeans' racist attitudes and condemnation of local traditions and customs. With the advent of World War I, many Malawians were distressed when the Europeans recruited them for a cause not theirs. A large death toll, combined with land problems and labor abuses on certain estates, produced in January 1915 an uprising against European control. The Chilembwe rising shook European complacency, resulted in an official government inquiry, and recommended, but never implemented, reforms.

During the interwar years, the British adopted a policy of indirect rule in which certain judicial powers were delegated to chiefs. They were permitted to hold court and were given various administrative responsibilities, such as levying taxes. In the 1920s and 1930s, the British attempted to raise the standard of living. Patterning their efforts after the Jeanes educationalists, they established centers in which community workers, chiefs, and headmen attended courses to promote the use of better hygiene, nutrition, child care, and agricultural methods. Addressing the critical land problem that plagued the protectorate, a 1936 Order in Council secured 90 percent of the land for African use, leaving the remainder for townships, forest reserves, Crown land, and that already alienated—legally transferred or occupied—by Europeans. The Abrahams Commission in 1946 designated more alienated land in the Shire Highlands for African use. Subsequent purchases of alienated land have been necessary since then to reduce the number of squatters.

Unlike its neighbors, Malawi did not have an abundance of minerals that drew many Europeans to its soil. European traders and planters wanted an assurance of good transportation, cheap labor, and land. The latter two were easily obtainable, but the rail system, developed at great expense to the protectorate, made transportation costs inordinately high. A classic underdevelopment case, Malawi had few industries, which forced its male population to seek employment in neighboring states that were more industrially advanced. Besides severely straining the family social structure, the Malawian migrant laborers influenced the economic development of Zambia, Zimbabwe, and South Africa, leaving Malawi without skilled labor. Men who were migrant laborers or recruits fighting in World War II returned from those travels with experiences that often left them dissatisfied with their own political status, living standards, and/or educational opportunities.

After World War II, the native associations drew together into the Nyasaland African Congress, and the very small but vocal European community was attracted to the possibility of uniting with a richer territory. The possibility of establishing a closer union among East and Central African territories had been bandied about since World War I and gained considerable support in the 1930s among the Europeans. However, agreement could not be reached before the onset of World War II, which placed dreams of amalgamation on hold. Finally in 1953, after many more months of discussion, the Federation of Rhodesia and Nyasaland was established. At no time were discussions about a closer union ever supported by the vast majority of Africans in Nyasaland. The Bledisloe Commission Report in 1939 recognized that the opposition to a federation was overwhelming. Whenever the associations, provincial councils, or chiefs were polled for African sentiment, the reply was always the same: the Federation would benefit Europeans, not Africans. Not surprisingly, Malawi did not benefit economically from the union. Along with total rejection of the Federation came the movement to end the union and become independent. Led by a generation of younger leaders such as Henry Chipembere and Kanyama Chiume, the followers of the Nyasaland African Congress became more militant in their demands to gain control of their own lives.

In 1958 Dr. Hastings K. Banda returned to Nyasaland to take over headship of the nationalist movement, to work for secession from the Federation, and to revise the constitution, providing for an African majority and independence from British rule. When the NAC allegedly advocated violence, Governor Robert Armitage declared a state of emergency (March 1959) during which unnecessary brutality was used against NAC members; Banda, Chipembere, and many others were sent to prison. The Devlin Commission of 1959 exonerated Banda and the NAC, which was now called the Malawi Congress Party (MCP). In the following year a constitutional conference was held in London with Banda, Chirwa and Chiume, three chiefs, and two Asian delegates in attendance. The MCP emerged from this meeting with a majority in LEGCO. In the election under the new constitution that was held in August 1961, all 20 lower roll seats were won by the MCP, which received 99 percent of the votes cast. The issues at the polls were to keep the Federation or become independent, to support Africanization of government positions, and to improve social conditions. Banda became de facto prime minister. The British agreed to permit Nyasaland to secede from the Federation and subsequently granted it independence on July 6, 1964.

Sovereignty obtained, Dr. Banda set about administering the new nation. Almost immediately, his efforts to directly control the entire government met with opposition from some of the younger men who had struggled with him for independence. Unable to reconcile their differences on domestic and foreign policy issues, the former cabinet ministers were forced to leave Malawi in what came to be known as the Cabinet Crisis. In 1966 Malawi became a republic and a one-party state. From the mid-1960s Dr. Banda nearly single-handedly governed his nation, often appealing to the people to trust him to rule in their interest.

The apparent political stability and positive economic climate in Malawi pleased foreign aid agencies, which oversubscribed loans and saw Malawi's economic growth rates at 5 percent annually. Some of the development money went to extend roads and railways to move produce from rural areas to markets within and outside the country. More schools were built and health programs were implemented. Most of the aid was allocated to the planning and execution of rural agricultural projects aimed at increasing productivity of the smallholder producer, thereby ensuring food security in the country. The results were mixed partly because the prices set by the Agricultural Development and Marketing Corporation (ADMARC), which had a virtual monopoly on market smallholder produce, were inadequate to make agriculture profitable to the farmers. On the other hand, the estate sector (mostly tobacco, tea, sugar) operated under more favorable conditions with the result that, throughout the 1970s and for most of the following decade, it experienced tangible growth.

Toward the end of the 1980s, the economy of Malawi was not in good shape. It was adversely affected by world market prices, it lacked diversification in its exports, and it increasingly experienced weaknesses in management, especially of the parastatal organizations that had become dominant features in the socioeconomic life of the country. The government accepted the structural adjustment program of the International Monetary Fund (IMF) and the World Bank, which involved, among many other measures, lifting subsidies on fertilizers and oil; consequently, the cost of most consumer goods rose. The program also liberalized the marketing of smallholder produce so that ADMARC no longer held the monopoly in this field.

Meanwhile, although Banda and the MCP continued to be intolerant of dissent, pressure was mounting for political reform. As the Soviet Union broke apart, Western nations that had hitherto supported Banda because of his anticommunist stance demanded change as a prerequisite for aid. For a period in 1992–1993, Malawi received little foreign assistance, and this badly affected the economy. Malawians in exile also called for immediate reform, and underground opposition within the country began to surface with open calls for multiparty democracy. In March 1992 the Catholic bishops issued a pastoral letter, which was read in their churches, criticizing the government's human rights record. Before the end of the year, two new political parties, the Alliance for Democracy (AFORD) and the United Democratic Front (UDF), were formed. In the face of heightening political agitation, Banda was forced to accept changes that a national referendum in May 1993 confirmed overwhelmingly. In June of the following year, the first general elections in over 30 years took place. Bakili Muluzi of the United Democratic Front defeated Banda and two other candidates; the UDF also won the majority of the seats in the expanded national assembly. Freedom of expression and association had returned to Malawi, and political tensions eased considerably.

Muluzi inherited an unstable economy and, like Banda, turned to donor agencies for assistance. The IMF and the World Bank advised on more structural adjustment programs, including a massive devaluation of the Malawi kwacha and an acceleration in the privatization of nearly all statutory organizations. In foreign affairs, Malawi extended friendship to Arab and Islamic nations, most of which the Banda government had shunned. Muluzi became a more active participant in inter-African affairs and even offered to contribute to an Africa-based peacekeeping force.

Although practically retired, Dr. Banda remained titular head of the MCP until his death on November 25, 1997; within a few months, Gwanda Chakuamba was elected to succeed him. In the general elections of June 1999, he was the presidential candidate for the MCP-AFORD partnership, and Chakufwa Chihana of the Alliance For Democracy stood as vice president. Muluzi won and his party also took the majority in the national assembly. Although the election results were hotly contested by the MCP-AFORD and by the smaller Malawi Democratic Party led by Kamlepo Kalua, it seemed clear that the culture of democracy was beginning to take root in Malawi.

The Dictionary

Note: Terms in boldface type refer to other entries.

– A –

ABDALLAH, YOHANNA BARNABA. Distinguished Christian worker and **Yao** historian. Abdallah was born in northern **Mozambique**. Ordained an Anglican priest at the Likoma Cathedral in 1898, he was briefly assigned to a church center in Zanzibar but spent most of his working life at the Unangu mission station, east of **Lake Malawi**. A noted Greek and Bible scholar, Abdallah visited the Holy Land in 1905, an event that heightened his devotion to Christianity. He was the author of *Chikala cha Wayao*, which was translated and edited by **Meredith Sanderson** and published in 1919 and 1973; the book was a pioneering study of the of the Yao and their homeland. Abdallah died in 1924.

ABRAHAMS COMMISSION. Appointed in 1946 to investigate the problem of land and tenancy, mainly in the **Shire Highlands**. Sir Sidney Abrahams, the commission's leader, was a 1906 British Olympian, a distinguished lawyer, and a privy councillor. In the 1920s he served as attorney general in the Gold Coast, Uganda, and Zanzibar; in the 1930s he was chief justice of Uganda and then of Ceylon. Although the matter of land had been the subject of inquiries such as the **Jackson Commission** of 1920, the **Ormsby-Gore Commission** of 1924, and the Bell Commission of 1938, it had never really been resolved. In 1943 and 1945, land-related riots occurred in **Blantyre** and **Thyolo**, respectively, proving that the issue remained explosive. The disturbances led to the appointment of the Abrahams Commission to recommend a permanent solution to the problem.

The commission recommended that the government purchase all cultivable land in the areas concerned and administer it as native trust land. Africans on European-owned estates were to be given three choices: move to the native trust land, vacate the estate in lieu of government compensation for loss of home and garden, or remain on the estate on the

1

condition of working for the landowner until the contract lapsed or the tenant became dissatisfied with the deal. A dissatisfied tenant could resort to the second option.

Although these recommendations were not fully implemented until 1952, Africans, by and large, reacted favorably to them. On the other hand, Europeans such as **Malcolm Barrow**, threatened by the possibility of labor shortages, were unhappy with aspects of the commission's findings.

ACHIKUNDA. *See* CHIKUNDA.

ADAM, OSMAN. Prominent Indian businessmen in 20th-century **Malawi**. Osman Adam started his commercial enterprises in **Blantyre** in 1894, becoming the first Indian to do so in the new British colony. In the early 1920s Adam became founding president of the **Nyasaland Indian Traders Association** and rose to leadership in the **Nyasaland Indian Association**. In 1943 he and C. K. Dharap, another leading Indian businessman, financed the establishment of the first Indian primary school in Blantyre. Dharap Primary School still exists today, the students being predominantly indigenous Malawians. *See also* ASIANS.

AFRICAN COOPERATIVE SOCIETY (ACS). Based at **Shiloh** (Chikunda), just outside **Blantyre**. The ACS was formed in 1900 by **Joseph Booth** as an answer to some of the financial problems that the Seventh Day Baptist Mission was encountering in the **Shire Highlands** and as a way of ensuring that Africans rendered unemployed by the failure of Booth's agricultural projects could earn a living. Under this scheme, Booth was able to secure porterage contracts that enabled about 500 workers to carry the **African Lakes Company**'s (ALC) goods, mainly between Katunga on the Shire and Blantyre. Booth took charge of the finances of the ACS, and consequently, when **Jacob Bakker** headed the mission in the latter part of 1901, he found it difficult to understand the management of the project. The ACS was virtually dead by early 1902 after Booth severed ties with the Sabbath Evangelizing and Industrial Mission of Plainfield, New Jersey, which sold some of the Shire Highland assets to the Seventh-Day Adventist Church.

AFRICAN LAKES COMPANY (ALC). Originally called the Livingstonia Central Africa Company. It changed its name to African Lakes Corporation before changing it again to African Lakes Company. It was a Glasgow trading and transportation business established in 1878 and managed by the brothers John and Fred **Moir**. Their motives in forming the company included expectations of profit, reducing the effectiveness of the slave trade, and promoting European influence. In 1890 it was absorbed by **Cecil Rhodes's British South Africa Company.** Popularly known as **Mandala** because John Moir wore glasses (*mandala*), the ALC had general trading establishments in almost all districts in the colony, its only competitors being **Indian** traders who dominated commerce in the rural areas. Today the firm's main business is car dealerships and insurance, including agency of Lloyds of London.

AFRICAN METHODIST EPISCOPAL (AME) CHURCH. Black American separatist church founded in the 19th century. AME stressed the right of black men and women to control their own lives. The first AME mission was started in Malawi in 1924 by **Hanock Phiri**, who had become a member during his stay in South Africa; a year later, the church's first school began. Dr. **Hastings K. Banda** was a member of the AME Church from 1922 to 1932, and the church partially funded both his passage from South Africa to the United States and his education at the Wilberforce Institute in Ohio.

AFRICAN NATIONAL CHURCH. Church formed in 1929 in the **Chilumba-Chitimba** area of **Malawi** by former elders of the **Livingstonia Mission**, principally **Simon Kamkhati Mkandawire, Paddy Nyasulu, Robert Sambo Mhango, Levi Mumba**, and Isaac Mkondowe. Accepting polygamy and, in time, becoming more tolerant of beer drinking, the church accepted members of other churches who had been expelled from the mainstream church on grounds of polygamy or adultery. Its adherents also included people who had never joined a Christian church because of polygamy or beer drinking. The African National Church strongly supported the aspirations of the **African welfare associations**, which sought to improve the welfare of indigenous peoples in the British colony. Within a few years of its formation, the African National Church had branches in many parts of Malawi, including **Zomba** and **Lilongwe**, and, through the efforts of Paddy Nyasulu, southern Tanganyika. By the 1960s, it had spread to **Zambia, Zimbabwe**, and southern Congo; in the 1960s the church also changed its name to the African International Church, partly to reflect its transnational character and partly because the Malawi government insisted on a different name because of the fear that its original designation would give the impression that it was the country's official church.

AFRICAN PROTECTORATE COUNCIL OF NYASALAND. Consisting of three members from each of the three Provincial Councils, the

African Protectorate Council was formed by the governor in 1946 as an assurance to Africans that their views could be discussed at high levels of administration. Considered by some as a way of minimizing the influence of the radical members of the new **Nyasaland African Congress** (NAC), the African Protectorate Council opposed both closer union of the Rhodesias and Nyasaland and the **Federation of Rhodesia and Nyasaland**. In 1949 the governor nominated two members of the Protectorate Council, **Ellerton Mposa** and **Ernest Alexander Muwamba**, to serve in the **Legislative Council** (LEGCO).

AFRICAN REFORMED PRESBYTERIAN CHURCH. *See* MKANDAWIRE, YAPHET.

AFRICAN WELFARE ASSOCIATIONS. Also referred to as native associations or voluntary associations, they were early pressure groups representing an African effort to work with the colonial administration. The first was the **North Nyasa Native Association** (NNNA), formed in 1912 at **Karonga** by, among others, Simon Muhango and **Levi Mumba**. It was followed by others, including those in **Mzimba** (Mombera), **Zomba**, **Chiradzulu** (started by Dr. **Daniel Malekebu**), **Mulanje**, and **Blantyre**. As local and regional groups, they kept the colonial government in touch with African public opinion, and they kept their districts well informed politically, explaining new legislation. The membership of the associations tended to be elitist, consisting mostly of teachers, ministers of religion, and civil servants. By 1933 educated Malawians had organized 15 such associations.

Associations sought recognition from the government and wanted it to consider several issues vital to the majority population. They argued for better postal service, bridges, and roads; they sought relief from high retail prices; they urged assistance in ensuring village sanitation; they asked for cooperation in protecting women from unwanted advances from European men; they were concerned over the harmful effects of labor migration; and they persistently requested more and better educational facilities. Throughout the 1920s and 1930s the associations unsuccessfully attempted to reason with an administration that was deaf to pleadings for reform. During the **Bledisloe Commission** hearings, the associations spoke frankly against any form of closer union or amalgamation with the Rhodesias.

Associations tended to shun mass participation in their groups and clung to constitutional methods in an effort to effect political change. In 1944 they played a major role in the formation of the first nationalist movement, the **Nyasaland African Congress** (NAC). Levi Mumba, its first president, had in 1929 initiated the formation of the Zomba-based Committee of Northern Province Associations. Similarly, **James Sangala**, a key person in the movement toward the formation of the NAC, had been active in associations in Zomba and Blantyre.

AFRICANIZATION. Phasing out expatriate civil servants and replacing them with Malawians. Unlike other African leaders, Dr. **Hastings Banda** resisted rapid Africanization, insisting that Africans would be promoted on their merit, not their skin color. Africanization also extended beyond public service into the commercial and industrial sector, where Asian retailers and European-owned businesses were affected. Among the industries nationalized was Malawi Railways, previously controlled by **Lonrho**. *See also* ASIANS; SKINNER REPORT.

AGRICULTURAL DEVELOPMENT AND MARKETING CORPORATION (ADMARC). The origins of ADMARC are found in the colonial period, when the government established various boards to regulate the marketing of crops produced by Africans. The Native Tobacco Board was established in 1926, and similar organizations were set up for **cotton** (1951) and for beans, **groundnuts**, and **maize** (1952). In 1956 the three agencies merged to form the Agricultural Production and Marketing Board (AP&MB). The director of agriculture became chairman of the board, and most of its employees were seconded from the Department of Agriculture and doubled in marketing and extension work. The government granted the board a monopoly to market all the crops in which it was involved. By 1960, the AP&MB had established markets in various parts of the colony, and it had capital installations worth £1.5 million and a turnover of approximately £3,500.000.

When Dr. **Hastings Banda** took over the agricultural ministry in 1961, he changed the organization's name to **Farmers Marketing Board (FMB)**. The FMB began to expand its activities to include buying freehold farms that some Europeans were voluntarily selling as they left the country. In the second half of the 1960s, the organization sold some of these farms, most of which were in the Southern Region, to individual Malawians through an arrangement by which the board assured such prospective buyers loans and even farm managers.

In April 1971 the FMB changed its name to Agricultural Development and Marketing Corporation (ADMARC). A statutory corporation owned by the government and directed by the Ministry of Agriculture and Natural Resources, ADMARC continued in the main to purchase (and process where necessary) crops produced by smallholder farmers, improve agricultural production standards, establish agro-industrial enterprises, and market the increased volume of exportable crops. The corporation posts a set of purchase prices for each commodity before the planting season, and it is mainly interested in maize, **rice**, cassava, cotton, **tobacco**, and groundnuts, the last three grown primarily for export. ADMARC maintains well over 50 storage depots for the various crops. Its agents at these bases also sell select seed, fertilizer, pesticides, and farm implements to rural farmers.

During the 1970s ADMARC made huge profits, largely because of the wide differential between its buying and selling prices for the smallholder crops such as fire-cured tobacco, whose farmers were paid less than one-third of the prevailing market price. The enormous profits enabled ADMARC to establish a diverse investment portfolio, which in the early 1980s included enterprises in most sections of the economy. In 1971 it became a major shareholder in the new Commercial Bank of Malawi and in the just constituted National Bank of Malawi, and it invested heavily in many of the companies controlled by **Press (Holdings) Ltd**. ADMARC was able to keep its substantial profits until 1979, when the central government required that the Treasury receive 40 percent of those profits. In the early 1980s the World Bank began working with the Malawi government, AID, UNDP, and other donors to strengthen ADMARC by focusing its activities on marketing, improving its management, and reducing its nonmarketing activities. When in the mid-1980s ADMARC was no longer making a profit and its liquidity problems became very serious, the government had to assist it to purchase smallholder crops. *See also* BANKING.

Beginning in the 1987–1988 growing season, the private sector was allowed to compete with ADMARC in the marketing of smallholder crops. Since 1988, ADMARC investments have been reduced to agrobased industries and agricultural activities, and the range of crop marketing has been expanded for the private sector. Except for one, all of ADMARC's estates have been sold to entrepreneurs, Malawians who have secured loans on easy terms. The privatization of ADMARC has had its problems, not all of them economic: delays in land transfers, finding markets and buyers for its holdings, and extricating its investment from **Lonrho,** a private multinational company that until 1996 had a monopoly on the sugar industry. More recently, ADMARC purchased Stagecoach, a transportation company formerly owned by British interests. However, because of the poor state of the roads, problems with spare parts, and competition from the mushrooming minibus business, Stagecoach has not been profitable. ADMARC is due to be privatized by 2003. *See also* AGRICULTURE.

AGRICULTURE. Lacking any significant mineral wealth, Malawi has always been an agricultural country. Throughout his political career, Dr. **Hastings Banda** maintained that agriculture had to be the country's first order of business; food production was primary whereas industry and its accompanying urbanization came much later. Nearly 90 percent of the population is engaged in agricultural activities. **Maize** is both the main subsistence and cash crop of the smallholder, whereas **tobacco, tea,** and **sugar** are the cash crops of the estate farmers. Agriculture provides approximately 37 percent of Malawi's gross domestic product. Subsistence production provides the largest and most stable element of crop production. Estate and smallholder cash crop production varies annually according to market demands and weather conditions.

Estate production, however, accounts for about 60 percent of domestic exports. Dating back to colonial days, when expatriate farmers were given freehold or leasehold titles to land, estate crops have been important. Most estates (about 400) survived after independence and the government supported the expansion of this sector. After 1964, President Hastings Banda was able to reward his most loyal supporters with profitable tobacco and tea estates that could be purchased by government loans. And legislation passed in 1965 gave him the power to issue leases for estates to his political allies. The economic patronage provided the president with years of unchallenged political support. Village headmen and chiefs were warned by government officials not to confiscate customary land and sell it to the estate sector or to withhold lands from smallholders. The World Bank also insisted on ending land transfers that continued to favor the estate sector's access to land.

Agricultural production has diversified in recent years. Maize, pulses (beans and peas), **rice**, and cassava are staple foodstuffs grown by smallholders for domestic consumption, whereas **groundnuts, cotton,** firecured tobacco, and to a certain extent **coffee** are key cash crops grown by smallholders for both home use and export. Most Malawian farms are small, averaging about 3 acres (1.2 ha.); only 2 percent of all farms are 12 acres (4.8 ha.) or larger. Sixty-three percent of all farmers cultivate 35 percent of the acreage on farms of 4 acres or less. Large holdings of 6 acres or more represent 19 percent of the farms and 42 percent of the total cultivated acreage.

Regional distribution of crops is complicated and may only be described in oversimplified terms. In general, maize, pulses, and groundnuts are grown throughout the country. Of the leading cash crops, tobacco and groundnuts have their areas of maximum production in the central region; cotton and tea in the south; rice in the north. Since the 1970s, there have been rice projects along the central shores of **Lake Malawi**, near Salima and Nkhotakota, and tobacco is now grown in the north, especially in **Mzimba** and **Rumphi** Districts and, to a degree, in **Chitipa**; cotton and coffee are also being revived in that region. Some coffee is also grown in the south and north.

The government's agricultural development program has been conservative. The largest projects were near **Lilongwe, Chikwawa**, and **Karonga** and were financed in part by the World Bank. Other projects concentrated on developing certain crops: cotton, rice, tea, and flue-cured tobacco. These integrated rural projects had mixed results, and their operations extended to only 10 percent of the population. Because of the limited impact and high costs, the rural projects were dropped in 1978 in favor of the **National Rural Development Programme** (NRDP). This program concentrated on a much larger number of families over two decades by assisting these farmers with credit and extension information. *See also* RURAL AGRICULTURAL PROJECTS.

Since the late 1980s the **Agricultural Development and Marketing Corporation** (ADMARC) has not had a monopoly on marketing smallholder produce. Individual entrepreneurs now purchase food and cash crops from smallholder farmers, and this has given the producers, especially the tobacco growers, more control and has increased their incomes.

Agricultural extension services have been expanded significantly since independence, and the ratio of extension officers to farmers has increased. Until 1973, when the Malawi government took over the expenditures, the extension services were financed by the British government. General shortages in skilled extension services staff have continued and, generally, such government aid is rendered only to farmers who have sufficient acreage to implement the suggested changes, including growing hybrid pure maize with proper amounts of fertilizer.

The post-Banda government has also emphasized agriculture as the central economic activity, and has continued to encourage an increase in the cultivation of maize, rice, cassava, sorghum, and millet. However, food security has been greatly threatened by factors such as drought and El Niño. At the beginning of the 1997–1998 season and, in late 1998, too much rain caused waterlogging, forcing the government to import maize from countries such as South Africa. Agricultural production has also been adversely affected by the devaluation of the Malawi **kwacha** and by the removal of subsidies on fuel and fertilizer, measures that have rendered the latter too expensive for most peasant farmers. *See also* CURRENCY. Cash crops, including tobacco, tea, and cotton, have remained key foreign exchange earners, except that they too have been badly affected by the same factors. Tobacco, which in the 1970s and 1980s had surpassed tea as the main export crop, has further suffered from the progressively low prices it has fetched on the auction floors. In 1998 a government deficit of 700 million kwacha (about US$16 million) led to a devaluation of the Malawi kwacha by 68 percent. Farmers in remoter areas such as Chitipa have been further hampered by the poor roads, as often the high cost of transporting the crop to the auction floors renders the activity unprofitable. *See also* TRANSPORTATION.

Another notable aspect of post-Banda agriculture is the promotion of less traditional cash crops in the hope that their earnings will offset the deficit created by the falling prices of tobacco. One such crop is pigeon peas, which in many parts of the country are part of the everyday diet. However, although Malawi is a major producer of this crop, earning as much as US$6 million annually from exporting it mainly to South Africa, India, and Holland, the Malawi government has until recently not considered it a significant foreign exchange earner. In 1999 a 150-acre hydroponic farm was opened in the **Blantyre** area with a view to greatly increasing the availability of fresh vegetables and fruits, thereby reducing their importation from **Zimbabwe** and **South Africa**. This US$6 million project is headed by the Africa Vegetable Corporation, operating in Malawi under the name of Africa Commodity Traders.

In addition to all this, reforms are being made to effect more effective land utilization and improve maize markets through incentives such as better pricing and storage. As part of the liberalization program, ADMARC is being privatized and commercialized, and the Strategic Grain Reserve (SGR) has been replaced by the independent National Food Reserve Agency (NFRA). All smallholder crop authorities are also part of the privatization program, as is the Malawi Rural Finance Company. A task force consisting of the railways, haulage firms, and private traders has been set up to establish means of reducing the cost of imported fertilizer.

AIDS. The first confirmed AIDS case in **Malawi** occurred in 1985. Early surveys at prenatal clinics and hospitals began to indicate a 2 percent HIV positive rate among expectant mothers and blood donors in urban areas. By 1987 this had risen to 8 percent, and to 19 percent and 23 percent in 1989 and 1990 respectively. This was to rise further in the 1990s, and by the end of the decade, 13 percent of the Malawian population (as opposed to only blood donors and expectant mothers) aged 15–47 were HIV positive.

Initially, the government did not actively campaign against the spread of AIDS. But as it became increasingly clear that AIDS was a reality in Malawi and as the World Bank and the World Health Organization (WHO) urged authorities to take the threat seriously, the government began to use radio and newspapers to educate the people about its dangers. Theater groups at the university and elsewhere in the country performed plays with an AIDS-related theme, and medical personnel attended workshops concerning AIDS. Testing of donated blood became routine, at first in the major hospitals and later in the district ones. Prostitutes and the most sexually active age-groups were also targeted for AIDS education, as well as other sexually transmitted diseases. The use of condoms, usually a taboo subject, was beginning to be discussed openly. The high-profile awareness campaign against AIDS also included posters and signs conspicuously posted in public places. It was vital to enlist the cooperation of traditional doctors because they remain popular and often use razor blades and other sharp objects to administer their medicines. Many such doctors falsely claimed that they had a cure for AIDS-related illnesses, thereby giving a false sense of security to those who consulted them and potentially leading to a further proliferation of the disease.

By the mid-1990s AIDS had become an epidemic and was devastating the workforce and family life as thousands of people in the 15–45 age-group died annually. The national economy lost thousands of workers in their most productive years: young adult wage earners and food producers. Orphanages became a necessity as surviving children of AIDS victims found that the extended family system could not always absorb them. The number of children born with the AIDS virus was also increasing at an alarming rate, and hospitals could not cope with the hundreds of AIDS patients who required treatment for multiple AIDS-related diseases. Expensive medications administered to AIDS sufferers in the West were beyond the reach of most Malawians and were not readily available in the country.

By the late 1990s Malawi had one of the highest incidences of HIV/AIDS in sub-Saharan Africa, reducing the life expectancy from 52 to 44 years. The Malawi government was widening its AIDS education program within the Essential Health Package (EHP) scheme. *See also* DISEASE; HEALTH SERVICES.

A. L. BRUCE ESTATES. *See* BRUCE, ALEXANDER LIVINGSTONE; BRUCE, ALEXANDER LOW; CHILEMBWE, JOHN; LIVINGSTONE, WILLIAM JARVIS.

AIR MALAWI. *See* TRANSPORTATION.

ALLIANCE FOR DEMOCRACY (AFORD). One of the main political parties in **Malawi** since September 1992. AFORD was born out of the United Committee for Multiparty Democracy (UCMD), formed by opposition groups that met in Lusaka, **Zambia**, in April 1992 to discuss effective means of bringing about political change in Malawi. Also attending this meeting was **Tom Chakufwa Chihana** who, upon his return to Malawi, chaired the Interim Committee for Democracy Alliance, an underground movement and a child of the UCMD. The Interim Committee grew into AFORD, which in September 1992 formally declared itself and registered as a political party. By that time President **Hastings Banda** had reluctantly come to accept the idea of multiparty democracy. Although imprisoned in April 1992 and not released until June the following year, Chihana became head of AFORD. Among other important officeholders were **Augustine Mnthambala**, **Denis Nkhwazi**, McNight Machika, legal scholar at **Chancellor College**, **Justin Malewezi**, **Morton Mughogho**, James Limbe, a businessman, **Aaron Longwe**, **Rodwell Munyenyembe**, and Simon Pamdule. At the time of the Referendum of 1993, they were joined by Zambia-based activists, including **O'Brien Mapopa Chipeta** and **Frank Mayinga Mkandawire**.

In the June 1994 **elections**, AFORD fielded candidates in most constituencies in the country. Although it won all the seats in the Northern Region, it completely failed in the Southern Region and managed only two in the Central Region. Later that year, AFORD joined the United Democratic Front government, and several of its senior politicians were given cabinet positions; T. C. Chihana (second vice president and irrigation minister), O. J. M. Chipeta (Agriculture), **Jimmy Mponda Mkandawire** (Physical Planning), F. M. Mkandawire (Environmental Affairs), **Matembo Nzunda** (Science and Research), and Rodwell Munyenyembe (Speaker of parliament). The coalition lasted only two years. Following the breakup, three AFORD ministers, Chipeta, Mayinga Mkandawire, and Nzunda, and two junior ministers, Chenda Mkandawire and Mervin Moyo, refused to leave the government; Munyunyembe also chose to remain Speaker. The leadership of AFORD regarded this attitude as rebellious and embarked on a campaign to discredit them. Some AFORD MPs such as Musyani of Chitipa Central also disagreed with the party. In the 1999 elections, AFORD and the **Malawi Congress Party** (MCP) formed an alliance; **Gwanda Chakuamba** (MCP) and Chakufwa Chihana (AFORD) stood as presidential and vice presidential candidates, respectively. Chakuamba lost narrowly to **Bakili Muluzi**. In the parliamentary elections all the AFORD rebels unsuccessfully stood as independents. The party took all but five seats in the Northern Region and won one in the Central Region.

AMBALI, AUGUSTINE. Born about 1856 in Uzaramo on the periphery of Dar es Salaam. Ambali was sold to slavers as a boy but freed by the British navy, which intercepted a boat carrying him and others from the mainland to Pemba Island. He ended up in the hands of the **Universities' Mission to Central Africa** (UMCA) at **Zanzibar**. He was in the group of freed slaves who constituted the core African Anglicans trained at St. Andrews, the UMCA school at Kiungani, Zanzibar. Ambali taught at Msumba in 1888 and remained there even after he was ordained deacon (in 1898) and priest (1906). In 1917 he went to Ngoo as priest in charge and five years later became the first African to be appointed canon of **Likoma** Cathedral. Regarded as one of the foremost preachers in the **Lake Malawi** area in the late 19th and early 20th centuries, Ambali died in 1931.

ANGLO-PORTUGUESE TREATY (1891). This convention established the arbitrary southern border of Malawi in June 1891. The confluence of the Ruo and **Shire River**s divided British and Portuguese colonial claims to the lands held by Makololo chiefs. In the years immediately preceding the treaty both colonial powers, following the diplomacy of the time, attempted to sign separate treaties with the chiefs. Each nation was on a "civilizing mission," which in fact was a power struggle over control of southern **Malawi**, which nearly ended in war in 1890. When the Portuguese backed away from the crisis, they effectively relinquished their influence in the region. Within a year, the British had accorded protectorate status to the area.

ARAB-SWAHILI WAR (1887–1889). The origins of this series of conflicts, more accurately termed the Karonga War, lie mainly in the struggle for commercial dominance in the **Lake Malawi** area. The **Swahili-Arabs**, led by **Mlozi bin Kazbadema**, had established themselves in the area in the late 1870s at about the time the **African Lakes Corporation** (ALC) led by the **Moir** brothers was also becoming active in the region. Initially, the ALC and the Swahili-Arabs in the **Karonga** area became partners in the ivory trade. When a **Ngonde** headman was killed by Swahili-Arabs in an otherwise trivial incident, mediation resulted in compensation to the Ngonde. Later, when the Ngonde attacked the Swahili-Arabs, the latter retaliated in what appeared to be an Arab bid for hegemony over the Ngonde. Soon the ALC and the missionaries joined the disagreement on the side of the Ngonde, thereby widening the conflict.

It now became mainly a physical combat between the Swahili-Arabs on the one hand and the ALC, the missionaries, and the Ngonde on the other. Supported by the British consul, the anti–Swahili-Arab party argued that Mlozi was a slaver and a danger to the local Ngonde people. Thirsty for power, Mlozi posed a problem to British designs in the area and, as a Muslim, would be an impediment to Christian missionary endeavors in the area. However, research has also shown that as the ivory trade became highly competitive in the wider African region, the ALC was beginning to face commercial problems and increasingly began to see the Swahili-Arabs under Mlozi as diverting its business.

Both parties, weakened by sickness and lacking vital supplies, succumbed to a peace treaty in 1889 presided over by Sir **Harry Johnston**, the newly appointed British consul for Mozambique and the Lake Nyasa (Malawi) region. In fact, the major significance of this conflict lies in the events that followed, that is, the considerable British interest in the region that led to the declaration of British rule in Malawi and eastern Zambia. *See also* SWAHILI-ARABS.

ARMITAGE, SIR ROBERT PERCEVAL. Sir Robert Armitage was governor of Cyprus before assuming the same position in **Nyasaland** in 1956, at a time when African nationalist politics were taking a more radical turn. Born in England in 1906 and educated at Oxford University, Armitage joined the colonial civil service in 1929, working first in Kenya, the Gold Coast, and Cyprus. However, although he had long experience in the colonies, particularly having worked in the Gold Coast during the colony's transition to a free nation called Ghana, Armitage seemed ill prepared to deal with mounting political pressure, especially after the return of Dr. **Hastings Banda** in July 1958. He refused to discuss the possibility that Nyasaland might secede from the **Federation of Rhodesia and Nyasaland** and further rejected all constitutional proposals suggested by **African National Congress** (NAC) members. On

March 2, 1959, Armitage declared a state of emergency, proscribing the NAC, and ordered the detention without trial of over 1,000 members of Congress during **Operation Sunrise**. The **Devlin Commission** into the disturbances of that year concluded that Armitage had overreacted. In April 1961 he retired and for some years worked for the Beit Trust; he died in England on June 7, 1990.

ARMY. The Malawi Rifles has about 10,000 men and includes three light infantry battalions, each divided into five rifle companies. The present forces have been trained according to British tradition, and the United Kingdom (UK) remains a primary source of military aid. Significant military assistance has also been received from the **United States**, France, Germany, and **South Africa**.

The origins of the army go back to 1896, when the Central African Rifles (CAR) was established. It consisted of six companies and by 1898 had developed to two battalions. In that year the CAR was renamed the Central African Regiment. These troops saw service in Mauritius, Somalia (against Mohammad Hassan, "the Mad Mullah"), and the Gold Coast (in 1901) against the Ashanti as the British attempted to establish direct rule over those they considered uncooperative. In 1902 all troops in British colonies in East and Central Africa merged to form the **King's African Rifles** (KAR) and, in Nyasaland, they were commanded by Brigadier **William Manning**, who later became governor of the colony. The two battalions of the CAR now constituted the First and Second Battalions of the KAR.

In the early days of colonial authority in **Malawi**, when pacification was still in progress and the civil service was not fully developed, the military performed the duties normally reserved for civilians. Among other things, they collected taxes and were magistrates, health workers, labor recruiters, and administrators. Established in various parts of the colony, the military stations were fortified, hence their African name, *boma,* which is a Swahili word, the local equivalents being *linga* and *tchemba*. As civilian district administrative centers developed, they came to be referred to as *bomas,* a designation that continues to be used throughout Malawi. An estimated 300,000 Malawians served as porters or soldiers in World War I. Forced participation in the war was despised, and one attempt to resist the wartime recruitment was the **Chilembwe uprising** in 1915. Many soldiers lost their lives through battle and disease, causing considerable hardship to families at home. Besides this, Malawians, like most African peoples, were expected to contribute to the war effort by, among other things, supplying tons of food. During World War II, over 30,000 men distinguished themselves in campaigns in northern Kenya, the Somali-Ethiopia region, Madagascar, the Indian subcontinent, and Burma, where they fought the Japanese. When the **Federation** became a reality in 1953, the KAR in the three territories (the Rhodesias and **Nyasaland**) became part of the federal armed forces.

At independence in 1964, the First Battalion of the KAR became the First Battalion of the Malawi Rifles. The headquarters remained at the Cobbe barracks in **Zomba**, named after Lieutenant Colonel Alexander Cobbe VC, the commander who had led the CAR into Ashanti country. However, in 1967, the Third Battalion was formed, and its home was to be the newly constructed Moyale barracks in **Mzuzu**. It was christened **Moyale** in memory of the site on the Kenya-Ethiopian border where a contingent of the Nyasaland KAR excelled by outmaneuvering their Italian enemy. In the early 1970s, the headquarters of the Malawi army moved to the new Kamuzu barracks in **Lilongwe**, which also became the home of the Second Battalion; Cobbe barracks continued to be the base of the First Battalion.

In the colonial period, an indigenous person could not expect to become a commissioned officer. This changed after the 1961 elections, when Malawians began to be sent abroad for training, mostly in the United Kingdom. Later some were trained in Kenya. In 1978 a new military institution, the Kamuzu Military College, opened in **Salima**, primarily to train soldiers of all ranks. Officers continued to be sent to military schools in countries such as the United Kingdom, the United States, and France for advanced and more technical training. Less than 10 percent of the national budget is spent on the military, and an estimated 561,000 males (aged 15–49) are considered fit for military service. Currently Malawi has three well-commanded, disciplined, and well-equipped battalions. Helicopters and transport aircraft have been added to the armed forces. There are also patrol boats on **Lake Malawi**, and a small army air wing is based at the **Zomba** airport.

Until the early 1970s, the British, as part of technical assistance, provided the leadership of the Malawian army in the person of the commander. They also attached commissioned and noncommissioned officers to the Malawian army to help with basic training. However, in 1972, Brigadier **Graciano Matewere** was promoted to the rank of major general and became the first local general officer commanding the Malawi army. Eight years later, he was replaced by General **Melvin Khanga**, a Sandhurst-trained officer, considered to be a very competent soldier and administrator. Since his retirement in 1992, the army has had a number of commanders, including Generals Yohane, Chigawa, Kelvin Simwaka, and Joseph Chimbayo. Yohane was forced to resign because his fellow officers felt he was incompetent; Chigawa was murdered by bandits in the Dedza area on the Zomba-Lilongwe road; Simwaka, originally appointed partly because he was the choice of other officers, was retired and assigned to an embassy abroad.

On the whole the Malawi army has kept out of politics, although during **Operation Bwezani** (November 1993), they seemed to indicate that they would be playing a more active role in the political destiny of the country. The army has also been involved in minor incidents including one on January 15, 1998, when some soldiers ransacked the offices of the *Daily Times* in **Blantyre** because of a story that they did not like. The paper took the case to court, but it was settled out of court when the army commander apologized, saying that the action of the soldiers had not been sanctioned by the command.

Surprisingly, the Malawi army has come to play a role in mediating international disputes. In 1987 it joined frontline forces in trying to contain the actions of the guerrilla movement **RENAMO** in **Mozambique**. The Malawi army was assigned the responsibility of guarding the Nacala-Malawi rail line in northern Mozambique. Companies of the army patrolled that region for three years. In more recent times the army has been part of the United Nations peacekeeping forces in Rwanda and in Eastern Europe. Malawi has confirmed its commitment to this aspect of international relations by offering its armed personnel to be part of a trained force which can be called upon to perform such duties anywhere in Africa. Malawi soldiers are involved in the Crisis Response Initiative (ACRI), a U.S.-sponsored program aimed at training African soldiers for peacekeeping, humanitarian, and similar emergencies. In the second part of 1999, 72 Malawi soldiers were part of the **Organization of African Unity's** Military Observer Force to the Democratic Republic of the Congo and, early in 2000, the air wing of the Malawi Army played a leading role in the rescue operations following the flood disaster that befell Mozambique. *See* TRANSPORTATION.

In late 1999 the Malawi army, for the first time in its history, started recruiting **women** into its ranks and, prior to this, had organized a workshop to sensitize officers on gender matters.

ASIAN CONVENTION. An umbrella political organization of the mainly **Indian** and Pakistani communities in **Nyasaland**, led by **Abdul Sattar**

Sacranie, a prominent **Blantyre**-based lawyer. Sacranie cooperated with the **Malawi Congress Party** (MCP) and, partly because of this, the convention tended to side with the African organization in the various constitutional talks leading to decolonization.

ASIANS. Most Asians in Malawi trace their origins to the Gujarat region of western India and Pakistan. Initially, they went to the Lake Malawi area in the service of the British colonial government, mainly as surgeons, noncommissioned military officers, and operators in the new railway system. Some of them returned home at the end of their contracts while other remained to become independent businessmen. They were joined by relations and friends, and soon the rural and urban retail trade was dominated by people from the Indian subcontinent. Today they are professionals, small traders, craftsmen, and commercial middlemen. *See also* TRANSPORTATION.

In 1970 the government ordered Asians to sell their stores in rural areas to Africans; the order restricted Asian traders to towns. Although the 1970 order did not limit the freedom of Asian residents and citizens to travel within the country, they had to reside and work in one of the four urban areas: **Lilongwe, Zomba, Mzuzu, Blantyre**. Within some of these urban centers, strict rules governing where Asians could own property resulted in limitations on where they could reside. Asian residents, whether Malawian citizens or not, were also compelled to transfer ownership of trucking businesses to Malawians of African origins. Asians remained free to expand into other areas of business, and industrial licenses for new Asian industries were routinely granted.

However, many Asians chose to leave the country, mostly for the United Kingdom (UK). Those who remained began to feel more pressure with the 1986 Immigration Act, which called on foreign residents to choose among the following options within two years: to emigrate from Malawi, to register as citizens of Malawi, a country that does not allow dual citizenship, or to apply for a permanent resident permit. It is estimated that by the early 1990s fewer than 13,000 Asians were still living in Malawi. After the 1994 **elections**, the situation changed in that the new government reversed the 1970 order. Asians were now permitted to return to the rural areas to live and engage in business.

A notable number of Asians had actively supported the move to multiparty politics and some of them, such as Krishna Achutan, became significant players in the **United Democratic Front** (UDF) party.

Asians have contributed much to Malawi culture, including vocabulary which has come to be assumed to be indigenous to the **Lake Malawi** region. Since initially the colonial **army** was manned by Indians, certain Indians words came to be popularized and were eventually adopted by Malawian languages. Among such words are *basi* (enough), *chai* (tea), *debe* (tin), *galimoto* (motorcar) *rupiya* (shilling), and *tchuti* (holiday); their Hindustan derivatives are *bas, chae, dubbi, gharri, rupee,* and *chuti.*

ASKARI. Of Swahili origins, in **Malawi** the term refers to soldiers. Its usage can be traced to the establishment of the first modern military force by Sir **Harry Johnston**. *See also* ARMY.

ASSOLARI, BISHOP ALESSANDRO. Catholic bishop of the **Mangochi** diocese. Assolari was born in Italy in 1928 and was a priest in Madagascar for six years before going to Malawi in 1961. Eight years later, he was appointed the first vicar apostolic prefect of Mangochi, the area mainly identified with Islam. In 1973 he became bishop of the new diocese of Mangochi. Assolari was a signatory of the **Catholic bishops' pastoral letter** of March 1992 that hastened political reform in Malawi.

ATONGA TRIBAL COUNCIL. Formed in 1932 by the district commissioner of **Nkhata Bay** with a membership of 32, this council consisted of all chiefs in the district and in effect collectively assumed the role of an unofficial paramount chief. The government took this unusual step ostensibly because it was a means of solving problems arising out of disagreements among chiefs as to who was senior. Initially the council chairman, elected by the chiefs, held office for a year. But later the period was shortened by half, apparently to avoid the emergence of particularly powerful individuals. Among matters discussed at council meetings were tax collection, immigrant labor, administration of justice, and improvement of **education** and **health**. The government was not keen for the Western-educated **Tonga** to join the council for fear of upsetting the status quo. Thus in 1934 when the chiefs voted to include people other than chiefs, the district commissioner vetoed the decision. This changed later as some commoners were coopted into the council. In February 1948 the government abrogated the council.

AUNEAU, BISHOP LOUIS. Second Catholic bishop of the Shire diocese. Louis Auneau was born in France in 1876, was ordained a priest in the Montfort order in 1900, and seven years later was posted to the Shire area of Malawi. He served at **Nzama** and Utale, and in 1910 he succeeded **Auguste Prezeau** as bishop of Shire. Louis Auneau is closely associated with the expansion of the **Catholic Church** in the southern region of **Malawi** and in parts of **Mozambique**: many primary schools were opened during his tenure as bishop; Zomba Secondary School and seminaries at Nankhunda and Likulezi were established under his general guidance; he started the Utale leprosarium; and he created two local religious orders of the Catholic Church, the Society of African Lay Brothers and the Diocesan Society of African Sisters. When Auneau retired in 1949, the Pope made him Assistant at the Papal Throne and bestowed on him the title of Roman Count. Bishop Auneau received other honors. The French government made him Order of the Legion of Honor, and the British conferred him with the Order of the British Empire (OBE). He died in 1959.

AURORA. Mission journal of the **Livingstonia Mission** at **Khondowe**. It was edited by one of the missionaries and printed at the mission. It described developments at Khondowe and all the major and satellite stations of Livingstonia. It also included contributions and commentaries on political developments as well as articles of an anthropological and historical nature. The series of publication is a major source of the history of early colonial **Malawi**.

– B –

BAKKER, JACOB. Missionary sent by the Sabbath Evangelizing and Industrial Association in the **United States** to assist **Joseph Booth** in his Seventh Day Baptist work in the **Lake Nyasa** area. Jacob Bakker, then 26 years old, arrived in the **Shire Highlands** in early 1901. A printer by training, Bakker did not fit in with Booth's plans, which required an educator and an accountant, and before long tension arose between the two men. Shortage of finances, health problems affecting Booth and his wife, and Bakker's lack of preparation for his work at the mission contributed to the tension. In July that year, the Booths departed for South Africa and the United States, leaving Bakker in charge of all the operations in the country. Bakker showed less enthusiasm for some of Booth's projects, such as the **African Cooperative Society**, and was to close other projects, including several schools. Politically more conservative than his predecessor, Bakker did not receive the same support and loyalty from African assistants that they had given to Booth. While Booth was in the United States later that year, arrangements were made to sell the

Plainfield Industrial Mission to the Seventh-Day Adventist Church, to which Booth had now become affiliated. Bakker returned to the United States in late 1902.

BALAKA. Rising commercial center in **Malawi** located on the **Zomba-Lilongwe** road and the **Blantyre-Salima** rail line. Until 1998 Balaka was a subadministrative *boma* within **Machinga** District; it has now become the substantive headquarters of the new Balaka District.

BANDA, ALEKE KADONOMPHANI. Prominent politician in the period leading to independence and in postcolonial **Malawi**. Aleke Banda was born on September 19, 1939, at Kwekwe, **Zimbabwe** (then **Southern Rhodesia**), where his father, a **Tonga** from **Nkhata Bay** District in **Nyasaland**, worked at Moss Mines. Banda went to Inyati School of the London Missionary Society in Bulawayo and there distinguished himself as a first-class student, a prefect, and an editor of the school magazine. He became a prominent leader in the Southern Rhodesia African Students Association (banned in 1959) and at 15 was elected secretary of the Kwe Kwe branch of the **Nyasaland African Congress** (NAC). Using his good writing skills, he published nationalist articles opposing the **Federation of Rhodesia and Nyasaland** and colonialism in general. When the state of emergency was declared in Southern Rhodesia in March 1959, Banda was arrested on his school premises and detained at the Khami prison, where some Nyasaland-based politicians had earlier been taken. Within a short time, he was deported to Nyasaland. There he worked for the London and Blantyre Supply Company while continuing with his anticolonial activities. He began to edit a trade union paper, *Mtendere pa Nchito,* and when **Orton Chirwa** founded the **Malawi Congress Party** (MCP) on September 31, 1959, Banda became its full time secretary-general. He also became, with **Thandika Mkandawire**, founding editor of the party newspaper, the *Malawi News,* which he continued to edit until 1966.

A tireless and enthusiastic party worker, Banda (no relation to **Hastings Banda**) was a member of the MCP delegation at the Nyasaland constitutional talks in London in July 1960. Later that year, he was part of the party's delegation at the **Lancaster House Conference**, which reviewed the future of the Federation. When **Dunduzu Chisiza** died in 1962, Banda once again became secretary-general of the Malawi Congress Party. In 1966 he was appointed minister of development and planning, and in the next two years he served as minister of economic affairs and minister of finance, respectively. Later, in a 1972 cabinet reshuffle, he took over the Ministry of Trade, Industry, and Tourism. A year later, President Hastings Banda dismissed him from the cabinet, ostensibly for a breach of party discipline, and for the next three years Aleke Banda lived in his village, becoming a notable farmer. After a well-publicized apology to President Banda, he was appointed managing director of **Press Holdings,** but within five years he lost this position and was placed under detention at **Mikuyu,** where he remained until 1991.

Upon his release, Banda joined the groups agitating for the democratization of Malawi, becoming a founder and vice president of the **United Democratic Front** (UDF). In the 1994 **elections** he stood for a Nkhata Bay constituency and, although he lost, he was appointed minister of finance; in 1997, he was transferred to the Ministry of Agriculture. In the 1999 general elections Banda stood as a UDF candidate for Nkhata Bay South but lost to Sam Kandodo Banda of **Alliance for Democracy** (AFORD). In spite of this result, he continued to be the first vice president of the UDF and was reappointed minister of agriculture and irrigation in the new cabinet; in a cabinet reshuffle later, Banda became minister of health and population. A prominent businessman, Banda's family owns the *Nation*, which was established in the early 1990s as a prodemocracy organ and remains one of the influential papers in the country.

BANDA, DR. HASTINGS KAMUZU. Malawi's former Life President. Banda was born Kamnkhwala Banda at Mphonongo in Chief Chilawamatambe's area in modern **Kasungu** District in about 1896. Since his mother, Akupinganyama, and his father, Mphonongo, wanted him to go to a good school, Kamnkhwala left his village school near **Mtunthama,** the site of present-day **Kamuzu Academy,** for his maternal grandparents' home at Chiwengo. This enabled him to attend the school at Chikondwa, where the Chayamba Secondary School stands today. In 1908 he moved to Chilanga mission station, where two years later Dr. **George Prentice** of the Free Church of Scotland baptized him as Akim Kamnkhwala Mtunthama Banda. He added two other names, Hastings and Walter, the latter of which he later dropped. Banda continued his schooling at Chilanga Primary School, whose teachers included his uncle, **Hanock Msokera Phiri.** In 1914 Banda passed Standard Three.

Three years later Banda set out for **South Africa,** apparently with a view to enrolling at **Lovedale,** the famous Scottish Presbyterian school. For a brief period he worked at Hartley, **Southern Rhodesia,** where he met his uncle who had gone ahead. The two proceeded further south, working at a Natal colliery before reaching Johannesburg. There Banda probably made friends with **Clements Kadalie** and learned of Garveyism. Although he changed his plans to go to Lovedale, Banda did not lose sight of his ambition to improve his education, and to this end he completed Standard Eight. He also became a member of the **African Methodist Episcopal Church** (AME), which agreed to underwrite his education in the **United States**.

Banda began his studies at the AME Church's Wilberforce Institute, Ohio, where he completed his diploma in only three years. Next he entered the University of Indiana, pursuing an early interest in medicine. He remained there for two years and then transferred to the University of Chicago, majoring in history and politics. After he received a bachelor's degree (1931), Banda entered Meharry Medical College in Nashville, Tennessee. In May 1937 he received his doctorate in medicine and decided to go to Scotland to attain qualifications to enable him to practice in the British empire, his plans being to return home as a medical missionary. Returning to **Nyasaland** became a long-term goal after the Church of Scotland and the government refused him positions in the colony. Instead, he established a practice in Liverpool in 1941. As a conscientious objector, he spent the remaining war years in Tyneside working at a mission for colored seamen and subsequently at the Preston Hospital, North Shields, near Newcastle.

After World War II, Dr. Banda established a practice in the London suburb of Kilburn and became more politically active, joining the Labour Party and the Fabian Bureau. He enjoyed the exchange of ideas with other African expatriates and future leaders such as **Kwame Nkrumah** and Jomo Kenyatta. Certainly at this juncture, Banda had the funds to return home but chose to stay in London. He generously supported the education of about 40 needy African students while maintaining a practice of several thousand patients. He remained in regular touch with Malawi, and, beginning with its founding, Banda encouraged, advised, and gave financial support to the **Nyasaland African Congress** (NAC). He also gave financial aid to a cooperative farm in Kasungu by purchasing land and equipment. This Kasungu agricultural scheme (1950) later served as a model for similar African-run developments in Malawi.

As the movement for the **Federation of Rhodesia and Nyasaland** advanced, Banda responded with a militancy not before exhibited by this rather conservative man. He campaigned against the Federation through the Fabian Bureau and sympathetic members of the British Parliament. Banda and the NAC opposed the Federation relentlessly, as both were vociferous in noting African objections to such plans. Despite this opposition, the decision was made to form a closer union, and in 1953 the Federation of Rhodesia and Nyasaland became operative. When the Federation became a reality, Banda felt betrayed by London. He also felt that he was responsible for the failure of the Kasungu farm project back at home. At this point in his life, he chose to leave London for the Gold Coast (later Ghana), where Nkrumah invited him to accept an administrative post in the government that had resulted from recent constitutional changes. However, Banda chose a more reclusive life in Kumasi, the Ashanti capital, where he lived with Mrs. **Margaret French**, his companion since the end of the war. Until 1957 he practiced medicine and ignored events at home. During this same period, the NAC floundered badly before being revitalized by **Henry Chipembere** and **Kanyama Chiume**. In 1956 both became members of the **Legislative Council** (LEGCO), where they exerted pressure on the government to dissolve the Federation.

A new militancy began in the NAC, and in 1957 Dr. Banda was informed of those developments. That same year, **Thamar Dillon Banda** (no relation) visited Dr. Banda in Kumasi and urged him to return home to head the NAC. Chipembere followed up by writing to Banda, emphasizing the need for a charismatic type leader who was qualified for the task. The time seemed propitious to Banda: the Federation news grew grim with talk of membership in the Commonwealth, and in Kumasi charges (later proven false and dropped) were made against Banda preventing his practice of medicine. Banda welcomed the invitation to return home and departed from Ghana, leaving Mrs. French there; he briefly stopped in London where he met old friends, made speeches, and prepared for his journey in July 1958.

Banda arrived in **Blantyre** prepared to wage a long struggle or, if his people did not want him, to return to London. However, on July 6, 1958, several thousand Malawians greeted him at Chileka airport, treating him like their savior from colonialism. In August the NAC elected Banda as their president, and he chose a cabinet consisting of Chipembere (Treasury), Chiume (Publicity), **Dunduzu Chisiza** (Secretary), and **Rose Chibambo** (Women's League). Banda then began a campaign to strengthen the NAC. In the next two months, he visited nearly every district, lecturing against the "stupid Federation," advocating immediate decolonization, and attacking tribalism and *thangata*. Everywhere he spoke of the virtues of unity, loyalty, obedience, and discipline. By the end of the year, Malawians were united as never before and were growing impatient with an inflexible protectorate government. Relations between the European settlers and the NAC worsened as the former dismissed the constitutional demand for African majorities in the Executive Council and LEGCO as absurd proposals.

In January–February 1959 the NAC began a campaign of nonviolence and noncooperation in which the detested agricultural regulations (malimidwe) were ignored. Banda opposed the use of violence as a political weapon but did not exclude the possibility if it ended the despised Federation. Fearful of the increased number of Congress meetings and speeches, the government reinforced its police staff with Southern Rhodesian troops and, on March 3, declared a state of emergency. Banda was aroused from sleep in his Limbe home, taken to Chileka airport in his nightclothes, and flown to Gweru prison in **Southern Rhodesia (Zimbabwe)**. In Gweru, Banda, with Chipembere and the Chisiza brothers, planned Malawi's political and economic future. During 13 months in detention, Banda also wrote his autobiography, which to date has not been published. In April 1960 Banda was flown home, but he did not stay long before embarking on short speaking engagements in the United Kingdom and the United States. *See also* ARMITAGE, ROBERT; OPERATION SUNRISE.

At home again, he concentrated on the **Lancaster House Conference** in July–August. At this constitutional meeting Banda, **Orton Chirwa**, Chiume, and **Aleke Banda** represented the **Malawi Congress Party** (MCP) which, during Banda's period in jail, had become the successor political organization to the NAC. **Michael Blackwood** represented the United Federal Party of European supporters, and **Nophas Kwenje**, **James Ralph Chinyama**, and Thamar Dillon Banda stood for a more moderate African position. Dr. Banda took an immediate hard line and repeated the demand for African majority rule, self-government, and the dissolution of the Federation. By the end of the conference, both sides had agreed to a dual-roll franchise, LEGCO having 28 elected members, and an Executive Council of 10 members, all of whom would have ministerial status. The new constitution was presented by Banda as a vital document leading to independence. However, moderates such as Kwenje were blamed for the failure to secure a universal franchise.

Shortly after the **Monckton** Report indicated that secession from the Federation could be permitted, Dr. Banda attended the Federal Review conference in London in December 1960. Also attending the conference and maintaining a hard line against the Federation were Joshua Nkomo of the National Democratic Party (NDP) of Southern Rhodesia and **Kenneth Kaunda** of the United National Independence Party (UNIP) of **Northern Rhodesia**. The conference accomplished little, but when Banda returned home he announced that the Federation was dead. He spent the next months preparing for the August 1961 **elections**. His campaign to enroll voters and ensure their support for the MCP was immensely successful. His appearances and speeches were very popular, and his control in and over the MCP was growing more complete. The election results were nothing less than spectacular, for Dr. Banda and his MCP swept the lower-roll seats (20) and obtained two higher-roll seats. The governor, **Glyn Jones**, appointed Dr. Banda minister of natural resources and local government. In this new capacity, Banda directed his energies to eliminating the abusive and detested thangata and *malimidwe*. From then (1961) on, Dr. Banda concentrated on the agricultural development of Malawi, with some notable results.

The interim period before the dissolution of the Federation in 1963 witnessed the gradual assumption of political power by Dr. Banda and his associates. Governor Jones had confidence in the ministers' abilities and was impressed by their eagerness to get on with the problems of government. The final preparations for self-government were formalized at Marlborough House, London, in November 1962; these negotiations resulted in the establishment of a cabinet and a legislature. The only point that remained nonnegotiable was Banda's determination to secede from the Federation. Finally, in December 1962, the right of Nyasaland to withdraw from the federal government was formally announced, although months before that it had been conceded by the British government. It would take a year to dismantle the Federation.

In February 1963 Kamuzu Banda was formally made prime minister, a role he had held, practically speaking, for over a year. Several months later he and Governor Jones negotiated the last of the constitutional changes made at Marlborough House. Accordingly, elections were held in April of the following year in which 50 MCP nominees were elected unopposed. Banda selected his cabinet shortly thereafter: Chipembere (Education), **Yatuta Chisiza** (Home Affairs), **Colin Cameron** (Works), **Willie Chokani** (Labor), and **John Msonthi** (Transportation). At independence on July 6, 1964, Chiume became minister of information and external affairs, and **John Tembo** became minister of finance. Dr. Banda assumed the portfolios of Trade, Natural Resources, Social Development, and Health.

In the decades following independence, Banda assumed even greater personal power and enjoyed wide popularity. Ambitious economic projects and government reorganization also characterized his administration, which had the paternalism of Frederick the Great of Prussia, the 18th-century enlightened despot. The Kasungu-born doctor reversed decades of British neglect and indifference with the result that Malawi's earliest loans were oversubscribed by foreign investors delighted with the positive economic climate and apparent political stability. Malawian entrepreneurs were encouraged to engage in commerce formerly run by **Asians**, and Banda sought some **Africanization** of large-scale industries such as railways. Banda also invested his party's money in Malawi, mainly in **Press Holdings Ltd**. The Cinderella protectorate, as Malawi was once dubbed, did emerge from the ashes but critics of his style of government often point out that economic development was skewed and was attained through authoritarian methods and greatly diminished political freedom.

The **Cabinet Crisis** was a catalyst for the reorganization of government and the further consolidation of Banda's personal rule. In September 1964 Banda dismissed several cabinet ministers, and three others resigned out of sympathy. He portrayed his former ministers as enemies of the state and expelled them from the MCP. At Banda's direction, Malawi virtually became a one-party state by mid-1965. In nearly every aspect of life in the country, the party complemented the state in political power; public criticism of the government was eschewed, and only private questions were tolerated by the Banda government.

The ministerial crisis also precipitated a revitalization of local or traditional institutions, long overlooked during the colonial period. Banda encouraged the return of traditional dancing and the use of one national language, ciChewa, which was also his mother tongue. His efforts to exert moral control over Malawian society included regulations on drunkenness, tight trousers, and short skirts. The traditional (local) court system was expanded, and Malawian jurisprudence was increasingly preferred over that inherited from the British, which Banda perceived as too permissive, allowing unacceptable numbers of criminals to escape because of clever lawyers or poorly presented evidence. The judiciary became less independent and more susceptible to political controls by Banda and the MCP. Extrajudicial measures, such as the Forfeiture Act (1966) permitting the government to seize property of "subversive" persons, became law. In 1971 presidential elections were not held, and the Malawi parliament declared Banda Life President, stipulating that on his death the functions of that office would be performed by a presidential council comprising two cabinet ministers and the secretary-general of the Malawi Congress Party.

Under Banda's leadership, Malawi's priorities were to expand agricultural production, especially the estate sector, to encourage industrial development, and to improve the nation's **transportation** system. Banda's economic influence was all-pervasive, mostly as a result of the economic statutory bodies, some of which he had inherited. Parastatals were created as a means for Malawi to control its economy and retain whatever expatriate resources were necessary to reach the proposed national goals. At independence, the nation lacked capital and an entrepreneurial class with management ability; the parastatal, or publicly owned holding company, sought to fill that vacuum, and Dr. Banda, by becoming general overseer of this corporate empire, extended his powers far beyond those provided by government. He allowed these organizations to function in the marketplace and used their resources for his own political purposes. Some of the most important of these statutory bodies were the **Malawi Development Corporation** (MDC), **Agricultural Development and Marketing Board** (ADMARC), **Air Malawi**, and the **Electricity Supply Commission of Malawi** (ESCOM); only the latter proved able to make a profit.

In addition to his office of president, Banda held as many as seven other ministries: Justice, Works, and Supplies, External Affairs, Agriculture, Women's Affairs, Home Affairs, and Defense; only in the last years of his rule did he relinquish some of them. He resided in Sanjika Palace in Blantyre and, when parliament was sitting, he would be at the State House in **Zomba**; he had other homes in **Lilongwe**, Kasungu, **Mzuzu**, **Karonga**, **Monkey Bay**, and the Lower Shire.

Entering the decade of the 1990s, the Life President fell victim to declining health, which reduced his public appearances, including his annual crop inspection tours. Even though the facade of a free government steadfastly met problems, Banda continued to insist that Malawians did not want change in their political system. In 1991 the president asked members of parliament to debate the need for a multiparty system; not surprisingly, the MPs, all members of the ruling party, supported a one-party government. Meanwhile pressure from within Malawi and from outside the country was mounting on Banda to initiate reforms leading to a full-fledged democratic system of government.

On March 8, 1992, the **Catholic bishops** of Malawi issued a pastoral letter detailing how the autocratic political system and the government's economic policies had led to suffering in the country. In the following month, **Tom Chakufwa Chihana**, secretary-general of the Southern Africa Trade Union Co-ordinating Council (SATUCC), announced that he would challenge the government by forming an alliance of groups opposed to the single-party system. Chihana's boldness and the pastoral letter encouraged people to openly defy the government and the MCP. University students protested, and workers went on strike demanding livable wages and better working conditions. In Blantyre, the strikers protested in the city center, and on May 7 the strike became violent. Looters struck, among other establishments, the main Peoples' Trading Center (PTC) shop, which was part of Banda's Press empire. On that same day, the **Malawi Young Pioneers** and the police, equipped with guns, intervened, resulting in the death of 40 people.

In the meantime, governments in Europe and North America, many of which had supported Banda during the Cold War, threatened to reduce and withhold aid unless he instituted reforms immediately. In a radio broadcast on July 5, he announced his willingness to embark on a process of sociopolitical changes, starting with forums at which all Malawians could engage in debate with government. This is how the **Presidential Committee on Dialogue** (PCD) and the **Public Affairs Committee** (PAC) came to be born. The first one was composed of cabinet ministers, and the latter consisted of the **Law Society of Malawi**, churches, and representatives of the business community. Three other developments took place later in 1992: the launching of the *Malawi Financial Post* as the first independent paper; the inauguration of two new political parties, the **Alliance for Democracy** (AFORD) in October and the **United Democratic Front** (UDF); and Banda's declaration on October 18 that a national referendum would take place on June 14, 1993, to enable Malawians to decide whether or not they wanted the one-party system to be replaced by a multiparty one.

Although very old and frail, Banda vigorously campaigned for the retention of his mode of rule. He and his party lost, however, when most areas of the country overwhelmingly voted for change. He disregarded calls for resignation but set in motion procedures for constitutional reforms leading to multiparty general elections. To create a good atmosphere and to enable everyone to participate in the new dispensation, exiles living abroad were to be allowed to return, and all political prisoners were to be freed. It was also agreed to have free elections on May 14, 1994, and two units, the **National Consultative Council** (NCC) and the National Executive Committee (NEC) of the MCP, were created to oversee the change to multiparty democracy. Meantime, Banda featured prominently in the campaign for the return to power of the MCP. Loyal party members used his name as a symbol of national unity and prosperity; he himself went on the campaign trail, which he had interrupted at the end of 1993 when he fell ill, was flown to the Garden City Clinic in Johannesburg, South Africa, and underwent brain surgery. After a period of convalescence, the infirm president returned to the campaign trail, but the end of his political life was near. Banda's party lost, forcing him to retire to Mudi House, which had been his government residence in Blantyre before 1975 when Sanjika Palace was completed. He remained head of the MCP but in 1996 withdrew from politics altogether, the presidency of the party going to **Gwanda Chakuamba**. With **Cecilia Tamanda Kadzmira** at his bedside, Banda died at the Garden City Clinic from cardiac complications and pneumonia on November 25, 1997. After lying in state in Blantyre and Lilongwe, Banda was given a national funeral on December 3 and was the first person to be buried at the Heroes' Acre in Lilongwe.

BANDA, JOHN R. First indigenous registrar of the **University of Malawi**. John Banda born in **Mzimba** District, went to **Blantyre** and Dedza Secondary Schools, and then proceeded to Makere University, Uganda, where in 1964 he was awarded a B.A. (Hons.). He worked as a government officer but after a short time joined the new university as administrative assistant. In the late 1960s Banda spent a year in Northern Ireland on attachment as a fellow of the Inter University Council. When the campus at Chichiri was christened **Chancellor College**, he became its registrar but soon moved to the central offices of the university as deputy university registrar. In 1971 he took over from Ivan Freeman as registrar of the University of Malawi, and in 1973 he and others were presiding when the university offices and Chancellor College were moved to **Zomba**.

In 1975 Banda was among the many professionals and academics who were imprisoned without trial during one of the bouts of **human rights** abuses in the country. Released two years later, he was employed by **Lonrho**. In 1979 he left for the University of Botswana, where he became senior assistant registrar; he occupied the same position at the University of Swaziland before he was appointed, in the late 1980s, registrar of the University of Bophuthatswana, later renamed the University of the North-West.

BANDA, KAPICHILA. Strongman of Dowa politics and a dedicated Dr. **Hastings Banda** loyalist. Kapichila Banda became MP in the 1970s and succeeded **Aaron Gadama** as the **Malawi Congress Party**'s (MCP) regional chairman and as minister for the Central Region. Banda had little Western education and was uncomfortable expressing himself in

English. He was considered the party's organizer par excellence, one who ensured his region's total loyalty to the fundamentals of the MCP. He is credited as the brain behind the rise and success of the Dowa Women League's singers, whose lyrics not only overpraised Banda and the party but also tended to advocate and celebrate violence directed at those in disagreement with the Life President. Banda died in 1988 of heart failure.

BANDA, MASANYA. Born in **Kasungu** District, Masanya Banda was one of the original broadcasters at the **Federal Broadcasting Corporation** (FBC) main station in Lusaka, where he and others such as Sylvester Masiye announced in ciNyanja. When the FBC opened a substation in **Blantyre**, later to be the **Malawi Broadcasting Corporation**'s (MBC) principal station, Banda moved to Blantyre. Considered as the most experienced broadcaster at the MBC, he headed the ciChewa section at the corporation; he retired in the 1980s.

BANDA, MTALIKA. Born in **Nkhata Bay** District, educated at **Bandawe** and the **Overtoun Institution, Khondowe**, Banda worked as a civil servant before becoming an activist in the **Nyasaland African Congress** (NAC). A confident and fiery speaker, he was secretary-general of the NAC for a brief time in the early 1950s. In 1959 he was detained and upon his release became an organizer of the **Malawi Congress Party** (MCP) at the district and regional levels. After the constitutional changes in 1961, Banda went to India to study cooperatives; he also became a member of parliament before being posted to a diplomatic office in the **United States**. He died in 1995.

BANDA, RICHARD. Chief justice of **Malawi** and first indigenous person to occupy this important position. Richard Banda spent his early childhood in **Northern Rhodesia**, where his parents worked from the 1930s to the 1950s. He returned to Malawi to attend primary school at **Ekwendeni** before going on to Dedza Secondary School. A keen sportsman and star player on the national soccer team, Banda worked in the civil service from 1960 to 1961, primarily as a sports administrator and coach. In 1961 he was one the first Malawians to attend the new Part 1 London Bar course at the Institute of Public Administration, Mpemba; he proceeded to London to complete his legal studies before being called to the bar at one of the Inns of Court.

Banda returned to Malawi as a barrister and worked in the Department of Justice, rising to the position of solicitor general. In the early 1970s he was appointed minister of justice and attorney general but soon fell out of favor with President **Hastings Banda**. After a few years of virtual confinement to his home area in **Nkhata Bay** District, he was appointed chief magistrate and was soon promoted to a High Court judge. Upon the retirement of Mr. Justice Skinner, Richard Banda became the chief justice of Malawi.

BANDA, THAMAR DILLON THOMAS. Born in 1910 in **Nkhata Bay** District, Banda went to **Bandawe** mission school and then to **Livingstonia**, where in 1930 he qualified as a teacher. For 10 years he taught at Bandawe and other schools in Nkhata Bay. In 1940 he went to **Southern Rhodesia**, where he worked as an accounts clerk. In 1946 Banda became a boarding master at Goromonzi Government School, and three years later he returned to **Nyasaland**. He worked briefly for the **Colonial Development Corporation** (CDC), which was establishing a major development scheme in the Nkhata Bay–**Mzuzu** area. In 1953 he was appointed clerk to the Council of Chiefs in Nkhata Bay, and from 1953 to 1956 he worked as an accounts clerk in the **African Lakes Corporation**'s establishment in the district. At the same time, he was active in politics, becoming chairman of the Chintheche branch of the **Nyasaland African Congress** (NAC) in 1952 and, two years later, Congress's organizing secretary for the Northern Region. In 1956 Banda was elected secretary-general of the NAC, and in the following year he became president-general of the nationalist movement. In that year, he and others drew up the Memorandum on Constitutional Changes, demanding, among other things, majority rule.

In the meantime, younger activists such as **Henry Chipembere** and **Kanyama Chiume** were growing increasingly unhappy with Banda's leadership, which they considered weak and ineffective. It is they who urged him to visit Dr. **Hastings Banda** (no relation) in Kumasi in March 1957 to try to convince him to return to Malawi to lead the nationalist struggle. However, even before Dr. Banda's return home, Banda was (in March 1958) suspended from the headship of the Congress. In May 1958 he formed his own political organization, the **Congress Liberation Party**, which, although joined by other older politicians, **Dunstan Chijozi**, **Nophas Kwenje**, and **James Ralph Chinyama**, did not have much support in the country. The Congress Liberation Party contested in but lost the 1961 general **elections**, marking the end of its short life; it was also the end of the political career of T. D. T. Banda.

BANDAWE. Located on the lakeshore in the southern part of **Nkhata Bay District**, it became the site in 1881 of a Free Church of Scotland mission and later a school. This was a successor to the first memorial mission, **Livingstonia**, which the church had initially established in 1875 at **Cape Maclear**. Although the main Livingstonia mission moved to **Khondowe** in 1894, Bandawe remained a major religious and educational center, its graduates occupying influential positions in **Nyasaland** and other parts of **Southern Africa**. Its numerous alumni include **Clements Kadalie**, **Eliot Kamwana Chirwa**, **Orton Ching'oli Chirwa**, **Wellington Manoah Chirwa**, and **Thamar Dillon Banda**.

BANDAWE, LEWIS MATAKA. Born in 1887 in **Mozambique**, Lewis Bandawe went to the **Shire Highlands** 12 years later and soon enrolled at the **Blantyre** mission school. In 1913 the mission employed him as teacher/evangelist and in the same year posted him to Mehaccani, Mozambique, to establish a mission station. When World War I broke out, he went to **Blantyre** for a brief period but soon returned to Mehaccani, where he remained until 1928. While in Mozambique, Bandawe wrote a **Lomwe** grammar book and translated the New Testament and Psalms into Lomwe. Upon his return to Malawi, he left the Blantyre Mission and joined the Judicial Department, where he rose to the position of senior clerk. In 1943 he founded the Alomwe Tribal Representative Association, which actively petitioned the British administration to purge its documents of the pejorative word "Anguru" and replace it with "Lomwe." Bandawe was one of the founders of the **Nyasaland African Congress** (NAC).

BANDAWE, SERGEANT MAJOR. A **Tonga** from the northern lakeshore. Bandawe was one of the first **Nyasaland** Africans to rise to the position of sergeant major in the new military force established by Sir **Harry Johnston**. He played an important part in the fight against the **Swahili-Arabs** in 1887–1889, personally capturing **Mlozi** and handing him to the authorities. *See also* ARAB-SWAHILI WAR.

BANKING. The history of modern banking in **Malawi** goes back to August 1894, when the **African Lakes Company** (ALC) began to provide the first banking facilities in **British Central Africa**, as Malawi was then called. However, dissatisfied with the services, European settlers invited the Standard Bank of South Africa to establish a local branch in the colony in 1901. By the beginning of the 1920s, it had branches in **Blantyre**, **Zomba**, and **Lilongwe**. Meantime, in 1918 the banking operations of the ALC were taken over by National Bank of South Africa, which in turn was replaced by Barclays Bank D.C.O. in 1929. The latter also had branches in Blantyre, Zomba, and Lilongwe. In 1971 Standard and Barclays amalgamated to form the National Bank of Malawi. The equities were held as follows: combined Standard and Barclays, 51 percent; **Press (Holdings) Ltd.**, 29 percent; **Agricultural Development and Marketing Corporation** (ADMARC), 20 percent. Further changes took place in 1977, when the Standard/Barclays shareholding was lowered to 20 percent while those of Press (Holdings) Ltd., and ADMARC were raised to 47.4 percent and 32.6 percent, respectively. At the same time Standard Bank and Barclays became service companies of the National Bank of Malawi. At the end of 1982, Standard Bank PLC bought Barclays' interests, and in October 1990 it assumed the name Standard Chartered Bank of Africa PLC, its shareholdings going up by 20 percent. As the service company, Standard Chartered furnished the National Bank with senior managers, including the chief executive officer and his deputy, advisers, and an assortment of technical experts. In June 1996 the service agreement elapsed, and later that year the Standard Chartered sold its shares to abiding shareholders on a pro rata arrangement.

The other major bank is the Commercial Bank of Malawi, established in April 1970, whose shareholders include local and foreign interests. The former consists of Press Holdings, ADMARC, and the **Malawi Development Corporation (MDC)**. By virtue of its majority shares, Press led the local block and dominated the appointment of the directors.

In post–**Hastings Banda** Malawi, international banks with no ties to the government have opened branches in the country, including the Merchant Bank and the Finance Bank. The Post Office Savings Bank has operated as a government-owned institution since colonial times and has been a major channel for mobilizing rural savings. The bulk of its resources are invested in government securities.

Another important financial institution is the Investment and Development Bank (INDEBANK), established in 1972, which has local and foreign shareholders (British, Dutch, German) and provides medium- and long-term credit to borrowers who want to invest in the economic development of Malawi.

The clearinghouse of the Malawian banking system is the Reserve Bank of Malawi, which was established in 1964 to act as banker and adviser to the Malawi government. The bank also issues legal tender and maintains external reserves to safeguard the international value of the currency. The Reserve Bank also acts as a depository in Malawi for the assets of the **International Monetary Fund** and **World Bank** Group. On a quarterly basis, it publishes the *Economic and Financial Review,* indicating trends in the economy. In 1971 **John Tembo** became the first Malawian governor of the bank and after 11 years was replaced by **Lyoond Chakakala Chaziya**. He was dismissed after four years, and his successor, Chimwemwe Hara, served for a shorter time. In 1989 President Hastings Banda appointed a West German, Hans Joachim Lesshaft, as the bank's chief administrator. He was replaced by his Malawian deputy, Francis Pelekamayo. When the **United Democratic Front** (UDF) formed the new government in 1994, President **Bakili Muluzi** chose Dr. Mathews Chikaonda as governor of the bank. After the 1999 general **elections**, Chikaonda became minister of finance, leaving the headship of the bank to Dr. Ellias Ngalande Banda who, like his predecessor, was formerly a university don.

BARRON, A. FRANCIS. A major European **tobacco** grower. Together with **Roy Wallace** and **Ignaco Conforzi**, Barron was a strong exponent of tenant farming. A. F. Barron emigrated to **Nyasaland** from Great Britain in 1913 and established a large estate at Makoka in **Zomba** District. In 1920 he started farming tobacco in the Central Region, where by the mid-1940s his holdings in three districts included six estates in **Lilongwe** totaling 9,752 acres; five estates in Dowa totaling 6,384 acres; and a 1,060-acre estate in **Kasungu**. His tobacco business consisted of three main parts. First, tobacco, mostly flue-cured, was grown on his estates by wage laborers. Second, flue-cured tobacco was produced by tenants on land that he provided and with seedlings and technical help that he also provided, on condition that it was sold to him. Third, fire-cured tobacco was grown by peasants on their own land but sold to European farmers. Within 15 years of commercial tobacco farming in the Central Region, Lilongwe and Dowa accounted for over half of the crop produced in the colony.

BARROW, MALCOLM PALLISER. Born in Surrey, England, in 1900, Barrow went to Malvern College and then to Clare College, Cambridge, before emigrating to **Nyasaland** in 1927. He became a **tobacco** planter in **Zomba** and later moved to Naming'omba in **Thyolo** District, where he developed major **tea, tung,** and tobacco estates. In 1940 he became a member of the Nyasaland **Legislative Council (LEGCO)** and a year later was appointed to the Executive Council, a position he held until 1953. In that year he became a member of the new federal parliament and was appointed minister of commerce and industry; two years later he was also assigned the Power portfolio. When **Roy Welensky** became prime minister of the **Federation of Rhodesia and Nyasaland**, he made Sir Malcolm deputy prime minister. Knighted in 1953 and one of the most powerful Europeans in the Federation, Malcolm Barrow also had major farming interests in Gadami, **Southern Rhodesia**. He died in Salisbury in 1973, a few months after his wife.

BEER HALLS. From the early 1940s, British policy reflected an acceptance of the African as a permanent urban dweller, and this meant, among other things, building long-lasting facilities to cater for residents of the new emerging towns. With financing provided by the **Colonial Development and Welfare Act**, dwelling houses for Africans were constructed. But so too were welfare and beer halls in the hope that Africans would spend their time and money there instead of going to bars and drinking houses, most of which were considered disreputable. It has been suggested that this policy was a means of social control used by colonial governments that were anxious to mold the new African townsman to fit their conception of a colonial dependent. In **Nyasaland**, social welfare and beer halls were built in **Blantyre/Limbe**, **Zomba**, **Lilongwe**, **Mzuzu**, and the larger district headquarters such as **Mzimba**.

BEIRA. Mozambican port. It was the principal port through which Malawi's overseas exports and imports passed before the rail connection between Nacala and **Malawi** was constructed in the 1970s. *See also* TRANSPORTATION.

BEMBA. Inhabitants of the region south of Lakes Mweru and Banguelu in present-day **Zambia**. The Bemba social structure is matrilineal and divided into chiefdoms. Their traditional paramount ruler assumes the title Chitimukulu. The Bemba are known as great hunters, and they successfully repelled the **Ngoni** attempt to settle in their area. From the end of the 19th century on, their country witnessed much Christian missionary activity, including that of the Free Church of Scotland and the **White Fathers**. The area also became a center of African nationalism; President **Kenneth Kaunda** and his first vice president, Simon Kapwepwe, were brought up in Bembaland. *See also* KAUNDA, DAVID.

BEMBEKE. Located on the western side of the Dedza mountain, this major Catholic center in a **Chewa/Ngoni** area was originally a substation of **Mua** and was used mainly as a base where priests could escape from the hot weather of the lakeshore. In 1910 it attained full station status. A school and training college were later established.

BENINGOMA. The word *beni* is derived from the English word "band," and *ngoma* refers to the drum and team dances that imitate a military brass band. Of all the variations of Beni, the Mganda dance of **Malawi** is most important. Whereas *beni* is still associated with the **Yao** peoples, *mganda* (or *malipenga*) remains popular with the **Ngoni**, the **Tumbuka**-speaking peoples, **Ngonde**, Lambya-**Nyiha**, **Ndali-Sukwa**, **Tonga**, and the **Chewa**. Aspects of *mganda/malipenga* resemble the parade of soldiers, and it is performed only by men.

Originating in the 1890s among Swahili Muslims imitating the Royal Navy regiment, these dance performances began in **Malawi** at the end of World War I. Resentful of their forced participation in the war, returning porters and soldiers introduced the military-style dances into their society. A mockery of British ceremony and discipline, the *mganda* reproduced the military drill, the brass band sound, and the officer hierarchy. Today the dance is still performed in most parts of Malawi. *See also* ARMY.

BINGHAM, MAJOR HUMPHREY F. First registrar/commissioner of cooperative societies in **Malawi**. Bingham was born in England and saw action in World War I. He worked in East Africa before transferring to **Nyasaland**. His work in the provincial and district administration included serving as district commissioner in the West Nyasa (**Nkhata Bay**) and **Blantyre** Districts. In 1938 he was assigned to start the Department of Co-operatives, which did not really come into existence until after he returned from the war. Bingham retired to England in 1955.

BIRTHRATE. In 1997 **Malawi**'s birthrate was estimated to be 40.79 births per 1,000, and the death rate was 25.08 per 1,000; the total fertility rate was 5.77 children born per woman. The infant mortality rate was 138.9 deaths per 1,000 live births. Life expectancy increased from 38 years (1960) to 42 years (1975) and then 48 years (1987) but has fallen to the present rate of 35.26 for the total population, 36.68 for females. This decline can largely be attributed to the **AIDS** epidemic. In 1997 the total population of Malawi was estimated to be 9,609,081, with a growth rate of 1.57 percent.

The infant mortality rate (per 1,000 live births) was 178, up from 150 in 1989; the under-five mortality rate was approximately 26 percent. Only 45 percent of births were attended by health personnel (U.S. = 99, Canada = 99, U.K. = 100), and 20 percent were identified as low birthweight babies (U.S. = 7, Canada = 6, U.K. = 7). The annual population growth rate for Malawi grew from 2.9 (1960–1988) percent to a projected 3.3 (1988–2000) percent. Comparable figures declined for the **United States** (1.1 to 0.7), Canada (1.3 to 0.7), and the United Kingdom (0.3 to 0.1). An estimated 7 percent are using contraceptives (U.S. = 68, Canada = 73, U.K. = 83). To improve this further, the government has developed an expanded primary care program that emphasizes family planning, **child spacing**, and child survival activities. *See also* HEALTH. The population in 1960 was 3.5 million; by the late 1970s it had grown to 5.5 million. In 1990 the population was over 8 million, with 5.3 million under the age of 16. In 1997 it was estimated that the population had risen to 9,609,081, and the breakdown was as follows: 0–14 years = 46 percent (male 2,210,871; female 2,190,564); 15–64 years = 51 percent (male 2,430,178; female 2,250,608); 65 years and over = 3 percent (male 109,010; female 147,850). With the rate of population growth outstripping real economic growth, the standard of living becomes more depressed, resources more strained, and the shortage of land more apparent. The presence of a million Mozambican refugees in Malawi between the mid-1980s and 1994 exacerbated an economy already in crisis. The population density doubled between 1966 and 1988: 43 persons per square kilometer in 1966 to 59 in 1977 and 85–90 in 1990. Less than 50 percent of the total land is arable and usable by the 86 percent rural population.

BISA. In precolonial times, these matrilineal people of northeastern **Zambia** were famous for long-distance commerce covering the area between the region east of the Luangwa River and the **Lake Malawi** area and beyond. In the 18th and 19th centuries they were particularly famous as traders of ivory, which they exported via the Indian ocean. Their main partners were the **Yao**, with whom they developed a joking relationship.

BISMARCK, JOSEPH. Born at Quilimane, **Mozambique**, around 1859, Bismarck was part of the second **Livingstonia Mission** expedition. In 1880 he was in the initial group of Africans sent by the **Blantyre Mission** of the Church of Scotland to study at **Lovedale**. Upon his return in 1884, he taught at the mission's schools. He made **Malawi** his home, and he became one of the first African church deacons of the Blantyre Mission. A colleague of Dr. **David Clement Scott**, Bismarck made a living mainly as a planter of **tobacco** and **coffee**, cultivating over 150 acres. A major opponent of *thangata*, Bismarck was very critical of this system when he presented evidence to the commission investigating the **Chilembwe uprising** of 1915.

BLACK MAN'S CHURCH OF GOD WHICH IS IN TONGALAND
(Mpingo wa Afipa wa Africa). *See* MWASE, YESAYA ZERENJI.

BLACKWOOD, MICHAEL HILL. Born in 1917 in Lancashire, England, Blackwood went to Ormskirk Grammar School and went on to
study law at Liverpool University. He qualified as a solicitor in 1939, and
after war service he joined a law firm in **Blantyre, Nyasaland**. Blackwood was one of the first members of the Nyasaland Law Society and
became active in European settler politics. He was mayor of Blantyre
from 1951 to 1952, and two years later he was elected to the **Legislative
Council** (LEGCO) on the settler ticket. He became deputy leader in
Nyasaland of the **United Federal Party** and in this capacity was one of
the leading advocates of the merits of the **Central African Federation**,
which the majority of African peoples detested. He attended the constitutional talks in London in the early 1960s, opposing transfer of power
to Africans and speaking on behalf of Federal interests. Regarded as the
most powerful European settler after Sir **Malcolm Barrow**, Blackwood
won the 1961 elections on the federal ticket, and after **Malawi** became a
republic in 1966, he assumed leadership of the nominated non-African
members of parliament. In 1971 he left Malawi to retire in England.

BLAKE, ROBERT. Ordained minister of the **Dutch Reformed Church
of South Africa**. Blake opened Dutch Reformed mission stations in 1894
in the **Ngoni** areas of **Msakambewa** and Kafanikhale, and at Chimbazi
near **Kongwe**, which was ruled by Msyamboza, a **Chewa**. At the latter
station, Blake and his wife established a school that in the 20th century
was named after him and developed into a major secondary school, producing some of the leaders of postcolonial Malawi. In 1897 Blake translated the Bible into ciChewa under the title *Mbiri Yakale*.

BLANTYRE. Malawi's largest city and commercial center. Blantyre has
an estimated population of 500,000 inhabitants (1966 = 109,000; 1977 =
228,000; 1990 = 332,000) and is the administrative headquarters of the
Southern Region. Originally home to mostly **Mang'anja** people, the city
was named after **David Livingstone**'s Scottish birthplace and was chosen as the site of a Church of Scotland mission in 1876. Two years later,
a Scottish firm, the **African Lakes Company** (ALC), set up headquarters at Blantyre; soon other companies followed, giving Blantyre an early
commercial start.

Blantyre was declared a town in 1894 and formed a chamber of commerce and a town council. The **Shire Highlands Railway** reached Blan-

tyre from Chiromo in 1908 amid much cheering by Europeans, who needed the railway for their commercial enterprises. Blantyre elected its first African mayor in 1967. It is also a major **education** center, boasting many primary and secondary schools, colleges of education, and the Polytechnic and the Medical School of the **University of Malawi**. Blantyre is also the home of the Queen Elizabeth Hospital, the country's major referral medical center. Its industrial activity continues to grow, although the development and expansion of **Lilongwe** has resulted in some industries going to the new capital city.

Blantyre is also the site of the spectacular Sanjika Palace, the principal residence of the president of Malawi. Although it has never been the political capital of Malawi, all government ministries have always maintained prominent suboffices in this city.

BLANTYRE AND EAST AFRICA COMPANY (BEA). One of the major European settler companies that were given large tracts of land in the **Shire Highlands** in the era of **certificate of claims** in the 1890s. With 107,000 acres under the company's control, its managers became particularly powerful in settler and colonial circles. Among its better-known general managers were **R. S. Hynde** and William Tait-Bowie, both of whom served on the **Legislative Council** (LEGCO).

BLANTYRE MISSION. In 1876 **Henry Henderson** and his guide/ interpreter, **Tom Bokwito**, began to build the Blantyre Mission of the Church of Scotland at a site given to him by **Kapeni**, the local **Yao** chief. In 1878 he was joined by other Scottish missionaries, including Rev. **Duff MacDonald**, who became its leader. The mission started badly, mainly because it adopted a civil administration policy that led to excessive behavior on the part of some of the missionaries. In 1881 a Foreign Mission Committee investigation led to the dismissal of MacDonald and other missionaries. A different approach was adopted by the new head, Rev. Dr. **David Clement Scott**, and his assistant, Rev. **Alexander Hetherwick**. Scott preferred working with African evangelists, and in 1893 three of his African colleagues, **Joseph Bismarck**, Rondau Kaferanjila, and **Donald Malota**, became deacons. Scott found little support for his "radical" views among European settlers. In 1898 he was forced to resign his post for health reasons, and Hetherwick assumed leadership.

In 1909 the Blantyre Mission opened the **Henry Henderson Institute**, which became an important education facility, training Africans in the same areas as the **Overtoun Institution**. In 1924 the Blantyre and Livingstonia Presbyteries agreed to form the **Church of Central Africa**

Presbyterian (CCAP), a move originally suggested by Dr. **Robert Laws** and later revived by Hetherwick. In 1926 the Dutch Reformed Presbytery joined the CCAP. The formation of the CCAP led to the appointment of African clergymen to various committees; for example, in 1933, Rev. **Harry Matecheta** became the first African moderator of the Blantyre Synod Presbytery. In the postwar period, expatriate missionaries, including Rev. **Andrew Doig**, Rev. **Tom Colvin**, and Rev. Andrew Ross, sided with African aspirations, in many ways continuing the tension between the colonial administration and the mission going back to the era of Sir **Harry Johnston** and Rev. **David C. Scott**. Within the mission station itself the transfer of power from foreign missionaries to the indigenous clergy and laity progressed, culminating in the 1962 appointment of Rev. **Jonathan Sangaya** as general secretary of the Blantyre Synod.

BLEDISLOE COMMISSION. Headed by Viscount Charles Bledisloe and appointed in 1938 to inquire into possibilities of the amalgamation of the Rhodesias and **Nyasaland**. The Bledisloe Commission published its report in the following year, concluding that the union was not possible at that time. Although it did not preclude a time when such arrangements might be possible, the commission argued that African policies in the three colonies were different, and, furthermore, that each territory had a distinct constitutional status. In addition, the three territories were unequal in financial resources and economic development. For the first time, however, the factor of African opposition to any closer union was noted. In practical terms, the responsibility of the Colonial Office for African interests was ignored in favor of a government dominated by white Rhodesians. Since the London government had failed to develop **Malawi** to any degree, such an arrangement assured the exploitation of Malawi's labor force by amalgamation supporters such as **Godfrey Huggins** (Lord Malvern) and Sir **Roy Welensky**. After World War II these protagonists convinced London that a **Federation of Rhodesia and Nyasaland** was the answer.

BOCARRO, GASPAR. Portuguese national. In 1616 Bocarro traveled from Tete in present-day **Mozambique** to Kilwa on the East African coast, recording and commenting on his observations. He was the first person to leave written evidence on the **Mang'anja/Nyanja**, the Shire, and other areas of southern **Malawi**.

BOKWITO, TOM. After a party of **David Livingstone** and Bishop **Charles Mackenzie** freed Tom Bokwito from slave captives somewhere in the **Shire Highlands**, they took him to **Magomero** Mission. Later he went to **South Africa** and studied at the **Lovedale** College. In 1875–1876 Bokwito accompanied the first **Livingstonia Mission** party, led by Dr. **James Stewart**, principal of Lovedale. He was assigned to **Henry Henderson**, and the two looked for a site for the **Blantyre Mission**, starting with **Zomba**, then Magomero, and finally **Kapeni**. The new Blantyre Mission marked the beginning of the modern city of **Blantyre**. Bokwito was familiar with this area and its peoples, and he became a guide and interpreter to Henderson and other missionaries who followed. He also distinguished himself as an evangelist and a teacher.

BOMA. Administrative station established by the British to govern the protectorate; usually it was the office of the Resident or **district commissioner** (DC), as it was later called. The first administrative headquarters in **Blantyre** had a thorn hedge surrounding it that was called *boma,* meaning stockade. *See also* ARMY.

BOOTH, EMILY. Born 1884 (–?), daughter of **Joseph Booth** and author of *This Africa Was Mine*. At the age of nine she accompanied her father to **Malawi**. **John Chilembwe** became her nurse as well as her father's cook and interpreter. She married E. B. Langworthy.

BOOTH, JOSEPH. Born in England in 1851, Booth went to **Malawi** in 1892 and was responsible for developing the **Zambezi Industrial Mission** at **Mitsidi**, near **Blantyre** and the **Nyasa Industrial Mission**. Within a year, he had encouraged enough Nyasaland Africans to plant **coffee** that there were over 30,000 acres of land under cultivation. Booth insisted that Africa was for the Africans and that they needed only the economic and political chance to achieve proper development. This pro-African view made Booth an outstanding person in times when other European missionaries generally held opposing viewpoints.

In 1897 he left for England and the **United States**, taking **John Chilembwe** with him. When he returned to Malawi in 1899, he set up a new mission station south of Blantyre and called attention to the several grievances Africans had about the protectorate. His petition suggested that the colonial administration revert to Malawian control in two decades and that higher **education** be provided to no less than 5 percent of the African populace. Commissioner **Alfred Sharpe** declared the proposals absurd and dangerous and threatened to deport Booth. Booth ignored government efforts to have him refrain from his "seditious remarks." A religious disagreement caused Booth to leave for **South**

Africa in 1902, but five years later he was barred from returning to Malawi. Although he corresponded with Chilembwe, it is unlikely that he knew of any plans for an uprising; still, the British suspected him of encouraging the rebellion. He died in England in 1932.

BOUNDARIES. In addition to its 26 district and three regional boundaries, **Malawi** shares political boundaries with **Zambia, Mozambique,** and **Tanzania**. Its relatively unrestricted western border with Zambia follows the irregular ridge line of plateaus and extends for about 500 miles. The Mozambique border is essentially the one that imperial governments of Britain and Portugal agreed to in the late 19th century. With the exception of **Nsanje** and **Chiromo,** most of this eastern and southern border is sparsely settled. In 1954 a British-Portuguese agreement led to a change in the demarcation of **Lake Malawi** from the eastern shore to a line running through the middle of the lake. However, the islands of **Likoma** and Chisumulu, which lie east of this line, were retained by Malawi. The northeastern border with Tanzania is mostly water and was in dispute in the mid-1960s. It is a line that Great Britain and Germany drew in the last century and was formalized in a League of Nations mandate after World War I.

BOURGET, PIERRE. French leader of the original party of Montfort missionaries who arrived in the **Lake Malawi** region in June 1901. Pierre Bourget was born in 1852 and ordained as a priest in 1878. For over 20 years he taught at seminaries in France and the Netherlands. In 1901 he offered to open the first Montfort mission station in the **Shire Highlands.** On his arrival in **Blantyre,** he consulted with some European Catholics working in the area and decided that he and his colleagues, Father **Auguste Prezeau** and Father **Anton Winnen,** a Dutchman, would establish the mission station at **Nzama,** part of the Maseko **Ngoni** country on the **Mozambique-Malawi** border.

BOWRING, SIR CHARLES CALVERT. Governor of **Nyasaland** from 1924 to 1929. Bowring was born in England in 1872 and educated at Clifton College before joining the Colonial Audit Bureau of the British Exchequer in 1890. He served in the Far East and in 1895 was posted to British Central Africa Protectorate (later Nyasaland). Four years later, he was transferred to Kenya and became auditor of the Kenya government and the Uganda Railway. In 1891 he was promoted to the position of treasurer of the Kenya colonial administration, and in 1911 he became chief secretary. In 1924 he returned to Nyasaland as governor.

In Nyasaland, Bowring became a friend to **Livingstonia** and to Rev. **Alexander Hetherwick** of the **Blantyre Mission**, but he was also an advocate of European planter views, urging estate owners to form the **Convention of Associations**, which was to give a major political voice to the several European farm groups in the colony. In 1929 he retired from the colonial administration; he died in 1945. *See also* MISSIONS.

BOYCE, DR. SORABJI. First medical doctor and one of the initial civil servants assembled by **Sir Harry Johnston** in 1891. Although recruited at **Zanzibar**, Boyce was from India and had qualified at Bombay. On December 15, 1891, barely six months after his arrival, he was on the gunboat *Domira* as part of an expedition against the **Yao** under **Makanjila**. When he went ashore to try to recover the body of Captain **Cecil Montgomery Maguire**, he too was killed.

BRANCH, THOMAS. Seventh-Day Adventist (SDA) missionary and first African American to work in **British Central Africa** (BCA). Thomas H. Branch was born in the 1860s and was employed in Pueblo, Colorado, just before leaving for Africa. Branch was assigned the task of heading **Plainfield Industrial Mission** when the Seventh-Day Adventist (SDA) Church bought it after **Joseph Booth** severed ties with the Seventh Day Baptists in 1901. In 1902 Branch arrived in the **Shire Highlands** accompanied by his wife, Henrietta, a nurse; daughter, Mabel, a teacher; and two sons of 11 and 7. Booth and the Branch family lived at Plainfield and the two men shared the responsibility of managing the mission center, with the former concentrating on administration, the latter on pastoral and educational work. By the end of the year, there was much tension between them, resolved only in 1903 when Booth left the colony for Cape Town, **South Africa**.

Branch and his family learned the local language and established good relations with the African peoples among whom they worked. Throughout the Branches' stay in BCA, the SDA Church in the **United States** had been concerned about the colonial government's unease with the presence of African Americans in the country, and especially their regular contact with indigenous peoples. The government's worry was based on the fear that **Ethiopianism** would be embraced by Africans through the agency of African Americans who, it was felt, strongly believed that Africa had to be ruled by Africans. The Bambanta rebellion in South Africa seemed to confirm this fear. Largely in response to such government attitudes, the SDA Church recalled Thomas Branch, in spite of his general conservatism, and replaced him with Joel C. Rogers, a white

American who had worked in South Africa, whose temperament and approach to Africans was more in tune with the Europeans in BCA.

BRITISH CENTRAL AFRICA. The British imperial authority's designation of Malawi from 1891 to 1907, when it became **Nyasaland**. It was known as Nyasaland until decolonization on July 6, 1964, when it became **Malawi**.

BRITISH CENTRAL AFRICAN CHAMBER OF AGRICULTURE AND COMMERCE. Formed in 1895 when the **Shire Planters' Association** and the Nyasaland Planters Association united. The chamber of commerce became the most effective mouthpiece of the European settler community in the colony, representing their interests on matters such as land and labor. Disagreements between farmers and businessmen led to the establishment in 1925 of the **Nyasaland Planters' Association**. In 1929 the various European associations formed an umbrella organization, the **Convention of Associations**.

BRITISH CENTRAL AFRICA COMPANY (BCA). Second largest (after the **British South Africa Company**) landholder in early colonial **Nyasaland**. It was owned by **Eugene Sharrer** and held about 373,000 acres granted to it under the **certificate of claim** scheme. Sir **Harry Johnston**, former commissioner of the colony and the mind behind the certificates of claim, became one of the company's directors. Like the **Blantyre and East Africa Company** and the **A. L. Bruce Estates**, its management strongly supported labor tenancy.

BRITISH CENTRAL AFRICA GAZETTE. Weekly publication founded by **Harry Johnston** to present the view of the colonial administration. It attempted to counteract the mission magazines, mainly the **Blantyre Mission**'s *Life and Work*, which tended to side with the position of Africans, many of whom faced land problems. *See also* NEWSPAPERS.

BRITISH CHRISTIAN UNION. Pacifist organization that aimed at promoting spirituality, peace, understanding, and good race relations among different peoples of the world. It was formed by **Joseph Booth** in Cape Town in 1912. John Dube, a founding father of the African National Congress of **South Africa**, as well as a regular visitor to Booth's house, was a member of the British Christian Union, which established active branches in the United Kingdom.

BRITISH COMMISSIONERS AND GOVERNORS OF BRITISH CENTRAL AFRICA/NYASALAND (1891–1964). Although the area immediately south and west of Lake Nyasa (**Lake Malawi**) became a British protectorate in 1891 under the name **British Central Africa**, there had been a low-key formal British presence in the region during the preceding ten years. The title of the official British representative was "Her Majesty's Consul to the territories of the Kings and Chiefs in the districts adjacent to Nyassa." The consul had no territorial jurisdiction. Those who served in this capacity were Captain C. E. Foot (1883–1984), Lawrence C. Goodrich (acting consul, 1884–1985), A. G. S. Hawes (1885–1889), **John Buchanan** (1889), and **Harry Hamilton Johnston** (1889–1891). When the status of the Lake Malawi area changed in 1891, the title and responsibilities of the representative of the British government also changed, assuming more definite administrative duties.

Commissioners/consuls-general included Sir Harry Hamilton Johnston (1891–1896) and Sir **Alfred Sharpe** (1996–1907). In 1907 British Central Africa became **Nyasaland**, and the commissioner and consul-general titles were changed to governor. Governors included Sir Alfred Sharpe (1907–1910), Brigadier Sir **William Henry Manning** (1911–1913), Sir **George Smith** (1913–1923), Sir **Charles Calvert Bowring** (1923-1929), Sir Thomas Shenton Whitelegge Thomas (1929–1932), Sir **Hubert Winthrop Young** (1932–1934), Sir **Harold Baxter Kittermaster** (1934–1939), Sir Henry Charles Donald Cleveland Mackenzie-Kennedy (1939–1942), Sir Edmund Charles Smith Richards (1942–1947), Sir **Geoffrey Francis Taylor Colby** (1948–1956), Sir **Robert Perceval Armitage** (1956–1961), and Sir **Glyn Smallwood Jones** (1961–1964). Sir Glyn Smallwood Jones served as governor-general from 1964 to 1966.

BRITISH COTTON GROWING ASSOCIATION (BCGA). A British organization formed in 1902 primarily to champion the production of **cotton** in the colonies in order to reduce reliance on imports from the **United States**. While remaining interested in purchasing African-produced cotton, it encouraged European settlement in the cotton-growing areas of the empire and even assisted such settlers with loans to make cotton farming easier for them. In many areas the association supplied most of the seeds, had the monopoly to buy the cotton, and therefore tended to control the prices; it also had a large share in the ginneries. In **Malawi** the association was particularly active in the Lower Shire region. At a time when cotton was the colony's top export, the BCGA had a powerful voice that the Nyasaland government could not always ignore.

BRITISH SOUTH AFRICA COMPANY (BSAC). The brainchild of diamond and mines multimillionaire **Cecil John Rhodes** (1853–1902). BSAC was formed and granted a royal charter in 1889. With a ruthless and fanatical zeal, Rhodes amassed his fortune and proceeded to use that awesome wealth as a power base in Central and **South Africa**. Rhodes had applied for a charter for the BSAC promising Her Majesty's Government that he could forestall a Portuguese presence in **Malawi** and could avoid quarrelsome ethnic problems while carrying out the responsibilities of government.

Shortly after the BSAC was formed, it acquired controlling stock of the **African Lakes Company** (ALC). In order to make good on promises to protect the mission and provide law and order, Rhodes paid **Sir Harry Johnston** £10,000 annually to administer the new region with the assistance of a police force recruited from India. Johnston also had the use of ALC steamers providing there was no interference with ALC trade. This was the arrangement from 1891 to 1895. By that time, **Lord Salisbury**, the British prime minister, wanted no further financial involvement in the **Lake Malawi** region.

In 1893 Rhodes's BSAC laid claim to one-fifth of Malawi's land. Nearly all of today's Northern Region (almost 3 million acres) was claimed as BSAC property until 1936, when it reverted to the protectorate government. However, until 1966, the company continued to retain the mineral rights for the region.

BROCKWAY, ARCHIBALD FENNER. (1888–1988) Left-wing member of the British Labour Party. An MP who was later elevated to the House of Lords, Brockway was one of the strongest supporters of decolonization. In parliament he spoke on behalf of nationalist causes and readily assisted politicians and political organizations in the colonies. During the state of emergency in **Nyasaland**, Lord Brockway vociferously spoke in defense of incarcerated politicians and the banned **Nyasaland African Congress** (NAC). He was also one of the people who advocated the appointment of the **Devlin Commission**.

BRUCE, ALEXANDER LIVINGSTONE. One of the influential European settlers of his time. Alexander Livingstone Bruce became owner of the **A. L. Bruce Estates** on the death of his father, **Alexander Low Bruce**, in 1893. He also became an unofficial member of the **Nyasaland Legislative Council** and tried to influence policy, especially that concerning labor on the estates. A hard-liner on labor tenancy, he consistently argued that commercial **agriculture** in the colony needed the system and that Africans who did not like the idea had to be evicted. **Magomero** estates, which he owned, was a major area of activity during the **Chilembwe uprising**. See also LIVINGSTONE, WILLIAM JERVIS.

BRUCE, ALEXANDER LOW. (1839–1893) A major holder of **certificates of claim** in the **Shire Highlands**, with holdings in **Zomba** (101,83 acres), **Blantyre** (27,858), and **Mulanje** (38,130 acres). When he died in 1893, his son, **Alexander Livingstone Bruce**, assumed ownership of the estates. Alexander Low Bruce was also a founder of the Imperial British East Africa Company, which controlled Kenya and Uganda in the 1880s and 1890s and had extensive economic interests in East Africa.

BRUCE ESTATES. See A. L. BRUCE ESTATES.

BUCHANAN, JOHN. One of the first laymen recruited by the Church of Scotland to work in the **Shire Highlands**. In 1880 he, **Duff Macdonald**, and **George Fenwick** were dismissed from the mission, after less than three years service, because the nature of civil administration that they had adopted resulted in indiscipline on the part of some missionaries. Buchanan, recruited as an agriculturalist, had actually been sent to work at a substation at **Zomba**, in the vicinity of the present-day **Church of Central Africa Presbyterian** (CCAP) school, and he remained there after he lost his job. Adjacent to the mission, especially along the Mlunguzi stream, he grew **coffee**, as he had done at **Blantyre**, and he is credited with introducing the crop into the country. On the lower side of the Mlunguzi, Buchanan grew **sugar**. In 1885 he brought coffee pulping machinery and a sugar mill for his Zomba operations from the United Kingdom. Buchanan also developed major land and business interests in Blantyre, becoming one of the most influential settlers in that town.

Between 1885 and 1891, Buchanan acted as British vice consul for the **Lake Malawi** region, and during the **British Central African** (BCA) administration, he was an unpaid vice consul, joining **Alfred Sharpe**, **Cecil Maguire**, and others in **Harry Johnston**'s team of administrators. As vice consul, Buchanan played a major role in the expansion and consolidation of British authority in that part of Africa.

Further up the slope on a site commanding good views including **Mount Mulanje**, he built a large and attractive two-story house that he used as a consulate. Johnston later turned it into the Residency and capital of the new British protectorate. On its grounds, Johnston established an impressive botanical garden. Since the 1980s it has been revived by the National Herbarium. The building, now protected under the National Monuments Act, is still much in use and is known as the Government Hostel.

BUNDA COLLEGE OF AGRICULTURE. This constituent college of the **University of Malawi** is located south of **Lilongwe** *boma*, near Bunda hill. It opened in 1966 and specializes in agricultural sciences to diploma and degree levels. *See also* EDUCATION.

BUTLER, ROBERT AUSTEN "RAB." Minister of home affairs in the United Kingdom. In March 1962 **Harold Macmillan** reassigned him to a new cabinet position specifically dealing with Central Africa, that is, the Rhodesias and **Nyasaland.** After visiting the region twice that year, he concluded that Nyasaland could leave the **Federation of Rhodesia and Nyasaland,** thereby effectively dismantling the controversial political union.

BWALO LA NYASALAND. Paper published in **Southern Rhodesia** in ciNyanja (ciMang'anja/ciChewa) by European settler interests. It was circulated in colonial **Malawi** with the sole purpose of advancing colonialism and the aims of the **Federation of Rhodesia and Nyasaland.**

BWANALI, EDWARD CHITSULU. Born in 1946 in **Blantyre** District and holding a diploma in public administration granted by the **University of Malawi,** Bwanali was **district commissioner** of **Mchinji** and then of Kasupe. In 1975 he became member of parliament (MP) for **Blantyre** North and minister of health. He also served as minister of transportation and communications, as well as Southern Regional chairman of the **Malawi Congress Party** (MCP). In 1989 he was dropped from President **Hastings Banda's** cabinet as minister of local government and MCP chairman. Subsequently, Bwanali "resigned" his parliamentary seat representing Blantyre North. In the early 1990s he reemerged as a force in the struggle for a new democratic dispensation. When the **United Democratic Front (UDF)** assumed power in 1994, he became minister of foreign affairs. He then moved to the Ministry of Health and finally to the Ministry of Water and Irrigation. Bwanali died on October 23, 1998.

BWANAUSI, AUGUSTINE. Born in 1930, Bwanausi was educated at **Blantyre** Secondary School, where he distinguished himself as a brilliant student. He went to Makerere College, Uganda, graduating with a bachelor of science degree. He returned to **Malawi** and became increasingly involved in nationalist politics while looking for a teaching job. In

1955 he completed a diploma in education at the University of Bristol, United Kingdom, and thereafter became a schoolmaster, teaching mathematics and sciences at Blantyre Secondary School. During the state of emergency in 1959, he was arrested and detained in **Southern Rhodesia**. Released in 1960, he returned to teaching but continued to play a major role in party politics.

In 1961 Bwanausi was elected to parliament as member for Blantyre and was appointed minister of internal affairs and development. Later he became minister of works before Dr. **Hastings Banda** dismissed him during the **Cabinet Crisis** in 1964. He went into exile in **Zambia**, returning to the teaching profession while also becoming a prominent member of **Henry Chipembere**'s Pan-African Democratic Party (PDP). In 1973 Bwanausi and two others were killed in a car accident on the Copper Belt while traveling to a PDP meeting in Ndola. With his death Malawi lost an intellectual and a leader.

BWANAUSI, HARRY. Leader of the United Democratic Movement (UDM). Harry Bwanausi, brother of **Augustine Bwanausi**, was educated at **Blantyre** Secondary School, Witwatersrand University, and the University of Natal, where he qualified as a medical doctor. On his return home, he worked in the government medical service but all the time was quietly active in nationalist politics. One of the handful of Malawian medical practitioners at independence in 1964, he was forced into exile after the **Cabinet Crisis** because he sided with the rebelling ministers. He spent the next 29 years in Lusaka, **Zambia**, where he practiced medicine, besides engaging in anti-Banda politics. He returned to **Malawi** just before the 1994 general **elections**, which he contested as leader of his party but lost. He was appointed chairman of the **University of Malawi** Council, a position he relinquished after just over two years.

BWEZANI, OPERATION. See OPERATION BWEZANI.

– C –

CABINET CRISIS (1964). Two months after **Malawi** attained independent status, differences between Dr. **Hastings Banda** and several cabinet ministers erupted into a serious and permanent break. There were important domestic and foreign issues separating the two. The ministers resented Banda's approval of the **Skinner Report** and wished to see it discarded. They also wanted Banda to adopt a more rapid **Africanization** policy in the civil service. The institution of a monetary charge (three pence) for hospital outpatients was loudly decried as well. In foreign affairs, Banda favored a policy of coexistence with Portugal, which was despised by ministers who wished to support the **Mozambique** liberation movement and thus minimize the political contact with Portugal.

Submerged beneath these frontal issues was a resentment of Banda's treatment of his ministers, whom he often referred to as "his boys." Ministers also felt that Banda trusted expatriates more than his cabinet. These grievances were stifled in favor of a united front, but Banda knew that differences existed. Apparently the ministers felt that compromise was possible with Banda, but he was insensitive to their feelings. Although the ministers remained personally loyal to Banda, he concluded that loyalty and acceptance of his policies were one and the same.

At an August 1964 cabinet meeting, several ministers challenged Banda's indecision on an aid offer from the People's Republic of **China**. Banda felt so threatened by these unprecedented "attacks," as he called them, that he offered to resign but was dissuaded by the governor, Sir **Glyn Jones**. The next day more amicable relations existed as Banda seemed willing to review points at issue: the Skinner Report, hospital charges, **foreign policy**. Soon Banda began believing rumors of a cabinet conspiracy, and he told the ministers that he had no more time for their grievances. The angered ministers wanted Banda to resign, but instead, on September 8, he dismissed three of them at an emergency cabinet meeting. **Augustine Bwanausi** (Housing and Development), **Orton Chirwa** (Justice), **Kanyama Chiume** (External Affairs), and **Rose Chibambo** (parliamentary secretary) were accused of disloyalty and of conspiring with a foreign power, China. Three other cabinet ministers resigned in solidarity with their colleagues: **Willie Chokani** (Labour), **Yatuta Chisiza** (Home Affairs), and, upon his return from a visit to **Canada**, **Henry Chipembere** (Education).

Reconciliation seemed possible as both sides voiced hope of finding a solution to the Cabinet Crisis. Expecting to gain constituent support for their demand that they be more involved in cabinet decisions, the ex-ministers returned to their districts. In their absence, Banda appointed new ministers to the cabinet, but he kept four positions vacant, stating he expected some former ministers to return. However, ministers such as Chipembere made less than temperate speeches in their home districts.

Enraged by their resoluteness and fearful of a broader plot against him, Banda expelled all the rebellious former ministers from the **Malawi Congress Party** (MCP) on September 16. In spite of this move, the ministers reaffirmed their loyalty to Banda, but he decided not to make any concessions or to allow Governor Jones to mediate the crisis.

By early October, it was becoming clear to the ex-ministers that their personal lives were in danger from party operatives. Five of them left Malawi for **Tanzania** and **Zambia**, and, under new security regulations adopted by Banda, Chipembere was restricted to his **Malindi** home. When Banda toured the Central and Northern Regions, he found support for his actions; only in the Southern Region were there minor disturbances in **Zomba** and **Fort Johnston** (**Mangochi**), primarily as a show of support for Chipembere. In February 1965 this localized support resulted in a rebellion in Fort Johnston District that was quickly ended by Banda's security forces. A less successful revolt occurred in September 1967 that was led by **Yatuta Chisiza**, who with a group of supporters tried to infiltrate Malawi through **Mwanza** District in the Southern Region. *See also* CHIPEMBERE, HENRY.

Soon after crushing the incident ruthlessly, Banda passed a series of security measures aimed at preventing a recurrence. Two years earlier, parliamentary amendments had made treason punishable by death and had allowed detention without trial of those persons deemed to violate the security of Malawi. The amendments also made it possible for MPs not representing the MCP to be dismissed; they further gave authority to the prime minister to appoint to ministerial positions persons outside parliament.

As a result of the 1964 Cabinet Crisis, Banda was able to strengthen his position as head of state and as leader of the MCP more quickly than might have been the case otherwise. Another consequence was the obvious loss of talented ministers and the unlikely possibility that members of the cabinet in the future would speak out against the president or his policies. The crisis had an ideological and generational basis, but it also had its ethnic implications and long-term effects. No ministers from the Central Region resigned, and during the following years the majority of people who were detained on suspicion of supporting or associating with the former ministers tended to be from the Northern and Southern Regions.

CAMERON, COLIN. A Scottish lawyer and sympathizer of the African cause in the fight for decolonization, Colin Cameron represented many African nationalists in trials following the declaration of the state of emergency in March 1959. In August 1961 he was elected to parliament on the higher roll and was appointed minister of works and transport. Although a firm supporter of Dr. **Hastings Banda**, he resigned his position as cabinet minister before the **Cabinet Crisis** primarily because Banda was planning to reintroduce a 1960 preventive detention act. For safety reasons he left **Malawi** for Scotland, where he continued to practice law.

CANADA. The founding member of the Commonwealth of Nations to which **Malawi**, as a former British colony, belongs. In the 1970s and 1980s Canada consistently provided aid to Malawi. The numerous projects financed with Canadian assistance include the Natural Resources College and **Malawi Institute of Management (MIM)**, both located in **Lilongwe** District, and the **Salima**-Lilongwe railroad extension. However, relations between Malawi and Canada predate the 1960s as a significant number of Catholic missionaries (priests and nuns) came from the province of Quebec.

CAPE MACLEAR. Located on the southwestern shores of **Lake Malawi**, Cape Maclear is one of the most beautiful spots on the lake. Most of Cape Maclear area falls within the Lake Malawi National Park, created in 1980 to protect the flora and fauna in the reservation, and the special marine life that is found in the bay area. With clear sands, Cape Maclear is easily the favorite destination of the majority of low-budget international backpacking visitors to Malawi who stay at the Steven's Rest House. Cape Maclear's fame dates back to 1876, when it became the site of the first **Livingstonia Mission**. Six years later, the mission moved to **Bandawe**, leaving Cape Maclear as an outstation. From 1949 to 1950, Cape Maclear was the main Malawi port for the Short Solent flying boats that the British Overseas Airways Corporation (today called British Airways) regularly operated between Southampton, England, and the Vaal Dam near Johannesburg, **South Africa**.

CAPRICORN AFRICAN SOCIETY. This society, which emerged in **Southern Rhodesia** and spread to **Nyasaland** and **Northern Rhodesia**, espoused multiracialism in the sense that it opposed separation of peoples on the basis of color while advocating a cultural bar. In 1956 the society held its meeting at a lake resort in **Salima**; delegates came from East and South Africa, including Alan Paton, famous for *Cry the Beloved Country*, among other books; Noni Jabavu, author of *Drawn in Colour* and daughter and granddaughter, respectively, of eminent South Africans John Tengo Jabavu and Professor D. D. T. Jabavu. Among the Nyasalanders who attended the Salima meeting was **Charles Matinga**, former president-general of the **Nyasaland African Congress** (NAC), who by that time had become a supporter of the **Federation of Rhodesia and Nyasaland**, which the Capricorn Africa Society hoped to sell to Africans in the three territories. From 1958 to 1963, when nationalism was at its height in Nyasaland, the term "capricorn" became a term of derision that was equated with duplicity.

CATHOLIC BISHOPS' PASTORAL LETTER. On March 8, 1992, a pastoral letter, *Living Our Faith*, issued by the seven Catholic bishops, was read in all their churches. It expressed major concern about the detrimental effects that lack of **human rights**, poverty, fear, and hunger, among other things, had on family life and social relations. While the government and the **Malawi Congress Party** (MCP) were very upset by this honesty, most Malawians were pleased and encouraged by the letter, which marked a turning point in the postcolonial history of the country. From that time on, the fervor for political reform was intensified, leading to the referendum and general **elections** of 1993 and 1994, respectively. The Catholic prelates had issued pastoral letters before, most of which were not taken notice of by the government because their messages were deemed innocuous. One such letter was *How to Build a Happy Nation*, issued in March 1961, just as Malawi was approaching its first major constitutional changes. In it the bishops dwelt on church–state relations and on the duties and rights of Christians in a nation-state and on the role of the Church in helping fulfill them. The letter had followed a period of tension between the Church and the Malawi Congress Party. Since 1994, the bishops have written other Lenten letters in which they again conveyed their disquiet, this time regarding continuing poverty, hunger, disease, and violent robberies. *See also* BANDA, DR. HASTINGS KAMUZU; KATSONGA, CHESTER; THEUNISSEN, BISHOP JEAN-BAPTIST.

CATHOLIC CHURCH. *See* CATHOLIC BISHOPS; MISSIONS.

CENTRAL AFRICAN AIRWAYS (CAA). The origins of the CAA can be traced to the Rhodesia and Nyasaland Airways Ltd. The latter was established in 1933 but was taken over by the Southern Rhodesia Air Services (SRAS) at the beginning of World War II and became a part of the war effort. In 1946 the CAA was born and assumed the assets of SRAS, becoming a joint enterprise of **Southern Rhodesia, Northern**

Rhodesia, and **Nyasaland**. With the creation of the **Federation of Rhodesia and Nyasaland** in 1963, the CAA became its airline. Ten years later, the Federation was disbanded, marking the beginning of the end of the CAA; in 1965, Malawi received 10 percent of its assets, the remaining shares going to **Zambia** and Southern Rhodesia. Two years later, it disbanded, leading to the formation of two national airlines, **Air Malawi** and Zambia Airways. *See also* TRANSPORTATION.

CENTRAL AFRICAN BROADCASTING SERVICES (CABS). Formed in 1941 in Lusaka, **Zambia**, as an entertainment and educational radio station for the emerging Westernized Africans in the Rhodesias and **Nyasaland**. The CABS broadcast in English, ciNyanya, ciBemba, ciTonga, ciLozi, ciShona, and Sindebele. The station became particularly popular after an affordable receiver, the "saucepan radio" (shaped like a saucepan), was introduced into the region in 1949. Programs included education-related ones; local plays, thereby giving rise and exposure to African playwrights; and most popular, *zimene mwatifunsa,* a request program, usually in the form of greetings to friends and relations in the wider Southern African region. Announcers and producers would regularly visit the three territories to record items for broadcast on the station and surveyed listener opinions regularly also.

It was through the CABS that most Africans received national and world news and became part of the world culture by listening to jazz and other popular music of the time. African musicians such as **Alick Nkhata**, **Enoch Evans**, and the **Paseli Brothers** became widely known mainly because of the CABS. Among the many popular African announcers was Sylvester Masiye, who belonged to the senior management team in the postcolonial broadcasting system in Zambia.

Until 1953 the CABS was little affected by racial views prevalent in the colonies. But when it was taken over by the federal government in 1954 and its name was changed to **Federal Broadcasting Corporation** (FBC), many Africans did not like the way it reported facts that they felt were distorted and propagandistic in nature. Michael Kittermaster, the director of broadcasting, resigned in protest against the direction the service was forced to take.

CENTRAL AFRICAN FEDERATION. *See* FEDERATION OF RHODESIA AND NYASALAND.

CENTRAL AFRICAN PLANTER. See NEWSPAPERS.

CENTRAL AFRICAN TIMES. See NEWSPAPERS.

CERTIFICATE OF CLAIM. An official document issued by the government to European settlers in **Nyasaland**, legally recognizing land that they had bought or taken possession of. During **Harry Johnston**'s tenure in **Malawi**, it was becoming increasingly obvious that land, especially in the **Shire Highlands**, would be a source of major problems. As more European settlers arrived in the country and bought land from traditional rulers, it became imperative for the government to regulate the transactions and confirm sales. Most of this land was sold on very generous terms, even though, as the government was to find out later, the chiefs had no right to sell this land, of which they were mere custodians.

CHAKUAMBA, GWANDANGULUBE. Born in **Nsanje** District in 1935, Chakuamba was educated at **Zomba** Catholic Secondary School and in Southern Rhodesia. He worked as secretary for the Port Herald (now Nsanje) branch of the **Nyasaland African Congress** (NAC) in the late 1950s and was briefly detained during the state of emergency. During the period leading to constitutional changes, he became particularly active in the **Malawi Congress Party**'s (MCP) Youth League. In 1961 he was elected to the **Legislative Council** (LEGCO) as a representative for Port Herald. During the **Cabinet Crisis** he remained a staunch supporter of Dr. **Hastings Banda**, who rewarded him with the position of minister of community and social development. In subsequent cabinet reshuffles, he was moved to local government, education, information and tourism, agriculture, youth and culture, and the Southern Region. For part of the 1960s and during the 1970s, Chakuamba was commander of the Young Pioneers, a position that made him one of the most powerful and feared people in the country. Not only did the Young Pioneer bases in all districts produce much food, the organization, regarded as the military wing of the MCP, had its own arsenal and intelligence gathering service, which was active as the **Special Branch** of the **police**. *See also* YOUTH.

In February 1980 Chakuamba was expelled from the MCP for "a gross breach of party discipline, illegal possession of firearms, uttering seditious words with the intent of raising discontent, and having copies of prohibited publications." Placed on trial in November 1980, the former chairman of the Central Committee and commander of Young Pioneers was found guilty and received a 22-year jail sentence.

When Chakuamba was released in 1992, he rejoined the MCP and became a campaigner, first for the retention of one-party rule and, after the referendum in May 1993, for the return to power of the MCP. He was elected vice president of the MCP and in 1997 became president of the party. This position was confirmed at a party convention held in **Mzuzu** in January 1999 when he defeated his deputy, **John Tembo**. Late in 1998 it was announced that in the general **elections** in the following year, the MCP would form an alliance with the **Alliance for Democracy** (AFORD) and that Chakuamba and **Chakufwa Chihana** of the latter party would stand as candidates for the offices of state president and vice president, respectively. Tembo disagreed with the decision but was overruled. In April and May 1999, the Electoral Commission went to the High Court of Malawi to issue an injunction to stop the two parties from working together in this manner. As it became obvious that the judges saw no legal impediments to such party cooperation, the commission withdrew the petition. Chakuamba and Chihana went on to campaign together, but when Chakuamba lost the elections to **Bakili Muluzi** of the **United Democratic Front** (UDF), he and his party went to court again to challenge the results, arguing that the governing party had rigged the process. *See also* ELECTIONS.

CHANCELLOR COLLEGE. Generally regarded as the main campus of the **University of Malawi**, this college opened in 1965 at the former Chichiri Secondary School in **Limbe**. It graduated its first students in 1969, and four years later it moved to new premises at Chirunga on the periphery of **Zomba** town. With about 1,600 students, Chancellor College offers undergraduate and graduate degrees in natural and social sciences, humanities, and education. It also has a law school and it issues diplomas in education and public administration, and certificates in library science.

CHANGALUME. Located 10 miles southwest of **Zomba** town, Changalume is the site of Malawi's main limestone mine and the factory that produces most of the cement used in **Malawi**.

CHATSIKA, LEWIS. Born in **Thyolo** District of Maseko **Ngoni** and **Lomwe** parentage. Chatsika went to **Blantyre** Secondary School and Goromonzi High School, **Southern Rhodesia**, before working as a civil servant in **Nyasaland**. After the general **elections** of 1961, the Institute of Public Administration at Mpemba began to prepare prospective advocates for Part 1 of the English bar examinations, and Chatsika was one of its first candidates. He proceeded to one of the Inns of Court in London, where he was called to the bar in 1965. Back in **Malawi**, he worked in the Legal Defense Department, and in 1968 he became the first Malawian director of public prosecutions. Two years later, he was appointed a judge of the High Court of Malawi, again, the first local person to occupy the position.

Regarded as one of Malawi's most brilliant and articulate lawyers and judges, Chatsika left the bench in 1980 to join the law faculty at the **University of Malawi**. Ten years later, he returned to the judiciary as a member of the Supreme Court of Malawi, and there he made many courageous decisions at a time when the country was going through unprecedented political changes. In 1994 he was appointed to head a commission of inquiry into the conditions of the civil service. Judge Chatsika died in 1997. *See also* CHATSIKA REPORT.

CHATSIKA REPORT. In 1994 and 1995 there were widespread civil service strikes, and the new **United Democratic Front** (UDF) government appointed a commission of inquiry led by Justice **Lewis Chatsika** to recommend solutions to the problems. The Chatsika Commission recommended sweeping changes aimed at improving the working conditions of civil servants; the latter included a major increase in salaries. Although salaries were indeed raised, workers felt that the Chatsika Report had not been followed to the letter.

CHAUTA. *See* CHIUTA.

CHAWINGA, CHIEF KATUMBI. From the 1940s to the early 1970s, he was the traditional ruler of the **Tumbuka**-speaking people of **Hewe**, northwestern **Rumphi** District. A committed modernizer, Chief Katumbi was determined to develop his area, and in the 1950s he made it available for an agricultural project sponsored by the **Colonial Development Corporation** (CDC). The scheme failed to materialize, but this did not discourage him from proposing various other projects to the colonial government. Courageous and articulate, Chief Katumbi was one of the traditional authorities who were always identified with anticolonial views, and he was an active member of the **Nyasaland Union**. In 1972 he and a few other chiefs supported the return of **Wellington Manoah Chirwa** to **Malawi**, and because of this he was deposed from his traditional position of chief.

CHAWINGA, DUNCAN "GOODNEWS." This soccer player and artist was famous for his cartoon, *njolinjo*, which appeared in the government newspaper *Msimbi* for most of the 1950s. Born in **Hewe**,

Rumphi District, and a member of the ruling family of the area, Duncan Chawinga was trained at **Livingstonia** before joining the Department of Information, where he retired as information officer.

CHAZIYA PHIRI, LYOOND CHAKAKALA. Born in **Lilongwe** in 1947, Chaziya was educated at Kanzimbi School and **Likuni** Boys Secondary School. He received his diploma in education from the **University of Malawi** and taught for some years. He was elected to parliament in 1977 and later was appointed minister of finance before becoming governor of the Reserve Bank of Malawi, a position he lost in 1987. Chaziya spent some time in political detention, and when the movement for multiparty democracy started in the early 1990s, he became an active member of what was to become the **United Democratic Front** (UDF). He returned to the **Malawi Congress Party** (MCP) for a brief period, but the UDF lured him back and he accepted a position in President **Bakili Muluzi's** cabinet, becoming minister of local government and sports. Chaziya died in 2000.

CHEEK, LANDON. Baptist pastor and one of the two African American missionaries to work at **John Chilembwe's Providence Industrial Mission** (PIM) headquarters at **Mbombwe**. Cheek was born in Canton, Mississippi, in 1871. He attended a black college in Jackson, Mississippi, before going on to study theology at Western College in the same state. Cheek had always been interested in mission work in Africa, and in 1899 he offered his services to the Baptist Convention, which was in the process of setting up operations in the **Lake Nyasa** area. With financial assistance from African American churches, Cheek sailed for Africa in January 1901, arriving in the **Shire Highlands** in May of the same year and proceeding to Mbombwe, where he immediately set out to help Chilembwe build a Christian center. Besides preaching and teaching, Cheek supervised construction work at Mbombwe as well as working on the mission's trial projects on **coffee, tea, rubber, cotton**, and pepper farming. He learned ciNyanja, and his relations with the local African peoples and local rulers such as Chiefs Kumtumanji and Malika were very cordial. Like other black Americans in the British colony, Cheek was regularly subjected to government surveillance because of fear that he would encourage anticolonial attitudes among the indigenous peoples. The government constantly worried that black Americans would help spread **Ethiopianism**, which would lead to dissent and disquiet in the colony. Cheek married Rachael, Chilembwe's niece, and by the time he returned to the United States in 1906, they had three children, one of whom, Ada, died in the Shire Highlands. Also returning with Cheek to the **United States** were the two sons of **Duncan Njilima**, **Frederick Njilima** and Matthew Njilima.

CHEWA. Inhabitants of most of the Central Region of **Malawi**, parts of the **Chipata** District of **Zambia**, and sections of Tete province of **Mozambique**. Their area constituted part of the core of the **Maravi** empire, with Kapiri-Ntiwa on the Dzalanyama Range as principal religious center. In 1967 Dr. **Hastings Banda** declared ciChewa, the language of the Chewa (which is basically the same as ciMang'anja/ciNyanja), as Malawi's national language. This was reversed by the **United Democratic Front** (UDF)–led government, which liberalized the language policy.

CHIBAMBO, MACKINLEY QABANISO YESAYA. The son of **Yesaya Mlonyeni Chibambo**, one of the first Africans to be ordained as a minister in the Free Church of Scotland. Chibambo was born in 1917 at **Ekwendeni** in **Mzimba** District. He went to school at Ekwendeni Mission and at **Livingstonia**, where he qualified as a bookkeeper. His first job was with the Nyasaland Tobacco Board, and in 1940 he entered the civil service as a clerk, rising to the position of head clerk, the highest an African could expect to attain. He served at different district headquarters, including the **district commissioner**'s office at **Fort Manning** (now Mchinji), before being transferred to **Lilongwe** in 1948. Having worked there before, Chibambo knew this provincial headquarters well, and soon he became involved in anticolonial politics, especially the mounting opposition to the **Federation of Rhodesia and Nyasaland**. In 1953 he was imprisoned for 15 months, and upon release in 1954 was placed under restriction at Port Herald (now **Nsanje**) at the southern tip of **Nyasaland**. He remained there until 1959, when, following the state of emergency in March that year, he was rearrested and taken to Khami in **Southern Rhodesia** with other detainees; later he went back to Kanjedza prison camp in **Limbe**.

Upon his release in September 1960, Chibambo was elected **Malawi Congress Party** (MCP) chairman for the Northern Region. In the following year he was elected MP for a **Mzimba** constituency, and in 1963 he became parliamentary secretary to the Ministry of Works and Housing. At independence, Chibambo was made minister for the Northern Region and later minister of works, development, housing, and health. In 1976 he ceased to be a government minister; later he worked as executive chairman of the Malawi Housing Corporation. He has since retired to Chibambo village near Ekwendeni. One of his sons, Ziliro, an activist in the prodemocracy movement of the early 1990s, became a **United Democratic Front** (UDF) cabinet minister and later served as ambassador to France and Mozambique.

CHIBAMBO, ROSE. Born Rose Ziba, in **Mzimba** District. She was a political activist in **Blantyre** in the 1950s. In 1958 she was a member of the **Nyasaland African Congress** (NAC) committee appointed by Dr. **Hastings Banda** to organize the Women's League, and she became leader of that wing of the NAC. In 1959 she was arrested and detained without trial, and in 1964 Chibambo was elected as MP for a Mzimba constituency and was appointed parliamentary secretary, a post she held until the **Cabinet Crisis** in September that year, when Dr. Banda suspended her and others from the **Malawi Congress Party** (MCP). She and her family, including her husband, Edwin Chibambo (son of **Yesaya Mlonyeni Chibambo** and brother of **Mackinley Chibambo**), took refuge in **Zambia**. When her husband died, she went to live in the **United States** but returned to **Malawi** after the demise of the Banda regime; she settled in **Mzuzu** and became a businesswoman.

CHIBAMBO, SAMUEL SONGELWAYO. Brother of **Yesaya Mlonyeni Chibambo**. Samuel was ordained a Presbyterian minister, along with **Charles Chinula** and **Peter Thole**, in October 1925.

CHIBAMBO, YESAYA MLONYENI. Born in 1887, Yesaya Chibambo attended mission schools at **Ekwendeni** and **Khondowe**. In 1920 he had the distinction of being the first mission alumnus to be awarded the honors schoolmaster's certificate. Known for his forthrightness, in 1921 he wrote to the powerful Mission Council pointing out the unfavorable working conditions for Africans employed by the **Livingstonia Mission**, the lack of respect accorded to them by their European counterparts, and their exclusion from the decision-making process of the establishment of which they were part. In 1924 he entered the theological college and was ordained four years later. When the Mbelwa Administrative Council began local commercial initiatives in the 1930s, Chibambo became secretary of a farm committee that managed two of the council's stock farms at Ekwendeni and Chitara.

A respected **Ngoni** historian and adviser to Ngoni chiefs, Chibambo wrote *Makani gha baNgoni* (The Story of the Ngoni) in 1932 and was a key informant and assistant of Margaret Read during her researches for, among others, *The Ngoni of Nyasaland* and *The Children of My Fathers*.

Earlier he had submitted written evidence to the commission investigating the **Chilembwe uprising**. In 1942 he published *My Ngoni of Nyasaland*. Chibambo died in 1944 and is buried at Ekwendeni.

CHIBUKU. A popular **sorghum/maize**-based beer brewed by a nationally organized company and sold in paper cartons in most parts of **Malawi**.

CHIDAWATI, SIMON. A prominent politician and member of the **Nyasaland African Congress**'s youth wing. Chidawati fell out of favor with Dr. **Hastings Banda** because he sided with the rebelling ministers during the **Cabinet Crisis** of 1964. Banda declared him one of the foremost enemies of the state and announced that he wanted him dead or alive. Chidawati escaped into exile.

CHIDYAWONGA. The Maseko **Ngoni** in the central and southern reaches of **Malawi** have their origin in **Mputa** and Chidyawonga, the sons of the Swazi chief, Ngwana. In a separate group from **Zwangendaba**, Mputa crossed the Zambezi in the 1830s and settled for a while in the grasslands of Domwe mountain. Fearing that the followers of Zwangendaba were too close, Mputa moved east and north of **Lake Malawi**, reaching the area of Songea (**Tanzania**). This area, like the Dedza area he left in Malawi, was cattle country. A segment of northern Ngoni who had separated and were led by **Zulu Gama** joined up with Mputa. After the deaths of Zulu Gama and Mputa, the Ngoni were driven out. Led by Mputa's brother, Chidyawonga, the Maseko Ngoni returned to the Domwe mountain, where the **Maravi** inhabitants were integrated into the new Ngoni state. Chidyawonga, an effective military strategist, consolidated and dominated east and west of Dedza and **Ntcheu**. After Chidyawonga's death, his nephew Chikusi became paramount chief, not Chidyawonga's son, Chifisi. Henceforth the Maseko were divided in two lines.

CHIDZANJA-NKHOMA, RICHARD BESTON. Appointed minister at large in July 1977. Chidzanja Nkhoma was born at Mtimuni in **Lilongwe** District in May 1921. He qualified as a vernacular grade teacher in the Dutch Reformed mission system and taught for some time before going to work in Southern Rhodesia and South Africa. On his return home, he vigorously campaigned against the **Federation of Rhodesia and Nyasaland** and throughout the 1950s became a leading politician and businessman. His hotel became the gathering point of most activists visiting Lilongwe. A local councillor, Chidzanja Nkhoma was one of the **Nyasaland African Congress** (NAC) officials who in 1957 sent a petition to

Dr. **Hastings Banda** in Ghana imploring him to return to **Nyasaland** to provide needed leadership in the fight for decolonization.

Following the declaration of the state of emergency in March 1959, Chidzanja-Nkhoma was detained but a year later was released. Soon afterward, he was appointed Central Region chairman of the **Malawi Congress Party** (MCP). After the first general **elections** in 1961, he became MP for Lilongwe, and following the **Cabinet Crisis** in 1964, he entered Banda's cabinet as minister of local government and minister for the Central Region. In the late 1960s Chidzanja-Nkhoma held diplomatic posts, and upon rejoining Banda's cabinet in 1969, he occupied a number of offices, including those of minister for **Organization of African Unity** (OAU) affairs and minister at large. Regarded as one the best party organizers at the grassroots level, he died of natural causes in April 1978.

CHIEFS UNION. Full name, Nyasaland Chiefs Union. Formed in 1952, the union was meant to be the mouthpiece of all the traditional rulers in the country, especially at a time when they were under pressure from the colonial government to support the introduction of the **Federation of Rhodesia and Nyasaland**. Activist chiefs such as **Philip Gomani**, **Lazalo Jere** (M'mbelwa II), **Kuntaja**, Kumsamala of **Balaka**, and Nsomba worked toward the formation of the organization, which was chaired by **Chief Mwase** of **Kasungu**. Through this organization chiefs, as a body, spoke with the **Nyasaland African Congress** (NAC).

CHIHANA, TOM CHAKUFWA. President of the **Alliance for Democracy** (AFORD) since its formation in 1992. Chihana was born at Lubagha in the Henga valley, **Rumphi** District. After secondary school he worked, becoming a leading trade unionist. In the early 1960s he was leader of the General Workers Union, which was allied to the **Malawi Congress Party** (MCP). However, from the middle of 1962 on, the trade unions and the MCP drifted apart, mainly because the former argued for more radical policies such as nationalization, a program that the new government did not favor. As a result, Chihana and **Suzgo Msiska** of the Allied Workers Union were suspended from the party and attacked by the *Malawi News*. This marked the beginning of the trade unions' decline and the government's increasing control of the labor movement.

From 1971 to 1977, Chihana was detained without trial. Not long after his release, he left **Malawi**, studied in Europe, and worked in Kenya, among other countries, before becoming secretary-general of the Southern Africa Trade Unions Co-ordinating Council (SATUCC). In this capacity he lived in Botswana and Lesotho. In 1989 SATUCC's headquarters were moved to Malawi, where within a short time Chihana also began to clandestinely involve himself in politics of reform. In April 1992 he was imprisoned for openly calling for political change and was not released until June 1993, just in time to campaign for the general **elections** scheduled to take place in the following year. While he was in prison, AFORD had formally come into existence, and the leadership had made him its president.

Chihana lost in the presidential elections, but when the coalition government of the **United Democratic Front** (UDF) and **Alliance for Democracy** (AFORD) was formed in late 1994, Chihana became second vice president and minister of irrigation. In 1996 his party withdrew from the arrangement, and he returned to his **Chiweta** base in the Rumphi lakeshore area and continued to head AFORD from there. In 1998 his party and the MCP established a partnership for purposes of the general elections in the following year. Besides standing as AFORD MP for Rumphi Central, Chihana was the vice-presidential candidate for the MCP-AFORD alliance. He easily won the former but lost the latter following the reelection of **Bakili Muluzi**. He and **Gwanda Chakuamba**, the MCP presidential candidate, challenged the results in court on grounds of vote rigging. *See also* BANDA, HASTINGS KAMUZU; POLITICAL PARTIES.

CHIJOZI, DUNSTAN W. This **NkhotaKota**-born politician was elected to the **Legislative Council** in 1956 on the **Nyasaland African Congress** ticket, at the same time as **Kanyama Chiume**, **Henry Chipembere**, **Nophas Kwenje**, and **James Chinyama**. Regarded as a moderate, he fell out of favor with the mainstream nationalist movement, and in the 1961 **elections** he unsuccessfully stood as a parliamentary candidate of **Thamar Dillon Banda**'s **Congress Liberation Party**, the organization he had earlier represented at the constitutional talks in London. As constitutional changes accelerated in **Malawi**, Chijozi faded from prominence.

CHIKANGA. One of the most successful witch finders in recent times. Chikanga, whose real name is Lighton Chunda, was born at Ihete in the mountainous area of southeastern **Rumphi**. A **Tumbuka** speaker, Chunda belonged to the **Church of Central African Presbyterian** (CCAP) and went to local Presbyterian primary schools. In the mid-1950s, probably while in his twenties, he fell ill but recovered after receiving treatment from a traditional doctor, Muzengerwa Simwaka. To Chunda, the nature of his illness pointed to the fact that his mission was to find and expose witches and sorcerers. Although he was suspended from the church because of this development, he continued with his new devotion. By 1960 his reputation had gone far beyond Rumphi, and he had changed his name to Chikanga, which in ciTumbuka means courage or perseverance. People anxious to be treated and to identify those responsible for their ailments and misfortunes arrived at Ihete in thousands and often had to wait for weeks for an audience with him. He did not charge for his services, and he built accommodation for the ever increasing numbers of arrivals from Malawi and other countries.

Chikanga's active involvement in witch and sorcerer finding was cut short when Dr. **Hastings Banda**, the new prime minister of **Malawi**, summoned him to tell him to stop practicing his trade. Apparently, Rev. Patrick Mzembe, general secretary of the Livingstonia Synod of the CCAP, had complained to the government about the detrimental effects that Chikanga's activities and reputation were having on rural societies. He was accused of usurping the powers of the chiefs in that he was becoming the administrator of justice instead of them, encouraging and spreading belief in witchcraft and thereby promoting distrust and tension in communities, and not paying attention to proper sanitation at his Ihete village, which did not have adequate water for his thousands of clients. The government was also unhappy with the security problems posed by large numbers of people entering Malawi, particularly after the **Cabinet Crisis** in 1964, when many politicians took refuge in **Zambia** and **Tanzania**. Chikanga was ordered to move to **Blantyre**, where security agents could observe him. But at some point, he moved to **Southern Rhodesia** (now **Zimbabwe**). He returned to Malawi later to lead a much quieter life.

CHIKANG'OMBE. The main religious shrine of the region under the jurisdiction of the **Chikulamayembe**, located at Chikangombe hill. The chief priest came from the Kachali clan, one of the established pre-Chikulamayembe groups in the area.

CHIKULAMAYEMBE. This is the title of the traditional rulers of most of what is today central **Rumphi**, and the clan name is Gondwe. Originally traders from Tanganyika, the Gondwe followed a migration route that took them across the lake; hence their praise name, *balowoka*. By the time the **Ngoni** arrived in the area, the Chikulamayembe dynasty had been established for about a century. During the rebellion against the Ngoni in 1880, Mujuma, the eighth holder of the title, was killed and the office was abolished. It was revived in 1907, when **Chilongozi Gondwe**,

a policeman, became the ninth Chikulamayembe. The seat of the Chikulamayembe is Bolero in the **Nkhamanga** plains, **Rumphi** District.

CHIKUMBU. Title of the ruler of a **Yao** chiefdom in **Mulanje** District.
Most of the occupants of this office are known by the term rather than by
their first or family name. An occupant of the office in the 1880s and
1890s fearlessly resisted the imposition of British authority in his area.
Scottish missionaries and administrators such as **Harry Johnston** and
Alfred Sharpe considered the Chikumbu a threat to the spread of Christianity, Western civilization, and the establishment of the Pax Brittanica
in the **Shire Highlands**, and they put much effort into subduing
Chikumbu's area. Originally in the Nsoni area, he moved east nearer to
Mulanje mountain, not far from **Fort Lister**, which the British built to
observe the traditional commercial route to Quilimane on the **Mozambique** coast. Chief Chikumbu (1960s–1970s) was appointed to the national traditional court.

CHIKUNDA. Indigenous people, including some former slaves, who were
employed by the Portuguese settlers, the *prazeros*, in pre-19th century
Mozambique as retainers and soldiers. They guarded *prazo* boundaries,
making sure that the Africans within did not flee, thus ensuring the availability of labor.

CHIKUNDA. Located on the outskirts of **Blantyre**, it was the main base
of **Joseph Booth**'s **African Cooperative Society**. *See also* SHILOH.

CHIKWAKWA, JOHN "JOMOH." Founding member of the **Malawi
Congress Party** (MCP) and former national chairman of the League of
Malawi Youth. Chikwakwa was born at Namitambo in **Chiradzulu** Dis-
trict in July 1937 and educated in local schools and at **Zomba** Catholic
Secondary School. In 1958 he joined the youth wing of the **Nyasaland
African Congress** (NAC) and a year later was in the group headed by
Orton Chirwa, which formed the **Malawi Congress Party** (MCP). Regarded as a militant, he was often compared to some of the young lead-
ership of the Mau Mau movement in Kenya; hence his nickname, Jomoh,
after Jomo Kenyatta, the first president of Kenya. In 1962 Dr. **Hastings
Banda** sent Chikwakwa and Kapombe Nyasulu, another Youth League
activist, to **Southern Rhodesia (Zimbabwe)** to organize support for the
MCP and to establish branches of the party in that country. In the following year, Banda arranged for the two youth leaguers to go to Ghana
to study at the Winneba Ideological Institute set up by **Kwame
Nkrumah**. At the beginning of 1964, five months into the course, they

were recalled home, apparently to take part in the preindependence **election** campaign. Upon arriving, however, they were suspended from the MCP for disobeying the order to return home weeks earlier than instructed. Reinstated after a few months, Chikwakwa was forced into exile soon after the **Cabinet Crisis** of 1964 because of his association with **Henry Chipembere** and his views. For most of the 1960s President Hastings Banda declared Chikwakwa a wanted person. Chikwakwa lived in **Tanzania** as a refugee until 1993, when he returned to **Malawi**.

CHIKWAWA. Capital (*boma*) of Chikwawa District in the Lower Shire area of **Malawi**. Chikwawa *boma* is also the furthest point of navigation on the **Shire River** as, above this site, are the Murchison cataracts, which make river navigation impossible until north of Matope. In the early colonial period Chikwawa became an important river port on the Shire River and a major center of activities. The **African Lakes Company** (ALC) had a trading store at Chikwawa and, in 1892, the British established a government station there. A main **cotton**-growing area, Chikwawa was most recently the site of an irrigated **rice** project and fish farms sponsored by **nongovernmental organizations** (NGOs). It is also the major **sugar**-growing part of Malawi, and thus the main operations area for the Sugar Company of Malawi (SUCOMA), which has recently been bought by the Ulova Sugar Company of **South Africa**. Not far from Chikwawa *boma* is a site where **Chewa** rulers resided in the past. *See also* SHIRE.

CHILD SPACING. This government-sponsored birth control program started in the early 1980s, mainly at the behest of the **World Bank** and donor agencies such as the United Nations Population Fund (UNPF). Afraid of offending traditional Malawian sensitivities to matters concerning reproduction, the government stressed adequate spacing between children, hence the name, Child Spacing Program. The emphasis was always the **health** and developmental advantages to mothers and their children of such an approach to child bearing. Based at all hospitals and health centers throughout the country, teams led by nurses talked to **women** about various forms of birth control and administered the appropriate medications. The teams also visited rural areas to do the same. *See also* BIRTHRATE.

CHILEMBWE, IDA. This extraordinary woman was married to **John Chilembwe** and was probably of **Sena** parentage. She was a teacher at the main day school at **Mbombwe, Chiradzulu**, where she taught weekly classes in sewing and European-style deportment to women and girls. In the early days of the **Providence Industrial Mission** (PIM) her principal assistant was **Emma DeLany**. With Bible in hand, she often visited **women** in nearby villages and tried to encourage them to learn to take a more equal place next to their husbands. Ida Chilembwe did not like the widely accepted practice of early marriage for young women because she felt they were merely children themselves when they became pregnant, and that they never got to enjoy their youth. She also argued that such marriages rarely led to happy lives and that it was important for women to attend schools. Educated women could be equal partners with their spouses and help their families financially. Despite her exemplary behavior, deep religious feelings, and her efforts to help her sisters, Ida Chilembwe obtained little or no help or consideration from neighboring European women, some of whom were themselves wives of pastors. She knew incredible hardship and bore a double burden of isolation from both European and African societies. She died in 1918 during the flu epidemic.

CHILEMBWE, JOHN. Leading early anticolonial leader. Chilembwe was born around 1870 of **Yao** parentage in **Chiradzulu** District and went to elementary school in **Blantyre**. In 1892 he met English missionary **Joseph Booth** at his **Mitsidi** Mission. Chilembwe became a servant in the Booth household and acted as nurse-companion to the Booth children. Chilembwe was strongly influenced by Booth and his teachings, particularly the missionary's egalitarian belief of Africa for the Africans. In 1897 Booth took Chilembwe to the **United States**, where the National Baptist Convention underwrote his education at Virginia Theological College, a black seminary in Lynchburg, Virginia. During Chilembwe's two years in the Theology Department he learned much about the experiences of American blacks. He also traveled in several American states before returning to **Malawi** as an ordained minister in 1900.

Chilembwe purchased about 90 acres of land near **Mbombwe**, Chiradzulu District, and built a mission patterned after an earlier concept by Booth. He called it the **Providence Industrial Mission** (PIM). Soon several black American Baptist missionaries came to Malawi to help Chilembwe's mission; **Landon Cheek** and **Emma DeLany** were among them. During their five-year stay, the PIM grew steadily with followers from Chiradzulu and **Mulanje** Districts. The mission began experimental planting of **cotton**, **tea**, and **coffee**. Chilembwe also established a series of mission schools at Namkundi, Matili, Ndunde, Tumbwe, Malika,

Sangano, and the main school at Chiradzulu. The British standard elementary subjects were offered at Chilembwe's schools. The PIM also offered practical agricultural courses. At the urging of Chilembwe, **women** were taught European-style deportment and dress. Chilembwe was convinced that if the members of his community experienced European-type success, they would develop more self-respect. He preached hard work and clean habits to his followers, whom he urged to be sober, industrious, and respectable. In 1913 he and his followers completed construction of the PIM church, a beautiful large brick structure. *See also* CHILEMBWE, IDA.

Prior to the 1915 uprising, Chilembwe had elected to work within the framework of the colonial government, a position that the **African welfare associations** and **the Nyasaland African Congress** (NAC) would also pursue for several decades after World War I. Chilembwe always sought to improve conditions for his African community, and he understood its burdens well. Although Malawians were compliant, Chilembwe realized that they resented the colonial government's imposition of power over traditional authorities, the increased hut tax rates, and the continued abuses of the *thangata* system. Additionally, the protectorate had experienced drought, and with subsequent crop shortages many Malawians starved during the famine of 1912–1913. Against the backdrop of these conditions, Chilembwe experienced personal frustration and suffering with his poor health (chronic asthma and growing blindness), heavy debts, and the death of his daughter Emma. Although all these factors were cumulative, the immediate event causing the revolt was World War I.

When Chilembwe articulated his complaints against the government in the *Nyasaland Times* of November 1914, he also reminded the British of the loyalty shown by Malawians since the commencement of their rule. In peacetime, he continued, the government had directed all its attention to the Europeans, but now in war, Africans had been recruited for a cause that was not theirs. Chilembwe became distressed at the intense recruitment demands for carriers *(tenga-tenga)* in his PIM area. By December, Chilembwe and his followers became more militant in their meetings, and by the next month, they had agreed to "strike a blow and die." Associated with these fatal expectations was Chilembwe's willingness to become a martyr for his people. To this end he conspired with **Filipo Chinyama** in **Ntcheu** District and he hoped for support from Mulanje District and perhaps from the Germans in East Africa **(Tanzania)**. However, none of these subplots materialized.

Chilembwe chose to begin his revolt on Saturday evening, January 23, apparently because he knew many Europeans were partying at the Blantyre Sports Club. He sent some of his followers to Blantyre, where they attempted unsuccessfully to burglarize the **African Lakes Company** (ALC) store and take its ammunition. Another contingent was sent to the **A. L. Bruce Estates**, infamous for harsh working conditions. The chief target on the estates was its unusually cruel manager, **William J. Livingstone**, who had burned down African tenant prayer houses, whipped and moved those tenants frequently and without reason, and paid them extraordinarily low wages. Livingstone was killed and beheaded, and two other European planters were speared to death. Following Chilembwe's strict orders, his army of 200 harmed no women and seized no property. Chilembwe was able to elude government forces until February 2, but his followers were rounded up earlier. Those who were not killed were jailed or went into exile.

Although most of his coconspirators had some Western education and were propertied African entrepreneurs, Chilembwe enjoyed support from areas beyond the PIM, including among the **Ngoni** of Ntcheu District. Few traditional authorities lent him support despite a common complaint against war recruitment for the **King's African Rifles** (KAR). The **Watchtower** group was also nonsupportive. Nevertheless, Chilembwe exhibited a unity against European rule and European abuses that the government had to acknowledge. Swept away was the European complacency that all was well with their African wards. In 1916 a commission of inquiry investigated the uprising and recommended reforms, but the government did not implement any.

CHILEMBWE UPRISING. *See* CHILEMBWE, JOHN.

CHILIBVUMBO, ALIFEYO. Former minister of sports in the first **United Democratic Front** (UDF) government. Chilibvumbo was born in Nkhotakota. He was educated locally and at **Blantyre** and Dedza Secondary schools before going to Makerere University, Uganda, where he majored in sociology. He went to the University of California, Berkeley, where he was awarded master's and Ph.D. degrees before returning to **Malawi** in 1968. Chilibvumbo taught at **Chancellor College** until 1974 when he fell afoul of the government and was detained without trial. Released just over two years later, he joined the faculty of the University of Zambia, and in the mid-1980s went to the University of the Transkei in the Eastern Cape, **South Africa**. He also briefly taught at the University of Swaziland before returning to Malawi in 1993 to join the prodemocracy movement. In the following year, Chilibvumbo was elected to parliament as a United Democratic Front member for a Nkhotakota constituency. He died in 1996.

CHILOBWE. This is a high-density, low-cost housing and lively township in western **Blantyre**. *See also* CHILOBWE MURDERS.

CHILOBWE MURDERS. Beginning in November 1968 and continuing for many months thereafter, a grisly series of murders took place in the **Blantyre** suburb of **Chilobwe**. These unsolved murders were accompanied by widely accepted rumors about the South African government, including one that the killings were to provide blood in payment for South African loans; another rumor concerned selling Malawians as slaves in **South Africa**. In 1969 several men were arrested, but due to insufficient evidence they were all acquitted of the charges. Early in 1970 another man, Kawisa, perhaps a member of a gang, confessed to some of the murders.

The events caused considerable apprehension in the **Hastings Banda** government, which blamed the cabinet ministers expelled in 1964 for trying to disrupt the progress **Malawi** was making. Within Malawi, **Gomile Kumtumanji**, a **Yao** chief and long-time **Malawi Congress Party** (MCP) chairman for the south, MP for **Zomba**, and senior cabinet minister, was accused of being associated with the incidents and, as a result, was detained without trial. More significantly, the event was also viewed as a challenge to Malawi's friendly relations with South Africa. Politically, Banda treated the incidents seriously because the rumors tied to the murders were accorded such high credibility and were indicative of an inordinate fear of South Africa.

CHILUMBA. Area on the southern **Karonga** lakeshore inhabited by the Henga, a **Tumbuka**-speaking people. Chilumba falls under the traditional authority of the Mwafulirwa. Cassava is their main staple, and fish constitutes part of their everyday diet. Prominent in the Chilumba area is Luromo, a peninsula, the home of the Ndovi clan, who in the past were significant players in the economic life of the northern section of **Lake Malawi**. Chilumba is also on the narrowest point on Lake Malawi and in precolonial times was an important crossing point to the eastern side of the lake. Ivory traders from the Luangwa area found Chilumba a most convenient way of transporting their merchandise to the Indian Ocean. The activities of **Swahili-Arab** traders led the early colonial government to establish a government post that was later moved to Karonga. The colonial authorities named the area Deep Bay because the section on the northern side of Luromo is the deepest bay north of **Nkhata Bay**. Even today, Deep Bay (now once again called Chilumba) is a main port of call for transport vessels on Lake Malawi.

CHILUMPHA, CASSIM. A respected national leader in the **United Democratic Front** (UDF). Chilumpha was on the law faculty at the Polytechnic in **Blantyre** as the agitation for political change mounted. He became a founding member and one of the legal advisers of the UDF, was elected to parliament in 1994, and joined the cabinet as minister of justice. In a 1997 cabinet reshuffle, he was given the finance portfolio that he retained in the government named after June 1999. A few months later Chilumpha was transferred to the Ministry of Education, Sports, and Culture but was dropped from the cabinet in November 2000, following a report of the Public Account Committee of parliament detailing mismanagement of finances in some government departments.

CHIMERA, JAMES. Popular fast-talking announcer and disk jockey. Chimera worked for the **Malawi Broadcasting Corporation** (MBC) for many years before accepting the position of deputy minister of broadcasting and information in the last days of the **Hastings Banda** government. After the **United Democratic Front** (UDF) was voted into power, Chimera became the publicity chief of the **Malawi Congress Party** (MCP). In March 2001, he joined the UDF.

CHIMOLE, BISHOP MATHIAS. Born in **Zomba** in 1917, Bishop Chimole went to **Nankhunda** and **Kachebere** seminaries. After his ordination, he worked mainly in the Zomba diocese. In 1970 Lawrence Hardman retired as bishop of Zomba and was succeeded by Mathias Chimole. Nine years later, he became bishop of **Lilongwe** in place of **Patrick Kalilombe**, who had resigned earlier. A significant member of the Bishops Conference, Chimole was a signatory of the **Catholic bishops' pastoral letter** of March 1992, which greatly contributed to political reform in Malawi. The bishop played other roles in Malawi, including that of chairman (1974) of the **Christian Service Committee of the Churches in Malawi**. In 1994 he retired as bishop of Lilongwe and was succeeded by Tarcisio Ziyaye.

CHIMTALI, FRED. Long-time minister of the **Zomba** town **Church of Central Africa Presbyterian** (CCAP) congregation and one of the most distinguished pastors of his generation. Chimtali was educated in Zomba and at the **Henry Henderson Institute** (HHI), where he qualified as a teacher. After teaching for some years, he trained as a teacher supervisor at **Domasi**, a course introduced in the mid-1930s. Later, Chimtali went to theological college at the HHI and then worked in a number of parishes before being appointed to the town of Zomba. Reverend Chimtali was one of the Malawians who gave evidence to the **Devlin Commission** of 1959. He died in 1984, having retired a few years earlier.

CHINA. Prior to Malawi's independence, the People's Republic of China (PRC) had obtained assurances from Dr. **Hastings Banda** that after July 1964 **Malawi** would extend diplomatic recognition and would press for China's admission to the United Nations. In return for ending a friendly policy toward Taiwan, Beijing offered Malawi US$6 million in aid. Banda made no decision, but his minister for external affairs, **Kanyama Chiume**, met with the Chinese ambassador, Ho Ying, in Dar es Salaam in August 1964. At this meeting, Ying raised the amount of aid offered to US$18 million. At the next cabinet meeting the subject of the latest Chinese offer became an issue, along with several internal grievances held by Banda's cabinet ministers; a political crisis ensued. *See also* CABINET CRISIS.

During early negotiations with the disgruntled ministers, Banda indicated that he merely needed more time to consider the Chinese question. As the crisis worsened, Banda implied that Ambassador Ying had provoked his ministers into a conspiracy. Although his suspicions of Chinese support for the former cabinet ministers continued, Banda supported China's admission to the United Nations during a December 1964 speech before the General Assembly. When Banda learned some weeks later that China had aided the ex-ministers, who had since fled Malawi, he reversed his support. From then on, Malawi officially favored Taiwan at the UN, and in 1966 Banda established diplomatic relations with the government of the Republic of China (Taiwan).

Taiwan established an embassy in Malawi and became active in the country mainly through the provision of personnel and technical assistance in rice agricultural schemes, and in numerous demonstration gardens. After the 1994 **elections**, the new **United Democratic Front** (UDF) government began to show an interest in reviewing its relations with the PRC, and for the first time Malawi cabinet ministers paid official visits to Beijing. There were indications that Malawi might follow **South Africa** in establishing diplomatic relations with the People's Republic, even if it meant breaking with Taiwan. However, at the start of 2000, the latter's presence in Malawi seemed as strong as ever, to the extent that it was in the process of building and equipping a modern hospital in **Mzuzu**, capital of the Northern Region.

CHINDE. Until the railway lines linking colonial **Malawi** and **Beira** were constructed, Chinde, on the mouth of the Zambezi River, was the main port of entry into the **Lake Malawi** region. The majority of Europeans who went to the latter area did so via river steamers from Chinde, up the Zambezi and the right on to the Shire.

CHINDIO. *See* CHINDE.

CHINKONDENJI, C. M. In 1959 Chinkondenji was nominated to the **Legislative Council** (LEGCO) and, with **Ernest Mtawali**, appointed to the Executive Council, the first Africans to hold such positions in the colonial administration. This made Chinkondenji most unpopular in African nationalist circles, where it was felt that he had betrayed his countrymen by joining a government that had just strongly frustrated African aspirations through the declaration of the state of emergency. After the general elections of 1961, Chinkondenji retired from politics.

CHINTHECHE. Located in the southern part of **Nkhata Bay** District, Chintheche is in the heartland of **Tonga** country. During the 1870s and 1880s it was heavily stockaded because of regular **Ngoni** raids into the area. Five miles north of **Bandawe**, the second site of the **Livingstonia Mission**, Chintheche fell in the immediate catchment area of the mission, resulting in a comparatively high rate of Western education among the Tonga. Many inhabitants of this locality distinguished themselves in different walks of life in **Nyasaland** and the wider Southern Africa region. When British colonial authority was established in the **Lake Nyasa** region, Chintheche became the *boma* of West Nyasa District and then of Chintheche District, before the main offices were moved north to Nkhata Bay, which also became the new name of the district.

Chintheche has not developed much physically, but in the 1970s the government hoped that it would be the site of the VIPCOR pulp and paper mill. Investors found it more expensive to get the trees out than expected, and with an impossible **transportation** situation, VIPCOR became a dead project. However, wood from this beautifully forested area is used locally, mainly for furniture and for building material. *See also* FORESTRY.

CHINULA, CHARLES CHIDONGO. A leading intellectual in the pre-1960 era of Malawian history. Charles Chinula was born at the end of

1885 in Mthimba village on the Kasitu River. At age 11, he started school at Hora, where he was taught by, among others, the **Lovedale**-educated lakeshore **Tonga**, David Marawanthu. In 1900 Chinula entered the more advanced school at **Ekwendeni**, where his teachers included **Muhabi Amon Jere** and Rev. **Donald Fraser**. Two years later, he went to the **Overtoun Institution** at **Khondowe**, and there he met **Charles Domingo**, who gave his own name to the younger man so that from then on he was to be referred to as Charles Chidongo Chinula. In 1907 he completed the Teacher Probationer's Certificate, passing first in a class of 11.

Even as early as 1908, when he was a teacher at **Loudon Mission**, Chinula was vehemently opposed to the missionary attitude toward African culture, especially their attempts to limit traditional African dances. He was ordained minister in 1925, and he soon developed a reputation as a powerful preacher and composer of about 21 church hymns, one of his most famous being "Hena mwana wa mberere" (See the Lamb of God). Impressed and influenced by **Yesayi Zerenji Mwase**, Chinula became a major advocate of African advancement and rights, including the insistence that mission education should be open to all children, even those who came from non-Christian families. Viewed by some as arrogant and militant, Chinula gave his opponents an opportunity to silence him. At a meeting of Presbytery in November 1930, Chinula, then a minister for the Hoho congregation, confessed to adultery; he was defrocked and his church membership was suspended. Within two years he regained membership and, at a reduced salary, was assigned to oversee and aid those who, like him, had committed church offenses.

When the repeated requests of his congregation that he be restored to the ministry failed, Chinula, encouraged by Zerenji Mwasi's success as an independent pastor, left the church in July 1934 and established his own, Eklesia Lanangwa (Church of Freedom), with the headquarters at Sazu Home Mission, a short distance from **Edingeni**, the seat of northern **Ngoni** authority. There he established a school and opened others in **Mzimba** District. However, without a proper source of finance, most of the schools closed eventually, leaving only the one at Sazu to survive into the 1990s. While waiting to be reinstated in the church, Chinula translated the *Pilgrim's Progress* into ciTumbuka; he also wrote a condensed version of the book and called it *Vyaro na Vyaro* (Lands and lands).

A year later, he, Zerenji Mwasi, and **Yaphet Mkandawire** formed a loose union of churches that they called the Black Man's Church in

Africa. In 1941 he unsuccessfully suggested to the **Livingstonia Mission** that there should be a mutual recognition and interchange of membership and communality between their respective churches.

When the **M'mbelwa African Administrative Council** was established in 1933, Rev. Chinula became adviser to M'mbelwa II, and in this capacity he was considered the new **Ng'onomo Makamo**, in spite of his **Tumbuka** roots. He held this distinguished post until 1961, when the M'mbelwa District Council replaced the Administrative Council. A committed nationalist, Chinula became founding secretary of the Mombera Native Association in 1920, and of the Representative Committee of the Northern Province Native Associations in 1924. As a close adviser to M'Mbelwa II, Chinula was the author of the memorandum that the Ngoni rural paramount presented to the **Bledisloe Commission**. When the **Nyasaland African Congress** was formed in 1944, he became chairman of the **Mzimba** District branch and vice president at the national level; he was also a member of the Northern Provincial Council.

A first-rate preacher and teacher, as well as a prolific composer of hymns, Chinula retired from active politics after 1950. In 1967 he returned to the Livingstonia Synod of the **Church of Central Africa Presbyterian** (CCAP), which had suspended him in 1930. Although his ministry was not restored, he preached many times, reminding his listeners of his oratory. Chinula died at home on November 3, 1971.

CHINYAMA, FILIPO. This **Ntcheu**-based clergyman, coconspirator of **John Chilembwe** and friend of **Alexander Makwinja** and **Peter Nyambo**. Chinyama became associated with the **Baptist Industrial Mission** from about 1903, when he studied at **Malamulo**, which **Joseph Booth** had just established. In 1908 John Hollis of the Church of Christ baptized Chinyama at **Chikunda**, and in the following year he went to the **Nyasa Industrial Mission** Training Institute in **Thyolo**, only to leave after a brief period in protest against the mandatory daily three hours manual labor for students. Between that time and 1911, he was a labor migrant in Bulawayo, Southern Rhodesia (**Zimbabwe**), but by mid-1911 he was once again active in church work in Ntcheu, reviving a church and school at Uchinda, also known as Ntinda, near Dzunje, which the Church of Christ had earlier vacated. Chinyama and Booth corresponded, and in this manner he received a copy of Peter Nyambo's petition to the British King. In November 1914 he spent over a week at **Mbombwe** as a guest of Chilembwe, and during that time they most likely discussed plans for the January 15 uprising. As Chilembwe's forces moved on to **Blantyre**, Chinyama and 300 supporters, armed with spears, descended on Ntcheu *boma*, aiming to seize the armory. The plan failed, and the government, led by its local representative, Claude Ambrose Cardew, pursued, captured, and executed Chinyama.

CHINYAMA, JAMES RALPH NTHINDA. Son of **Filipo Chinyama**. James was a **Lilongwe**-based businessman who from the 1940s was active in nationalist politics. In 1950 he replaced **Charles Matinga** as president-general of the **Nyasaland African Congress** (NAC) but was voted out three years later for providing ineffective leadership in the struggle against the **Federation of Rhodesia and Nyasaland**. In the elections of 1956, Chinyama and **Dunstan Chijozi** were elected to represent Africans in the Nyasaland **Legislative Council** (LEGCO). After Dr. **Hastings Banda** returned to the colony in 1958, James Chinyama came to be identified with the less progressive politicians, and eventually he was forgotten.

CHIONA, BISHOP JAMES. Archbishop of **Blantyre** since 1968 and one of the signatories of the **Catholic bishops' pastoral letter** of 1992. Chiona was born in **Zomba** District, where he attended the **Nankhunda** seminary before proceeding to **Kachebere** Major Seminary. After ordination he served in different parishes, and in 1968 he succeeded **Jean-Baptiste Theunissen** as senior Catholic prelate in **Malawi**. In 2001 James Chiona announced his retirement from the archbishopric.

CHIONA, PETER. A senior office bearer of the **Malawi Congress Party** (MCP) in the post-**Hastings Banda** era. Peter Chiona was born in Misuku, **Chitipa** District. He went to Bulambya Primary school, **Zomba** Catholic Secondary School, and the **Domasi** Teachers Training College. After teaching at Iponjora, Misuku, and at Soche Hill Secondary School, he proceeded to Oxford University in England, graduating in 1968 with a B.A. degree. On his return to **Malawi** he joined the Planning Department at the Ministry of Education headquarters, and in October 1969 he went to Paris to study education planning. Two years later he returned to the Ministry of Education, but within a short time he joined the teaching staff of the Soche Hill College, a constituent institute of the **University of Malawi**. In 1973 Chiona relocated to Zomba because his institution became part of the expanded **Chancellor College** at its new campus at Chirunga Farm.

In 1976 he was one of the hundreds of people who were victims of arbitrary political detentions but was released at the end of the year. He became unemployed but was reemployed by the university in 1978. A year later, he joined the United Nations Economic Commission for Africa (ECA) in Addis Ababa, Ethiopia, where he specialized in education planning. In the early 1990s, retired from the ECA, he became a **Mzuzu**-based businessman but also began to be active in politics. In 1997 he was appointed secretary-general of the Malawi Congress Party (MCP) and two years later second deputy president of the party. In that capacity he was instrumental in forging the partnership between his party and the **Alliance for Democracy** (AFORD). At the same time he became one of the two vice presidents of the MCP. In the 1999 general elections, Chiona was elected MCP MP for Chitipa East, one of the few non-AFORD MPs in the northern part of Malawi. *See also* MUWALO-NQUMAYO, ALBERT; GWEDE, FOCUS.

CHIPATA. *See* FORT JAMESON.

CHIPATULA. A **Kololo** chief who lived at **Chiromo** in the Lower Shire region. Chipatula, like many Kololo, grew sesame which, with ivory, he sold to Europeans. His relations with Portuguese officials, businessmen, and their associates was tense, and, much to the liking of the British, he sought to curtail Portugal's influence in the area. Chipatula had a good working relationship with the British, who found him to be temperamental; the indigenous **Mang'anja** regarded him as a despot. In 1884 Chipatula was shot dead by **George Fenwick**, who was in turn killed by the dead chief's subjects. His son and successor, Chikuse, had equally bad relations with the Portuguese and their associates. For some time they considered the **African Lakes Company** (ALC), Fenwick's employers, responsible for his father's death. *See also* KOLOLO; KASISI.

CHIPEMBERE, CATHERINE. This **Likoma**-born teacher played a significant behind-the-scenes role in the days leading to decolonization. After the **Cabinet Crisis**, she joined her husband, **Henry Chipembere**, in **Tanzania** and later in the **United States**, where she and their children remained even after his death in 1975. She returned to **Malawi** to contest the 1994 **elections** for a **Mangochi** constituency, and, upon the formation of the **United Democratic Front** government in June 1994, she was appointed junior minister, first for education and later for health. In 1999 she retired from active politics.

CHIPEMBERE, CANON HABIL. A priest in the Anglican Church (UMCA). Canon Chipembere, father of **Henry Masauko Chipembere**, worked in many parts of the **Lake Malawi region**, including **Ntchisi**, **Nkhotkota**, **Machinga**, and **Mangochi** Districts. In World War II, he served as chaplain to the **King's African Rifles** (KAR) and in this capacity went as far as India. In the mid-1950s Habil Chipembere was promoted to the position of canon, and from 1961 to 1963 he was MP for **Fort Johnston** (later renamed Mangochi), a seat he handed to his son when he was released from prison. He returned to full-time priesthood, but his life was disturbed in 1964 when the government hounded him out of the country because of his association with his son, who was at the time regarded as an enemy of the state. Canon Chipembere went into exile in **Tanzania**.

CHIPEMBERE, HENRY BLASIUS MASAUKO. One of Malawi's foremost nationalists, popularly known as "Chip." Of **Nyanja** and **Yao** parentage, Henry Chipembere was born on August 5, 1930, at Kayoyo, **Nkhotakota** District, where his father, **Habil Chipembere**, a priest in the Anglican Church, was stationed. Later the family moved to **Malindi** Mission in **Mangochi** District (then known as Fort Johnston), where Chipembere went to school before going to Malosa and on to **Blantyre** Secondary School. He then proceeded to Goromonzi High School near Harare, **Zimbabwe**, where he distinguished himself as an excellent student. The **Nyasaland** government awarded him a bursary to study at **Fort Hare** University, **South Africa**, majoring in history and political science. He graduated in 1954 and became assistant district commissioner at **Domasi** but resigned from the civil service to become a political activist in the **Nyasaland African Congress** (NAC).

At its 1955 general meeting at **Lilongwe**, the NAC demanded the right to secede from the **Federation of Rhodesia and Nyasaland** and urged the resignation of Federal Assembly representatives **Wellington Chirwa** and **Clement Kumbikano**. Both Chipembere and **W. Kanyama Chiume** were behind this more militant stand of the NAC as well as responsible for reorganizing and increasing the membership in the Congress. In 1956 he ran for and was elected to the **Legislative Council** (LEGCO), where he and four other African members began a vigorous parliamentary campaign (1956–1959) that criticized the Federation with a severity not witnessed before. Chipembere, Chiume, and other young politicians were responsible for revitalizing the NAC, for encouraging Dr. **Hastings K. Banda** to return home, and for relentlessly pursuing freedom for his homeland. Chipembere was probably Banda's most militant lieutenant.

In 1957 the annual meeting of the NAC took place at **Lilongwe**. At the behest of Chipembere, Chiume, **Dunduzu Chisiza**, and others, it was decided to contact Dr. Banda, then living in Ghana, urging him to return home, to become the leader of the Congress, and to provide a savior/hero figure for the nationalist movement. Chipembere actually wrote to him, detailing the message. The new militancy in the NAC and the outspokenness of its members in LEGCO were positive factors in Banda's decision to return to Malawi. In July 1958, Banda had demanded and received from Chipembere guarantees that upon his return he would be president of the NAC and could direct the movement as he thought best. In August 1958 Banda chose Chipembere to be NAC treasurer, Chiume as publicity secretary, Chisiza as secretary-general, and **Rose Chibambo** as leader of the **women**'s section of the NAC. Over the next several months, the Congress harassed the government with speeches and assemblies and occasional outbreaks of violence. Security forces had their hands full, Southern Rhodesian troops were called in and, finally, on March 3, 1959, the government declared a state of emergency. *See also* OPERATION SUNRISE.

Chipembere was jailed from March 1959 to September 1960. Upon his release, Banda, at a large rally in Nkhotakota, reinstated him as treasurer of the Congress, by that time renamed the **Malawi Congress Party** (MCP). In February 1961, four months later, the government found Chipembere guilty of sedition and incitement on account of a speech he had made at **Rumphi** and sentenced him to three years in **Zomba** prison. Although promised by Banda that he would exert pressure on the governor, **Glyn Jones**, for an early release from prison, Chipembere received no such help, perhaps because Banda found it calmer and easier to rule without his young cohort. Early in 1963 Chipembere was released and was greeted with enthusiasm and much excitement. Banda immediately assigned him the Ministry of Local Government, and in early 1964, he became minister of education, which he retained after Malawi became an independent nation on July 6, 1964.

From August to September 1964, ministerial dissent erupted into the **Cabinet Crisis** in which Banda dismissed (on September 7) **Augustine Bwanausi**, Rose Chibambo, **Orton Chirwa**, and Chiume. When Chipembere arrived (September 8) home from a visit to **Canada**, he learned of the difficulties of the past two weeks. Like **Yatuta Chisiza** and **Willie Chokani**, who had resigned in sympathy, so too did Chipembere. But he remained conciliatory in his speeches in parliament, and he endeavored to have Glyn Jones mediate the rift. Reconciliation hopes were dashed in the next week as Banda replaced the vacated posts in the cabinet and the ex-ministers took a firmer stance, especially when

Chipembere attacked Banda's slow **Africanization** policy. Although Chipembere and the other ministers had declared their loyalty to Banda, he called them irresponsible and refused to negotiate. Chipembere had been restricted to his Malindi home by police. Banda had banned public meetings and restricted the "conspirators." In February 1965 Chipembere led about 200 armed men from Malindi to Mangochi, where they seized rifles and proceeded to Liwonde. There government reinforcements forced a retreat to Malindi.

Chipembere then fled to the **United States**, where he studied for a master's degree at the University of California at Los Angeles (UCLA). Encouraged by old friends to return to Africa, Chipembere lived in **Tanzania** from 1966 to 1969. In addition to his teaching duties at Kivukoni College, Chipembere worked with Malawian refugees and exiled leaders. He also led his party, the Pan-African Democratic Party of Malawi. After Eduardo Mondlane was assassinated, Chipembere, having experienced several attempts on his own life, again left East Africa for the West Coast of the United States. He also needed to be near better facilities for the treatment of diabetes from which he had suffered for some time. He and his family settled in Los Angeles, where he taught at California State University while also pursuing his Ph.D. studies at UCLA. His death on September 24, 1975, cut short that last ambition just as events had denied his creative leadership in Malawi. His wife, **Catherine Chipembere**, and their seven children remained in exile until 1993, when she returned to Malawi, joined the **United Democratic Front** (UDF), successfully contested for a Mangochi constituency, and was appointed deputy minister of education in the new government headed by **Bakili Muluzi**.

CHIPERONI. Moist and cool winds that blow into southeastern **Malawi** from the Indian Ocean through **Mozambique**, bringing with them enough rain to render **tea** growing possible in **Mulanje** and **Thyolo** Districts. In the 1960s a popular **sorghum/maize** beer, basically the same as **chibuku**, was named after this weather condition.

CHIPETA, O'BRIEN MAPOPA. Second minister of external affairs in the first **United Democratic Front** (UDF) government. Chipeta was raised in **Mzimba** District and went to the local secondary school before attending the **University of Malawi**, where in 1979 he earned a B.A. with honors, majoring in history. He joined the Antiquities Department, and between 1981 and 1986 he was a graduate student at Dalhousie University, **Canada**, which awarded him M.A. and Ph.D. degrees in history.

He returned to the Antiquities Department but left after 18 months to work as a research officer at the Southern Africa Political and Social Research Trust in Harare, **Zimbabwe**.

In 1992 Chipeta took a leave of absence to devote time to campaign for political reform in **Malawi**. With colleagues such as **Frank Mayinja Mkandawire**, he began to clandestinely send literature advocating multiparty democracy into Malawi. They also published a weekly newsletter, *The Democrat*, which was also sent to Malawi, much to the anger of the **Malawi Congress Party** (MCP) and its government. Late in 1992 Dr. **Hastings K. Banda** accepted the reality of political reform, leading Chipeta and other political activists abroad to return to Malawi in the following year. By this time he had identified himself with **Alliance for Democracy** (AFORD), and the *Democrat* had become the organ of the party. He became one of AFORD's leading ideologues and in 1994 was elected to parliament as a member for Mzimba West.

When the UDF and AFORD formed a coalition government in late 1994, Chipeta was appointed minister of agriculture. Two years later, he replaced **Edward Bwanali** as minister of external affairs and remained in that position until the 1999 general **elections**. In the meantime, he had fallen out of favor with AFORD for refusing to leave the government when the leadership decided against continuing with the coalition arrangement. In June 1999 he contested the Mzimba West seat as an independent but lost to Loveness Gondwe, an AFORD candidate.

CHIPOKA. Natural port on **Lake Malawi**. Since the mid-1930s, when the railway line was extended north of **Blantyre**, Chipoka has been a crucial element in the commercial life of the country. It is here that most of the cargo from the railway is transferred to lake transport for consignment to the northern parts of **Malawi**. Similarly, at Chipoka southbound goods are transferred from boat transport to the railway. *See also* TRANSPORTATION.

CHIPUNGU, A. W. Thyolo-based nationalist of the 1950s and early 1960s. Chipungu was elected to parliament in the 1961 general **elections**. Later he was appointed parliamentary secretary in the Ministry of Health. In the late 1960s Chipungu fell out of favor with Dr. **Hastings K. Banda** and was forced out of active politics.

CHIRADZULU. Name of the district northeast and southwest of **Blantyre** and of **Zomba**, respectively; it is also the name of the *boma*, the district headquarters. A subdistrict of Blantyre until the 1950s, Chiradzulu, a densely populated area, was one of the European settler farming regions of the country and was greatly affected by land problems and the accompanying labor tenancy, *thangata*. This was the home of the **A. L. Bruce Estates**; **John Chilembwe**'s **Providence Industrial Mission** (PIM) had its headquarters at **Mbombwe** in the district, which was also the center of the **Chilembwe uprising** of 1915.

CHIRADZULU NATIVE ASSOCIATION. An early interwar welfare association formed by Dr. **Daniel Malekebu** in 1929. *See also* AFRICAN WELFARE ASSOCIATIONS.

CHIRIMBA. Residential area in the northwestern section of the city of **Blantyre**. Chirimba was associated with the emerging Malawian entrepreneurial class and political activists until the 1960s. Today, part of Chirimba is a low-density housing zone of Blantyre.

CHIRNSIDE, ANDREW. Member of the Royal Geographical Society. On a visit to the **Lake Malawi** region in 1879, he heard of the nature of civil administration adopted by the Church of Scotland Mission at **Blantyre** and its substations such as that at **Zomba**. Since July 1878, the mission had been headed by Rev. **Duff Macdonald** who, following the original instructions of the Foreign Mission Committee to, inter alia, act as the settlement's magistrate, had presided over indiscipline and unethical behavior on the part of some of his Scottish assistants. Such behavior included burning the houses of suspected culprits and flogging and executing people accused of stealing and murder. Some of these incidents were reported in great detail by Andrew Chirnside in *The Blantyre Missionaries: Discreditable Disclosures* (1880). In response, the Foreign Mission Committee appointed Rev. Dr. Thomas Rankin and Alex Pringle to investigate the allegations, most of which they confirmed. As a result of the Rankin–Pringle inquiry, Macdonald and two of the artisans, **John Buchanan** and **George Fenwick**, were dismissed from the mission.

CHIROMO. Town in the Lower Shire. Chiromo was once the official port of entry into **Malawi** via river transport, and in 1892 it became an important government station. In 1902 the Foreign Office agreed to build a railway from **Blantyre** to Chiromo, which became the **Shire Highlands Railway**. The rail bridge at Chiromo was converted in 1977 to auto traffic, thus ending the ferry service across the Shire River.

CHIRWA, ELIOT MUSOKWA KAMWANA. Generally known as Eliot Kamwana, both of which were actually first names. Eliot Musokwa

Kamwana Chirwa was one of the most colorful and traveled religious leaders in colonial **Malawi**. Born in about 1872 as his **Tonga** parents were returning to the lakeshore after escaping **Ngoni** authority, Eliot went to local schools, including **Bandawe**, before proceeding to the **Overtoun Institute, Khondowe**. He left the latter in 1901 after only three years and after passing the Standard 3 examinations. Dissatisfaction with the church, including a delay in baptizing him, seems to have convinced him to leave the Scottish mission and join the **Plainfield Seventh Day Mission** (later renamed **Malamulo**) in **Thyolo** District, where he was baptized the following year.

Chirwa briefly taught at one of the Seventh Day Mission schools before going to **South Africa,** where for three years he worked as a hospital assistant at Main Reef Mine, Johannesburg, and studied and preached, mainly to compatriot immigrant workers. In 1907 he joined **Joseph Booth** at Sea Point, Cape Town, spending most of the time receiving instructions on the **Watchtower** teachings of Pennsylvania pastor Charles Taze Russel. Russel's message emphasized the imminent apocalypse, which would be the final judgment call to heaven to the Kingdom of God. The teachings were also social and political in that they referred to the rise of the masses who would replace injustice with justice. It was the type of message that suited Booth, a recent convert from the Church of Christ, and Kamwana, whose dealings with Scottish missionaries had not always been pleasant. The message was easy to absorb for most Africans in colonial Africa, where nonwhites were second-class citizens.

In 1908 Kamwana returned to **Nkhata Bay**, where he preached to large audiences and baptized hundreds of people, Tonga, **Tumbuka** speakers, and Ngoni. He attacked the Church of Scotland missionaries for their policies governing (as well as their methods of) baptism and for charging school fees. He accused the colonial government, which he referred to as Babylon, of injustice and of taxing people. He predicted that Europeans would be forced out, leaving Africans to take control of the affairs of the country. In late 1909 Kamwana was deported to South Africa. When he returned in the following year, he was confined to **Mulanje**, where the government could watch him closely. Toward the end of 1910, William W. Johnston, a professor from Glasgow, Scotland, sent by the Watchtower Society to establish and report on the situation of the movement in **Nyasaland**, took Kamwana to South Africa. When the South African authorities refused to allow him to disembark at Durban, he returned to **Mozambique**. After a month's imprisonment early in 1914, he returned to **Mulanje**, again closely observed by the government.

In 1915, just before the **Chilembwe uprising**, the government deported Kamwana, his wife, and his close lieutenants and brother, Eliot Yohane Chandaka Chirwa, and another confidant, William Mulagha Mwenda, to Mauritius and, after some time, to the Seychelles. When his wife died on the island, his disciples at home found him another and sent her to join him in exile. Kamwana remained in Seychelles until the coronation of King George VI in 1937. Mercy was granted to him, and he was allowed to return home in August of that year. With the aid of his followers, other converts, and people such as **Charles Domingo**, the Watchtower movement grew in all parts of the country.

However, within a short time of his heroic return, Kamwana was embroiled in an ideological conflict with his supporters. He now insisted on strict observation of certain limitations, including prohibitions on smoking and ornaments such as beads. His proposal to raise church funds through a contribution of one penny upset some of the Watchtower adherents. Within Nkhata Bay itself some people were displeased when he transferred the movement's headquarters from Chirwa in the south to Mdyaka, north of Chintheche and the Luweya River. All this led to a split in the organization. Those who opposed the move called theirs the Watchtower Society of Chifira; Kamwana's came to be known as the Watchtower Healing Mission Society or the Mlonda Healing Mission Society. The major difference with his original organization was belief in spiritual healing, not spirit possession, rather than medicine.

Starved of funds, Kamwana's new center did not develop according to plan. The years of exile seem to have reduced Kamwana's interest in politics, since he talked increasingly of differentiating what belonged to Caesar from that which belonged to God. Some Watchtower followers, especially those in the Thyolo-Mulanje area, were unimpressed by the change in emphasis, and they ignored his plea to adopt the new approach to preaching. By the time he died on July 31, 1956, his political influence had long been superseded by **African welfare associations**, the **Nyasaland African Congress** (NAC), and, nearer home, the **Atonga Tribal Council**. His religious influence had also greatly diminished, leaving him with an estimated 4,000 followers.

CHIRWA, JONATHAN. In 1897 Jonathan Chirwa, a **Tumbuka-Ngoni**, was preacher and teacher in charge of the Free Church station at Hora in the heartland of Ngoni territory. In May 1914 he was one of the first three

Africans to be ordained a full minister and was immediately posted to **Loudon Mission** as assistant to Rev. **Donald Fraser**. Two years later, he was transferred to **Mwenzo** in **Northern Rhodesia**, but in July 1918 he resigned from the ministry and was suspended from the church for admitting to adultery. Christians and coworkers in Ngoni, led by **Rev. Andrew Mkochi** and Rev. Donald Fraser, continuously and vigorously called for his restoration, which finally took place in 1924. He was reposted to Loudon, and four years later he scored another first by being elected as the first African moderator of a Presbytery. Chirwa, an accomplished composer of church hymns, remained at Loudon where, as the years passed, he came to be regarded as *"an eminence grise"* (T. J. Thompson 1995, 207). He died in the mid-1930s and is buried in a Ngoni-style cattle kraal, in the same grave in which the remains of Donald Fraser were laid to rest in 1935.

CHIRWA, ORTON EDGAR CHING'OLI. Born in **Nkhata Bay** District in 1919, Chirwa was educated at **Bandawe, Khondowe** (Livingstonia), and at St. Francis College, Natal, before going to **Fort Hare University** College, where in 1950 he obtained a B.A. degree with philosophy as his major. He returned to **Malawi** to lecture at the **Domasi** Teachers Training College. Besides his teaching duties, two other things preoccupied him at this stage: preparation for Part 1 of the English bar examinations and his disappointment with the policies and organization of the **Nyasaland African Congress** (NAC), especially at a time when the **Federation of Rhodesia and Nyasaland** was being imposed on the Africans of **Nyasaland**. He left the party only to return to it after a brief period. In 1955 Chirwa resigned from government service, went to England to complete his legal studies, and in May 1958 was called to the bar, thereby becoming Malawi's first indigenous barrister.

On his return he entered private practice and also became the NAC's legal adviser. On March 6, 1959, he was arrested, sent to Khami prison in **Southern Rhodesia**, and was released eight months later. In September of that year, Chirwa and other free activists such as **Sydney Somanje**, Chechwa Bwanausi, **Augustine Mnthambala**, and **Aleke Banda** formed the **Malawi Congress Party** (MCP) with a view to continuing the work of the banned NAC. The new party immediately began to campaign for the release of political detainees and for a boycott of the **Monckton Commission**, which was due to arrive in the country in 1960 to review the future of the Federation of Rhodesia and Nyasaland.

When Dr. **Hastings K. Banda** was released in April 1960, Chirwa handed him the presidential reins of the MCP. During the next several years Chirwa was a key aide to Banda, serving him at the numerous constitutional conferences where self-government and independence were negotiated. After the 1961 general **elections**, Chirwa became parliamentary secretary in the Ministry of Justice; later he was appointed minister of justice and attorney general. In this capacity, he was responsible for initiating the nation's local court system. Chirwa split with his chief over Banda's slow **Africanization** policy of government positions. The prime minister reacted by accusing Chirwa of collusion with the Chinese in **Tanzania**. Chirwa was dismissed in September 1964, and for security reasons he left the country to live in exile in **Tanzania**. He taught law at the University of Dar es Salaam, and later he and his wife, Vera, also a lawyer, moved to Lusaka, **Zambia**, where for a time they were on the law faculty at the university in that city.

Chirwa also started a political party, the **Malawi Freedom Movement (MAFREMO)**, aimed at organizing the overthrow of the Banda government in Malawi. He had been in exile for 17 years in December 1981, when he, Vera, and their son, Fumbani, were enticed to visit the **Chipata-Mchinji** area on the Zambia-Malawi border. They were subsequently abducted by agents of the Malawi government and placed under arrest. From July 1982 to February 1983, the trial was held in the national traditional court to ensure that the verdict would favor the government. In May 1983 they were sentenced to death for treason, for having conspired to overthrow the government, and were confined to the maximum security prison in **Zomba**, where they were not allowed to communicate. Both Amnesty International in London and the Church of Scotland protested the trial and urged Dr. Banda to grant a reprieve of their sentence. In June 1984 the death sentence was commuted to life in prison; five months earlier, Dr. Banda had ordered the release from "protective custody." Fumbani reported that he had been held in solitary confinement in Zomba prison in a section reserved for political prisoners. Dr. Banda is said to have later regretted the commuted sentences, particularly after a MAFREMO attack on the northern police post north of Kaporo in January 1987.

In 1992 Orton Chirwa died in jail. Since the agitation for political change had by that time become a fact of life, the government gave the rare permission that he be buried in Nkhata Bay, his home district. Much to the government's dismay, it became a national funeral, attended by people from all walks of life and from all the three regions of the country.

Bakili Muluzi, head of **United Democratic Front** (UDF) and future president of Malawi, also attended. However, Chirwa's wife, Vera, still in prison, was not allowed to view his body or accompany the funeral party.

CHIRWA, ROBSON WATAYACHANGA. Secretary-general of the **Malawi Congress Party** (MCP) in the 1980s. Robson Chirwa was born in 1931 in Mabilabo's area in southern **Mzimba.** He went to local mission schools and to Dedza Secondary school, where he completed the Cambridge School certificate. He then studied for the advanced teacher's certificate at the **Domasi** Teachers' Training College. He taught in schools in Mzimba, was promoted to assistant school inspector and then inspector. In the mid-1960s he spent a year in England studying education administration. In the late 1960s Chirwa was appointed education attaché at the Malawi High Commission in London. He returned to **Malawi** early in 1971 and worked as district education officer. Later that year, he entered parliament and in 1972 was appointed parliamentary secretary in the Ministry of Transport and Communications. Subsequently, he served in several ministries as full minister, including the position of regional minister of the north. In 1987 he became minister without portfolio and administrative secretary of the MCP. Three years later, he was appointed minister of trade, industry, and tourism, a post he held until the MCP lost power in 1994. An articulate "supporting player" and generally well liked, Chirwa was not particularly ambitious for higher office and so was never regarded as a serious contender as successor to President **Hastings K. Banda.** Chirwa has virtually retired from politics, lives in **Mzuzu,** and now concentrates on farming and other businesses.

CHIRWA, VERA. Politician, lawyer, academic, **human rights** activist, and wife of **Orton Ching'oli Chirwa,** Vera Chirwa (née Chibambo) was a founding member of the **Malawi Congress Party** (MCP) and a national leader of the **League of Malawi Women.** Born at Chibambo Village in **Ekwendeni, Mzimba** District, Vera trained as a lawyer. After the 1964 **Cabinet Crisis** she and her husband went into exile, first to **Tanzania** and then to Lusaka, where she taught law at the University of **Zambia.** In 1982 agents of the Malawi government kidnapped her with her husband, Orton Chirwa, and son, Fumbani, and put them in **Zomba** prison. Although their son was later released, they were tried by the national traditional court, found guilty, and condemned to death. Their sentences were commuted to life; Orton Chirwa died in prison in 1992, and his wife was released in the following year. Upon her release she became a campaigner for political reform and a nonpartisan **human rights** activist. At the heads of state summit of the **Organization of African Unity** (OAU) held in Algeria in July 1999, Chirwa was one of the persons elected to the African Human and People's Rights Commission.

CHIRWA, WELLINGTON MANOAH. Born in **Nkhata Bay** District in 1916, he went to school at **Bandawe** and **Livingstonia**, where he qualified as a teacher. He taught in local schools, became a headmaster, was clerk to the **Atonga Tribal Council**, secretary of a teacher's association, and chairman of the West Nyasa Native Association. In 1938 Chirwa went to **Southern Rhodesia**, where he worked as a teacher and served as principal of the Gloag Ranch mission school. For a brief period (1945–1946), he was a journalist. All this time, he furthered his education by correspondence and in 1948 was admitted to **Fort Hare University** College, graduating in 1952 with a B.A. degree and a teaching certificate. From 1952 to 1953, Chirwa taught at the **Henry Henderson Institute** in **Blantyre**. Since he was developing an increasing interest in politics, however, he turned his entire attention to that field.

Chirwa became an active member of the **Nyasaland African Congress** (NAC) and joined the opposition to the **Federation of Rhodesia and Nyasaland**. However, unlike many of his contemporaries, he decided to fight it from within its structures. Against the wishes of many Africans, Chirwa and **Clement Kumbikano** were elected, with the blessing of the NAC, to the new Federal Assembly in 1954 as representatives of the Nyasaland African provincial councils. In the Federal Assembly he spoke against the Federation and was a member of the African Affairs Board. Although established to protect African interests, the board proved to be quite ineffective, much to the disappointment of Chirwa. In 1957 the opinions of **Henry Chipembere** and **Kanyama Chiume**, as well as a memo from Dr. **Hastings K. Banda**, persuaded the NAC to insist that Chirwa and Kumbikano resign from the Federal Assembly or be expelled from the Congress. The latter course was taken in July 1957.

Chirwa was a member of the **Monckton Commission**, which he joined in February 1960 only after he received assurance that Dr. Banda would be released. The minority report, signed by Chirwa, among others, demanded a quick dissolution of the Federation on the grounds of its unpopularity among Africans. However, in spite of these views and his sharp mind, which could have benefited postcolonial **Malawi**, Chirwa was vilified for having identified himself with federal institutions. Soon after the constitutional changes began to be implemented, he left Malawi to live in Southern Rhodesia.

In 1965 Chirwa tried to return but was refused entry; he tried again in 1968, but he was asked to leave the country after only a week in Nkhata Bay. In 1972 Chirwa sent feelers to Dr. Banda expressing his desire to return to Malawi. Banda had the matter discussed at the annual convention of the **Malawi Congress Party** (MCP), which that year was held in **Lilongwe**. His expectation was that delegates would be totally opposed to the request, thus giving him an excuse to turn it down. A number of delegates, including some chiefs from all the three regions, saw no problem with Chirwa's wish. But this response annoyed Banda, who stormed into the convention hall to express his disappointment with the people who had been sympathetic to Chirwa's request; he told the convention that such an approach indicated that they were unappreciative of the work he had done for Malawi since his return in 1958. Following Banda's unexpected outburst, the convention turned against those who had offended the president and, amid abuse and shouting, asked them to leave the venue of the meeting and return to their homes. The chiefs were expelled from the MCP and deposed from their traditional authorities. Chirwa remained in exile in London. In recent years he has actively supported multiparty democracy and from his London base has been involved in charity work that aims at raising money to assist development in Malawi.

CHIRWA, YURAIAH CHATONDA. One of the most distinguished of the initial alumni of **Livingstonia Mission**. Chirwa was born in modern **Nkhata Bay** District, went to school at **Bandawe**, and was already a teacher when **Robert Laws** sent him and **Charles Domingo** to **Lovedale** for further education in 1891. He returned three years later and spent most of his working life at **Khondowe**, where by the 1920s he was a senior assistant at the **Overtoun Institution**, Khondowe. A founding member and vice president of the **North Nyasa Native Association**, Chirwa also presented evidence to the commission of inquiry into the **Chilembwe uprising**. Although politically active, he was considered a moderate, certainly compared with Domingo and **Levi Mumba**, also one of his contemporaries. *See also* AFRICAN WELFARE ASSOCIATIONS.

CHISIZA, DUNDUZU KALULI. Chisiza was born in 1930 in **Karonga** and educated at **Livingstonia**. From 1949 to 1950, he worked as a clerk in the

Tanganyika Police Department. In 1950 he went to Uganda to further his education at the Aggrey Memorial College. In 1953 Chisiza left for **Southern Rhodesia**, where he worked as editor of the information bulletin at the Indian High Commission in Salisbury. He became involved in local politics and, with young activists such as George Nyandoro and Robert Chikerema, founded the Rhodesia African National Youth League, forebear of the Rhodesia African National Congress.Chisiza's activism led to his deportation in September 1956. Back in **Nyasaland**, he became a member of the **Nyasaland African Congress** (NAC), but in October of the following year he went to study economics at Fircroft College, part of the Selly Oak Colleges in Birmingham, England. He returned to Malawi in September 1958, and Dr. **Hastings K. Banda** immediately appointed him secretary-general of the rejuvenated NAC.

Chisiza became a key organizer of the Congress and was part of the inner circle that met on January 24–25, 1959, to discuss the future program of action. These meetings discussed, among other matters, a change of approach from nonviolence to violence where necessary. Not long after the deliberations, there were incidents of violence in some parts of the country, including Fort Hill (now **Chitipa**), **Karonga**, Dowa, and **Ntcheu**. As outbreaks of violence increased, the governor, Sir **Robert Armitage**, declared a state of emergency, which gave him extraordinary powers to effect his authority in the colony. Chisiza was arrested on March 4 and taken to Gweru prison, Southern Rhodesia, where he was confined with Dr. Banda, **Henry Chipembere**, and **Yatuta Chisiza**, his brother. Chisiza was released in September 1960 and once again became secretary-general of the **Malawi Congress Party** (MCP), the successor to the NAC. He was a delegate to the **Lancaster House Constitutional Conference** in December 1960 and to the **Federal Review Conference** later. After the MCP won the **elections** in 1961, Chisiza became parliamentary secretary in the Ministry of Finance, a position he had been preparing for many years. A fine theoretician, Chisiza was perceptive of the problems facing his nation and produced a plan of economic development for Malawi. But he never saw it through; in September 1962 a car accident at Thondwe bridge on the **Blantyre-Zomba** road tragically took his life. There are many who doubt the circumstances of his death, even four decades later. However, there is no doubt that the death robbed Malawi of a leading economist, a courageous person, and a pragmatic and broad-minded leader, one who was not afraid of Dr. Banda, soon to become dictator of Malawi.

CHISIZA, DUNDUZU, JR. Malawi's leading professional actor. Dunduzu was a baby in 1962, when his famous father, **Dunduzu Kaluli Chisiza**, died. After completing secondary education at the **Henry Henderson Institute** (HHI) Secondary School, he went to college in the **United States**, where he specialized in theater arts. On his return to **Malawi** in the mid-1980s, he formed the Wakhumbata Theatre Ensemble and became the director and principal actor. Based in **Blantyre**, the group made regular tours to different parts of the country, in the process establishing itself as the best known of such theater companies in Malawi. Although many plays that he wrote and acted in tended to include an antigovernment commentary, Chisiza surprised many Malawians when he joined the Malawi cabinet in 1993 at the height of the agitation for political reform. He became minister of youth and culture, and he contested and lost **elections** in 1994, when he returned to full-time acting. Dunduzu Chisiza Jr. died in 1999.

CHISIZA, YATUTA KALULI. Born in 1926 in **Karonga** and educated at **Livingstonia**, Yatuta Chisiza was the older brother of **Dunduzu Chisiza**. In 1948 he joined the Tanganyika police and advanced to the rank of inspector, becoming one of the very few such senior officers in the colony. In 1956 his brother, Dunduzu, encouraged him to return to **Nyasaland**, where the struggle for decolonization was gathering momentum. Yatuta based himself in **Blantyre**, where he became a businessman and politician. When Dr. **Hastings K. Banda** returned to Malawi in July 1958, Chisiza was one of the politicians who took Banda to different parts of the country to introduce him to the people he was about to lead on the road to decolonization. Taking advantage of his experience as a police officer and of his large physical stature, the party appointed Chisiza as Banda's bodyguard and head of security. He also became Banda's private secretary.

Chisiza was arrested during **Operation Sunrise** and, with Banda, **Henry Chipembere**, and Dunduzu, was detained in Gweru, **Southern Rhodesia**. In September 1960 he was released. Like many other senior politicians in the banned **Nyasaland African Congress** (NAC), he became a key player in the **Malawi Congress Party** (MCP), where he held the position of administrative secretary. When his brother died in September 1962, Yatuta became MP for Karonga and was promoted to parliamentary secretary. At independence, he became minister of home affairs. He broke with Banda during the **Cabinet Crisis** of September 1964 and then went into exile in **Tanzania**.

In 1967 Chisiza assembled some of his closest supporters and had them trained in guerrilla warfare. In October of that year they entered Malawi through **Mwanza** with a view to overthrowing Banda's government. The local officer in charge of **police** informed headquarters of reports of the infiltration. Within hours, the Malawi **army** was led to the camp of Chisiza and his followers, who were equipped with weapons such as bazookas and AK-47 assault rifles. In the ensuing combat Chisiza and some of his people were killed. Others ran away, and one shot himself as the Malawi security forces approached him; others were captured, taken to **Zomba**, and executed. Although the government was silent on its losses, it is reported that many soldiers were killed in this short operation.

CHISSANO, JOACHIM. President of **Mozambique** since 1986. Chissano was born in southern Mozambique in 1939 and was educated locally and in Portugal. In 1962 he abandoned his legal studies to join **FRELIMO** and in the following year became a member of the Central Committee of the organization. From 1969 to 1974, he was FRELIMO's chief of security as well as its chief representative in Dar es Salaam, **Tanzania**. Chissano was prime minister of Mozambique during the transition to independence, and when the Portuguese handed complete power to the people of Mozambique, Chissano became foreign minister in a government headed by President **Samora Machel**. When Machel died in 1986, Chissano became president of the former Portuguese territory and immediately started working to improve relations between Mozambique and **Malawi**, which had become particularly strained due to suspicion that Malawi was aiding RENAMO in its attempt to overthrow the FRELIMO government.

CHISUMPHI. A northern **Chewa** designation for High God; it a proto-Chewa theological tradition predating the rise of the Phiri, the rulers of the **Maravi** state, to political dominance. Chisumphi's principal functionaries came from the Banda clan, and Makawena was a title of the High God's ritual "wife."

CHISUSE, MUNGO MURRAY. Of **Yao** affiliation, Chisuse was one the first students of **David Clement Scott** at the **Blantyre Mission**. He went on to train as a printer and even spent two years in Scotland studying the trade. He became the printer in charge at the **Henry Henderson Institute**, printing mission publications as well as those of the government and commercial firms.

CHITALO, EDDA. Born in **Blantyre** in 1932. After primary school, Chitalo went to teachers college, where she qualified in 1951. She taught at Blantyre Girls School, later becoming headmistress. Chitalo became a member of parliament for Blantyre in 1971 and within two years was appointed a junior minister. In the early 1980s she was expelled from the **Malawi Congress Party** (MCP), lost her position, and virtually retired from active politics. In the early 1990s she returned to politics as an advocate of reform. She was reelected to parliament in May 1994, this time on a **United Democratic Front** (UDF) ticket; she was appointed minister of health and later moved to the Office of the President.

CHITENJE. Popular colorful cotton prints, about two meters long, usually wrapped around the waist to cover the lower part of the body. Often a chitenje is worn over a dress or skirt to protect it from becoming dirty. Sometimes dresses, skirts, and men's shirts are made from chitenje material. Most of the chitenje cloth is made locally by David Whitehead & Sons, but some of it is imported from other parts of Africa and from Holland. During the **Malawi Congress Party** (MCP) rule, the **League of Malawi Women** had uniforms of chitenje printed with special party colors that included a prominent image of Dr. **Hastings K. Banda**. Since every woman was expected to belong to the league and the uniform was mandatory, immense profit accrued from the sale of it, adding much to the party's treasury.

CHITIMBA. Known as Florence Bay in colonial days, Chitimba lies on the northeastern point of the lakeshore area of **Rumphi** District. For many years this was the main port for the **Livingstonia Mission** at **Khondowe**, which was approached through a dramatic 22–hairpin turn road.

CHITIPA. Built in 1896 to guard the road to **Northern Rhodesia** and Tanganyika, Chitipa is located in the northernmost section of **Malawi**. The British named the place Fort Hill, in honor of Sir Clement Hill, a senior officer in the Foreign Office. During World War I, it was an important military base, strategic in its nearness to Tanganyika, then known as German East Africa. For most of the colonial period, Fort Hill was significant only as a customs and immigration post. However, as a result of widespread antigovernment activity, accompanied by some violence in early 1959, Fort Hill became the headquarters of the Fort Hill subdistrict, which encompassed all the upland section of **Karonga**. In 1965 Fort Hill was renamed Chitipa, actually reverting to its original Lambya name. It also became the *boma* of the new Chitipa District.

Chitipa District falls within the Karonga Agricultural Development Division and is noted for **maize**, beans, **coffee**, and cattle production; in recent years it has also proved to have potential as a **tobacco**-growing area, except that its very poor **transportation** links with the rest of the country make commercial **agriculture** an unprofitable proposition. Until the 1960s, Chitipa town was the site of a labor recruitment office for **Witwatersrand Native Labour Association** (WENELA) of **South Africa**. The organization's catchment area included southern Tanganyika and **Northern Rhodesia (Zambia)**. In previous decades it had also been the recruiting center for the Rhodesia Native Labour Bureau, locally known as Mthandizi or Untuli ("the helper"). Chitipa was also one of the early training bases of the Young Pioneers, which, like all other similar establishments, have now been closed. *See also* YOUTH.

CHITSULO, BISHOP CORNELIO. First Malawian to become a Catholic priest. Chitsulo was born at Njoro village on the periphery of **Mua** Mission. In 1920 he joined the Minor Seminary at Mua, and seven years later he went to Kipalapala Major Seminary in Tanganyika, where he spent 10 years studying for the priesthood. In 1937 he was ordained at Mbembeke, and in 1956 he became the first African apostolic vicar and was charged with the responsibility of the new Dedza vicariate, which became a diocese in 1959. Bishop Chitsulo held that office until 1984, when he was replaced by Bishop G. M. Chisendera.

CHITUKUKO CHA AMAI MU MALAWI (CCAM). Formed in 1984–1985 at the behest of **Cecilia Kadzamira**, this organization acted as a vehicle for the socioeconomic development of the **women** in **Malawi**. Central to its agenda was the self-sufficiency of women. Its method of attaining this goal was for women in each locality to think of means of generating income that would be used to improve conditions in their areas. Among the numerous projects were communal agricultural plots and sewing and knitting schemes. This idea was interesting, considering President **Hastings K. Banda**'s hatred for all things socialist. CCAM did not flourish because at times it was difficult to distinguish it from the **League of Malawi Women**. Many women, especially those with employment, felt that the CCAM was interfering with their work and the time they usually spent with their families. Enthusiasm for it was limited because most saw it as an idea imposed from the top, an idea with a political agenda. Given the dominance of the party, they had no choice but to reluctantly be part of the project.

CHIUME, MURRAY WILLIAM KANYAMA. Prominent nationalist who worked for **Malawi**'s independence. Born in 1929 at **Usisya** in the northern lakeshore area of **Nkhata Bay** District, in 1938 Chiume left with his uncle for Dar es Salaam, Tanganyika, where he attended primary school before going on to Dar es Salaam Central School and completing Standard Eight (form two or grade eight). In 1946 he qualified to enter Tabora Senior Government Secondary School, then the most select high school in the colony, He passed his Cambridge University Higher Certificate Examinations (A Level) and in 1949 was admitted to Makerere University College, Kampala, Uganda, with a science focus. Makerere, like **Fort Hare** in **South Africa**, was a major breeding ground for future leaders of the decolonization movement. In 1951 Chiume was admitted to the medical school but changed within a year to science education, which he found more to his liking.

While at Makerere, Chiume also found time to return home, where in 1950 he was made secretary of the **Nyasaland African Congress** (NAC) conference at Nkhata Bay. At the end of 1953, he was awarded his diploma in education, and early the following year he began teaching at the Alliance Secondary School, Dodoma, Tanganyika. In September of that year he resigned, and in January 1955 he returned to **Nyasaland**, where he became actively involved in the NAC, joining other recent graduates such as **Henry Chipembere**, **Harry Bwanausi**, and **Vincent Gondwe**. This group of young men also started the Nyasaland College Association to raise funds to enable more indigenous people to go to universities abroad.

In 1955 Chiume became a small-scale **coffee** farmer in Chikwina, an area not far from **Mzuzu**, the new northern provincial headquarters. The government had just introduced coffee growing in the area, but because people were increasingly suspicious of government projects, Chiume noticed resistance to the adoption of this cash crop. However, convinced that they needed a dependable cash crop in order to tackle poverty and promote self-reliance, he campaigned for it. In October of that year, he was elected to the Nkhata Bay District Council, which in turn elected him to the Northern Province Council. In that same year, a new constitution allowing five Africans to be elected to the **Legislative Council** (LEGCO) was introduced in the colony. Chiume stood as the NAC candidate for the north, and on March 15, 1956, he was duly elected to the LEGCO. Chipembere also won elections in the south, and the two became the most effective advocates of decolonization in the LEGCO as well as outside it. They were also among the senior Congress members who called on Dr. **Hastings K. Banda** to lead the nationalist movement. When Dr. Banda assumed the headship of the NAC, Chiume was made publicity secretary-general of the movement, and he also became its chief foreign affairs spokesperson, participating in many pan-African conferences as well as tours on behalf of Banda and the Congress.

When the state of emergency was declared on March 3, 1959, Chiume, unlike other ranking politicians, escaped arrest and detention because he was abroad seeking support for the party. He was to spend most of 1959 and 1960 in the United Kingdom as the party's ambassador at large, making several trips to Africa and Europe to explain the aspirations of the NAC. At the Lancaster House constitutional talks in 1960, he joined the **Malawi Congress Party** (MCP) delegation, and on his return to **Nyasaland** he resumed his position as publicity secretary-general of the MCP. In 1961 he was elected MP for **Rumphi** and was appointed the first African minister of education, to which ministry the portfolios of Information and Social Development were added. In 1964 he was returned unopposed, this time as member for Rumphi East. At independence, Chiume became minister of foreign affairs. But he was soon sacked from office because of his opposition to Banda's policies and his subsequent role in the **Cabinet Crisis** of 1964. Threatened by party zealots and afraid of political detention, Chiume sought refuge in Tanganyika, where he became a businessman and resumed his old interest, journalism. He also wrote several books and became a co-owner of the Pan-African Publishing Company. Chiume remained politically involved and was the president of the **Congress for the Second Republic** of Malawi (CSR), a party that was active mainly among Malawian exiles in **Tanzania** and **Zambia**.

Meantime, in **Malawi**, Dr. Banda and the MCP were determined that Chiume would never return to lead anything. As time went by, he became the most maligned political exile. The party faithful and youth leaguers were instructed to look for him and, if possible, kill him should he try to enter the country; he was portrayed in political speeches as evil and an enemy of the country. Anybody indicating any association with his name or party was arrested and imprisoned without trial. He was so vilified in popular MCP songs that the generation of Malawians born after the **Cabinet Crisis** came to identify his name with infamy. In 1994 Chiume arrived back in Malawi for the first time in nearly 30 years. His party contested the elections for a new multiparty parliament. Although he was a popular and flamboyant speaker, all his party's candidates lost. The new

United Democratic Front government made him chairman of the Malawi Book Service, but after this parastatal agency was privatized in 1996, Chiume lost that office. He now lives mainly in Mzuzu and maintains his business interests in Tanzania.

CHIUTA (CHAUTA). Among the **Tumbuka** and **Chewa/Mang'anja**, name of the Supreme Being to the extent that it is also applied to the biblical God.

CHIWANDA-GAMA, ALFRED. Born in March 1933 at **Mulanje**, he was educated at the **Henry Henderson Institute** in **Blantyre** and at **Malamulo** Seventh-Day Adventist Mission, where he completed primary school before going on to qualify as a carpenter. After a period of self-employment, he went to **Southern Rhodesia (Zimbabwe)** to work and became involved in politics, becoming the organizing secretary of the Msasa branch of the **Nyasaland African Congress** (NAC). In 1959 Chiwanda returned to Southern Rhodesia but within a year was back in **Malawi**. This time, he based himself in the Mapanga area, just outside **Limbe**, where in 1960 he was elected chairman of the **Malawi Congress Party** (MCP) branch. In 1962 he became a member of the Blantyre District Council, and in 1963 he was elected to two chairmanships—of the council and of the district MCP. In 1964 he went to parliament on the MCP ticket and four years later was appointed minister of labor; he also served as regional chairman of the MCP and regional minister for the Southern Region. By the early 1980s, Chiwanda had lost his positions in the party and had practically retired from politics.

CHIWANGA, DAVID. Born in 1942 in **Blantyre**, Chiwanga attended the **Henry Henderson Institute** in Blantyre, Tuskegee Institute in Alabama, and the University of London. From 1968 to 1973 he was the assistant **cotton** officer for the Southern Region; later he was the area's development officer for the **Shire Valley** Agricultural Development Project (1973–1976). He entered parliament in 1976. In May 1983 Chiwanga, along with John Sangala, **Dick Matenje**, and **Aaron Gadama**, was killed in an auto "accident" in **Mwanza** District. In the post–**Hastings Banda** period, the "accident" was the subject of a judicial inquiry. Although it resulted in confessions of the actual murderers, it was inconclusive on matters relating to the person or persons who ordered the actions. *See* MWANZA ACCIDENT AND TRIALS.

CHIWETA. Formerly one of the most isolated locations on **Lake Malawi**. Before the road that winds down from the northern Viphya Mountains to the lakeshore at Chiweta was constructed, a road described as commanding some of the most spectacular scenery in the world, Chiweta was little known. Just off Chiweta lies the **MV Viphya**, a passenger steamer that sank in 1946.

CHIWODA. A popular traditional dance usually performed by women, mostly in the lakeshore areas and nearly all districts of northern **Malawi**. In the decades immediately preceding independence, the Chiwoda was a vehicle for celebrating nationalistic songs and raising political consciousness. In President **Hastings Banda**'s time, Chiwoda's songs were used to praise the achievements of government.

CHIZUMILA, COLLINS. Prominent legal personality and politician. Chizumila was born in Misuku, **Chitipa** District, and qualified as a lawyer at the **University of Malawi**, after which he worked in private practice. In the early 1990s he became a leading prodemocracy advocate, was a member of the **Public Affairs Committee** (PAC), and became part of the founding leadership of the **United Democratic Front** (UDF). Although he lost in the 1994 parliamentary **elections**, he was appointed to the cabinet, first as transportation minister and later as minister of justice and attorney general. He died in 1997.

CHIZUMULU. Island adjacent to **Likoma** that constitutes part of **Nkhata Bay** District. Like Likoma, it was a center of the **Universities' Mission to Central Africa** (UMCA) activities and has one of the highest literacy rates in the country.

CHOKANI, WILLIE. Born in 1930 and educated at **Blantyre** Secondary School, he received his B.A. with honors, M.A. (history), and B.Ed. in Delhi, India. In 1957 he returned to Malawi and became founder-teacher of the **Henry Henderson Institute** Secondary School; he was also appointed headmaster of the school, the first African in the colony to hold such a position. A politically minded person, one who had witnessed the detrimental effects of colonial agricultural and agrarian policies on his people in **Chiradzulu**, Chokani actively campaigned for decolonization. In March 1959 he was arrested and taken to Khami in **Southern Rhodesia**. Upon his release in 1960, he continued his political activism and was considered one of the leading intellectuals in the **Malawi Congress Party** (MCP). In 1961 he was elected MP for Chiradzulu and was one of the MCP delegates to the Marlborough House Constitution Conference, which discussed self-government for **Malawi** and led to the elevation of Dr. **Hastings K. Banda** to the status of prime minister. Chokani was minister of labor until the **Cabinet Crisis** of 1964. With **Yatuta Chisiza** and **Henry Chipembere**, he resigned from the cabinet in sympathy with the four sacked colleagues. In September 1964 he went into exile in **Zambia**, where he became the first African headmaster of a an ex-federal school, which also meant that, among other things, he had to preside over its desegregation. He quickly and smoothly localized the student body and the teaching staff. Subsequently Chokani worked at the Northern Technical College, Ndola, in the Copper Belt. While doing all this he also managed to complete a master's degree (education) of the University of Leeds, United Kingdom.

In exile Chokani remained active in politics, mainly as treasurer of the Pan-African Democratic Party formed by Henry Chipembere after he moved to **Tanzania**. For the first time in 20 years, he returned to Malawi in August 1993 and became a member of the **National Consultative Council** (NCC), which oversaw the transition from dictatorship to a democratic dispensation. After the **United Democratic Front** formed the government in 1994, Chokani was appointed Malawi's ambassador to the **United States**, and he remained in that position until 1999, when he became ambassador to Ethiopia.

CHOLERA. The first cases of cholera were reported in **Malawi** in 1970, the epidemic entering the country from **Mozambique** and initially attacking **Nsanje**. It followed the railway and the **Shire River** north and then affected the entire lakeshore. By 1974 all parts of Malawi had been touched. It was identified as a **disease** that occurred in the rainy season. **Health** workers also began to educate people about hygiene as the best means of dealing with it. It has recurred many times but, due to education, is less of a menace than it was in 1970, when it was virtually new to the area.

CHOLO. *See* THYOLO.

CHRISTIAN COUNCIL OF MALAWI. This is an organization of all Protestant churches in **Malawi**.

CHRISTIAN HOSPITAL ASSOCIATION OF MALAWI (CHAMA). Formerly known as the Private Hospital Association of Malawi (PHAM), this organization was formed in 1965 and is composed of 15 denominations with 21 hospitals, 38 primary **health** care centers, 76 subcenters, and 13 health-related training schools. From 1978 the **Malawi** government assisted with the salaries of Malawian professional staff, enabling CHAMA members to employ properly trained people in their establishments. However, in the late 1990s, the government announced that it would no longer subsidize salaries, and some of the hospitals and health centers wondered whether they would survive as a consequence.

CHRISTIAN SERVICE COMMITTEE OF THE CHURCHES IN MALAWI (CSC). This ecumenical organization was originally established in 1965 as a service division of the **Blantyre** Synod of the **Church of Central Africa Presbyterian**. It assumed its current name in 1968 when it became a joint effort of the Christian Council of Malawi (Protestant) and the Episcopal Conference of Malawi (Catholic). Basically a Christian endeavor to address problems of poverty, famine, **disease**, and hunger, the CSC plans and executes development projects aimed at fulfilling this objective. Central to its operations is the involvement of the rural communities concerned; the latter initiate the requests, provide the labor, and generally work with the CSC, which provides technical expertise, equipment, and finance. Its funds come from donor agencies mainly in Europe and North America, and some of its most active supporters have been DANIDA, Christian Aid, the World Council of Churches, and Birt fur World. Among the numerous projects of the CSC are improvements in rural water supply, construction of health clinics and school buildings, primary health care, and vocational and distance education.

CHRISTIAN SOCIAL DEMOCRATIC PARTY (CSDP). This short-lived political organization was formed in October 1960 by **Chester Katsonga**, a businessman and former **Nyasaland African Congress** (NAC) activist. The new **Malawi Congress Party** (MCP) strongly condemned its formation, accusing it of causing confusion when unity in the nationalist movement was needed. Katsonga was a Catholic, and the MCP in a famous editorial in its organ, the *Malawi News*, further accused the Church, especially Archbishop **Jean-Baptist Theunissen**, of supporting the CSDP.

CHULU. Area in northern **Kasungu** that takes its name from the dynasty that ruled it for over four centuries. The original Chulu was part of the **Maravi** expansion north, and it included, among others, **Kaluluma** and **Kanyenda**.

CHUMA. With Susi and others, Chuma was one of **David Livingstone**'s servants, carriers, and guides recruited in the **Shire Highlands** of

Malawi. He was also part of the group that in 1873 carried Livingstone's embalmed body and private papers for 1,500 miles, from Chitambo, Ilala, in modern **Zambia**, to **Zanzibar**, where they handed it over to the British authorities. The journey took them two months. Later he and Susi were taken to England, where the Royal Geographical Society presented them with its bronze medal. They also helped **Horace Waller** edit Livingstone's last journals (1874).

CHURCH OF CENTRAL AFRICA PRESBYTERIAN (CCAP). Formed on September 17, 1924, the **Blantyre** and **Livingstonia** Presbyteries of the Church of Scotland combined to form the Synod of the Church of Central Africa Presbyterian. Two years later, the Mkhoma Synod of the Dutch Reformed Church joined the CCAP. By the late 1960s, they had a theological college at Mkhoma. With other members of the Christian Council, they moved the college to **Zomba**.

COCKERILL, WALTER. American missionary who went to **Nyasaland** in 1914 to revive the work of the Seventh Day Baptist movement started by **Joseph Booth**. Cockerill was born in New Berlin, Wisconsin, in 1886, and was a member of the Seventh Day Baptist church in that town. His ambition was to work outside the United States, and in 1913 he dropped out of college and joined the Seventh Day Baptist Church at Plainfield, New Jersey, through which he was able to identify Nyasaland as a possible destination. In January 1914 he left for the British colony, arriving in **Blantyre** on March 31, and set himself up at **Shiloh**. He began to establish contact with some of the local people who had worked with Booth, particularly during his affiliation with the Seventh Day Baptist Church. **Alexander Makwinja**, who had continued some of Booth's education projects, became one of Cockerill's principal associates. In early August that year, Cockerill left Blantyre for the north and spent a brief time in **Ntcheu** to acquaint himself with **Filipo Chinyama**, who had worked with both Booth and Chilembwe. He proceeded to **Nkhata Bay**, where there were many followers of **Eliot Kamwana**, and then on to **Mzimba**, where **Charles Domingo** was still the principal Seventh Day Baptist leader. While he was on this journey, World War I started. Fears of increased messianic fervor and the refusal of the **Ngoni** paramount, Inkosi **Chimtunga Jere**, to assist in recruiting conscripts caused H. C. MacDonald, the colonial government's representative at Mzimba, to force Cockerill back to Blantyre. From there he was to go to **Zomba** to be interviewed by the governor himself, Sir **George Smith**. The meeting took place on October 19, and as a result Cockerill was confined to the **Shire Highlands**. In January 1915 the **Chilembwe uprising** took place; many of Booth's and now Cockerill's religious friends, including Chinyama and Makwinja, were implicated. Cockerill's outspokenness, as well as his indirect association with Booth and some of the leading followers of Chilembwe, rendered him easy prey to the colonial administration, and in April 1915 he was deported from Nyasaland.

COFFEE. Although not as significant a cash crop as **tea** and **tobacco**, coffee has been grown in **Malawi** since the establishment of colonial rule. Introduced to the colony by Scottish missionaries, it was expected to be the main cash crop in the colony and became the principal preoccupation of some of the early European commercial farmers in the **Shire Highlands**. By 1900 it was apparent that this bean had poor prospects of succeeding, and as a result it greatly diminished in importance. The few Europeans who grew it did so for domestic consumption. In the 1920s the **Livingstonia Mission** embarked on a project to encourage African coffee production in the Phoka country and in north Viphya. At the same time, Africans in the Misuku hills, **Chitipa**, began to grow it with much enthusiasm. However, because of problems, mainly with **transportation**, this experiment did not succeed either. In the 1950s Africans in places such as Chikwina near **Mzuzu** grew coffee, again not with very good results. In the 1960s the **Commonwealth Development Corporation** began to promote growing by small-scale farmers. The main areas of the scheme were the **Thyolo/Mulanje** region and the **Viphya Highlands**. Since the mid-1990s, smallholder farmers in the latter area, including those in Msisuku and Phoka, have been producing and exporting Arabica coffee under the brand name Mzuzu Coffee. In the 1980s some European commercial farmers in the Shire Highlands were returning to coffee production, especially as the international prospects of tobacco were becoming increasingly cloudy.

COLBY, SIR GEOFFREY FRANCIS TAYLOR. Governor of Nyasaland from 1948 to 1956. Colby was born in England in 1901. He attended Cambridge University and then joined the colonial civil service, his first posting being to northern Nigeria in 1925. By 1945 he had risen to the position of administrative secretary in the secretariat, Lagos, and in 1948 he was appointed governor of **Nyasaland**. Colby is credited with developmental plans hitherto not experienced in Nyasaland; **agriculture** was at the center of the schemes. Awarded KCMG. He retired in 1956 and died two years later.

COLLECTOR. In the early colonial period, collector designated the head of the district administration, with the collection of revenue as its central responsibility. The name collector was later changed to Resident and then to **district commissioner**.

COLONIAL DEVELOPMENT CORPORATION (CDC). Established in 1948 as a vehicle for harnessing agricultural and mineral development in the British empire. the Colonial Development Corporation was largely financed by public sources, including those made available to it by the **Colonial Development and Welfare Act** of 1940. The CDC's first major project in **Nyasaland** was the development, from the late 1940s to the early 1960s, of **tung** estates in the **Viphya Highlands** and a subsidiary one, the Limpasa Dambo project in **Nkhata Bay**. The latter scheme was to concentrate on **rice** production to feed workers in the tung-growing region. Although both projects failed, **Mzuzu** grew out of the tung project, to the extent that in 1954 it replaced **Mzimba** as the headquarters of the Northern Region. As the British empire declined, the corporation changed its name to the Commonwealth Development Corporation. It extended its activities in Malawi, but this time as a joint investor with local interests. Among the current projects are **coffee** and **tobacco** production.

COLONIAL DEVELOPMENT AND WELFARE ACT. Passed by the British Parliament in 1940, it empowered the use of public funds for purposes of production and distribution and for promoting social welfare programs in the colonies. The act was revised several times in the 1940s and 1950s. *See also* COLONIAL DEVELOPMENT CORPORATION.

COLONIAL DEVELOPMENT AND WELFARE FUND. Funds made available to the colonies for the use of development projects. In **Nyasaland** programs such as the agricultural cooperatives and the **Master Farmers Scheme** of the 1950s benefited from the fund. *See also* COLONIAL DEVELOPMENT CORPORATION.

COLONIAL GOVERNORS. *See* BRITISH COMMISSIONERS AND GOVERNORS OF BRITISH CENTRAL AFRICA/NYASALAND (1891–1964).

COLVIN, REV. THOMAS. Scottish Presbyterian minister who joined the Blantyre Synod of the **Church of Central Africa Presbyterian** (CCAP) in 1954, serving mostly in **Blantyre**. Upon his return from leave in 1959, the **Nyasaland** and federal governments refused him reentry into the colony because of his anticolonial and pro-African views. Between 1959 and 1964, Colvin was a missionary in Tamale, Ghana, but returned to the Blantyre Synod in the year **Malawi** attained its independence from British authority. In 1968 he founded the **Christian Service Committee**, which he served as executive secretary until retiring to the United Kingdom in 1974. In 1984 he went to work in **Zimbabwe**, and three years later he returned to Malawi in the service of another **nongovernmental organization** (NGO). In 1990 Colvin retired to Scotland; he died in 2000.

COMMON MARKET FOR EASTERN AND SOUTHERN AFRICA (COMESA). COMESA grew out of the **preferential trade area** for Eastern and Southern African States (PTA), an association of states with the purpose of promoting a free trade area, a customs union, a common market, and ultimately an economic community with some uniformity in economic policies. Although discussions leading to the formation of PTA go back to 1977, the foundation dates to December 21, 1981, when the heads of state of participating countries, meeting in Lusaka, **Zambia**, signed the Preferential Trade Treaty detailing its aims and programs. At that stage the signatories were the Comoro Islands, Djibouti, Ethiopia, Kenya, **Malawi**, Mauritius, Somalia, Uganda, and Zambia; in the following year, they were joined by Burundi, Lesotho, Swaziland, and **Zimbabwe**. Rwanda became a member in 1984, the year of the organization's formal launching. In that year, the PTA instituted its Multilateral Clearing Facility (clearinghouse) to handle settlement claims originating from deals between member states. But this department has been operationally problematic from the beginning. The UAPTA (unit of account of the PTA) through which intraregional commerce was to be articulated, which was equivalent to the Special Drawing Rights (SDR) of the **International Monetary Fund** (IMF), was introduced in the early 1990s but proved to be unpopular.

Under a new treaty of 1994 the PTA was replaced by the Common Market for Eastern and Southern Africa (COMESA), and by that time the membership had increased to include **South Africa**, Uganda, Zaire (Democratic Republic of Congo), and Angola. Malawi hosted COMESA's summit conference in December 1994, and President **Bakili Muluzi** has served a term as chairman of the organization. Malawian **Bingu wa Mutharika** replaced Bax Nomvete, the first secretary-general of the PTA, in 1989 and oversaw its transition to COMESA; in 1997 he returned to Malawi and founded the **United Party**.

COMMONWEALTH DEVELOPMENT CORPORATION. *See* COLONIAL DEVELOPMENT CORPORATION.

COMMUNICATION SERVICES. Malawi's communications network has expanded considerably since independence. Telecommunications services include telephone, telex, and telegraph. Most investments in equipment, plant, and buildings are in the major urban centers and are funded by British and Danish government loans. Virtually all districts in **Malawi** now have telephone facilities. Most rural exchanges are manually operated, but replacement by automated exchanges is continuing. International service improved greatly in 1976 with the introduction of direct satellite circuits to the United Kingdom and **South Africa**. That same year in **Blantyre**, a telecommunications training school began operation under the sponsorship of the United Nations' International Telecommunication Union. Students from Malawi, Botswana, Lesotho, and Swaziland attended courses. The most recent international assistance has been used to fund the expansion of the rural telephone network, the Blantyre-**Lilongwe** microwave link, and the development of a national mail sorting and storage center.

The postal service enjoys a fine reputation because its deliveries are exceptionally prompt. Post offices are located in every region, with postal boxes being used almost exclusively. Post Office Savings Bank deposits are also collected at post offices; interest is paid and deposits are free of all taxes.

There is also now an increasing use of electronic mail (e-mail) in Malawi. Malawi.Net, a parastatal organization, was established in 1996 as the main provider of Internet services. However, there are other servers, including the Lilongwe-based Epsolom Omega; many Malawians are also connected to international servers such as Hotmail and Yahoo. *See also* TRANSPORTATION.

CONFORZI, IGNACO. One of the most successful **tea** and **tobacco** growers and businessmen in Malawi. Conforzi was born into a landed family just north of Rome, Italy, in 1885. He trained in agricultural science, and in 1907 he became a manager in **Nyasaland** of one of the tobacco estates belonging to the British and East Africa Company. Two years later, Conforzi started his own tobacco plantation in **Thyolo** (Cholo) and other parts of the **Shire Highlands**. By the end of World War I, he was a major producer, selling most of his tobacco to the **Imperial Tobacco Company** (ITC). During the interwar period, Conforzi, with **A. F. Barron** and **Roy Wallace**, opened up large estates in the Central Region, where they pioneered growing tobacco through the tenant system. Besides selling tobacco to the ITC and later to Gallaher Ltd. of Belfast, Northern Ireland, he and other Italians started a tobacco brokerage company, Clagget, Brachi & Co., which operated from England. Conforzi also established major **tea** estates in Thyolo, becoming one of the major tea producers in the country. In addition he became a leading blanket manufacturer, the brand name, Chiperoni, being particularly identified with the Conforzi family business.

CONGRESS FOR THE SECOND REPUBLIC. Formed in 1964 by **William Kanyama Chiume**, not long after he sought exile in **Tanzania**. The party, whose membership is difficult to determine, was the subject of regular infiltration by Malawi's security agents. In 1994 Chiume returned to **Malawi** to contest the presidential **elections**. He and all his parliamentary candidates lost. He was not a candidate in the 1999 general elections, and the Congress for the Second Republic seems to be near extinction.

CONGRESS LIBERATION PARTY (CPL). Formed on May 4, 1958, by **Thamar Dillon Thomas Banda**, former secretary-general and president-general of the **Nyasaland African Congress** (NAC). Its agenda was generally similar to that of the main nationalist movement: one-man one-vote, independence, no color bar, free **education**. However, it also reflected the moderate views of its founder: continuation and respect for the power of the chiefs, and respect for private property. Although the party did not achieve notable support, Thamar Banda attended the **Federal Review Conference** in London in 1960, and, unlike African delegates from the three territories of the **Federation of Rhodesia and Nyasaland**, he attended the full conference. The CPL contested the 1961 general **elections** but lost, marking the effective demise of the party.

CONVENTION OF ASSOCIATIONS. This was the coordinating body of all European settler organizations in **Nyasaland**. Such associations included the Planters Associations of **Zomba** and **Mulanje**, the Cholo Settlers Association, the Nyasaland Council of Women, and the Cholo Tea Association. It became a particularly powerful organization and had direct influence on the colonial government. In time, associations of residents who did not identify themselves as Africans also joined the convention. Organizations in the latter category included the Indian Employees Association, the Sikh Association of Nyasaland, and the Anglo-African Association of Nyasaland.

COOPERATIVES. As early as the 1920s a European cooperative shop existed in **Blantyre**, and during the interwar era African credit unions and brick-making cooperatives were a feature of urban centers such as Blantyre-**Limbe**, **Zomba**, and **Lilongwe**. However, agricultural cooperatives were a postwar phenomenon, part of the colonial government's policy of encouraging self-sufficiency and discouraging labor migration to the farms and mines of the Rhodesias and **South Africa**. Among the successful agricultural cooperatives were the **Kilupula Rice Growers Co-operative Union**, the **Ulambya Ghee Producers Co-operative Union**, the **Kasitu Valley Ghee Producers Co-operative Union**, and the Shire Valley Rice Growers Co-operative Union. Three years after independence, the government decided to disband all such organizations; it also closed the Department of Co-operatives, which had been in existence since 1945.

COTTON. In early colonial Malawi, cotton was one of the major export crops and was grown primarily in the Lower and Upper Shire, **Karonga** and **Salima** Districts. Although some European settlers grew cotton, many indigenous people also produced it. Even after it was replaced by **tobacco** in importance, it remained a significant cash crop throughout the colonial period. Today cotton is extensively, but not exclusively, cultivated by farmers in the rural agricultural development projects in **Karonga**, Lower Shire, and central lakeshore. Production of medium-staple cotton by the smallholder sector is bought by the **Agricultural Development and Marketing Board** (ADMARC) and sold to the local textile industry, with any surplus cotton being exported. In the early 1980s, when producer prices favored **maize**, farmers lost interest in cotton. The cotton market remains extremely depressed. Neighboring **Zimbabwe** has increased medium-staple cotton exports, thereby increasing competition in Malawi's regional market. The number of cotton growers is still on the decline, although there are limited alternatives for crop production in the Lower Shire. A 10 percent increase in producer prices did not encourage farmers to increase their acreage in cotton. *See also* BRITISH COTTON GROWING ASSOCIATION.

CROSS, DAVID KERR. Ordained Scottish medical doctor who went to the **Lake Malawi** region in 1884 to work at the **Livingstonia Mission**. Kerr Cross was posted to Ncherenje in **Mweniwanda, Ulambya**, in today's **Chitipa** District, where he joined Rev. A. J. Bain. Chosen partly because it was on the Stevenson road joining Lakes Malawi and Tanganyika, the site was not a particularly healthy one, and in 1886 his wife,

Christina, died. When the mission was abandoned in 1889, he moved to **Karonga**, where he was pastor and doctor. In 1896 he joined government service, working in **Zomba** and **Blantyre** before going to **South Africa** in 1902. Dr. Kerr Cross was the first person to produce a medical report on the Karonga lakeshore. Among the common **diseases** he encountered were malaria, smallpox, goiter, and syphilis (which he mostly associated with the **Swahili-Arabs**), epilepsy, and meningitis; he also saw some cases of elephantiasis and filariasis, but no cases of tuberculosis.

CURRENCY. In 1971 **Malawi** adopted a modern decimal system and dropped the use of British pounds/shillings. The main unit of currency is now the **kwacha**, which is divided into 100 tambala. Decimal coins have been issued: 1t, 5t, 10t, 20, 50t, and 1K. Since the early 1980s, Malawi has experienced nearly yearly currency devaluations in order to become more competitive in the export market and obtain additional assistance from the **International Monetary Fund (IMF)**. Each time the kwacha was devalued— by 12, 15, and even 20 percent. The average exchange rate of 1989–1991 was MK2.75 per US$, in 1993 MK4.4 per US$, in 1997 MK18.28 per US$, in 1999 MK43 per US$, and toward the end of 2000 MK77.00 per US$. *See also* FINANCIAL AND ECONOMIC DEVELOPMENTS.

– D –

DAOMA, ANN. In 1861 a tiny girl was found lying beside her dead mother following an attack by **Universities' Mission to Central Africa (UMCA)** on the **Yao** in an attempt to rescue the **Mang'anja**, just captured into slavery. Bishop **Charles Mackenzie** personally carried the girl to **Magomero**, where she was baptized and named Ann. When **Horace Waller** left the mission for **South Africa** en route to Great Britain, he took with him a number of rescued Mang'anja, including Daoma, who was left at the St George's Orphanage in Cape Town. Daoma attended school there, trained as a teacher, and worked in that part of Africa; she died in 1936.

DAYARAM, PRANLAL. Asian businessman. In 1949 he became a member of the **Legislative Council** (LEGCO) representing the interests of his community. In that year, he was also appointed to the Food and Distribution Advisory Committee, which played a major role in sorting out problems arising out of the **famine** of 1949.

DEEP BAY. *See* CHILUMBA.

DELANY, EMMA B. Born in Florida in 1871, DeLany was educated at Spelman Seminary (now Spelman College) in Atlanta, Georgia. After she worked as a matron at the Florida Institute in Live Oak, the National Baptist Convention sponsored her as a missionary to the **Lake Malawi** region. She arrived in the **Shire Highlands** in 1902 and began work at **John Chilembwe's Providence Industrial Mission** (PIM). The preceding year, two other black American missionaries had come to PIM: **Thomas Branch** and **Landon Cheek**. With help from **Ida Chilembwe**, DeLany developed programs that included sewing classes for **women**. She was popular with the PIM congregation, and when she left in 1905, one of her devotees, **Daniel Malekebu**, followed her back to America. DeLany, with Cheek, helped Chilembwe organize his mission effectively.

DELEZA, WADSON BINI. Born in **Chiradzulu** and educated at **Zomba** Catholic Secondary School, Deleza became interested in politics while at school. Between 1958 and 1959, he was a prominent member of the Youth League, organizing support for the **Nyasaland African Congress** (NAC) and its successor, the **Malawi Congress Party** (MCP), among the **youth** of the country. In the early 1960s Deleza went to the Haille Selassie University, Addis Ababa, Ethiopia, and received a M.Sc. degree in crop science from the University of Southern Illinois in the **United States.** From 1965 to 1971, he worked as a research officer in the Ministry of Agriculture. In 1971 he became a nominated MP for Chiradzulu and minister of labor. Two years later, he was transferred to the Ministry of Transport and Communications, a post vacated by the dismissed **Aleke Banda**. Subsequently, he served as minister of trade, industry, and tourism but later returned to the Ministry of Labour. By the mid-1980s, Deleza had become a senior cabinet minister and one of the more influential politicians in Malawi; he had Dr. **Hastings K. Banda**'s confidence and was even appointed administrative secretary of the MCP. Considered a hawk in matters regarding the democratization of **Malawi**, Deleza lost his seat in the 1994 **elections**, and he retired from politics to become a full-time businessman. He died in 1998.

DEMOCRAT. The *Democrat*, or the *Malawi Democrat*, was originally a prodemocracy newsletter published by advocates of change based in Lusaka, **Zambia**, and secretly transported to **Malawi**. Behind the paper were **O'Brien Mapopa Chipeta** and **Mayinga Mkandawire**, both of whom were associated with the **Alliance for Democracy** (AFORD).

When the two moved to Malawi to campaign for multiparty democracy, they took with them the paper, which came to be identified with AFORD. A popular and hard-hitting publication, it became a tabloid and was closed in 1996.

DEPARTMENT OF ANTIQUITIES. This branch of government was created in 1967. The department is responsible for preserving local monuments, researching local history, and establishing site museums. It is particularly active in publishing the results of archaeological excavations, especially those of Late **Stone Age** and **Iron Age** sites. The director of antiquities is an ex-officio member and secretary of the national Monuments Commission. Manned by highly trained local personnel, the department has on its staff archaeologists, palaeontologists, and historians, and is considered to be one of the most professionally organized and effective in Africa. Since 1987, the Department of Antiquities has fallen under a wider department headed by the commissioner of culture; the other three sections of the latter department, Archives, Cultural Affairs, and Museums, are each headed by a director.

DEVLIN COMMISSION. Chaired by Sir Patrick Devlin, this commission was appointed to examine the incidents following the declaration of a state of emergency in March 1959. In its report, made public in July 1959, the colonial government in **Nyasaland** was discredited for its autocratic behavior toward **Nyasaland African Congress** (NAC) members, some of whom, the commission admitted, had pursued violent actions. Although the commissioners stated that they had no evidence of a plot to massacre Europeans in the colony, apparently there was informal talk among a few Congress members to murder some European officials if Dr. **Hastings K. Banda** was killed. The commission found that no formal plan existed and that Banda was not aware of any such plot. The Devlin Report was particularly embarrassing for the government, as it detailed instances of illegal force and unnecessary brutality. After interviewing Banda, the commissioners not only absolved him of any responsibility for the violence but declared him an outstanding and dedicated leader of his people. Many members of the British Conservative Party were not impressed by the report, and it is said that it may have cost Sir Patrick Devlin, a senior and highly respected judge, promotion to higher office.

DEVLIN REPORT. *See* DEVLIN COMMISSION.

DHARAP, M. G. This leading Indian general trader, founding member of the **Nyasaland Indian Traders Association** and the **Indian Chamber of Commerce**, was originally a wholesaler. By the 1950s, he had established retail shops in almost every district of **Malawi**.

DIET. Most Malawian diets are based on the subsistence crops that they grow. A thick, warm-to-hot **maize** flour (in some areas, cassava flour) porridge *(nsima)*, usually served with a spicy relish, is common at a village meal that rarely includes any meat, which is beyond people's means. In urban centers the traditional diet is often supplemented with eggs, milk, bread, and meat. In the lakeshore areas and other places with established markets, fish—dry and fresh—is a regular companion of *nsima*. Beer, often made from finger millet, is popular in both rural and urban areas. The necessity of balanced diets and good nutrition is being promoted in government educational programs, especially the radio broadcasts of the MBC. *Nsima,* in all its varieties, is also the main diet in most parts of sub-Saharan Africa. Many Malawians also eat **rice**, especially in areas such as **Karonga** and **Nkhotakota**, where it is grown. **Sorghum** and millet, once the staples, are now insignificant in the diet of the **Lake Malawi** region. *See also* NUTRITION.

DISEASE. The disease pattern found in **Malawi** is common to many African countries, which have limited **health** facilities. Pneumonia, malaria, gastroenteritis, anemia, measles, and tuberculosis are the leading causes of death in **Malawi**, where average life expectancy at birth is 47 years. **AIDS** is also prevalent. Sanitation conditions are not always good. Waste disposal tends to be unsatisfactory and water supplies are often contaminated. The Ministry of **Health** program to teach principles of sound **nutrition** and good hygiene is frequently hampered by widespread illiteracy and poverty. Additional constraints include population growth (3.2 percent annually) and budgetary limits on the part of the Malawi government. In the past **Malawi** has allocated 92 percent of its health expenditure to urban hospitals; it is hoped that the new emphasis on primary health care will lead to serving many more people.

Through multilateral and bilateral aid, and the assistance of **nongovernmental organizations** (NGOs) such as OXFAM and the **Christian Service Committee**, more attention is being paid to family planning services and child health as well as to training Malawi health personnel in the prevention of common diseases. Particularly emphasized are childhood immunization, diarrhea control, malaria prevention, and nutrition monitoring. *See also* CHOLERA; JIGGERS; PLAGUE.

DISTRICT COMMISSIONER (DC). From the 1930s, the principal district administrators were called district commissioners. Besides maintaining law and order and presiding over the collection of taxes, they were also the magistrates of their divisions. District commissioners had to learn, and pass a test in, a designated Malawian language, usually ciNyanja (ciChewa). The DC's house would be the largest at the *boma*. Since he was the senior government official in his area and therefore also representative of the British Crown, a flag would be hoisted on his car whenever he was on official duty. The term "district commissioner" and the prestige associated with it continued into the postcolonial era. *See also* COLLECTOR.

DIXON, ALAN. A leading European politician and sisal producer, Alan Dixon was also the general manager of the **British Central Africa Company** (BCA) and chairman of the European Land Owners Association. Dixon's BCAC had shares in the Nyasaland Railways, and Dixon was a notable member of the chamber of commerce. In 1953 he replaced **Malcolm Barrow** as an unofficial member of the **Legislative Council** (LEGCO) and four years later became unofficial member of the Executive Council of the **Nyasaland** government, effectively making him principal spokesman of the European settler community in Nyasaland. Dixon strongly opposed decolonization and supported Sir **Robert Armitage**'s declaration of the state of emergency in 1959. As a director of the Blantyre Printing and Publishing Company, he used the *Nyasaland Times* to publicize his views and to reflect the opinion of the European settlers in Nyasaland. He and **Michael Blackwood** represented European settler interests at the constitutional talks in London; as the transfer of power to Africans approached, Dixon left the country for **South Africa**.

DOIG, REV. ANDREW. Scottish missionary in service of the Blantyre Synod of the **Church of Central Africa Presbyterian** (CCAP) who sympathized with African nationalist aspirations. In 1951 he was nominated to the Nyasaland **Legislative Council** (LEGCO) to represent African interests. Although opposed to the establishment of the **Federation of Rhodesia and Nyasaland**, he was also nominated by the governor to represent the same interests in the federal parliament. There he became a member of the African Affairs Board but in 1958 resigned from it and from the federal parliament and returned to **Blantyre Mission**, where he became secretary-general of the synod until 1962, when he switched positions with Rev. **Jonathan Sangaya**, who had been his deputy. Doig was one of the people who persuaded Dr. **Hastings K. Banda** to return to **Malawi** sooner than he had planned, arguing that his age and experience qualified him for the leadership that the people of **Nyasaland** required at that crucial stage of their political history.

DOKOWE, BAZA. Of the Nyirongo clan, Baza Dokowe was a minor chief in **Tumbuka** country around Mount **Hora**, an area that had come under the authority of the **M'mbelwa Ngoni**. Sometime between 1877 and 1878, Baza led an uprising against the Ngoni. Some historians argue that Baza's action was prompted by the success of the **Tonga** rebellion against the Ngoni fifteen months earlier; others contend that the reason was economic in the sense that Baza refused to surrender the ivory that the new rulers demanded. The Ngoni then besieged Mount Hora, where many of the indigenous people had gathered, attacking and killing many of them. Baza and his wife were saved by narrowly escaping at dawn and taking refuge in **Mwase Kasungu**'s area further south. Baza Dokowe died in Kasungu in 1924.

DOMASI. Located 10 miles north of **Zomba** town, Domasi is the seat of **Malemia,** the Yao ruler who in the late 1860s conquered the indigenous **Mang'anja** and established authority over them. Within two years of its establishment in the **Shire Highlands**, the **Blantyre Mission** set up a major substation in western Domasi, where the initial missionaries included **R. S. Hynde**, who was to become an influential European businessmen in **Nyasaland**. Domasi became particularly famous after 1929, when the government opened the **Jeanes Training Centre** in the central section of the area. The center trained community workers, chiefs, government clerks, and teachers. Domasi continues to be associated with **education**. It is the home of the Malawi Institute of Education and Domasi Teacher's College.

DOMINGO, CHARLES. Domingo was born in Quilimane in **Mozambique** and was brought to **Malawi** in 1881 by **William Koyi**. He worked as a servant for Dr. **Robert Laws**, who sent him to **Lovedale** for further education in 1891. He returned in 1894 and, when the theological college started at the new **Livingstonia Mission** at **Khondowe**, Domingo became one of its first students, completing the course in 1900. A talented and effective teacher, Domingo became increasingly frustrated by the delay in his ordination. In 1903 he became a "licentiate," a status that allowed him "to preach the Gospel" but not entirely fulfill the duties of a minister. Although normally a licentiate would have expected ordination within six months, Domingo continued to wait for the occasion. In the same year, he was sent to Chinyera in **Ngoni** country, and in 1907 he was transferred to **Loudon Mission**, also in a Ngoni-dominated area. Although the Kirk at Loudon was impressed by him and made it known to officials that they wanted him to be one of their full ministers, Domingo's position did not change. Frustrated by the length of his probation, he resigned in 1909. He had already been in touch with **Eliot Kamwana Chirwa**, **John Chilembwe**, and **Joseph Booth**, and he came to be identified with Booth, who at this time was in **South Africa** as a representative of the Seventh Day Baptist Church.

From 1910 to 1916, Domingo was the principal organizer of the African Seventh Day Baptists in **Mzimba** District, acquiring several thousand adherents by 1912. He also edited the Malawi version of the *African Sabbath Recorder* while Booth remained its chief editor in the Cape. Funded by Booth and the home church in the **United States**, Domingo set up his base near Mzimba *boma* and from there preached and disseminated literature, some of which came from Eliot Kamwana Chirwa's **Watchtower** Society. Furthermore, he established numerous village schools, in which, as in many of his unpretentious mud churches, political and other issues were discussed. He talked about fairness, equality of human beings, and the autocracy of the colonial government.

Although there was no evidence to directly implicate Domingo in the 1915 **Chilembwe uprising**, his views and message were similar to those of Chilembwe, Booth, and Kamwana Chirwa. He was not arrested but in 1916 was deported from **Nyasaland** after the authorities intercepted a letter to Booth in which he stated, among other things, that "the world should have equality of representation in the respective Legislative Assemblies or councils and should be fully eligible to all sorts of loveliness in the commencement of the New Heaven [on] Earth" (quoted in R. Rotberg 1965, 72).

DUPONT, JOSEPH. Head of the **White Fathers** order of the Catholic Church in the **Bemba** country, **Northern Rhodesia**, in the 1890s and early 1900s, and first vicar apostolic of **Nyasa**, Bishop Dupont was responsible for establishing the Catholic presence in the **Lake Nyasa** region. In 1889 he directed other White Fathers to set up a mission station at **Mponda** at the southern end of Lake Malawi. Later he also recommended to the Montfort Fathers that they found their own stations in the region.

DUTCH REFORMED CHURCH OF SOUTH AFRICA MISSION (DRC). Following the 1886 founding of the Minister's Missionary Society by some pastors of the Dutch Reformed Church of Cape Town, a decision was made to send a mission to the **Lake Malawi** region. In 1888 Rev. **Andrew C. Murray** became the first missionary of the Dutch Reformed Church, the initial plan being to establish stations among the **Ngonde** and the **Nyakyusa**. However, discouraged by the instability in the area because of the conflicts between the **Swahili-Arabs** and the British, Murray moved south to work with Rev. **Angus Elmslie** among the M'mbelwa **Ngoni** for some months before finally deciding to set up stations among the **Chewa** further south. In 1889 Murray and Rev. T. C. B. Vlok, who had joined him earlier, established their first mission station at **Mvera** in Chief **Chiwere Ndhlovu**'s area, midway between **Lilongwe** and **Salima**. Other missionaries, including **Robert Blake, William Murray**, Martha Murray, and Koos du Toit, joined the DRC mission, establishing newer centers at **Kongwe, Nkhoma**, and **Mlanda**, among other locations. Between 1895 and 1900, the **Livingstonia Mission** handed their stations at **Livulezi** and **Cape Maclear** to the DRC; in 1924, a similar transfer took place in **Kasungu**. Further expansion took place to the Ngoni and Chewa areas of Portuguese territory in **Mozambique** and the southern Luangwa area in **Mpezeni**'s country. By the beginning of World War I, the DRC was the dominant Protestant sect operating in the Central Region of Nyasaland.

In 1926 the DRC Mission, under the umbrella of the Nkhoma Synod, joined the **Church of Central Africa Presbyterian** (CCAP). The mission was active in training a local laity, and in 1924 it ordained its first ministers, **Namon Katengeza** and Andreya Namkumba. Compared with the **Blantyre** and Livingstonia Missions, the other partners in the CCAP, the DRC's educational policy tended to be less active in promoting Western education among Africans, preferring to emphasize **agriculture** and artisan work. It was also more reluctant than the other two in handing over authority to the local clergy.

DWANGWA. The Dwangwa River drains from the **Lilongwe** plain and Rift Valley into **Lake Malawi**, and it was the northern limit of the **Maravi** Confederation. The river delta is the site of an irrigated **rice** project begun in 1972, and the Dwangwa Sugar Corporation began production in the area in 1979.

– E –

ECONOMY. *See* FINANCIAL AND ECONOMIC DEVELOPMENTS.

EDINGENI. Located between **Mzimba *boma*** and **Loudon Mission**, Edingeni is the headquarters of the northern **Ngoni** and the residence of their ruler, Inkosi ya makosi **M'mbelwa**. This was the home of the **M'mbelwa African Administrative Council** and is the main base of the M'mbelwa District Council.

EDUCATION. In precolonial times, formal and informal education took different forms, depending on individual societies. Western education was introduced in Malawi by Christian missionaries in the last quarter of the 19th century as an essential part of proselytizing. Christian organizations that were responsible for Western education included the **Livingstonia Mission, Blantyre Mission**, the **Universities' Mission to Central Africa** (UMCA), the **Dutch Reformed Church of South Africa** (DRC), the **White Fathers** and Montfort Missionaries, Baptists, Church of Christ, the **Zambezi Industrial Mission**, and the Seventh-Day Adventists. Through its Quranic schools, **Islam** also played a role in education in **Malawi**. Although in areas of Islamic influence Western education went hand in hand with the Muslim one, generally the former required some time to take root.

After World War I, government involvement in education increased. In 1923 the British government established the Advisory Committee on African Education in Tropical Africa, which, in conjunction with the **Phelps Stokes Commission** of the United States, visited Malawi in 1924 to study education in the colony. The latter committee, supported by other commissions, urged, among other things, the establishment of a local advisory board on African education. In 1926 the colonial government appointed the first director of education; the Advisory Committee on African Education was also formed, and two Africans, **Levi Mumba** and **Charles Matinga**, became members in 1933 and 1937, respectively.

In 1929 a government college to train teacher supervisors was opened at **Domasi**. Christened the **Jeanes Training Centre,** in honor of the American philanthropist and educationist Anna T. Jeanes, and funded by the government and the Carnegie Corporation, the college was to train teachers whose main duty was to supervise teachers in rural/village schools and thus ensure good standards of education. From 1934 on, selected chiefs would complete a four-month course at the Jeanes Centre, concentrating on community and rural development. After World War II, the center expanded its mission to include training teachers at higher levels, that is, students who had received some secondary school education. In 1937 Protestant missionaries started a secondary school in **Blantyre**, which opened its doors to students in 1940–1941. Blantyre Secondary School was followed a year later by Zomba Catholic Secondary School. Although after World War II a few more secondary schools were opened in places such as Dedza, **Livingstonia**, Mtendere, Mzedi, **Nkhata Bay**, **Kongwe**, and **Mzuzu**, further development in this field was generally slow. In 1961 there were only four secondary schools that enrolled students up to the School Certificate (O level) grade. Access to secondary schools had remained restrictive because of slow expansion attributable partly to inadequate financial assistance to Christian missions, which had continued to dominate education at this level. The same applied to teacher training colleges.

In the early 1960s, two commissions were appointed to review the matter. The Phillips Commission, which reported in 1962, recommended a major expansion of primary and secondary education; it also recommended limited involvement of voluntary agencies in primary education, and greater control by local government. It further recommended that as primary schools became the responsibility of local communities, government's spending on secondary education must increase. In 1963 the second commission, under the auspices of the American Council on Education, concentrated on professional and tertiary education. In 1964 it submitted its findings, the Johnston Report. While agreeing with the Phillips Commission on the importance of primary and secondary education, it recommended, among other things, the establishment of the **University of Malawi**, which was duly founded in that same year. Four institutions not directly part of the University of Malawi were established in the 1980s. They are the **Kamuzu Academy** in **Kasungu** District, the Malawi College of Accountancy in Blantyre, the Institute of Education at Domasi, and the **Malawi Institute of Management** (MIMS) in Lilongwe.

Complementing the formal school system are vocational training and nonformal education programs. For instance, six technical schools offer vocational training for carpenters, welders, mechanics, and bricklayers. The Malawi Correspondence College (MCC) was established in 1965 essentially to absorb primary school graduates who could not find openings in the secondary schools. In conjunction with the **Malawi Broadcasting Corporation**, MCC has provided radio programs to primary and secondary schools. Many such centers were later turned into Distance

Education Centers (DEC), each accommodated in modern facilities and headed by properly trained high school teachers.

In 1994 the **United Democratic Front** (UDF) government introduced free primary education as pledged in its party manifesto. Although a shortage of trained teachers forced the government to introduce a crash course in teaching, the student-teacher ratio remained very high. Whereas in 1983, only 53 percent of primary school-age pupils actually attended school, 85 percent did so in 1995. Associated with this problem is classroom space, lack of textbooks, and low teacher salaries. The enlargement of primary education has meant a greater demand for space in secondary schools, which have increasingly faced the same problems as those of the lower tier. One result of all this has been the proliferation of private schools at all levels; many such schools have been established as business enterprises. For its part, the Malawi government has transformed 315 of the distance education centers into community day secondary schools. It is also building more regular secondary schools, besides those sponsored by the **World Bank**, the African Development Bank (ADB), and the Japanese International Co-operation Agency (JICA). Boarding schools are being phased out and replaced with day institutions. Furthermore, teacher training colleges, including the Domasi Secondary Teacher Training College, will increase their intake.

A new government-sponsored university opened at Mzuzu at the end of 1998. Housed in the former teacher training college, it will initially focus on science education and thus assist in solving the shortage of secondary school teachers. Other developments include the establishment of private externally funded tertiary institutions, mainly associated with religious organizations. *See also* CHANCELLOR COLLEGE; UNIVERSITY OF MALAWI.

EKWENDENI. Located 14 miles from **Mzuzu** on the Mzuzu-**Rumphi** road, Ekwendeni is one of the principal bases of the **Livingstonia** Synod of the **Church of Central Africa Presbyterian** (CCAP). Opened in 1889 after Inkosi **Mtwalo I** approached Rev. **Walter Elmslie** with a request for missionary activity in his domain, it became the second important Livingstonia mission station in **Ngoni** country after **Njuyu**. Elmslie supervised its development from his Njuyu post, but it was Peter McCallum and his wife who oversaw its initial growth into a major educational and health training center, producing some of the leading people in Nyasaland, including **Mtwalo II** (Amon Jere), **Yesaya M. Chibambo**, **Hezekeya M. Tweya**, **Levi Z. Mumba**, **Isaiah Mopho Jere**, **Edward**

K. Gondwe, **Vera Chirwa**, and Chief Justice **Richard Banda**. Today, Ekwendeni has the biggest CCAP hospital in northern Malawi, a major girls' boarding high school, and a facility to train lay church workers.

The **London & Blantyre Supply Company** had its northern head-quarters at Ekwendeni until the late 1950s, when it was moved to Mzuzu. Before the **Africanization** of **Asian** businesses in most parts of Malawi, Ekwendeni was a major Asian trading center.

ELECTIONS. The first elections in which Africans participated took place in 1956 under the 1955 Constitution, according to which the provincial councils, consisting mainly of chiefs, were to elect members of the **Legislative Council** (LEGCO). The Southern and Central Regions were each to elect two members, and the Northern Region, one member.

The first general elections based on free adult suffrage took place in August 1961 following the constitutional talks at **Lancaster House Conference** the year before. The majority of the voters (107,076) registered on the lower roll (African) seats, and 4,401 voters, of which 471 were Africans, registered for the higher roll. The total poll was 95.1 percent, and the **Malawi Congress Party** (MCP) won all 20 seats on the lower roll; there were eight seats on the upper roll: the MCP won two, an independent with African and Asian support won the third, and the rest went to the United Federal Party (UFP).

The next general elections were set for in May 1964 but did not take place because all the 53 nominated candidates were returned unopposed. Of these, 50 belonged to the MCP and were to contest the 50 general roll seats; the **Nyasaland Constitutional Party** (formerly the UFP) took the three special roll seats reserved for Europeans. In 1966 the MCP ran an unopposed slate of candidates; they were up for re-election in 1971, but Dr. **Hastings Banda** called off the elections and chose 60 members of parliament (MPs) nominated at MCP conferences. The next election was held in June 1978, when registered Malawi voters went to the polls to cast ballots for MPs. Thirty-three candidates were returned unopposed based on earlier nominations. Write-in ballots were disallowed with only designated candidates accepted for balloting. Registered voters were required to show age and residence certificates. Seven constituencies were left vacant in this 1978 election as 80 MPs were sworn in. A new feature of this election was that candidates without high school certificates had to pass an English competency test in order to qualify. The test had to be set and administered by the vice chancellor of the **University of Malawi**.

In the June 1983 general elections, the membership of the National Assembly was increased to 101 elective seats. Eleven were presidential appointments. Of the 101 seats, 75 were contested within the one-party system, the rest being returned unopposed. Five had failed the English competency test.

The elections of May 1987 were for 112 seats in the National Assembly. However, more than 200 stood for election, 38 were returned unopposed, and 53 lost their seats. With 11 appointed by the president, there was a total of 123 parliamentarians. There was a high turnout at the 1987 elections, which took place without incident. In June 1992, 675 candidates contested for 141 seats, of which 45 were returned unopposed and five were not filled because of the disqualification of candidates. The turnout was low.

The May 1994 elections were the first in which parties other than the MCP fielded candidates. For the first time, there were presidential candidates as well as those for parliament. **Bakili Muluzi** of the **United Democratic Front** (UDF) won the presidential contest as follows: Muluzi of the UDF, 47.3 percent; H. K. Banda of the MCP, 33.6 percent; **Chakufwa Chihana** of the **Alliance for Democracy** (AFORD), 18.6 percent; **Kamlepo Kalua** of the **Malawi Democratic Party** (MDP), 0.5 percent. The results of the parliamentary elections were as follows: UDF, 85 seats; MCP, 56; AFORD, 36. The following parties did not win seats: the **Malawi Democratic Party** (MDP), the **Congress for the Second Republic** (CSR), the United Party for Multi-Party Democracy (UFMD), the Malawi National Democratic Party (MNDP), the Malawi Democratic Union (MDU).

In the May 1999 presidential and parliamentary elections, the results were as follows: Bakili Muluzi (UDF), 2,432,685; **Gwanda Chakuamba** (MCP/AFORD alliance), 2,106,790; Kamlepo Kalua (MDP), 67,856; Rev. Daniel Kamfozi Mnkhumbwe (CNU), 24,737; **Bingu Wa Mutharika** (UP), 22,073. The results for the much enlarged National Assembly were as follows: AFORD, 29: 28 (North), 1 (Center); MCP, 66: 4 (North), 54 (Center), 8 (South); UDF, 93: 1 (North), 16 (Center), 76 (South). For the first time since 1961, four independents were elected to parliament; however, by mid-August they had all joined the UDF party. International observers declared the elections generally free and fair.

The results of the presidential elections were bitterly contested by the MCP/AFORD partnership, which accused the UDF of vote rigging; it also criticized the electoral commission for announcing the results before investigating charges of irregularities. The MCP/AFORD partnership unsuccessfully took the commission to the High Court of Malawi, insisting that the results be annulled. There were reports of loss of two lives, violence against Muslims, and burning of mosques in the Northern Region. It was also reported that some property belonging to the MCP/AFORD partnership had been destroyed in **Mangochi** District. In August 1999, Against War in Africa, the Botswana-based African Conference for NGOs, announced that former Tanzanian president **Julius Nyerere** was to chair a peace conference in Malawi in October with a view to reconciling those aggrieved with the results of the elections and the subsequent violence. Nyerere was taken ill and died before undertaking the Malawi mission, and in 2000 a judge of the High Court of Malawi ruled that Bakili Muluzi was indeed the winner of the 1999 presidential elections.

In November 2000 local government elections took place for the first time in many years. The turnout was very low, especially in the Northern and Central Regions, but the UDF won overwhelmingly.

ELECTRICITY. Malawi's electric capacity is about 224 megawatts (mw), over 95 percent of which is produced from hydropower stations, mainly on the Shire River. The first such power station was opened in 1966 at Nkula Falls on the **Shire River** with a capacity of 24 mw; a second phase added 36 mw and served 10 rural districts by 1985. Further downstream at Tedzani Falls, another station was opened in 1973 with a 20 mw capacity. By 1978, stage two of Tedzani was completed; this provided an additional 20 mw. Commissioned in 1983, a third hydro plant providing 100 mw was completed by 1986.

The generation and supply of electricity is the responsibility of a public statutory body, the Electricity Supply Commission of Malawi (ESCOM). Even in the late 1990s, it was the only parastatal performing with a profit, but problems arising out of difficulties of access to spare parts have adversely affected it. There have been other problems as well, including increasingly frequent rainfall shortage. The demand for fuel and relaxation in forest patrols have led to significant deforestation in catchment areas. These factors have meant that not enough water is flowing into **Lake Malawi** and on to hydro plants down the Shire River. To solve the problem of shortages, the Malawi government has investigated the possibility of importing electricity from neighboring countries such as **Mozambique**, **South Africa**, and **Zimbabwe**.

ESCOM's initial rural electrification project funded by the African Development Bank is near completion, with ESCOM now supplying electricity to the extreme east, west, and south of the country: power lines have been built from Nkula station to **Lilongwe**, **Mangochi**, **Mulanje**, and along the lakeshore to **Salima**, **Nkhotakota**, **Mzuzu**, **Ekwendeni**, and **Rumphi**. There is also in progress a line to **Chitipa boma**. Power transmission lines have been constructed with financial assistance from the German government, which also financed a smaller hydro-generating plant in **Chilumba**, **Karonga** District.

Rural areas are still largely without electricity because of the high costs of line extensions and low customer loads. Most of ESCOM's electricity demand comes from the urban centers of Lilongwe and **Blantyre**, but it is exploring the feasibility of extending its electric grid system into the flue-cured **tobacco**-growing areas in northern and central Malawi. The bulk of Malawi's future electricity demands, however, will most likely continue to came from large industries and government institutions.

ELECTRICITY SUPPLY COMMISSION OF MALAWI (ESCOM). *See* ELECTRICITY.

ELMSLIE, WALTER ANGUS. Livingstonia medical missionary who served at **Njuyu** and **Ekwendeni** for many years. Elmslie was born in 1856, qualified as a medical doctor at Aberdeen University, and went to **Malawi** in 1885. He translated parts of the Bible and produced a grammar of **Tumbuka**. In 1901 he published *Among the Wild Ngoni*, a personal history of his work in the **Livingstonia Mission** in the last two decades of the 19th century. After serving for nearly four decades, most of them as second in command to Dr. **Robert Laws**, Elmslie returned to Scotland, where he died in 1936.

ENVIRONMENT. For many years Malawi's environment has been declining because of multiple factors. Since most Malawians depend on wood for fuel, woodland areas have increasingly come under attack. People living in rural areas use firewood, and many in urban centers depend on charcoal that is derived from wood, deliberately cut for the purpose. Charcoal is prepared in the rural areas and transported to towns by vendors. Even forest reserves are being cut, especially now that many casual laborers who guarded the forests were retired as part of the program to reduce the civil service and cut government expenditures. The expansion of the **tobacco** industry has also contributed to the depletion of forest areas in **Malawi**. Burley tobacco, grown by most smallholders, is dried in sheds constructed of wood and grass. Usually they are replaced every two to three years. Deforestation is also adversely affecting the lakes of Malawi in two main ways. First, deforestation at the source and along the course of the rivers that feed the lakes is causing some rivers to dry, thus reducing the amount of water flowing into the lake. Second, because of soil erosion upstream, rivers deposit alluvium into the lakes that covers algae and other nutrients, thus badly affecting the ecology of fish. *See also* FINANCIAL AND ECONOMIC DEVELOPMENTS; FISHING.

An increase in the population of Malawi has had an impact on land use, especially as people have claimed even forest areas and wetlands. This and other problems are now the domain of the Ministry of Environmental Affairs, created in the early 1990s. The ministry's program is guided by the Environmental Management Act of 1996, which aims, inter alia, at an efficient use of resources, tackling the problems of deforestation, marine life, land use, climatic changes, endangered species, and industrial pollution.

ETHIOPIANISM. A phrase used to note religious African nationalism in the late 19th and early 20th centuries. Racism and cultural administrative differences led black ministers to establish their own churches; this separatist movement absorbed much of the African disaffection with European rule. This term for black nationalism has also been applied to the **Chilembwe uprising**. *See also* INDEPENDENT AFRICAN CHURCHES.

ETHNIC GROUPS. About 50 percent of Malawi's population are **Chewa-Mang'anja** peoples, the descendants of those Africans whom early 16th-century Portuguese travelers called **Maravi**. The Chewa are numerically greater and live in the Central Region along with some **Ngoni** peoples. The Mang'anja, or **Nyanja** ("people of the lake"), live in the Southern Region, especially along **Lakes Malawi** and **Chilwa** and in **Blantyre**, **Zomba**, and **Chikwawa** Districts. They live side by side with Ngoni, **Yao**, **Lomwe**, and **Sena**. Both groups are matrilineal and share the same language, ciChewa/ciMang'anja.

Some 20 percent of the population are Lomwe and live in southeastern Malawi, especially in **Mulanje**, **Thyolo**, **Phalombe**, and **Chiradzulu** Districts. Their language is ciLomwe, and their matrilineally based social organization is similar to that of the Yao and Mang'anja. Also in the south, particularly the Lower Shire, live the Sena, many of whom trace their origins to **Mozambique**. They have a patrilineal system of marriage and inheritance and are active in commerce and politics.

The Yao originated in the northeastern part of Mozambique and migrated to Malawi in the last half of the 19th century. For 200 years prior to that, they were the trading allies of the **Swahili-Arabs**, participating in the east coast ivory and **slave trade**. Many Yao adopted **Islam** because of their contact with the Swahili-Arabs, and the two often intermarried. The Yao live mostly in **Mangochi, Balaka, Machinga, Zomba**, and **Chiradzulu** Districts.

Unlike most other ethnic groups inhabiting Malawi, the Ngoni are patrilineal and were part of the *mfecane* of the 19th century. The descendants of the followers of **Zwangendaba** are found mainly in **Mzimba** district and in **Mchinji** (belonging to the **Mpezeni** section); those associated with Ngwane and **Mputa Maseko** live in **Ntcheu** and Dedza. Today their paramount ruler is Willard, **Gomani III**, whose headquarters are Lizulu in Ntcheu district. There are also pockets of the Ngoni in **Dowa, Salima**, and **Thyolo** Districts.

In the northern reaches of Malawi live numerous ethnic groups of varying sizes. The **Tumbuka**-speaking peoples, many of whom are of diverse origins, are in the majority and are found in all districts of the region, as well as in northern **Kasungu**. Other peoples of the region are the **Tonga**, who inhabit most of **Nkhata Bay** District, the **Ngonde** in a large section of **Karonga** District, and the **Nyiha-Lambya** and **Sukwa-Ndali** in **Chitipa** District. CiTonga is linguistically related to ciTumbuka.

EVANS, ENOCH. From the late 1940s to the early 1960s, Enoch Evans, an accomplished acoustic guitar player, was one of the most popular singer-songwriters in **Nyasaland** and **Northern Rhodesia**. His recorded songs, mainly commentaries on contemporary events, were regularly played on the **Federal Broadcasting Corporation** (FBC) radio, at social gatherings (including **beer halls**), and in private houses. One of his more popular compositions, *infa yilibe citsoni*, refers to the unpleasant way in which the colonial government treated Inkosi Zintonga Philip, **Gomani II** of **Ntcheu**.

EXECUTIVE COUNCIL (EXCO). This elite group of four, formed in 1907, consisted of the governor, the attorney general, the treasurer, and the government secretary. Appointed at the same time as the **Legislative Council** (LEGCO), the Executive Council did not include any European unofficial members of the legislative body until 1939. The first Africans were not added until 1959: **C. M. Chinkondenji** and **Ernest M. Mtawali**. The EXCO ended with the dissolution of the **Federation of Rhodesia and Nyasaland**. It was replaced in February 1963 by a cabinet headed by a prime minister.

EXILES. Although nationalists of the late colonial period presented people such as Dr. **Hastings K. Banda** as having lived in self-imposed exile, this phenomenon is mainly a postcolonial one. A handful of the politicians who had supported Federal institutions left to live in exile because they felt insecure in a decolonized **Nyasaland**. Among such politicians were **Wellington Manoah Chirwa**, who went to the United Kingdom, and **Ernest Mtawali**, who emigrated to **Southern Rhodesia**. However, following the **Cabinet Crisis** of 1964, many people who supported or were deemed to support the rebelling cabinet ministers feared political persecution and fled, mostly to **Zambia** and **Tanzania**, where they sought refuge. Some sought employment in their new homes, and many continued with opposition politics in the hope of returning to Malawi. During his brief stay in Tanzania, **Henry Chipembere** started a new party, the Pan-African Democratic Party, which many exiles in that country and in Zambia joined. Later, **Kanyama Chiume** also started his own party, **Congress for the Second Republic**. However, one of the most active exile political organizations was the Socialist League of Malawi (LESOMA), which from 1975 was headed by Dr. **Attati Mpakati**. LESOMA even claimed to have formed a military wing of guerrillas having the ability to launch an attack on Malawi, given the right circumstances. When Mpakati was assassinated in 1983, Grey Kamunyambeni took over the leadership of LESOMA.

Orton Chirwa headed the **Malawi Freedom Movement (MAFREMO)**, but when he was kidnapped and imprisoned in Malawi, Edward Yapwantha became the new leader. Yapwantha studied law at the University of Zambia and at McGill University in **Canada** before assuming MAFREMO leadership in 1983. In 1988 the sale of MAFREMO T-shirts in Malawi was strongly opposed by the government and the distribution source of the Yapwantha-imprinted shirt was investigated. Yapwantha was asked to leave **Zimbabwe** in December 1989 and was presumed to have left for Uganda.

In mid-1991, the exiled parties formed an alliance in Lusaka called the United Front for Multi-Party Democracy (UFMD). It consisted of MAFREMO, LESOMA, and the Malawi Democratic Union (MDU), the latter headed by **Adamson Akogo Kanyaya**. The umbrella organization called for the immediate resignation of Banda, amnesty for exiled Malawians, respect for **human rights**, and the lifting of the state of emergency and the ban on **political parties**. It campaigned mainly through newspapers and information sheets, some of which were circulated clandestinely in Malawi. During the move toward multiparty democracy in 1992–1993, the advocates for change argued for the return home of all the exiles so that they could take part in the transformation process.

EXTERNAL TRADE. Malawi's main trading partner is **Great Britain** followed by **South Africa**, Germany, Japan, France, the **United States**, **Zimbabwe**, the Netherlands, Taiwan, Thailand, Singapore, and Vietnam. Trade has increased with the 17 **Preferential Trade Area** (PTA) countries, a group of East and South-Central African nations determined to promote more trade and cooperation among its members. In the late 1980s, the PTA introduced a common monetary unit (Uapta), but by the mid-1990s it had virtually disappeared from circulation. By the mid-1990s, over 40 percent of regional trade was being conducted through the PTA.

Malawi's main exports are **tobacco**, **tea**, **sugar**, **goundnuts** (peanuts), and wood products. It has run a deficit trade balance since 1966. This trade balance is governed by world market prices and the level of production of major export crops such as tobacco, sugar, and tea. The serious **transportation** difficulties increase the cost of imports, since these goods must travel greater distances than is cost-effective. Imported commodities include food, consumer goods, spare parts and tools, equipment, petroleum products, and transportation equipment. The balance of trade is sometimes small, often large, but never favorable. In 1996 the total value of exports was MK1.805 billion (US$435 million), whereas that of imports was MK22.704 billion (US$528 million). The devaluation of the **kwacha** in the 1990s has made the cost of imports particularly high. *See also* CURRENCY; FINANCIAL AND ECONOMIC DEVELOPMENTS.

– F –

FACHI, PETER. After graduating in law at the **University of Malawi**, this son of a prominent Lower Shire businessman went into private practice. A leading member of the **Law Society of Malawi**, he became interested in, among other things, **human rights** and, when calls for political reform started in the early 1990s, Fachi emerged as one of its main advocates. He was one of the founders of the **United Democratic Front** (UDF). In 1994 he was elected to parliament and appointed minister of land. In 1996 he became attorney general and minister of justice, a position he retained after the 1999 general **elections**.

FAMINE. Famines occur in **Malawi** at regular intervals for a variety of reasons, including prolonged droughts, poor drought management, excessive rains, a shortage of good cultivable land, and misuse of land. The most famous famine in Malawi occurred in 1949–1950; however, there have been other major famines in the 20th century; in 1903 and 1922 many people from **Mozambique** were forced to migrate to the **Shire Highlands.** Notable famines took place in the 1790s, 1830s, 1860s, and 1890s.

FARMERS MARKETING BOARD (FMB). *See* AGRICULTURAL DEVELOPMENT AND MARKETING BOARD (ADMARC).

FEDERAL BROADCASTING CORPORATION (FBC). As soon as the **Federation of Rhodesia and Nyasaland** was established, the **Central African Broadcasting Services** became a statutory body of the federal government and changed its name to Federal Broadcasting Corporation (FBC). While continuing many of its programs, it also became a major propaganda tool for the federal government.

FEDERAL REVIEW CONFERENCE. Called to review the future of the **Federation of Rhodesia and Nyasaland**, it took place in London between December 5 and 16, 1960. The three leading African nationalists, Joshua Nkomo **(Southern Rhodesia)**, **Kenneth Kaunda (Northern Rhodesia)**, and **Hastings Banda (Nyasaland)**, attended reluctantly and on December 12 walked out. In the end the conference achieved little of significance, except to prove to the British government that, with the wide gap between African and European views on the Federation, the arrangement had no realistic future.

FEDERATION OF RHODESIA AND NYASALAND. From 1953 to 1963, **Nyasaland** was a reluctant member of an association that included **Northern Rhodesia** (presently **Zambia**) and **Southern Rhodesia** (now **Zimbabwe**). Although the governmental machinery for Federation was not established until the 1950s, the movement to create such an association originated decades earlier.

During World War I the **British South Africa Company** (BSAC) had suggested an amalgamation, but European settlers were not then enthusiastic. However, white settlers began to feel that their way of life was threatened when, through the Devonshire Paper of 1923 and the **Passfield** Memorandum of 1930, the Colonial Office declared its policy of trusteeship and paramountcy of African interest. In 1935 the government heads of the three territories met to consider possible union in matters of trade and tariffs, **education**, and defense. In the following year, a second meeting continued the agitation for union. At this point the British government assigned the **Bledisloe Commisssion** with the task of determining the feasibility of closer cooperation in all three territories. When the Bledisloe Report was published in 1939, amalgamation was not immediately recommended but was considered a possibility for the future. During the three-month tour, the commissioners were left under no doubt about the vehement opposition of Nyasalanders to any association. Leaders of **African welfare associations**, village chiefs, and even Scottish missionaries unanimously rejected schemes of amalgamation. Upon returning to England, the commissioners also received a memo from Dr. **Hastings K. Banda** indicating his opposition.

The outbreak of World War II stifled amalgamation talks as priorities were placed on the war effort. A council formed in 1941 allowed the three territorial administrations to consult each other on nonpolitical matters. But, as its functions were expanded in 1944, the advocates of amalgamation exploited the council. When the postwar Labour Party opposed an amalgamation of the Rhodesias, Stewart Gore-Browne, a settler member of the Northern Rhodesia **Legislative Council** (LEGCO), suggested a federation among the three territories that ostensibly would preserve African rights. Other white settlers supported the concept, including **Roy Welensky** and **Godfrey Huggins**. At the latter's initiation a small group of settlers met in February 1949 at Victoria Falls and agreed to try to create a Federation of Rhodesia and Nyasaland. Welensky openly admitted that he expected the plan would rid Northern Rhodesia of the Colonial Office. As for the Southern Rhodesia delegates, their expectations were linked to Northern Rhodesia's copper, and the Nyasaland settlers hoped for an improved economic situation. In May 1949 Dr. Banda and **Harry Nkumbula**, then the leading African nationalist in Northern Rhodesia, wrote a memorandum detailing opposition to this federation plan. The Banda-Nkumbula memo warned that Nyasaland and Northern Rhodesia could expect to be dominated by Southern Rhodesia with its detested segregationist policies and its antipathy toward the African populace. The partnership concept advanced by Federation supporters was just a facade and therefore the plan must be rejected, the memo concluded. Africans relaxed momentarily when the colonial secretary, **Arthur Creech Jones** (Labour Party), indicated that there would be no move toward federation at that time and no abrogation of responsibilities.

In late 1950 and early 1951, events changed in favor of the profederationists. James Griffiths (Conservative), who succeeded Creech Jones as colonial secretary, agreed to reinvestigate the federation issue. When Griffiths toured the protectorate, he became aware of Africans' intense opposition to any closer association. Responding to this resistance, Griffiths insisted that Africans be represented, for the first time, at a Federation conference in September 1951. The Nyasaland delegates—**Edward K. Gondwe, Clement Kumbikano, Chief Mwase Kasungu, Ellerton Mposa**, and **Alexander Muwamba**—refused to consider federation. The conference ended abruptly to provide time for the British general elections to be held. The Conservatives were returned to power, and immediately the new colonial secretary, Oliver Lyttelton, announced that his government favored federation and that Africans would have to accept it.

Both in Nyasaland and in England, the British government was reminded of its earlier promises not to transfer its obligations to the African populace. In Malawi, ordinary people, village chiefs, Scottish missionaries, and the **Nyasaland African Congress (NAC)** registered their opposition and reminded the British government of promises made earlier. In England, Dr. Banda, in a series of speeches, pleaded against any move toward federation. Dubbed as agitators by the advocates of federation, Africans and their supporters were ignored and further concessions were made to the followers of Huggins and Welensky. Dr. Banda suggested the NAC begin a campaign of civil disobedience, but some Congress members found the move too radical and a split in the NAC ensued. Federation forces advanced at this critical time when Congress lacked unity. When the Nyasaland LEGCO voted on federation in April 1953, its African members, Muwamba and Mposa, walked out in protest. Further petitions and noncooperation did not alter the course of events, and the Central African Federation officially commenced on August 1, 1953.

The Federation held few surprises for the African population that had so vehemently opposed its creation. The new federal government spent more money on Europeans than on Africans. The impact of taxation weighed significantly on Africans as cheap cigarettes and clothes of the type purchased more by Africans than whites were taxed more heavily. Most of the Federation capital available for investment was used in Southern Rhodesia, that is, on Kariba Dam. Disparities existed in educational facilities and in hospital services (8 beds per 1,000 for Europeans, 1 bed per 1,000 for Malawians). Politically, no partnership existed. The color bar was discriminatory and attempts by Africans to reach administrative levels in the civil service had dismal results: only nine candidates in all of the Federation in as many years. Representation in the Federal

Assembly was a near sham. Out of a total of 35 seats, Africans were permitted only six seats, two representatives from each territory. Malawi's Assembly representatives were **Wellington Manoah Chirwa** and Clement Kumbikano. When the federal constitution was revised, Africans obtained 12 of the 59 Assembly seats.

Events leading to independence took an abrupt turn after the overwhelming victory achieved by the **Malawi Congress Party** (MCP) in the August 1961 elections. The MCP had won all of the lower roll and a quarter of the upper roll seats in LEGCO. The governor, **Glyn Jones**, soon granted 10 seats on the Executive Council to the MCP. In November 1961 Welensky was informed that Nyasaland would be permitted to secede from the Federation, and in December the British government formally announced that Nyasaland was to be allowed to withdraw. During the two-year apprenticeship (1961–1963), Banda and his ministers made reforms and industriously planned for the future. As minister for natural resources, Banda was in a position to negate the abusive, abhorred agricultural practices conducted by the protectorate government. And **Dunduzu Chisiza**, parliamentary secretary to the minister of finance, outlined a five-year economic development scheme. Not only did the new African ministers wish to govern, but Glyn Jones encouraged their initiative and allowed them to make decisions that officially were in the governor's province. In February 1963 Banda was sworn in as prime minister, **Orton Chirwa** as minister of justice, **Henry Chipembere** as minister of local government, and **Augustine Bwanausi** as minister of housing.

The Federation was dissolved quietly at the end of that year, and the following July was set for independence. In April 1964 general elections allowing the enlargement of LEGCO were held in which all 50 MCP candidates won on the general roll and three Europeans were elected on a special roll. The following month Banda announced the ministers he had selected for the independence cabinet: **Yatuta Chisiza** (Home Affairs), **John Msonthi** (Transport), Bwanausi (Housing), Chipembere (Education), **Kanyama Chiume** (External Affairs), and **John Tembo** (Finance). In addition to serving as prime minister, Banda kept the following portfolios for himself: Health, Natural Resources, Social Development, Trade, and Industry. On July 6, 1964, Malawi became free of colonial rule, and two years later it was declared a republic.

FENWICK, GEORGE. Among the first Scottish laymen at **Blantyre Mission**, Fenwick is particularly identified with unethical and ruthless behavior, including the flogging of Africans. Conduct such as his led the Foreign Mission Committee of the Church of Scotland to send Rev. Dr. Rankin to Blantyre to investigate. The inquiry confirmed the unscrupulous behavior of some missionaries at Blantyre, and it resulted in the dismissal of Fenwick and others in 1880. Fenwick joined the **African Lakes Company** (ALC) as an elephant hunter. Four years later, the Kololo killed him for shooting their chief, **Chipatula**.

FIDDES, GEORGE STEVENSON. Leading **Limbe**-based European entrepreneur. Fiddes was born in County Tyrone, Northern Ireland, in 1879, studied engineering at Herriot Watt College in Scotland, and in 1903 went to **Nyasaland** as an employee of the **British Central Africa Company (BCAC)**. He worked as an assistant manager, a plantation manager, and, for 29 nine years, as joint general manager. In 1932 he became an independent businessman, milling, making soap and shoes, and tanning. He also had a butchery in Limbe and was involved in the **tobacco** and **tung** industries. He is said to have introduced tractors for agricultural purposes, and he used them at his Namitembo estate in **Thyolo** District. An active member of the chamber of commerce and the Nyasaland Tobacco Association, Fiddes was a one-time Limbe town councillor and was a founding member of the Limbe Country Club and the **Blantyre** Sports Club. He died in March 1952. His son, a graduate of Edinburgh University, held senior posts in the Ministry of Education and was the first executive secretary of the Malawi National Examinations Board in the early 1970s.

FINANCIAL AND ECONOMIC DEVELOPMENTS. Until the late 1970s, **Malawi** maintained a stable economy, achieving average annual rates of growth of over 5 percent. But the Malawi economy was affected by a series of exogenous shocks beginning in 1979, including disruption of its key **transportation** routes to the Indian Ocean, deterioration in the terms of trade, and poor climatic conditions. These events were exacerbated by weaknesses in the economy, including a narrow export base, limited growth potential for smallholder **agriculture**, and dependence on energy imports, as well as weaknesses in economic management centered on agricultural pricing, industrial price controls, budget management, and inefficiencies within the parastatal sector. Despite the government's advocacy of free enterprise, controls of input and output markets were widespread.

To deal with these problems, the government implemented structural adjustment programs that were designed to encourage diversification of output and exports, improve agriculture production, and restructure the key institutions. To this end, incentives to smallholders were increased, steps were taken to improve the efficiency of parastatals, exchange and interest rates were adjusted according to supply and demand, and external borrowing was restrained and debt payments were made in a timely fashion. With more favorable weather and better export prices, as well as the change in policy orientation, the Malawian economy began to respond. Recovery was slowed in 1985 as the terms of trade deteriorated 20 percent and bumper harvests in neighboring countries cut the export possibilities of Malawi's **maize** crop.

Malawi's rate of growth continued to be modest because of serious constraints that the country still faced: extremely high transportation costs, rapid population growth, and low per capita income. The objectives of the government were to double economic growth between 1989 and 1991 and to reduce inflation from approximately 15 percent in 1990 to 5 percent in 1992. The **World Bank** estimated that Malawi would need US$1.2 billion in foreign funding from 1990 to 1994; at the time, the bank held over half of the nation's long- and medium-term debts. In its May 1990 report, the World Bank identified poverty reduction as the main focus of its lending program which would involve an expansion of food production, expansion of credit to smallholders, elimination of the poll tax, and expenditure increases on primary **health** care and **education**.

Malawi found it particularly hard to implement even part of the recommendations largely because, between 1991 and 1993, Western donors withheld aid as a way of forcing President **Banda** to institute political reforms. In response, the Malawi economy, which had relied heavily on development aid since independence, contracted sharply, the cost of living rose, and imported commodities became very scarce.

Between 1993 and 1997, the performance of the economy was mixed. Real gross domestic product (GDP) per capita rose from US$564 to US$689, and the agriculture sector, employing 85 percent of the workforce, continued to be the largest contributor (45 percent) to GDP. Although the foreign exchange reserves increased by 184.2 percent to US$162 million, the external debt in 1996 was US$2.312 billion, and the annual servicing of it US$89 million, representing 18.7 percent of export goods and services. The inflation rate decreased, but the Malawi **kwacha** was devalued from US$ = MK4.4 to US$ = MK18.28; in 1997 the budget deficit was 12.4 percent of the GDP. In 1996, when imports were worth US$528 million, exports were only valued at US$435 million. *See also* EXTERNAL TRADE.

Since 1998 the Malawi government has been working with the World
Bank and the **International Monetary Fund** (IMF) in the context of the
enhanced structural adjustment facility (ESAF) to reduce financial im-
balances and strengthen economic performance. As a result of the large
fiscal deficits, tobacco export prices decreased by nearly 20 percent in
1998 from what they were in 1997; the kwacha was further depreciated
to US$ = 25.623 in 1998, to US$43.00 in 1999, and to US$75.00 in 2001.
Also contributing to the devaluation of the kwacha was the poor **maize**
yield in 1997, which decelerated the growth of GDP to 5 percent. At the
recommendation of the IMF, the government embarked on a major privatization program involving planned divestiture of most of the parastatals, including the **Agricultural Development and Marketing Board**
(ADMARC) and Malawi Railways. To improve the efficiency of tax collection, the Malawi Revenue Authority (MRA) was established to replace the Department of Taxes. This was one of the measures taken to en-
hance fiscal discipline and reduce expenditures. In 1999 the Malawi
government also initiated discussions with its external creditors aimed at
tackling the country's high debt service burden. During 1998–2001, the
external financial requirements will be US$1.602 million (in 1998–1999
alone US$911 million), and it is anticipated to be partly paid from offi-
cial loan transfers and from budgetary and balance of payments support.
In 1999 the main balance of payment loans were from the World Bank
(US$215 million), Japan (US$50 million), the African Development
Bank (US$32), and the IMF under the ESAF program; grant aid is ex-
pected mostly from the United Kingdom (US$37 million), European
Union (US$37 million), and USAID (US$34 million). *See also* CUR-
RENCY; FISHING; FORESTRY; MANUFACTURING; MINING.

FISHING. Malawi is able to cover all its domestic demand for freshwater
fish and is now exporting it in increasing quantities. Although fish are
exported to neighboring **Zambia**, **Zimbabwe**, and **Mozambique**, most
are consumed locally. Fish provide three-quarters of Malawi's annual
protein intake. The four main fishing waters are **Lakes Chilwa, Malawi**,
and Malombe, and the **Shire River**. Commercially, five varieties are important: catfish, chambo (tilapia), usipa, chisawasawa, and utaka; however, over 225 different fish species exist in Lake Malawi alone. More
than 20,000 people are directly involved in fishing, with thousands more
indirectly working in the industry. Many of these people have been
trained at Mpwepwe Fisheries Training School in **Mangochi**, a project
largely financed by the British government. Other projects include

taxonomy research, the freshwater prawn hatchery at **Domasi**, and fish farming extension services. The government's Fisheries Department has also introduced trawling techniques in Lake Malawi and has established fishing centers supplied with refrigeration and processing machinery.

When exchange problems occurred in the 1980s, export earnings declined, forcing 25 percent of the smaller fishermen out of business. The United Kingdom (UK) and European Union (EU) provided monies to reverse this trend. In its budget, the Malawi government allocated more money to fisheries to make loans available for equipment, boat building, and fisheries research.

The ability to earn a living from fishing in a situation of economic instability has led to increased numbers of fishermen (30,000) in Malawi waters and in turn has greatly contributed to overfishing, thereby threatening the ecology of fish. Fishermen who could not afford big boats continued to use traditional dugout canoes, which forced them to concentrate in the shallower waters, also the main breeding areas for fish. Fishermen resisted attempts by conservation officials to stop the practice. As the catch of the popular varieties declined with overfishing, fishermen turned to the less popular species, even when they were not fully developed. They also began to use nets with small meshes so that they could maximize their catch, which many times included the immature of the larger favored species.

The following statistics demonstrate some of the effects of overfishing. In 1987 the commercial catch was 88,586 tons, of which 101 tons were exported; in 1991, 63,000 tons were caught and only 3 tons were exported; in the following year, the catch was 69,500 tons, all of which were consumed locally. Similarly, in the 1980s, Lake Malombe's annual yield was 5,000 tons, but in 1991 it was 500 tons. The situation did not really improve in the rest of the 1990s, except that the Department of Fisheries and aid agencies, particularly the Food and Agriculture Organization (FAO) adopted a new approach to the problem. Fishing communities are now involved in enforcing policy through elected natural resources committees, assisted by officials of the Ministry of Natural Resources and Environmental Affairs. Another problem affecting the biodiversity of Lake Malawi is the large amount of alluvium that is carried into the lake every year as a result of soil erosion along the course of the rivers that feed the lake. As the sediment is deposited into the lake, it conceals all the food nutrients, thus disturbing the natural growth of the fish. The rivers also take into the lake toxic forms of fish food, which further affects their healthy development.

Since Malawi shares the lake with **Tanzania** and Mozambique, the problem has to be tackled at a regional level. With the assistance of the **Southern African Development Community** (SADC), United Nations Development Program (UNDP), FAO, Danish International Development Agency (DANIDA), and Canadian International Development Agency (CIDA), experts from the three countries are coordinating their efforts to solve the problems of fish in Africa's third largest lake.

Fish farming has also been expanding since 1986, and the Department of Fisheries is providing extension services to smallholders, exploring ways to reduce fish losses, and is conducting fish pond research. There are research fish farms in all three regions of Malawi. **Nongovernmental organizations** (NGO) such as the International Living Aquatic Resource Management Centre (ICLARM) have been working with the government to promote aquaculture in Malawi.

FLAG. The **Malawi** flag is a tricolor black, green, and red. A red rising sun is superimposed over the black horizontal stripe; the sun represents the dawn of freedom and the black depicts the people of Africa. A stripe of green represents the evergreen nature of Malawi and the red stripe the blood of martyrs for African freedom.

FLORENCE BAY. *See* CHITIMBA.

FOOT, SIR DINGLE. Distinguished British lawyer and politician from a famous political family. Dingle Foot was legal adviser to Dr. **Hastings K. Banda** during the state of emergency (1959–1960). Foot was on the team that defended **Flax Katoba Musopole**, who was accused of sedition, among other charges.

FOOTBALL. Football, or soccer, is the most popular entertainment sport in **Malawi** and is played in every district, area, and village. The Football Association of Malawi (FAM) governs football in the country, and all leagues have to be affiliated with it and abide by its rules. It is a member of the Federation of International Football Associations (FIFA) and the Confederation of African Football Associations (CAFA), through which it takes part in contests leading to the World Cup Football competitions, the African Nations Cup, and the African Clubs Championship Cup. In 1984 Malawi reached the final 16 of the African Nations Competition and in the previous 10 years had twice won the East and Central Africa championship. In the 1990s the national team did not distinguish itself as well as it did in the 1970s and 1980s. However, clubs such as the **Blantyre**-based **Wanderers**, Bata

Bullets, MDC United, ADMARC Tigers, and **Lilongwe**-based Silver Strikers fared better.

FOOTMAN, CHARLES WORTHINGTON FOWDEN. From 1947 to 1951, Footman was financial secretary to the government of **Nyasaland** and from 1951 to 1960 was chief secretary, effectively the deputy governor of the colony. He held the latter position at a crucial time for the future of the colony. As chief secretary, he was in charge of security matters. Like Sir **Robert Armitage**, he was strongly associated with the state of emergency in 1959 and the imprisonment of hundreds of nationalist politicians. In 1960 Footman was transferred to Tanganyika, where he became chairman of the Public Service Commission. Later he worked in the Commonwealth Relations Office and the Ministry of Overseas Development, London. Footman died in 1996.

FOREIGN AID. Since becoming independent in 1964, **Malawi** has received a substantial amount of aid, particularly from the United Kingdom (UK). The new nation needed external support to maintain the government on a daily basis; British direct grants supported not only the budget deficits but also the new rural development programs.

In the 1960s and 1970s, Malawi gained a good reputation among foreign investors because it maintained political stability and was guided by fiscally conservative policies. It used loans successfully and honestly, which appealed to many donors. As British aid changed to grants from soft loans, the **World Bank** supported the country with additional aid.

In general, aid had beneficial results in Malawi, as it did not inhibit efforts at self-reliance. With the exception of South Africa, almost all of its donors have provided aid on easy terms. Aid has originated from noncommunist nations, mostly the United Kingdom, **Canada**, Japan, West Germany, Denmark, the **United States**, Israel, Taiwan, South Africa, and the World Bank group. South African loans, on relatively harder terms, financed the Nacala railway extension and the new capital at **Lilongwe**. Canada has also aided railway development and the renovation of existing lines. Taiwan has sponsored **rice**-growing projects, and the fisheries industries have benefited from Danish, Israeli, and Japanese aid. German aid has financed highway building, and American aid has been used for **roads**, **education**, and community development.

Military aid primarily has come from the British in the form of materials as well as financial aid. The Royal Engineers assisted in road building on the **Chitipa** side of the **Nyika Plateau** and in **Mangochi** District, an area Dr. **Hastings Banda**'s government considered troublesome because of local dissidents and **FRELIMO** guerrillas. Additional equipment has also been acquired from Australia, Belgium, and South Africa. France and Germany have trained pilots and supplied equipment to the air wing of the Malawi army. Some military aid has also come from the United States.

United Nations development projects planned at the end of the decade totaled over US$43 million and ranged from policy planning, **tobacco** research, **forestry** and fisheries training, development of rural housing, commercial and secretarial training, business advisory services, training engineers, trade promotion, primary teacher education and curriculum development, vocational training, and rehabilitation.

In 1991–1993, foreign aid to Malawi was reduced sharply because donors tied it to political reform, with the exception of assistance for humanitarian purposes. Aid resumed in 1993 after President Banda permitted free elections to take place for the first time in nearly 30 years.

Even before this pressure was exerted on the Banda government, some changes had occurred among donors. West Germany and Canada, among Malawi's top donors in the 1970s and 1980s, had greatly reduced their assistance by the early 1990s. Bilateral aid from countries such as the United Kingdom, United States, and Japan continued, but there was a significant shift to multilateral aid through organizations such as the European Union and the World Bank.

Nongovernmental organizations (NGOs) increased their presence in the country, but they, like other donors, were concerned with indications of lack of fiscal discipline and corruption in the public service. *See also* FINANCIAL AND ECONOMIC DEVELOPMENTS.

FOREIGN POLICY. Throughout Dr. **Hastings K. Banda**'s period as head of state, Malawi's foreign policy was pro-Western. From late 1964, when Dr. Banda took control of external affairs, Malawi has had few contacts with nations other than those in Western Europe, the **United States**, and several Asian states. At the United Nations, which it joined at independence, Malawi almost always voted with the West. Besides the United Nations and its specialized agencies, Malawi is also a member of the **Organization of African Unity** (OAU) and the British Commonwealth of Nations. During Banda's time, the country enjoyed a respected status at the **World Bank** and **International Monetary Fund** (IMF).

Three principles governed Malawi's foreign policy according to Dr. Banda: not interfering in the affairs of other nations; judging each individual country on its own merits; welcoming any country willing to aid

Malawi. In fact, Banda maintained a strongly anticommunist stance and **foreign aid** was accepted only from Western sources. As head of state of a landlocked and poor nation, Dr. Banda chose to place Malawi's economic welfare above political considerations. At independence in 1964, he elected to establish a coexistence accord with white-ruled regimes in **South Africa**, **Southern Rhodesia (Zimbabwe)**, and the then Portuguese-controlled **Mozambique**. What's more, Malawi's president actively cultivated friendly relations with the Lisbon government, insisting that he pursued this strategy out of economic necessity. Respecting the military might of South Africa and the limited chance that his or any other African state could defeat apartheid forcibly, Dr. Banda established diplomatic relations with Pretoria in September 1967.

Whereas another nation might have reasoned that a policy of neutrality was best vis-à-vis powerful neighbors, Banda hoped that he could make **Malawi** the "bridge" between black and white rule in Africa. He argued that in adopting a position of open dialogue with South Africa, he was not implying any support for apartheid or the repressive South African rule, a situation he had experienced firsthand as a young man. Banda expected to bring about political changes that he could not conceive as occurring by brute force or economic sanctions. He consistently maintained his opposition to apartheid, and his speeches, which publicly criticized the South African government, had the same theme: anti-apartheid, anticommunist, and pro-West.

A shift in Malawi's foreign stance took place in 1985 when it recognized Romania and Albania; three years earlier North Korea had received diplomatic recognition. Despite these overtures to the East, the policy had no real impact on the parties concerned. Malawi remained strongly pro-West and refused to permit any communist nation to have an embassy in Malawi. While the recognition of these two Eastern European countries probably made Malawi feel more important, it was in fact window dressing.

Banda's attitude toward white-ruled Southern Africa was not well received at the OAU, which expected all members to actively support the liberation movements in overthrowing colonialism. As a general rule, Banda was not supportive of OAU policies and specifically disdained embargoes or violence as a solution to the Southern African problem. This stance did not ingratiate him with many African leaders, and it tended to place Malawi in an isolated position within the continent. In spite of this, however, in 1980 Malawi was a founding member of the Southern Africa Co-ordination Conference (SADCC) and the **Preferential Trade Area** (PTA), both of which did not originally include South Africa.

Post-Banda foreign policy remained friendly to the West. Unlike his predecessor, President **Bakili Muluzi**, a Muslim, has established close relations with Islamic countries, including Libya. Malawi under Muluzi has also become an active participant in African affairs, fully embracing the OAU and even contributing to an African peacekeeping force. Since 1994, contingents of the Malawi **army** have served as part of the United Nations observer forces in Rwanda, the Congo, and Eastern Europe. Muluzi attends all meetings of SADCC (now renamed SADC [Southern African Development Community]) and the PTA, and he has already served terms as chairman of both organizations.

FORESTRY. The Forestry Department manages over 1.9 million acres (769,000 hectares) of forest reserves and protected hill slopes. Malawi has considerable forestry potential and has a reforestation program designed to eventually make the nation entirely self-sufficient in the construction grades of timber. These efforts are critical in a nation where timber provides approximately 90 percent of the country's energy. Although pulpwood is confined to the Viphya Plateau, timber production is concentrated at Chongoni, **Zomba**, **Mulanje**, Dzalanyama, and **Blantyre**.

When economic constraints prohibited the use of the softwood Viphya Plantation as feed stock for paper production, an outlet was found with the establishment of a plywood sawmill (VIPLY). Softwood wastes from the government plantation were applied as feedstock for a charcoal production project. It is the largest of its kind in sub-Saharan Africa and has a capacity of 9,500 tons per year. More significantly, it is a feasible alternative to coal and other fuel wood for household cooking and **tobacco** curing. In the heavily populated Southern Region, where in the past resources have been taxed by the influx of **refugees** from **Mozambique**, stands of wood have been replaced by crops of **maize** needed to feed the expanded population. Reforestation programs are in place, particularly legislation to protect indigenous trees.

Shortages in newsprint in the mid-1980s and in packaging materials in the early 1990s led the Malawi government once more to request that Viphya Pulpwood Corporation (VIPCOR) investigate the establishment of a pulp mill at **Liwonde**. That too fell through.

Demand for cooking fuel, charcoal in the urban areas and firewood in rural areas, continues to be a threat to Malawi's forests. Similarly, the use of wood to build sheds for tobacco remains a threat to forests. The reduction of the civil service as part of the expenditure reduction program has also affected forests as many of the personnel who guarded them against bush fires and human predators have been laid off. At the beginning of 2000, there was ample evidence of unprecedented deforestation in many parts of rural Malawi. *See also* ENVIRONMENT.

FORT HARE UNIVERSITY. Located in Alice, Eastern Cape, **South Africa**, and founded by Presbyterians in 1916 to provide tertiary education to black people. Fort Hare University was the alma mater of many future leaders of Southern Africa, including **Henry Chipembere**, **Orton Chirwa**, **Wellington Manoah Chirwa**, and the former South African president, Nelson Mandela.

FORT HILL. *See* CHITIPA.

FORT JAMESON. Now called Chipata, this Zambian town near the border with **Malawi** developed near the seat of Inkosi **Mpezeni**, one of the sons of **Zwangendaba**. The British defeated the Mpezeni **Ngoni** in 1898, and in the following year Robert Codrington of the Northern Rhodesia administration moved there from **Zomba**, turning it into a regional headquarters of the **British South African Company** (BSAC).

FORT JOHNSTON. Named after Sir **Harry Johnston** and renamed **Mangochi** after independence, this district headquarters is located at the southern tip of **Lake Malawi** very near the point where the **Shire River** flows out of the lake. It was a British fort in the late 1880s and in the 1890s at the height of the establishment of Pax Britannica in the area. Fort Johnston became a defensive and an offensive post against the **Yao** chiefs **Mponda**, **Makandanji**, **Makanjila**, and **Jalasi**, all of whom strongly resisted the new British authority. Part of the memorabilia relating to the period of British pacification is currently displayed at the Mangochi museum at the *boma*.

FORT LISTER. Renamed **Phalombe** and located in the valley northwest **of Mulanje mountain**. Fort Lister was a British post in the fight with **Yao** chiefs, especially **Chikumbu**.

FORT MAGUIRE. *See* CECIL MAGUIRE.

FORT MANGOCHE. Located in the mountainous area west of **Mangochi** (Fort Johnston) *boma*, this was a fort that the British used in the 1890s and early 1900s to extend their authority in the mainly **Yao**-dominated area in the border region with **Mozambique**.

FORT MANNING. Renamed Mchinji and located in **Chewa/Ngoni** country, Fort Manning was built in 1898 during campaigns against the

Mpezeni Ngoni. In January 1898 Captain **William Manning** of the **King's African Rifles** (KAR) launched his attacks on **Mpezeni** from this fort, and it was here that the defeated Mpezeni was held prisoner for a year. About 12,000 cattle from Mpezeni's area were also taken to Fort Manning. In recent years the fertile lands in this district have become major **tobacco-** and **maize**-growing areas, and the large estate owners included Dr. **Hastings K. Banda** and several of his ministers. **Groundnuts**, tobacco, and maize are grown in the district. The district headquarters is also the Malawi railhead for a rail line extending from **Lilongwe** to the **Malawi-Zambia** border.

FORT MLANGENI. Located on the **Malawi-Mozambique** border, between **Ntcheu** *boma* and **Lizulu**, this fort was a British post in the campaigns against the Gomani **Ngoni**. Later, Fort Mlangeni became a major recruiting center of the **Witwatersrand Native Labour Association** (WENELA). Later still, it became a training center for the Young Pioneers and the Police Mobile Force. *See also* GOMANI I.

FRASER, DONALD. Born in 1870, he came to **Nyasaland** in 1897, joining senior colleague Rev. **Walter Elmslie** at the **Livingstonia Mission** at **Ekwendeni**. Later, with his wife Agnes Robson, he was stationed at **Loudon**. With Fraser's arrival came a more sympathetic attitude toward African culture. He attempted to reform the more puritanical church restrictions on dancing, polygamy, and beer drinking and emphasized the writing of **Ngoni** hymns and the similarity between existing Ngoni and **Tumbuka** religious beliefs and Christianity. Among the books he wrote are *Winning a Primitive People* (1914), *African Idylls* (1923), *Autobiography of an African* (1925), and *The New Africa* (1927). He left Malawi in 1925 and died in 1933. He was buried at **Loudon Mission**, **Mzimba**, next to Rev. **Jonathan Chirwa**. *See also* ROBERT LAWS.

FRELIMO. This is the abbreviated name for Frente de Libertacao de Mocambique, the ruling party of **Mozambique** since 1975. FRELIMO was formed in 1962 and by the end of the 1960s had become the leading nationalist liberation movement, waging guerrilla warfare against Portuguese authority in Mozambique.

FRENCH, MARGARET. This British woman became **Hastings K. Banda**'s friend, lover, and companion during his stay in London and Ghana. The two met in northeast England when Margaret's husband was serving in World War II. She became Banda's landlady, and when Banda moved to London and bought his own house, she, her son, and husband joined him. Later her husband left and successfully filed for divorce, citing Banda as the corespondent. When Banda left for Ghana in 1953, she went with him, leaving her son with his father. However, when he decided to return to **Malawi** in 1958, she remained in Ghana and eventually went back to London; contact between them was minimal at first and soon terminated completely. Mrs. French died in 1976.

– G –

GADAMA, AARON. Born in 1934 near **Kasungu**, Gadama went to local primary schools before proceeding to St. John's Bosco Teacher's College, **Lilongwe**, where in 1959 he received the primary school teacher's certificate. While teaching at a number of schools in the Central Region, he studied by correspondence to upgrade his basic **education**. He became headmaster of Kasungu Primary School but continued to further his education. The mid-1960s were a busy time for Gadama: he was awarded a British government bursary to study education for a year at Morray House, Edinburgh; he spent some time in Australia studying education and received a certificate in modern mathematics from Nairobi.

An articulate, intelligent, and entertaining person, he became an MP for Kasungu in 1971. Gadama was quickly promoted by Dr. **Hastings Banda** to minister of community development. In the mid-1970s, he was appointed minister without portfolio before moving on to become minister for the Central Region. In the latter capacity, he was also chairman of the **Malawi Congress Party** (MCP) in the Central Region. In May 1983 Gadama was one of the four cabinet ministers and members of parliament who died in a car "accident" in **Mwanza** District. A commission of inquiry established in the post-Banda period has been told that the police killed the ministers on orders from the top, and it is no longer a matter of speculation that he may have been involved in a power struggle involving the issue of succession to the aging Banda. *See also* MWANZA ACCIDENT AND TRIALS.

GHAMBI, KWACHA. Very wealthy and controversial businessman whose behavior and constant clashes with police led him to be regarded as the most notorious outlaw in post-Banda **Malawi**. Born in **Karonga** District in 1967, Ghambi attended local schools, and then the Polytechnic in **Blantyre**, and lived in Great Britain for some time before becoming an import-export businessman. From his base in Blantyre, he imported, among other items, cars from **South Africa**, some of his merchandise being of suspicious origins. Police in both countries followed his business trails continuously, and in 1997, his South African-born wife was killed under doubtful circumstances. In early July 2000, Ghambi was arrested and taken to the maximun security prison in **Zomba**. On July 6, he was fatally beaten by prison warders, following a quarrel with one of them. The manner of Ghambi's demise became national news and was taken up by **human rights** activists, and in October that year, seven officers were charged with the death of the businessman. His lifestyle and the way he died have already contributed to turning Ghambi into one of the legends of modern Malawi.

GLOSSOP, REV. ARTHUR G. B. A missionary of the **Universities' Mission to Central Africa** (UMCA) who was posted to **Likoma** Island in 1893 and for 50 years continued to work in the **Lake Malawi** area. As the high Anglican archdeacon in the UMCA, Glossop was the sole cleric representative on the Commission of Inquiry on the **Chilembwe uprising**. In the Commissioners Report (1916) Glossop's bias against small independent missions was apparent; he believed Africans needed discipline, not the kind of individualism seen in Chilembwe and his followers.

GOMANI I, INKOSI CHITAMTHUMBA. In September 1891 Gomani succeeded his father, Chikuse, as the leader of the Maseko **Ngoni**. Within a few years, a civil war commenced between his followers and those of his cousin, **Kachindamoto**, grandson of **Chidyawonga**. With the assistance of the **Yao** chief **Mponda**, Gomani forced Kachindamoto to the lakeshore area, where he established a base at Mthakataka, a famous railway station and Christian mission center. In November 1894 the two warring leaders reconciled at a meeting on Dedza Mountain.

Peace attracted many foreigners to the area, and they included missionaries, hunters, businessmen, and colonial administrators, a development that concerned some of Gomani's followers who became convinced that their ruler had lost a grip on his domain. To prove the contrary, Gomani sent his security forces to the area between the Kirk Ranges and **Liwonde** to punish villages that had offended his administration. Convinced that this was a challenge to the colonial government and seeing a chance to humiliate an African ruler considered recalcitrant, the colonial government sent soldiers to remind Gomani that he was answerable to it. Defiant, he reminded the government party led by Captain Stewart and Acting Consul Grenville that he and his people would never submit to the British. When Kachere, a bodyguard, tried to prevent Gomani's arrest, his head was severed from his body; on October 27, 1896, Gomani was taken away by the army and, midway between Dombole and Chiole, was killed and buried. His subjects found his body and re-buried it about five miles north of present-day **Ntcheu** district headquarters; the grave has become a major symbol for all the Maseko Ngoni.

GOMANI II, INKOSI ZINTONGA PHILIP MASEKO. A descendant of **Mputa** and Chikuse, paramount chief of the Maseko **Ngoni** of **Ntcheu** District from 1921 to 1954, and one of the few traditional rulers to stand firm against the establishment of the **Federation of Rhodesia and Nyasaland**, Znintonga Gomani was born in 1894 at Chipiri on the **Mozambique** side of **Malawi**. After mastering the basic elements of reading and writing, Zintonga went to the **Henry Henderson Institute** (HHI), **Blantyre**, and was baptized at Ntcheu in 1921, the year he succeeded his father, **Chitamthumba Gomani**, as chief. Under the District Native Ordinance of 1933, Zintonga, now using his Christian name, Philip, became officially recognized as paramount chief of Ntcheu District. In 1934 he was among the first chiefs to attend a course for traditional rulers at the **Jeanes Training Centre, Domasi**. Ten years later he was appointed to the Provincial Council and to the **African Protectorate Council**, a position that gave him the opportunity to meet and know other chiefs and leading Nyasalanders outside his district.

Totally opposed to the **Federation of Rhodesia and Nyasaland**, Chief Gomani was to be part of the delegation of Nyasaland chiefs who went to London to oppose its institution. However, because of poor health, his son, Willard, went instead. When the Federation was imposed in 1953, Gomani began to pursue peaceful resistance by ignoring official agricultural and conservation regulations, many of which were highly unpopular in the colony. In reaction, the government suspended and then withdrew its recognition of his chiefly authority; on May 26, 1953, the police, led by the Deputy Commissioner Geoffrey Morton, tried to force Gomani out of the district but failed because the thousands of people gathered at the chief's **Lizulu** headquarters made it impossible. The chief then hid near Villa Coutinho on the Mozambican side of the border, where he was arrested by the Portuguese authorities, which handed him over to the Nyasaland police. His arrest was followed by major disquiet throughout the colony. In June the case against him was due to start in the **Zomba** magistrate court, but the chief could not appear because he was ill at the Seventh-Day Adventist Hospital, **Malamulo, Thyolo**, where he died on May 12, 1953. He was buried at **Lizulu** two days later, his funeral attended by thousands of people, including leading nationalist politicians such as **James Sangala**, **Charles Chinula**, and **James Chinyama**.

GOMANI III, INKOSI WILLARD MASEKO. Born in 1915 at **Lizulu** in **Ntcheu** District, son of Inkosi Zintonga Philip, **Gomani II**, Willard went to Seventh-Day Adventist schools. During World War II he was a signaler in the **King's African Rifles**. Upon demobilization in 1943, he joined government service as a clerk. By the time he became acting chief in 1952, he had risen to the rank of head clerk, the highest position an African could attain in the colonial civil service. Like his recently deposed father, Inkosi Willard strongly opposed the **Federation of Rhodesia and Nyasaland**, and in 1952–1953 he was part of a delegation of six chiefs that went to London to oppose its institution. Unimpressed by all this, the colonial government not only refused to accept Willard as the successor to his father when the latter died in 1953 but even imprisoned him for seven months. When he was released, still only acting chief, he continued to support nationalist causes to the extent that during the state of emergency in 1959, he was detained for eight months.

In 1961 Inkosi Gomani stood as **Malawi Congress Party** (MCP) candidate for Ntcheu and was duly elected to parliament, which he left four years later to devote his attention to his traditional role as leader of the **Ngoni** in the Ntcheu/Dedza area.

GOMBERA, THOMAS. The first African detective in the **Nyasaland police** and the first African to attain the rank of police inspector. Gombera was born in 1896 in Southern Rhodesia. From 1912 to the beginning of World War I, he served in the British South African Police Force and for four years saw war service in East Africa as part of the Rhodesia Native Regiment. Upon demobilization in 1919, he went to Nyasaland to join the police force that was about to be formed. In 1920 he became one of the first recruits of Major **Francis Stephens**, the first police commissioner with whom he had served in Rhodesia and East Africa. From January 1921 to his retirement in 1961, Gombera was in the Criminal Investigation Division of the Police Department. A recipient of five police medals, including the Colonial Police Medal for Meritorious Service in 1947, he was promoted to the rank of Inspector in the Police Force in February 1959.

GONDWE, CHILONGOZI. Former government policeman who in 1907 became **Chikulamayembe**, the traditional ruler of the **Tumbuka**-speaking peoples in **Rumphi** District. This position had disappeared after the M'mbelwa **Ngoni** ransacked the area in the 1870s; the colonial government reinstituted it after a long and well-organized campaign by the Tumbuka speakers associated with the Chikulamayembe dynasty.

GONDWE, EDWARD KAYIONANGA. One of the most senior and respected civil servants in **Nyasaland**. Edward Gondwe was born in 1906 at Enukweni in **Mzimba** District. He went to the local Presbyterian mission school and to **Ekwendeni** Primary School before proceeding to the **Overtoun Institution** at **Khondowe**, where he completed the Primary Teachers Certificate. He taught at several schools, including Ekwendeni, where he became a headmaster. He was also active in his church, holding the position of church elder. As part of a program to improve the quality of primary education, the colonial government in Nyasaland identified some of the best indigenous teachers and educational administrators to become school inspectors and, when required, tutors at the **Domasi** Training Center. Gondwe was such a candidate and in 1948 was among the first Nyasaland teachers to attend an 18-month course at the Institute of Education, University of London. Upon his return, he was appointed inspector of schools, mainly for **Rumphi, Karonga**, and parts of **Mzimba** Districts. In 1958 he became education officer, the highest position occupied by an African without a university degree. One of the most respected civil servants in colonial Malawi, Gondwe retired from government service in the mid-1960s. *See also* EDUCATION.

Throughout his working life, Edward Gondwe played other significant roles in public life. In 1951 he was a member of the African delegation to the **Lancaster House Conference**, at which the **Federation of Rhodesia and Nyasaland** was discussed. With other African delegates from Northern Rhodesia and Nyasaland, Gondwe did not in the end attend the official talks because of the feeling that such an action would have identified them with the advocates of the Federation. In 1960 he was a member of the **Monckton Commission** appointed to review the Federation. Even though his membership in this commission convinced some people that he did not side with Malawian nationalist aspirations, Gondwe and two other Africans produced a minority report not favorable to the Federation. In fact, when Malawi became independent in 1964, Gondwe was recalled from retirement and requested to serve in the Malawian mission to Germany. He later retired from the foreign service and returned to **Mzuzu,** where he died in 1993.

GONDWE, GOODALL. Head of the Africa Department at the **International Monetary Fund** (IMF) from 1998 to 2001. Gondwe was born in 1936 and went to **Ekwendeni** Primary School and **Blantyre** and Dedza Secondary Schools before proceeding to the University of Rhodesia and Nyasaland and then to Makerere University in Uganda, where he graduated in 1965, majoring in economics. He worked in Malawi, occupying senior positions in the Reserve Bank of Malawi and the Ministry of Finance. He then joined the African Development Bank in Abidjan, Cote d'Ivoire, which he later headed. In 1981, he joined the IMF, which in 1998 appointed him head of its Africa Department.

GONDWE, KANYOLI. In 1879 Kanyoli Gondwe and **Kambondoma Mhango** led the resistance to M'Mbelwa **Ngoni** authority over, and encroachment into, the Nkamanga and Henga valleys, both **Tumbuka**-speaking areas in modern northern **Malawi**. Much feared and respected as warriors, they formed the Kwenda and Sikwaliwene regiments, which were headed, respectively, by Kanyoli and Kambondoma, and calling themselves **Majere-Henga**, in 1879 rebelled against the Ngoni. When the rebellion failed, Kanyoli Gondwe, a member of the **Chikula-mayembe** family, sought refugee among the **Ngonde** in the **Karonga** lakeshore area.

GONDWE, MASOPERA. Born in **Rumphi**, Gondwe was assistant general secretary of the **Nyasaland African Congress** (NAC) during the presidency of **James Sangala**. He was disappointed when the leadership tacitly approved of **Wellington M. Chirwa** and **Clement Kumbikano** when they entered the federal parliament. In August 1955 he lost the senior position in the party as a disciplinary measure for remonstrating with Chirwa without official permission. In reaction, Gondwe formed his own organization, the Congress Peoples Party (CHIPIPI), which was short-lived because of a lack of money and a poor membership. Generally regarded as an honest man, he was also viewed by some as a maverick. Clearly, the government took him seriously; while he was still in the NAC, the colonial authorities in **Northern Rhodesia** banned him from entering the colony, where he had planned to attend a meeting of the Pan-African Congress.

GONDWE, TIJEPANI DOROTHY. Political activist and one of the leading members of the **League of Malawi Women** of the **Malawi Congress Party** (MCP). Tijepani Gondwe was born at Mpoda village in north **Karonga** on March 24, 1924. She attended schools in **Malawi** and Tanganyika, got married, was widowed, and returned to Malawi in the 1950s. Within a short time she joined the **Nyasaland African Congress** (NAC) and became an activist in Karonga. In 1958 she was elected organizing secretary for the district. She also became a prominent member of the Women's League and even attended the secret bush meeting that the NAC leadership called in February 1959 to plan a program of action. In the period leading to the declaration of the state of emergency on March 3, Gondwe and **Flax K. Musopole** worked day and night to inform people that should Dr. **Hastings K. Banda** be arrested, they should take up arms against the government. As people were detained, they crossed the **Songwe** into Tanganyika, where they were arrested in August and taken back to Malawi. Gondwe was taken to prison and stayed until the following year.

In the mid-1960s Gondwe went to England to study community and social work. Upon returning in 1969, she worked for the government. However, within two years, she had fallen out of favor with the authorities and was dismissed from her job. She returned to Karonga to farm and was not fully rehabilitated into the Malawi Congress Party until 1992, when she was appointed to its National Executive Committee, in the hope that she could sway opinion toward retention of the status quo. Gondwe campaigned against political reform and in 1994 tirelessly campaigned for the MCP.

GONDWE, VINCENT. Former senior civil servant, ambassador, and international civil servant. Vincent, son of **Edward K. Gondwe**, attended **Blantyre** Secondary School and **Fort Hare University, South Africa**. He then studied for a teacher's diploma at Bristol University and became a teacher at Dedza Secondary School. In 1964 he was appointed Malawi's first ambassador to Ghana and in 1967 became permanent secretary in the Ministry of Education, the first Malawian to occupy such a senior civil service position. Gondwe served as ambassador to Ethiopia and the **Organization of African Unity** (OAU). After retiring from government service, he worked for the Food and Agriculture Organization (FAO). He died in 1991.

GOVERNMENT. On July 6, 1964, **Malawi** became independent from British rule after 73 years of protectorate status. Two years later, it became a republic within the Commonwealth of Nations. The president, elected every four years, is executive head of the state and is assisted by a deputy and cabinet ministers, normally appointed from members of parliament of the ruling party. The principal officer in the president's office is the secretary to the president and cabinet and is also the head of the national civil service. Each cabinet minister is in charge of one or more government departments and is advised by a principal secretary, who is also the head civil servant in the ministry.

The country is divided administratively into three regions, Northern, Central, and Southern. During the **Hastings K. Banda** government one-party system, each was headed by a cabinet minister. The regions are further divided into districts, each headed by a **district commissioner** who is a civil servant and is answerable to the Office of the President in **Lilongwe**. Local government is carried out in 26 districts. In addition to the district councils there are city and town councils, all of which are supervised by the minister of local government. Although councils are elected and act as vehicles for development at the local level, the national government is able to exert control over them by its budget approval and the allocation of national monies for regional needs.

As recommended by the **International Monetary Fund** (IMF) and the **World Bank**, the local government system is being strengthened by, among other measures, granting it more financial independence. This will necessitate a reorganization of the district administrative system, probably leading to the abolition of the district commissioner's office.

GOVERNORS. *See* BRITISH COMMISSIONERS/GOVERNORS OF BRITISH CENTRAL AFRICA AND NYASALND, 1891–1964.

GREAT BRITAIN. Malawi's close ties with Great Britain go back to the 19th century, when Dr. **David Livingstone** first visited the region in the late 1850s. Three Christian **missions** were established: the **Universities' Mission to Central Africa** (UMCA) and then the **Livingstonia** and **Blantyre Missions.** The first major European firm to trade in the Lake Malawi area was the Scottish **African Lakes Company** (ALC). By the time British rule was established between 1889 and 1891, more traders and planters had arrived from Great Britain. The system of **education** that the missionaries introduced in the colony was modeled on the British one. At independence in 1964, Dr. **Hastings K. Banda** retained many British civil servants, pointing out that he would not replace the expatriates until fully qualified Malawians were prepared to fill their positions. This deliberate **Africanization** policy met with more British approval than Malawian, and it was a factor in the 1964 **Cabinet Crisis**.

Banda's commitment to capitalism ensured a continuance of British economic interests in **Malawi**, although other foreign interests have since entered the market. Great Britain remains the dominant European trading partner of Malawi, and the strong Britain–Malawi friendship has been further sustained by generous foreign assistance grants. Budgetary deficits for several years after independence were covered by British grants-in-aid, and British development loans regularly were provided for projects in **agriculture, education**, housing, and **forestry. Human rights** groups, religious organizations, and other **nongovernmental organizations** (NGOs) based in Great Britain were supportive of the political reform movement in the 1990s, and the warm relations between the peoples and governments have continued into the post–Hastings Banda era. *See also* EXTERNAL TRADE; FOREIGN AID; FOREIGN POLICY.

GROUNDNUTS. Grown throughout the country but more commonly in the Central Region, until the late 1980s groundnuts (peanuts) were purchased from smallholders and marketed only by the **Agricultural Development and Marketing Board** (ADMARC). **Malawi** is the largest exporter of the large, hard-shelled confectionery grade, accounting for over 50 percent of the world sales of this type. The groundnuts are machine graded in an ADMARC factory in **Liwonde** and sold directly to overseas processors. In the late 1970s drought reduced production levels and ADMARC purchases declined from 31,000 to 9,000 metric tons. In 1985–1986 the trend was reversed when the authorities increased producer prices by 89 percent. There was a record output of groundnuts and record purchases of the crop by ADMARC.

To meet the need for more **maize**, **Malawi** has in the recent past exchanged tons of surplus groundnuts for tons of South African maize. In the late 1990s groundnuts continued to be a major export, and it was hoped that more people would grow crops such as groundnuts instead of tobacco, as the price of **tobacco** declined yearly. Efforts to develop production of both cashew and macadamia nuts for export have fallen short of expectations.

GUDU, WILFRID. Founder of the Ana a Mulungu (The Children of God) Church. Gudu was born in **Thyolo** District in the late 1880s or early 1890s. Of **Mang'anja** ethnic affiliation, Gudu became a Seventh-Day Adventist in 1906, when he went to school at the **Malamulo** Mission. Between 1911 and 1918, he worked for the mission as a teacher and preacher, but due to illness he was out of a job until 1921, when he was reemployed by Malamulo. His relations with the white missionaries were not always cordial. In 1935 he queried the manner in which they had settled an adultery case. Although the boy in question was not suspended from the church, Gudu was disciplined for protesting against what he viewed as an injustice. In response, he left the church altogether and established his own, Ana a Mulungu.

Gudu and his followers lived in Chief **Ntondeza**'s area, where they planned to grow **maize** to sell to nearby **tea** plantations. The plan failed because the chief accused them of using land that did not belong to them. In 1937 Gudu unsuccessfully appealed to the local **district commissioner** (DC) to intervene on his behalf. In turn, Chief Ntondeza, assisted by government police, expelled the Ana a Mulungu adherents from his area. Gudu then informed the DC that he and his disciples would no longer pay taxes and accused the government of not following the teachings of God as detailed in the Bible. In February of the following year, two attempts to arrest him failed. But in March he and some of his people were sentenced to three months imprisonment at the **Zomba** Central Prison. They refused to wear the prison uniform because, for them, it was ungodly. Later in 1938 Gudu was back in Zomba prison for a further six months and was then ordered to remain in the district. In 1942 he returned to Thyolo, and although he paid taxes this time, he continued to preach and to talk against colonial rule and settler greed. Gudu died in March 1963.

GWEDE, FOCUS. Former head of the Police Special Branch. Gwede was born in **Ntcheu** District, where he attended primary school before joining the **police** force. After some years as a regular policeman, he transferred to the **Special Branch**, the security division of the force, of which he became the head in the early 1970s. Regarded as a hard-hearted and overzealous man, Gwede was directly associated with the indiscriminate political detention of hundreds of Malawians, mainly from 1974 to 1976. In 1976 he and **Albert Muwalo-Nqumayo** were arrested and charged with a plot to overthrow the government, and in the following year they were tried in the national traditional court. Muwalo-Nqumayo received the death sentence and Gwede was given a life sentence. After the **United Democratic Front** (UDF) came to power in 1994, Gwede was released from prison.

GWENGWE, JOHN. This educator, author, and politician trained as a teacher at the William Murray Teachers Training College, **Lilongwe**, and the **Jeanes Training Centre, Domasi**. He taught at several schools in the Central Region before becoming an inspector of schools in the early 1960s. In 1966 he was appointed junior minister in the Ministry of Education; later, he became minister of trade and industry. In 1970 he fell out of favor with Dr. **Kamuzu Banda** and retired from politics. Gwengwe is best known as an author of short stories and novels in ciChewa, and as a major promoter of local **literature**.

– H –

HALL, AUBREY VICTOR. Founder of Hall's Holdings Limited, Aubrey Hall went to **Nyasaland** from the United Kingdom in 1923 in the service of the Central African Transport Company (CATCO). Ten years later, he founded Hall's Garage, which sold and serviced cars; this business developed into a larger enterprise, Hall's Holding Ltd., which by the late 1960s had branches in the Central and Northern Regions of **Malawi**. A prominent member of the European settler community in Malawi and a founding member of the Nyasaland Society, Aubrey Hall served as mayor of **Blantyre**, president of the chamber of commerce, chairman of the Nyasaland Society for the Blind, president of the Blantyre Sports Club, and president of the Nyasaland Golf Union.

HARA, SAMUEL. Preacher from Emawoleni village, **Mzimba** District. Hara translated, without assistance, the Holy Bible from Bishop Colenso's Zulu version into ciTumbuka, which was published posthumously. This was the first time such a task had been undertaken in the **Livingstonia** Synod, and it remained in regular use until the 1960s.

HAYES, GEORGE DUDLEY. Businessman and conservationist, Hayes was born in Kent, England, in 1904. As a young man, he went to **Malawi**, where he became a planter, working for the **A. L. Bruce Estates** at **Magomero**. In 1931 he became an independent contractor, working on roads and locust control, and guarding farms from ravaging elephants. Later he joined the civil service as an agricultural supervisor and was posted to **Chikwawa**, marking the beginning of a long association with the **Lengwe National Park**, of which he was made warden in 1939. During World War II, he served with the **King's African Rifles** (KAR) and, in 1945 he established Antipest, a pest control company. A keen environmentalist and conservator, in 1947 he became founding secretary-treasurer of the National Fauna Preservation Society of Malawi and continued to lead the organization until early 1981. Another major interest was the **Society of Malawi**, of which he became a committee member in 1951. He became its vice chairman and chairman in 1963 and 1973, respectively, and edited its journal, the *Society of Malawi Journal*, from 1951 until his death in 1981. George Hayes wrote the *Guide to Malawi's National Parks and Game Reserves* (1979).

HEALTH SERVICES. Christian missionaries introduced Western medicine into the **Lake Malawi** region in the 19th century. Until that time, matters of health were the sole domain of indigenous specialists. Although men tended to dominate the field, **women** too distinguished themselves as doctors; generally, childbirth was the preserve of female experts. It was strongly believed that in many cases the ability to heal was hereditary, passing from generation to generation, so much so that particular families were known as healers. One could also train in healing by apprenticeship to a healer. Famous healers would receive patients from far afield and, because of this, they would provide accommodation for their wards. Even with the increasing popularity of Western medicine in the 20th century, traditional medical practice continued to feature prominently in most Malawian societies. In some situations, it functioned parallel to modern health systems and, in others, the two worked hand in hand.

Missionaries and **mission** stations were the first point of contact between Western medicine and Malawian societies. Besides a church and a school, almost every mission station had a health clinic. The first doctors to work in Malawi were missionaries; they were also the first to conduct surveys of the various **diseases** that afflicted the people. Doctors in this category include **Robert Laws**, the **Elmslies**, **Kerr Cross**, **George Prentice**, **Jane Waterston**, **William Murray**, and **William Wigan**. The first Malawian medical personnel were trained at mission hospitals such as **Blantyre**, **Nkhotakota**, **Nkhoma**, and **Livingstonia**, and they formed the core of medical support staff in the government health system. Although the beginnings of the latter can be traced to June 1891, when Dr. **Sorabji Boyce** was appointed as government doctor, only in the early 1900s did the government build facilities where people could seek medical help. At the start of World War I, there were five hospitals in the colony: **Karonga**, 2 beds; Fort Johnston **(Mangochi)**, 6; **Zomba**, 46; Blantyre, 12; Port Herald **(Nsanje),** and Dedza. In 1930 the **Colonial Development Fund** allocated £78,284 for the expansion of the health system, and four years later new hospitals were built at Karonga, 50 beds; **Mzimba**, 30; **Kasungu**, 30; Nkhotakota, 50; Dowa, 30; **Lilongwe**, 30; **Fort Manning** (Mchinji), 30; **Chiradzulu**, 30; Zomba, 100; **Mulanje**, 50; **Thyolo**, 50; and **Chikwawa**, 30. Wards were added to the units at Dedza, Fort Johnston, and Port Herald. This development increased hospital beds from 170 to 634. In Blantyre, Zomba, and Lilongwe there were hospitals specifically for Europeans.

Health services were disrupted during the two world wars as medical personnel, European and African, were seconded to the army. After the war, few hospitals were built but more day health centers manned by African medical assistants were established in many rural areas. By 1950 the population of **Nyasaland** was 2.5 million and the number of beds in government medical facilities for Africans had increased to 1,115. The special psychiatric hospital built at Zomba before the end of World War

I was expanded, and a new leprosy residential treatment center was in the process of being built at Kochilira in **Fort Manning** (Mchinji) District. Campaigns against smallpox (started at the end of the 19th century) continued, and with advancement of medicine there was also a more effective treatment of malaria, yaws, and tuberculosis.

After 1953 the health services became the responsibility of the federal government. This increased the budget, leading to the construction of additional wards in hospitals, and by 1957 there were 1,797 beds in government hospitals. In spite of this, overcrowding remained a feature at all hospitals in Malawi, including those managed by Christian missions, which at the time had a combined total of 1,600 beds. In 1958 the Queen Elizabeth Hospital opened in Blantyre. It was well equipped, had 412 beds, and it replaced Zomba Hospital as the principal referral hospital in the country.

As a result of the dissolution of the **Federation of Rhodesia and Nyasaland** in 1963, the Medical Department reverted to the Nyasaland government. Many doctors, including specialists, returned to **Southern Rhodesia**. At independence in July 1964, Malawi had an acute shortage of doctors; there were only 14 doctors working for the government and of these only one was a Malawian. Foreign doctors were recruited, mainly from Israel, the United Kingdom, and Netherlands, as part of aid programs to Malawi. In the meantime it was expected that Malawian medical students training abroad since the early 1960s would return in 1969. In fact, very few did and by 1972 there were only 12 Malawian doctors in government service. The reliance on foreign doctors and those working at mission hospitals continued. Meantime, while Zomba hospital remained the base for the school for state-enrolled nurses, a new school to train state registered nurses opened at Queen Elizabeth Hospital in 1965. In addition, the medical assistants' college at Lilongwe and the numerous mission hospitals, which also trained state-enrolled nurses, provided the medical personnel that still form the backbone of health care in Malawi.

In the 1970s a plan for the development of health services was worked out on the basis of World Health Organization (WHO) recommendations, and it called for the expansion of health facilities in areas of agricultural projects, the replacement and renovation of existing antiquated hospitals, and the establishment of a network of basic health centers from which to conduct preventative health services. In 1977 a new 250-bed general hospital was opened in Lilongwe, as well as the new Medical Auxiliary Training School, which greatly relieved staff shortages of clinical officers and pharmacy and laboratory assistants. Four new hospitals were completed (1986–1987) at **Salima**, Mchinji, Karonga, and **Ntchisi**. Doctors continued to be trained outside Malawi, and the several government and mission schools also continued to train nurses, midwives, medical/health assistants, and health inspectors. As the population of Malawi grew in the 1980s, the shortage of doctors became evident: one doctor for every 52,961 persons. It was largely in response to this problem that the **University of Malawi** established a new medical college in Blantyre in 1988. It is hoped that doctors will stay to work in Malawi and not be attracted to better remuneration outside the country, as has been the case throughout the postcolonial period.

In the early 1990s the Malawi government embarked on an ambitious ten-year health plan through which it expects to establish a primary care center (rural hospital) for every 50,000 persons, a health subcenter for every 10,000, and a health post for every 2,000. Expanded health services for maternal and child care is also a critical need being addressed in the plan. In 1989 the infant mortality rate was 150 for every 1,000 live births; this had been projected to drop to 110, but the expectation was dashed with the publication in 1990 that malnutrition, **AIDS**, and malaria had resulted in a rise in the mortality rate to 178 in every 1,000. Health officials no longer anticipated the decline to occur soon. The number of maternal deaths was expected to drop from 16 to 10 by expanding pre- and postnatal services. The plan also included the use of contraceptives, the usage of which was expected to increase to 10 percent.

Although Malawi received foreign assistance to execute these programs, the economic situation within the country restricted their full implementation. The post-Banda government tried to effect the projects but was hampered by personnel shortages and inadequate finances. The devaluation of the Malawi **kwacha** led to a rise in the cost of equipment and medicine, most of which is imported. Some hospitals and health centers did not even have the basic medicine to treat malaria or the common cold. However, there were also accusations of corruption and mismanagement on the part of some health authorities. By 1998 the new government had modified the plans. While it would continue to emphasize primary health care services, it would provide them through the Essential Health Package (EHP), a cost-effective approach that would involve, inter alia, enlarging immunization, reproductive health, and nutrition programs. As part of the EHP, the per capita annual budget allocated for drugs and vaccines would be maintained at US$1.25 per person, and a revolving Drugs Fund, managed by the rural communities themselves, would be established at clinics, thereby ensuring that the 20 percent of the population not covered hitherto would have access to health facilities. A system would be introduced to recover costs at district and specialist hospitals, as well as a more effective method of collecting fees from patients in private wards at government hospitals. The problem of AIDS is also to be addressed under the EHP. *See also* DISEASE.

HENDERSON, HENRY. Founder of the **Blantyre Mission**, a Scottish layman who had briefly worked in Queensland, Australia. In 1875 he volunteered to be the Established Church of Scotland's representative accompanying the Free Church of Scotland, which set out to establish a mission in the **Lake Malawi** region in memory of **David Livingstone**. In 1876 Chief **Kapeni** gave a site to Henderson on which to develop the Blantyre Mission of the Church of Scotland. The period between 1876 and 1880 was particularly difficult because of the unrealistic policies that guided the mission's relations with the local people and because of the indiscipline of some of Henderson's colleagues at **Blantyre**. In 1881 some missionaries were dismissed from service, including Rev. **Duff Macdonald**, who had headed the Blantyre Mission since 1878. When the mission started afresh under Rev. **David C. Scott**, Henderson continued to work at Blantyre and played a major role in the establishment of substations at **Zomba**, **Domasi**, and **Mulanje**. He died at Quilimane, **Mozambique**, on February 12, 1891, while on the journey back to Scotland. A river steamer, the *Henry Henderson*, purchased by the mission in 1892, was named in his honor. The steamer, operating on the **Shire**, was used as a floating school and church, and was manned by African graduates of the Blantyre Mission. An educational establishment, the **Henry Henderson Institute** (HHI), was also named after him.

HENDERSON, MAJOR DAVID. A survivor of the **Moyale** campaign in Northeast Africa. Henderson became a successful dairy and **tobacco** farmer at his Mpalangaga estate, two miles south of the quarry on the **Zomba-Blantyre** road. He maintained his interest in the welfare of retired servicemen, and when he died, the Malawi army gave him a military-style funeral. *See also* ARMY.

HENRY HENDERSON INSTITUTE (HHI). Fondly referred to as the HHI, this is an educational establishment at the **Blantyre Mission** of Church of Scotland mission station named after **Henry Henderson**. The mission developed a primary school, a teacher training college, a theological college, and a center concentrating on technical subjects such as carpentry, bricklaying, printing, and later mechanical skills. The institute was also the home of the mission's print department, which was responsible for printing a variety of publications, including religious materials, school textbooks, and government and private **newspapers** and weeklies. Like its counterpart, the **Overtoun Institution** of the **Livingstonia Mission**, the HHI played a most significant role in religious, educational, and political developments in **Malawi**. In the late 1950s, a secondary school was added at the institute.

HERBALIST ASSOCIATION OF MALAWI (HAM). Formed in 1963 as the Traditional Mediciners of Central Africa (in ciChewa, Ochiritsa), the HAM is the largest umbrella organization of the practitioners of traditional African medicine. Guided by a constitution, the HAM is registered with the Ministry of Health and determines the fees that its members charge for the various ailments they treat. The **University of Malawi** encourages HAM members to take samples of their plant medicines for testing of their biological composition, and those who do so are awarded testimonials. As a way of gathering information on health activities in rural areas, the Ministry of Health requests HAM members to complete forms detailing their activities. *See also* HEALTH SERVICES.

HETHERWICK, ALEXANDER. In 1899 Dr. Hetherwick succeeded Rev. **David C. Scott** as head of the **Blantyre Mission**. He was highly regarded throughout the protectorate and from 1907 to 1913 was the missionary representative in the **Legislative Council** (LEGCO), where he often spoke on behalf of African interests. A supporter of British rule, Hetherwick perceived the mission's role as the conscience of the administration. His views of Africans, regularly printed in the mission publication *Life and Work*, tended to be paternalistic: the European was there to govern and to teach the African. He retired in 1927.

HEWE. Situated in northwestern **Rumphi** District on the border with Luangwa valley, **Zambia**, this area falls under the traditional authority of the Katumbi of the Chawinga clan. Hewe is in the location of the Vwaza marsh, which it shares with Zambia and is home to large herds of elephants.

HILTON YOUNG COMMISSION. Appointed in 1927 and chaired by Sir Edward Hilton Young, the commission sought to determine whether a closer union in East Africa was possible and whether a closer association might be sought between the Rhodesias and **Nyasaland**. Commissioners toured **Northern Rhodesia** and Nyasaland, listening to a variety of petitioners. In their 1929 report members of the commission stated that any closer association should be one that benefited the Africans, not merely the settler element. The settlers felt no responsibility toward the Africans and argued that it was up to the British government to protect their African wards. Last, the commission reported that, while there might be economic advantages to linking the protectorates, the British government should not make any plans tying together the Central African territories, especially at that time. The settlers rejected the African paramountcy concept and in the 1930s began efforts to try to amalgamate the territories. *See also* FEDERATION OF RHODESIA AND NYASALAND.

HORA. This mountain in central **Mzimba** is associated with some of the Early **Stone Age** settlements in the **Lake Malawi** region. In 1975 it was the site of a **Tumbuka** rebellion against **Ngoni** authority; **Baza Dokowe**, the leader of the Tumbuka, fled to **Kasungu**. Hora was also to become one of the important outstations of the **Livingstonia Mission**.

HUGGINS, GODFREY MARTIN. First prime minister and minister of defense of the **Federation of Rhodesia and Nyasaland**, Godfrey Huggins was born in England in 1883 and trained as a medical doctor before emigrating to Southern Rhodesia (**Zimbabwe**) in 1911. In 1924 he was elected to parliament as a member of the segregationist Reform Party of which he became leader. A strong believer in closer union between the Rhodesias and **Nyasaland**, Huggins rose to be prime minister of Southern Rhodesia and from that position spearheaded the campaign for a federation of the three British colonies. In 1953 he became the prime minister of the Federation. He relinquished the position three years later and was given a life peerage under the title of Lord Malvern.

HUMAN RIGHTS. For most of the postcolonial era, Malawi's record in human rights and respect for civil liberties has been poor in many respects. First, according to the constitution adopted at independence in 1964, there is no state religion and there are no restrictions on religious observances that do not impinge on government authority. However, during Dr. **Hastings K. Banda**'s presidency, the **Jehovah's Witnesses** came under pressure to identify with the program of the **Malawi Congress Party** (MCP); when they refused to conform, they were persecuted. Some were imprisoned, others went underground, and many others sought refuge outside the country. Freedom of speech and the press were also curtailed during the rule of the MCP. Criticism of the government and its policies was not tolerated, and this extended to parliament, where expression of total loyalty to the president was expected. The media (radio stations and at the time two newspapers) operated under informal but strict self-censorship; journalists were jailed for publishing articles that met with official displeasure. At the university level, freedom of inquiry existed but did not include explicit criticism of the government. Freedom of assembly was also limited in Dr. Banda's **Malawi**. Individuals and organizations were generally free to meet and associate, provided the purpose was not to speak against the government. *See also* POLITICAL DISSIDENTS.

External and internal travel were also affected by the regulations of the government and the MCP. For most of the postcolonial period, civil servants and others working for parastatals could not leave the country, even for officially sponsored conferences and seminars, without the permission of the government. Legal provision existed for restricting the movement of those convicted of criminal or political offenses. Formal emigration was neither restricted nor encouraged, and, with the exception of a small group of political dissidents and the Jehovah's Witnesses, there was no outward flow of Malawi **refugees** from the country. Until 1987 Malawi did not accord official refugee status but allowed private voluntary organizations to provide medical and other relief to the large number of displaced persons who had come into Malawi fleeing the fighting and hunger in **Mozambique**. Approximately a million Mozambicans crossed Malawi's border to avoid harassment and insurgency forces. In the post-Banda period, Malawi has received refugees from countries such as Rwanda, Somalia, and even Sierra Leone.

More serious was the situation regarding arbitrary arrest and detention. Under the Preservation of Public Security Act, the president could order the arrest, search, and detention of any person whom the government deemed capable of causing trouble in Malawi. A person arrested under this law could be detained by the **police** without trial in a court of law. At any given time a number of individuals were detained arbitrarily for real or perceived offenses against the party or government. Political detainees were often beaten and the length of confinement was uncertain; the usual cause was suspected disloyalty to the president and the MCP. Forced labor was not normally practiced but at times could be used as a form of criminal punishment.

Those charged with criminal offenses could not count on a fair trial. They might be tried in the traditional or modern court system; lawyers were not permitted to assist defendants in the former, but legal counsel was permitted in the latter. The right of appeal existed in both courts. The modern judiciary was, and still is, independent of the executive branch, although the president appoints the chief justice, who in turn is involved in the appointment of the other justices. On the other hand, National Traditional Court justices were appointed by the president. There is little executive interference in traditional court cases, which are conducted without publicity, as are executions. However, certain political cases were always directed to the traditional court system because, without the normal strict rules of evidence, a progovernment result was predictable. The post-Banda parliament has abolished the traditional courts justice system.

Moreover, the death penalty is mandatory for murder and treason and can be imposed for armed robbery. Beatings by the police at the time of detention or arrest, though not officially condoned, occur. Prison terms of hard labor are the norm for common criminals; during Banda's rule political detainees usually received less harsh and degrading treatment. Prison conditions are generally very poor, and human rights organizations such as the Red Cross have been critical of this aspect of the **United Democratic Front** (UDF) government. In recent times, some prisons, including the Central Prison in **Zomba** and that at Chichiri in **Blantyre**, have not had enough food to feed the inmates. In 1998 and 1999, the British government offered money to buy food for prisoners.

The matter of general human rights in Malawi came to the fore in early 1991–1993, when some foreign donors reduced aid to Malawi on the grounds that the Banda government's record in this area was abysmal. This action played a significant role in forcing Banda to accept the principle of multiparty democracy, leading to the free **elections** in 1994. In the post-Banda order, freedom of speech and association is recognized as a right: there are two daily **newspapers** and several weeklies, and all have editorial policies as dictated by the ownership; there are five political parties, and many active **labor unions**. Another feature of the post-Banda period is the number of active human rights and civil rights organizations operating freely in the country. They include the Civil Liberties Committee, the Legal Resources Center, the Consumer Association of Malawi (CANA), and the Malawi Institute of Democratic and Economic Affairs.

HYNDE, R. S. He originally came to **Nyasaland** as a Church of Scotland missionary assigned to **Domasi** but soon engaged in **agriculture**, planting **tea** and **tobacco**. As general manager of the **Blantyre and East Africa Company** (1901–1918), Hynde vigorously encouraged the cultivation of tobacco. He was editor of the *Central African Planter*, renamed the *Nyasaland Times* in 1907, and often expressed his pro-European planter views in these publications. Politically active, Hynde also served on the **Blantyre** Town Council.

– I –

ILALA I. Named after Ilala on the shores of Lake Banguelu, the place where **David Livingstone** died, this was a steamer that the first Free Church of Scotland party led by **Edward D. Young** used to transport themselves from the **Mozambique** coast on to the **Shire River** via the Zambezi and on to **Lake Malawi**. As its Scottish designers had planned, it was disassembled at the Murchison Falls and then reassembled up the river. From then on it was used as the main form of transport between the Upper Shire and the northern Lake Malawi area. In 1882 the *Ilala* was bought by the **African Lakes Company** (ALC), which employed the same engineers who had worked for the missions.

ILALA II. Built in Glasgow, Scotland, and named after the place where **David Livingstone** died in 1873, it has been the main transport vessel on **Lake Malawi** since 1951.

IMPERIAL TOBACCO COMPANY (ITC). Popularly known as the ITC, this British-owned company opened its factory in **Limbe** in 1908, the same year the railway line to the latter city was completed. As the company expanded its activities to include **tobacco** farms in **Blantyre**, **Zomba**, and elsewhere, its Limbe headquarters became one of the major employers of labor in the Blantyre-Limbe area. In the late 1960s, the company was reorganized and its name was changed to the Imperial Tobacco Group (ITG). However, by the late 1990s, it had closed its operations in **Malawi**.

INDEPENDENT AFRICAN CHURCHES. The independent African Churches are those that broke away from the mainstream denominations such as the Church of Scotland, the Dutch Reformed Church, the Seventh-Day Adventists, and the Seventh Day Baptists. The first independent church, the **Providence Industrial Mission** (PIM), was founded by **John Chilembwe** in 1900. Influenced by **Joseph Booth**, who took him to the **United States**, and by the Negro Baptists in Virginia, John Chilembwe adopted some of the functions of the American black independent churches. The preachers, Chilembwe observed, were active politicians whose churches were converted into political organizations sustained by religious enthusiasm. Returning to Malawi, Chilembwe created an impressive industrial mission that sought the betterment of Africans economically as well as intellectually. The PIM was African controlled and gave expression to such African grievances as low wages, long hours, and general mistreatment. After the **Chilembwe uprising** in 1915, the church was discontinued. In 1926 **Daniel Malekebu** reinstituted the mission.

On the eve of World War I the independent churches consisted of Chilembwe's PIM, **Eliot Musokwa Kamwana**'s **Watchtower**, **Charles Domingo**'s Seventh Day Baptists, and **Filipo Chinyama**'s **Ntcheu** Mission. For those Africans unhappy with the older established European missions, these independent churches provided opportunities for leadership, respectability, and social advancement; they also were a means through which economic, political, and social grievances could be aired. As an alternative path, these independent churches often drew converts from those who were refused entrance into one of the Presbyterian churches without long probation or were unable to afford the school fees that were levied on members. Domingo and Kamwana appealed to the less privileged members of the African community.

During the era between the wars, a new group of independent churches emerged, particularly between 1925 and 1935. In 1925 **Jordan Msumba** formed the Last Church of God and His Christ, which permitted polygamy. Three years later, the **African National Church** (ANC) was established by several **Livingstonia** church elders and pastors, including **Simon Kamkhati Mkandawire**, **Levi Mumba**, Isaac Mkhondowe, and **Paddy Nyasulu**. The African National Church retained most of the Presbyterian principles but permitted polygamy and alcohol consumption. In 1935 three Livingstonia ministers, **Yaphet Mkandawire**, **Yesaya Zerenji Mwasi**, and **Charles Chinula**, who had left the **Church of Central Africa Presbyterian** (CCAP) only a year or two before, joined forces to form the **Black Man's Church in Africa** (Mpingo wa Afipa wa Africa). Ironically, perhaps, the Livingstonia Mission had taught and encouraged its students to be of an independent mind and conscience. The evolution of independent churches was related to the ineffectiveness of the European missions in dealing with such moral problems as evil, witchcraft, and divisiveness. The new church leaders were activists, engaging in the work of local **African welfare associations** and encouraging the development of African schools. In the field of **education**, it was Daniel Malekebu's PIM, and to a lesser extent Chinula's projects, that enjoyed the greatest success in the interwar period.

Most often individuals who sought an independent path were acting out of a sincere love for the Christian church. When differences arose in regard to traditions and customs, reconciliation was sought but not always achieved. Differences were sometimes concerned with which day was the Sabbath, which method should be used for baptism, and how long a period of preparatory training was necessary for admission to a church. Generally, they were fundamentalist in their interpretation of the Bible. Most desired more control over their own lives and beliefs and a lessening of European authority. *See also* ETHIOPIANISM.

INDIAN CHAMBER OF COMMERCE. Formed in August 1936 to protect and further the interests of Indian wholesale merchants in **Malawi**, this organization worked hand in hand with the **Nyasaland Indian Traders Association**, and many Indians belonged to both bodies.

INDIANS. *See* ASIANS.

INDIRECT RULE SYSTEM. This system of colonial administration was originally espoused by Lord **Frederick Lugard** in his numerous publications, including the *Dual Mandate in Tropical Africa* (1922). It sought to rule the African peoples through their indigenous political institutions. In **Malawi**, aspects of the system were introduced under the District Administration (Natives) Ordinance of 1912, but it was not until the **Native Authorities Ordinance** of 1933 that a more serious attempt was made to effect the spread of this method of rule.

INTERNATIONAL MONETARY FUND (IMF). *See* FINANCIAL AND ECONOMIC DEVELOPMENTS.

IRON AGE. *See* PREHISTORY.

ISLAM. It is estimated that 20 percent of Malawians profess to be Muslims, as compared with 75 percent who acknowledge Christianity as their religion. **Swahili-Arabs** brought their Islamic religion with them when they arrived in the area in the 19th century. As trader-merchants, they were not active proselytizers; the most numerous conversions occurred after **Harry Johnston** ended the **slave trade** in the 1890s. In addition to the Arab-Swahili traders, two Muslim teachers, Shaykh Abdallah Mkwanda and Shaykh Sabiti Ngaunje, are identified with the spread of

Islam in **Malawi**, most of the conversions taking place among the **Yao** and the lakeside **Chewa**.

Conversion to Islam required observance of the Ramadan feast, acceptance of circumcision, and the imitation of some rituals and prayers. Islam offered an advance in social status beyond traditional faith, and it provided an alternative for those Africans seeking some status vis-à-vis the Europeans. Converts who became teachers *(waalimu)* often settled in villages where they earned money tutoring students. Some Muslim villages had Quranic schools, but instruction was often superficial because of poorly prepared teachers.

Islam was viewed by Christian missionaries as a threat. Missionary tracts often referred to Islamic aggression, which could unite Africans into hostile groups. Their concern that Islam would encourage uprisings turned into near hysteria at the outset of World War I, when the colonial government was already apprehensive over German attempts to turn Muslim followers against their British rulers. As the Germans lost the East African campaign, however, the Muslim scare subsided. The number of Islamic schools and mosques was nevertheless limited by the protectorate government in the belief that Muslims had encouraged the **Chilembwe uprising**. Throughout the colonial period, therefore, Islam developed slowly.

The situation has changed since the early 1980s, when money from Islamic countries, mainly Saudi Arabia and Kuwait, helped establish a major center of learning near Mpemba, outside **Blantyre**; smaller educational bases were set up in other locations, including **Balaka** and **Mangochi**. Through such centers, Islamic literature was disseminated. Modern mosques were also built in different parts of the country, including **Chitipa**, where the Muslim presence had until then been insignificant. In addition, some Malawian Muslims were sent to North Africa and the Middle East to further their education. Even though Dr. **Hastings K. Banda** was not particularly friendly to the Islamic world, he allowed the proliferation of Islamic activities on condition that there was no interference in Malawian politics.

Islamic nations gave some financial backing to the **United Democratic Front** (UDF) party headed by **Bakili Muluzi**, the first Muslim to be elected president of a Southern African country. Since Muluzi became president, some Christian denominations have complained of the increasing influence of Islam in a country that since the late 19th century has been primarily identified with Christianity. Mosques and

Muslims were subjects of violent acts in parts of northern Malawi because some people attributed the success of President Muluzi and the UDF in the elections to financial aid emanating from external Islamic sources. The violence was condemned by many, including the Anglican bishop of **Mzuzu**, who contributed US$1,000 toward the reconstruction of the mosques.

– J –

JACKSON REPORT. This was the report of the Land Commission of 1920, headed by Judge Edward Jackson and appointed to inquire into the problem of land, especially in the **Shire Highlands**. From the days of Sir **Harry Johnston**, European settler farmers had come to occupy the best arable land in the area between **Zomba** and **Mulanje**, limiting the ability of the growing African population to expand agricultural activities. After the war, more European settlers arrived, expecting land in the same area; some Europeans, including the older residents, were even applying for land that had been reserved for African use. Meantime, it was feared that African unhappiness with the evolving situation would lead to political unrest; the government was also concerned that many indigenous people would join the labor force across the Zambezi. The Jackson Commission recommended solutions to the problem, including fixed tenure for Africans as opposed to the usual communal ownership of land. It also recommended that, since scarcity of land was a fact, Africans should be allowed tenancy on European estates on favorable terms. However, it also considered labor tenancy inevitable.

JAFU, GEORGE. The first Malawian head of Civil Service and secretary to the president and cabinet, Jafu was born and raised in **Mangochi** District. After completing secondary school, he worked in the civil service and in 1964 became one of the first students to attend an eight-month crash course for administrators at the Institute of Public Administration, Mpemba. He also spent a year at Oxford University and upon returning occupied several senior positions in the civil service before taking over from **Bryan Roberts** as secretary to the president and cabinet. In 1975 he was replaced by **John Ngwiri** and he joined **Lonrho**, where he was to be its chief executive in **Malawi**.

JALASI. Jalasi is an area in **Mangochi** District ruled by **Yao** chiefs of the same name. In the late 19th century, Jalasi strongly fought off British authority in his area. In 1891 he defeated British troops, and in February 1895 he, **Kawinga**, and **Matipwiri** joined to remove the British from the Shire. But later that year, he and other chiefs north of **Zomba** were forced to surrender to colonial rule.

JARDIM, JORGE. Politically astute Portuguese businessman based in **Beira, Mozambique,** and a close confidant of the Portuguese leadership, including Dr. Antonio Salazar. Jardim is credited with turning (in late 1961) Dr. **Hastings K. Banda**'s hard-line views on settler colonialism in Southern Africa to accommodation and cooperation. He secretly met Banda in **Blantyre** initially, but later, in 1962, he arranged for the Malawi leader to visit Portugal, where relations between the two countries were strengthened. Jardim's plan was to ensure that Banda withdrew support for the Mozambican liberation movements, thereby ensuring that they did not use Malawi as a launching pad for attacks on the Portuguese colony. For his part, Banda was assured of continued access to Beira and, even more, of building a rail connection with the northern Mozambique port of Nacala. It is said that discussions took place concerning possibilities of ceding part of northern Mozambique to Malawi. Jardim was closely connected with the Resistencia Nacional Mocambicana (**RENAMO**), and his influence on Banda continued even after he left Mozambique following the successful war of independence.

JEANES TRAINING CENTRE. *See* EDUCATION.

JEHOVAH'S WITNESSES. Fundamentalist religious sect that rejects any allegiance to a political party or a government. It was considered subversive during colonial rule, and in Dr. **Hastings K. Banda**'s time it was banned and subjected to violence. As the **Malawi Congress Party** (MCP) prepared for independence in 1964, Witnesses refused to register as voters and tried to dissuade others from joining the MCP. In **Mulanje** District, violence broke out between the Witnesses and the Youth Leaguers. In 1967 the Witnesses were again subject to harassment. They still refused to join the party, they continued to proselytize those who were not interested, and they attempted to dissuade people from paying **taxes.** When the Witnesses opposed party efforts to register voters and renew party membership cards, the **Malawi** government retaliated by allowing Leaguers to assault Witnesses. *See also* YOUTH.

The sect was banned in October 1967, and violence followed, with charges of arson, rape, and assault levied against Youth Leaguers. Until 1973 the Jehovah's Witnesses were not interfered with, but their continued opposition to the MCP resulted in a wave of persecutions that drove nearly 20,000 adherents into **Zambia** and **Mozambique**. Unfavorable world publicity and the fact that Zambia found them equally unwelcome led to their repatriation. In 1975 about 2,000 were arrested and jailed for belonging to a banned organization. Two years later, nearly all of the Witnesses were released. In 1991 several hundred Mozambican **refugees** were deported because of their affiliation with the Witnesses. The post-Banda government has respected freedom of association, including religious affiliation, with the result that the Jehovah's Witnesses have practiced their faith undisturbed.

JERE, GWAZA. A respected *nduna* (counsellor, minister) of **Zwangend-aba** whose wise counsel helped the **Ngoni** through the difficult period following the death of their leader in about 1848. A succession dispute arose, which led to a split among the Ngoni; Gwaza kept the main party together by acting as a regent while the problem was solved and by presiding over the peaceful emergence of **Mhlahlo M'mbelwa Jere** as the rightful successor. He was installed in the Henga Valley c. 1857.

JERE, INKOSANA ISAIAH MURRAY MOPHO. A highly respected **Ngoni** historian, political activist, and church elder, Mopho Jere was born near **Ekwendeni, Mzimba** district, and educated at the local mission station. In 1928 he became a clerk in the medical department, **Zomba**, where he became secretary of the Representative Committee of the Northern Province Native Association (RCNPNA) and, as the church of **Central Africa Presbyterian**'s (CCAP) representative elder in zomba, of Christians from the area dominated by the **Livingstonia Mission**. In the 1930s Jere also served as president of the RCNPNA. He died in April 1979.

JERE, MAXON, INKOSI M'MBELWA III. Son of **Lazalo Jere**, **M'mbelwa II**. He succeeded his father as *inkosi ya makosi* (king of kings) in 1960 and guided the northern **Ngoni** through some of the most tense years in the postcolonial history of **Malawi**. Following the **Cabinet Crisis** of 1964, he made sure that peace reigned in his domain, in spite of the number of his subjects who fell victim to President **Hastings K. Banda**'s abuse of **human rights**. In 1970 he was appointed to the National Traditional Court. But his refusal to be on the panel hearing the case of **Orton** and **Vera Chirwa**, on the grounds that he was disqualified because Mrs. Chirwa was his subject, displeased the government and the **Malawi Congress Party** (MCP). He died in 1983.

JERE, MBALEKELWA CHIMTUNGA, INKOSI. Originally known as Mbalekelwa, Chimtunga succeeded his father, **M'mbelwa I**, in April 1897. Generally considered weak when compared with his father and with his son who was to succeed him, Chimtunga was the **Ngoni** ruler when **Alfred Sharpe** succeeded in bringing the northern Ngoni under British jurisdiction in 1904. In spite of this, the colonial government remained suspicious of the Ngoni, especially, their fierce independent-mindedness and their unity under Chimtunga. The opportunity to deal with them came at the beginning of World War I, when Chimtunga refused a government request to contribute to the war effort by providing carriers and food. H. C. Macdonald, the local **district commissioner** (DC), accused him of siding with the Germans and **John Chilembwe**. In January 1915 Chimtunga was arrested, dethroned, and exiled to Chiromo in the Lower Shire, where he remained under detention until 1920. In the meantime, the government reduced and then withdrew financial assistance to Ngoni chiefs, all of whom had stood by Chimtunga. Much to their displeasure, the government then applied to their area the District Administration (Native) Ordinance of 1912, which meant that the authority of the Ngoni leader was now greatly diminished. Upon his return to **Mzimba**, his official title was that of village headman, a much lesser designation than what he had held before his detention. He died in 1924.

JERE, MHLAHLO, INKOSI M'MBELWA I. Mhlahlo, as he was known before he took the name M'mbelwa, was the son of **Zwangendaba** by his wife **Munene Nzima** who had become the *inkosikazi* (chief wife) after **Soseya**, mother of Mputo (**Mpezeni**), was disgraced because of suspicion that her family of the house of Lompetu wanted to poison her husband. Most likely born in 1840 at Mabili in the vicinity of Embangweni during the **Ngoni** journey north, M'mbelwa was installed as the successor to his father in 1857 in the area of Ng'onga in the Henga valley, this time during their southward movement. With him as the new leader, the main Ngoni group moved to several places, including Choma (not far from **Mzuzu**) and **Njuyu** before establishing their headquarters at **Edingeni** in central **Mzimba**.

However, even before the emergence of Edingeni, M'mbelwa and his advisers began to organize the Ngoni and the conquered into six chiefdoms, each headed by a descendant of Zwangendaba: **Mtwalo, Mpherembe, Mzukuzuku, Mabilabo, Chinde,** and **Mzikubuola.** M'mbelwa remained as the paramount ruler. They expanded further and by the late 1870s, when the **Livingstonia** missionaries first established contact, their new territory was vast, covering almost all the present-day Mzimba district. It was M'mbelwa who handled the sensitive task of dealing with the missionaries, and also had to tackle the more difficult diplomatic problem of fending off the colonial government's determination to establish authority over the Ngoni. By the time of his death in August 1891, the British had still not succeeded in this ambition. M'mbelwa was buried near Njuyu, and his grave site has been declared a national monument.

JERE, MKHOSI LAZALO, INKOSI M'MBELWA II. Son of **Chimtunga Jere,** Mkhosi Lazalo was born at Mzalangwe in 1894. He went to school locally and then to **Khondowe,** where he passed standard six, then the highest educational qualification an African could attain in the colony. In 1913 he was employed as a clerk at the **district commissioner's** office at **Mzimba,** and from 1917 to 1919 was a clerk at Chiromo in the Lower Shire. For the next nine years he was a clerk in the **Rhodesia Native Bureau** office at **Fort Jameson in Northern Rhodesia.** On May 11, 1928, four years after the death of Chimtunga, **Ngoni** kingmakers installed Mkhosi Lazalo as their traditional leader, with the government title principal headman.

However, this was not enough for the Ngoni. Like the Maseko, they wanted their ruler to assume the government-recognized title of paramount chief. **Charles Chinula,** Mkhosi Lazalo Jere's principal adviser on matters concerning the colonial government, together with the Mombera **Native Association,** actively campaigned for their chief's status to be changed. They got their wish: under the **Native Authority Ordinance** of 1933, the government acknowledged M'mbelwa as the supreme (paramount) chief of the northern Ngoni; similarly, **Gomani II** became paramount chief in **Ntcheu** district. In fact, the two were the only traditional authorities in the colony to have this designation. At the suggestion of Rev. **Andrew Mkochi** and the newly formed **M'mbelwa African Administrative Council,** Lazalo assumed the title *inkosi ya* *makosi* (chief of chiefs or king of kings). The success of the council (1933–1961) was largely due to the guidance and administrative abilities of M'Mbelwa II.

Throughout his reign, M'mbelwa II played an active role in matters of national importance. In 1938 he presented evidence to the **Bledisloe Commission** opposing the amalgamation of the Rhodesias and **Nyasaland**. In 1944 he visited Nyasaland soldiers in the East African Command, and three years later he went to Salisbury (now Harare) to meet the British monarch. In 1952–1953 he and other chiefs traveled to England to register their opposition to the **Federation of Rhodesia and Nyasaland**. Although a recipient of six medals from the British Crown, M'mbelwa II was a strong opponent of colonialism and always identified himself with nationalist sentiments. *Inkosi ya makosi* M'mbelwa II died in 1959.

JERE, INKOSI MTWALO I. Son of **Zwangendaba** and brother of **Mhlahlo M'mbelwa**, Mtwalo was born in about 1838 during the **Ngoni**'s epic journey north. He was a pillar of Ngoni stability during the uncertain years before the installation of Mhlahlo as successor to Zwangendaba, and he was a reliable adviser to the latter in the period leading to the settlement of the main party in present-day **Malawi**. Assigned the northern section of their new domain, Mtwalo had his headquarters at **Ekwendeni**, later replaced by Ezondweni. Known for his lack of enthusiasm for Christian missionary work and his hard-hearted attitude toward the indigenous peoples among whom the Ngoni settled, Mtwalo died in 1890, only a year before M'mbelwa.

JERE, MUHABI AMON, INKOSI MTWALO II. Son of **Mtwalo I**, Muhabi Jere was born in 1873 at Uswesi, **Ekwendeni**, and succeeded his father as *inkosi* (chief) on June 15, 1896. When, in 1886, the **Ngoni** gave official sanction to the Scottish missionaries, to embark on their work, Muhabi and his elder brother, Yohane, were among the first pupils to attend the school at Ekwendeni. He went to **Livingstonia** and, after completing standard six, trained as a teacher. Meantime, in 1896, he married another Christian convert, Emily Nhlane, daughter of **Chipatula Nhlane**. Not only was he the first Ngoni chief to marry according to Christian rituals, but he was the first to be married at Ekwendeni Mission.

In the same year, Amon Jere succeeded his father's chiefship, taking the title Mtwalo II. In 1903 he was suspended from the church for taking another wife; he also stopped teaching and concentrated on his chiefly duties. When the Ngoni country finally came under British rule in 1904, Mtwalo, like all other Ngoni chiefs, began to receive a government stipend. Amon Jere was a founding member of the Mombera **Native Association** and was its president in 1922–1923 and in 1924–1925. When he died on April 1, 1970, he was 97 years old, had lived in precolonial and postcolonial Malawi, and had been *inkosi* for 74 years. Since he had no children, he was succeeded by his nephew (son of Yohane), Baiwell Jere, who on his installation in September 1971, assumed the title Mtwalo III.

JERE, TIFAPI, INKOSI MZUKUZUKU. A descendant of one of the sons of **Zwangendaba**, Tifapi Jere is one of the five inkosi under M'mbelwa. Educated at **Loudon Mission**, this chief, noted for his oratory and organizational ability, worked as a protocol officer in the Ministry of External Affairs before retiring to his Ephangweni headquarters to concentrate on his chiefly duties. In **Hastings Banda**'s time, Inkosi Mzukuzuku was frequently the leader of the **Mzimba** Ingoma dancers who often entertained him and whom the president regarded as the "real warriors." Inkosi Mzukuzuku was a justice in the National Traditional Courts system, which has since been abolished.

JERE, ZWANGENDABA, M'MBELWA IV. Son of Maxon and grandson of **Mkhosi Lazalo,** Zwangendaba Jere was educated at **Edingeni** Primary School and **Mzuzu** Secondary School before working for **Press Holdings**. In December 1984 he succeeded his father as head of the **Ngoni** in northern Malawi, a position that is well respected nationally.

JIGGER. Known as *matekenya*, this sand flea was first reported in **Malawi** in the early 1890s. It almost certainly entered the region following the trade routes linking **Lake Nyasa** and East Africa, where they had arrived from West Africa. By 1910 jiggers had spread to nearly all parts of Malawi, causing sores and sometimes ulcers in the toe and foot areas as the fleas burrowed and deposited their eggs. Jiggers were greatly reduced after World War II when DDT and gammexane were used to control them, as well as ticks and mosquitoes. *See also* DISEASE.

JOHNSON, WILLIAM PERCIVAL. Archdeacon of Nyasa with **Universities' Mission to Central Africa** (UMCA) and author of *My African Reminiscences, 1875–1895* (1924). William Johnson first went to **Malawi** in 1880. But within a short time illness forced him back to **Great Britain**. He returned in the following year, this time with another missionary, Charles Janson, who died from malaria in February 1882. Two years later, Johnson went to England and raised money to buy a steamer, the *Charles Janson*, to be used as a floating mission station for the UMCA. He was stationed at **Likoma** and in 1886 was joined by **Chauncy Maples**, who had spent 10 years working on the eastern side of the lake. In 1895 Maples, newly appointed bishop of Nyasa, died in a drowning accident. In 1901 Johnson added another steamer to those owned by the mission, which he called the *Chauncy Maples* in honor of his friend. The *MV Chauncy Maples* is now owned by Malawi Railways and still carries passengers and cargo on **Lake Malawi**.

JOHNSTON, SIR HENRY "HARRY" HAMILTON. British consul to Mozambique (1889–1891) and Her Majesty's Commissioner and consul-general to the territories under British influence north of the Zambezi (1891–1996). Johnston was singularly responsible for creating the administrative machinery of the British protectorate established in the **Lake Malawi** area in 1891. Born in Kennington, London, in 1858, he was trained as an artist but had a wide range of serious interests, including botany, zoology, history, geography, and linguistics, and published extensively in all these fields.

Johnston had worked as consul-general in the Oil Rivers region of Nigeria before assuming his appointment as consul to **Mozambique** in 1889. In that year, he met **Cecil Rhodes**, who was immediately impressed by the young Johnston. Rhodes hired him to represent his company in the Lake Malawi area, which Johnston was about to visit in his capacity as British consul to Mozambique. On his way to **Blantyre**, Johnston met and hired **Alfred Sharpe** as his vice consul. Together with another assistant, John Nicoll, they entered into several treaties with the Kololo and **Yao** chiefs. When the Foreign Office designated the area of Malawi as a British protectorate in 1891, Johnston was appointed commissioner and consul-general; by that time he had gathered a staff devoted to the task of developing an administration. Within a year, he had established European-type courts of justice and several departments, including police, medical, and postal services, as well as engineering and financial units. Johnston first divided the country into four districts, but in 1893 he reorganized it into 12 administrative units. By the next year, Johnston had an armed force consisting of 370 regulars. His commandant was Major C. A. Edwards, who was assisted by Captain **William Manning**. Using his army during a series of small wars between 1891 and 1895, Johnston extended British rule and established a network of *bomas*. *See also* BRITISH SOUTH AFRICA COMPANY.

During his 1894 administrative leave Johnston succeeded in securing the financial takeover of the protectorate by the British Treasury. Until that time, Rhodes paid Johnston £2,000 to begin his work in Central Africa. Two years later, Rhodes and his company agreed to pay £1,000 annually to Johnston to maintain a **police** force. Johnston was also allowed the use of the lake steamers belonging to the **African Lakes Company** (ALC), a firm in which Rhodes's BSAC owned a controlling interest. In 1893 Rhodes increased his subsidy to £17,500 annually in exchange for BSAC absorption of all Crown rights to land in Malawi. This financial hold of the BSAC finally ended with an agreement with the Foreign Office (1895) in which the Treasury assumed full financial control over the area.

The Johnston administration was preoccupied with raising local revenue to help run the government and with working out a land policy for the protectorate. In 1892–1893, Johnston, assisted by Sharpe and Lieutenant Bertram Sclater of the Royal Engineers, reviewed every land and mineral claim for authenticity and proper compensation. Funds to finance the new administration included those raised internally, such as postal fees, import duties, license fees, stamp duties, and hut taxes. The latter tax, of three shillings per year, was first imposed in the Southern Region but by 1896 included all districts of Malawi in which British rule obtained.

Johnston was not always popular with the European missionaries, planters, and merchants who had preceded the British administration. Traders and planters, free from any government regulations for years, objected to paying **taxes** and to the enforcement of laws. With the exception of Dr. **Robert Laws**, for whom he had great respect, Johnston disliked most missionaries. **Missions** too had enjoyed the exercise of "governmental" powers for several years, but now British rule had made them subordinate to Commissioner Johnston. Johnston left the British protectorate in 1896. A prolific writer and fine naturalist, he personally illustrated his encyclopedic *British Central Africa* (1897). Previously, during his 1894 leave in England, he had produced a *Blue Book* detailing the first three years of his administration. In 1923 he published his autobiography, *The Story of My Life*. Johnston died in 1927.

JONES, ARTHUR CREECH. Member of the British Labour Party and the Fabian Society. Jones was shadow minister of colonial affairs when Clement Atlee was the leader of opposition in the United Kingdom. He became secretary for colonies in the postwar Labour government, which also presided over the establishment of the **Colonial Development Corporation**. In 1947 he met with Dr. **Hastings Banda** and a deputation from the **Nyasaland African Congress** (NAC). As a result of the meeting, funds were made available to the **Nyasaland** government for the establishment of the Dedza Secondary School and for the **Domasi** Teacher's College. Creech-Jones was strongly opposed to the **Federation of Rhodesia and Nyasaland**, and he assured Nyasalanders that they would not be part of any such association. After he left office, he campaigned widely against it. However, his successor, James Griffiths, was more sympathetic to the Federation scheme.

JONES, SIR GLYN SMALLWOOD. Chief secretary to the **Nyasaland** government (1960–1961), governor (1961–1964), and governor-general (1964–1966). Jones and **Hastings K. Banda** established a good working relationship after the release of **Malawi Congress Party** (MCP) members, including Banda himself, detained in prison during **Operation Sunrise** in 1959. In July 1964 Glyn Jones became governor-general and, during the **Cabinet Crisis** of 1964, he advised Prime Minister Banda to solve the rift instead of resigning from office; he also advised Banda to seek a parliamentary vote of confidence, which he was duly given. In 1965 Glyn Jones demanded that more humane treatment be given to political prisoners detained by Banda as a consequence of the **Cabinet Crisis**. On his retirement from colonial service in 1966, Sir Glyn Jones worked for the Malawi government as the head of the London-based Buying and Trade Agency. He died in 1992.

JUMBE. The term refers to the leader of the **Swahili-Arabs** at **Nkhotakota** on the western shore of **Lake Malawi**. The first Jumbe, Salim bin Abdallah, established his commercial base at Nkhotakota in the 1840s. He and successive Jumbes were often able to establish cordial relations with the **Chewa**, **Ngoni**, **Tonga**, and **Yao** chiefs of the area, as well as with the Scottish missionaries and later with British government officials.Nkhotakota was conveniently located for the Jumbe to conduct his lucrative east-west caravan trade The Jumbe and his retinue were well armed and had large quantities of cloth that they traded for slaves and ivory destined for the east coast. Until Commissioner **Harry John-**

ston's time, no one had the strength to oppose the Jumbe's political-economic power. During their half-century of rule in Malawi, the Jumbes brought in coastal trade goods, introduced Islamic culture in the area, and cultivated **rice** and coconuts in the region for the first time. *See also* ISLAM; SLAVE TRADE.

– K –

KABULA STORES. *See* SHARRER, EUGENE.

KABUNDULI. Title of a chief and name of a chiefdom in **Nkhata Bay** district that traces its origins to the **Maravi** empire. As the latter expanded, Kabunduli went north into **Tonga** country beyond the Luweya River, where he and his party were later joined by the Kapunda Banda, a **Chewa** matrilineage.

KACHAMBA BROTHERS BAND. Famous Malawian band that popularized its own version of the South African township *kwela* flute (pennywhistle) jive music. Its founder, Daniel Kachamba, and his younger brother, Donald, were born in **Blantyre** district in the 1950s. From 1957 to 1962, they lived in Harare (Salisbury), where their father, like many Malawians of the time, worked. This was the era when Kwela music was at its height, with records of artists such as Elias and the Zig-zag Jive Flutes, Lemmy Special Mabaso, and Spokes Mashiyane, the "king of *kwela*," playing in all urban areas of Southern Africa.

The Kachamba brothers learned to play the pennywhistle at an early age, and when they returned to Malawi in 1962, Daniel formed the Kachamba Brothers Band. Initially they played in and around Chileka, their home area just north of Blantyre. Things began to change in 1967, when they met the Austrian musicologist, Dr. Gerhard Kubik, who became interested in their music. Their repertoire now included the *Mbaqanga* of **South Africa**, as popularized by Simon Mahlathini Nkabinde. Their instruments included the pennywhistle, guitar, mouth organ, rattle, and a one-string band. In 1970 and 1973 Kubik and the Kachamba brothers toured many parts of Africa, Europe, and South America. Daniel died in the mid-1980s.

Donald continued to play in the tradition of the Kachamba Brothers Band. In 1999–2000 he was musician in residence at the Department of Ethnomusicology, University of California at Los Angeles. Donald died in January 2001.

KACHAMBA, DANIEL. *See* KACHAMBA BROTHERS BAND.

KACHAMBA, DONALD. *See* KACHAMBA BROTHERS BAND.

KACHASU. This is a spirit distilled, mostly by **women**, from husks of **maize**. Colonial authorities banned it because of its alcoholic potency and on the grounds that it led to prostitution, venereal diseases, crime, and absenteeism. However, the postcolonial government encouraged the distillers to sell it to the Malawi Distilleries Ltd., the company that produces, among other drinks, Malawi gin.

KACHEBERE. Located on the **Malawi-Zambia** border in **Ngoni**-Senga country. During the last quarter of the 19th century this area fell under the rule of Inkosi **Mlonyeni**, a subordinate of Inkosi **Mpezeni**. In May 1903 the **White Fathers** established a station on the Bua River, and within a few years it became an important Catholic center. In 1939 the Kachebere Major Seminary to train indigenous priests from Zambia and Malawi was established not far from the mission station, and it continued to fill this function until the early 1980s when St. Peters Seminary was established in **Zomba**.

KACHINDAMOTO. Located in Dedza district, this is one of the main centers of the Maseko **Ngoni**. Kachindamoto is also the title of the chief of the area, the original holder having been the son of **Chidyawonga**, one of the early leaders of the Maseko.

KACHINGWE, AUBREY. This author, journalist, broadcaster, and businessman was born in **Ntcheu** district in 1926 and educated in **Malawi** and Tanganyika. In 1955, his employer, the East African Standard Group in Nairobi, sent him to England on attachment to the *Daily Herald* newspaper. Later he joined the Information Department in **Nyasaland** and in 1963 returned to London, this time on attachment to the British Broadcasting Corporation (BBC). Upon his return, Kachingwe became head of the News Department at the **Malawi Broadcasting Corporation** (MBC.). On his retirement, he became a businessman based in **Blantyre**. Kachingwe is the author of a novel, *No Easy Task* (1966), in the Heinemann African Writers Series.

KADALIE, CLEMENTS. Founder of the Industrial and Commercial Workers Union of South Africa. Kadalie was born Lameck Koniwaka Kadalie Muwamba at Chifira village, near **Bandawe**, in **Nkhata Bay** in April 1896. His father, Musa Kadalie Muwamba, was the son of Chief Chiweyu, who met **David Livingstone** when the Scottish doctor visited the Chikali beach area in 1863. Lameck attended school at Bandawe Mission where his uncle, Alick Banda, was a teacher. In 1908 he went to **Overtoun Institution** at **Khondowe**, where he established himself as an able, articulate, and confident student. Dr. **Robert Laws** appointed him as his assistant and to preside over the YMCA at **Livingstonia**. In 1913 he passed the teachers examinations with distinction. By this time he had changed his name to Clements Kadalie in honor of his uncle, Isaac Clements Katongo, then a civil servant in Northern Rhodesia. Kadalie was posted to a school headed by Rev. **Yesaya Zerenji Mwasi**.

In 1915 Kadalie left Malawi and journeyed to **South Africa** via Mozambique and Southern Rhodesia. In 1918 in Cape Town, a chance encounter with politician and trade unionist Arthur Batty led Kadalie to form an association of African dockworkers in the following year. In February 1919 Kadalie became the national secretary of the Industrial and Commercial Workers Union (ICU), the first African trade union in South Africa. In December 1919 he organized the first major dock strike, which virtually shut down Cape Town harbors for nearly three months. The strike ended only after management agreed to meet the demands of the union. In November 1920 Kadalie was ordered to leave South Africa, but the deportation order was withdrawn in January of the following year after the Church of Scotland mediated the dispute. Two years later, the ICU began to publish its own newspaper, *The Worker's Herald*.

By 1926 the ICU had a total membership of 150,000, and during most of the 1920s the union became the main vocal critic of the government, replacing the African National Congress (ANC), which was particularly inactive at the time. In May 1927 Kadalie attended the International Labour Conference in Geneva as the representative of the ICU, giving him the opportunity to establish contacts with labor activists from different parts of the world. The visit to Europe was backed by **Arthur Creech Jones**, head of the Fabian Society in the United Kingdom. Although his influence waned in the 1930s, he remained a political firebrand and continued to criticize white rule in Africa. Author of *My Life and the I.C.U.*, he died in East London, South Africa, in 1951.

KADUYA, DAVID. One of the principal leaders in the **Chilembwe Uprising**, Kaduya and **Stephen Mkulitchi** led an armed party of men from **Mbombwe** to the **African Lakes Company** (ALC) headquarters at Mandala, **Blantyre**, on Saturday evening, January 23, 1915. At Mandala, they rendezvoused with **Duncan Njilima**'s group. The joint party attacked the company store and took five rifles before the establishment was defended.

On Sunday morning Kaduya and his men engaged a contingent of the **King's African Rifles** (KAR); his leg wounded, he was carried away to safety in the Chikomwe hill area. After the rebellion ended, he was captured and taken to Chikonja, near one of the **A. L. Bruce Estates**, and was executed in the presence of the farm's workforce.

KADZAMIRA, CECILIA THAMANDA. Malawi's "official hostess" during the leadership of Dr. **Hastings K. Banda**. Cecilia Kadzamira was born in Dedza district in 1938 and raised in Southern Rhodesia (**Zimbabwe**), where her father worked as a medical orderly. In the mid-1950s she returned to **Malawi** to train as a nurse at the **Zomba** General Hospital. When Banda set up a small medical practice upon his return to Malawi in 1958, Kadzamira became one of his employees. Soon her position was changed to personal nurse and assistant, making her a particularly influential person. After independence she became the official government hostess, Banda being a bachelor. The position, which was equivalent to principal secretary, enabled her to wield considerable power behind the scenes. In 1984 she formed the **Chitukuko Cha Amai Mu Malawi** (CCAM). Her relatives were also politically well placed: her sister, Mary, was Banda's secretary; her uncle, **John Tembo**, was a very powerful politician throughout Banda's time; her brother, **Zimani D. Kadzamira**, was a senior administrator in the **University of Malawi** and in 1991 became Malawi's first ambassador to Japan; her other sister, Esnat J. Kalyati, was the first woman to become principal secretary in a government ministry.

After Banda lost to **Bakili Muluzi** in 1994, Kadzamira remained close to Banda and nursed him until his death in November 1997. A successful farmer and businesswoman, Kadzamira retired from active politics but continues to influence the **Malawi Congress Party** (MCP).

KADZAMIRA, ZIMANI DAVID. Former principal of **Chancellor College**. Zimani Kadzamira was raised in Southern Rhodesia (**Zimbabwe**), where his father worked as a hospital orderly. He returned to **Malawi** to go to school at **Blantyre** and Dedza Secondary Schools before proceeding to Princeton University, where he graduated with a B.A. degree in political science. Back in Malawi, he joined the teaching faculty of the university and in 1969 went to Manchester University, England. Five years later, he was awarded a Ph.D. degree. In 1981 he was appointed principal of Chancellor College and in 1990 was transferred to **Bunda College of Agriculture** to occupy the same position. Two years later he was appointed ambassador to Japan but was recalled when the **Malawi Congress Party** lost power in 1994. He returned to teach at Chancellor College.

KAHUMBE, CHARLES. Medical doctor, businessman, and one of the founders of the **United Democratic Front** (UDF). Kahumbe was born into one of the most established families in **Blantyre** district. Educated in the district, he went to India and qualified as a doctor. On his return, he worked for the government medical service and later opened a private practice in Blantyre. Dr. Kahumbe is the personal physician of President **Bakili Muluzi** and serves as one of the president's advisers.

KAINJA, KATE. Academic and politician born in the **Lilongwe**-Dedza area. Kainja emerged in the mid-1990s as one of the leading negotiators in the **Malawi Congress Party** (MCP) hierarchy. Kainja taught home economics at **Chancellor College, University of Malawi**, until the early 1990s, when President **Hastings K. Banda** appointed her to his cabinet. In 1994 she was elected to parliament and returned in 1999. She is a member of the central executive of the MCP and one of its main strategists.

KAKHOBWE, SAM. Born in **Lilongwe** in 1938, Kakhobwe went to Dedza Secondary School and the University of Lesotho, Botswana, and Swaziland at Roma, Lesotho, where he graduated with a B.A. degree. He joined the civil service in 1968, received successive promotions, and served in the foreign service before becoming secretary of the Treasury. In 1985 Kakhobwe succeeded **John Ngwiri** as secretary to the president and cabinet, his duties including headship of the civil service. Upon his dismissal from the civil service in 1987, Kakhobwe joined Farmingand Electrical Services, a large commercial firm in **Blantyre**. After the 1994 **elections**, the government appointed him to head a development commission.

KALESO, REV. PETER. Activist church minister of the **Blantyre** Synod. Kaleso went underground for some time, fearing arrest by President **Hastings K. Banda**'s security forces. Later he was to be a member of **Public Affairs Committee** (PAC), a founder of the **Alliance for Democracy** (AFORD), and then a leading official of the **United Democratic Front** (UDF) party. In 1994 he was appointed ambassador to **South Africa**, and five years later he was elected to the National Assembly as member for **Mulanje** South-East.

KALILOMBE, REV. W. F. PATRICK AUGUSTINE. The first Malawian clergyman to join the **White Fathers** order of the Catholic

Church. Patrick Kalilombe was born near **Mua** in Dedza district. He lectured in Scripture at Kachebere Major Seminary and later became rector of the institution. In 1972 he became the first African bishop of **Lilongwe**, replacing Bishop Joseph Fady, who had headed the Lilongwe diocese since 1951. In 1976 Patrick Kalilombe went on leave to lecture and study. Three years later, he resigned as bishop of Lilongwe and began lecturing at the Selly Oak Colleges in Birmingham, England. A frequent commentator and prolific writer on Christian churches in Africa, Bishop Kalilombe remains one of the most highly respected theologians in Africa.

KALIMBUKA. This low-density residential area in **Zomba** town is one of the historical links with Chief Kalimbuka, a subordinate of **Malemia** whose headquarters were at **Domasi**. Kalimbuka's residence was in the vicinity of the parliament buildings, where he played host to **Henry Henderson** and **Tom Bokwito** in 1875. Kalimbuka, with Malemia, gave permission to the Church of Scotland to build a mission station at Zomba.

KALINGA, JATO VINCENT MSULA. The first Malawian executive secretary of the **Christian Service Committee of the Churches of Malawi** (CSC). Jato Kalinga was born in **Ulambya**, **Chitipa** district, in 1922. He attended local schools before going to Mwenilondo in **Karonga** and **Livingstonia**, where he qualified as a teacher. He taught at Livingstonia and in Chitipa. In 1949 he was in the early group of the new Higher Grade teachers course at **Domasi**. After graduating two years later in 1951, he was appointed headmaster of Ulambya Primary School, the only full primary school in the old Karonga district. In 1955 Kalinga became assistant inspector of schools, first stationed at **Mzuzu** and a year later at Karonga. From 1957 to 1958, he studied at Bristol University, England, and for the next six years he was the first inspector of schools for Karonga district, and then district education officer. He also worked at **Mzimba** and at the Ministry of Education Headquarters before becoming regional education officer for the Northern Region; he served in the same capacity in the Central and Southern Regions. In 1972 Kalinga retired from the civil service and joined the Christian Service Committee as administrative secretary; two years later he took over the headship of the organization from Rev. **Thomas Colvin**. He retired from the CSC in 1978 to farm in Chitipa.

KALONGA. The title of the rulers of the **Maravi** state system. In everyday ciChewa, it means leader.

KALUA, KAMLEPO. Former employee of **Malawi** Hotels Limited. Kalua became famous in 1991 and 1992 when, as an exile in **South Africa**, he used Channel Africa of the South African Broadcasting Corporation to campaign against Dr. **Hastings K. Banda**'s government. He became leader of the **Malawi Democratic Party** (MDP) and ran as its presidential candidate in 1994, receiving 0.52 percent of the vote. In 1999 he stood again as the MDP candidate for the presidency. As in 1994, only a small percentage voted for him.

KALULUMA. Located in northern **Kasungu** district, this area is ruled by chiefs of the same name. The original Kaluluma, part of the **Maravi** expansion in the 17th century, settled among **Tumbuka** clans, including the Kanyinji, Nyirongo, and Zimba, all of whom lived without central authority. In spite of resistance, Kaluluma eventually succeeded in establishing himself as the new ruler of the area.

KAMBONDOMA. *See* GONDWE, KANYOLI.

KAMENYA BROTHERS. This was an a cappella group from Dedza district composed of diehard **Malawi Congress Party** (MCP) loyalists who would sing for Dr. **Hastings K. Banda** whenever he toured the Central Region. Almost always their lyrics threatened death to people, especially those like **Kanyama Chiume**, who were in exile and were suspected of plotting against Banda and his MCP government.

KAMUNGU, LEONARD MATTIYA. One of the first African clergymen of the **Universities' Mission to Central Africa** (UMCA). Kamungu was born in 1877 at Mayendayenda in Chia, on the eastern side of **Lake Malawi**. When the UMCA opened a school at Chia in 1887, Kamungu was among its first pupils, and one his teachers was **Augustine Ambali**. He later went to the **Likoma** Island school, recently established by Rev. **Chauncy Maples**. In 1890 he was baptized and took the name Matthias; in the same year, he and a group of other African students left for St. Andrews, Kiungani, **Zanzibar**, for further education. He completed his studies at St. Andrews in 1897 and returned to Likoma as an assistant to Rev. **Arthur Glossop**, who had arrived on the island four years earlier.

Toward the end of the following year, Bishop John Edward Hine made him Reader, and in 1899, Kamungu and a few others returned to Kiungani to prepare for the deaconate. He returned from Zanzibar at the end of 1900 and was posted to **Mponda**'s area at the southern tip of Lake Nyasa to teach and gain some pastoral experience. In November 1902

Bishop Gerard Trower ordained Kamungu as deacon, the ceremony taking place at Chia. Thereafter he worked at Lungwena and **Fort Maguire**, mainly **Yao** and Islamic areas, **Nkhotakota**, and from 1911 at Msoro near **Chipata** in the Luangwa Valley, Northern Rhodesia. A few years before going to Msoro, Kamungu had been ordained priest. Throughout his life, he stuck to the vows of celibacy that he had taken before Bishop Hine when he became deacon. On February 27, 1913, Father Leonard Kamungu and his cook died, apparently from poisoning; the Anglican community still regards him as one of the most devoted clergymen to work in the **Lake Malawi**-Zambezia region.

KAMUZU ACADEMY. Located at **Mtunthama**, **Hastings K. Banda**'s birthplace, named after him and modeled on English public schools, the academy was established as a high school for exceptional students. In Banda's time, one girl and two boys from each district of the country were selected to attend the school, and the fees were paid by the government. Students had to pass the national primary school examination with a very high grade. Others had to write an entry examination set by the school. Built with government money, its board of governors, the headmaster, and the teaching staff had to be personally approved by Dr. Banda. The board, always headed by a Malawian, was international in composition but the teaching staff was exclusively of European origin, mostly British, because Banda believed that most Africans did not understand Latin and ancient Greek, a prerequisite for an appointment to a teaching job. Banda insisted that students at the academy had to be taught classics, which he argued were an essential part of good **education**. The salaries of teachers and the general conditions of employment were much better than those of teachers in other government schools and even the **University of Malawi**.

Since the change of government in 1994, the Kamuzu Academy has received less government subvention, has Malawian teachers, and charges very high fees. Students still write qualifying examinations, but it is becoming a school for the elite, since only those who can afford fees apply for places.

KAMUZU COLLEGE OF NURSING. *See* EDUCATION.

KAMWANA, ELIOT. *See* CHIRWA, ELIOT MUSOKWA.

KAMWANA, MAC J. The first Malawian head of the Malawi **police** force. Son of a respected Dutch Reformed Church clergyman, Mac Kamwana was born at Kamwana, Dowa district, on June 26, 1935. He went to local primary schools before attending Kongwe Secondary

School and going on to the Police Training College (PTC) in 1953. A bright and dedicated policemen, he became a tutor at the police school from 1957 to 1962. Mac Kamwana served in various districts before returning to the PTC four years later, this time as supervisor of the Advanced Training Wing. In 1967 he was promoted to the rank of superintendent and was also appointed deputy commandant of the college. In the following year, he completed a course at the Scottish Police College at Tulliallan. Upon returning to Malawi, he took command of the PTC, becoming the first Malawian to do so.

In 1969 Mac Kamwana was promoted to senior superintendent and moved to the Southern Division as second in charge. He was awarded another promotion in 1970, to acting commissioner of police for force administration. After attending a command course in the United Kingdom later that year, he received yet another promotion, to deputy commissioner of police. In 1972 Mac Kamwana was appointed commissioner of police, the first Malawian to head the nation's police force. By the time he retired in 1982, the position of commissioner had been redesignated inspector general of police. Mac Kamwana died in 1984.

KAMWENDO, JOHN. Born in April 1936, Kamwendo became a youth activist in the **Nyasaland African Congress** (NAC) and its successor, the **Malawi Congress Party** (MCP). Later he worked for the MCP headquarters and even managed the party newspaper, the *Malawi News*. In 1967 Kamwendo was elected mayor of the city of **Blantyre**, becoming the first African to occupy this position. He was also group general manager of the **Press Holdings Group** of Companies. When he lost that position in late 1974, he became an independent businessman.

KAMWENDO, MIKE. Educated in the **United States**, Kamwendo returned to Malawi in 1972 to work as a producer for the **Malawi Broadcasting Corporation** (MBC). In 1976 he joined the Blantyre Newspapers; a year later, he was made editor of the *Malawi News*. In January 1979 he was appointed managing editor of the Blantyre Newspapers, which now included the *Daily Times* and the *Malawi News*. In the mid-1980s Kamwendo became an independent journalist, although he returned to the Blantyre Newspapers for a brief period. In the late 1990s he was once again appointed editor of the *Daily Times*.

KANADA. Head of the guerrilla-type force that was behind **Henry Chipembere**'s attempt to overthrow **Hastings K. Banda**'s government in 1965. Government forces found Kanada, like **Medson Silombela**, elusive. They captured him only when he killed a man at his girlfriend's home.

KANDODO. A chain of retail stores which, by the late 1950s, had been set up in most parts of Malawi, competing with the **Mandala** stores of the **African Lakes Company** (ALC). Kandodo's parent group was the **London & Blantyre Supply Company**, a general dealers import and export firm, which started operating in Malawi in the mid-1920s. In the early 1970s most Kandodo stores were taken over by **Press Holdings, Ltd.**; the exceptions were those in **Blantyre-Limbe**, **Zomba**, and **Lilongwe** and **Mzuzu**.

KANSILANGA, REV. MISANJO. Former senior clerk of the synod to the General Synod of the **Church of Central Africa Presbyterian**. Kansilanga became a major player in the democratization of **Malawi** in the early 1990s. As secretary of the **Public Affairs Committee** (PAC), he was central in the communications between the government, on the one hand, and the churches and the general public, on the other.

KANTIKI, MATHIAS. This educationist and Catholic layman was born in **Ntcheu** district and was one of the first students at the Catholic Secondary School in **Zomba**. He trained as a teacher and in 1948 was among the first Malawians to attend an **education** course at the Institute of Education in London. On his return, he was appointed inspector of schools, and he served in the Department of Education until he retired in a senior capacity in 1972. Kantiki also served as education secretary-general for the Catholic Church in Malawi.

KANYAYA, ADAMSON AKOGO. Politician and leader of the **Malawi Democratic Union** (MDU). Kanyaya was born in Mulare, **Karonga** district. In the late 1950s, he became an activist in the **Nyasaland African Congress** (NAC) and was detained following **Operation Sunrise**. Upon his release, he was employed by the **Kilupula Rice Growers Cooperative Union**. In 1962 Kanyaya studied in the United States and two years later was elected MP for Karonga. Following the **Cabinet Crisis** of 1964, he went into exile in **Zambia**. Later he trained in guerrilla warfare and in 1967 was one of the people who formed the **Yatuta Chisiza** party that wanted to overthrow **Hastings K. Banda**'s government. He escaped capture and returned to Zambia. In 1993 Kanyaya returned to Malawi as leader of the Malawi Democratic Union and contested the elections in the following year. He lost but was appointed to the cabinet for just over two years.

KANYENDA. Rulers of the northern lakeshore area of **Nkhotakota** district. The original Kanyenda arrived in the area toward the end of the 16th century or early 17th century as part of the **Maravi** expansion. He and **Kabunduli** went north. The latter moved beyond the Luweya River to the region bordering the **Viphya Highlands**, settling among the **Tonga** and some **Tumbuka** speakers. Kanyenda settled in the southern Tonga area.

KAPALEPALE. *See* LIKAYA-MBEWE, SMART.

KAPENI. A township in **Blantyre**. It derives its name from the **Yao** chief Kapeni, who ruled the Blantyre area in the years before the Europeans arrived. It was Chief Kapeni who played host to **Henry Henderson** and guide **Tom Bokwito** in 1876, and it was he who directed them to the site where the **Blantyre Mission** was built. Of the **Mangochi** section of the Yao, Kapeni himself had in the late 1860s wrestled free from the indigenous **Mang'anja** ruler, Kankomba.

KAPHWITI. Sometime in the 16th century, Kaphwiti and his sibling, **Lundu**, spearheaded the **Maravi** expansion south to the Lower Shire region. Initially Kaphwiti, senior to Lundu, set up his headquarters at Malawi-ya-Kaphwiti on the Mkurumadzi River but later moved to Mbewe-ya-Nyungu, from which he ruled most of the Lower Shire valley. However, from the last quarter of the 16th century, Kaphwiti lost most of his authority to Lundu, who, probably in an attempt to control the ivory trade, expanded west to the Lolo and Makua country in the west and the **Sena** area south toward the confluence of the Shire and Zambezi Rivers.

KAPOCHE. The region around this tributary of the Zambezi River constituted the core of Undi's authority.

KARIM, ZEENAT JANET. Fearless journalist and founding editor of the *Independent*. Janet Karim, daughter of diplomat **W. Nyemba Mbekeani**, accompanied her father to different parts of the world. In the 1970s she attended the **University of Malawi**, graduating with B.A. and B.A. (Hons.) degrees. She then worked for various organizations. When the political atmosphere in **Malawi** began to change, Karim founded the *Independent*, which became a major critic of government policies.

KARONGA. Home of the **Ngonde** people and located on the northwestern shores of **Lake Malawi**. The name Karonga derives from one of the principal houses of the Ngonde royal family. Karonga is the name of the district as well as that of the *boma*. In the southern section of the district live the **Tumbuka**-speaking peoples under the Mwafulirwa; other Tumbuka-speaking peoples live in the Kaporo area in the north and near the *boma* itself. In the 1880s Karonga became a trading base of **Mlozi bin**

Kazbadema, a **Swahili-Arab**; it also became the site for a Free Church of Scotland mission station, a major commercial post of the **African Lakes Company** (ALC), and the eastern terminus of Stevenson Road, which connected Lakes Malawi and Tanganyika. Karonga was also the site of the conflict between the British and the Swahili-Arabs. The **North Nyasa Native Association,** the first welfare and political organization in the country, was formed at Karonga in 1912. A major **rice-** and **cotton**-growing district, Karonga was also the home of the **Kilupula Rice Growers Co-operative Union.** In recent years, it has been the location of the Karonga Rural Development Project, which seeks to improve yields of rice, **maize,** cotton, and **groundnuts.** *See also* ARAB-SWAHILI WAR; AFRICAN WELFARE ASSOCIATIONS.

KARONGA WAR. *See* ARAB-SWAHILI WAR.

KASISI (RAMAKUKAN). Kasisi, also known as Ramakukan, was one of the **Kololo** from Barotseland recruited by Dr. **David Livingstone** in the 1850s. Eventually he was left in the Lower Shire, where he emerged as a major political force in the area, establishing authority over the indigenous **Mang'anja.** Like **Chipatula,** he became very involved in economic activities such as the ivory trade, selling most of the elephant tusks to the **African Lakes Company** and other British businesspeople who were operating in the region from the 1870s. Kasisi's relations with the Portuguese and their **Chikunda** retainers were uneasy, and in the 1880s he sided with the British in their struggle with the Portuguese over control of the **Lake Malawi-Shire** area.

KASITU VALLEY GHEE PRODUCERS CO-OPERATIVE UNION. Association of several ghee-producing cooperative societies in central and northern **Mzimba** Districts. It was formed in 1952 and had its headquarters at Kafukule. From the early 1950s to 1968, when it ceased to operate, it and the Bulambya Ghee Producers Cooperative Union were the largest producers of ghee in the country.

KASUNGU. Located about 80 miles northwest of **Nkhotakota,** Kasungu is the birthplace of Dr. **Hastings K. Banda,** the first president of Malawi, and of Rev. **Hanock Phiri,** founder of the **African Methodist Episcopal (AME) Church** in Malawi. Kasungu District is one of the major **tobacco**-growing areas of Malawi. West of the Kasungu *boma* is the Kasungu National Park, the largest game reserve in Malawi. Kasungu is also the home of the **Kamuzu Academy.**

In the 19th century, Kasungu was on the main ivory–**slave trade** route between Nkhotakota on **Lake Malawi** and the Luangwa Valley. Chulu, the most senior **Chewa** ruler in Kasungu, was defeated by **Zwengendaba** during the **Ngoni** journey north. Chulu's defeat led to the emergence of **Mwase Kasungu** in the 1850s as the powerful chief of the area because he showed that he was prepared to provide protection when Chulu was unable to do so. In 1863 **David Livingstone** visited Mwase, and in 1890 **Karl Wiese**, representing the Portuguese, was a guest of the chief; it was Mwase who signed a treaty with **Alfred Sharpe**, the British vice consul, following his defeat by British forces in 1895.

KATENGA, BRIDGER. Former diplomat and senior civil servant. Bridger Katenga was born in **Nkhata Bay** South in 1926 and attended the Hofmeyr School of Social Welfare in Johannesburg. Subsequently, he worked as a welfare officer and probation officer in the colonial civil service. Upon independence in 1964, Katenga was appointed Malawi's ambassador to Ethiopia and later to the **United Nations**. On his return to Malawi he became permanent secretary for community development and social welfare; his last position was general manager and chief liaison officer of the Malawi-Canada Railway project, which oversaw the building of the railway line between the lakeshore at **Salima** and the new capital at **Lilongwe**. He died in 1975.

KATENGA-KAUNDA, REID WILLIE. One of the founders of the **United Democratic Front** (UDF) and chief of staff at **Sanjika Palace**, Katenga-Kaunda was a senior civil servant and a highly regarded diplomat before he fell from President **Hastings K. Banda**'s favor. In the early 1990s, he was among the major advocates of change, and later he unsuccessfully stood for the national assembly as a UDF candidate. He became secretary-general of the UDF and a political adviser to President **Bakili Muluzi**.

KATENGEZA, REV. NAMON. In 1924 Namon Katengeza was one of the first Africans to be ordained minister of the Dutch Reformed Church. He served in many parts of the Central Region of Malawi, including **Lilongwe**, the district of his birth. In 1944 Katengeza dictated to **Samuel Ntara** notes on **Chewa** history, and they formed the basis of *Mbiri ya Chewa* (1965).

KATENGEZA, RICHARD DEVELIUS. Politician, businessman, farmer, administrator, and son of Rev. **Namon Katengeza**. Richard

Katengeza was born in **Lilongwe** District and went to local primary schools before working for Du Toit and Du Preeze Flour Mills. Katengeza was an active member of the **Nyasaland African Congress** (NAC) and in 1956 unsuccessfully attempted to secure the party's nomination for a seat in the **Legislative Council**. In 1961 he was elected to parliament, but after a short time he was appointed chairman of the **Farmers Marketing Board**, the first Malawian to hold the position. Later still he became chairman of Malawi Railways. Katengeza died in the early 1980s. *See also* AGRICULTURAL DEVELOPMENT AND MARKETING BOARD.

KATSONGA, CHESTER. This flamboyant businessman and controversial politician was one of the numerous **Blantyre-Limbe** based African entrepreneurs who emerged in the postwar period. Katsonga was mostly in the grocery and catering business, supplying food at meetings of the Provincial Council and opening food outlets in places such as the Nyasaland Railway station, Blantyre, and at the central market in that city. In 1953 he branched into the bar business, becoming the first African to own a legally sanctioned bar in urban **Nyasaland**. Later he opened the famous Helen's Bar outside **Zomba**. Like most Blantyre businessmen, Katsonga became active in nationalist politics, rising to the position of branch chairman of the **Nyasaland African Congress** (NAC). In 1960 he formed the **Christian Social Democratic Party** (CSDP), for which he was much criticized and ostracized by the mainstream nationalist politicians. The Catholic Church was accused of supporting Katsonga, and consequently was strongly attacked by the **Malawi Congress Party** (MCP) newspaper, the *Malawi News*. Katsonga's party lost the 1961 elections, marking its virtual demise. From then on, he concentrated on his commercial interests and his drinking establishments, such as the Chester Bar on the periphery of **Zomba** town, which became particularly popular. He died in the early 1980s.

KAUNDA, DAVID JULIZYA. Father of **Kenneth Kaunda**, Zambia's first president. David Kaunda was one of the first residents of **Nyasaland** trained at the **Overtoun Institution** to be sent to Northern Rhodesia as evangelists and teachers. Son of Mtepa Kaunda and NyaChirwa, David was born in 1878 in modern **Nkhata Bay** district. When he was 17, his mother, widowed when her husband died in battle, took her children to Elangeni, an important **Ngoni** settlement that had also become a major center of **Livingstonia Mission** activity. One of the lay missionaries in the area was South African **William Koyi**. David went to school at Elangeni and **Ekwendeni** before attending the Overtoun Institution, where he trained as a teacher and met a Karonga girl, Helen Nyirenda, sister of **Robert Gwebe Nyirenda**. They married in 1905 and eventually had eight children, the youngest being Kenneth, who was born in 1924. In 1904 David Kaunda had been sent to Chinsali area in **Bemba** country, Northern Rhodesia, an area in which the Livingstonia Mission had been active since 1894, when they opened a mission station at **Mwenzo** in nearby **Namwanga**/Mabwe region. In 1927 David Kaunda went back to the Overtoun to train as a minister and was ordained three years later. He died at his **Lubwa** base in 1932.

KAUNDA, KENNETH DAVID. First president of Zambia. Kenneth Kaunda, youngest child of **David Kaunda** and his wife, Helen, was born in 1924 at **Lubwa** Mission in Northern Rhodesia (**Zambia**). After attending school at Lubwa, he went to Munali Secondary School before training as a teacher and returning to the mission to teach. Besides serving as a headmaster (1944–1947) of the mission school, he was an athletics coach and a scoutmaster. In 1949 he and a school friend, Simon Mwansa Kapwepwe (later to be vice president), became active in the Chinsali Welfare Association, and a year later he became its secretary. The welfare association, being a branch of the Northern Rhodesia African National Congress, enabled Kaunda to have contact with the national movement, which elected him as its secretary-general in 1953.

Disenchanted with **Harry Nkumbula**'s leadership, in October 1958 Kaunda formed a breakaway organization, the Zambia African National Congress, which the government banned in March 1959. Kaunda was arrested and then imprisoned until January of the following year. Upon his release, he was elected president of a new party, the United National Independent Party (UNIP), which in 1952 won the first parliamentary elections, leading to his appointment as minister of local government. In January 1964 the UNIP won the general elections. Kaunda became prime minister and on October 1924 president of an independent Zambia. A committed pan-Africanist, Kaunda bitterly opposed the settler colonial states in Southern Africa, and he played host to the African liberation movements in the region. Zambia suffered periodic physical attacks, mainly from Rhodesia and **South Africa**; the country's economy was also adversely affected by his determination to boycott relations with his wealthier southern neighbors, whose economies were better developed and historically tied to Zambia.

In 1991 Kaunda's party lost the elections to Frederick Chiluba's Movement for Multiparty Democracy (MMD). Within two years he retired from politics, only to return in 1996. This caused much division within the UNIP, however, and Kaunda decided to withdraw from national politics.

KAUNDA, WEDSON CHALULUMA. Politician and former sergeant at arms in the first African-dominated parliament. Kaunda was born at Lusangazi, near **Mzuzu**, in 1921 and educated at **Ekwendeni** and **Livingstonia**, where he qualified as a teacher in 1943. He taught briefly and then left for **South Africa**, where he worked as a clerk in the city of Port Elizabeth. On his return in 1949, he joined politics, becoming secretary of the **Nyasaland African Congress** (NAC) at Ekwendeni and five years later a member of the Northern Province Provincial Council. In 1956 he lost the NAC candidacy for the **Legislative Council** (LEGCO) to **Kanyama Chiume** but remained active in provincial politics. A close confidant of **Mkhosi Lazalo Jere**, the *inkosi ya makhosi* M'Mbelwa II, Kaunda became deputy and then full sergeant at arms in 1961. Three years later, he trained as a magistrate, a position he held until his retirement in the 1970s. He died in 1985.

KAWINGA. Of the Machinga branch of the **Yao**, the Kawingas settled in the area east of Lake Malombe. But their authority extended to most of today's **Machinga** District and the southern part of **Mangochi** district. From his seat at Chikala hill, Chief Kawinga strongly resisted British rule in the 1880s and 1890s, at times fighting the British directly and at times joining forces with other Yao chieftaincies. After the British defeated **Makanjila** in 1894, Kawinga, **Jalasi**, and **Matipwiri** jointly mounted an attack on the British in February of the following year, with a view to expelling them from the region. In September, however, Sir **Harry Johnston** and his Sikh soldiers fought back, ending the Yao aspirations.

KAWOMBA. Chewa chieftainship in **Kasungu** District established during the expansion of the **Maravi** state. In 1973 President **Hastings K. Banda** deposed Chief **Mwase Kasungu** as the senior chief in the area and replaced him with Kawomba. Mwase, as well as Themba Katumbi and Kyungu **Raphael K. Mwakasungula**, lost his position as traditional ruler because he had supported the return of **Wellington M. Chirwa**. Banda went further by directing that Mwase be replaced by someone from a ruling house other than that of the Mwase Kasungu. According to Banda's understanding of **Chewa** traditions, the house of Mwase Kasungu was junior to that of Kawomba; for Banda, the change was also determined by historical fact.

KAYIRA, REV. ANDREW. Church minister at **Karonga** from 1950 to the late 1970s. Andrew Kayira was born in Wenya, **Chitipa** District. He trained as a teacher at the **Overtoun Institution** and taught at several schools, including Mwenelondo, Karonga. In the late 1940s he completed theological courses and in 1950 was appointed to the Karonga mission station. In 1959 the governor nominated Rev. Kayira to the **Legislative Council** (LEGCO). Although he did not accept the post, he drew the anger of some nationalist political activists. They burned the manse house down, and he lost most of his property. He remained pastor in charge of the Karonga congregation until the late 1980s, when he returned to Wenya, his home.

KAYIRA, LEGSON. Malawian author born in Wenya, **Chitipa**. Kayira went to local schools and the **Overtoun Institution**. Later he graduated from University of Washington in the **United States**, majoring in political science. In the mid-1960s he won a scholarship to Cambridge University, where he studied history for two years and then worked in London. His books include *I Will Try* (1965), *The Looming Shadow* (1967), *Jingala* (1969), and *The Civil Servant* (1971), all in the Heinemann African Writers Series.

KAZIWIZIWI. Located southwest of **Khondowe** and forming part of the Nyika Highlands, since the 1980s Kaziwiziwi has become one of the main coal-producing areas in **Malawi**.

KERR CROSS, DAVID. *See* CROSS, DR. DAVID KERR.

KETTLEWELL, RICHARD WILDMAN. Director of agriculture from 1950 to 1959 and secretary for natural resources from 1959 to 1962. Kettlewell was one of the most influential civil servants in late colonial Malawi. Born in England in 1910 and educated at Cambridge University, Kettlewell joined the colonial service in **Nyasaland** as an agricultural officer in 1934. Like many government employees, he saw service in World War II. He served in different parts of the colony, and in 1951 Governor **Geoffrey Colby** appointed him to head the Agriculture Department. In 1959 he was appointed secretary for natural resources, from which position he retired in 1962. From 1957 to 1962, Kettlewell also served as a member of the **Executive Council**. His *Agricultural Change in Nyasaland* remains one of the most useful publications on the history of **agriculture** in colonial Malawi. Kettlewell died in 1994.

KHANGA, MELVIN MALUDI. Born in **Ntcheu** District and educated at **Malamulo**, Khanga was trained at the Royal Military College,

Sandhurst, England, where in the early 1960s he was commissioned as a lieutenant, becoming one of the first local officers in the Malawi **army**. Known as a hard-working, professional soldier, he served as aide-de-camp to President **Hastings K. Banda** and quickly rose through the ranks. By the late 1980s, he was a full general, and in 1980 he took over from General **Graziano Matewere** as commanding officer of the Malawi **army**, a position he held until he retired in 1991. Independent minded and highly respected by officers and men, Lieutenant General Khanga steered the army through difficult times, including its involvement in guarding the Nacala rail line from **REN-AMO** guerrilla fighters. In 1994 he was appointed chairman of the board of **Air Malawi**; he died two years later.

KHONDOWE. In 1894 Dr. **Robert Laws** decided to locate the **Overtoun Institution** of the **Livingstonia Mission** of the Free Church of Scotland on the **Khondowe** plateau, east of Nyika, overlooking **Lake Malawi**. This was to be one of the largest, most productive, and influential educational centers in Southern Africa.

KHONJE, NELSON. Speaker of the National Assembly from the mid-1970s to the early 1980s. Khonje was born in 1923 in **Mwanza** District and attended local Seventh-Day Adventist schools. After completing a teachers' course, he taught at several schools in the Southern Region. In the early 1960s he spent a year studying in Scotland. He taught at Masongola Secondary School, **Zomba**, and in 1965 became headmaster of Ntcheu Secondary School; he was later transferred to Ntchisi Day Secondary School. In 1971 Khonje entered parliament as member for Mwanza and was subsequently appointed deputy speaker of parliament; he became speaker of the National Assembly in 1975. By the late 1980s Khonje had virtually retired from active politics.

KHULUBVI. M'bona shrine on the west bank of the **Shire River**, near **Nsanje** *boma*, originally established by the **Kaphwiti** dynasty but later taken over by **Lundu**. *See also* M'BONA CULT.

KILEKWA, PETRO. Remarkable **Universities' Mission to Central Africa** (UMCA) priest. Kilekwa was born in Chilekwa, probably in the Lake Banguelo area of **Zambia**. As a young boy he was captured by slavers and taken to the east coast. There he and other captives boarded an Arab dhow bound for the Persian Gulf. A British patrol boat, the HMS

Osprey, rescued them on the third day of the voyage; they were taken to **Zanzibar**, where on September 30, 1887, he and other boys were handed over to St. Andrews College, the UMCA establishment at Kiungani. Two years later, Chilekwa was baptized Petro Kilekwa. In 1895 he was posted to teach at Masasi in southern Tanganyika, but within a short time he returned to assist at the school at Kiungani. In January 1897 he married Beatrice Myororo, a **Yao** who had been rescued from a slave dhow in 1881, and was taken care of by women missionaries of the UMCA at Nkunazini and Mbwini. She too was a teacher, having qualified in the same year as Petro. After their marriage, Kilekwa expressed interest in working in the **Lake Malawi** region, and the Kilekwas arrived on **Likoma Island** in April 1899. Petro was sent to a school at Ntonya in Nkhotakota; in 1906 he passed the reader's examinations and five years later became a deacon. Between 1915 and 1917, he was at Likoma studying for the priesthood, and after his ordination he became priest at Kayoyo. Kilekwa served in other parishes before retiring at Mkope Hill.

KILUPULA, CHIEF. *See* MWANJASI, JOSEPH.

KILUPULA RICE GROWERS CO-OPERATIVE UNION. This union of six **rice**-producing **cooperative societies** in Chief Kilupula's area, **Karonga** District, was formed in 1953. Throughout the 1950s, it was the largest rice-producing organization in the country, most of its grain being consumed locally but a significant amount being exported to neighboring territories. Its first secretary was Kelvin Nyirenda, son of **Robert Gwebe Nyirenda**. Throughout the life of the union its chairman was **Joseph Mwanjasi**, Chief Kilupula.

KIMBLE, DAVID. British political scientist and head of the **University of Malawi** from 1977 to 1986. David Kimble was born in 1921 and was educated at Reading University (B.A.) and the University of London (Ph.D.). He spent almost all his working life in Africa: University of Ghana, 1951–1961; University of Dar es Salaam, 1961–1969; CAFRAD, Morocco, 1969–1971; National University of Lesotho, 1971–1977. Kimble became vice chancellor at a time when the institution's morale was low, after many of its local faculty had fallen prey to **Hastings K. Banda**'s overzealous security **police**; some of the university teachers had even been taken as political detainees. Kimble established good working relations with the government and in the process restored morale somewhat. Faculty were able to travel abroad to attend conferences and seminars. Subject to censorship laws, they were also able to undertake and publish research. Beginning in 1978, Kimble was given the responsibility of setting and supervising English exams to all prospective MPs, and this exercise involved most faculty traveling to district headquarters to administer the examinations. Kimble is also known internationally as the founding editor (1960–1997) of the prestigious publication, *Journal of Modern African Studies* (Cambridge University Press).

KINGA. Inhabitants of the Livingstone (Kinga) Mountain range on the northeastern shores of **Lake Malawi**. From precolonial times to the early 1960s, the Kinga, most famous for their beautifully decorated pots, traded their wares with the **Ngonde** in exchange for food, which was always plentiful in their country.

KING'S AFRICAN RIFLES (KAR). *See* ARMY.

KINYAKYUSA. Language of the **Nyakyusa**; basically the same as **Kyangonde**.

KIRK, SIR JOHN. Surgeon, botanist, photographer, traveler, and administrator. This graduate of the Edinburgh Royal Infirmary joined **David Livingstone**'s Zambezi expedition in 1858, at the age of 26, as a plant collector for the Royal Botanical Gardens, Kew. Kirk visited Zomba Mountain and **Lake Chilwa**, and in September 1859 he, Livingstone, and a few others walked up the **Shire River** and then sailed around **Lake Malawi** as far as **Usisya** in the north. Besides his botanical interests, Kirk collected many samples of Lake Malawi fish, and he is reported to have been the first person to clinically describe Black Water Fever, which hitherto had been misidentified as Yellow Fever. In 1870 Kirk was the British consul-general at **Zanzibar**, and during the 1880s and 1890s he was a key adviser to the British Foreign Office.

KIRK RANGE. Mountain range named after Dr. **John Kirk**. From the **Ntcheu** area it stretches in a southeasterly direction.

KITTERMASTER, SIR HAROLD. The governor of **Nyasaland** from 1934 to 1939, when he died in office at **Zomba**. Kittermaster is much identified with the **Lacey Commission** and the introduction of the **Native Trust Lands** of 1936, which transferred most of the Crown land for the sole use of Africans.

KOLOLO. Also known as Magololo, they were a group of people whom Dr. **David Livingstone** took from Barotseland to the Lower **Shire valley**

of Malawi where they settled, becoming significant players in the political and economic life of the area. Originally Sotho from the area west of the Maluti Mountains, which they had left in 1823 during the *lifaqane*, led by the Fokeng chief, Sebetuane, they migrated north to Barotseland, western Zambia, where for a brief period they ruled the area. In 1855 Sebetuane's son and successor, Sekeletu, recommended 112 porters to David Livingstone, who left them at Tete while he proceeded on leave to England. On his return in 1858, he found that many had occupied their time working for the Portuguese in several capacities: canoemen, elephant hunters, gold diggers, and porters, among others.

In 1861 some of the Kololo, led by Moloka and **Kasisi** (also called Ramakukan), decided to remain in the **Chikwawa** area of the Lower Shire and make it their home. The Kololo had guns, most of which they had received in lieu of pay, and they used them to gain power in the **Mang'anja** region, which was particularly unstable because of the **slave trade** and also because of the **famine** of the 1860s. By 1870 they had established political control in the area between **Chiromo** in the south and Manthiti Falls in the north, and divided it into six chieftaincies.

The Kololo stopped slave raids in the area, and they became active elephant hunters and ivory traders and farmers, growing sesame seeds that they sold to Europeans. They had tense relations with the **Chikunda** and Portuguese on their western borders but, in the main, had cordial dealings with the British. Both the **African Lakes Company** (ALC) and the Scottish missionaries made treaties with the Kololo; the former depended much on Kololo ivory. However, at times, mutual distrust led to conflict, as in the incident involving **George Fenwick**. During the scramble for Africa in the late 1880s and early 1890s, the British exploited the Kololo dislike of the Portuguese to keep the latter out of the southern **Lake Malawi** area. A significant number of the Kololo were among the first students at the **Blantyre Mission**, and some of them became notable residents of the emerging town of **Blantyre**. *See also* CHIPATULA; ANGLO-PORTUGUESE TREATY.

KONGWE. Located in Dowa District, this is the site of one of the major mission centers of the Dutch Reformed Church established between 1889 and 1891. Today it is the home of the Robert Blake Secondary School.

KOTA KOTA RICE GROWERS CO-OPERATIVE UNION (KKRGU). Formed in 1962, when the **Kota Kota Rice Trading, Ltd.** closed. The KKRGU, with the **Kilupula Rice Growers Co-operative Union**, became the largest rice producer and exporter in the **Federation**

of Rhodesia and Nyasaland. Like most government-affiliated agricultural cooperatives in Malawi, the KKRGU was liquidated in 1968.

KOTA KOTA RICE TRADING, LTD. Planned in 1938–1939, and commencing operations in 1945, this government-backed commercial concern bought paddy rice from producers in the Kota Kota **(Nkhotakota)** District and processed it for sale within the colony and for export, mainly to Southern and Northern Rhodesia. Using modern machinery, it also often processed paddy rice for the **Kilupula Rice Growers Co-operative Union** when their own equipment could not handle the quantities they produced. In 1961 it was converted to a cooperative union of the various **rice**-growing associations in the district.

KOYI, WILLIAM MTUSANE. Of Ngqika ethnic affinity and therefore a Xhosa speaker, William Koyi was born in the Thomas River area in 1846. In 1871 he became a student at **Lovedale**, and in 1876 he was one of the several black South Africans who offered to accompany Dr. **James Stewart** to the **Lake Malawi** region to set up the **Livingstonia Mission**. Koyi's ability to communicate in both Xhosa and Zulu was an advantage that the missionaries fully utilized in their determined effort to establish their presence among the **Ngoni**. Koyi, an all-around handyman, was to play many roles: interpreter, adviser on Ngoni and African customs, diplomat, teacher, and preacher. Although three European missionaries were residing in Ngoni country, Koyi, later based at **Njuyu**, was effectively the principal missionary to the court of **M'belwa** and other Ngoni chiefs between 1878 and 1885, when Dr. **Walter Elmslie** arrived in the area. Much loved by the Ngoni and respected by all who knew him, Koyi died of tuberculosis in 1886. He was the best known of the Lovedale missionaries; the others were **Shadrack Ngunana**, **Isaac William Wauchope**, **Mapas Ntintili**, and George Williams.

KUBWALO, JOSEPH. This professional photographer was a founding member of the **United Democratic Front** (UDF) and minister of defense. He was also MP for **Blantyre** from 1994 to 1999.

KUFA, JOHN GRAY. John Chilembwe's second in command. Kufa was born at Kongone on the Zambezi River, where in 1885 he joined a party of missionaries bound for **Blantyre**. In 1892 he was one of 11 Africans to be ordained deacons, and within a few years he became the first African to train as a medical assistant, passing his elementary surgery examinations with distinction. He assumed the position of chief medical assistant in the **Blantyre Mission** dispensary. In 1896 Kufa was posted to Mulumbo in **Mozambique** to start a substation of the Blantyre Mission. When the Portuguese authorities successfully claimed the area as part of their colony in 1900, the Church of Scotland recalled Kufa, closing down the young church establishment.

Kufa left the mission and for a time worked at the **A. L. Bruce** dispensary at **Magomero**. However, he was now also preoccupied with the 140-acre estate he started at Nsoni, growing **cotton, maize**, and **tobacco** and employing 27 workers. He also grew fruits and raised livestock. Kufa had maintained his contact with Mulumbo, and as the number of **Lomwe** from that side of the Nyasaland border migrating into the **Shire Highlands** increased, some of them settled in his Nsoni neighborhood. Many of the Lomwe immigrants knew him, and many converted to **John Chilembwe**'s religious and political beliefs. Kufa and Chilembwe were long-time friends and belonged to the group of close confidants who planned the 1915 uprising. Kufa was captured on January 28, five days after the uprising started and, along with **Stephen Mkulitchi**, was hanged in Blantyre in February.

KULUNJIRI, KINROSS W. Businessman and politician. Kulunjiri was president-general of the **Nyasaland African Congress** (NAC) for a brief period in the early 1950s.

KULUUNDA, BIBI. Yao female chief in the lakeshore area of **Salima** District.

KUMBIKANO, CLEMENT. Leading **Nyasaland African Congress** (NAC) politician. Kumbikano became a member of the Federal Parliament in December 1953 and refused to withdraw from it when his party asked him to do so. In 1952 he had been part of the delegation of **Nyasaland** Africans to attend the London conference on the **Federation of Rhodesia and Nyasaland** and, with others, boycotted the official talks at the advice of Dr. **Hastings K. Banda**. Expelled from the NAC in 1957, he and **Wellington Manoah Chirwa** remained in the Federal Assembly until the early 1960s. The **Malawi Congress Party** (MCP) shunned and demonized them, making sure that they had no place in independent **Malawi**. Consequently, both went into **exile**.

KUMBWENZA, JEREMIA T. Former regional minister of the Central Region, Kumbwenza was born at Mitundu, **Lilongwe** District, in 1925. He attended local Dutch Reformed Church Schools and studied bookkeeping by correspondence while working as a timber salesman. In 1951 he joined the **Nyasaland African Congress** (NAC). When the **Malawi**

Congress Party (MCP) was formed in 1959, he was vice treasurer of his locality. In 1961 he became an MP and three years later was appointed parliamentary secretary in the Ministry of Trade and Industry. In 1964 he was promoted to the cabinet as full minister in the latter ministry. Within a short time, he became regional minister for the Central Region, a position he held until the mid-1970s, when he virtually retired from politics.

KUMTUMANJI, GOMILE WILANICHILAMBO. Southern Region chairman of the **Malawi Congress Party** (MCP) throughout the 1960s and regional minister for the south in the late 1960s. Kumtumanji was born in the ruling family of the Kumtumanji chiefdom in western **Zomba** the District. After basic education he worked outside **Malawi** for a period. Upon his return, he became involved in the politics of decolonization, playing an active role in the **Nyasaland African Congress** (NAC) in the district. In 1959 Kumtumanji was among the hundreds of people arrested during **Operation Sunrise**. After being released, he was elected chairman of the new MCP for the south. In 1961 he was elected to parliament and appointed junior minister. In 1964 Kumtumanji was promoted to the cabinet and remained there until 1970, when he was arrested on charges that he was associated with the **Chilobwe** murders. He died in prison in 1989.

KUMWENDA, SWEETMAN. Born in **Mzimba** District, Sweetman Kumwenda was a senior police officer and prospective first African head of the Malawi **police**. In the late 1960s Kumwenda served as a diplomat in the United Kingdom, but in 1970 he was arrested and imprisoned without being charged of an offense. He died in custody.

KUNDECHA, REV. STEPHEN. One of the first Africans to be trained at **Blantyre Mission** and in 1911 the second African to be ordained as a minister. Kundecha, like **Harry Kambwiri Matecheta**, had worked with Rev. **David Clement Scott** and was a major force in African evangelization and **education**. He was responsible for training other prominent African pastors such as **Harry Mtuwa**, Joseph Kaunde, and **Thomas Maseya**. Kundecha was also a very outspoken critic of the *thangata* system, making his views public whenever possible.

KUNTAJA, CHIEF. Born in **Blantyre** District in 1916, Chief Kuntaja was educated at village schools before going on to the **Henry Henderson Institute** (HHI) in **Blantyre**, where he completed his primary school certificate examination. He was employed as a clerk until 1942, when he joined the **King's African Rifles** (KAR). He distinguished himself and was promoted to the rank of staff sergeant. He left the **army** in 1947 and briefly returned to work as a clerk. In the following year he was installed as Chief Kuntaja. He became a popular and hard-working chief, always seeking ways and means of improving the economic and social well-being of his people.

Chief Kuntaja strongly opposed the **Federation of Rhodesia and Nyasaland** and was one of the six chiefs, including **Philip Gomani III**, **M'Mbelwa II**, and Katumbi, who went to London in 1953 to make their position known to the British government. Chief Kuntaja visited London again in June 1958, this time in the company of **Henry Chipembere** and **Hastings K. Banda**, to argue for immediate constitutional changes. In July 1960 he returned to London as part of the **Malawi Congress Party** (MCP) delegation to the Lancaster House constitutional talks. After a new government took over in 1961, Kuntaja continued to support the MCP and remained a chief committed to his traditional duties.

An earlier Kuntaja (1870s–1880s) ruled the area adjacent to the **Blantyre Mission** and seems to have been junior to Chief **Kapeni**.

KWACHA. In all Malawi languages, *kwacha* means "dawn," and in 1955 nationalists adopted it as a rallying slogan to signify the dawn of "freedom" from colonial rule. All Malawian politicians, including Dr. **Hastings K. Banda**, would start their speeches at political gatherings with the slogan, as Kenyatta and Kenyans did with *harambe*. Even after independence *kwacha*, symbolized by a cockerel, continued to be widely identified with the **Malawi Congress Party** (MCP).

In 1952 the **Nyasaland African Congress** (NAC), under the influence of **James Sangala**, began to publish a newsletter to keep its membership and the general public abreast of its programs. Called *Kwacha,* the newsletter also counteracted government propaganda published in *Msimbi* and *Bwalo la Nyasaland*. In August 1955 *Kwacha* became a broadsheet and played a major role in mobilizing Congress supporters in the 1956 elections. It folded soon because of lack of advertisers. Since 1971 *kwacha* has also been the unit of **currency** of Malawi.

KWENJE, NOPHAS DINNECK. Journalist and politician. Kwenje trained as a teacher at the **Henry Henderson Institute** (HHI) and served as headmaster at one of the schools in the Southern Region before going to Southern Rhodesia, There he worked at a variety of jobs, as a photographer, teacher, postal worker, and police detective. Before returning to **Nyasaland** in 1956, he edited the famous Bulawayo publication, the *Bantu Mirror*, of which he also became business manager. In 1956 the first Africans were about to be elected to the **Legislative Council**

(LEGCO); Kwenje successfully stood as one of the **Nyasaland African Congress** candidates for the Southern Region. Compared with **Henry Chipembere** and **Kanyama Chiume**, Kwenje and other African members of the LEGCO were considered moderates and did not feature in the **Malawi Congress Party**–dominated parliament. However, unlike **James Chinyama** and **Dunstan Chijozi**, who were vilified by the MCP, Kwenje later became acting general manager of *Malawi Press,* a ruling party–related position.

KYANGONDE. Language of the **Ngonde**; basically the same as **Kinyakyusa**, which is spoken on the Tanzanian side of the **Songwe River**.

KYUNGU. Traditional title of the **Ngonde** rulers; the Kyungu family established political authority in the northern **Karonga** lakeshore around 1600.

– L –

LABOR UNIONS. The trade union movement in Malawi was a post–World War II development. The first central union, the Nyasaland Trades Union Congress (TUC), was formed in 1956, but its affiliation with the International Confederation of Free Trade Unions (ICFTU) stimulated the creation of a dissenting organization: the National Council of Labor. The TUC and the Council merged and then dissolved in 1961. Beginning in 1962, unions lost influence and many union leaders took government or **Malawi Congress Party** (MCP) jobs. Labor unions were also closely supervised by the Ministry of Labour and were generally ineffective. Collective bargaining was limited and strikes, although guaranteed, rarely took place, except for the **tea** estates, where they occurred occasionally.

The situation began to change in the early 1990s. First, in 1989, President **Hastings K. Banda** allowed the Southern Africa Trade Union Coordinating Council (SATUCC), then led by **Chakufwa Chihana**, to move its headquarters from Maseru, Lesotho, to **Lilongwe**. This tended to encourage the revival of trade unionism in **Malawi**. Chihana was a leading advocate for political reform in Malawi, and unions played a major role in political liberalization. In the post-Banda period, labor unions are a feature of civil society, the Malawi Congress of Trade Unions (MCTU) being the largest umbrella organization.

LACEY COMMISSION. A 1935 committee led by Travers Lacey and appointed by the **Nyasaland** government to look into the problem of labor recruitment in and migration from Nyasaland. Europeans in Nyasaland had complained against recruiting, as they were concerned that they would lose labor to other parts of Southern Africa. Missionaries had also strongly criticized the practice, pointing to their detrimental effect on family and community life. The commission advised the government against interference in the movement of individual laborers; however, it also strongly recommended that the government enter into an agreement with the countries interested in Malawi labor so as to return to government-regulated recruitment. In this regard it also recommended a quota system to govern the movement of laborers; the enforcement of all conditions of labor recruitment; that all governments involved coordinate matters concerning taxation, deferred pay, family remittances, and repatriation at the end of contracts; and that Nyasaland establish resident labor commissioners in all the recipient countries. The commission recognized the deleterious effects of labor migration as detailed by missionaries in their presentations, and they argued that the only solution to the problem was for the internal economy to be able to absorb potential migrants. However, it also pointed out that labor migration was an important source of revenue for the government.

LADY NYASSA. A small steamer belonging to the **African Lakes Company** (ALC), in service from 1898.

LAKE CHILWA. Third largest lake in **Malawi**. Located in western **Zomba** District on the Malawi-**Mozambique** border, Lake Chilwa has always been a source of fish in the area. Some 335 villages, inhabited by 60,162 inhabitants, in the proximity of the lake, are involved in fishing. Today the yearly catch is about 17,000 metric tons worth over US$3 million. With the assistance of the Danish International Development Agency (DANIDA), extensive work will be carried out in the catchment area to ensure that the lake, an inland drainage system, does not dry up. The project aims at maximizing the usage of the wetland surrounding it. The Lake Chilwa region has always been identified with rice production, and in the late 1940s and early 1950s the colonial government unsuccessfully tried to turn it into a major **rice**-growing one.

Another goal of the DANIDA scheme (1900–2003) is to increase the productive capacity of this potential rice-producing wetland. For ornithologists and bird watchers, the area is said to have more than 161 species of birds. It is expected that the project will improve the quality of the environment of the area to the benefit of its communities and its fauna.

LAKE CHIUTA. Fishing area on the **Malawi-Mozambique** border that is inhabited mostly by **Yao** speakers.

LAKE MALAWI. Lake Malawi is Africa's third largest lake and forms the southern part of the Great African Rift Valley. It is 363 miles long and 10 to 50 miles wide. It covers 11,430 square miles, lies 1,500 feet above sea level, and is 2,310 feet deep in its northern section, especially the portion between the Livingstone Mountains of **Tanzania** and the Nyika and **Viphya Highlands** on the Malawi side.

A freshwater lake, it is fed by rivers such as the **Songwe**, the North and South Rukuru, the Luweya, Dwangwa Bua, and Linthipe. Through the **Shire River** it drains into the Zambezi and eventually into the Indian Ocean. Because of the ready supply of water, the fertile soils around it, and its many species of fish, the lake has from time immemorial attracted people to its shores. Parts of its littoral have the largest concentration of population in Malawi, and they include the **Karonga** plains, **Usisya** and southern **Nkhata Bay** District, and **Nkhotakota**. The lake has two main islands, **Likoma** and Chizumulu, which since the late 19th century have been centers of the **Universities' Mission to Central Africa** (UMCA).

Malawi shares the lake with **Mozambique** and Tanzania, where it is still called Lake Nyasa, the name Dr. **David Livingstone** gave to it in 1859, itself a misnomer because *nyasa* is the **Mang'anja** word for lake. Long before the arrival of Europeans the lake was an important transport avenue, providing the principal link between the various parts of the region. It is not surprising that *bomas* were established on the shores of the lake, and they include **Fort Johnston** (Mangochi), Nkhotakota, **Chintheche** (later **Nkhata Bay**), and Karonga. Lake Transport continues to play a major role in the economic life of Malawi. *See also* FISHING; TOURISM; TRANSPORTATION.

LAKE NYASA. *See* LAKE MALAWI.

LANCASTER HOUSE CONFERENCE. *See* HASTINGS KAMUZU BANDA; ELECTIONS.

LANGUAGES AND LANGUAGE POLICY. Throughout colonial rule English was the official language of communication. Nevertheless, expatriate government officers in provincial and district administration had to learn ciNyanja (basically the same as ciChewa) and pass a required examination. CiNyanja was taught in schools, and government papers such as **Msimbi** had ciNyanja sections; it was also one of the principal broadcast languages in the period before and during the **Federation of Rhodesia and Nyasaland**. CiTumbuka was taught in schools in the Northern Region.

The situation did not change until 1968, when ciChewa, basically the same as ciNyanja, was officially declared Malawi's national language. CiTumbuka ceased to be taught in schools in the north and no longer appeared in the print and broadcast media. English continued to be the official language. After the **Malawi Congress Party** (MCP) government was defeated in 1994, the **United Democratic Front** (UDF) government greatly modified the language policy. While the status of English remained unchanged, ciChewa lost its position as the national language in that others, including ciYao, ciLomwe, ciTumbuka, ciSena, and ciTonga, began to be broadcast on the radio; they had already been used in the opposition papers from 1992 to 1994. CiChewa/ciNyanja continues to be taught in schools and is one of the subjects at the Malawi School Certificate (MCE), or O' level. *See also* ETHNIC GROUPS.

LAST CHURCH OF GOD AND HIS CHRIST. *See* NGEMELA, ISIWANI BEN; MSUMBA, JORDAN.

LAUDERDALE ESTATE. Located near **Mulanje Mountain**, this was the first estate to seriously grow **tea** in Malawi. In 1891 the **African Lakes Company** (ALC), owners of the estate, employed Henry Brown to open Lauderdale as a **coffee**-growing venture. Having been recruited from Ceylon (Sri Lanka), where tea was gradually replacing coffee, years later Brown started to experiment with tea planting, initially using bushes from the **Blantyre Mission** gardens. Within a few years, the **Thyolo-Mulanje** area was established as the main tea-producing region of Malawi. Later Henry Brown opened his own Thornwood Tea Estate, not far from Lauderdale.

LAW SOCIETY OF MALAWI. This organization regulates the standards, ethics, and practices of the legal profession in **Malawi**. As a professional body, it can also initiate debate on legislature emanating from the National Assembly. In the early 1990s it played a major role in advocating for political reform and in pressing for a return to respect for **human rights**; the society was represented on the **Public Affairs Committee** (PAC). In the post-**Hastings Banda** era, the Law Society has continued to guard against any infringements of human rights.

LAWRENCE, ISA MACDONALD. Founding treasurer-general of the **Nyasaland African Congress** (NAC). Together with **James Sangala**

and **Levi Mumba**, Lawrence was a leading light in the new organization; he was responsible for changing the name from Nyasaland African Council to Nyasaland African Congress. A widely read man, through publications such as **Clement Kadalie**'s *Worker's Herald* and Marcus Garvey's *Negro World*, he had for some time followed the progress of black organizations in Africa and America. In the 1920s the colonial government had taken him to court for possessing this type of **literature**, which it deemed dangerous and illegal.

LAWS, ROBERT. Born on May 28, 1851, this founding member of the **Livingstonia Mission** party that arrived in the **Lake Malawi** area in 1875 qualified as a medical doctor at Aberdeen University and was ordained a minister of the Free Church of Scotland after attending the United Presbyterian College in Edinburgh. Reverend Dr. Robert Laws served in **Nyasaland** for over 52 years and exercised considerable influence on the socioeconomic, cultural, educational, and political life of the British colony. Although initially Dr. **James Stewart** of **Lovedale** was the official leader of the Livingstonia Mission, in practice, Laws was the effective head from the beginning, overseeing its work from the **Cape Maclear** base, supervising its relocation to **Bandawe** in 1881 and moving its headquarters to its permanent site at **Khondowe** in 1894. At Khondowe he established the **Overtoun Institution**, for a long time one of the best educational centers in colonial Africa. Laws envisaged the institution playing a major role in the socioeconomic development of the region through the training of teachers, clergy, and government clerks, as well as apprentices in technical skills. At one stage he even seriously entertained the idea of a university at Livingstonia.

His belief that training in European skills was a prerequisite to African development drew opposition. **Donald Fraser**, for one, feared the destruction of village life. Fraser also objected to the **education** of a few, preferring a mass education approach. By the 1920s others were questioning the relation of fine industrial training to the village way of life. Despite the strict rules affecting their lives at Overtoun, many Malawian apprentices were trained and were employed by Europeans in **Malawi**, other parts of Southern Africa, and nearby **Tanzania** and **Zambia**. Although Laws's Overtoun Institution has been criticized as an object to promote the colonial (not African) economy, the institution was responsible for producing many articulate and politically adept graduates who became leaders in local **African welfare associations** and later the **Nyasaland African Congress** (NAC). Laws was supportive of these groups, believing that an outlet for political expression was necessary.

In the 1880s and 1890s Laws encouraged the **Moir** brothers to expand their **African Lakes Company (Mandala)** stores in an effort to promote legitimate trade to compete with the growing influence of the **Swahili-Arab** traders in the **Lake Malawi** area. His views were valued by early protectorate governors such as Sir **Alfred Sharpe**, who respected the missionary's judgment and counsel. In 1912 Laws was appointed a member of the **Legislative Council (LEGCO)**, and it was he who requested an inquiry into the origins of the **Chilembwe Uprising** in 1915, in part because Livingstonia and other missions were under attack for educating Africans and inciting them to protest European rule.

Laws wrote several school primers in local languages and was instrumental in translating the New Testament into ciTumbuka. He also published a mission magazine, *Aurora,* and later wrote his memoirs, *Reminiscences of Livingstonia* (1934). Laws and his wife, Margaret Gray, left Malawi in 1927; he died in August 1934.

LEAGUE OF MALAWI WOMEN. This wing of the **Malawi Congress Party** (MCP) was initiated by Dr. **Hastings K. Banda** and organized by **Rose Chibambo** in 1958. At the same time, Banda organized the Youth League. Both wings acted as a political vanguard to the Malawi Congress Party, and they zealously supported Dr. Banda for most of his presidency. Banda listened to the league, and in noncontroversial matters it had an influence on the Life President. The league enjoyed a monopoly on the sale and distribution of a millet brew, the money going to the Women's League for its projects and charities. The Women's League was encouraged to maintain the strength of the MCP by urging people to renew their party membership cards. They appealed to league members to attend party meetings, enroll in home-craft and literacy classes, and practice traditional dances in their local areas. *See also* YOUTH.

Referred to as Banda's *mbumba* (female members of his family), these **women** had to buy special Women's League uniforms and perform at every official appearance of the president. Their compositions always praised him, describing them as their guardian and Malawi's savior. Modern houses were constructed for senior party *mbumba*, especially single and widowed women, as a reward for their loyalty and diligence, and their utility bills were paid for them by **Press Holdings**. The league had branches in every town and district, and it had chairwomen appointed to oversee the many social activities and charitable functions engaged in by the membership. The league reached every rural part of

Malawi; women farmers, who may not have seen or known an extension service officer, knew the league chairwoman in their village. Women who for some reason did not want to attend MCP functions or did not have the money to buy the party uniform were often subjected to unpleasantness.

Since the fall of the MCP government, the Women's League has become an insignificant wing of the party. Many members, remembering the manner in which they were forced to attend party functions, have deserted the party for new ones, such as the **United Democratic Front** (UDF) and the **Alliance for Democracy** (AFORD).

LECHAPTOIS, REV. ADOLPHE. In 1889, at age 36, Adolphe Lechaptois led the first Roman Catholic mission to the **Lake Malawi** area. Of the **White Fathers** Order, he was ordained in 1878 and worked in Algeria before being assigned to South Central Africa. His first station was **Mponda** at the southern end of Lake Malawi. After an uneasy time in the area, the mission moved to Northern Rhodesia. Lechaptois later moved on to Tanganyika, where he became vicar apostolic. *See also* MISSIONS.

LEGISLATIVE COUNCIL (LEGCO). In 1907 the Legislative Council was created as the consultative and legislative body in **Nyasaland**. Generally, the power to initiate legislation lay with the governor, who also appointed the members. LEGCO members included the governor, three ex-officio members of the **Executive Council** (the chief secretary, attorney general, treasurer), and three (six in 1911) members of **nongovernmental organizations** nominated by the governor. The unofficial members consisted of European planters, traders, and missionaries. The missionary members of LEGCO acted as the representatives of African interests, not African persons. Many missionaries accepted their role with sincerity and spoke out against *thangata*, hut taxes, labor migration, and the sale of African land.

Until 1949 no Africans (or **Asians**) had direct representation in LEGCO, despite the fact that **African welfare associations** and the **Nyasaland African Congress** (NAC) had made such a request. Earlier, in 1944–1945, the government established the mainly African Provincial Councils, dominated by traditional authorities. From the three councils, 20 people were chosen to form a **Protectorate Council**. The Protectorate Council was permitted (1949) to submit the names of five Africans to the governor, who chose two (three from 1953) to become LEGCO members. In 1949 **E. A. Muwamba** and **K. Ellerton Mposa** were the African representatives and **P. Dayaram** was the Asian representative. Europeans had appointed their first females to LEGCO just prior to that: Mary Tunstall Sharpe (daughter-in-law of Sir **Alfred Sharpe**) in 1946 and Marjorie Barron in 1947.

During the **Federation** (1953–1963), Europeans in LEGCO gained the right of direct election, thus eliminating the nominating process by the governor. In the 1955 Constitution a common roll for Europeans and Asians and a separate roll for Africans were created. At the same time, the unofficial membership of LEGCO was increased to include five Africans (to be elected by Provincial Councils) and six Europeans. Following this, the NAC won all five African seats, and the members were **Henry Chipembere, Kanyama Chiume, Dunstan Chijozi, James Chinyama**, and **Nophas Kwenje**. By 1960 there were seven African members in LEGCO, of whom three were elected and four nominated by the Protectorate Council. In the 1961 **elections**, the **Malawi Congress Party** (MCP) won all 20 lower-roll seats and two of the eight upper-roll seats in LEGCO. Two years later, LEGCO was renamed the Legislative Assembly and reconstituted to include 53 members, 50 elected from a general roll and three from a special roll.

LEMANI, DUMBO. Minister in the **United Democratic Front** (UDF)–led government formed after the 1999 elections. Previously Lemani had served as minister of state in the Office of the President, and in 1994 he was appointed minister of energy. Born and raised in **Zomba** District, Lemani spent part of the 1960s in prison because of his association with **Henry Chipembere** and other cabinet ministers who had rebelled against Dr. **Hastings K. Banda**'s policies and style of rule. After his release, he worked in **Blantyre** and became famous nationally as a first-rate **football** organizer and club manager. In the late 1980s, he became a pastor, and when the agitation for political reform surfaced in 1992, Lemani became a founding member of the UDF. In 1994 he was elected to the National Assembly and served as, among other things, minister of energy. In the 1999 **elections**, Lemani was returned as member for Zomba **Thondwe**, retained his position as UDF director of campaigns, and was appointed special adviser to President **Bakili Muluzi**. In November 2000 he became minister of state for presidential affairs.

LENGWE NATIONAL PARK. Covering about 50 square miles and located in **Chikwawa** District in the area south of the Mwanza River and west of the Shire, Lengwe was declared a game reserve in 1928. In 1963 the government's Forestry Department assumed responsibility for wildlife conservation, and consequently 20 miles of connecting roads were constructed and a rest house was built.

LEPROSY RELIEF ASSOCIATION (LEPRA). In 1963 the British Leprosy Relief Association (LEPRA) established the Malawi Leprosy Control Project at the Queen Elizabeth Central Hospital in **Blantyre**. Through its expatriate and locally trained staff and through the use of modern medicine and methods, LEPRA aimed at treating large numbers of leprosy suffers; in the process it hoped to eradicate the **disease** from the country. Initially the project covered an area of 2,000 square miles with a population of 1,000,000 people and 10,000 to 12,000 leprosy patients. The association's innovative method was to use mobile treatment units located in Blantyre, **Zomba**, and **Mulanje** to visit treatment centers in the rural areas. This way, patients remained near their homes, and the cost of treatment was reduced. Later the area of the project extended to other parts of the country. In 1978 LEPRA began an intensive study of the epidemiology of leprosy, using **Karonga** District as a starting point. From 1986 on, trials for a multidrug therapy of Dapsine, Lamprene (Clofazamine), and Rifampicin commenced in Karonga and lasted for 8 to 15 years. In the mid-1990s it was said that the project had succeeded in dealing with the leprosy problems. However, in early 2001, the Queen Elizabeth Central Hospital in Blantyre announced an increase in leprosy patients.

LEVER BROTHERS. Malawi's main producer of cooking oil, detergent, and soap. It is based in **Limbe** and linked to the international conglomerate Unilever. Lever Brothers has dominated the economy of **Malawi** since the 1950s.

LIBRARIES. *See* NATIONAL ARCHIVES; NATIONAL LIBRARY SERVICE.

LIFE AND WORK. The official magazine of the **Blantyre Mission**, founded by Rev. **David Clement Scott**. Missionaries used it as a vehicle to oppose government policies, especially those concerning land and labor.

LIKAYA-MBEWE, SMART. Entertainer whose stage name, Kapalepale, is synonymous with popular culture in Malawi from 1966 to 1992. *Kapalepale* was actually the title of a 30-minute ciChewa play aired on Radio Malawi every Saturday evening. Until the late 1970s, the plays centered on issues concerning everyday life with which people could easily identify: feuds between neighbors in an urban context, a person from a remote village mesmerized by life in a city he or she is visiting for the first time, an adulterous village headman, and so on. It was the most popular program on the radio, making the main character, Kapalepale (Likaya-Mbewe), a household name. His rise from a simple messenger at the MBC to a national personality enhanced his reputation as, for many, he became a role model. However, from the early 1980s to the 1990s, the play became influenced by **Malawi Congress Party** (MCP) politics, and it became identified with the ruling party's propaganda. *See also* MALAWI BROADCASTING CORPORATION.

LIKHUBULA. Located on the Likhubula stream, near the **Mitsidi**, on the periphery of **Blantyre**, this was the headquarters of **Joseph Booth**'s **Zambezi Industrial Mission** (ZIM).

LIKOMA. Largest island on **Lake Malawi**, originally inhabited by **fishing** communities related to peoples on both sides of the lake. From 1885 to the middle of the 20th century, Likoma was the main center of the **Universities' Mission to Central Africa** (UMCA), and it was from there that Anglican missionary activities spread to the rest of the Lake Malawi region. Many people from the Mozambican and Tanzanian hinterlands migrated to Likoma and the neighboring Chizumulu after the missionaries set up operations there. One of the results of Likoma's long association with Western **education** is that it has the highest literacy rate in Malawi. Likoma is also famous for its majestic cathedral, completed and consecrated in 1911, as the largest building in **Malawi**.

LIKULEZI. A major Catholic center in the Southern Region and the location of two seminaries. It is the home of the **Oblates of the Holy Family**, a Malawian order of Brothers; it is also the mission station where the Diocesan Society of African Sisters are trained. In 1969 it became the site of the Catechetical Training College directed by Father **Matthew Schoffeleers**. The curriculum included pastoral anthropology, Malawian culture, and **Africanization**.

LIKUNI. Likuni, in the heartland of **Chewa** country, became one of the main Catholic missions of the **White Fathers** in 1903. A few miles southwest of **Lilongwe** city, it is now a major Catholic educational center, boasting a girls' and a boys' secondary school, a printing establishment, and a big hospital.

LILONGWE. With a population of over a quarter of a million, Lilongwe has been the capital of **Malawi** since 1975. Located in the heartland of

Chewa country, Lilongwe became the site of a *boma* in 1902, after the local chief, Njewa, requested its establishment. At the time, the area was called Bwaila, and the new *boma,* was named after the nearby river, Lilongwe. In 1904 it became the district headquarters, and within two years the first **Asian** traders arrived at the *boma,* the **African Lakes Company** (**Mandala**) having already established its presence there. Lilongwe became even more important in 1909, when a trunk road was constructed connecting it with **Fort Manning** in the west and **Fort Jameson** in Northern Rhodesia. The connection with Dedza had been built four years earlier. In 1910 the area was separated into Dedza District and Lilongwe District. At that time Lilongwe town boasted a boma, a growing population of Africans, Asians, and Europeans, a Mandala store, a post office, and a **White Father**'s mission at nearby **Likuni**. Even at this early date, Lilongwe was the junction of the major north-south and east-west roads.

Although local **tobacco** *(labu)* had been grown in **Lilongwe** District, its commercial growth was encouraged only after World War I, and in 1930 the **Imperial Tobacco Company** opened a factory. Major European planters such as **A. F. Barron** and **R. F. Wallace** established large plantations in the area; Lilongwe also became a major area of operations for the **Native Tobacco Board** (NTB) and later for other tobacco organizations. The city has the largest tobacco floors in the country.

In 1964 Dr. **Hastings K. Banda** announced that his Gwelo Plan no. 2 was to begin, which included the construction of the lakeshore road, establishment of the **University of Malawi**, and relocation of the capital from **Zomba** to Lilongwe. When the British government refused to fund the new capital plan, the Malawi government turned to the **South African** government for loans. In 1968 the Capital City Development Corporation was established to build the capital city, which was officially inaugurated in 1975. Many commercial businesses in **Blantyre** now have branches in Lilongwe. In keeping with the expansion of the city as the national capital, the new Lilongwe International Airport opened in 1983, and work on a new state house was completed in the early 1990s. The post-Banda government did not use the state house for its original purpose, leaving a decision on its fate to parliament. Lilongwe is also the home of educational institutions such the **Kamuzu College of Nursing** and the **Malawi Institute of Management** (MIMS).

LIMBE. Located nearly five miles east of **Blantyre**, Limbe developed primarily as an important terminus of the railway into Nyasaland. Limbe also became the headquarters of the **Imperial Tobacco Company** (ITC), which depended heavily on rail **transportation** and, like the rail company itself, became a major employer of local labor. By 1905 Limbe had grown enough to be declared a town, guided by a mayor and a town council. Limbe also came to be associated with **Asian** business, as many people from the Indian subcontinent settled there. In 1956 Limbe and Blantyre joined under one mayor, and in 1959 the Amalgamated Council was transformed into the municipality of Blantyre and Limbe. *See also* TRANSPORTATION.

The road to **Zomba** begins in Limbe and passes through some of the main **tobacco**-producing areas in the country. Limbe is also on the routes to **Thyolo** and **Mulanje** Districts, the principal **tea**-growing regions of Malawi. To the immediate southeast of the town is the Mzedi Catholic Mission, home to St. Patrick Secondary School. Limbe boasts two other educational institutions, Soche Secondary School and Our Lady of Wisdom Secondary School, situated next to the Limbe Catholic Cathedral. Limbe is the headquarters of the **Agricultural Development and Marketing Corporation** (ADMARC), seat of **Lever Brothers** and the Chiperoni blanket factory, and home of numerous light industries. The central sorting post office is located in Limbe, as is the **Shire Highlands Hotel**, one of the oldest hospitality establishments in the country.

LIPENGA, KEN. Author and minister of education and culture in the post-1999 **United Democratic Front** (UDF) government. Lipenga graduated from the **University of Malawi** before doing graduate work at the University of Leeds (M.A.), United Kingdom, and the University of New Brunswick, **Canada**, where he was awarded a Ph.D. degree in English literature. He taught at the **University of Malawi** until the mid-1980s, when he was appointed editor in chief of the *Daily Times,* a position he relinquished in the period of the agitation for political reform. Subsequently, he became an activist in the UDF party, and after the 1994 elections he became President **Bakili Muluzi**'s political adviser and speechwriter. In 1997 he successfully contested for parliament as member for a **Phalombe** constituency and was appointed deputy minister of foreign affairs. In 1999 he was returned to the National Assembly and was appointed minister of education and culture. During a cabinet reshuffle in November 2000, he became minister of tourism and public works.

LITERATURE. In addition to the rich tradition of oral family and clan histories and accounts of the migration of groups such as the **Maravi, Chikulamayembe**, **Ngoni**, and **Kyungu**, Malawi has a modern literary tradition. In the colonial period, this tradition was nurtured by missionary organizations, almost all of which had printing presses. Individual missionaries took an interest in the writers and encouraged them to publish their manuscripts. Reverend Charles Stuart encouraged **Yesaya Mlonyeni Chibambo** to publish his *Makani gha baNgoni;* J. P. Brewer and Rev. **T. Cullen Young** encouraged **Samuel Josiah Ntara**, and J. L. Pretorius, **Yesaya Mwasi**. Among other early authors are Steven Kumakanga, *Nzeru a Kale* (1932), E. W. Chafulumira, *Kazitape* (1950), *Kantini* (1954), and *Mfumu Watsopano* (1962).

Since the 1960s, a strong tradition of writing in English has developed. Despite President **Hastings K. Banda**'s censorship, the Writers Workshop at **Chancellor College** of the **University of Malawi** has contributed immensely by encouraging prospective writers to realize their ambitions. Some members of this group began to publish their literary anthologies, and in 1977 nine plays written for the National Theatre of Malawi were published. Writers who have belonged to this group include Steve Chimombo, Christopher Kamlongera, **Ken Lipenga**, **Blaze Machila**, **Jack Mapanje**, Felix Mnthali, Lupenga Mpande, Anthony Nazombe, James Ng'ombe, Patrick O'Malley, and Paul Zeleza, all of whom are household names in Malawian literary circles. In its own way, the Writers Corner program at the highly politicized Radio Malawi of the **Malawi Broadcasting Corporation** (MBC) also played a notable role in nursing the ambitions of writers.

Many Malawian authors have published overseas in series such as Heinemann's African Writers Series, and a similar one by Longman. However, local publishing houses, including Popular Publications in its Malawian Writers Series, have been the main publishers of Malawian literature in English. During the rule of the **Malawi Congress Party** (MCP), writers had to be careful about the contents of their stories and about the **language** they used. The Censorship Board had to approve manuscripts before they were published, and an author who ignored the requirement could be imprisoned.

The first Malawians to write in English include **Legson Kayira**, *I Will Try* (1965), *Looming Shadow* (1967), *Jingala* (1969) and *Civil Servant* (1971); **Aubrey Kachingwe**, *No Easy Task (*1966); and **David Rubadiri**, *No Bride Price* (1967).

LIVINGSTONE, DR. DAVID. One of the most famous British missionaries and travelers of the 19th century. Livingstone was born at Blantyre, near Glasgow, Scotland, in 1813. As a boy he led a difficult life that included working in the coal mines of Scotland. But as he grew, his ambition was to become a missionary in China. After qualifying as a medical doctor in 1840, however, he changed his mind, joined the London Missionary Society, and left for Southern Africa to work with Rev. Robert Moffat, his future father-in-law, who was then stationed in Griqualand. Besides missionary work, Livingstone traveled extensively, culminating in the 1856 journey that took him from Angola to **Mozambique** on the east coast of Africa.

After he published *Missionary Travels and Researches in South Africa* (1857), he commenced his Zambezi expedition (1858–1963). This brought Livingstone up the **Shire River** and into southern and central Malawi. With Livingstone's retinue in the 1850s were several **Kololo** from the upper Zambezi area who subsequently stayed in the Lower Shire region and established themselves as chiefs there. In 1859 he made three journeys. One was to **Chikwawa** and another to **Lake Chilwa**, and they allowed him to observe firsthand the ravages of the **slave trade**. His third trip brought him to the shores of **Lake Malawi**. In 1861 Livingstone made another lake trip, visiting **Nkhotakota** and **Bandawe**. That same year he also helped the **Universities' Mission to Central Africa** (UMCA) settle in at their ill-fated **Magomero** mission site. During Livingstone's visit to the Lake Malawi region in 1863, he and his party traveled along the lakeshore and then west to **Kasungu**. The travel pattern set by Livingstone would be followed by succeeding European travelers: from the Zambezi River, north and up the Shire to the Murchison Cataracts, overland to Matope, and returning to the Shire until reaching Lake Malawi. Only the rail system that was built in the 20th century changed this earlier pattern.

In 1866 Livingstone returned to Malawi, traveling from Tanganyika along the east coast of Lake Malawi, turning south to Lake Malombe and then west into the Dedza Highlands. On this journey, as on earlier ones, he fought tirelessly against the slave trade. He did, however, show considerable tolerance and often had friendly relations with the **Swahili-Arab** traders. He died at Chitambo, **Zambia**, in 1873, and his body was carried to **Zanzibar** by Africans, led by Susi and **Chuma**, the servants he had recruited in the **Shire Highlands**. In the United Kingdom, his death roused much interest in missionary work, resulting in the establishment of the **Livingstonia Mission** in 1874. The **African Lakes Company** (ALC) was also a response to Livingstone's call for Christianity, commerce, and Western civilization in Africa. **Blantyre**, Malawi's largest commercial city, is named after Livingstone's birthplace. *See also* MISSIONS.

LIVINGSTONE, WILLIAM JERVIS. Distant relation of Dr. **David Livingstone** and manager of the 169,000-acre **A. L. Bruce Estates** at

Magomero. On the night of January 23, 1915, Livingstone was beheaded by his workers, most of whom were followers of **John Chilembwe**. Born on the Island of Lismore in western Scotland, Livingstone was recruited in 1894 by A. L. Bruce initially to grow **coffee** on the estate. He failed, as did many other Europeans in the **Shire Highlands**, but Livingstone showed that the area could produce **cotton** profitably. However, as the commission of inquiry into the **Chilembwe uprising** showed, William J. Livingstone was a particularly harsh manager who abused the *thangata* system in the extreme. He ignored the laws regulating the employment of labor. Laborers were forced to work for tax for two months and for tenancy for another two to three months; the working hours were long and the wages very poor. Livingstone would evict tenants without notice, causing much hardship to families, and he burned the churches John Chilembwe built on his estate.

LIWONDE. City named after Liwonde, a **Yao** chief, and located at the point where the **Zomba-Lilongwe** road crosses the **Shire River**. Liwonde is a small but thriving commercial center that is known for its **fishing** industry and the barrage on the Shire. Increasingly, however, it has become famous for the Liwonde National Park, which opened in the mid-1970s and is known for its rare species of flora and the game that live there.

LIVINGSTONIA MISSION. *See* EDUCATION; MISSIONS.

LIVULEZI. First mission station (1887) of the **Livingstonia Mission**. Located in a valley in northeast **Ntcheu** District in a region under the influence of the Maseko **Ngoni**, the area was primarily a **Chewa** one but was already recognizing the authority of the Ngoni Chief, Chikusi. For the Scottish missionaries, a foothold in this area was an important step toward establishing their presence in Maseko Ngoni country.

LIZULU. Traditional headquarters of the Maseko **Ngoni** and the seat of the **Gomani** authority. It is located near the **Blantyre-Lilongwe** road, halfway between Dedza and **Ntcheu**.

LOMWE. Ethnic group that inhabits mostly **Mulanje, Phalombe, Thyolo, Blantyre, Chiradzulu**, and parts of **Zomba** District. For a number of reasons, including drought and **famine**, and the hardship of living under Portuguese authority, the Lomwe emigrated from southern **Mozambique** between the 1880s and the 1920s. Many of them were victims of *thangata*, and a significant number joined **John Chilembwe's Provi-**

dence Industrial Mission and supported his uprising. Many Lomwe also joined the **police** and the **army**.

LOMWE TRIBAL SOCIETY. Short-lived society (1943–1945) chaired by **Lewis Mataka Bandawe**. Its principal aim was to improve the image of the **Lomwe** and raise their ethnic consciousness. One of their major successes was convincing the government to cease referring to the Lomwe by the somewhat pejorative name Anguru.

LONDON & BLANTYRE SUPPLY COMPANY. Mother company of **Kandodo** and one of the major European import and export companies established at the beginning of the 20th century.

LONG, PETER. Commissioner of **police** of Malawi from December 1964 to 1972. Long joined the Metropolitan Police in England in 1936. He worked in the Jamaican constabulary from 1938 to 1951, when he was reassigned to the **Nyasaland** police. As superintendent, he was charged with the task of improving the Criminal Investigation Division (CID). He was rapidly promoted, and by August 1963 he was deputy commissioner of police. When J. V. Mullin left Malawi in November of the following year, Peter Long took over the headship of the police of independent **Malawi**. He is credited with adding a dog section and a marine wing to the police force.

LONGWE, REV. AARON. Human rights activist, vocal advocate of political reform, and member of the **Public Affairs Committee** (PAC). Aaron Longwe was trained as a pastor in **Malawi** and worked in the Synod of **Livingstonia**. He studied further in Scotland and, on his return, became one of a new generation of politically aware church ministers. Later he helped establish the Foundation for Justice and Peace through which he promoted human rights. Several times in 1992, Longwe was arrested and released. When the **Alliance for Democracy** (AFORD) was formed, he became one of its spokesmen. He later left the party because of disagreements with its leadership. Longwe died in 1997.

LONGWE, BAGEYA. A female witch finder from Mphongo in Lundazi District, **Northern Rhodesia**. Longwe's fame spread to the **Nyasaland** side of the border. She was particularly active during World War II. Hundreds of people in the two colonies went to her with their ailments; she was also invited away from her home to cure the sick and detect sorcerers. In 1942–1943 she cured nyaGama, the *inkosikazi ya makhosikazi* (principal wife) of M'mbelwa II, after she had returned from a Western hospital still ill. The result was that more people flocked to Bageya, and M'mbelwa gave an unofficial green light to her presence in his area. Disturbed by her popularity, the **district commissioner** (DC) at **Mzimba** summoned M'mbelwa and accused him of aiding disorder and unlawful activities. In the magistrate's court, the paramount chief, advised by **Charles Chinula**, successfully argued that Bageya was a legitimate healer, even though some thought she was not a genuine witch finder. M'mbelwa was acquitted, but Bageya was sent to **Zomba** Central prison for one year.

LONGWE, JANET. Nkhata Bay District chairman of the **League of Malawi Women** from 1961 to 1968. Longwe attended primary school in the district and worked as a medical attendant for some time before becoming a full-time **Malawi Congress Party** (MCP) activist. In 1968 she became MP for Nkhata Bay South but left the National Assembly a few years later.

LONRHO. Short for London and Rhodesian Mining Company. Lonrho was taken over by Roland "Tiny" Rowland (1917–1988) an English businessman in 1963. Although based in England, earlier he had worked in **Southern Rhodesia.** Lonrho grew into a major commercial empire with interests in the United Kingdom, the Middle East, and Africa. In **Malawi,** Lonrho became involved in engineering, car dealerships, and agro-business, mainly **sugar** production at Nchalo in the Lower Shire and at Dwangwa in **Nkhotakota**. Rowland became particularly close to Dr. **Hastings K. Banda**, and this made him and his companies particularly powerful in Malawi. In the early 1990s Lonrho began to withdraw from Malawi and sold its sugar interests to a South African firm based in Durban.

LOUDON MISSION. Located at Embangweni, near the seat of Inkosi **Mzukuzuku**, the mission was established in 1902 with the aid of £1,000 donated by the widow of Dr. Loudon of Hamilton, a friend of **David Livingstone**. This became one of the two major **Ngoni**-based Church of Scotland Missions in Ngoniland. The mission, headed in its formative years by the liberal **Donald Fraser**, produced distinguished Malawians such as **Charles Chinula** and **Mkhosi Lazalo Jere**. The station had a hospital and later a teachers college, which in the early 1980s was converted into the **Robert Laws** Secondary School.

LOVEDALE MISSIONARY INSTITUTE. Major educational center in the Eastern Cape, **South Africa**. Later known as Lovedale College and usually referred to simply as Lovedale. The Missionary Institute was established by the Free Church of Scotland in the 19th century. Dr. **James Stewart**, the first head of the **Livingstonia Mission** in the 1870s, was the principal of Lovedale during the last quarter of the 19th century. Livingstonia was partly modeled on Lovedale, and in the 1880s and 1890s some of the students who had distinguished themselves at Livingstonia and even at **Blantyre** were sent for further training at Lovedale. In the early 1900s Lovedale was headed by James Henderson, formerly of the **Overtoun Institute** at **Khondowe**.

LUBANI, LALI. Prominent **Blantyre** businessman. From the 1940s to his death in July 1966, Lubani strongly supported the nationalist cause. Having little Western education, Lubani worked for the Central Africa Transport Company (CATCO) as a driver-mechanic. In 1948 he resigned to become a full-time businessman, mainly as a transporter and brick maker. Always generous with his money, Lubani, a devout Muslim, used some of his profits to establish a school that offered Islamic and Western **education** to children of African Muslims. He regularly gave financial assistance to **Nyasaland African Congress** (NAC) leaders to ease administrative and transport problems. In 1960 he became one of the most respected members of the National Executive Committee of the **Malawi Congress Party** (MCP); he also held important positions in local and national Islamic organizations.

LUBWA. Located in **Bemba** country on the western shores of Lake Bangweulu, Northern Zambia, this was the site of the **Livingstonia Mission** station. It was initially headed by **David Julizya Kaunda**, father of **Kenneth Kaunda**, first president of **Zambia**. Kenneth Kaunda was born in Lubwa and brought up there.

LUCHENZA. Located in the center of the **tea**-growing area, Luchenza sits on the border of **Thyolo** and **Mulanje** Districts. In August 1953 it was the scene of a conflict between Basil Tennent, a planter, on the one hand, and African employees and a local chief, on the other. The underlying cause of the problem lay in long-standing land issues. The incident attained national proportions partly because it coincided with the introduction of the **Federation of Rhodesia and Nyasaland** and unpopular agricultural and conservation measures. Luchenza is also widely known as the home of the Luchenza Flying Club, which was established in 1933 and was still in existence in the 1990s.

LUGARD, LORD FREDERICK DENHAM. One of the major empire builders in the 19th and 20th centuries. Lugard's initial serious contact with Africa was the **Lake Malawi** area, which he visited in 1887 while on sick leave from his Norfolk Regiment based at Gibraltar. During a brief stop in **Mozambique**, Lieutenant H. E. O'Neill, the British consul there, convinced him to go to the Lake Malawi area to help fight the Swahili-Arabs at **Karonga**. Although Captain Lugard left the region two years later without subduing **Mlozi**, the Swahili-Arab leader, the British army officer had begun to develop an interest in British imperial expansion in Africa. He left military service and devoted himself for the next 50 years to imperial issues, becoming known as the foremost theorist in British colonial policy. He served in Hong Kong and in other parts of Africa, including Uganda and Nigeria, the structure of which he created. Lord Lugard died in 1942, having become a baron. Among the books he wrote are *The Rise of Our East African Empire,* vols. 1–2 (1893), *Political Memorandum* (1906), and the *Dual Mandate* (1929). *See also* ARAB-SWAHILI WAR; INDIRECT RULE SYSTEM.

LUNDU. Dynasty of **Mang'anja** chiefs located in the Lower Shire. These chiefs trace their origins to the original **Kalonga**, the founder of the **Maravi** state. Like other dynasties associated with the expansion of the Maravi in the 16th century, Lundu belonged to the Phiri matriclan. Strongly associated with the M'bona religious order, the original Lundu headquarters were at Mbewe-ya-Mitengo. From there, in an attempt to control the ivory trade, they expanded south toward the Zambezi River and west to the Lolo and Makua region.

LUNGU, MORDECAI MALANI. Born in 1930 near Euthini, **Mzimba** District, Lungu graduated from **Domasi** Teacher's College, became MP for Mzimba North in 1966, and three years later was assigned to the Ministry of Education. In July 1977 he was appointed regional minister for the Northern Region, and in the early 1980s, he was appointed Speaker of parliament, a position he held until his death in 1993. A loyal party man, he resisted changing to multiparty democracy. He became an active spokesman for the **Malawi Congress Party** (MCP) during the 1991–1993 period, as the country moved toward the first free **elections** in over 30 years. He died in 1993.

LUNGUZI, MACWILLIAMS. Born in Dedza District, where he also went to school before attending the Police Training School. After regular duties he joined the **Special Branch** (security), and for some time he was attached to Malawi embassies abroad. He had a meteoric rise in the **police** force, and in 1990 he was promoted to inspector general. He remained in that position until the **United Democratic Party** (UDF) party formed a new government in July 1994. Lunguzi, who had already been identified with the **Malawi Congress Party** (MCP), now became a full-time official of the party and was considered an effective organizer. He died in a car accident on the **Kasungu-Lilongwe** road in 1997.

– M –

MABILABO. The southernmost **Ngoni** chief under the M'mbelwa. His area, bordering on **Kasungu** District, is also known as Mabilabo.

MACDONALD, REV. DUFF. In July 1878 Duff Macdonald arrived in the **Shire Highlands** to assume the headship of the Church of Scotland Mission, which **Henry Henderson** had established at **Blantyre** two years earlier. The mission became involved in the civil administration of the mission station, leading to abuses such as village burning and corporal punishment. The mission did not have a large budget and had to depend on lay missionaries such as **George Fenwick** who were unfit for missionary work. In 1881 Macdonald and other missionaries, including Fenwick and **John Buchanan**, were dismissed from mission service after a Foreign Mission Committee inquiry showed that the **Blantyre Mission** had been badly managed. In the year of his dismissal, Macdonald published *Africana*, a two-volume work dealing with the early history of the mission and with the customs of the African peoples among whom he had worked.

MACDONALD, SIR MALCOLM. Secretary of state for the colonies in the late 1930s. Macdonald accepted the inevitability of decolonization and opposed the amalgamation of the Rhodesias and **Nyasaland** because he feared that it would not be in the interest of the Africans. In the early 1960s Malcolm Macdonald became the governor and high commissioner to Kenya.

MACHEL, SAMORA MOISES. First president of **Mozambique**. Samora Machel was born in the Gaza region in 1933 and attended Catholic schools before training as a nurse. In 1963 he went into exile in **Tanzania**, where he became an active member of **FRELIMO**, gradually rising through the ranks until 1970, when he became head of the liberation movement. In June 1975 he became president of the newly decolonized Mozambique. But by the end of the 1970s his country was at war with **RENAMO**, the antigovernment guerrilla movement at first supported by Rhodesia and later by **South Africa**. Machel accused

Dr. **Hastings K. Banda**'s government of giving logistic assistance to RENAMO and threatened to bomb important installations in **Malawi**. Machel died in October 1986, when his plane crashed into the Libombo Mountains on the South African side of the Mozambique border.

MACHILA, BLAZE. College professor who taught at **Chancellor College** from 1976 to 1988. Machila was born in **Thyolo** District and educated at the **University of Malawi**, the University of Wisconsin, and the Australian National University. A close associate of **Jack Mapanje**, Machila was so disturbed by the imprisonment of his friend that he would often walk to the **Zomba** police station, and even the state house, to demand an explanation for the government action. In 1988 he himself was detained at **Mikuyu**, in spite of the fact that by that time he was suffering from a psychiatric illness. He died a few years later.

MACHINGA. Formerly known as Kasupe, this district was once a division of **Zomba** District. Machinga *boma*, the district headquarters, is scenically located on the southern slope of the Zomba range of mountains facing the Rift Valley, where the **Shire River** flows south. Machinga *boma* was originally established as a post to guard against the **Yao** chiefs **Kawinga** and **Liwonde**.

MACKENZIE, BISHOP CHARLES FREDERICK. Head of the first **Universities' Mission to Central Africa** (UMCA) party. Mackenzie was born in 1825 and educated at Caius College, Cambridge, where he also taught for a brief period. In 1852 he was ordained as a priest, after which he worked as a minister in the Cambridge area. Two years later, he became archdeacon of Natal, **South Africa**. His return to England in 1859 coincided with efforts to assemble the first UMCA mission party. The UMCA was a response to **David Livingstone**'s famous speech at Cambridge University in December 1857, appealing to the British to follow up his work in Africa. The Universities of Cambridge, Oxford, Durham, and Dublin set up a joint mission that they called the Universities' Mission to Central Africa. Mackenzie was appointed its head, and in 1860 the party set off for Africa. They stopped in Cape Town, where on New Year's Day, 1861, Mackenzie was consecrated bishop "to the tribes dwelling in the neighborhood of Lake Nyasa and the River Shire." From Kongone the vessel carrying the UMCA group, the *Pioneer*, traveled up the Zambezi River and then the Shire until they reached a group of **Mang'anja** villages under Chief Mankhokwe, who ruled the area as far north as **Lake Chilwa**. Since the chief would only allow them a brief stay in his area, they moved on further north to the country of the more friendly Chibisa and then finally to **Magomero**, which they reached on July 19 and made their headquarters.

Magomero was then at the center of the **slave trade**, the Mang'anja being the main subjects of **Yao** raiders. Mackenzie saw it as his duty to intervene whenever occasion called. Soon Magomero became a home for **refugees** escaping from the slavers, and Mackenzie and his colleagues even engaged in battles with the Yao, who viewed the mission as interfering in their business. In January 1862 Mackenzie accompanied his colleague, Henry Burrup, to the Lower Shire, where they were to meet the latter's sister. By the time they got to the mouth of the Luo, both were ill with diarrhea and malaria, which they were unable to treat because they had lost their medicine chest on the way. Mackenzie died there on January 31 and was buried at **Chiromo** on the left bank of the **Shire River**. Three weeks later, Burrup died at Magomero. Mackenzie's body was later exhumed and transferred to the **Blantyre** church named after him.

On April 25 the remaining UMCA party left Magomero for Chibisa's area. When **William Tozer** arrived in June the following year to take over as the new bishop, the mission moved further south to Mount Morambala. The new site was no better than Magomero, and in 1864 the UMCA moved to **Zanzibar**, where it trained most of the Africans who were to take part in the renewed mission efforts in the Lake Malawi region 20 years later. *See also* AMBALI, AUGUSTINE; EDUCATION; KILEKWA, PETRO; MISSONS.

MACLEOD, IAIN. Harold **Macmillan**'s secretary of state for the colonies from early 1959 to October 1961. Macleod ordered the release of Dr. **Hastings K. Banda** from prison in Gweru, **Southern Rhodesia**, and met him in **Zomba** on April 1, 1960. He then arranged for the **Lancaster House** Constitutional talks, set the timetable for the first general **elections** in 1961, and replaced Sir **Robert Armitage** as governor with Sir **Glyn Jones**, thereby creating a more friendly atmosphere for political change in the colony.

MACMILLAN, MAURICE HAROLD. British prime minister from January 1957 to October 1963. Macmillan appointed **Iain Macleod** as colonial secretary and appointed the **Devlin Commission** and the **Monckton Commission.** In his famous 1960 "winds of change" speech during his visit to **South Africa**, he warned the South African government to accept the inevitability of change. In February of that year, he stopped briefly in **Nyasaland**. While he was attending a luncheon at the **Ryall's Hotel**,

Malawi Congress Party (MCP) protestors reacted to police action, leading to a minor scuffle that in turn led to the **Southworth Commission of Inquiry**. In 1963 Macmillan retired from active politics, and in 1984 he became first Earl of Stockton. He died in 1986.

MAFINGA MOUNTAINS. Lying in a north-south direction, this range of mountains forms part of the border between northeastern **Zambia** and **Malawi**. It is an important source of water for many people in northern Malawi, especially those in **Chitipa** District.

MAGOMERO. Site located in north **Chiradzulu** District. Magomero features prominently in the history of 19th- and 20th-century **Malawi** as the site of the first **Universities' Mission to Central Africa** (UMCA) mission, as the home of the **A. L. Bruce Estates**, and from the 1960s to the early 1990s as the location of the **Nasawa** Young Pioneer Training Base. *See also* CHILEMBWE, JOHN; MACKENZIE, CHARLES.

MAGUIRE, CECIL. Brother of Rochfort Maguire, **Cecil Rhodes**'s private secretary. Captain Maguire was the first commander of the military force established by **Harry Johnston** in 1891. The force consisted of 71 Indian soldiers, over half of whom were Sikhs, a few **Zanzibar** citizens, and later some local people. Maguire became central to Johnston's plans for establishing the Pax Britannica in the **Lake Malawi** region, but in December 1891 he was killed in action against the **Yao** chief, Makanjila. The British built a fort in the area, named it after him, and used it as a staging area to subdue **Makanjila** and **Makandanji** in 1894.

MAIZE. Maize remains the staple food crop in **Malawi** as well as the principal crop of the smallholder sector. Some farmers grow hybrid varieties for sale to the **Agricultural Development and Marketing Board** (AD-MARC) and other markets. But with rising fertilizer prices, the acreage devoted to high-yielding maize varieties tended to decline. Large increases in its producer price resulted in sizable marketed surpluses and effectively turned maize into an export commodity. Export was relatively easy and profitable in 1983 and 1984, when drought affected a number of neighboring countries. Maize exports peaked in 1984, but excessively heavy rains in 1985 meant that maize production was 3 percent below the 1984 record crop. A hot spell affecting the 1987 maize harvest forced the government to import a quantity of maize, not an easy decision considering the nation's campaign for food self-sufficiency. To meet the widespread shortages, especially in **Nkhata Bay**, **Chikwawa**, and **Nsanje** Districts, a free food distribution program began in late 1987.

Weather problems (drought, heat, dry spells, flooding) continued to plague the nation's main staple. In 1990 maize production again had fallen and the severe shortage had to be met with government distribution of tons of relief maize. Nsanje District lacked sufficient food, although the government denied its people were starving. In addition to the vagaries of nature, maize production is hampered by the fact that 60 percent of Malawi's smallholders have insufficient land on which to grow maize. They have to survive by wage employment and depend on the market for their food. Additionally, 80 percent of all smallholders have no access to credit, and only a quarter have access to or use fertilizer. With massive devaluations of the Malawi **kwacha** in the 1990s, the price of fertilizer has risen, making access to it more difficult.

In the 1990s two droughts adversely affected the production of maize, forcing the government to import from **South Africa** and **Zimbabwe**. *See also* AGRICULTURE; FINANCIAL AND ECONOMIC DEVELOPMENTS.

MAJERE-HENGA. *See* GONDWE, KANYOLI .

MAKAMO, NG'ONOMO. A **Zansi Ngoni** of Thonga origins. Ng'onomo was the most powerful *induna* (counsellor) of the **M'mbelwas** in the late 19th and early 20th centuries. Ng'onomo was a key policy formulator and, after the M'mbelwa, the most dominant person in Ngoni country. Generally considered an uncompromising hawk, he was the mastermind of continued raids into the Nyika-**Karonga** area and east into the Luangwa region, long after the Ngoni had given up their warlike tendencies. Ng'onomo was suspicious of Western influence, strongly resisted British authority, and was prepared to send Ngoni warriors to assist other Africans, including **Mpezeni** and **Mwase Kasungu**, in staving off European rule. Missionaries found him difficult to deal with, and on several occasions he warned them not to interfere with the Ngoni way of life, which he was determined to protect. Ng'onomo Makamo died in 1907.

MAKANDANJI. One of the **Yao** chiefs who strongly resisted British rule in the 19th century. In 1894 he and **Zarafi** went to the assistance of **Makanjila**, but the British, led by Captain Edwards and fighting from nearby **Fort Maguire**, defeated them.

MAKANJILA. Mountainous area in northeastern **Mangochi** District named after its **Yao** ruling family. Of the Masaninga section of the Yao, the Makanjila of the 1880s and 1890s mobilized his people and strongly resisted the extension of British authority in the region. In turn, he and several other chiefs became subjects of British punitive expeditions. During one such action in 1891 Makanjila's men killed Captain **Cecil Maguire**, the British commander. In 1894 Makanjila was defeated and his subjects were forced to accept British rule.

MAKATA. Of the Mangoche section of the **Yao**, this chief and his people settled in the **Blantyre** area in the 1860s.

MAKATA, LAWRENCE. Successful **Blantyre**-based **Yao** businessman. Makata was a political activist and belonged to the central executive of the **Malawi Congress Party** (MCP). For most of the 1940s, Makata was a driver-mechanic in the employ of Hall's Garage, resigning in 1948 to become an independent businessman. Like his close associate, **Lali Lubani**, he became a brick maker and transporter and maintained close links with nationalist politicians. He too regularly supported the **Nyasaland African Congress** (NAC) financially. Makata died in an automobile accident in 1962.

MAKHUMULA, JAMES LEANERD. One of Malawi's most successful businessmen, Makhumula was born and raised in **Zomba** District. He worked for the government as a mechanic and motor vehicle examiner before retiring from the civil service in the 1970s. In the early 1980s he started the Yanu Yanu Bus Company, which was the first nationally operated **transportation** concern owned by a Malawian. In the 1990s he became active in the political reform movement. A founding member of the **United Democratic Front** (UDF), he was elected to parliament in 1994 and was appointed to the cabinet. In 1999 he was reelected to the National Assembly as member for the Zomba Nsondole constituency. This time he did not become a government minister but remained national treasurer of the UDF and an influential member of the central executive of the party. In 2001 Makhumula resigned from the UDF.

MAKHUMULA-NKHOMA, PEARSON. Former minister for the Southern Region. Makhumula-Nkhoma was born in **Zomba** District in 1933 and was educated at the **Henry Henderson Institute** and Zomba Catholic School. He qualified as a teacher at **Domasi** Teachers College and later attended Bristol University for one year. As a teacher–education officer he taught in the Southern Region, served as an educational attaché at the Malawi Embassy in Washington, D.C., and in 1971 entered the National Assembly as MP for Zomba. In the following year, President **Hastings K. Banda** appointed him minister of local government. In 1977 he became minister for the Southern Region, but in the early 1980s he fell out of favor with the **Malawi Congress Party** (MCP), losing his positions in the party and government. Subsequently, he became a director of the **Yanu Yanu Bus Company**, one of the most successful indigenous enterprises in Malawi. He died in 1998.

MAKWINJA, ABITI DOROTHY. Chair of the **League of Malawi Women** in **Zomba** District from the early 1970s to the early 1980s. With Mrs. Tsamwa of **Blantyre** and **Hilda Manjamkhosi** of **Lilongwe**, Makwinja was one of the most powerful **women** in Malawi. Like the two others, she had direct access to President **Hastings K. Banda**, who valued her views and took action accordingly. Abiti Makwinja was a recipient of housing built for some Women Leaguers at Banda's direction.

MAKWINJA, ALEXANDER. Early Seventh Day Baptist Church convert and student of **Joseph Booth**. Makwinja was a **Yao** born near **Blantyre**. He met Booth in the 1890s, and in 1909 became one of the first students at a school that Booth established at Park Hotel in Pretoria, **South Africa**. When he returned to **Nyasaland** in 1910, he became a member of the **Watchtower movement** and an associate of **Eliot Musokwa Kamwana Chirwa**. He headed the Watchtower office at **Shiloh** near Blantyre. In 1915 he was arrested on suspicion of being an associate of **John Chilembwe**. In 1925 he began to preach again, but the Seventh Day Baptists in the **United States** rejected his attempts to work with them. By the time they changed their position in the 1940s, he had decided to work independently of external support.

MALAMULO. Located in **Thyolo** District, the home of the first and the largest station of the Seventh-Day Adventist Church in **Malawi**. Established in 1902 as the **Plainfield Industrial Mission**, Malamulo became the major center for Seventh-Day believers, training African teachers, religious leaders, and hospital workers. From Malamulo, local church workers left to establish outstations such as Matandani and **Mwanza** in the Southern Region and Mombera, Luwazi, and Chambo in the Northern Region. In all these rural areas, schools and **health** clinics were opened. Malamulo has a large hospital that is one of the best-equipped health facilities in the country.

MALAWI. Etymologically meaning "fire flames," the term has been historically associated with the southwestern lake region. Malawi, or **Maravi**, is also an ethnic designation referring to peoples who inhabited an area north of the Zambezi River and south of **Lake Malawi**. One hypothesis holds that the Phiri clan was called Maravi, or "people of the fire flames." It appears that **Chewa** speakers have used the term "Malawi" to indicate Phiri clan members. Although the term has been associated with peoples as well as places, today it refers to the independent nation in south-central Africa that was previously known as **Nyasaland**.

MALAWI AGAINST POLIO (MAP). This charitable organization campaigns to eradicate polio in **Malawi** and to assist its victims in overcoming their affliction. Formed in 1979 by Dr. Jan A. Borgstein, chief of surgery at the Queen Elizabeth Hospital, and His Grace, Donald Arden, then archbishop of Central Africa, it is very involved in the rehabilitation of polio patients. MAP relies on voluntary service and raises money through donations and help from **nongovernmental organizations** (NGOs) and governments to pay its professional staff.

MALAWI BROADCASTING CORPORATION (MBC). The Malawi Broadcasting Corporation (MBC) took over the studios and most of the personnel of the of the **Federal Broadcasting Corporation** (FBC) at the breakup of the **Federation of Rhodesia and Nyasaland**. New local experts were employed and trained mainly with British, German, and American assistance. These countries have at various times also provided studio equipment and transmitters. In its programming, the MBC airs Malawi Correspondence College courses, instructional programs on **agriculture**, and informative school programs that supplement the curriculum. Broadcasts also include the plays and poetry of local writers, and a variety of other programs, including news and music.

During the **Malawi Congress Party** (MCP) government, the autonomy of the MBC was much compromised. The senior management tended to be political appointments, and programs were expected not to conflict with the views of the party and government. Dr. **Hastings K. Banda**'s speeches and attendance of ceremonies, no matter how long, were broadcast live, and then repeated in the evening, to ensure that everyone listened to them. This was sanctioned by the Malawi Broadcasting Corporation Act, which in effect restricted access to Malawi airwaves to those opposed to government. In the period leading to the referendum, the MBC remained an organ of the MCP government and refused to allow debate between the various parties.

After the change of government in 1994, discussions took place regarding the repeal of the act and its replacement by the Communications Act, which would allow for the establishment of the Malawi Communications Regulatory Authority (MACRA), an independent body that would control **communications services** by way of license providers. It was hoped that the MBC would be truly autonomous and open to different political views. However, by 2000, the bill to effect these changes was still to be passed. The MBC Act remained operational with the effect that the MCP and other opposition organizations complained of the **United Democratic Front** (UDF) government's domination of the broadcasting corporation.

MALAWI CHAMBER OF COMMERCE AND INDUSTRY. Umbrella organization of business and industry in Malawi. During the rule of the **Malawi Congress Party** (MCP), the chamber of commerce had a low profile. With the liberalization of the economy and politics in the post-1994 period, however, it has become one of the most influential associations in the country. Its pronouncements on **Malawi**'s economy are taken seriously by the government and **nongovernmental organizations** (NGOs), and its secretariat, manned by highly trained personnel, regularly produces reports on economic trends in the country.

MALAWI CONGRESS PARTY (MCP). On March 2, 1959, a state of emergency was declared in **Nyasaland**; the **Nyasaland African Congress** (NAC) was banned and its leadership jailed. In September of that year, the released Congress members were permitted by the protectorate government to form another political organization. Accordingly, in September 1959 **Orton Chirwa**, lawyer for the NAC, having been released early, founded the Malawi Congress Party and became its acting president, with **Aleke Banda** as secretary-general. Dr. **Hastings K. Banda**, still in Gwelo prison, was kept informed of Congress activities. Membership in the MCP grew quickly and an aggressive broadside, the *Malawi News*, propagated the party's position. The MCP refused to negotiate with British officials until Dr. Banda was released from prison. When Banda left Gweru in April 1960, he found that the administrative skills of the Chirwa-Banda team had provided him with an efficient political machine.

One of the early actions of the MCP was the effective mobilization of African opinion against the **Monckton Commission**, which most Malawians proceeded to boycott. The **Lancaster House Conference**, called by the British government in London in July 1960, agreed to a new constitution and designated **elections** for the following year. In the months of preparation for those elections, Dr. Banda worked closely with local MCP members, choosing the candidates carefully. In the election campaign the MCP had promised voters advancement in the civil service, modernization of **agriculture**, better **education**, and a neutral **foreign policy**. When the August 1961 election results were announced, the MCP had won every (20) lower-roll seat and one-quarter of the upper roll, for a total of 23 seats in the **Legislative Council** (LEGCO). Dr. Banda assumed the post of minister of natural resources. Governor **Glyn Jones** soon granted 7 out of 10 of the **Executive Council**'s seats to the MCP.

The most serious break in the unity of the Malawi Congress Party has been the **Cabinet Crisis** of September 1964. As a direct result of the challenge to power represented by that event, the MCP convention in October 1965 adopted a constitution that made Malawi a one-party state. Furthermore, the new constitution, effective in 1966, established Malawi as a republic with a president who was the head of the government and **army**. The National Assembly, which in theory was the seat of authority, could be called into session or dissolved at the president's will. Consequently, power lay with the president and the ruling party. Candidates in the 1966 election ran unopposed, and in 1971 the election was aborted by Banda and all nominated candidates were considered elected.

The president's control over the MCP permitted him to exert immense influence over the MPs. Disagreements with the president have resulted in a loss of party membership; by law, no one may retain a parliamentary seat who is not a member of the MCP. A 1973 victim of this law was Aleke Banda, who had been a loyal supporter of the president for many years. Since the MCP was the only party permitted in Malawi and because it was effectively controlled by the Life President, most Malawian citizens regarded the government and the party as synonymous. In the 1974 party Constitution it was stated that the MCP was the government of Malawi; subsequently, party officials were given priority over equally ranked government officials. Party control was held by Dr. Banda and his executive committee, assisted by regional and district committees, and at the base of the political pyramid, area and local committees. Whereas the district committees met monthly, the area and local committees met biweekly and weekly, respectively. Often at the regional level, the government ministers and party officials were one and the same. Through **Press Holdings Ltd.**, the MCP and Banda, who was chairman and major shareholder, managed to control a significant segment of Malawi's economy. Press Holdings had investments in **tobacco** estates, an oil company, the Commercial Bank of Malawi, a chain of supermarkets, the **manufacturing** industry, and many other ventures.

The MCP was able to use its considerable authority to enlist community support for the success of rural self-help schemes or new government projects. When there were citizen grievances, the MCP would alert the government on behalf of the populace or, conversely, monitor it for antigovernment activities. In this regard the **League of Malawi Women**, the **Youth League**, and the **Young Pioneers** played a major role as guardians of what the party stood for.

From 1992 to 1994, the MCP strongly resisted moves toward multiparty politics, arguing that such a step would encourage disunity in the country. It lost the referendum in 1993, and in the following June it lost power to the **United Democratic Front** (UDF). Banda retained the presidency of the MCP but, in effect, **Gwanda Chakuamba**, the vice president, led the organization. After Banda's death, Chakuamba was elected president of the party amid signs of disunity, as some would have preferred **John Tembo**. In the 1999 elections the MCP allied itself with the **Alliance for Democracy** (AFORD) but lost to **Bakili Muluzi's** UDF. However, it gained some seats in the Northern and Southern Regions, especially in **Nsanje** District, the home of Chakuamba.

MALAWI COUNCIL FOR THE HANDICAPPED (MACOHA). In 1972 the Malawi parliament passed an act enabling the formation of an organization with a specific mission to handle problems associated with the handicapped. This was the birth of MACOHA. Besides vocational training and rehabilitation, the council raises funds to help it further its aims, and the International Labour Organisation (ILO) is one of its major supporters. MACOHA has a tie-dye workshop in **Lilongwe** but is more famous for its weaving factory at Bangwe, near **Limbe**, which produces, among other items, mats, bedspreads, and wall hangings. In 1997 the factory caught fire, leading to loss of property and jobs for the many disabled who manned it.

MALAWI DEMOCRAT. See DEMOCRAT.

MALAWI DEMOCRATIC PARTY (MDP). One of the political parties formed in 1992 to exert more pressure on President **Hastings K. Banda** to liberalize politics in Malawi. The founder of the party, **Kamlepo Kalua**, campaigned for political reform from **South Africa**, where he used Channel Africa of the South African Broadcasting Corporation to transmit his views to Malawi. Compared with the **United Democratic Front** (UDF), **Malawi Congress Party** (MCP), and the **Alliance for Democracy** (AFORD), the MDP remains a small party. Although it is not represented in the National Assembly, it continues to be vocal, especially on issues such as corruption, **human rights**, **education**, and **health**.

MALAWI DEVELOPMENT CORPORATION (MDC). This holding company, established in 1964 with direct responsibility to the president of Malawi, is charged with developing new enterprises in **mining**, commerce, **agriculture**, and industry. Initially funding was from the United Kingdom, but later the government controlled the shares of this holding company, which until recently had equity in nearly 60 enterprises. Between the MDC, **Press Holdings**, and the **Agricultural Development and Marketing Board** (ADMARC), an intricate, often confusing, interlocking directorate existed, as each parastatal owned a portion of the other and its subsidiaries.

By the mid-1980s, the MDC was so badly managed that the European Community had to assist in its restructuring and reduced by half its equity interest portfolio. By the end of the decade, the MDC was enjoying rising profits. In the post-Banda era some of the enterprises directly controlled by the MDC were privatized.

MALAWI FINANCIAL POST. In 1992 this weekly was the first alternative publication to appear in Malawi, thereby breaking up the domination of the pro-Banda **Malawi Congress Party**/*Malawi News* and the *Daily Times*. The weekly quickly identified itself with the advocates of political reform, particularly the **United Democratic Front** (UDF) party. Its editor, **Alaudin Osman**, had previously edited the *Daily Times* and had worked as senior journalist in Botswana for most of the 1980s. He later became President **Bakili Muluzi**'s chief press spokesman.

MALAWI FREEDOM MOVEMENT (MAFREMO). *See* CHIRWA, ORTON.

MALAWI INSTITUTE OF MANAGEMENT (MIMS). Located just outside **Lilongwe** on the road to the international airport, the Malawi Institute of Management was established with the assistance of the Canadian government in the late 1980s. It serves as an in-service training center for middle and upper-level management personnel.

MALAWI INVESTMENT PROMOTION AGENCY (MIPA). This **Lilongwe**-based agency was created in 1991 by an act of parliament, and it is charged with the responsibility of promoting private and foreign investment in the country. The MIPA helps create an attractive atmosphere for investment by, among other things, ensuring that investors do not contend with bureaucratic and minor impediments in their endeavors.

MALAWI NATIONAL EXAMINATIONS BOARD (MANEB). Organization established by parliament to undertake and oversee the testing and examinations process in the school systems of **Malawi**. Initially mandated for high school level only, in the mid-1980s, it took over all responsibilities concerning examinations formerly administered by the ministry of education.

MALAWI PRESS. See PRESS HOLDINGS LTD.

MALAWI RIFLES. *See* ARMY.

MALAWI YOUNG PIONEERS. *See* YOUTH.

MALEKEBU, DANIEL SHARPE. Born in about 1890 in **Chiradzulu** District. In 1905 Daniel Malekebu became the first Malawian graduate of **John Chilembwe's** mission to study abroad in the **United States**. After graduating from the North Carolina Negro College, now North Carolina Central University, he entered the Meharry Medical College in Nashville, Tennessee, qualifying as a medical doctor in 1917. He went on to study theology so he could go back home as a medical missionary. He returned in 1926, his homecoming having been delayed because the colonial government in **Malawi** feared the possibility that his arrival would rekindle pro-Chilembwe sentiments. Malekebu reorganized and administered the **Providence Industrial Mission** (PIM) for over 30 years, placing emphasis on training nurses and teachers. He was a key personality in the Chiradzulu Native Association in the 1930s, bringing serious cases of injustice to the government's attention and generally working to promote a better quality of life for those to whom he ministered.

MALEMIA. Area in **Zomba** District deriving its name from **Yao** chiefs who have ruled it since the late 1860s, when they were forced to move from Chikala hills to **Domasi** by the actions of the ambitious **Kawinga** and by the push of the Maseko **Ngoni** into the **Shire Valley** area. It was Malemia with whom the Scottish missionaries had to negotiate with before they could establish stations at Zomba and Domasi.

MALEWEZI, JUSTIN. Vice president of **Malawi** since 1994. Malewezi was born in **Ntchisi** District, educated in the **United States**, and taught for many years before becoming an education administrator, rising to the rank of chief education officer. Later he became a principal secretary and was promoted to the position of secretary to the president and cabinet, the highest civil servant in the country. In 1991 Malewezi fell out of favor with the **Hastings Banda** government and lost his job. In the following year, he became a founding member of the executive committee of the **Alliance for Democracy** (AFORD). However, by the end of 1993, he had joined the **United Democratic Front** (UDF). After the 1994 **elections**, he became vice president of Malawi, an office he retained in June 1999, when the UDF was returned to power. He was elected to the National Assembly as the member for Ntchisi Northeast and had added responsibilities as minister in charge of privatization.

MALINDI. Site located a few miles northeast of **Mangochi**. Malindi was one of the most important centers of the **Universities' Mission to Central Africa** (UMCA). Later Malindi became the home of the St. Michael's Teachers College and then St. Michael's Secondary School. It also has a large mission hospital.

MALINKI, JAMES. Leading pastor in the Seventh-Day Adventist Church, and son of **Morrison Malinki**. James was a missionary in the Belgian Congo (now Democratic Republic of the Congo) for many years and is credited with pioneer work for his church in northern Malawi. He established mission stations at Luwazi in the **Nkhata Bay** District and at Mombera in **Mzimba**, both of which became major religious and educational centers. In 1952 Queen Elizabeth II awarded Pastor Malinki the Certificate of Honour.

MALINKI, KALINDE MORRISON. Educator, evangelist, and friend of **John Chilembwe**. Morrison Malinki's family were **Ngoni** taken into slavery by the **Chikunda** in the Tete area, where he was born around 1870. His mother escaped to **Mwanza** on the **Malawi-Mozambique** border, taking her children with her. Later they moved to Mpemba near **Blantyre**. In about 1884 Malinki became a student at the **Blantyre** mission school. In 1892 he joined **Joseph Booth**'s **Zambezi Industrial Mission**, where he befriended John Chilembwe and **Gordon Mataka**.

In 1897, already a teacher and preacher, he became a founding member of the African Christian Union, whose main objective was to champion African interests. In this regard he began establishing schools in which he emphasized self-reliance and sound **education** based on Christian principles. Chileka, north of Blantyre, became his main area of activity. In 1902 he affiliated with the **Plainfield Industrial Mission** at

Malamulo, Thyolo, thereby becoming a member of the Seventh-Day Adventist Church. From 1904 to 1920, he was the church's inspector of schools, covering the entire Southern Region. He became mission leader at Monekera in the Chileka, Blantyre, area, and in 1927 he was ordained pastor. Unlike his friend Chilembwe, he advocated moderation and shunned militancy. However, despite these differences, and although he did not support the **Chilembwe uprising**, Malinki was briefly arrested in 1915, mainly because of his association with the **Providence Industrial Mission** (PIM) leader. Pastor Malinki died in 1957.

MALOTA, DONALD. In 1878 Malota became an employee of Jonathan Duncan, one of the lay missionaries at **Blantyre Mission**. Malota was one of the mission employees whom Mrs. Christine Duncan taught privately in her house. Upon her death in 1883, Malota began to take care of the Duncans' baby daughter and accompanied the bereaved family to Scotland, where he attended school for a year and was baptized. On his return he taught at the mission and was regarded as an exemplary member of the African staff. In the late 1880s, Malota became involved in the ivory trade. Many European settlers, including former mission employees such as **John Buchanan**, were also involved in it. Soon he chose to devote his time to business, obtaining the lease of 200 acres of land in the **Nguludi** area and establishing D. Malota & Bros. By 1900 he had planted 80 acres of **coffee**; he also grew **maize** and raised livestock, mainly cattle, goats, and sheep, and built a large, modern house.

Besides all this, Malota was employed by **Eugene Sharrer** and received a good salary. His job involved recruiting labor in the **Ntcheu** and Dedza area for European planters in the **Shire Highlands**. This was a highly competitive, violent business that often included beatings, raiding and burning villages, rape and murder. In February 1901 Malota and his assistant, Mbatata, were charged with murder and condemned to death. But in April he escaped while on the way from **Zomba** to **Blantyre**, where he was due to be executed. He was never recaptured. In 1903 his Nguludi estate was sold to the Montfort Marist Fathers, a Roman Catholic order that had just arrived in the country. His other property was sold to European settlers and Indians.

MALVERN, LORD. *See* HUGGINS, GODFRY MARTIN.

MANDA, EDWARD BOTI. This articulate clergyman trained as a teacher at **Livingstonia** and, after teaching at the **Overtoun Institution** for some years, qualified as a minister in 1916 and was ordained two years later.

In 1925, while a minister at **Karonga**, he was suspended from the church after being convicted of misappropriating funds. He regained church membership a year later and was reinstated to the ministry in July 1929. A fiery, politically alert, and widely read preacher with a great interest in history, Manda had followed the fate of black Americans and their progress after emancipation. Manda is also associated with the re-emergence in the 1930s of the **Chikulamayembe** paramountcy over the **Tumbuka**-speaking peoples north of the **South Rukuru** River. With **Saulos Nyirenda**, he was a principal adviser to the movement for the recognition of the Chikulamayembe as the principal traditional authority of what was later to be **Rumphi** District. In this struggle Manda was pitted against the M'mbelwa of the **Ngoni**, whose advisers included **Charles Chinula** and **Yesaya Chibambo**.

MANDALA. This word means spectacles in ciMang'anja and was a nickname given to **John Moir** of the **African Lakes Company** (ALC) because he wore glasses. In time, *mandala* came to be used interchangeably with the ALC. Mandala was also the name of a chain of shops that the ALC established in many corners of **Malawi**, dominating the retail trade in the country.

MANG'ANJA. The Mang'anja are the original inhabitants of the **Shire Highlands** and the **Shire Valley**, and they constitute the southern section of the **Maravi** peoples. Their language, ciMang'anja (ciNyanja), is basically the same as **ciChewa**. In the second half of the 19th century, most of the Mang'anja in the Shire Highlands fell under the rule of the various **Yao** chiefdoms that established themselves in the region.

MANGOCHI. Located at the southern end of **Lake Malawi**, Mangochi was called Fort Johnston until the mid-1960s. In 1964–1965, **Mangochi**, **Henry Chipembere**'s home district, was a center of resistance to Dr. **Hastings K. Banda** and the **Malawi Congress Party** (MCP). Anti-government forces attacked the *boma*, killing a senior policeman's wife, and proceeded toward **Zomba** but failed to cross the **Shire River** at **Liwonde**.

Mangochi District is notable for **Malindi**, one of the major centers of the Anglican Church, situated northeast of the *boma;* its beaches and resorts; its **fishing** industry; and its **tobacco** cultivation.

MANGWAZU, TIMOM. **Kasungu**-born and Oxford University–educated leader of the Malawi National Democratic Party (MNDP) and its presidential candidate in 1994. Mangwazu spent a major part of the post colonial period as an ambassador, serving in, among other countries, the United Kingdom, West Germany, and the **United States**. In 1994 he lost his bid for the presidency of **Malawi** but was included in **Bakili Muluzi**'s first cabinet.

MANJAMKHOSI, HILDA. Malawi Congress Party (MCP) loyalist and long-time chair of the **Lilongwe** District **League of Malawi Women**. Manjamkhosi openly opposed the democratization of **Malawi** and was one of the people angered by the **Catholic bishops' pastoral letter**, *Living Our Faith*, to the extent that she and others advocated punitive action against the clerics.

MANKHAMBA. On the banks of the Linthipe River, this is the location of the first Phiri **Kalonga**, who established the **Maravi** state. It became their religious center.

MANNING, WILLIAM. Former governor of **Nyasaland**. Manning went to **British Central Africa** in 1894 as an army captain and was heavily involved in the extension of British rule in the Lake Malawi region. He is particularly associated with the campaign against the **Ngoni** chief **Mpezeni**. The fort he used in this action was later named after him. Manning rose to the rank of brigadier and commander of the **King's African Rifles** (KAR), and he was governor of Nyasaland from 1910 to 1913. *See also* ARMY; FORT MANNING.

MANTHIMBA. Located in present-day **Salima** District, Manthimba (or Maravi) was the headquarters of the **Maravi** state and became a major commercial center with links to the east coast, west to **Bisa** country, and south and southwest to the Zambezia region.

MANUFACTURING. This relatively small sector accounts for 30 percent of the gross domestic product (GDP) and employs about 4.6 percent of the labor force. Because it is heavily dependent on the processing of agricultural products, it is extremely seasonal. Under colonial rule industries processed agricultural commodities such as **cotton**, **tea**, **tobacco**, and **sugar** for local consumption or export. This industrial pattern did not change until the 1960s and 1970s, when the production of import-substitution consumer goods was introduced into the economy, including cigarettes, household utensils, soap, soft drinks, beer, shoes, edible oils, and textiles. This industrial policy has continued, as well as those directed toward expanding food processing industries and establishing small-scale rural industries. However, in the 1990s, the textile industry, particularly David Whitehead, faced challenges, mostly from imported second-hand clothes, and unsuccessfully tried to get government protection.

Incentives promoting industrial development included protected markets, generous depreciation allowances on capital expenditure, customs duty exemptions, low-cost industrial sites, and popular liberal provisions for the repatriation of profits and capital. In the 1970s and 1980s, industrial activities were affected by external influences: worldwide inflation and the closure of the **Mozambique** border, both of which resulted in higher costs for raw materials, equipment, and spare parts.

The government recognized that regional development had to be balanced, and it promoted new industries in **Lilongwe** and, to a lesser degree, **Liwonde**. As **Asians** moved into designated areas of urban **Malawi** in the 1970s, Malawians wishing to take over Asian businesses had access to government training in basic management skills. Through the **Malawi Development Corporation** (MDC) and the Investment and Development Bank of Malawi (INDEBANK), the government tried further to stimulate industrialization. In the late 1990s, the Malawi government began to privatize some of the industries managed by parastatals, even those directly associated with the MDC.

MAPANJE, JACK. Scholar of linguistics and a leading Malawian writer/poet. Mapanje was born in **Makanjila**'s area, **Mangochi** District, in 1944. He went to local primary schools, to **Zomba** Catholic Secondary School, and to Soche Hill College, where he qualified as a teacher. After teaching for some years, he entered **Chancellor College, University of Malawi,** where he majored in English. In 1971 he went to the University of London, and two years later he was awarded an M.Phil. in linguistics. He returned to teach at the University of Malawi, but in three years he was back in London at University College to complete his graduate studies and earned a Ph.D. degree. He then taught at the University of Malawi and was head of its English Department until September 25, 1987, when he was arrested and confined at **Mikuyu** prison without being charged. His arrest caused much international protest from individuals and organizations such as PEN.

Mapanje was released from prison in 1991. He and his family then left for England, where they have been living since then. Mapanje has received many literary honors, including the Poetry International Award, and is author of (among others) *Of Chameleons and Gods* (1981), *The Chattering Wagtails of Mikuyu Prison* (1993), and *Skipping without Ropes* (1998). He has also held many important offices, including chair of the Linguistic Association of Southern Africa Development Coordination Conference (SADCC) Universities. Mapanje and his family have lived in Great Britain since 1991.

MAPANTHA, JOHN GRAY KUFA. *See* KUFA, JOHN GRAY.

MAPLES, BISHOP CHAUNCY. A missionary at Masasi and Newala in the region east of **Lake Malawi** for 10 years. In 1886 he was transferred to **Likoma** as archdeacon of **Nyasa**. A graduate of the University of Oxford, Maples worked with Father **William P. Johnson** to establish many schools on the eastern shores of the lake and at Likoma and Chizumulu. In June 1895 he was consecrated bishop of Likoma, but he drowned in **Lake Malawi** when the boat taking him to Likoma capsized.

MARAMBO. Located in a major elephant area greatly favored by **Swahili-Arab** ivory traders, Marambo, with Chasefu, became one of the important **Livingstonia Mission** stations in the Luangwa country inhabited by the Senga and **Tumbuka**-speakers.

MARAVI. A state system established in the **Lake Malawi** area in the 16th century. Led by the Phiri matriclan, the headquarters of the state was at **Manthimba** or Maravi, not far from the southwestern shores of **Lake Malawi**. With the title of **Kalonga**, the Maravi rulers expanded south to the Lower Shire, west to the Luangwa-Zambezi valley regions, and north to **Tumbuka** and **Tonga** countries.

MASEKO, MPUTA. Son of Ngwana Maseko of the Swazi section of the Nguni peoples. Mputa led (in the 1830s) the northward migration of the Maseko **Ngoni** to the Songea area across the Rovuma River, where they came in conflict with **Zulu Gama**'s successors. Under the leadership of Mputa's brother, **Chidyawonga**, and later Mputa's son, Chikusi, the Maseko Ngoni settled in the **Ntcheu**-Dedza region in the 1860s and 1870s.

MASEKO NGONI. *See* MASEKO, MPUTA; NGONI.

MASEYA, REV. THOMAS MPENI. Maseya was one of the first students at the **Blantyre** mission school and was also one of the initial lay preachers. In 1894 he and other deacons, including **Harry K. Matecheta** and **John Gray Kufa Mapantha**, went to **Lovedale** for further training. Later he was ordained minister and served in various parts of the **Shire Highlands**. Maseya was an active member of the Blantyre Welfare Association and the Southern Province Welfare Association.

MASSINGIRE UPRISING. *See* MATEKENYA (PAUL MARIONO II).

MASTER FARMERS SCHEME. This 1950s government project aimed at creating a yeoman-type farmer who would receive extension services, including basic loans. Their success, it was hoped, would be an example to other growers who would try to follow their examples. The Master Farmers Scheme was attacked by nationalist politicians, partly for being elitist and partly because it was identified with unpopular agricultural and conservation regulations introduced at about the same time as the project.

MATAKA, GORDON. Of **Yao** affiliation, Gordon Mataka joined **Joseph Booth** at **Mitsidi** in 1892. With **John Chilembwe, Morrison Malinki,** and others, he became one of the early Africans to be associated with the **Zambezi Industrial Mission** (ZIM). In 1896 he was one of the local people involved in Booth's African Christian Union, including the proposed Mlonda estate. In the same year, Mataka accompanied Booth to Durban, **South Africa.** While they were there, however, their relations changed. The Yao, influenced by Zulu opinion, became increasingly, suspicious of Europeans as collaborators. Mataka and Booth never regained their former warm relationship.

MATAKENYA (PAUL MARIANO II). This leading *prazero* was a dominant player in the politics and economy of the Lower **Shire Valley** and the **Shire Highlands** for a major part of the 19th century. Paul Mariano II built on a foundation laid by the first Paul Mariano, a Goanese from India, who used Quilimane as a base and had traded in ivory, gold dust, and slaves in **Mozambique.** In 1854 Paul Mariano II and his brother, Bonga, led a successful conquest expedition to the **Shire River** region, and from then to the 1880s, he and his offspring were to dominate the area between the confluence of the Zambezi and the Shire Rivers in the south, and the upper Ruo River near **Mulanje.** Behaving like a chief, Mariano changed his name to Matakenya; he and his **Chikunda** assistants engaged in the **slave** and ivory trade, and they terrorized local people opposed to him.

Matakenya's relations with the Portuguese were tense, largely because he seemed to be claiming dominance in an area that was theirs. In 1858 the Portuguese authorities imprisoned him twice, on a variety of charges; during the second imprisonment he escaped and proceeded to reorganize his army of Chikunda retainers. In 1861 he fought off a Portuguese attempt to arrest him. With guns already in his possession and those he seized from soldiers sent to arrest him, Matakenya and his well-equipped army moved further north to the Chironje area of the Shire. From there he stepped up his slave raiding activities, this time in the mainly **Mang'anja** territory. In 1862 he defeated **Chief Tengani**'s army, killing the chief and ransacking the **Khulubvi** of M'bona. Although Matakenya died in the following year, his followers continued to be a menace in the Shire region as far north as Mulanje.

Both of Matakenya's successors, Paul Mariano III and Paul Mariano IV, took the name Matakenya. In the main they behaved much as he had done, trading in ivory and slaves, and, with the help of guns, imposing themselves on local populations. Like him, they were always keen to co-operate with incoming Europeans in an attempt to isolate the Portuguese. It was not long before the **Kololo** and the Matakenya clashed. As the former moved into Massingire (Matchinjiri) (as the area under Matakenya came to be known), the hitherto invincible *prazero* could not contain them. Unimpressed by this poor show of confidence, the Chikunda surrendered Paul Mariano IV to Portuguese officials, and in 1881 he was killed at Mopea en route to Quilimane. The Portuguese now went to the aid of the Chikunda in Massingire and in May 1882 raised a flag at Pinda, next to the Kololo area. Portuguese authority was short-lived, however, as in 1884 the people of Massingire rebelled, citing excesses of Portuguese rule, including the tax system, lack of respect for local custom and tradition, and meddling in the appointment of chiefs such as Paul Mariano's successor. They destroyed Portuguese property, stole some of it, and proceeded to do the same to other Europeans, including the **African Lakes Company** (ALC).

The Massingire uprising forced the ALC to strengthen its alliance with the Kololo; the missionaries and the British government used it as an excuse to pay closer attention to Portuguese expansionist ambitions into the **Lake Malawi** region, which many British were beginning to consider as falling within their "sphere of influence." On their part, the Portuguese began to establish closer links with the **Yao**, whose relations with the missionaries were at times cool.

MATAPWIRI. Yao chief. In the 1860s he settled in the area between **Mulanje** and Matapwiri, from which he controlled trade between the east coast and the **Shire Highlands**. He became a major foe of the British, whose authority he resisted until his defeat in 1895. His successors assumed the same chiefly name.

MATECHETA, REV. HARRY KAMBWIRI. Distinguished church minister and one of the first Malawian members of the **Blantyre**

Mission, even before it was sited. As **Henry Henderson** and **Tom Bokwito** stopped in his village while looking for a place to build the mission, Matecheta joined them, becoming one of the early converts to Christianity and one of the first students at Blantyre. At his baptism, he added Harry to his names, and upon completing his schooling, he became a teacher and preacher. In 1893 he established a substation at Nthubi in the country under the Maseko **Ngoni**. He returned to the area in 1898 and was there for many years, becoming known as the **Yao** missionary to the Ngoni. He gained the confidence of Inkosi **Gomani I**, ruler of the Maseko Ngoni, and was a frequent visitor to their **Lizulu** headquarters. In 1907 he became a student at the new theological school in **Blantyre**, completing the course in 1911. On April 9, 1911, he was ordained minister, four days before **Stephen Kundecha**, thereby becoming the first Malawian clergyman in the Church of Scotland. In 1951 he published a history of the Blantyre Mission, *Blantyre Mission: Nkhani ya Ciyambi Cace*.

MATENJE, DICK. Educator turned politician. Matenje was born near **Blantyre** in 1929 and was educated at the **Henry Henderson Institute** (HHI) and Blantyre Secondary School and qualified as a higher grade teacher at **Domasi** Teachers College. He also furthered his education at the University of Bristol, England, University of Ottawa, **Canada**, and University of Western Australia, Perth. He served as headmaster of Soche Day Secondary School. Later he was assigned to the Ministry of Education headquarters. In 1971 he became MP for Blantyre and in the following year was appointed minister of education. After a few years, he was transferred to the Ministry of Finance and later to Trade, Industry, and Tourism. In the late 1970s he returned to the Ministry of Education, to which portfolio was added Youth and Culture. More significantly, in 1981, Matenje became minister and administrative secretary of the **Malawi Congress Party**. In 1983 he and three other politicians were killed in **Mwanza** District. *See also* MWANZA ACCIDENT AND TRIALS.

MATEWERE, GRAZIANO. First Malawian **army** commander, promoted in 1972 to major general. Matewere joined the **King's African Rifles** in 1947 and at the time of independence was a lieutenant. In 1969 he was appointed deputy army commander; subsequently, he was promoted to commander. He has since retired from the army.

MATINGA, CHARLES. A member of the Blantyre Native Association who became vice president of the **Nyasaland African Conference** (NAC) in

1944. On the death of **Levi Mumba** a few months later, Matinga took over the leadership of the party. He resisted Dr. **Hastings K. Banda**'s efforts to streamline the administrative and financial ends of the Congress and in 1948 was relieved of his position for alleged mismanagement of Congress funds. He later left to live in Southern Rhodesia **(Zimbabwe)**.

MAUDLING, REGINALD. British Conservative Party politician. In October 1961 he succeeded **Iain Macleod** as secretary of state for the colonies. He and **Robert Butler** later came to accept the breakup of the **Federation of Rhodesia and Nyasaland** as inevitable.

MAXWELL, WILLIAM ALEXANDER. Cotton planter and owner of a ginnery. Maxwell was born in 1883 in Dumfrieshire, Scotland, where he was trained as a carpenter. In November 1902 he went to **Nyasaland**. In the following year the **African Lakes Company** (ALC) employed him as a carpenter and miller and from 1908 as a general handyman, a position that took him to most parts of the colony where the company had property. Just before World War I he became a cotton planter in the Ngara-Nyungwe area of southern **Karonga** District. During the war he joined the Nyasaland Field Force and was part of the contingent that engaged the Germans at Karonga. After the war he concentrated on cotton and on operating a ginnery that had originally belonged to the **British Cotton Growers Association** (BCGA). Maxwell died in **Blantyre** in 1963 and was buried at his Nyungwe farm.

MBANDE HILL. Sacred hill and ritual center of the **Ngonde**. In the past the area around it was the traditional headquarters of the Ngonde rulers; earlier it was the seat of the Simbowe, whom the **Kyungu** dynasty overthrew at the beginning of the 17th century.

MBEKEANI, JANET. *See* KARIM, ZEENAT JANET.

MBEKEANI, WALES NYEMBA. Respected public servant, businessman, and politician. Mbekeani was born in **Ntcheu** District and trained as a social welfare officer. He was also active in the politics of decolonization, and after independence in 1964 he became a diplomat, serving as ambassador at several of Malawi's missions. In the early 1970s he returned to **Malawi** and became general manager of the Malawi Housing Corporation. In the early 1980s he retired, becoming a farmer and a businessman. In the early 1990s President **Hastings Banda** appointed him to the cabinet as minister of commerce and industry, a position he retained until the elections in 1994, when he resumed his life as a businessman.

MBOMBWE. Home of the **Providence Industrial Mission** (PIM), established by **John Chilembwe** in 1900. Located just south of **Chiradzulu** *boma*, it was a catchment area for European labor seekers, including the nearby **A. L. Bruce** Estate managed by **William J. Livingstone**, and was also in the heartland of *thangata* country. When **Daniel Malekebu** returned to **Malawi** in 1926 to take over leadership of the PIM, Mbombwe remained the headquarters of the church.

M'BONA CULT. Territorial religious cult. Its chief shrines are located in **Thyolo** and at **Khulubvi**. M'Bona is concerned with the larger good of the community, including prevention of droughts, epidemics, and floods. For centuries the M'Bona cult has been associated with the **Mang'anja** people now in the Lower **Shire Valley**. In the 14th century the Mang'anja peoples intruded upon the indigenous inhabitants and seized their shrine. Shortly thereafter the Phiri clan imposed its seniority, the shifts of power within the Phiri hierarchy giving way in the 16th century to paramountcy by the **Lundu**. Each political takeover of the area included the appropriation of the cult and all its myths and ritual. Christian missionaries in the 19th century viewed the cult negatively, despite parallel beliefs in a creative and powerful God, specialized priests, and prophetic traditions.

MBUMBA. In matrilineal societies *mbumba* refers to dependents within the matriclan. The *nkoswe* is the guardian of the *mbumba*. In patrilineal society *mbumba* would refer to dependents within the patriclan. President **Hastings K. Banda** viewed himself as the *nkoswe* (guardian) of all the **women** in Malawi and thus he called them his *mbumba*.

MCHAPE. This witchcraft eradication movement began in the **Mulanje** District and swept through **Malawi** in 1933. The leader in Mulanje was Bwanali Mpulumutsi (Bwanali the savior); he and others like him conducted mass-cleansing ceremonies in villages for the purpose of eradicating or purging areas of all evil. Those villagers declared to be witches or sorcerers were given a medicine to cleanse them of their sins. The movement, which spread to neighboring **Zambia** and Tanganyika, was apparently fed, in part, by the failure of various Christian churches to vanquish evil. Newly initiated Christians believed that their new religion would end the rivalries and differences in their society. As **AIDS** has become a factor in the lives of many communities in Malawi, *mchape*-like personalities claiming to possess the ability to cleanse society of the evil of AIDS have appeared. *See also* MISSIONS.

MCHINJI. *See* FORT MANNING.

MHANGO, KAMBONDOMA. With **Kanyoli Gondwe**, Mjuma, and Mwendera, Kambondoma led the Kamanga and Henga rebellion against M'mbelwa **Ngoni** authority in 1879. He and Kanyoli formed the Kwenda and Sikwaliweni regiments, which they headed respectively. Having served under Ngoni command, the **Majere-Henga**, as the rebels came to call themselves, had learned the best in warfare with the result that their former rulers found them particularly difficult to subdue. In fact, the Ngoni succeeded only after **Mwase Kasungu** rendered them some assistance. When the rebels realized that they were about to lose, they sent their families to the **Karonga** lakeshore; the rebel leaders were to follow them later, marking the migration of the **Tumbuka**-speaking people to **Ngonde** areas such as Kaporo and central Karonga.

MHANGO, MKWAPATILA. Malawian journalist. Mkwapatila Mhango was murdered along with his family in Lusaka in 1989. Active in the **Malawi Freedom Movement** (MAFREMO), Mhango was critical of Dr. **Hastings Banda** and the **Malawi Congress Party** (MCP). The Mhango family, like **Attati Mpakati** a few years earlier, was killed by Malawi intelligence officials.

MHANGO, ROBERT SAMBO. Founding member of the **North Nyasa Native Association**. Mhango was born and educated in **Karonga**. He worked in **South Africa** before returning to **Nyasaland** in 1912, two months after the formation of the South African Native National Congress. In 1928 he and **Simon Kamkhati Mkandawire** became founders of the African National Church.

MICHAEL, IAN. First vice chancellor of the **University of Malawi**. Ian Michael was born in England and educated at the Universities of Reading and London. He taught at the University of Bristol for many years before becoming professor of education at the University of Khartoum, Sudan. In 1964 he was appointed chief executive of the new University of Malawi. In 1973 he resigned from the university to become deputy director of the Institute of Education, University of London.

MIGRANT LABOR. Since colonial days many Malawians have sought work outside their national borders, particularly in **South Africa**, **Zimbabwe** (Southern Rhodesia), and **Zambia**. With the introduction of taxation in 1892, it was increasingly important to earn enough money to pay **taxes** and to pay for a Western **education**, as well as purchase European goods. Even before migrant laborers began leaving Malawi for neighboring territories, they had moved about internally, seeking money to pay Europeans. Of all migrant workers, 75 percent were men, 10 percent were women, and the remainder were juveniles, mostly boys.

Although Dr. **David Livingstone** is the first known European to employ Malawi laborers, the **African Lakes Company** (ALC) was really the first to systematically recruit workers for other European business interests. In 1886 **Tonga** porters enlisted by the company to transport goods within the country so impressed the planters in the **Shire Highlands** that soon they began to employ thousands of them on their estates. No labor regulations existed pertaining to hours of work, wages, or conditions until 1895, when the **Harry Johnston** administration began to codify some rules, according to which workers could not be employed for more than 12 months at a time; workers also had to receive travel money to return home. In addition, laborers were to be housed and fed, and their medical needs taken care of by the employer. The planters were most unhappy about the government regulations, arguing that they only aggravated the labor shortage facing them at the time. In fact, European planters sought labor in the planting season when the Africans preferred to cultivate their own land; it was also a fact that Europeans paid very minimal wages to their African employees.

When a labor bureau was established in 1901 to recruit and distribute workers, there were even more abuses, particularly when recruiting agents obtained the cooperation of the European government **collector**, who would hand over African tax defaulters to them. The treatment that these farm workers and porters received was shockingly poor even at that time, and it did not improve in the early 20th century, when the railway company began to recruit workers to build its line. News of the railway's ill-treatment of its workers reached the Colonial Office after the governor, Sir **Alfred Sharpe**, personally wrote about abuses he had observed.

Attempts to stop organized labor recruitment by the South African Chamber of Mines were led by missionaries, especially Dr. **Alexander Hetherwick** of the **Blantyre Mission**. With the men absent, village life was disrupted and the women had to do both their work and the men's. Many deserted families experienced incredible hardship. There was additional strain in villages of Catholic conversion because the **missions** refused to recognize divorce, even though traditional law permitted it in cases of desertion. Mission opposition to labor migration proved futile as workers continued to leave on their own to work in mines or on farms or perform domestic labor. By 1914 about 40,000 Malawians were working in mines in

South Africa and Southern Rhodesia (Zimbabwe). The numbers of workers exceeded 100,000 by the 1930s, with as many as one-third never returning home. At this time the protectorate government acknowledged the vast emigration and its effect on the remaining families. An effort was made in a series of agreements with neighboring countries to repatriate laborers after two years and to provide more suitable camp and travel arrangements. Even as the Malawi migrant was strongly influencing the economic development of Zimbabwe, he was also contributing to the underdevelopment of his homeland, severely straining the territory's social structure.

From the 1920s to the mid-1960s, **Northern Rhodesia** (Zambia) was another destination for Malawian labor, despite the fact that there were no recruiting agencies for the country. The development of the Copper Belt attracted Malawians into that country, and some of them even went beyond to Katanga, Belgian Congo (Democratic Republic of the Congo), where copper was also being mined. When Zambia became independent in 1964, recruitment of Malawian laborers was discouraged because of the local unemployment problem.

When Dr. **Hastings Banda** became the head of government, he discouraged Malawians from going to South Africa, saying that they would be too far from their families and would be exposed to the harsh urban life of the region. He tried to convince them that they could earn a living by cultivating cash crops. Despite Banda's efforts, Malawian labor continued to leave the country in large numbers. In 1970 the **Witwatersrand Native Labour Association** (WNLA), popularly known as WENELA, recruited 90,000 workers and the **Rhodesia Native Labour Bureau** (RNLB) 2,000 for South African and Southern Rhodesian employers, respectively. The Malawi government forbade further recruitment after 1974, when a WENELA airplane crashed and killed 75 homeward-bound Malawian mine workers. Until mid-1977, the number of laborers was few, as low as 200 in early 1977. However, the Banda government responded to numerous requests by WENELA to resume recruitment, and about 20,000 trained workers were permitted to leave, far fewer than the 130,000 who were working in South Africa at the time of the crash.

In the early 1980s, the name WENELA was replaced by TEBA (**Temporary Employment Bureau of Africa**), which continued to recruit on two-year contracts to South Africa, the South African mining industry being the largest user. In 1988, believing that hundreds of Malawi's migrant miners were infected with **AIDS**, South Africa sent them back to Malawi. Although the Malawi government has responded to this **health** crisis, mine owners continue to restrict Malawian labor in South Africa. In fact, the African National Congress governments led by Nelson Mandela and his successor, Thabo Mbeki, now completely restrict nonskilled Malawian labor from the country, pointing out that, with high unemployment within their country, they have to take care of their citizens first before they can think of foreigners. However, since the change of government in South Africa, skilled and professional Malawians have been going there to work in considerable numbers. Until 1994 most Malawians in this category tended to go to Botswana, where the expanding economy was able to accommodate them.

MIKUYU. Located eight miles west of **Zomba** town, where there is a prison by the same name. During the 1970s and 1980s it was used as a detention center for political prisoners. People such as **Jack Mapanje,** **Aleke Banda,** and **Brown Mpinganjira** spent time at Mikuyu. In the post–**Hastings Banda** period, there has been a move to turn the prison into a museum to remind people of the evils of dictatorship.

MINING. Until the 1980s, the major mineral production in **Malawi** was quarrying tons of marble for the manufacture of cement. In 1985 a state-owned company started mining coal at Kazibizibi and Mchenga in **Rumphi** District; experts have described the deposits there as high in quality but low in quantity. The French government funded a laboratory in **Lilongwe** for the analysis of coal; the French also sponsored the geological mapping of the Lengwe and Mwabvi coalfields in southern Malawi to make it easier to select sites for drilling. A drilling project conducted by the Malawi Government Geological Survey Department at Mchenga in northeastern Rumphi helped to increase production in the country. Until that stage, over 80 percent of domestic needs came from the Kaziwiziwi mines near **Livingstonia,** which had significantly increased its output of high-quality coal (26,000 tons annually), meaning that less coal had to be imported from neighboring **Zimbabwe, Zambia,** and **Mozambique.** The Malawi government's parastatal Mining Investment and Development Corporation (MIDCOR), aimed at ending all coal imports by the late 1990s.

The Portland Cement Company has worked the limestone at Changalume near **Zomba** since 1960. The quarry at Malowa hill potentially could produce 15,000 tons annually in meeting domestic demands. MIDCOR's recent license to produce lime for a Bwanje Valley quarry in **Ntcheu** District has been assisted by Canadian and South African commitments of equipment for the construction of a plant.

Of the 20 minerals confirmed at present in Malawi, none has been exploited commercially to any extent. The most valuable find is the bauxite deposits in the **Mulanje**, but earlier surveys by **Lonrho** indicated that smelting those limited reserves would be very costly and would have detrimental effects on the area's **environment**. In 2001 the Malawi government grated permission to a South Africa-based firm to survey Mulanje with a view to commence mining. Environmentalists remained totally opposed to the project.

Some commercial concerns continue to investigate deposits of monazite in **Machinga** District and vermiculite near Mpatamanga gorge. Some gems, including garnet, aquamarine, and ruby, are exported to overseas dealers by private dealers who obtain licenses from the Ministry of Energy to engage in this trade.

MISSIONS. It would be difficult to overestimate the influence of missionaries, especially the Scottish, who entered Malawi in the late 19th century. They preceded the establishment of the British protectorate in Malawi and, predictably, supported the advent of British rule. Three societies, responding to **David Livingstone**'s plea for Christianity and commerce, had sent delegations by 1875: the **Universities' Mission** to **Central Africa** (UMCA), the Free Church of Scotland **(Livingstonia Mission)**, and the Established Church of Scotland **(Blantyre Mission)**. Three other Protestant missions were established between 1889 and 1892: the **Dutch Reformed Church** (DRC), the **Zambezi Industrial Mission** (ZIM), and **Nyasa Baptist Industrial Mission** (NIM). Roman Catholics did not establish permanent missions until the early 20th century. The Montfort Marist Fathers arrived in 1901 and the **White Fathers** reestablished in 1902 what they had failed in 13 years before.

Set up in England in 1859, the **Universities' Mission to Central Africa** (UMCA), an Anglican mission headed by Bishop **Charles F. Mackenzie**, chose **Magomero** in 1861 to be its main base. From the beginning, it faced immense problems arising from its location. Magomero was in the midst of a region in which the **Yao** looked for slaves, and the missionaries became involved in local politics, including anti-Yao activities. When Mackenzie died in January 1862, the rest of the missionaries moved further down the **Shire Valley**, where they were joined by the new head, Bishop **William Tozer**. In 1864 it was decided to transfer the whole operation to **Zanzibar**, where it remained until 1885, when **Likoma** Island was chosen as the new UMCA headquarters. At the urging of **William P. Johnson**, the mission acquired a steamer to service the missions situated along **Lake Malawi**. By the end of the century the mission had a string of schools along the lake. In 1899 it established the St. Michael's College to train local teachers. In 1911 the impressive Likoma Cathedral was finished.

In 1875 the party of Livingstonia Mission of the Free Church of Scotland, headed by Dr. **James Stewart** and **Robert Laws**, established its base at **Cape Maclear**; in 1881 it was relocated further north to **Bandawe**. In addition to the Christian message, the Livingstonia Mission concentrated on formal Western **education**, including technical and commercial training. In 1894 Dr. Laws founded the **Overtoun Institution** at **Khondowe**, where teachers, clergymen, bookkeepers, clerks, masons, and carpenters were trained. The most active mission in education, the Livingstonia schools by 1900 taught most postprimary students and well over 50 percent of Malawi's primary pupils.

In 1876 **Henry Henderson** and his guide/interpreter, **Tom Bokwito**, began to build the Blantyre Mission of the Established Church of Scotland at a site given to him by **Kapeni**, the local **Yao** chief. In 1878 he was joined by other Scottish missionaries, including Rev. **Duff Macdonald**, who became its leader. The mission started badly mainly because it adopted a civil administration policy that led to excessive behavior on the part of some missionaries. In 1881 an investigation by the Foreign Mission Committee of the church led to the dismissal of Macdonald and other missionaries. A different approach was adopted by the new head, Rev. Dr. **David C. Scott** and his assistant, Rev. **Alexander Hetherwick**. Scott preferred working with African evangelists, and three of his African colleagues became deacons in 1893: **Joseph Bismarck**, Rondau Kaferanjila, and **Donald Malota**. Scott found little support for his "radical" views among European settlers. In 1898 he was forced to resign his post for health reasons, and Hetherwick assumed the leadership. In 1909 the Blantyre Mission opened the **Henry Henderson Institute** (HHI), which became an important educational facility, training Africans in the same areas as the Overtoun. In 1924 the Blantyre and Livingstonia Presbyteries agreed to form the **Church of Central Africa Presbyterian** (CCAP), a move originally suggested by Laws and later revived by Hetherwick. In 1926 the DRC Presbytery joined the CCAP. The formation of the CCAP led to the appointment of African clergymen to various committees; for example, in 1933 Rev. **Harry K. Matecheta** became the first African moderator of the Blantyre Presbytery.

Although **Mvera** (1889) in Dowa District was the first mission station of the Dutch Reformed Church (DRC) of South Africa, **Nkhoma**, in **Li-**

longwe District, became the main center of this missionary society. Established by **William H. Murray** in 1896, Nkhoma developed into a major educational and **health** center, where teachers, church ministers, and health workers were trained. From Nkhoma, the DRC expanded to other parts of Central Malawi, including **Mlanda** and **Mchinji**, and had stations in **Mozambique**, **Zambia**, and **Zimbabwe**.

In 1889 the White Fathers Order became the first Roman Catholic missionary group to arrive in Malawi, setting up a base at **Mponda** on the southern tip of Lake Malawi. After two years, they left for northern Zambia but returned in 1902. By 1904 the White Fathers had three permanent stations at **Kachebere**, **Likuni**, and **Mua**, and the Montforts had two missions, at **Nguludi** and **Nzama**. In the late 1930s the White Fathers established stations in the Northern Region, starting with Katete in **Mzimba** District. Most of the White Fathers were French and, among the early leaders, were Bishops **Louis Auneau**, **Joseph Dupont**, and Mathurin Guilleme. It was not until 1937–1938 that the first Malawian priests were ordained: **Cornelio Chitsulo**, Alfred Finye, and Andrea Makoyo.

There were some differences between the Catholic missions and the Protestant ones, the former being more hierarchical and authoritarian than most of the latter. There was not much movement among African priests to break away and form independent churches, such as happened at Livingstonia and Blantyre. At Roman Catholic missions, women worked more successfully. Nuns, being single, worked full-time with Malawian women and children, not just occasionally as the wives of Protestant missionaries were able to find time. Although the Roman Catholic missions were noticeably less able to recruit African males to the celibate priesthood, the convent life offered by the sisterhood had its appeal to Malawian women. Female recruits enjoyed status, good education, and more independence than was allowed in a male-dominated secular society.

Scottish missionaries, more than other missionaries, were early in encouraging African aspirations and, in this way, greatly contributed to nationalism. *See also* BOOTH, JOSEPH; CHILEMBWE, JOHN; MALAMULO.

MITSIDI. Located just northwest of **Blantyre**, Mitsidi became the headquarters of **Joseph Booth**'s **Zambezi Industrial Mission** (ZIM). Today Mitsidi is part of Greater Blantyre.

MKANDA. Located east of the Luangwa valley and southwest of **Mwase Kasungu**, Mkanda was one of the more powerful **Chewa** chiefdoms in the 19th century. A century earlier, Mkanda, also the title of the ruler, was subordinate to the Undi dynasty but had managed to gain autonomy. The military genius who was responsible for the growth of the chiefdom was Mkanda Chapongolera Mbewe, whose main reputation was his ability to protect people by, among other things, housing them in large stockaded settlements. Mkanda directly controlled the center of the kingdom but assigned adjacent areas to other groups, allowing them to collect tribute from **Tumbuka**, Chewa, and **Nsenga** populations. The ivory trade was also a factor in the growth of the Mkanda chiefdom.

MKANDAWIRE, DONTON. Educator and politician. Donton Mkandawire was educated at **Zomba** Secondary School, **Domasi** Teacher's College, and the University of Western Australia, Perth. After teaching at Soche Hill Secondary School, he went to the University of Pittsburgh, where he completed a Ph.D. in educational testing. Upon his return in 1984, he joined the Malawi Examinations and Testing Board (MCTB), which he soon headed. When the **Kamuzu Academy** was established in 1981, Mkandawire was appointed to its board and became its chairman. In 1987 he was removed from the directorship of the Examination Board, and after a year he left for the University of Botswana; three years later, he was appointed professor of education at the University of Namibia. In 1993 the **Malawi Congress Party** (MCP) government recalled him and offered him a cabinet position, minister of information and broadcasting. Not long after the **elections** he joined the **United Democratic Front** (UDF) and briefly became Minister of Education; later he headed a government-sponsored educational research organization. In June 1999 he unsuccessfully stood as UDF candidate for a **Mzimba** constituency, and in the following year he replaced **Mtembo Nzunda** as clerk of the **Lilongwe** City Assembly.

MKANDAWIRE, FRANK MAYINGA. Founding member of the **Alliance for Democracy** (AFORD) party and with **Mapopa Chipeta**, its principal organizer while it was based in Lusaka, **Zambia**. Raised in **Rumphi** District, Mkandawire went to local schools and to the **University of Malawi** but went into political **exile** in Zambia, completing his studies at that country's main university in Lusaka. In 1991–1993 he became actively involved in the movement for political reform; he and Mapopa Chipeta clandestinely sent literature demanding change into Malawi. Through a newsletter, the *Malawi Democrat*, later to be AFORD'S organ, they further articulated the need for immediate reform. In 1993 Mayinga Mkandawire returned to Malawi and was elected to parliament a year later. Under the coalition arrangements that the **United Democratic Front** (UDF) and AFORD worked out in late 1994, Mkandawire was appointed minister of forestry, fisheries, and environmental affairs. In 1996 he was one of the AFORD people who refused to leave government when requested to do so by his party. In 1999 he stood as an independent candidate in the **Rumphi** Central constituency but lost to **Chakufwa Chihana**, the leader of AFORD.

MKANDAWIRE, GRANT MIKEKA. Leading **Blantyre**-based African businessmen, active member of the **Nyasaland African Congress** (NAC), and minister without portfolio in the first cabinet following the general **elections** of 1961. Mikeka Mkandawire was born at **Chikwawa** in the Nkhamanga area of **Rumphi** and educated locally. In the 1940s he worked for the Central African Company (CATCO) and for the Trevor Construction Company in Blantyre. In 1949 he became a businessman, building a grocery store at Chichiri where some of his associate businessmen, including **Lali Lubani**, **Lawrence Makata**, and James Mpunga also operated. When Africans were forced to move out of the Chichiri area in 1956–1957, Mkandawire established his business at Kanjedza, not far from where the **Church of Central Africa Presbyterian** (CCAP) church stands today. This time, he added a hotel to his grocery enterprise. Mkandawire, like most other African entrepreneurs, was actively involved in nationalist politics. Associated with the radical wing of the NAC, he was, in the mid-1950s, president of the Shire Province of the party. He opposed the **Federation of Rhodesia and Nyasaland** and **Wellington Manoah Chirwa**'s and **Clement Kumbikano**'s nomination to, and entry into, the federal parliament. His Mikeka's Hotel was a venue of numerous party gatherings and was patronized by many African nationalist activists.

Like many NAC activists, Mikeka Mkandawire was arrested and imprisoned without trial in 1959, and in 1961 was elected to parliament on the higher roll as a representative of the Northern Region. He was appointed minister without portfolio but resigned before independence to study in Scotland. He returned a few years later and lived quietly in northern Malawi.

MKANDAWIRE, JIMMY BILLY MPONDA. Influential **Alliance for Democracy** (AFORD) MP for **Karonga** North. Son of the late Mponda Mkandawire, a prominent local businessman and rice and cotton farmer, Mkandawire was born in 1943 at Kaporo, Karonga, and attended the Mwanjasi Primary School and **Blantyre** Secondary School. In 1963 he went to the **United States** to study civil engineering. Unable to return to **Malawi** because he had become identified with opposition politics, Mkandawire worked in the United States and continued his studies, graduating with a Ph.D. degree in civil engineering. A committed supporter of political reform, he joined forces with AFORD and in 1993 returned to Malawi to campaign for the party. In the following year, he was elected to parliament, and under the coalition arrangement with the **United Democratic Front** (UDF), he was appointed minister of works. When the working arrangement between the two parties broke down, Mkandawire left government but has remained an AFORD MP. In 1999 he was reelected to the National Assembly.

MKANDAWIRE, MATUPI. Born in Nkhamanga in Western **Rumphi**, where he was educated to primary level, Mkandawire worked in **Southern Rhodesia** for most of the 1940s and early 1950s. In 1955 he was deported back to **Nyasaland** because of his involvement in politics. He continued his political activism and in 1956 was elected to the Rumphi District Council as a representative for **Nkhamanga** Ward. Mkandawire worked hard to set up branches of the **Nyasaland African Congress** (NAC) in Rumphi District, and became a close ally of **Kanyama Chiume**, the MP representing the Northern Region. He was briefly detained during the state of emergency in 1959, and after the constitutional changes two years later, he became one of the north's public relations officers for the **Farmers Marketing Board**. Within two years be became MP for Rumphi West, but following the **Cabinet Crisis** of 1964, he supported the expelled ministers, was taken as a political prisoner, and died in detention, apparently soon after receiving the news that his twin brother had died at home. As a village chief, Mkandawire had traditional authority and the respect that went with it. He was also an active member of the African National Church.

MKANDAWIRE, SIMON KAMKHATI. Founder of the African National Church. Mkandawire was born at **Chitimba**, **Rumphi** District, educated at the **Overtoun Institution** up to Standard Six level, before going to work in the Belgian Congo. In 1928 he, **Robert Sambo Mhango**, and **Paddy Nyasulu** also originally associated with the **Livingstonia Mission**, founded the African National Church, which retained all the characteristics of a Presbyterian church, except for their lack of tolerance of polygamy. The African National Church strongly supported the aspirations of the **African welfare associations**. Today the church is known as the International African Church and has adherents in, among other countries, **Zambia**, Republic of the Congo, **Zimbabwe**, and **Tanzania**.

MKANDAWIRE, THANDIKA. Leading Malawian and African social scientist. Mkandawire spent his early years in **Southern Rhodesia**, where his father worked. He attended school at **Zomba** Catholic Secondary School, and in 1959–1960 he became an activist in the youth wing of the new **Malawi Congress Party** (MCP). He, **Aleke Banda**, and others founded the party's organ, the *Malawi News,* becoming a member of its editorial staff. Later he went to study at Ohio State University and completed his graduate studies in Sweden, where he earned his Ph.D. degree in economics. Mkandawire taught at universities in Europe, Africa, and the **United States** and for some time worked at the Zimbabwe Institute of Development Studies. From the mid-1980s to late 1996, he headed the Council for the Development of Economic and Social Research in Africa (CODESRIA) in Dakar, Senegal. In 1997 Mkandawire became head of research at the Institute of Economic and Social Research in Geneva, Switzerland.

From the time of the **Cabinet Crisis** to 1993, Mkandawire was a wanted man in **Malawi**, primarily because the government and the MCP regarded him as a sympathizer of the exiled ministers. Dr. **Hastings Banda** personally denounced Mkandawire as a dangerous person, forcing him to remain abroad.

MKANDAWIRE, YAPHET. Upon his ordination in 1918, Yaphet Mkandawire worked at **Khondowe** directly under Dr. **Robert Laws**. In 1927 he attained the distinction of being the first African treasurer of the Presbytery, and in the following year he became minister to the Hara and Mlowe congregations, in the border region of modern **Karonga** and **Rumphi** Districts. In July 1932 the hierarchy of the mission was informed that Mkandawire had been administered *mphemba,* a medicine that was believed to offer protection from poison or bewitchment. Later that year, a committee set up to inquire into the report concluded that he had indulged in an evil act. Despite his good record as a minister and some recommendations that he only be reprimanded, Mkandawire was defrocked and suspended from the church. He reacted by resigning from the church and establishing his own, which he called the African Reformed Presbyterian Church.

MKANDAWIRI, JAPHET BAMININGO. This first secretary-general of the Rhodesia Native Association was a **Nyasaland Tonga** migrant who moved to the famous Epworth Mission in **Southern Rhodesia** after marrying a girl from there. He then converted from the Dutch Reformed Church to the Methodist Church. Although he remained in his employment as a clerk in Salisbury, he became a preacher and an activist in African politics.

MKOCHI, REV. ANDREW. One of the leading **Ngoni** teachers, evangelists, and pastors in the **Livingstonia Mission**. In 1897 Mkochi was the first person to open a school at M'mbelwa **Chimtunga Jere**'s headquarters, with the new Ngoni leader as one of its students. In 1902 he was among the initial group of Ngoni-based evangelists appointed by Rev. **Donald Fraser**. Later in the same year, he represented **Hora** at the North Livingstonia Presbytery. In 1914, he finished theological training at the **Overtoun Institution**, was licensed a year later, and was posted to Chinsali in **Northern Rhodesia**. Mkochi returned in 1917 and was ordained at **Loudon** in November that year. In 1924 he was a member of the Livingstonia delegation to the **Blantyre** Synod, leading to the establishment of the **Church of Central Africa Presbyterian**. Five years later, he was called to the Milala congregation at Engalaweni, just west of **Mzimba** *boma*. He was the moderator of the extraordinary Presbytery that suspended **Charles Chinula** from his ministry.

An influential member of the M'mbelwa council, Rev. Mkochi suggested the title *Inkosi ya Makosi* (kings of kings) for the Ngoni paramount ruler.

MKULITCHI, STEPHEN. A close associate of **John Chilembwe** and planner of the uprising. With **David Kaduya**, Mkulitchi attacked the **African Lakes Company** (ALC) stores on Saturday evening January 23, 1915. It was to his house that the European women and children from **Magomero** were taken to spend the night before they were rescued by the **King's African Rifles** (KAR). Mkulitchi hid in the **Lake Chilwa** area but was caught and shot.

MLANDA. Located almost halfway between Dedza and **Ntcheu**, not far from **Lizulu**, Mlanda became one of the major outstations and educational centers of the **Dutch Reformed Church**, training many future leaders of **Malawi**.

MLANGA, HARVEY. Born in **Blantyre** in 1928, Mlanga attended **Henry Henderson Institute** (HHI) and Blantyre Secondary School. In the mid-1950s he went to Salisbury (now Harare, **Zimbabwe**), where he joined the African Newspapers Group and became editor of *African Weekly*. He transferred to Blantyre, and in the 1960s he worked for the **Malawi Broadcasting Corporation** (MBC). In 1972 he joined the Blantyre Newspapers and eventually rose to the position of managing editor. Mlanga died in February 1979.

MLANGA, MARGARET JEAN NANYONI. Teacher and politician. Mlanga was born in 1927 near **Blantyre** and was educated in local schools and at the Women's Teacher Training College at the **Blantyre Mission**. She led the **League of Malawi Women** from the mid-1960s to 1975, when she was dismissed from the **Malawi Congress Party** (MCP) and imprisoned for some time. Mlanga also served as MP for Blantyre West and as parliamentary secretary in the Office of the President.

MLELEMBA, PETER. Generally known as Haya Edward Peters. Mlelemba was one of the most successful African entrepreneurs in colonial Malawi. Born in **Blantyre**, he was educated at the **Blantyre Mission** and the **Mitsidi** headquarters of the **Zambezi Industrial Mission** (ZIM). In 1905 **Eugene Sharrer** employed Mlelemba in one of his establishments, but he left to become an independent businessman. First, in a joint venture with Mr. Ryalls, he tried to mine mica in the Kirk Mountains. But the enterprise failed, and he then became a farmer, leasing land at Nangafungwe Estates of the **British and East Africa Company**, on the northern side of Ndirande hill. Although his main occupation there was the timber business, Mlelemba also planted **tobacco** and chilies. He called his new firm the PT Company. While pursuing business interests, he bettered himself by registering at a correspondence college in London, and he urged other Nyasalanders to also improve their **education**. In 1909 he was a founding joint secretary (with **Mungo Chisuse**) of the Native Industrial Union, formed to help emerging African entrepreneurs in the area. Among the other members were **Joseph Bismarck**, **John Gray Kufa Mapantha**, **Harry K. Matecheta**, and **Thomas Maseya**.

A close friend of **John Chilembwe**, Mlelemba, also an ivory trader, was out hunting elephants in **Mozambique** when the 1915 uprising broke out. Realizing that his association with its leader would not spare him from trouble, he fled to **South Africa**. Deported from the latter country on charges of political activism, he returned to **Nyasaland** in 1933. Mlelemba could not resume his businesses at Nangafungwe because they had been confiscated in his absence. For a brief period during the war, he worked at the Blantyre *boma* as a military head clerk, but he remained a poor man. Always politically aware, he was present at the founding of the **Nyasaland African Congress** (NAC) in 1944. Mlelemba died on June 24, 1945.

MLONYENI. Title of the **Ngoni** chief in the area of the same name in **Mchinji** District. The original Mlonyeni was the son of Somfula, a kinsman of **Zwangendaba** who had accompanied **Mpezeni** to the Luangwa valley region; he was assigned the area south of the Bua River, Mchinji, on the **Malawi-Zambia** border, which he ruled as Mpezeni's junior. It was in this area that the British built **Fort Manning**, from which they launched an attack on Mpezeni. Mpezeni was imprisoned in Fort Manning for over a year. Although traditionally the office of Mlonyeni remains junior to Mpezeni, in practice they are independent of each other, the former living in Malawi and the latter in Zambia.

MLOZI BIN KAZBADEMA. A **Swahili-Arab**. Mlozi achieved fame as the main adversary of the British in the **Arab-Swahili War**. In 1879 Mlozi's partners in the Luangwa valley asked him to set up operations in the **Ngonde** country on the **Karonga** lakeshore, from which they could transport their merchandise across **Lake Malawi** to the east coast of Africa. His relations with the Ngonde were initially cordial, but the situation became complicated when the British began to establish their presence in the region. By the late 1890s, conflicts had arisen between the Swahili-Arabs, on the one hand, and the British and Ngonde, on the other. On December 6, 1894, the British defeated Mlozi and executed him.

MLUMBE. Area on the western side of Zomba mountain ruled by **Yao** chiefs of the same name. The original Mlumbe settled in this **Mang'anja** region in the 1860s after he and **Malemia** had ran away from the more powerful and combative **Kawinga**, whose seat of power was in Chikala hills.

M'MBELWA. Title of the rulers of the **Ngoni** of northern **Malawi**, adopted after **Mbalekelwa Chimtunga Jere** succeeded his father, **Zwangendaba**.

M'MBELWA AFRICAN ADMINISTRATIVE COUNCIL. Born out of the Jere Chiefs Council, the M'mbelwa Administrative Council was established in 1933 and was chaired by the paramount **Ngoni** ruler, M'mbelwa II. One of the most successful native authorities in colonial Malawi, the council consisted of the M'mbelwa, the six Ngoni chiefs *(amakosi),* and five councillors *(iziduna).* The council had its own treasury, school system, and, within the provisions of the **Native Courts Or-**

dinance of 1933, judicial system. It also developed business interests in commerce, **agriculture**, cattle, and the ghee industry. The M'mbelwa Administrative Council existed until 1961, when it was replaced by the M'mbelwa District Council.

M'MBELWA NGONI. *See* JERE, MHLAHLO; NGONI; ZWANGEND-ABA.

MNTHAMBALA, AUGUSTINE. Educator, founding member of the **Malawi Congress Party** (MCP), and first vice president of the **Alliance for Democracy** (AFORD). Augustine Mnthambala was educated in India and taught at Kongwe Secondary School, Dowa District, before he was arrested and imprisoned without charge. Upon his release, he worked for the American embassy in **Lilongwe**. In 1992 he became a founding vice president of the AFORD. Later he left the party and was appointed high commissioner to Namibia and transferred to the Malawi mission in Paris, where he became ambassador.

MOANO. Located on the **Kapoche** River, a tributary of the Zambezi, Moano was the headquarters of the Undi state.

MOIR, FREDERICK, AND JOHN MOIR. Scottish brothers who were joint managers of the Livingstonia Central African Company, which arrived in the **Lake Malawi** area in 1878 and set up its headquarters about a mile from the Church of Scotland Mission in **Blantyre**. The Scottish company had been formed in response to **David Livingstone**'s call for Christianity and commerce in Africa. The company and its headquarters came to be known as **Mandala**, spectacles, because John wore them. Its name was later changed to African Lakes Corporation (ALC) and then **African Lakes Company**.

MONCKTON COMMISSION. This was a commission of inquiry appointed by the British government to review the future of the **Federation of Rhodesia and Nyasaland**. Chaired by Sir Walter Monckton, the 26 commissioners, including five Africans, spent the period from February to May 1960 gathering evidence in different areas of the Federation. Most Africans boycotted the commission because they assumed that the white majority on it would turn in a report favorable to the Federation. In fact, the opposite occurred. The Monckton Report noted the long-standing and widespread opposition to the Federation and added that the union could not work without some measure of goodwill. The report recommended that, since the Federation was so disliked in its existing form, the British government ought to retain control over the future of the union, including the possible secession of any of its territories. This latter point sounded the death knell for the Federation. The report was unexpectedly attacked by Sir **Roy Welensky**, the federal prime minister.

MONKEY BAY. Scenic bay known for its abundance of monkeys. Located near the southern tip of **Lake Malawi**, Monkey Bay is the main dry dock and operations headquarters of the principal lake transport system in Malawi. To its southeast and southwest are located many traditional **fishing** villages, holiday resorts, and lakeside cottages.

MOTSETSE, KGALEMAN T. Former president of the Bechuanaland People's Party. Motsetse was born in Bechuanaland (Botswana) and educated in **South Africa** and at the University of London, where he graduated with B.D., B.A., and M.A. degrees. In the mid-1940s he taught at the **Blantyre Mission** and became influential in **Nyasaland** African politics, encouraging **James Sangala** to form the **Nyasaland African Congress** (NAC). He also encouraged Sangala to contact the South African trade unionist William G. Ballinger and his wife, Margaret Hodgson Ballinger, a member of the **South African** parliament.

MOXON, PETER. British farmer and supporter of African nationalist aspirations in **Nyasaland**. Moxon visited Dr. **Hastings Banda** in Ghana in 1957 and was one of the people who convinced the doctor to return to Nyasaland to lead the struggle for decolonization. In 1961 he stood as a higher-roll **Malawi Congress Party**–backed independent candidate for Shire North. Following the **Cabinet Crisis** in 1964, Major Moxon left the country, since he was associated with the dismissed members of the cabinet.

MOYALE. Located on the Ethiopia-Kenya border, this was the site of a major Italian siege of a **King's African Rifles** (KAR) contingent consisting mainly of a detachment of the **Nyasaland** battalion. The **Nyasa** soldiers distinguished themselves during the siege (July 1–15, 1940). It is in honor of this battle that Moyale barracks, **Mzuzu**, the home of the Third Battalion of the **Malawi Rifles,** is named. *See also* ARMY.

MOZAMBIQUE. The Anglo-Portuguese Treaty of 1891 established the boundaries between Britain's claim on **British Central Africa** and Portugal's "province" of Mozambique. As a result of the agreement, nearly half of Malawi is surrounded by Mozambique, and many Malawians have families across the border. As the gateway to **Nyasaland** by sea, Mozambique was to play an important role in the **transportation** system of Malawi throughout the 20th century. **Beira**, on the Mozambique coast, became the major port of Malawi when the Trans-Zambesia Railway was completed in 1922. As Malawi approached independence from British rule, the **Malawi Congress Party** (MCP) policy was to attack Portuguese colonialism in Mozambique, particularly when it became clear that decolonization was not on Portugal's agenda.

This intense hostility against the Antonio Salazar government in the early 1960s was ameliorated by **Jorge Jardim**, an envoy of the Lisbon government who began meeting with Dr. **Hastings Banda** on a regular basis. In 1962 Banda announced that although the Portuguese system was to be abhorred, he considered a policy of coexistence possible, much like the one the British and Americans had with the Soviet Union. By 1964 Banda had appointed Jardim as Malawi's honorary consul at Beira. The Portuguese responded by negotiating a mutual trade pact and by permitting the construction of the Nacala Railway, which was to open in June 1970. These activities between Banda and Portugal were condemned by several of Banda's cabinet ministers and were a factor leading to the **Cabinet Crisis** in 1964.

As cooperation between **Zomba** and Lisbon grew, so did Portuguese investment in **Malawi**, particularly in the banking and petroleum fields. In 1967 the Malawi government sold its shares in the Trans-Zambesia Railway and its rights to the Zambezi Bridge to the Portuguese government for nearly US$3.4 million. Three years later, the Portuguese provided a US$2.5 million loan to build a highway.

The Frente de Libertacao de Mocambique **(FRELIMO)**, the Mozambican liberation movement, was allowed to have an office in **Blantyre**, but it was admonished not to use Malawi as a base of operations for raids into Mozambique. However, in 1972, the Malawi army could stop neither FRELIMO units nor pursuing Portuguese forces from trespassing on Malawi soil. Although relations with Lisbon were often strained at this time, Portugal did not press Banda. When FRELIMO won the war of independence in 1974, Malawi applauded the change and supported Mozambican independence. Relations between Malawi and Mozambique were tense throughout the 1970s and for most of the 1980s because of the suspicion that Banda's government was supporting the guerrilla activities of the Resistencia Nacional Mocambicana **(RENAMO)**. Originally supported by the former Rhodesian white regime, the RENAMO forces came to be dependent on Pretoria and former Portuguese colonialists. Aiming to overthrow the FRELIMO leadership of President **Samora Machel** of Mozambique, the RENAMO was responsible for the closure of the railway to Beira in 1983. This line carried 60 percent of Malawi's exports, and subsequently Malawi had to reroute its traffic through **South Africa** and Dar es Salaam, **Tanzania**. Malawi drew the ire of Mozambique as well as **Zambia** and **Zimbabwe** when it refused to take a stand against RENAMO. Instead, Banda chose to walk a tightrope with Mozambique and not make his neighbor's rebel troubles his business. Even when Malawi argued that it never sanctioned or assisted RENAMO troops, it was accused of being lax and unable to properly police its borders.

The ill will that had grown out of RENAMO guerrilla activities worsened in 1986. When President Machel died in an airplane crash in October that year, demonstrations against Malawi occurred in both Harare and Maputo. Student demonstrators, presuming South African complicity in Machel's death and noting Malawi's warm relations with South Africa, damaged Malawi property, mainly embassies, in both Mozambique and Zimbabwe. However, Malawi went on to establish a firm basis of cooperation with the new president, head of FRELIMO, and commander in chief of Mozambique, former foreign minister **Joachim Chissano**. A high-powered Malawi-Mozambique committee was established to discuss matters of mutual interest, and Mozambique refrained from making open allegations against Malawi, which agreed to send some of its troops into Mozambique to protect the Nacala Railway.

Malawi also bore the brunt of a million Mozambique **refugees** on its soil. Beginning with a few thousand who filled the refugee centers such as Mankhokwe camp in the Lower **Shire Valley**, within a short time, other camps mushroomed on the Malawi side of the border. Relief measures have come from many quarters: the Red Cross, Save the Children, Oxfam, and the Food and Agriculture Organization (FAO). In 1988 the United Nations High Commissioner for Refugees established an office in Malawi. When the conflict between FRELIMO and RENAMO ended in 1992, the process of repatriation, which was already in operation, was accelerated.

Mozambique-Malawi relations continued to normalize throughout the 1990s. The cessation of the civil war in Mozambique in the early 1990s promoted cordiality between the two countries to the extent that when a group of **Young Pioneers** hid in Mozambique following **Operation Bwezani**, the two governments immediately cooperated in resolving the problem. The election of a new government in Malawi in July 1994 further improved Mozambique-Malawi relations. Joint security and trade commissions have continued to meet regularly. Presidents Joachim Chissano and **Bakili Muluzi** also meet regularly, mainly through their active participation in meetings of the **Southern Africa Development Community** (SADC) and the **Common Market for Eastern and Southern Africa** (COMESA).

MPAKATI, ATTATI. Chiradzulu-born and Scandinavian-trained political scientist, academic, and leader of the Socialist League of Malawi (LESOMA). Attati Mpakati was assassinated during a visit to Harare, **Zimbabwe**, in March 1983 by agents of the **Malawi** government. Three years earlier, a parcel bomb had blown off his hands. Grey Kamuyambeni replaced him as head of LESOMA.

MPASU, SAMUEL. Leading **United Democratic Front** (UDF) politician and Speaker of parliament after the 1999 general **elections**. Mpasu was born in **Ntcheu** District in 1945 and educated at Dedza Secondary School. In 1969 he graduated from the **University of Malawi** with a B.A. degree. He joined government service and became a diplomat serving in Ethiopia. In the mid-1970s he worked for the **Viphya Pulpwood Scheme**. In 1975 he was arrested and placed in detention, remaining there for over two and a half years. Upon his release he worked for a variety of organizations, including the **Malawi Chamber of Commerce**, of which he became general manager. In the early 1990s Mpasu was among the leading advocates of political reform and a founding member of the UDF party. In 1994 he was elected to parliament, becoming minister of education; later he was transferred to the Ministry of Information, Broadcasting, Post, and Telecommunications. In 1999 he was returned to the National Assembly as member for **Ntcheu** Central.

MPEZENI. Also known as Ntuto. Mpezeni was the eldest son of the **Ngoni** leader **Zwangendaba** by his once favored wife, **Soseya** Nqumayo. Born in 1833 in today's **Zimbabwe**, Mpezeni was 15 when his father died in 1848. Following a succession dispute, he and his brother **Mpherembe** parted from the main group in southern Tanganyika and moved west toward **Bemba** country. Mpherembe rejoined the main group, now settled in the region west of **Lake Malawi**, but Mpezeni proceeded southeast, finally settling in the **Chipata** area east of the Luangwa River in about 1866. From there he extended his authority to include most of present-day **Mchinji** District, where he placed his subordinate, **Mlonyeni**. In 1885 Mpezeni granted a **mining**

concession to a German adventurer, **Karl Wiese**, who in 1896 sold it to the **North Charterland Exploration Company**, a division of the **British South Africa Company**. Mpezeni did not like the de facto extension of British rule and resisted it. In December 1897, his eldest son, **Nsingu**, rose against the increasing presence of the British in his father's territory. The British sent troops of the British Central African Rifles (later **King's African Rifles**) to subdue Mpezeni, his son, and his supporters. After a month of fighting, Nsingu was captured, court-martialed, and shot on February 5, 1898. His father surrendered four days later and was imprisoned at the new **Fort Manning**, where he remained until 1900. He died that year. His successors maintained relations with their cousins, the M'mbelwa **Ngoni**, in northern Malawi, and attended each other's installation ceremonies.

MPHEREMBE. Area located in northwestern **Mzimba** District. Its name is derived from Mpherembe, the **Ngoni** ruling family. The original Mpherembe was a son of **Zwangendaba** and brother of **Mpezeni**. After leaving the main Ngoni party to go west with his brother, he rejoined M'mbelwa and other children and followers of Zwangendaba, and was allocated the area south of Lake Kazuni and northwest of **Mtwalo**'s area. This is also a Ngoni area in which ciNgoni, a version of Zulu, is still the major language.

MPINGANJIRA, BROWN JAMES. Journalist, member of the **United Democratic Front**'s (UDF) Central Committee, MP for **Mulanje**, and influential cabinet minister in the post-**Hastings Banda** government. Mpinganjira was the Malawi government's deputy chief information officer until 1986, when he was arrested and imprisoned without being charged at **Mikuyu**. He remained in detention until the momentum for political reform began to gain pace, and he became a leading ally of **Bakili Muluzi**. After the 1994 **elections**, he was appointed minister of transport, communications, and information, but in a cabinet reshuffle he was transferred to the Ministry of Education. In 1999 he was reelected to the National Assembly as MP for Mulanje Central, retained his position as national organizing secretary of the UDF, and was appointed minister of foreign affairs and international cooperation. Later he became minister of public works but was dropped in a cabinet reshuffle in November 2000 as a result of a report of the Parliamentary Public Accounts Committee, which detailed cases of financial mismanagement in some government departments. In January 2001 Mpinganjira formed the National Democratic Alliance (NDA), which he hoped would develop into a major political party. Within three months the NDA was forging alliances with other opposition parties, and was winning support in various areas of **Malawi**.

MPINGO WA AFIPA. *See* MWASI, YESAYA ZERENJI.

MPONDA. Title of **Yao** chiefs who, since the early 1860s, have ruled the area around the southern tip of **Lake Malawi**. The first Mponda (1866–1986), son of Msamala the founder of the lineage, gave permission to the Free Church of Scotland to establish the **Livingstonia Mission** station at **Cape Maclear** in 1875. A convert to **Islam**, Mponda actively engaged in the ivory and **slave trade** with contacts on the east coast of Africa. Mponda II had tense relations with the **African Lakes Company** (ALC) but in 1889 allowed the **White Fathers** to set up a station near his village. He did not give them much freedom of action, and he continued with his trading activities, which the Catholic missionaries did not approve of. Five years later, the missionaries left the area for **Northern Rhodesia (Zambia)**. Mponda, like many other chiefs, resisted British rule but was finally defeated in 1896.

MPONDA, ANDREW JONATHAN. Former secretary-general of the **Nyasaland African Congress** (NAC). Mponda was a founding member of the organization and earlier of the Blantyre Native Association. In 1948 he accompanied **Charles Matinga** to England where, with Dr. **Hastings Banda**, they made representations to the British government on the conditions of Africans in **Nyasaland**. Within two years of their return, Mponda and Matinga lost their senior positions in the NAC because of charges of financial mismanagement and ineffective leadership.

MPONDA, JIMMY MKANDAWIRE. *See* MKANDAWIRE, JIMMY MPONDA.

MPOSA, J. ELLERTON. Appointed to the **Legislative Council** (LEGCO) in 1949. Mposa and **Ernest Muwamba** became the first Africans to sit in that body. Active in African nationalist politics, Mposa was a founding member of the Blantyre Native Association and of the **Nyasaland African Congress** (NAC). A critic of the **Federation of Rhodesia and Nyasaland**, Mposa, allying himself with the NAC, consistently spoke against its establishment.

MPUTAHELO, CHIMWEMWE. Journalist and politician born in December 1968. Former editor of the **United Democratic Front** (UDF)–allied *Mirror*, and later publicity secretary-general of the **Malawi Democratic Party** (MDP). In 1995–1996, Mputahelo was accused, with other members of the party's Central Executive Committee, of threatening President **Bakili Muluzi**, but they were cleared by a court of law. In September 1996 Mputahelo was accused of another plot, this time as a prospective hitman of **John Tembo** in a plot to kill **Brown Mpinganjira**, **Aleke Banda**, and **Peter Fachi**. He escaped to **South Africa** and wrote a long memorandum copied to many people including Muluzi, exonerating himself and charging that in fact the plot was to kill him and some **Malawi Congress Party** (MCP) officials. He returned to **Malawi**, was tried, imprisoned and later released. Mputahelo died in early 2001.

MSAKAMBEWA. Son of **Gwaza Jere**. Msakambewa accompanied **Chiwere Ndhlovu** to the **Kongwe** area not far from Lingazi River in present-day Dowa District. There Msakambewa established political authority, becoming one of the very few northern **Ngoni** to become chief in a **Chewa** area. The **Dutch Reformed Church** established a station and a school in his jurisdiction.

MSIMBI. Colonial government weekly published by the Department of Information in English and ciNyanja. Besides covering news favorable to the government, the publication sought to explain policy and in the 1950s acted as a major propaganda vehicle for issues such as the **Federation of Rhodesia and Nyasaland**. Many Malawians remember *Msimbi* for its cartoon character, Njolijo. *See also* CHAWINGA, DUNCAN "GOODNEWS."

MSISHA, MORDICAI CHIWEREWERE. Leading lawyer and **human rights** activist. Msisha was born in 1950 in **Southern Rhodesia (Zimbabwe)**, where his Malawian parents worked and went to primary school before attending Chaminade Secondary School at **Karonga**, northern Malawi. He read law at the **University of Malawi**, and upon graduation in 1975 he joined the Ministry of Justice as a legal aid counselor. From 1977 to 1979, he studied for a master's degree in law at the University of Toronto, **Canada**, and on his return to Malawi worked briefly as a prosecutor before joining the law firm Savjani & Company. Since 1990 he has been a partner in the Nyirenda & Msisha legal practice.

Msisha's name is closely identified with political reform in **Malawi**. From 1991 to 1994, he was actively involved in the struggle for multiparty democracy. As a member of the **Law Society of Malawi** and the **Public Affairs Committee** (PAC), he played a major role, including campaigning outside Malawi, in the events leading to the general **elections** in 1994. Originally identified with the **Alliance for Democracy**

(AFORD), he fell out of favor with **Chakufwa Chihana**, the party leader, and, just before the elections, withdrew from active politics and concentrated on his legal work.

MSISKA, REV. STEPHEN KAUTA. Theologian, scholar, and former principal of the **Church of Central Africa Presbyterian** (CCAP) Theological College at **Nkhoma**. Kauta Msiska was born near Mhunju, **Rumphi** District, in about 1914. He completed his education at the **Overtoun Institution, Khondowe**, trained as a teacher, and then returned to Khondowe to train for the church ministry, graduating in 1945, also the year of his ordination. He served in many parishes and in the late 1950s was moderator of the **Livingstonia** Synod. He spent the 1961–1962 academic year at the Divinity School of the University of Edinburgh. Upon his return, he was appointed tutor at the Theological College, Nkhoma, of which he was to become principal, the first African to hold the position. However, in 1974, he offended the **Malawi Congress Party** (MCP) when he advised his students to dress plainly during their conduct of worship, which also meant that they had to avoid wearing the MCP badge with Dr. **Hastings Banda**'s head on it, a permanent feature of the outfit of most party loyalists. For this he was unceremoniously dismissed from his position, threatened with death, and banished to his village in **Rumphi**, marking his virtual retirement from active church duties. A keen student of local history and customs, in 1997, Rev. Msiska published *Golden Buttons: Christianity and Traditional Religion among the Tumbuka*.

MSISKA, SUZGO. Leader of the Transport and General Workers Union (TGWU) in the early 1960s. Suzgo Msiska was also an active and radical member of the **Malawi Congress Party** (MCP). In 1962 **Rumphi**-born Msiska, like **Chakufwa Chihana**, resisted the efforts of the new MCP-dominated government to control the labor unions, resulting in his suspension from the party and the loss of his position as head of the TGWU.

MSONTHI, JOHN DUNSTAN. Teacher, politician, and former cabinet minister. John Msonthi was born at Kayoyo, **Ntchisi** District, in 1922. Son of a priest in the Anglican Church, Msonthi attended **Likuni** Catholic School before proceeding to **Zomba** Catholic Secondary School in 1945. Three years later, he wrote and passed the Cambridge School Certificate examinations (O levels), achieving the distinction of the being one of the first two Nyasalanders to sit for this type of examination. In the early 1950s he won the government of India Cultural Scholarship, which enabled him to study at St. Xavier's College and at the University of Bombay, where he was awarded B.A. and B.Ed. degrees, respectively.

Msonthi returned home in 1958 and taught at his old school in Zomba. He also became active in the **Nyasaland African Congress** (NAC) and was detained in March 1959. Upon his release, he taught at St. John's Teachers College in **Lilongwe**. In 1961 he was elected MP for Ntchisi (Visanza), and a year later he was appointed minister of trade and industry. In 1964 Msonthi became minister of transport and communications and in the early 1970s served as minister of education. Throughout this time, Msonthi was also Dr. **Hastings Banda**'s interpreter at political rallies held in the **Chewa/Nyanja**-speaking areas of Malawi. In 1973 he fell out of favor with Banda and was banished to his home in Ntchisi. Five years later, he was rehabilitated and appointed chairman of the Grain Milling Corporation, a position he held until his death in 1982.

MSOSA, ANASTASIA. High Court judge and chairman of the Electoral Commission of Malawi from 1993 to 1998. Anastasia Msosa graduated from the **University of Malawi** and served as a magistrate in several courts before she was promoted to the High Court. In 1998 the government removed her from the Electoral Commission and replaced her with Judge James Kalaile.

MSUMBA, JORDAN. Founder of the Last Church of God and his Christ. Jordan Msumba was born at **Usisya**, **Nkhata Bay** District, and by the early 1900s had been to local **Livingstonia Mission** schools. Between 1907 and 1909 he was converted to **Eliot Kamwana Chirwa**'s **Watchtower Society**. In 1909 he followed Kamwana to **South Africa**, where he also met **Joseph Booth**, under whom he was to study while also holding regular employment. He became a Baptist but returned to the Watchtower Society. In 1920 he was forced to return to **Nyasaland**, probably because of his association with activists such as **Clements Kadalie**. Back at home in Usisya, he began to meddle in chiefly politics, leading to his deportation in 1924 from the Nkhata Bay District.

A year earlier, Msumba had been excommunicated from the Watchtower and had founded the Last Church of God and His Christ. Similar to Watchtower practices, his adherents were baptized by immersion soon after confessing their sins, making its process faster than that of the Livingstonia Mission. Unlike Livingstonia or even the Watchtower, the Last Church allowed polygamy. In August 1925 Msumba officially inaugurated his church and went to **Karonga** to win more converts. There he met **Iswani ben Ngemela** and Tigone Munthali, both of whom became pastors of his new church. In December that year, Msumba proceeded to Tanganyika, working in **Mwanza** and Shinyanga, but he was not very successful in converting people to his denomination. In 1934 he returned to Nkhata Bay only to find that Isaac Kaunda, whom he had left to organize the Last Church in the district, had started his own church, Covenant Church (Chipangano Church), taking many people with him. From that time on, Msumba and Kaunda engaged in a war of words and competition for adherents, resulting in a major erosion of the followership of the Last Church.

MTAFU, ANDREW GEORGE NGA. For many years Malawi's only neurosurgeon. Mtafu was born at **Likoma** and trained at a medical school in Germany. In the 1980s he returned to **Malawi** and was based at the Queen Elizabeth Hospital in **Blantyre**. In February 1989, Mtafu was arrested and imprisoned without trial for making a statement disagreeing with President **Hastings Banda**'s pronouncements. Upon his release in 1991, he became active in reform politics, later associating himself with the new **United Democratic Front** (UDF) party. In 1994 he was elected to the National Assembly as member for **Nkhata Bay** East (Likoma) and was appointed minister of health. In 1999 Mtafu was reelected to parliament and became minister of tourism, national parks, and wildlife. In November 2000 he was appointed minister of education.

MTAWALI, BRAIN. Agriculturalist, diplomat, and last Speaker in the **Malawi Congress Party**–dominated National Assembly. Brain, son of **Ernest Mtawali**, was educated at **Livingstonia** and at **Zomba** Catholic Secondary School before going to India, where he graduated from University of Madras with a B.Sc. in agriculture. On his return, he joined the civil service and rose to the position of principal secretary. Upon his retirement, Mtawali was appointed high commissioner to **Canada** and in the early 1990s became Speaker of the Malawi parliament. After the general elections of 1994, he became a businessman in **Mzuzu**.

MTAWALI, ERNEST M. Member of the **Executive Council** from 1959 to 1961. Ernest Mtawali was born at Mlowe, **Rumphi**, and educated at **Overtoun Institution**, where he trained as a medical assistant. He worked at various health centers, establishing himself as one of the most experienced, efficient, and popular clinical officers. In 1959 he was appointed to the Executive Council, in effect the cabinet of the colonial governor. African nationalists strongly opposed his accepting the new position during the state of emergency and at a time when most activists were under arrest; they felt betrayed and Mtawali became a target of their anticolonial propaganda. After the 1961 **elections**, he went to live in **Southern Rhodesia (Zimbabwe)**.

MTEGHA COMMISSION. Appointed by the new **United Democratic Front** (UDF)–led government to inquire into and report on the 1983 **Mwanza accident**, this commission was headed by Justice Michael Harris Mtegha of the Supreme Court of Malawi. From July 11 to December 14, 1994, the commission heard evidence in camera to protect witness confidentiality and in January the following year released its two-part report, *Mwanza Road Accident Report*, Limbe, December 1994; and *Mwanza Road Accident: Verbatim Report of Proceedings* (not dated). The report established that four politicians, **David Chiwanga**, **Aaron Gadama**, Twaibu Sangala, and **Dick Matenje**, were assassinated. It traced the chain of events from their arrest at the roadblocks in **Zomba** following the Easter session of parliament in 1983 but found it difficult to identify the person or persons responsible for issuing the order for the murders. However, on the basis of the report, the government proceeded to prosecute **Hastings K. Banda**, **Cecilia Kadzamira**, and **John Tembo** on the grounds that, since they were the ultimate decision makers in **Malawi**, they must have known of the plans to kill the four politicians.

MTEMANYAMA, CHARLES. One of the early indigenous businessmen based in **Blantyre**. Mtemanyama was a married to Bela, daughter of **Joseph Bismarck**. Charles and Bela were a **Blantyre Mission**–educated, respected, churchgoing couple who had worked in Tanganyika before embarking on their laundry enterprise in 1922. For two years Mtemanyama's business was based at the **Ryall's Hotel** in the center of Blantyre, most of his customers being Europeans. In 1924 he moved to his own building at Michiru, just outside Blantyre, but he continued to use the Ryall's Hotel and other locations in Blantyre and **Limbe** urban areas as collecting points. By the late 1930s Mtemanyama was beginning to face competition from others entering the laundry business.

MTEWA, MEKKI. Academic and deputy minister of foreign affairs and international cooperation in the **United Democratic Front** (UDF) government of the post-1999 elections. Mekki Mtewa was born in **Mangochi** District and was educated in **Malawi** and the **United States**, where he obtained a Ph.D. degree in political science. In the 1970s he became one of the most reviled Malawians in **exile**, mainly because of his association with the views of **Henry Chipembere**. His father was imprisoned without trial, and his name was the subject of many songs sung by the **League of Malawi Women**. Mtewa taught in colleges in the United States and in the early 1990s was a founding member of the **Alliance for Democracy** (AFORD), becoming one of the party's leading theorists. However, before the elections in 1994, he fell out of favor with the leadership of the party and crossed over to the UDF, whose new government appointed him as a roving ambassador. In 1999 he was elected MP for Mangochi and was appointed deputy minister of foreign affairs and international cooperation.

MTIKA, EFFIE FUYIWE. Born in 1931 in **Mzimba** District, Effie Mtika joined the Malawi civil service in 1964 as a community development officer. Two years later, she went to the **United States**, where she trained further in community development at the University of Missouri. In June 1971 Mtika was nominated to parliament as member for Mzimba, and in the following year she became parliamentary secretary in the Ministry of Community Development and Social Welfare. She left parliament after a few years.

MTUNTHAMA. Located west of **Kasungu** *boma*, this is the site of the first school that **Hastings Kamuzu Banda** attended, in commemoration of which the **Kamuzu Academy** was built. Banda's official residence of Hastings Banda in **Lilongwe** was known as Mtunthama House.

MTUWA, REV. HARRY. One of the early **Blantyre Mission** teachers, Mtuwa was ordained minister in 1916 and became a most successful evangelist in the Blantyre Synod of the **Church of Central Africa Presbyterian** (CCAP).

MTWALO I. *See* JERE.

MTWALO II. *See* JERE, MUHABI AMON.

MUA. This major Catholic mission station is located in the eastern section of Dedza District, just below the escarpment that descends into the Rift Valley of which **Lake Malawi** is part. When the **White Fathers** missionaries returned to the Lake Malawi region in 1902, Mua became the main center from which they spread their activities to parts of the Central and Northern Regions. Mua is also the home of a large cultural and arts center, the KuNgoni Arts and Crafts Center, established in the 1980s.

MUGHOGHO, MORTON CHIPIMPHA. National chairman of the **Alliance for Democracy** (AFORD) from its inception. Mughogho was born in 1922 in Nthalire, **Chitipa** District, and went to local schools before qualifying as a teacher at the **Overtoun Institution, Khondowe**. He taught at home, and then for several years in **Southern Rhodesia (Zimbabwe)**. Back in Malawi he became headmaster of Nthalire Primary school, and in 1956 he was promoted to assistant inspector of schools. After serving in **Mzimba** and **Karonga** Districts, he spent the 1959–1960 academic year at Bristol University, England. On his return, he was posted to **Zomba** District as inspector of schools. In 1962 he became inspector of primary education for the Central Region, but following the **Cabinet Crisis** of 1964 he was detained without trial. Upon his release two and a half years later, he became headmaster of **Rumphi** Secondary School and then joined the inspectorate division at the Ministry of Education headquarters. He spent another brief period in detention and after his release became a **tobacco** farmer in Rumphi. In 1981 he became chairman of the **Phwezi Education Foundation** and headmaster of the Phwezi Secondary School in Rumphi District. In the early 1990s he was a founding member of AFORD and in 1994 was elected MP for Chitipa South; he retained the seat in the 1999 **elections**.

MULAGA, ENEAH FERDINAND "SUPER." A leading educator and one of the early graduates of the **Jeanes Training Centre, Domasi**. Mulaga was born in 1906 in **Ulambya, Chitipa** District. After attending local schools, he trained as a teacher at the **Overtoun Institution** and by the early 1930s was supervising teacher. Later he attended the new teacher inspector course at the Jeanes Training Centre and for the next 20 years was deeply involved in the expansion of schools in the upland section of **Karonga** District, to the extent that his name has remained associated with Western **education** and the type of Western values that Jeanes College sought to inculcate in the African mind. He retired in 1967 and died in 1993. Eneah Mulaga's brother, Rev. Adam Mulaga, played a significant role in education and evangelization in the district.

MULANJE. Located in southeast **Malawi** on the border with **Mozambique** and inhabited mainly by **Lomwe** and **Yao** speakers, this is one of the most densely populated districts in Malawi. The district is known for its **tea** plantations on the southern side of **Mulanje Mountain**. Fertile soils between Mulanje and the **Shire Highlands** support a large agrarian population, the majority of whom were subjected to the *thangatha* system during colonial rule. Just north of Mulanje was the site of Fort Lister, which overlooked the old slave caravan route between Mulanje Mountain and **Lake Chilwa**. With Phalombe becoming a district in 1996, the size of Mulanje has been reduced.

MULANJE MOUNTAIN. Located in **Mulanje** District on the Malawi-**Mozambique** border, Mulanje Mountain is the highest massif in South Central Africa. Sapitwa, its peak, is 10,000 feet high.

MULLINS, J. V. Born in Britain in 1909, Mullins served in British Guiana, Mauritius, Uganda, and **Zanzibar**. In Zanzibar he was commissioner of police from 1955 to 1958, when he was transferred to **Nyasaland** to occupy a similar position. As head of **police** from 1958 to November 1964, Mullins had to deal with many volatile situations, including the return to the colony of Dr. **Hastings Banda** and its political ramifications, the state of emergency, the **Monckton Commission**, the first general **elections** in 1961, independence in 1964, and the **Cabinet Crisis** later that year. On his retirement, he joined the faculty of the Police College, United Kingdom, where he became director of overseas studies.

MULUZI, ELSON BAKILI. President of the Republic of Malawi since 1994. Bakili Muluzi was born in **Machinga** District on March 17, 1943. After attending local schools, he joined the colonial civil service as a clerk. He became a political activist, and after independence he joined the **Malawi Young Pioneers** (MYP), becoming a technical instructor. Through the sponsorship of the MYP, he attended courses at Thirsted Technical College in Denmark and Huddersfield Technical College in the United Kingdom. In 1973 he was appointed principal of **Nasawa** Technical College near **Magomero**, **Chiradzulu** District. Two years later, he became MP for Machinga and in 1977 was promoted to the cabinet as minister of education. Within a short time he became minister without portfolio and secretary-general of the **Malawi Congress Party**, a position he held until 1982. Subsequently, he became a full-time businessman, among other things, growing **tobacco**. He was elected national chairman of the Malawi chamber of commerce, a position that allowed him to have contact with many businessmen, some of whom joined him in the early 1990s in the campaign for political reform.

In 1992 Muluzi became leader of the **United Democratic Front Party** (UDF) and ran as its presidential candidate in 1994. He won the **elections**, and his party had the majority seats in the new National

Assembly. He became president and formed a cabinet; a few months later, the **Alliance for Democracy** (AFORD) joined the government, with **Chakufwa Chihana** becoming the second vice president of Malawi. Two years later, the coalition ended. In June 1999 Muluzi and his party were returned to power.

In the main, Muluzi's economic policies are not radically different from Dr. Banda's, especially considering the fact that he too has continued to rely on **foreign aid** for budgetary purposes. Furthermore, Muluzi's government took over the liberalization program to which Western donors agreed, led by the **World Bank** and **International Monetary Fund** (IMF) on the one hand and the Malawi Congress Party (MCP) government on the other. The program includes the privatization of parastatal industries and the removal of subsidies on fertilizer and fuel. The latter measure has adversely affected food production and has contributed to a higher cost of living as the cost of fuel has greatly increased. *See also* FINANCIAL AND ECONOMIC DEVELOPMENTS.

In **foreign policy** the UDF-led government is nonaligned and has good relations with governments that Dr. Banda considered unfriendly or communist oriented. Muluzi, a Muslim, has established relations with Libya and many Arab states in the Middle East, most of which had no diplomatic links with Banda's regime. The UDF and the Islamic community in Malawi have benefited financially from strong connections with nations such as Libya. Muluzi has also been more active than Dr. Banda in African and world affairs, participating in regional and British Commonwealth heads of state summits, among others.

In the field of **human rights** Muluzi has radically departed from Dr. Banda's policies. Multiparty democracy is putting down deep roots, as the general **elections** of the 1990s show. In the post-Banda period, parliament is respected as an elected legislative body, and freedom of expression has become an accepted fact, as evidenced by the numerous newspapers and magazines published in Malawi. Similarly, freedom of association has become a major feature of life, with trade unions and other organizations operating freely within the law.

However, as a 2000 report of the Parliamentary Public Accounts Committee states, serious cases of misappropriation of funds by government officials have increased since Muluzi and the UDF won power in Malawi in the mid-1990s. Corruption in the public sphere has also become widespread.

MUMBA, LEVI ZILILO. One of the founders of the **Nyasaland African Congress** (NAC) and a highly regarded educator and civil servant. Levi Mumba was born, most likely, in 1884 at Chidakalala village, near **Ekwendeni, Mzimba** District. Of **Ngoni** and Senga origins, he went to one of the numerous schools being established in **Ungoni** by the **Livingstonia Mission**, distinguished himself as a brilliant pupil, and by 1902 had completed the highest level of education then attainable at the **Overtoun Institution, Khondowe**. He worked as an office assistant to **Robert Laws** and two years later became one of the first students at the new commercial school at the institution, graduating with distinction. After working for the mission for some time, he joined the civil service, serving in **Karonga, Zomba**, and **Lilongwe**, among other places. He rose to the position of head clerk, then the ceiling for Africans in government service.

Mumba also established himself as a notable political activist. He was a founder of the **North Nyasa Native Association,** the Southern Province Native Association, and the Committee of Northern Province Associations. With **James Sangala** and others, he formed the **Nyasaland African Congress** (NAC) in 1944, becoming its first president-general. In 1929 Mumba, Isaac Mkondowe, and **Paddy Nyasulu** formed the African National Church, which later spread to the rest of **Nyasaland** and beyond. Also in 1929 Mumba was the first African to be appointed to the Education Advisory Committee and fought relentlessly for improvement in African **education**. He died at Mzimba on January 23, 1945. *See also* AFRICAN WELFARE ASSOCIATIONS.

MUNTHALI, MARTIN MACHIPISA. Political activist and one of Dr. **Hastings Banda**'s bodyguards in the preindependence period. Munthali was a political prisoner from 1965 to 1992 and is known locally as the Nelson Mandela of Malawi. Arrested for supporting the views of the dissident ministers during the **Cabinet Crisis** of 1964, he was charged with illegal possession of arms. After serving his sentence, he was detained without trial and held at **Mikuyu** prison until the clamor for political reform started in 1992. After his release he tirelessly campaigned for multiparty democracy, presenting himself as a living symbol of oppression. Later Munthali successfully took the government to court for having deprived him of his civil liberties for 27 years. In the 1999 general **elections**, he stood as **United Democratic Front** (UDF) parliamentary candidate for **Rumphi** East but lost to Gowa Nyasulu of the **Alliance for**

Democracy (AFORD). He contested again in the local government elections in November 2000 and was elected to the Rumphi District Council as UDF member for Mlowe Ward.

MUNYENYEMBE, RODWELL WATAYACHANGA. Born in 1936 at Lukomo village, Nthalire, in **Chitipa** District. Munyenyembe studied at **Domasi** Teacher Training College and qualified as a teacher in 1960. He also trained as a special education teacher in Manchester, England. He has held several ministerial positions, including Information and Broadcasting, Community Development, and Social Welfare. In 1974 he was appointed minister of education as well as deputy regional chairman of the **Malawi Congress Party** (MCP) for the Northern Region. But four years later he fell out of favor with Dr. **Hastings Banda**, losing his cabinet post and his seat in parliament. He virtually retired from politics and concentrated on **tobacco** farming in **Rumphi** District. He was later elected chairman of the **Tobacco Association of Malawi** (TAMA) and vice chairman of the Tobacco Control Commission. In the early 1990s he reemerged as a prominent player in the political reform movement and identified himself with the **Alliance for Democracy** (AFORD). In 1994 he was elected to parliament as member for Chitipa South. In the initial working arrangements between AFORD and the **United Democratic Front** (UDF), he was elected Speaker of parliament, a position he held until 1998. In 1999 he stood for the Chitipa Wenya constituency as a UDF-backed independent candidate but lost to AFORD. Although he lost the **elections**, President **Muluzi** appointed him minister of state for presidential affairs, and a few months later he became minister of defense.

MURRAY, ANDREW C. Born in **South Africa** to Scottish parents, Andrew Murray was the pioneer missionary from the **Dutch Reformed Church (DRC) of South Africa**. Secretary of the newly formed Stellenbosch-based Students' Missionary Society, Murray went to the **Lake Nyasa** area in 1888 and worked with Livingstonia missionaries for a time while seeking a site for his church's mission station. In the following year, Rev. T. C. B. Vlok joined him, and they established a mission station near Chief **Chiwere Ndhlovu**'s village, west of present-day **Salima**. Murray was influenced in his methods by the **Livingstonia Mission** and especially by Dr. **Walter A. Elmslie**. He tried to pattern the **Mvera** ("obey") mission station on Livingstonia, which was further north. Murray retired in 1900.

MURRAY, WILLIAM H. One of the pioneer missionaries of the **Dutch Reformed Church (DRC) of South Africa**. Andrew C. Murray was born in **South Africa** in 1866. He qualified as a doctor in Edinburgh, Scotland, and received theological training in **South Africa**. A cousin of **Andrew C. Murray**, William was the second of numerous members of the Murray family to work in the DRC in Malawi. In 1894 William Murray journeyed to **Lake Malawi**, traveling with Albert van der Westhuysen, a missionary-farmer who started the DRC agricultural work program at **Mvera**. Murray was assigned to **Livulezi** mission station, south of Mvera, which the **Livingstonia Mission** handed over to the DRC in 1895. In agreement with the Livingstonia Mission, the DRC was responsible for Livulezi and **Cape Maclear** in the central area, and Livingstonia was to confine its work to northern Malawi. In 1896 **Nkhoma** mission was founded, As additional missionaries arrived, more stations and schools opened. In 1900 Murray married Elizabeth Duckitt. They had two children, both of whom became missionary doctors in Central Africa. In 1925 Murray was appointed to the **Legislative Council** (LEGCO), and in 1937 he resigned after 43 years of mission work.

MUSOPOLE, FLAX KATOBA. One of the most feared African nationalists in late colonial **Malawi**. Katoba Musopole was born in the Misuku area, **Chitipa** District in 1919. He attended local schools and Mwenilondo school in **Karonga** lakeshore before emigrating to **South Africa**. There, while working, he studied by correspondence and passed the South African matriculation examinations. In 1953 he was admitted to the University of Cape Town but left after two academic years. While in South Africa, he became an atheist and was influenced by leftist thought. He became a strong advocate of anticolonialism and even corresponded with Dr. **Hastings Banda** in London. By late 1957, he was back in **Nyasaland**, where, in a fiery manner, he began to speak against colonialism and the **Federation of Rhodesia and Nyasaland**. When Dr. Banda returned to Nyasaland in 1958, Musopole was one of the politicians who accompanied him during his introductory visit to the Northern Region. During the state of emergency of 1959, Musopole was accused of organizing and promoting violence in **Karonga** District, and security forces hunted him relentlessly without success. So elusive and effective an organizer was he that newspapers nicknamed him "General." He was finally captured in Tanganyika, brought back to Nyasaland, and charged with sedition. He was defended by the distinguished British lawyer and Labour Party politician **Dingle Foot**, assisted by **Orton Chirwa**. He served his sentence in **Zomba** Central Prison for two years, and upon his release was appointed clerk of the Karonga District Council. In the preindependence elections of 1964, he was elected to parliament as the first member of the new Karonga West (later Chitipa) constituency and was appointed parliamentary secretary in the Ministry of Community Development. In 1967 he was assigned to the Malawian mission to the United Nations but after two years was sent to the Malawi Labour Office in Botswana. Within a short time, he was back in Chitipa, where he became a businessman. Musopole died in 1989.

MUSOPOLE, REV. YORAM. Bible scholar and translator, and former chairman of the Bible Society of Malawi. Musopole was born in Misuku, **Chitipa** District. He went to school in Misuku, **Karonga**, and at the **Overtoun Institution**, where he qualified as a teacher. In the post–World War II period, he returned to the Overtoun Institution to train for the church ministry and was ordained in 1949. He served a number of congregations as pastor, including **Ulambya**, and in 1960 he became a member of a team of Lutenganyo (southern Tanganyika)–based church scholars translating the Bible into **Kyangonde**. For the remainder of his career, he was stationed at **Khondowe** and Karonga, where he continued to work on Bible translation. In the early 1970s he retired to farm **coffee** and raise chickens in Misuku. Musopole died in 1994.

MUSSA-GAMA, ELIAS AMIN. Prominent Muslim and politician. Mussa was born in 1926 at Chindamba, **Zomba** District. Educated in **Malawi** and **South Africa**, he set up a tailoring business in 1954. He was active in the **Nyasaland African Congress** (NAC) in the 1950s and spent a year in prison for his political involvement. In 1961 Mussa was elected district chairman of the **Malawi Congress Party** (MCP) at Zomba, and two years later he became Zomba's first African town clerk. In 1970 he entered the National Assembly as one of the members for Zomba District and remained in parliament until the early 1990s when he retired from active politics.

MUTHARIKA, BINGU WA. Economist Bingu Wa Mutharika formed the **United Party** (UP) in 1997, soon after returning to **Malawi** from his position as secretary-general of the **Preferential Trade Area** (PTA) of East and Central Africa. In the 1999 general elections, he unsuccessfully stood as presidential candidate for the UP. Bingu wa Mutharika had offered himself as leader of the **United Democratic Front** (UDF) in the 1994 **elections** but was shunned by the party. In 2001 Bingu wa Matharika disbanded his party, joined the UDF, and was appointed deputy-governor of the Reserve Bank of Malawi.

MUWALO-NQUMAYO, ALBERT. One of the most powerful persons in Malawi between 1964 and 1976. Albert Muwalo-Nqumayo was born on June 23, 1927, at Baleni village, **Ntcheu** District. He attended Gowa primary school before going to **Blantyre** Secondary School, and in 1947 he qualified and practiced as a medical assistant. In 1956 the Nyasaland African Medical Association elected him as its secretary-general, a powerful position, especially when medical services were under the Federal government, which was disliked by most Africans. He became the association's spokesman and increasingly was drawn into national politics. Muwalo was detained during the state of emergency in 1959. In 1962 he was elected Chairman of Ntcheu District Council and a member of the Central Committee of the **Malawi Congress Party** (MCP). After a three-month tour of Ghana studying **Kwame Nkrumah**'s party organization and management of the press, Muwalo became administrative secretary of the MCP. In September 1964 Dr. **Hastings Banda** appointed him minister of information. Two years later, he became minister of state in the President's Office, where he remained for a decade. This placed him in a particularly strong position in the Malawian power structure. With **Focus Gwede**, he virtually controlled matters of national security for most of the 1970s. In September 1976 the two were arrested and charged with treason, and in 1977 Muwalo was found guilty, sentenced to death, and executed. *See also* HEALTH.

MUWAMBA, ERNEST ALEXANDER. Distinguished public servant and first African member of the **Legislative Council** (LEGCO). Muwamba was born in **Nkhata Bay** in 1892. Son of **Yakobi Msusa Muwamba** and a cousin of **Clements Kadalie**, Alexander Muwamba completed his education at **Livingstonia** and in 1913 went to **Northern Rhodesia (Zambia)**, where he worked as a civil servant and became a head clerk, the highest position that an African could achieve. He was a founding member of the Ndola Native Welfare Association. Upon his return to **Nyasaland** in 1944, he maintained his interest in African nationalist activities. In 1949 he was nominated to the **Legislative Council** (LEGCO), becoming one of two Africans to join the body, the other African being **Ellerton Mposa**. In 1952 Muwamba was on the African delegation to the Federal conference in London, where he explained his views opposing the **Federation of Rhodesia and Nyasaland**. After independence in 1964, the Malawi government appointed him to the Public Service Commission, which he chaired. He died in 1970.

MUWAMBA, ISAAC KATONGO. Highly respected civil servant and political activist. Isaac Muwamba, son of chief Chiweyu Muwamba, was born in **Nkhata Bay** District in about 1890, went to **Bandawe** and to the **Overtoun Institution**, where he completed primary school. In 1912 he went to **Northern Rhodesia,** where he distinguished himself as an efficient clerk, rising to the position of head clerk and High Court interpreter. During World War II, many Europeans in the Northern Rhodesia colonial service joined the war effort, enabling Muwamba to act as a **district commissioner**, a very rare occurrence for an African in those days. An active member of the Lusaka Native Welfare Association of which he was a founding member, Muwamba returned to **Nyasaland** in 1949, and, like his cousin **Ernest Muwamba**, he became involved in the political well-being of Africans at home. He died in 1953.

MUWAMBA, JAKE. Social welfare officer and distinguished diplomat and businessman. Jake, son of Ernest Alexander Muwamba, was born in **Northern Rhodesia (Zambia)**. He was educated there and in **South Africa**, where he trained in social welfare work at the Jan Hofmeyr School of Social Work in Johannesburg. He worked as a social welfare officer in **Malawi** and in 1969 was appointed director of tourism. In 1975 he became ambassador to the United Nations On his return to Malawi in the early 1980s, he became a consultant and businessman; he was also appointed chairman of the Designated Schools Board. In the early 1990s he was a founding member of the **United Democratic Front** (UDF) and campaigned for change. After the general **elections** of 1994, he returned to the diplomatic service, this time as Malawi's high commissioner to the Court of St. James, London. In 1999 he returned to private business in **Malawi**.

MUWAMBA, YAKOBI MSUSA. Born in the Chintheche area of **Nkhata Bay** District, Yakobi Muwamba was one of the first students at the **Bandawe** school. With **Charles Domingo**, he was also the one of the first students to complete the theological course at the **Overtoun Institution, Khondowe**, in 1900. Passing the course with credit, Muwamba had earlier obtained a teacher's certificate from the institution but was never ordained, as he died before he could start his probationary period. His son **Ernest Alexander Muwamba** became one of the most distinguished public servants in **Northern Rhodesia (Zambia)** and in both colonial and postcolonial **Malawi**.

MVERA. This major educational center located in Dowa District was the first mission station for the **Dutch Reformed Church** (DRC). At the advice of the **Livingstonia** missionaries, Rev. **Andrew C. Murray**, assisted by Rev. T. C. Vlok, set up operations at Mvera (obey) in 1888, primarily because it was the home of Chief **Chiwere Ndhlovu**, the **Ngoni** who had earlier split from M'mbelwa's main party and established his own authority in **Chewa** country. From Mvera the DRC mission was to extend to various parts of central Malawi, including **Kongwe**, **Nkhoma**, and **Mlanda**.

MWAKASUNGULA, REV. AMON. Of the **Ngonde** ruling family, Amon Mwakasungula was ordained in 1924 and served in various parts of **Karonga** and **Chitipa** Districts before retiring in the early 1960s. A composer of church music, he translated John Bunyan's *Pilgrim's Progress* into **Kyangonde**.

MWAKASUNGULA, PETER MWANGALABA, KYUNGU. Traditional ruler *(kyungu)* of the **Ngonde** from 1927 to 1966. After receiving a basic mission education in **Karonga**, Peter was employed by the **African Lakes Company** (ALC) and by other Europeans operating in his home area. He became a major **cotton** grower, successful retail trader, and owner of large herds of cattle, making him a very wealthy individual. His brother, Fwangalubilo Mwangalaba, was the *kyungu* from 1904 to 1926, but Peter was the effective ruler for most of the 1920s. In 1927 he was installed *kyungu*. When the **North Nyasa Native Reserves Commission** visited Karonga, he presented a strong case against the **British South Africa Company**'s claims to land in his domain. Under the **Native Courts Ordinance** of 1933, his office changed from principal headman to **native authority** (NA), giving him power of jurisdiction of customary matters over most of the old **Karonga** District, with the exception of the area under the Mwafulirwa. Rather cool to nationalist aspirations in the late colonial period, the **Malawi Congress Party** (MCP) government tended to ignore him, preferring **Joseph Mwanjasi**, Chief Kilupula. Kyungu Peter Mwakasungula died in 1966.

MWAKASUNGULA, RAPHAEL KAPOTE. Musician, politician, and broadcaster. Son of Rev. **Amon Mwakasungula**, Raphael Kapote was born in **Karonga** and received his education there and at the **Overtoun Institution**. Although he worked in various capacities, his love was always music, and he composed many songs, some of which were featured on local radio. In the 1950s he became active in the **Nyasaland African Congress** (NAC) and was one of the principal grassroots organizers in Karonga in the period leading to the state of emergency in March 1959. In 1961 he became a social and community affairs official, but in two years he went to England on attachment to the British Broadcasting Corporation (BBC) African Service. On his return, he joined the **Malawi Broadcasting Corporation** (MBC) as a producer/announcer. In 1967 he became *kyungu*, the senior ruler of the **Ngonde**. He occupied that until the 1972 MCP convention, when he was deposed because he supported the return to Malawi of **Wellington M. Chirwa**. *See also* CHAWINGA, CHIEF KATUMBI.

MWALARE, NDICHE. Disabled banjo and guitar player who was an icon of Malawi popular culture in the 1950s and 1960s. Ndiche, as he was fondly called, played music from his wheelchair, his lyrics commenting on the life of Malawian immigrant workers in **Southern Rhodesia (Zimbabwe)**, the urban social scene in **Malawi**, and clashes between custom and modernity in rural areas. In the 1960s Ndiche worked for the **Malawi Broadcasting Corporation** (MBC) as a record librarian.

MWAMULIMA, PATRICK RUTHERFORD. Classmate of **Charles Chinula** at **Khondowe**. Mwamulima was a delegate to a meeting in **Blantyre** that led to the formation of the Church of Central Africa Presbyterian (CCAP), and member of the special Presbytery that met at Loudon on November 2, 1930, to consider the future of Charles Chinula after allegations of adultery. Mwamulima was also a prominent member of the **North Nyasa Native Association**, the first **African welfare association** to be formed in colonial Malawi.

MWANJASI, JOSEPH, NTEMI KILUPULA. Traditional ruler of **Ngerenge**, northern **Karonga**, from the 1940s to the early 1980s. Chief Kilupula went to local mission schools before briefly working in Tanganyika. He was a very progressive ruler, keen to modernize his area, a major **rice** and **cotton** grower. Mwanjasi was a key factor behind the formation in 1952 of the **Kilupula Rice Growers Co-operative Union**, one of the most successful **cooperatives** in the country. Joseph Mwanjasi was the union's chairman throughout its life (1952–1968). Highly respected by his people, he was a strong supporter of the nationalist cause. When the traditional courts system was established, he became a member of the National Appeals Court. He died in the early 1980s.

MWANZA. District west of **Blantyre** through which the Blantyre-Harare road passes via Tete in **Mozambique**. It is also a major orange-producing area. A few miles south of Mwanza *boma* was the site of the 1983 **Mwanza accident** involving three cabinet ministers and one member of parliament.

MWANZA ACCIDENT AND TRIALS. On the night of May 18, 1983, four leading Malawian politicians were murdered in **Mwanza** District: **Dick Matenje**, MP for **Blantyre**, secretary-general of the **Malawi Congress Party** (MCP), and minister in the Office of the President; **Aaron Gadama**, MP for **Kasungu** and minister for the Central Region; Twaibu Sangala, MP for Dedza and minister of health; and David Chiwanga, MP for **Chikwawa**. On the previous day, they had been arrested near the Likangala Bridge on the **Zomba**-Blantyre road as they drove to the latter city after attending parliament. They were taken to the Eastern Division's police headquarters in Zomba and then to **Mikuyu** prison for the night. On the following day, the four were taken to the MCP offices at Chichiri and then to the **Special Branch** center in John Abegg House, **Limbe**, where they were interrogated. That evening, they were transported in a blue Peugeot to the Thambani road in **Mwanza** District, where they were murdered.

The killing squad, led by Aaron Mlaviwa, head of the Police Mobile Force, deliberately executed their mission in a manner indicating a road accident. The bodies were placed in the car, which was then overturned. Directing the entire exercise was Macpherson Itimu, head of the Special Branch. According to evidence provided to a commission of inquiry into the incident, Itimu's actions had been authorized by then inspector-general of police, **Mac J. Kamwana**. The government issued press releases to the effect that the politicians had died in a road accident while escaping to **Mozambique**. Meantime, their burials, supervised by the **police**, were restricted to family members only, causing more suspicion in the general public.

The matter was never discussed in public until 1992–1993, when freedom of expression was beginning to return to Malawi. In 1994 the new **United Democratic Front** (UDF) government appointed Judge Harris Mtegha of the Malawi Supreme Court to head a commission of inquiry into the Mwanza incident. Evidence was heard in chambers, but the report was made public in January 1995. The government followed this by prosecuting former President **Hastings Banda**, **John Tembo**, and the government "official hostess," **Cecilia Kadzamira**, on grounds that they, as a powerful "inner circle," had to have been aware of the plans to murder the four politicians. The government team was led by the director of public prosecutions, Kamudoni Nyasulu. The defense's lead lawyer was Clive Stanbrook, QC, whom the MCP had hired in England. The judge was Maxon Mkandawire of the High Court. Banda never appeared in court in person because a medical report indicated that he was unfit to do so; Kadzamira was also not required to go to court in person. Things were different for Tembo. He had been arrested earlier and spent some time in prison before being bailed out. He had to be present in court in person. The trial was attended by international observers, including the vice president of the World Council of Churches, Benjamin Masilo of Lesotho, and Craig Baab of the American Bar Association. Toward the end of 1995, Banda, Kadzamira, and Tembo were all acquitted because of insufficient evidence incriminating them. The government said it would appeal but by mid-2000 had not done so. *See also* MTEGHA COMMISSION.

MWANZA, NELSON PETER. First Malawian principal of **Chancellor College, University of Malawi**. Mwanza was born in northern **Mzimba** and was educated locally at **Zomba** Catholic Secondary School and at Goromodzi High School in **Southern Rhodesia (Zambia)**. He studied at the University College of Rhodesia and Nyasaland and then at Ohio State University, which awarded him M.Sc. and Ph.D. degrees in botany. In 1966 he joined the faculty at Chancellor College, becoming its principal in 1971. In July 1975 Mwanza was dismissed from his job and later that year was arrested and detained without trial. Released in 1977, he joined the United Nations Environmental Program (UNEP) in Nairobi, Kenya. A few years later he became an employee of the United Nations Economic Commission for Africa (UNECA) in Addis Ababa, Ethiopia. In the 1980s he retired to **Mzuzu**, where he chaired the committee preparing the groundwork for the new University of Mzuzu. In July 2000 he was appointed vice chancellor of the university.

MWASE, GEORGE SIMEON. Civil servant, political activist, and author. Mwase was born about 1880 near **Chintheche** and was educated at the Free Church of Scotland school at **Bandawe**. In 1905 the colonial government hired him as a postal clerk at **Chiromo**. He resigned a year later and moved to **Northern Rhodesia**, where he worked for the government until 1920. Upon returning to **Nyasaland**, he was employed as a tax clerk before becoming a store manager and politician. He organized the Central Province Native Association in 1927. Between 1931 and 1932, he wrote *A Dialogue of Nyasaland: Record of Past Events, Environments, and the Present Outlook within the Protectorate,* an account of the **Chilembwe uprising** and life in **Malawi**. This typescript was discovered in the Malawi archives in 1962 by Professor Robert Rotberg and subsequently was published as *Strike a Blow and Die* (1967). Mwase played an active role in the **Nyasaland African Congress**, serving on its Executive Committee. He later became alienated from his Congress friends and in the late 1950s came out in favor of the **Federation of Rhodesia and Nyasaland**. Mwase died in 1962.

MWASE KASUNGU. Mwase Kasungu's **Chewa** kingdom developed in the 18th century as the influence of the **Kalonga** declined. The Mwase dynasty, centered at **Kasungu**, grew in power, reaching its zenith between 1830 and 1890. It exchanged salt for **cotton** and iron hoes. Engaging in the ivory and **slave trade** with the Portuguese brought considerable prosperity and influence in the 19th century. Mwase's territory bordered the Luangwa valley, a major elephant region and therefore a favorite of **Swahili-Arab** traders. The most convenient route to the east coast via **Nkhotakota** passed through Mwase's area. He established good commercial relations with the Swahili-Arabs and bought guns from them to ward off **Ngoni** raids. However, when these trading partners tried to avoid the fees charged for passing through his domain, Mwase quickly isolated them. He made a defensive pact with the Ngoni, who disliked the Swahili-Arabs and were not interested in trading with them. Soon the Swahilis' attempt to bypass the shrewd Mwase failed. In 1863 **David Livingstone** visited Mwase, and in 1890 **Karl Wiese**, in the service of the Portuguese, also visited the Chewa chief. Mwase resisted British rule until 1895, when they defeated him.

Between 1937 and 1972 the office was occupied by one of the most remarkable traditional rulers in 20th-century **Malawi**. In 1939 Chief Mwase spent some time at the School of Oriental and African Studies, University of London, as research assistant in ciNyanja. At this time he met a distant relative, Dr. **Hastings Banda**, who had been in the United Kingdom for two years. When the **Nyasaland African Congress** (NAC) was formed in 1944, Mwase became a member and, with chiefs such as **Zintonga Philip Gomani**, **Mkhosi Lazalo Jere** (M'mbelwa II), and **Kuntaja**, came to be identified with African political aspirations. In 1952 he became founding president of the Nyasaland **Chiefs Union** and, through it and the NAC, campaigned against the establishment of the **Federation of Rhodesia and Nyasaland**. Throughout the 1950s, Mwase remained a strong supporter of the NAC, siding with the radical wing of the party led by **Henry Chipembere** and **Kanyama Chiume**. In 1961 he attended the **Lancaster House Conference** as a representative of the chiefs. When the Traditional Courts System was instituted in postcolonial Malawi, Chief Mwase was appointed chairman of the Traditional

Court of Appeal, the highest court in that particular system. In 1972 Mwase was deposed and replaced by **Chief Kawomba** because he and a few other traditional authorities supported the return to Malawi of **Wellington Manoah Chirwa**.

MWASI, YESAYA ZERENJI. One of the first three Africans to be ordained church minister in the **Livingstonia Mission** and founder of **Mpingo wa Afipa wa Africa**. Yesaya Zerenji Mwasi was born in **Nkhata Bay** around 1869 and was educated at **Bandawe** and the **Overtoun Institution, Khondowe**, where by 1901 he was session clerk. In 1902 he completed the theological course, was licensed five years later, and in 1910 was a delegate to the **Blantyre** meeting at which the formation of the **Church of Central Africa Presbyterian** (CCAP) was discussed. In May 1914 he, **Jonathan Chirwa**, and **Hezekeya Tweya** became the first Africans to be ordained pastors in the Livingstonia Mission. A highly independent thinker, one who was prepared to challenge the superiority complex of some European missionaries, Mwasi was initially assigned to Bandawe, where in February 1915 Dr. William Y. Turner suspended him for insubordination. Eighteen months later, the Sanga congregation just north of Bandawe invited Mwasi to be its minister. In 1918 he was elected moderator of Presbytery, the first African to hold the position, and three years later became temporary clerk.

Mwasi's conviction that the missionaries applied double standards in their relations with the African clergy and African Christians never changed. He argued that all people were to be treated equally and different opinions had to be discussed even if they did not please European missionaries. From 1932 he began to threaten that he would resign if the Scottish missionaries did not change their attitudes, and in September 1933 he executed his threat, announcing the formation of his Mpingo wa Afipa wa Africa, or Black Man's Church of God. He detailed all his ideas for an African-based church in his *My Essential and Paramount Reasons for Working Independently* and proceeded to organize his new church, taking with him many in his Sanga congregation. Influenced by Garveyism, Mwasi emphasized African self-reliance, which he argued could be partly attained through independent African schools and colleges. He hoped to obtain financial assistance from **Tonga** immigrant workers in other parts of Southern Africa. He also established working relations with **Charles Chinula** of Eklezia Lanangwa. Mwasi was a founder of the West Nyasa Native Association (WNNA) in 1920, and in the 1930s and 1940s he became active in **Nkhata Bay** politics, which were to contribute to the demise of the **Atonga Tribal Council**. Mwasi died on July 17, 1955.

MWAVI. Ordeal by poison used in many African societies to establish a person's guilt or innocence. The assumption is that a guilty party does not survive it, whereas an innocent person vomits the poison.

MWAYA. Located on the shores of **Lake Malawi** in **Nyakyusa** country, Mwaya has for a long time served as the northern terminus of the **transportation** system on the lake. For a long time it was the main entry into Tanganyika (**Tanzania**).

MWENISONGOLE, REV. ARAM NDOLEZI. Educator and church minister. Mwenisongole was born in **Chitipa** in 1903 and attended local schools before going to the **Overtoun Institution, Khondowe**, where he passed the standard six examinations and then qualified as a teacher. Around 1940 he completed the institution's theological course and after ordination worked in the **Karonga** lakeshore area. In the late 1940s he was appointed manager of schools and minister in charge of Karonga Mission (Old Mission), the first African to head this station. In 1950 he transferred to **Ulambya**, but four years later he was defrocked. He left the **Livingstonia Mission** and became a teacher at **Edingeni**, the seat of the M'mbelwa **Ngoni** authority. In 1958 he fell ill and sought medical assistance at Mbeya, Tanganyika, where he died.

MWENIWANDA. Located in **Ulambya** plains in **Chitipa** District. In 1881 the Ncherenje section of Mweniwanda became the site of the Free Church of Scotland Mission. Chosen because it was on the road connecting **Lakes Malawi** and Tanganyika, Mweniwanda was headed by Rev. J. Alexander Bain. In 1886 he was joined by Hugh Mackintosh, Dr. **Kerr Cross**, and soon the latter's wife, Christina. On December 31, 1888, Christina died, followed by Mackintosh a day later. Dr. Kerr Cross abandoned the Mweniwanda Mission and moved to Lutenganyo in **Unyakyusa** and then to **Ngerenge** in **Ngonde** country.

MWENZO. Located in Namwanga country in northeastern **Zambia**. In 1894 Mwenzo became one of the stations of the **Livingstonia Mission**. The first missionary there was Rev. Alexander Dewar, assisted by a **Tonga** evangelist, Yohane Afwenge Banda, whose stipend was paid by the **Bandawe** congregation. He worked at the mission until after World War I, establishing himself as the longest-serving missionary at Mwenzo.

MZIKUBOLA. Ngoni chiefdom located south of **Mzimba** *boma* and ruled by the house of the same name, with its headquarters at Emchakachakeni. The original Mzikubola was the son of M'mbelwa I and thus grandson of **Zwangendaba**. The Inkosi Mzikubola of the later 20th century was educated in Ghana, graduating with a B.A. degree. He worked as a civil servant in Malawi and for over 10 years was a diplomat attached to the Malawi mission in the **United States**. Inkosi Mzikubola died in 2000.

MZIMBA. Name of the *boma* of the largest district in the Northern Region of **Malawi** (also called Mzimba). The district covers the area under the **Ngoni** paramount rulers, M'mbelwa, who originally established themselves in the region in the 1860s. Mzimba *boma* was the administrative headquarters of the Northern Region until 1954, when **Mzuzu** took over this position.

MZUZU. Administrative headquarters and principal commercial center of the Northern Region. With a population of just under 100,000, Mzuzu lies on the **Mzimba** side of the border with **Nkhata Bay** and Mzimba Districts. Its origins go back to 1945, when the colonial government decided to establish a major **tung**-growing area in the **Viphya Highlands** and appointed Charles Boardman as tung development officer. Two years later, Boardman identified a site on the Mzuzu stream as the nucleus of the tung project, which was to develop under the full auspices of the **Colonial Development Corporation** (CDC). As the number of expatriate staff increased, and as many Africans moved to the area to seek employment, Mzuzu grew into a small urban center. In 1954 the provincial administrative headquarters moved from Mzimba *boma* to Mzuzu, further swelling its population and size. The Catholic Church also transferred offices of the diocese from Katete in southern Mzimba to Katoto on the periphery of the new town. In 1958 Mzuzu Government Secondary School opened on the Nkhata Bay road. In the early 1960s, the Catholic Church built the Mary Mount Girls Secondary School, the Mzuzu Technical School, and St. Luke's Hospital, which until 2000 was the only health facility in the city. In the late 1970s the headquarters of the **Livingstonia** Synod moved from **Khondowe** to Mzuzu.

In 1986 Mzuzu became a city that today boasts a major hotel and numerous motels and rest houses, and is accessible via paved **roads**. It has an airport and is the site of two new projects, the University of Mzuzu and a large modern hospital built by the Taiwanese government.

NAMIWAWA, BLANTYRE • 287

– N –

NAKANGA, WENHAM. Lawyer and founding member of **United Democratic Front** (UDF). Nakanga was elected to parliament and appointed to the cabinet in 1994. He died shortly afterward.

NAMADZI. Located on the Namadzi stream on the **Zomba-Blantyre** road, this small retail trading center was until the 1970s dominated by **Asian** businessmen who were forced to move to the larger urban areas because of **Africanization.** Adjacent to **Magomero**, Namadzi is inhabited by the **Mang'anja**, **Yao**, and **Lomwe**, and it is surrounded by **tobacco** estates, most of them owned by European planters.

NAMALAMBE, ALBERT "DON." **Mang'anja** teacher and preacher, the first African convert of the **Livingstonia Mission**. Namalambe first went to the mission at its **Cape Maclear** base in the late 1870s as a servant of one of **Ramakukan**'s sons, who was a pupil at the school. He became a student and an assistant at the mission, was baptized in March 1881, and then moved to the new mission headquarters at **Bandawe**, where he became a teacher and preacher. In 1884 he returned to Cape Maclear to take charge of the school and station. He remained there until 1908, when he died. Namalambe played a major role in improving relations between the Maseko **Ngoni** ruler, Chikusi, and the Scottish missionaries. He helped convince the Ngoni to allow the establishment of a mission station at **Livulezi**.

NAMBUMA. This area in **Lilongwe** District is one of the leading **tobacco**- and **maize**-producing areas in **Malawi**. In the colonial period it was part of the sharecropping region dominated by European planters such as **A. Francis Barron**, **Roy W. Wallace**, and **Ignaco Conforzi**. The area is also a major center of the **Agricultural Development and Marketing Corporation** (ADMARC).

NAMITETE. Located on the **Lilongwe-Mchinji** border, Namitete is a **tobacco**-growing region of Malawi, a site of the **Agricultural Development and Marketing Corporation** (ADMARC), and a major Roman Catholic mission station, with a large school and a hospital.

NAMIWAWA, BLANTYRE. This low-density suburb of **Blantyre** is located on the western side of the city between the city center and **Mitsidi**. Namiwawa is a common place-name in **Malawi**, and it refers to a mahogany tree stream.

NAMOKO, ALAN. This singer, popular mostly in the 1970s and 1980s, is famous for his compositions, which include messages of a social nature.

NAMWANGA. Cultivators and cattle keepers. The Namwanga live in northeastern **Zambia**. In precolonial times they were famous as iron smelters and smiths who traded with other peoples, including the **Nyiha** and Lambya, in today's **Malawi**. Groups of Namwanga settled in the **Chitipa** area.

NAMWERA PLANTERS ASSOCIATION. Organization of European **tobacco** growers in Namwera, Fort Johnston **(Mangochi)** District. Like other such associations, the Namwera Planters Association strongly supported closer union with the Rhodesias and made its views known to both the **Hilton Young Commission** of 1929 and the **Bledisloe Commission** 10 years later.

NANGALEMBE, JOSEPH. A popular singer in the 1970s and 1980s. Nangalembe was raised in **Mulanje** District. He is known mainly because of the satirical nature and social content of his songs.

NANKHUNDA. This major Roman Catholic mission station, located on the western side of the **Zomba** mountain, was established in 1912 by Bishop **Louis Auneau**. In February 1928 the Montfort priests vacated Nankhunda in order for the first Minor Seminary to be established there, the initial 50 students coming from the **Nguludi** Normal School in **Chiradzulu** District. Before the seminary at **Kachebere** was established in 1930, most of the early Catholic clergy went to the Kipalapala Major Seminary in Tanganyika to complete their studies.

NAPOLO. According to Malawian belief, a python that resides below the **Zomba** mountain. Occasionally it travels underground to **Lake Chilwa** via the Mulunguzi River, which flows from the mountains into the Likangala, a main supplier of water to the lake. It is believed that Napolo's movements can be detected by certain environmental changes, including sudden drops in lake levels, which could indicate its migration back to the mountain.

In recent times the name Napolo has been associated with the powerful cyclone that stalled over the **Zomba** area while tracking west from the Indian Ocean through **Mozambique**, bringing much rain and causing death and considerable damage to property and roads. The cyclone hit Zomba on Friday afternoon on December 13, 1946, and did not move on until Sunday, December 15, when 20 inches of rain had been recorded in the town. Landslides demolished two villages on the western side of the mountain, killing 20 people; water overflowed the Mulunguzi and other streams, bringing with it massive boulders and trees. Nearly all bridges and culverts in Zomba town were destroyed, and the water supply and the **electricity**-generating plant on the slopes of the mountain were disrupted for several days.

Napolo has been immortalized by, among others, the **Paseli Brothers** in their popular composition, "Napolo Wachabe" (Napolo the Bad), and by Steve Chimombo in his collection of verse, *Napolo Poems (1987)* and the *Napolo and the Python* (1992).

NASAWA. This site in the northern part of **Chiradzulu** District was once part of the **A. L. Bruce Estates**. From the 1960s to the early 1990s it was famous as the main training base of the **Malawi Young Pioneers** (MYP). Nasawa was also the home of the MYP Technical College, where more able youth leaguers were trained in vocational fields such as masonry, joinery, and motor mechanics.

NATION, THE. A leading paper in post–**Hastings Banda** Malawi. *The Nation* was founded by **Aleke Banda** in 1992 as a voice for political reform in the country. In the period leading to the 1994 **elections**, the paper strongly championed the **United Democratic Front** (UDF) party, Aleke Banda's political affiliation, which formed the new government in June that year. After Aleke became a cabinet minister, his family took charge of *The Nation*. Although it has criticized the government's actions occasionally, it has continued to support its policies.

NATIONAL ARCHIVES OF MALAWI (NAM). Located in **Zomba** and established in 1947 as part of the Central African Archives. The National Archives of Malawi were reorganized under the National Archives and Publications Act of 1974. The NAM principally functions as a main depository and manager of government records, as well as any other **literature** concerning **Malawi**. Many other records and manuscripts, including those of private individuals, major and minor firms, the **Universities' Mission to Central Africa** (UMCA), the **Livingstonia Mission**, and the **Blantyre Mission** are deposited at the NAM. The National Archives Library is the national library of Malawi and the main collector, recorder, and preserver of literature pertaining to Malawi.

NATIONAL CONSULTATIVE COUNCIL (NCC). *See* PRESIDENTIAL COMMITTEE ON DIALOGUE (PCD); PUBLIC AFFAIRS COMMITTEE (PAC).

NATIONAL DEVELOPMENT COUNCIL (NDC). Established in 1968 to coordinate the planning and implementation of Malawi development projects among the various government departments and parastatal organizations. Constituting the NDC were the departments of finance, trade, and industry; works and supplies; agriculture, forestry, and natural resources; and two government agencies, the **Agricultural Development and Marketing Corporation** (ADMARC) and the **Malawi Development Corporation** (MDC). The council was active in the initial four years, producing the *Statement of Development Policies, 1971–1980*. After 1972, however, it became inactive, leaving other branches of the government to maintain a dynamic interest in development matters.

NATIONAL ECONOMIC COUNCIL (NEC). Under the **United Democratic Front** (UDF) government, this council is involved in coordinating economic development, very much in the manner of the original **National Development Council** (NDC). In 1999 **Mapopa Chipeta**, formerly minister of foreign affairs, was appointed head of the council.

NATIONAL LIBRARY SERVICE (NLS). Created under the National Library Service Act of 1967 as a statutory body to ensure library access to all peoples in all corners of **Malawi**. The act provided for a board to direct NLS policy. The board members, drawn from the general public, are nominated by the Ministry of Education and serve for a given time. The headquarters of the organization and the main library are in **Lilongwe**, but it has a major presence in **Limbe**, **Blantyre**, **Zomba**, and **Mzuzu**, and it serves all the districts in the country.

NATIONAL PARKS. There are five national parks in Malawi: **Kasungu, Lake Malawi, Lengwe, Liwonde**, and **Nyika**. All of them are administered by the **Malawi** government through its Department of National Parks and Wildlife. *See also* TOURISM.

NATIONAL RURAL DEVELOPMENT PROGRAM (NRDP). Under this ambitious program the entire nation was expected to benefit from the introduction of more intensified rural services. Evolving from discussions between the Ministry of Agriculture and the **World Bank**, the program had the following aims: to increase the level of smallholder production of cash crops for export as well as for the growing urban centers; to provide pesticides, fertilizers, and improved seed to enable smallholder production increases; to preserve natural resources by reforestation, by conserving key watershed areas, and by encouraging high standards of crop husbandry and soil conservation.

The **Malawi** government hoped to increase the efficiency of its **transportation** system and expand its extension services. The Marketing and credit would be improved as the **Agricultural Development and Marketing Corporation** (ADMARC), rural markets, and informal village markets would be more accessible. **Women**, in particular, were, and still are, active in the latter. Despite their prominent role in farming, however, there was no significant attempt to involve them in the agricultural education process. Whereas men had access to improved technology, information, and training, women were only taught how to cook some of the new crops.

The NRDP divided the country into nine management units (MU) that administered an equal number of agricultural development divisions (ADD). Each ADD was subdivided into development areas covering the whole of Malawi, the plan being to involve over 80 percent of smallholders in the NRDP. The Northern Region rural development programs (RDP) have provided over 56,000 Malawians with better credit facilities, new **health** centers, and improved **roads** and bridges. The **Karonga-Chitipa** RDP, sponsored by the World Bank, has concentrated on **cotton**, **maize**, **groundnuts**, and **rice**. Under the **Lilongwe** RDP, also sponsored by the World Bank, maize, **tobacco**, groundnuts, and some cattle ranching have benefited. German aid has promoted the **Liwonde** and **Salima** RDPs, both of which have concentrated on cotton, rice, and maize. British Overseas Development Administration (ODA) money sponsored the maize, cotton, and smallholder **tea** crops in the **Blantyre** RDP; and European Union aid has been responsible for the **Kasungu** RDP (groundnuts, maize, and fire-cured tobacco) and **Mzuzu** RDP (groundnuts and maize). The Malawi government assumed the administration of the RDP in the Lower Shire at Ngabu, where cotton and rice are produced.

At the end of its first decade the Malawi government characterized the program as a success, but its financial backers were more critical, indicating that the costs of agricultural services were too high and that smallholder output was sluggish. Donor disenchantment led to a shift from the NRDP concept and further structural adjustments. The needs of the subsistence farmers, and those without enough land to even qualify as subsistence farmers, were to be better taken care of. More technical personnel were to reach the poorer peasants to encourage them to effectively participate in a more meaningful smallholder program. *See also* AGRICULTURE.

NATIONAL STATISTICAL OFFICE (NSO). Although formally established under the 1967 Statistics Act, the NSO had been in existence since the immediate postindependence months in 1964. Based in **Zomba**, this government department regularly collects, compiles, analyzes, and publishes statistical information, thus making it readily available to other branches of government, **nongovernmental organizations** (NGOs), and the private sector. There are five main subject divisions of the NSO: Economic Statistics, which concentrates on national accounts and balance of payments, industry, retail prices, **external trade**, employment, and **tourism**; Agricultural Statistics; Demography and Special Surveys; Transport Statistics; and Statistical Common Service. Through the latter, the NSO renders service to other government departments by way of attaching its professional staff to those agencies. In this manner, the coordination of statistics and the uniformity of the system are assured. A case in point is the Data Processing Unit of the Accountant General Department, which operates in conjunction with the NSO to provide up-to-date information on government accounts.

NATIONALIZATION. Throughout his tenure as prime minister and president of Malawi, Dr. **Hastings Banda** publicly espoused pragmatism rather than adherence to political and economic ideologies, which he argued would lead to policies such as nationalization. However, in practice, his government nationalized many aspects of Malawi's **economy**, the rationale being to **Africanize** rural retail trade and to localize control of large-scale commerce and industry. As early as 1961, the first African majority government inherited the African Produce and Marketing Board (AP&MB), which marketed crops grown by Africans. Under the **Malawi Congress Party** (MCP) government, the AP&MB changed its name to **Farmers Marketing Board** (FMB) and finally to **Agricultural Development and Marketing Corporation** (ADMARC). The latter and the **Malawi Development Corporation** (MDC), the holding statutory body created in 1964, played a leading role in shaping the economy of independent **Malawi**.

In 1966 the government nationalized Malawi Railways, which had been owned by **Lonrho**. Four years later, the MDC and **Malawi Press**, in partnership, bought majority shares in Bookers (Malawi) Ltd., a division of Bookers Group of London, which dominated the retail, wholesale, and distribution business in the country. Bookers (Malawi) Ltd., which owned McConell's and **London & Blantyre Supply** (**Kandodo**), now became the National Trading Company. In the same year, the National Insurance Company was established, and in the next 20 years it absorbed most other insurance firms in the country. The MDC was involved in many other ventures, including the Carlsberg Brewery, Gilbery and Mathieson Distillery, and David Whitehead, the textile company. The Malawi government also nationalized the two banks, Barclays and Standard, creating the National Bank; through **Press Holdings Ltd.** and ADMARC, government also developed a new one, the Commercial Bank of Malawi, which set up branches in most corners of the country. In the 1990s government shares in National Bank were greatly reduced, and the ownership was virtually assumed by private interests. *See also* BANKING.

In the mid-1990s the **United Democratic Front** (UDF) government began to privatize most nationalized industries at the behest of the **International Monetary Fund** (IMF) and the **World Bank**, and it established a privatization company to supervise the sale of the statutory bodies. *See also* FINANCIAL AND ECONOMIC DEVELOPMENTS.

NATIVE ASSOCIATIONS. *See* AFRICAN WELFARE ASSOCIATIONS.

NATIVE AUTHORITIES (NA). A designation developed under the **indirect rule system** referring to traditional rulers—chiefs. Under the **Native Authority Ordinance** and the **Native Courts Ordinance**, chiefs were granted a wide range of administrative and judicial powers. Only a select group of traditional rulers were conferred with the title "native authority,"most of the chiefs being recognized only as sub–native authorities. In 1961 the African majority government recognized all chiefs as NAs.

NATIVE AUTHORITY ORDINANCE, 1933. This act formally recognized chiefs, or traditional African rulers, as **native authorities** (NA). The act gave powers to NAs to make rules to enable them to administer their areas for purposes of "peace, good order, and welfare." At the same time the Native Courts Ordinance was passed, to enable the NAs to establish Native Courts through which to enforce civil and criminal justice. Native Treasuries were also instituted to enable the NAs to raise revenue locally. These measures were at the core of the **indirect rule system** introduced in 1933, and it was through these ordinances that bodies such as the **M'mbelwa African Administrative Council** were established.

NATIVE COURTS ORDINANCE, 1933. *See* NATIVE AUTHORITY ORDINANCE.

NATIVE DEVELOPMENT AND WELFARE FUND. Controlled by the colonial government, this was a fund consisting of surplus money from the sale of African produce, mainly **cotton, maize,** and **tobacco**. The fund financed government-backed projects such as **cooperative societies, roads,** bridges, and **newspapers,** including *Msimbi.*

NATIVES ON PRIVATE ESTATES BILL, 1928. This law dictated that Africans living on private estates had to pay rent to the estate owner or work for wages. If they chose the former, the landlord could assign them a plot of land on which to grow crops that the landlord would then buy to generate the income needed for the rent. Default in payment of rent or behavior deemed unacceptable by the landlord could, according to the ordinance, result in eviction after six months notice. Although the ordinance also authorized the government to reserve more land for those evicted, the problem of land in the **Shire Highlands** was to remain unresolved until the postcolonial period. *See also* ABRAHAMS COMMISSION; AFRICAN TRUST LANDS.

NATIVE TOBACCO BOARD (NTB). In 1926 the government established the Native Tobacco Board to oversee the production and marketing of tobacco on **native trust land**. The board therefore had the responsibility for all African-grown tobacco in the colony. Chaired by the director of agriculture, its membership included **W. Tait Bowie, A. Francis Barron**, and **Ignaco Conforzi**. *See also* ROY W. WALLACE.

NATIVE TRUST LAND. By the Nyasaland Protectorate (Native Trust Land) Order in Council of 1936, all Crown land designated as unleased (i.e., land controlled by the government) was, with a few exceptions, to be converted into "native trust land" for use by the indigenous peoples of Malawi. Although the secretary of state for the colonies was the ultimate custodian of the native trust land, in practice, Nyasaland's governor, through his appointed trust board, was its main steward. This land was not to be sold or leased to nonindigenous people of **Nyasaland** without the permission of **native authorities**. However, the governor could authorize sale of such land without due consultation with the native authorities as long as the transaction was deemed to be in the interests of the Africans of the colony. *See also* ABRAHAMS COMMISSION; JACKSON REPORT.

NATIVE WELFARE ASSOCIATIONS. *See* AFRICAN WELFARE ASSOCIATIONS.

NCHALO. This area south of **Chikwawa** *boma* has been associated with **sugar** production since the mid-1960s. Originally a joint partnership between the Malawi government and **Lonrho**, the sugar plantations were privatized in 1997 and sold to a consortium dominated by the Ilovo company of Natal, **South Africa**. *See also* PRIVATIZATION.

NCOZANA, REV. SILAS. General secretary of the Synod of **Blantyre** of the **Church of Central Africa Presbyterian** (CCAP) from 1985 to 1995. Ncozana spent his early life in **Southern Rhodesia (Zimbabwe)**, went to theological school in **Malawi**, and later studied at the University of Aberdeen, which awarded him a Ph.D. degree. At the height of the agitation for political reform in the early 1990s, Ncozana played a significant role behind the scenes and through the **Public Affairs Committee** (PAC), thus ensuring a smooth transition from dictatorship to a democracy in Malawi. Two years after political change, Ncozana accepted a teaching job at the University in Durban.

NDALI. Name of a people and a language spoken by people in the Misuku hills in **Chitipa** District. The Ndali migrated from **Undali** in southern Tanganyika, settling among the indigenous **Sukwa**. The language of the Ndali, ciNdali, and ciSukwa, spoken by the Sukwa, are mutually intelligible.

NDEMA, G. E. Former minister of local government. Ndema was born at Naisi in **Zomba** District. After receiving an elementary education, he worked in **Southern Rhodesia (Zimbabwe)**. He was deported in 1959 because of his involvement in African politics. Back home he became an activist in the **Malawi Congress Party** (MCP), and in 1964 he was elected to parliament, later becoming minister of local government. In 1970 he was imprisoned without trial because he was suspected of being in league with **Gomile Kuntumanje**, who was accused of complicity in the **Chilobwe murders**. Ndema lost his property, which was not returned to him after his release in 1977. In the early 1990s the MCP unsuccessfully attempted to persuade him to rejoin the party so that he could help stem the tide of reform in Zomba District.

NDHLOVU, CHIWERE. Former *induna* (counselor). Chiwere Ndhlovu broke away from the main M'mbelwa **Ngoni** group after the death of **Zwangendaba**, taking with him two princes, Msakambewa Jere and Vuso Jere, and settled near **Mvera** in Dowa, heartland of the **Chewa**. He assumed political authority in his new area, and it was he who gave permission to the missionaries of the **Dutch Reformed Church** to establish their presence in the region.

NDIRANDE. High-density area below Ndirande mountain. One of the elevations in the **Blantyre-Limbe** area, Ndirande was originally inhabited by the **Mang'anja** before the area was conquered by the **Yao** in the early 1860s. When the **Blantyre Mission** was established in 1876, the area had several Yao-led villages, including those of the Mataka, Masangano, and Mlanga, all under the jurisdiction of Chief **Kapeni**. As Blantyre Mission and **Blantyre** itself grew into a major town, attracting labor into the area, many African newcomers went to live in Ndirande. Although, technically, Ndirande fell under **native trust land**, it was subject to the authority of the town and country planning section of the municipality of Blantyre. Today, Ndirande is part of the city of Blantyre and is subject to its bylaws. However, there are sections of it that can best be described as dominated by informal and unregulated building structures. Residents of Ndirande fondly call their township "republic of Ndirande," mainly because of its "wild" nature and independence of action. During the state of emergency in 1959, the area was particularly hostile to colonial authority, and many activists hid there; during the **Cabinet Crisis** of 1964 and for months after, Ndirande was noted for its antigovernment opinion. In the early 1990s it was strongly identified with the political reform movement.

NDOVI, RABAN PEMBA. Politician and first organizing secretary-general of the **Malawi Congress Party** (MCP). Ndovi was born in **Chilumba, Karonga** District. After receiving a basic education, he left **Nyasaland** in the early 1950s, finally arriving in England, where he became interested in the politics of decolonization. Soon after the MCP was formed in 1959, he returned home, where **Orton Chirwa** appointed him national organizing secretary of the new party. Ndovi adopted a very militant approach to Malawian nationalist politics, often advocating the burning of bridges and an uncompromising attitude toward the government and Europeans working in **Malawi**. When **Hastings Banda** was released from prison in Gweru in April 1960 and took over leadership of the party, he dismissed Ndovi from his position. Ndovi formed his own Convention of African National Union, which attracted only a few left-wing people. By 1964 Ndovi had left Malawi to live in **exile**.

NENO. Area in **Mwanza** District known for producing some of the best oranges in **Malawi**. Neno is also one of the earliest Roman Catholic mission stations in the country, dating to 1906.

NESS, J. R. Chairman of the **Settlers' and Residents' Association of Nyasaland** (SARAN). Ness's father was a former chairman of the **Imperial Tobacco Company** who had helped hunt for **John Chilembwe** following the rebellion in 1915. Educated in **South Africa**, a country of which he was a citizen until 1947, when he returned to **Nyasaland**, Ness was active in European settler politics, especially in the determination to maintain European authority in the area. In 1961 he and others founded SARAN, which sought to fight constitutional changes in Malawi. With decolonization, Ness left the country.

NEWSPAPERS. The first news-oriented periodical in **Nyasaland** and the Zambezia region to be published at regular intervals was *Life and Work,* founded by Rev. **Clement Scott** in 1888 and produced at the **Blantyre Mission** Press. The initial production staff of Scott and his students, led by **Mungo Chisuse**, assembled the printing press with the help of manuals and then taught themselves to operate it. *Life and Work* contained articles covering a variety of fields, including mission work, botany, **agriculture**, and anthropology. It almost invariably contained news of a political nature, especially in regard to the establishment of British authority in the area. In 1892 *Life and Work* changed its name to *Life and Work in British Central Africa*; at about that time, Dr. **Robert Laws** of the **Livingstonia Mission**, further north, started a similar magazine, the *Aurora*.

In the meantime, anxious to counteract the influence of **Blantyre** missionaries whose consistent criticism of his policies and style of rule did not please him, Sir **Harry Johnston**, head of the British administration in the **Lake Malawi** area, established his own publication, the *British Central Africa Gazette (BCAG)*. Financed by the government and ostensibly to communicate its ideas and programs, the *BCAG* tried to promote disunity within the Blantyre Mission and between the latter and other mission societies in the region. As time progressed, the *BCAG* reverted to printing public notices and announcing legislature and government notices.

In 1895 **R. S. Hynde**, a former Blantyre Mission layworker based at **Domasi** who had become a businessman and planter, started the first real newspaper, the *Central African Planter*, which championed imperialism and European settler business in the country. Two years later, Hynde changed the paper's name to the *Central African Times* and published it fortnightly. In 1909 it became the *Nyasaland Times*, a name it retained until 1964, when it changed to the *Malawi Times*; by this time, it was appearing twice a week. Throughout the colonial period, the *Nyasaland Times* supported the government as long as it protected the interests of Europeans in the country. On the other hand, until the 1960s, the paper always opposed African aspirations for independence. Its ownership changed at various times. At one stage it was part of the chain of papers owned by Lord Thompson of Fleet Street. Major changes began to take place to the paper in April 1969, when President **Hastings Banda** personally bought 49.7 percent of shares in the Blantyre Printing and Publishing Company (BP&PC), owners of the paper. From then on, the *Malawi Times* toed the government line, and by the early 1980s, when Banda had a much greater control of the PB&PC, the paper had became completely identified with the views of the government. It became a daily newspaper and increased its coverage of international news.

In 1959 the **Malawi Congress Party** (MCP) founded the *Malawi News,* and by the 1980s the paper was also printed by BP&PC and published on Saturdays. This meant that the only national newspapers in the country were controlled by the MCP and its government. During the agitation for democratization of Malawi, both papers campaigned for the status quo. However, by the end of 1992, the prodemocracy organizations had established their own papers. The *Malawi Financial Post*, edited by **Alaudin Osman**, a journalist of wide experience, was the first to appear. It was followed by many others: the *Malawi Democrat*, which was the official paper of the **Alliance for Democracy** (AFORD), *The Nation*, the *UDF News*, the *Monitor*, the *Michiru Sun*, the *Financial Observer*, the *New Express*, the *Citizen*, and the *Tribune*, all of which supported the **United Democratic Front** (UDF). The *Guardian* leaned toward the MCP, and, while committed to political reform, the *Independent*, edited by **Janet Karim**, lived up to its name. Some of these papers were printed by the Blantyre Printing and Publishing Press, an uncomfortable arrangement in view of the fact that the firm was owned by Banda and published the *Malawi News* and *Daily Times*. The *Malawi Democrat,* the *Michiru Sun*, and the *Malawi Finacial Post*, among others, folded within a few years of the defeat of the MCP government. The *Nation* became stronger and, with the *Daily Times,* emerged as Malawi's established daily newspaper; others, such as the *Chronicle, Inquirer, Weekly Digest, UDF News, Weekly News,* and *Malawi News*, remained weekend papers.

Also typical of the era of political reform was the emergence of fearless cartoonists whose sketches expressed serious or satirical commentaries of a political, social, and economic nature. Among the cartoons that began to appear at this time are *Zabweka, Takataka, Country Rat and Town Rat, Che Maliosi*, and *Gossip Computer*. Freedom of expression was beginning to be accepted in Malawi.

It should be pointed out that in both late colonial and postcolonial periods, some Christian **missions** published weekly newspapers, including the Presbyterian *Kuanika*, issued in **ciChewa**, and the Catholic *Moni* and *The African*, published in English and **ciChewa**.

NGAMWANE, CHIEF. Chief in **Thyolo** District. In August 1953 Chief Ngamwane was arrested and briefly detained in **Blantyre** following a conflict between some of his people and Basil Tennent, a planter at **Luchenza**. He was released only after his subjects rioted, damaging property belonging to the government and European planters, and barricading roads leading to Thyolo *boma*. The commission of inquiry set up by the governor, Sir **Geoffrey Colby**, to establish the cause of the riots concluded that the instability of the "native administration" in the district was to blame for the unrest, exacerbated by the increasing shortage of land in the area. *See also* NTONDEZA, CHIEF.

NGEMELA, ISWANI BEN. Early convert to the Last Church of God and His Christ. Of **Nyakyusa** and **Ngonde** parentage, Ben Ngemela became one of **Jordan Msumba**'s main pastors in **Karonga**. In the 1920s and 1930s, Msumba and Tigone Munthali were largely responsible for spreading the church's beliefs in the **Karonga** District and across the **Songwe** in **Unyakyusa**. In both areas the Last Church of God and His Christ is often referred to as *ichalichi cha* Ngemela (Ngemela's church).

NGERENGE. Ngonde area in north **Karonga**. Traditionally ruled by the **Kilupula**, Ngerenge is one of the major **rice**-producing areas in Malawi. Ngerenge, home of the **Kilupula Rice Growers Co-operative Union**, is also a noted **cotton**-growing region. In 1892 Dr. **David Kerr Cross** opened a station at Ngerenge, thereby establishing a **Livingstonia Mission** presence in the border region of **British Central Africa** and German East Africa.

NGONDE. Inhabitants of the northwestern shore of **Lake Malawi**. The Ngonde are related by language (**Kyangonde**) and customs to the **Nyakyusa** of southern Tanganyika. Around 1600 the Ngonde kingdom emerged in the area between the **Songwe River** and **Chilumba**, and it was in existence when the British colonized the area at the end of the 19th century. The traditional rulers still use the title **Kyungu**. A major cattle-keeping people, the Ngonde are better known as producers of **rice;**

the **Kilupula Rice Growers Co-operative Union** was based in northern **Ungonde**, as the Ngonde country is called. The Ngonde are also associated with **cotton** production.

NGONDOYI. Son of **Ntabeni**, brother of **Zwangendaba**, leader of the **Ngoni**. Ngondoyi was, according to one theory, identified by Zwangendaba as his successor. However, upon his death, the claim was disputed, and the disappointed Ngondoyi, accompanied by his principal adviser, Njenje, and their supporters, proceeded north, never to be heard of again.

NGONI. Deriving from the South African term "Nguni," this word refers to the descendants of **Zwangendeba** and **Mputa Maseko** and their followers. Those led by the former settled mainly in **Mzimba** and in **Chipata**, **Mchinji**, and Dowa Districts. The ones in Mzimba constituted the main group of Zwangendaba's followers, and they were led by **Mhlahlo Jere**, who took the name M'mbelwa, which became the title of the rulers of the **Ngoni** in this region. M'mbelwa's people came to be known as M'mbelwa Ngoni. Those who went to Chipata and Mchinji are called the **Mpezeni** Ngoni. Mputa Maseko's group, usually referred to as the **Maseko** Ngoni, settled mainly in **Ntcheu** and Dedza Districts; a small section moved to **Thyolo** District.

NGULUDI. Located in **Chiradzulu** District, this was one of the main sites of **Donald Malota**'s enterprise, which was sold to the Montfort Marist Catholic missionaries in 1903. The mission developed it into a major educational and **health** center.

NGUNANA, SHADRACH. One of the first assistants from **Lovedale** who joined the **Livingstonia Mission** at **Cape Maclear** in 1876. His work at the mission involved mostly teaching at the school, which he headed until he died of consumption in 1877.

NGWIRI, JOHN JAMES. Secretary to the president and cabinet (SPC) from 1975 to 1985, John Ngwiri came from **Ntcheu** District but spent most of his early life in East Africa, first in Dar es Salaam, Tanganyika, where his father worked and, later, in Uganda and Kenya, where he worked for the East African Community. He returned to Malawi in the early 1960s, and at independence he joined the foreign service, serving in Malawi missions abroad. In 1970 he became principal secretary in the Ministry of External Affairs. Five years later he replaced **George Jafu** as SPC and head of the Malawi civil service. An astute person who mixed easily with all ranks of the civil service, he was instrumental in establishing the Civil Service Club, of which he became an active member. Ngwiri also rose to be a very influential adviser to President **Hastings Banda**. In 1985 he fell out of favor with Banda and was replaced by **Sam Kakhobwe**. He retired to his farm in Ntcheu, where he died in 1991. His name featured prominently in the Mtegha Report and in the **Mwanza** trials, since the death of the four politicians in Mwanza took place in 1983 during his tenure as SPC. There was much speculation as to the role he may have played in the chain of events leading to the murders.

NHLANE, CHIPATULA. Influential hard-line **Ngoni** *induna* (councillor). During the Ngoni settlement in northern Malawi, Chipatula Nhlane was assigned by **Mhlahlo Jere** (M'mbelwa I) to the eastern section of their new domain, which at that time was supervised from Kaning'nina, just east of **Mzuzu**. In this capacity he was in charge of the **Tonga** who had been forced into Ngoni jurisdiction. Soon after his death in 1877, the Tonga revolted and returned to their homes. In September 1878 Chipatula's successor was the first notable "northern" Ngoni to be contacted by the **Livingstonia** missionaries, Dr. **Robert Laws**, **William Koyi**, **Fred Zarakuti**, and **James Stewart**. It was also the head of the Chipatula village who in turn established contact between the missionaries and the rest of the Ngoni hierarchy. Although the Nhlane village was to move west to Hoho in central **Mzimba**, the Chipatula Nhlane family continued to play a major role, not only in the consolidation of the Ngoni rule in the northern **Lake Malawi** area but also in the development of the often difficult relationship between the Ngoni and the Europeans.

NHLANE, DANIEL. Son of **Chipatula Nhlane**. Daniel was one of the early M'mbelwa **Ngoni** converts to Christianity. In 1887 he and **Andrew Mkochi** opened the first school at **Chimtunga Jere**'s village, a step regarded as a major advance in missionary effort in the area, especially since Chimtunga himself attended classes. Nhlane's involvement in the **William Zeil** incident in 1899 shows the extent to which he had become committed to missionary work but also demonstrates his determination to protect Ngoni paramountcy in the area. In 1902 Daniel Nhlane, his brother, Simon, and Andrew Mkochi were appointed as evangelists, and two years later they attended the new evangelist course at **Khondowe**, the headquarters of the **Livingstonia Mission**. A great preacher and composer of church hymns, Daniel completed the theological course at Khondowe but served a long period of probation while waiting to be ordained. He pleaded with the mission to relax its unnecessarily strict ordination rules for Africans so that he and others could become ministers. In 1915 he implored, "Let us be ordained before we die." But that was not to be; he died two years later, still not a minister.

NJILIMA, DUNCAN. A businessman and planter in **Chiradzulu**. Njilima was one of the most committed followers of **John Chilembwe**. Njilima was educated at **Blantyre Mission** and, sometime between 1892 and 1894, was a house servant of Bishop Wilfred Hornby, **Nyasaland**'s head of the **Universities' Mission to Central Africa** (UMCA). He briefly worked at Broken Hill, **Northern Rhodesia**, and on his return to Nyasaland became a major planter at Nsoni, **Chiradzulu** District. There he had two estates, one of well over 100 acres, and the second, which he jointly owned with Gordon and Hugh **Mataka**, was also 100 acres. On his larger holding, he had a labor force of about 30 people who helped him grow **cotton, maize**, and **tobacco**. Njilima also had general stores at Nangundi, Chiradzulu District, and at Ntumbi, **Ntcheu** District; he also owned property in **Blantyre**. Like other African businessmen of the time, Njilima felt that the labor laws discriminated against him in that his employees, unlike those of his European counterparts, could not transfer money from the unpopular labor tax. As a consequence of the law, labor costs were high for African entrepreneurs.

On the night of January 22, 1915, Njilima's party of mainly house servants and overseers working for Europeans in Blantyre was to meet at a rendezvous with other rebelling groups led by **David Kaduya, Stephen Mkulitchi**, and **John Gray Kufa**. Kaduya, Mkulitchi, and Njilima and their men met as arranged, and together they attacked the Mandala General Store in the town. Njilima was arrested within a few days and executed. His two sons, Fred and Matthew, were given an education in America, where they had been taken by **Landon Cheek**. Frederick later became active in the Southern Province Association. *See also* AFRICAN WELFARE ASSOCIATIONS; DELANY, EMMA.

NJILIMA, FREDERICK. Businessman, soldier, and intrepid adventurer. This son of **Duncan Njilima** was born in about 1897. In 1907 his father requested **Landon Cheek**, who was returning to the **United States**, to take along his two sons, Frederick and Matthew, so that they could receive an advanced education in that country. Financed by the Negro National Baptist Convention, **John Chilembwe**'s affiliate organization, they attended the Natchez College High School in Mississippi. Frederick went on to study at Lincoln Ridge College, Lincoln, Kentucky, and in 1915 he entered Kentucky State Industrial University.

When their father was executed following his part in the **Chilembwe uprising**, Matthew felt bitter and wanted nothing to do with colonial **Nyasaland**. However, Frederick was interested in pursuing his education at St. John's College, Cambridge University, and in furthering his father's business interests. Bishop Wilfred Hornby, formerly of Nyasaland and for whom his father, Duncan, had worked as a house servant in the 1890s, advised Frederick that he had to atone for his father's role in the Chilembwe uprising before he could recommend him to St. John's. The best way to do that was join the British army. Frederick duly volunteered as Frederick Gresham and was trained in the Irish Rifles. He was posted to the Machine Gun Corps at Ypres and served bravely in France for three years. Wounded on May 27, 1918, he was repatriated to the Cambridge Hospital, Aldershot, England, and received the Military Medal for bravery and a letter of commendation from the British Crown.

In October 1919 Njilima returned to Nyasaland. The government followed his movements, opened his letters, and was uncooperative in all his endeavors aimed at reviving his father's business. In the following year, Frederick unsuccessfully applied to lease 150 acres of Crown land in **Lilongwe**, where he could grow **tobacco**. He farmed in **Chiradzulu** and turned his attention to local politics. In 1922 he became an active member of the Southern Province Native Association and, in the late 1920s, was a founding member of the **Chiradzulu Native Association**, headed by Dr. **Daniel Malekebu**. Although he had an army pension of eight shillings a week, Frederick took up a job as a tutor at the Native Service School and later became a clerk in the Treasury Department. In the early 1930s he left the country again. After a brief stay in **Southern Rhodesia** and **Mozambique**, he went to Dar es Salaam, Tanganyika, where he taught at a school and became actively involved in the Tanganyika African Civil Servants Association. Later he taught at three of the leading African schools in that colony: Tabora Secondary School, Malangali, and Lorenza Girls School, Mbeya.

NJOBVUYALEMA. In 1901 this **Ngoni** chief subordinate of the Maseko supremo, **Gomani**, hosted the first Montfort mission station in the **Lake Malawi** region. *See also* NZAMA.

NJULI. Located in **Chiradzulu** District on the **Blantyre-Zomba** road, Njuli, a mainly **Mang'anja** and **Lomwe** area, was in the European planter zone. **Cotton**, **coffee**, and **tobacco** were grown at various times. *Thangata* was practiced here, and many supporters of **John Chilembwe** came from this area.

NJUYU. Located in the west-central part of **Mzimba** District, this was one of the early capitals of the M'Mbelwa **Ngoni** before they finally settled at their present seat at **Edingeni**. It was also one of the first **Livingstonia** mission stations in M'Mbelwa Ngoni country. In 1882, the mission posted **William Koyi** to Njuyu, where he was joined by other missionaries, including James Sutherland and Peter MacCallum. Three years later, Rev. Dr. **Angus Elmslie** arrived to take charge of the station. In the 1930s and 1940s, Njuyu was under the charge of Rev. **Peter Thole**.

NKHAMANGA. Plains immediately northwest of **Rumphi** *boma* and usually identified as the center of the **Chikulamayembe** power. It is one of the major **maize**- and bean-producing areas of **Malawi**.

NKHATA, ALICK. Leading broadcaster and one of the cultural icons of the northern Zambezia region. Alick Nkhata was born in Kasama, **Zambia**, in 1922, of a Malawian father from **Nkhata Bay** District and a **Bemba** mother. After attending local schools in Zambia, he qualified as a teacher and saw service during World War II. Upon demobilization, he became a full-time musician, composing and playing music that commented on the everyday life of the peoples of Zambia and **Malawi**. In 1950 he was part of the Hugh Tracey team, which toured the area from Kenya to **South Africa** recording African music. After this project, Nkhata founded a quartet and the Lusaka Radio Band, with which he recorded many popular songs in ciBemba and ciNyanja.

At the same time, Nkhata became an announcer in the vernacular division of the **Central African Broadcasting Service**. In the early 1960s Nkhata, a close friend of **Kenneth Kaunda**, wrote and played songs in support of the United National Independence Party, which was campaigning for decolonization. In 1964 he became director of broadcasting and cultural services. On his retirement 10 years later, he went to farm in Mkushi, where in 1978 he was killed by the Rhodesian Air Force during its raid on a camp of the Zimbabwe People's Union located in the area. His records remain popular in Malawi and Zambia.

NKHATA BAY. District west of **Mzimba**, home of the **Tonga** of Malawi. Dr. **David Livingstone** visited Nkhata Bay in 1859. The *boma*, also called Nkhata Bay, is one of the most picturesque district headquarters in **Malawi**, with one of the deepest natural ports on **Lake Malawi**. In the early period of colonial Malawi, the district was called West Nyasa and its *boma* was at **Chintheche** further south. In 1958 Nkhata Bay was the site of the conference of the **Nyasaland African Congress** (NAC), which chose Dr. **Hastings Banda** as the organization's president. On March 3, 1959, it was the scene of considerable violence as over 20 political activists were killed by security forces in one day.

In the early 1950s the **Colonial Development Corporation** (CDC) embarked on a major scheme to grow **rice** in the Limpasa Dambo in Nkhata Bay District. The project failed. The district is also known for other major agricultural schemes, **tea** and **rubber** production. From the 1950s to the 1980s, Nkhata Bay was one of the main tea-growing areas in Malawi. The tea estate has now been replaced by rubber trees following the **African Lakes Company**'s (ALC) revival of rubber production in the area.

NKHOMA MISSION. *See* MISSIONS.

NKHOTAKOTA. Called Kota Kota by Europeans and located on the western shore of **Lake Malawi**. Nkhotakota was a principal **Swahili-Arab** commercial center in the second half of the 19th century. Ivory and **slaves** were traded here, and in the 1870s nearly 10,000 slaves are reported to have passed through Nkhotakota annually on their way to the east coast of Africa. **Salim bin Abdalla**, the **Jumbe** of Nkhotakota, established a trading post here in the 1840s and came to enjoy immense political and economic power. Later, Nkhotakota became a major center of the **Universities' Mission to Central Africa** (UMCA); it also became the headquarters of the district of the same name. The district is in one of the major **rice**-producing areas in Malawi, and it was the location of the **Kota Kota Rice Trading Company** and the **Kota Kota Rice Growers Co-operative Union**. *See also* COOPERATIVES.

As a successful trading and UMCA center, Nkhotakota came to attract people from the east coast of Africa, **Mozambique**, and the Luangwa valley in the west. The immigrants lived among the indigenous inhabitants of this area, the **Chewa** and **Tonga**, turning the district into a complex mixture of African peoples.

NKHWAZI, DENIS. Founding member of the **Phwezi Educational Foundation** and the **Alliance for Democracy** (AFORD). Nkhwazi was born in **Rumphi** and received primary and secondary schooling in Malawi before going to Germany, where he studied political science. Upon earning his doctoral degree, he returned to **Malawi**, joined the civil service, and was posted to **Lilongwe** as assistant **district commissioner**. However, within a short time he was arrested and detained. When he was released over five years later, he became a **tobacco** grower in Rumphi.

In the early 1980s Nkhwazi and **Morton Mughogho** established the Phwezi Educational Foundation. Ten years later, Nkhwazi became active in the politics of reform, and in 1992 he helped found AFORD and became its secretary-general. In 1994 he was elected to parliament as the AFORD member for Rumphi East. In the coalition arrangement later that year, he was appointed minister of transport. Nkhwazi died in 1996.

NKONJERA, ANDREW. Karonga-based **Livingstonia Mission** employee. Nkonjera one of the first people to record and publish the history of the **Chikulamayembe** dynasty of the **Nkhamanga** area in **Rumphi** District. He also recorded the oral traditions of the peoples whom the Chikulamayembe ruled. The last section of Nkonjera's history deals with the tense relations between the **Ngonde**, the **Swahili-Arabs**, the **Tumbuka**-speaking peoples, and the Europeans at the end of the 19th century, as witnessed by the author. All this was published in two parts as "History of the Kamanga Tribe of Lake Nyasa: a Native Account," *Journal of the Royal African Society* 10 (1911); 11 (1912).

NKOPE BAY. This bay in the fishing area located on the southwestern tip of **Lake Malawi** is home to many holiday cottages belonging to firms and wealthy people in **Malawi**. The rocky section of Nkope is a major archaeological site. Pottery from it indicates that it was inhabited by iron-working people between the third and fifth centuries A.D. Ceramics from Nkope are similar to those found at sites in eastern **Zambia** and northern **Mozambique** that date to between the third and 10th centuries A.D. This type of ware is now officially referred to as the Nkope group. Archaeologists have determined that this Early **Iron Age** group is contemporaneous with the Kalambo group of northern Zambia.

The **Universities' Mission to Central Africa** (UMCA) was active in the Nkope region from the late 19th century, and today the area is still strongly identified with the Anglican Church.

NKRUMAH, FRANCIS KWAME. First president of Ghana and one-time friend of **Hastings Banda**. Nkrumah was born in Nkroful, Western Ghana (then the Gold Coast) in 1900. He attended Catholic mission schools before proceeding to Achimota College, where he trained as a teacher, qualifying in 1930. He taught in primary schools until 1935, when he left for Lincoln University in Pennsylvania. He graduated four years later with majors in economics and sociology. Nkrumah went on to graduate school at the University of Pennsylvania, and in 1945 he registered at the London School of Economics, University of London. In

London he became active in Pan-African politics and was a joint secretary at the Fifth Pan-African Conference in Manchester in 1945. While in London he also became friends with many future African leaders who were studying or working in England, and among them Dr. **Hastings Banda**.

When Banda became angry over the establishment of the **Federation of Rhodesia and Nyasaland** in 1953, he left England for Ghana and lived there for five years. By 1953 Nkrumah's Convention People's Party was the majority party in the **Legislative Council** (LEGCO), and in 1957 Ghana became independent, followed by republican status in the British Commonwealth three years later. In 1966 Nkrumah was overthrown by a military junta. He died in exile in Romania in April 1972. Before his death, Nkrumah's relations with Banda had cooled because of differences on **foreign policy**, particularly Banda's close relations with the settler colonies of Southern Africa. Nkrumah, a strongly committed Pan-Africanist, advocated the formation of an African military force to help the African peoples in those regions regain independence.

NKUDZI BAY. Located immediately south of **Nkope Bay** in **Mangochi** District, Nkudzi Bay forms part of the fishing areas of **Lake Malawi** and has many holiday homes owned by companies and individuals. The bay area is also an archaeological site identified with the Late **Iron Age**.

NKULA. *See* ELECTRICITY.

NKUMBULA, HARRY MWAANGA. Early nationalist leader in **Zambia**. Nkumbula was born in Namwala District, completed the teacher's course in 1934, and for 12 years taught in this area's schools and in the Copper Belt region of that country. In 1942 he went to England to study advanced teacher education and also attended the London School of Economics. In London he began to play an active role in Pan-Africanist activities, working with future leaders such as Jomo Kenyatta, **Kwame Nkrumah**, **Hastings Banda**, and West Indian George Padmore, whom he had admired since his youth. Nkumbula strongly campaigned against the **Federation of Rhodesia and Nyasaland**, and in 1951 he and Banda wrote *Federation in Central Africa,* detailing their opposition to the proposed union.

In that year, Nkumbula returned to Zambia (then called Northern Rhodesia) and within a short time became leader of the Northern Rhodesia African Congress, renaming it the African National Congress. In January 1955 the government accused Nkumbula and **Kenneth Kaunda**, the party's secretary-general, of distributing banned **literature** and imprisoned them for two months. Three years later he and Kaunda parted company when the latter formed his own Zambia African National Congress, which later became the United National Independence Party (UNIP) and went on to win the elections leading to independence on October 24, 1964. Although Nkumbula's African National Congress attempted a major revival in 1968, it was defeated in the general elections of that year. In 1973 he joined UNIP and five years later unsuccessfully contested for its leadership. Nkumbula died in 1983.

NONGOVERNMENTAL ORGANIZATIONS (NGOS). More than a hundred NGOs operate in Malawi. Nonprofit, private, and voluntary agencies with no ties to government, NGOs have been active in **Malawi** throughout the postcolonial period. Until the political reforms in the early 1990s, they were mostly concerned with economic development, adequate supply of clean water, poverty alleviation, and general **health** improvement. Some are religious, others secular. Some, including Oxfam, World Vision, Medecins Sans Frontieres, and Save the Children Fund, are divisions of international organizations with headquarters outside Malawi; others are Malawian in origin but depend on funds and some technical assistance from abroad. Typical of these is the **Christian Service Committee**. Besides its own development projects, it allocates some of its funds to other NGOS such as Christian Hospital Association of Malawi (CHAM). Still others solicit external financial and technical assistance but also rely heavily on funds raised within Malawi and on local volunteers; among such NGOs are the Red Cross, the **Malawi Council for the Handicapped** (MACOHA), and the **Leprosy Relief Association** (LEPRA). **Human rights** NGOs such as Amnesty International and Africa Watch were never allowed to work in President **Hastings Banda**'s Malawi, and the reports that they wrote on the country were based on, among other sources, confidential stringers based in Malawi, contacts in the diplomatic corps, and religious organizations. Since the early 1990s, human rights and civil liberties agencies have become an accepted part of Malawi's civic society.

NORTH CHARTERLAND EXPLORATION COMPANY. London-based company formed in 1895 in which the **British South Africa Company** (BSAC) had a 30 percent share. North Charterland bought the **mining** concessions that **Karl Wiese** had secured from **Mpezeni**, the **Ngoni** chief. In 1896 Mpenzeni granted the company permission to prospect for gold in his area. But increased European activity in the area and the possibility of losing their independence to the British worried the Ngoni. When these suspicions led to the death of some European prospectors, Karl Wiese asked for assistance, which came from the British Central African Administration in **Zomba**. Colonel **William Manning** led the British Central African Rifles to fight the Ngoni under the command of Mpezeni's son, **Nsingu**. The latter were defeated and the area came under the administration of the company, which proceeded to divide most of the prime land among European settlers. The company also established new administrative headquarters at **Fort Jameson**.

NORTH NYASA NATIVE ASSOCIATION. The first organization seeking to improve the social and economic welfare of localities; founded in 1912 at **Karonga** *boma*. Although traditional rulers such as **Peter Mwakasungula**, future *Kyungu* of the **Ngonde**, were founding members, its leadership and active membership consisted of Western-educated people, mostly clerks, teachers, and preachers. Among its founders were **Levi Mumba**, **Robert Sambo Mhango**, and Peter Mwakasungula, who was also its first president. Among its non-African supporters were Dr. **Meredith Sanderson**, medical officer at **Karonga**, and Dr. **Robert Laws**, head of the **Livingstonia Mission**.

NORTH NYASA NATIVE RESERVES COMMISSION, 1929. This commission was appointed in 1929 to settle the matter of three million acres of land in North Nyasa District (most of the current **Rumphi**, **Karonga**, and **Chitipa** Districts) given to the **British South Africa Company** in the era of **Harry Johnston**'s **certificates of claim**. On this land lived many indigenous people, and among the possibilities facing the commissioners was to remove the African occupants to enable the company to lease it to Europeans or to leave Africans to use it for their own socioeconomic development. In the end the commission recommended that the company abandon its claim to freehold of the land on the assurance of retention of the mineral rights.

NORTH RUKURU. One of the main sources of **Lake Malawi** waters, the North Rukuru River rises in the slopes on **Nyika plateau**, passes through Nthalire descending to the **Karonga** lakeshore at Mwankenja and empties into the lake near Karonga *boma*. In the past, the banks of the Karonga section of the river were lined with banana plantations; in recent times bananas have been replaced by **cotton** and **maize** fields.

NORTHERN CO-OPERATIVE UNION. Umbrella organization of all the cooperative unions in the Northern Region of Malawi. It was formed in 1951 and had its headquarters at **Rumphi** *boma*. It had lorries that transported the union's produce within the province, ghee-packaging machinery, and a shop that sold clothes and other items to the public.

NORTHERN RHODESIA. Designation of the modern Republic of **Zambia** until independence from the British in 1964. It was named after **John Cecil Rhodes**, founder of the **British South Africa Company**, which had major territorial and commercial interests in the area north of the Zambezi. The whole of Northern Rhodesia fell under direct British rule in 1924.

NORTHERN RHODESIA AND NYASALAND JOINT PUBLICATIONS BUREAU. Established in 1948 to replace the African Literature Committee and the Northern Rhodesia Publications Bureau. The Joint Publications Bureau has published short books, mostly in African languages, in fields such as fiction, folklore, history, dictionaries, grammar of African languages, proper manners, home economics (then called domestic science), and school textbooks. The bureau published many books on **Malawi** and by Malawian authors, including **Ntara**'s *Mau Okuluwika* (1964).

NSANJE. Located in the southernmost part of Malawi and called Port Herald in colonial times, Nsanje became the administrative headquarters of the Lower Shire District in 1891. Nsanje was the main entry into the **Lake Malawi** region for those using the Zambezi-**Shire** Rivers. In 1904 the **Shire Highlands Railway** was extended from **Chiromo** to Nsanje and then to the Zambezi by 1915. A major **cotton**-producing district, Nsanje is the lowest point above sea level and one of the hottest areas in **Malawi**. Nsanje is also the site of **Khulubvi**, the shrine of the **M'bona**, an important part of the **Mang'anja** religious belief.

NSENGA. Name of the people who live in Petauke District and parts of the **Chipata** District of Zambia. It is also the name of their language, parts of which are incorporated in the ciChewa spoken in sections of **Mchinji** District. In precolonial times the Nsenga were noted **cotton** growers and produced cloth; like the **Bisa** to their north, they were famous ivory traders. When **Mpezeni** and his **Ngoni** settled in the Luangwa valley, they colonized the Nsenga, intermarried with them, and within a short time adopted the language of the indigenous peoples.

NSIMA. This is the staple food of all Malawian peoples, as it is of most Africans in sub-Saharan Africa. It is made of **maize** or cassava flour or a combination of the two, which is boiled until it forms a very thick porridge that is traditionally eaten with the hands. The *nsima* is served with vegetables, fish, or meat. In times when millet and **sorghum** were extensively grown in Malawi, flour from these grains was popularly used for *nsima*.

NSINGU. *See* FORT MANNING; MPEZENI; WIESE, KARL.

NTABA, HETHERWICK MAURICE. Minister of external affairs in President **Hastings Banda**'s last government. Ntaba was educated at **Blantyre** Secondary School before going to the **United States**, where he qualified as a medical doctor. Later he went to England, where he specialized as a surgeon. Back in Malawi he rose rapidly, becoming head of the **health services**, and in 1990 he was nominated to parliament and appointed minister of health. In the period leading to political reform Ntaba became the chief spokesperson for the **Malawi Congress Party** (MCP) and minister of external affairs. In 1994 he was elected to parliament as a member for **Lilongwe** and five years later was returned to represent Lilongwe Southeast. Regarded as the most articulate member of the MCP Executive, Ntaba strongly supported his party's partnership with the **Alliance for Democracy** (AFORD) in the 1999 general **elections**.

NTABENI. Brother and close adviser of **Zwangendaba**. Ntabeni became regent when the **Ngoni** chief died at Mapupo around 1848, holding together the migration group. He too died not long afterward, leading to the first major split: his son Ngodoyi and his principal *nduna* (councillor) went north toward Lake Victoria and were not heard of again. *See also* ZWANGENDABA.

NTARA, SAMUEL JOSIAH. Educator, author, and leading historian. Ntara was born at **Mvera** on September 24, 1905. His father, Josiah Kamfumu, one of the first students at the **Dutch Reformed** mission school at Mvera, qualified as a teacher at **Livingstonia Mission**, and taught at Mvera for many years. Samuel Ntara himself attended the Mvera school to standard three level, after which he became a teacher in local village schools. He studied privately and in 1927 went to **Nkhoma** Mission and qualified as a third class teacher. After attending further short courses at Nkhoma, he was awarded a second teacher's certificate, the highest teaching qualification he could expect to obtain. Thereafter, he taught at various schools in **Lilongwe** District, and in 1932 he was transferred to Nkhoma, where he enrolled for the South African Junior Certificate (Grade 8) through Union College, which offered a variety of professional and academic courses by correspondence. In 1944 Ntara went to teach at **Kongwe** School, and two years later he became a member of the Dowa District Council. He was also a member of the Teachers Association, and an active elder of the **Church of Central Africa Presbyterian** (CCAP). With **Levi Mumba**, Gresham Masanghe, and **George Simeon Mwase**, he was part of the Lilongwe delegation to the first meeting of the **Nyasaland African Congress** (NAC) in 1944. In 1951 he was transferred back to Nkhoma Mission, and in the early 1960s he retired to his home near Kamphata in Lilongwe District. In 1968 Ntara was appointed to the Censorship Board and in 1975 became the first chairman of the National Monuments Advisory Council. Ntara died in 1976.

Ntara is most famous as an author and a historian. In 1932 he entered a literary competition organized by the International Institute of African Languages and Cultures in London. His entry, *Nthondo*, a fictional biography, won the biography division of the contest. Reverend **Thomas Cullen Young** translated the manuscript into English, and Julian S. Huxley, the respected scholar, wrote a foreword to *Nthondo*, which the Bible and Tract Society, London, published in 1933 as *Man of Africa*. Ntara went on to write other books, including *Mbiri ya Achewa*, based on notes dictated to him by Rev. **Namon Katengeza** in 1944; the Dutch Reformed Church published the book that year. In the late 1960s Kamphandira Jere translated *Mbiri ya Achewa* into English; Harry Langworthy later edited it, and in 1973 Franz Steiner Verlag published it under the title *History of the Chewa*. In 1949 Longman, Green published *Nchowa*, a fictional story of a lady of Nyasaland, considered the female complement to *Nthondo*. In the same year, Nkhoma Mission Press published *Msyambozya*, the story of a Chimbazi village headman who lived near **Kongwe** from about 1830 to 1926. Although a biography, it is also a social and political history of today's central Malawi. Cullen Young translated *Msambozya* into English, and Lutterworth Press published it in 1949 as *Headman's Enterprise: An Unexpected Page in Central African History*. In the early 1950s Nkhoma Mission commissioned Ntara to write a biography of Namon Katengeza, which the mission press published in 1964 as *Namon Katengeza*. In that same year, Ntara's *Mau Okuluwika*, a collection of Nyanja **(Chewa)** idioms, was published by the **Northern Rhodesia and Nyasaland Joint Publications Bureau**.

NTCHEU. Designation of the *boma* and district bordering **Mozambique** on the west, **Mangochi** on the east, Dedza on the north, and **Mwanza**

and **Balaka** on the south and southeast. Ntcheu is strongly identified with the Maseko **Ngoni**, who have dominated the area since settling there toward the end of the 19th century. **Lizulu**, the seat of the **Gomani** dynasty, is in the northern part of the district. Christian missions such as the Church of Scotland, the Roman Catholic Church, and the **Zambezi Industrial Mission** (ZIM) have been present in the district since the 1880s and the 1890s. Consequently, many people in the district have been exposed to Western education longer than in most areas of Malawi. The Maseko Ngoni are also identified with resistance to British authority; they did not easily accept British rule in the 1890s. **John Chilembwe** had significant support in Ntcheu, a district that was also a center of civil disobedience in 1953. *See also* CHINYAMA, FILIPO; GOMANI I; GOMANI II; LIVULEZI.

NTCHISI. The name of the *boma* and district formerly known as Visanza. It is located in the mountainous region southwest of **Nkhotakota** District and was one of the first areas to which the **Universities' Mission to Central Africa** (UMCA) expanded out of **Likoma**. The district produces citrus fruits and **coffee**, both of which are consumed within the Malawi market.

NTHOLO, ALICE. Politician born in December 1945 in **Kasungu** District. Ntholo went to local schools, and in 1968 she completed domestic science courses in Dowa and at Tuchila Farm Institute in **Mulanje**. She then worked as a home craft assistant, and in 1972 she was appointed home craft supervisor in the **Lilongwe** municipality. Two years later, Ntholo went to parliament as nominated member for **Kasungu**.

NTIMAWANZAKO, NACHO. One of the first students at the **Blantyre Mission** and a contemporary of **Mungo Chisuse** and **Joseph Bismarck**. Nacho Ntimawamzako became a teacher and a leading evangelist. As adviser to Rev. **David Clement Scott** on the **Mang'anja** dictionary, Ntimawanzako accompanied the pastor to Scotland in the mid-1880s and stayed there for two years. On his return in 1887, he became a teacher and evangelist and served at different stations, including **Mulanje**, which he managed for some time.

NTINTILI, MAPAS. One of the first **Lovedale** evangelists in the service of the **Livingstonia Mission**. Ntintili worked at **Cape Maclear** and for a brief period at Kaning'ina. In 1880 he and other Lovedale missionaries went home on vacation. Ntintili, however, did not return to the **Lake Malawi** area.

NTONDEZA, CHIEF. Traditional ruler in **Thyolo** District. In the late 1930s Chief Ntondeza was in conflict with **Wilfrid Gudu** and his Ana a Mulungu adherents, finally banishing them from his territory. In September 1953, Chief Ntondeza was at the center of another dispute, this time with his own people. After accusing him of supporting the **Federation of Rhodesia and Nyasaland**, they threatened to depose him and proceeded to destroy property including that belonging to nearby European plantations. The troubles in Thyolo, as in the rest of the country in that year, have been attributed to the Federation, the introduction of unpopular agricultural and conservation measures, and the *thangata* system.

NUNAN, JOHN JOSEPH. First judge and chief justice of **Nyasaland**, appointed by Sir **Alfred Sharpe** in 1900. Nunan laid the foundation of the judicial system in the colony and was instrumental in codifying its laws. A Catholic of Irish origins, Nunan was very helpful to the early Catholic missionaries—the **White Fathers** and the Montforts—in their attempts to establish themselves in the colony at a time when the Presbyterian and the **Dutch Reformed Churches** claimed the area to themselves. In 1905 Nunan was appointed solicitor-general of Guyana, and Charles Griffin became the new chief justice of **Nyasaland**.

NYAKYUSA. The people immediately north of the **Ngonde**. The Nyakyusa are closely related to the Ngonde, many of whom migrated from **Unyakyusa**. **Kinyakyusa**, the language of the Nyakyusa, is primarily the same as **Kyangonde**, that of the Ngonde.

NYAMBADWE. Low-density suburb of **Blantyre** located between the **Blantyre Mission** in the south, **Ndirande** in the east, and Chirimba in the north. Nyambadwe is the site of a government house that in the late colonial period was the official residence of the provincial commissioner for the Southern Region. In postcolonial Malawi it came to be known as Nyambadwe House and was used mainly to accommodate important foreign dignitaries visiting the country as guests of the government.

NYAMBO, PETER. Missionary, teacher, preacher, political activist, and traveler. Nyambo was born in **Ntcheu** District around 1884, and between 1895 and 1900 he attended school at **Blantyre Mission**. Two years later, Nyambo joined **Joseph Booth** at **Plainfield**, **Thyolo**, where he received more education. At the beginning of the following year, Booth and his family went to England via **South Africa**, taking along Nyambo, who spent the rest of 1903 at a school in Matlock, Derbyshire, where the

Booths also resided. For eight months in 1904 he was at the African Institute, Colwyn Bay, North Wales, an establishment directed by W. Hughes, whom a year earlier Booth had coopted into an abortive training scheme for Christian workers in the **Lake Malawi** area. In 1905 and 1906 he was at Duncombe Hall, a Seventh-Day Adventist college in Holloway, London, where he was baptized into the faith. Nyambo also spent part of 1906 touring Great Britain, Germany, and Switzerland, attending and speaking at 160 meetings. Toward the end of 1906, he was a member of a party of British missionaries setting up an Adventist presence at Kisumu in western Kenya. He remained there until December 1907, when he went back to **Nyasaland**, arriving in the **Shire Highlands** early in 1908.

Since leaving the British colony in 1903, Plainfield, the mission in Thyolo, had been given a **Mang'anja** name, **Malamulo**, that is, Commandments. **Thomas Branch**, the African American head of Plainfield, had been replaced by Joel Rogers, an American with South African experience. After a period at Malamulo, Nyambo was posted to Matandani northwest of **Blantyre**, where he and S. M. Konigmacher founded a new mission. At the time, Adventist schools did not go beyond the standard three level, and only at Malamulo was English taught. The vernacular was the only medium of communication at the satellite stations. The confident Nyambo found the environment in the Adventist Mission conservative and stifling, and in 1911 he left for Ntcheu, his home district. Toward the end of that year Booth, now in South Africa and a Seventh Day Baptist, reestablished contact with Nyambo, who had returned to **Shiloh** in Thyolo District. Back in Ntcheu, Nyambo opened many independent schools, mainly manned by teachers from the **Zambezi Industrial Mission** (ZIM). At the beginning of 1912, Nyambo, **Alexander Makwinja**, and others left for South Africa. By the following year, Nyambo had become Central African secretary of the **British Christian Union**, which Booth had established in Cape Town.

In March 1913 the *South African Spectator* published Nyambo's article critical of white authority in Nyasaland and the rest of Southern Africa. This was followed by other protests against segregation and land problems in the region, but it was his Rhodesias Nyasaland Appeal of May 1914 that identified him as a significant political activist. In this petition, signed by, among others, Booth and South African members of the legislature, he appealed to the British Crown to intervene in the situation in the Rhodesias and Nyasaland because of the manner in which Africans were being treated by the colonial government. Booth seems to have played a part in the petition and seems to have sent copies to **Filipo Chinyama**, **John Chilembwe**, and the *Nyasaland Times*. A copy was also sent to the high commissioner in Cape Town for transmission to the United Kingdom and the governor of Nyasaland.

In May 1914 Nyambo went to England. Contrary to his expectations, however, the King did not receive him nor did the British government acknowledge his presence in the country. He and Booth spent some time addressing meetings, mostly associated with churches, explaining the subject of the petition. Later that year Booth returned to South Africa, proceeding to Lesotho and carrying on with his plans for African education and economic development. Nyambo remained in England until 1917, when he sailed back to South Africa. When Nyambo finally returned to Malawi in 1943, he founded a church, **Calici ca Makolo**, or Church of Ancestors, which was strongly influenced by the creed of Sri Ramakrishma. Nyambo lived for another 25 years.

NYANGU. The mother of **John Chilembwe**. In **Maravi** tradition, Nyangu is the powerful perpetual mother of all the Phiri chiefs, including the **Kalonga**, Undi, **Kaphwiti**, **Lundu**, and **Kanyenda**.

NYANJA. Often also referred to as ciMang'anja and basically the same as ciChewa, this is the language of the indigenous peoples of the Upper and Lower Shire regions and of the **Shire Highlands**. Nyanja also means lake. *See also* MANG'ANJA; LANGUAGES AND LANGUAGE POLICY.

NYASA. Name that **David Livingstone** gave to **Lake Malawi**. It was a misnomer because his informants were merely telling him that Nyasa, or Nyanja, means the great waters. In effect, he called it lake lake. **Tanzania** still refers to the lake by its old name, Lake Nyasa. In 1907 **Nyasaland** was adopted as the official name of the colony hitherto called **British Central Africa**; in 1964 Nyasaland became **Malawi**. Throughout the colonial period, people from Nyasaland were generally called the Nyasa; this is how labor migrants in **Southern Rhodesia (Zimbabwe)** and **South Africa** were referred to.

NYASA INDUSTRIAL MISSION (NIM). Established by **Joseph Booth** in 1893, the Nyasa Industrial Mission had its headquarters near the source of the **Likhubula** stream, immediately northeast of **Mitsidi**, the location of the seat of the **Zambezi Industrial Mission** (ZIM), also founded by Booth. The new mission was initially staffed by Australian missionaries, and Booth saw it complementing the ZIM. Unlike the latter, which was interdenominational, the NIM was Baptist in dogma. When Booth was expelled from the ZIM in 1894, he concentrated on the NIM, seeking new backers in the United Kingdom. By 1897 Booth had loosened his links with the NIM, which was now expanding to other parts of the **Shire Highlands**.

NYASALAND. The name of Malawi between 1907 and July 6, 1964, when the British colony became an independent nation. From 1891 to 1893, the country was known as the Nyasaland Protectorate, and from 1893 to 1907, its designation was **British Central Africa**.

NYASALAND AFRICAN CONGRESS (NAC). Political organization founded in 1944, when the various **African welfare associations** joined together to form the NAC as the principal mouthpiece of African aspirations in the colony. It was banned in March 1959 and was succeeded in the following September by the **Malawi Congress Party** (MCP). From 1944 to 1959, the NAC changed from a narrow-based organization to a mass movement in pursuit of national independence. Until the mid-1950s, when its leadership was challenged, the Congress followed moderate policies. When the NAC committed itself to a more militant position, it persuaded Dr. **Hastings Banda** to return home in 1958 and lead the struggle for decolonization.

The person most responsible for the formation of the congress was **James Sangala**, a teacher and a government civil servant. An early nationalist, Sangala knew the necessity of united action. He received encouragement from the European settler **W. H. Timke** and support from the members of the Blantyre Native Association. In August and September 1943, Sangala and his associates convened meetings in **Blantyre** that resulted in the formation of the Nyasaland Educated African Council. Anxious to have an all-embracing organization, they removed the word "educated" from the name, and it became the Nyasaland African Council. In October 1944 another meeting approved a constitution and another change of name, this time to Nyasaland African Congress. The office bearers were **Levi Mumba** (president-general), **Charles Matinga** (vice president-general), **Charles Wesley Mlanga** (secretary-general), James Dixon Phiri (vice secretary-general), Harry Tung'ande (second vice secretary-general), **Isa M. Lawrence** (treasurer-general), and H. B. Dallah (vice treasurer-general). Among the executive committee members of the NAC were **George Simeon Mwase**, **Charles Chinula**, B. Namboyah, Raphael Mbwana, A. Mbebuwa, and Alexander Phambala. The meeting agreed to make several demands on the government: the right to hold seats in the **Legislative Council** (LEGCO) and not be represented by the missionaries; the right to form **labor unions**; and the right to have access to the best educational facilities and responsible civil service positions. As a result of these demands, Sangala found himself under government surveillance, but several months later his new umbrella organization represented 20 associations.

The first year of the young congress was a difficult one, partly because its treasurer, Isa Lawrence, and its president, Levi Mumba, died. Furthermore, the government did not acknowledge any of the resolutions passed by the congress. Although the congress received funds and advice from Dr. Hastings Banda, who was practicing medicine in England, it remained a victim of its own internal weakness. The central leadership had no effective hold on the autonomous branches. Full-time officers of the Congress were not paid. The Executive Committee met infrequently, resulting in a distinct lack of communication between senior members of the organization. The NAC's income was raised locally and was not centralized which meant that the several branches retained financial autonomy as well. In 1948, a scandal in the Congress pointed out its financial inefficiencies: Charles Matinga embezzled Congress funds to cover personal debts. The already weak leadership exhibited in the organization was allegedly also corrupt. When Dr. Banda attempted to reform the Congress financially and organizationally, the NAC leadership ignored his pleas.

The issues faced by the Congress in the 1940s and 1950s were serious, but the tactics employed were largely unsuccessful. The most absorbing problems were the land situation, the colonial imposition of new farming methods, and the revival of the federation concept. In the first instance population pressure in the **Shire Highlands** had increased, reaching a density of nearly 200 people per square mile. The treatment of African tenants on European estates had grown intolerable, with white owners in some instances prohibiting the cutting of timber or building of huts. Ill-feeling between Africans and Europeans was spotlighted in **Thyolo** District in 1953, when a petty larceny incident on a **Luchenza** estate mushroomed into a rumored murder and resulted in weeklong disorders. Shortly thereafter, the government initiated a program to repurchase land from European owners. *See also THANGATA;* NGAMWANE, CHIEF.

At the same time, the government was imposing unpopular agricultural policies on rural farmers. Inefficient cultivation and a rising population had led the government to seek an end to soil erosion. For most African farmers, forsaking a traditional procedure for an uncertain experiment was not a worthwhile risk. Sometimes what British agrarian experts demanded made more work for the African farmers; such demands included digging embankments for contouring before the first rains had softened the soil, and work of this nature often had to be undertaken with hand tools. The government was convinced that only coercion would succeed, and so fines and imprisonment soon followed. African resentment of the Europeans grew and African fears for their land deepened. The third issue, which resulted in massive disaffection, was that of federation. Africans were convinced that any closer association with **Southern Rhodesia (Zimbabwe)** would result in a loss of land. Many of Malawi's men had seen for themselves the amount of land alienation while working there. These observations by migrant workers intensified African concern over the possible loss of more land.

The NAC response to these grievances was ineffectual. Like the associations that preceded the formation of the Congress, the leadership insisted that patient prodding of the government would yield results. Since the NAC chose to operate within a colonial frame of reference, two weaknesses persisted. First, the NAC failed to develop a popular following and, second, the inefficient internal structure continued with a leadership that saw no need to change or grow. Although Africans were articulate in their opposition to the **Federation of Rhodesia and Nyasaland** as well as the land situation, the NAC was unable to transform those thoughts into action. In the mid-1950s the congress gave up its verbal campaign against the Federation and announced hopes to utilize appropriate constitutional procedures. Congress members, mostly church ministers, teachers, and civil servants, rejected the need to transform the organization into a mass movement.

A decided change in attitude began to evolve in the mid-1950s, particularly with the influence of **Henry Chipembere**, **Kanyama Chiume**, and **Dunduzu Chisiza**. The trio was a motivating force behind the NAC's eventual commitment to national independence and to the development of a popularly based political organization. The Congress was seriously divided as differences of opinion separated moderates and radicals. The year 1957 was critical to the NAC. At its annual convention, it voted to invite Dr. Banda to return to Malawi and to work for self-government and the end of the despised Federation. In July 1958 Banda assumed the presidency of the NAC. By early 1959 the NAC was a disciplined, centralized, authentic national movement. That same year the NAC adopted a new name, the **Malawi Congress Party**.

NYASALAND AFRICAN PROGRESSIVE ASSOCIATION. Formed in 1953 and led by **Charles Matinga**, **Andrew Mponda**, and **Orton Chirwa**, all considered moderates. This association supported African aspirations but opposed militant action, which had recently taken place in many parts of the colony, including **Thyolo**, **Mulanje, Domasi**, and **Ntcheu**. Chirwa left the group to join ranks with the mainstream nationalist movement. By 1958 the association had died, mainly due to lack of support.

NYASALAND BLACK MAN'S EDUCATIONAL SOCIETY. This organization was founded by **Yesaya Zerenji Mwasi** in August 1934 to promote educational, economic, and social development among black people in **Nyasaland** and other parts of the world. Influenced by Marcus Garvey's Pan-Africanist ideas, the society envisaged the advancement of black people being guided by black leadership and financed primarily by contributions from migrant workers in the Rhodesias and in **South Africa**. The society planned to establish educational institutions, including a college, which would train Africans in fields such as medicine, teacher **education**, and **agriculture**. The society did not attain its aims partly because its hopes for financial assistance never materialized and partly because it did not receive due recognition from the government education departments in Nyasaland and **Northern Rhodesia**, where many of its potential supporters were based. Within **Nkhata Bay** itself, the **Atonga Tribal Council** was antagonistic to the society. The schools in Nkhata Bay, and those set up by **Charles Chinula**, his colleague in the **Black Man's Church** (Mpingo wa Afipa), failed to fully develop when the lack of adequate financing prevented them from recruiting properly trained teachers and superintendents. *See also* CHINULA, CHARLES; MWASI, YESAYA ZERENJI.

NYASALAND CONSTITUTIONAL PARTY. The name of the United Federal Party (UFP) in **Nyasaland** after the **Federation of Rhodesia and Nyasaland** broke up. **Michael Blackwood** continued to lead the renamed party.

NYASALAND INDIAN ASSOCIATION. The Nyasaland Indian Association was formed in 1938 to represent the interests of all **Indian** residents of colonial Malawi, regardless of occupation. At the time the **Bledisloe Commission** was about to visit the region. Worried about the possible amalgamation of **Nyasaland** with the Rhodesias, Indians, like the Africans of the colony, wanted to make the commission aware of their opposition to the scheme. **Southern Rhodesia** had strict immigration laws with regard to Indians, and those in Nyasaland feared that amalgamation would lead to uniform legislative measures in the newly expanded political structure.

NYASALAND INDIAN TRADERS ASSOCIATION (NITA). Organization representing the interests of the Indian commercial community in **Nyasaland**. Formed in the early 1920s, thee NITA was the main negotiator in the fierce competition that existed among powerful European businessmen and associations. Initially, the NITA was dominated by Indian traders based in the **Blantyre-Limbe** area, and among its leaders were **Osman Adam**, president, **M. G. Dharap**, secretary, and Ismail Nurmahamed, treasurer. By the 1930s the NITA had evolved into a body representing Indian retailers, most of the wholesalers having formed the **Indian Chamber of Commerce** in 1936. The two organizations worked hand in hand to protect the interests of Indian business.

NYASALAND PLANTERS ASSOCIATION. Organization led by **John Moir** that was formed in December 1892 as a rival to the **Shire Highlands** Planters Association, chaired by **Eugene Sharrer**, established three months earlier. In 1895 the two associations joined to form the **British Central Africa** Chamber of Agriculture and Commerce, which became a powerful voice for the European settler and business community. In 1925 the Nyasaland Planters Association was formed and became another influential organization representing the views of European agriculture and commerce.

NYASALAND RAILWAY COMPANY. *See* TRANSPORTATION.

NYASALAND TEA ASSOCIATION (NTA). Formed in April 1934, the NTA was a response to the international **tea** restrictions instituted under the International Tea Agreements of 1933. Convinced that the existing Nyasaland Tea Research Association did not have the ability to deal with the emerging situation, Nyasaland planters led by, among others, **Malcolm Barrow**, established the NTA to represent more ably their interests in colonial and imperial government circles, at the International Tea Committee, and at all levels of international business. Barrow chaired the NTA for 19 years. In the 1960s the NTA changed its name to the Tea Association of Malawi. Among its other responsibilities, it owns the highly regarded Tea Research Station in **Mulanje**. *See also* TEA.

NYASALAND TIMES. See NEWSPAPERS.

NYASULU, ALEC MJUMA. Former MP for **Mzimba** South, cabinet minister, and Speaker of parliament. Nyasulu was born in **Rumphi** in 1918, was educated at the **Overtoun Institution**, and saw service in World War II. After demobilization Nyasulu taught at local schools, and in 1948 he became one of the first **Nyasaland** Africans to attend the new teacher education course at the Institute of Education, University of London. Upon his return, he became a tutor at the **Domasi** Training Centre, and in 1956 he was posted to Rumphi as Inspector of Nyasulu Schools. In 1961 Nyasulu was elected to parliament as **Malawi Congress Party** (MCP) member for Mzimba South. Between 1964 and 1975 he served in various capacities, including Speaker of parliament and minister of education. In late 1975 he fell out of favor with Dr. **Hastings Banda**, who dismissed him from the speakership of parliament and suspended him from the MCP. Nyasulu spent some time in prison without trial, and upon his release he became a major **tobacco** farmer in Rumphi and northern **Mzimba**. In the early 1980s he was restored to membership in the party and appointed chairman of the Malawi Housing Corporation. Alec Nyasulu died in 1987.

NYASULU, GEORGE. Evangelist in the **Livingstonia Mission**. During and after World War I he worked in the **Nyakyusa** and Kinga regions of Tanganyika, which had hitherto been the domain of the Berlin Missionary Society. Nyasulu entered the theological course at the **Overtoun Institution** in 1913. In spite of his proven record, especially in Tanganyika, he was never ordained. In 1932 Nyasulu lost his position as evangelist because he advised his fellow Christians to consult the *mzimu,* the miracle-performing prophet.

NYASULU, PADDY. One of the founders of the **African National Church**. Nyasulu, a Henga, worked as a teacher and storekeeper for the **Livingstonia Mission** before becoming a government clerk. A church elder, Nyasulu was excommunicated because of polygamy. With **Simon Mkandawire** and **Robert Sambo Mhango** and others, he started the **African National Church** in 1927. The new church's main departure from the Church of Scotland was that it permitted polygamy and alcohol. Most of its adherents were drawn from the latter church and from people who had been unable to join mainstream churches because of the prohibition of alcohol and polygamy.

NYAU. Cult associated with **Chewa** and **Mang'anja** societies. Many people view Nyau simply as a cult of fierce-looking men who wear animal masks to hide their identities during dance performances known as *gule wamkulu* (the great dance, nyau). In actuality, nyau is a serious aspect of Chewa/Mang'anja culture and history. It is full of religious ideas relating to the genesis of the world and humankind and to the evolution of indigenous social and political institutions. Chewa/Mang'anja myths of origins have it that, before the invention of fire, a harmonious relationship existed among human beings, animals, and spirits. In this context the Nyau, like other religious practices, attempts to reestablish that close linkage. The animal masks and the spirits that they represent have to be seen in this setting. The Nyau dance is performed as part of the rites of passage relating to birth, female and male initiation, and death.

Over the centuries, Nyau, as secret societies, have resisted any intrusion by alien institutions, particularly the Christian missionaries who found the male behavior both noisy and obscene. To its followers, the Nyau cult has religious and social significance, and it reflects and supports traditional society. Unlike the territorial cult **M'bona**, Nyau cult interests have been at the village level and have not played any nationalist role, except in parts of the Central Region, where it was used to intimidate people into maintaining their loyalty to the **Malawi Congress Party** (MCP). Throughout Dr. **Hastings Banda**'s presidency, censored versions of Nyau dancers were featured at Independence Day celebrations on July 6 and at MCP public rallies whenever he visited Central Malawi.

NYERERE, JULIUS KAMBARAGE. One of the most respected statesmen in Africa, Julius Nyerere was president of Tanganyika from 1963 to 1964 and of Tanzania from 1964 to 1985, when he retired. Committed to the eradication of settler colonialism in Southern Africa, Nyerere assisted African liberation movements in establishing majority governments in that region. This was contrary to President **Hastings Banda**'s **foreign policy**, which stood for dialogue with white-ruled Southern Africa. This factor, in addition to the fact that Tanzania hosted many Malawian political exiles, led to tension between **Malawi** and **Tanzania** in the period from 1964 to 1985. Nyerere died in a London hospital on October 14, 1999. *See also* CABINET CRISIS; EXILES.

NYIHA. Name of the people and language of the inhabitants of Kameme in the northwestern section of **Chitipa** District, the Chisenga-Ibuluma area of the district, Mbozi District of **Tanzania**, and parts of northeastern **Zambia**. The language is very closely related to that of the Lambya; in fact, historians are of the opinion that the Lambya and the **Nyiha** were originally the same people.

NYIKA PLATEAU. Located in northern **Malawi** and shared by three districts—**Chitipa**, **Karonga**, and **Rumphi**. **Zambia** lies along its western border. Nyika plateau is considered one of the most scenic areas of Southern Africa. With a temperature rarely above 70 degrees Fahrenheit, it is also the broadest and highest plateau range in Malawi, covering an area of about 900 square miles, with an elevation ranging between 7,000 and 8,000 feet at Nganda, the summit. The forests on its slopes have increasingly given way to brachystegia woodland, and the main plateau is mostly montage grassland interspaced by patches of forests and pine plantations. Other flora include many species of orchids, some specific to the area, and a variety of wildflowers. Nyika is also home to numerous species of animals: bushbuck, reedbuck, warthog, duiker, eland, blue monkey, and, on the slopes, elephant and buffalo; lions and cheetahs are occasionally seen in the area. The plateau is particularly known for its large population of zebra and for having the largest concentration of leopard in Malawi, Zambia, and **Zimbabwe**. Nyika is also home to diverse species of birds and has become a favorite area for bird watchers. The dams and numerous perennial streams are populated with trout, making the plateau particularly attractive to anglers. The indigenous inhabitants of the plateau are the **Phoka**, who in the past were famous ironsmiths. Archaeological work carried out in the area, especially at Fingira and Chowo, show human settlement and activity dating to between 175 B.C. and 120 B.C. In 1965 Nyika became a national park, and many of its human inhabitants were relocated. Thirteen years later, the park was expanded, making it the largest in Malawi. The park's main camp is at Chelinda from which visitors can walk or drive to many corners of the plateau. The Zambian part of the plateau also has a camp that is located near the Chowo forest.

Nyika has fascinated Europeans since 1893 when it was first visited by Richard Crawshay of the British colonial administration. But it was writer Laurens van der Post who popularized it in his *Adventure into the Interior* (1951).

NYIRENDA, BAZAAR. Long-time **Malawi Congress Party** (MCP) treasurer for the Northern Region and MP for **Mzimba** East. Bazaar Nyirenda was one of the diehard supporters of Dr. **Hastings Banda**. From the 1960s to the early 1990s, this prominent **Mzuzu**-based businessman held important positions within the ruling party and was known as a fearless and occasionally ruthless organizer. Since 1994 he has virtually retired from politics, concentrating on his business interests.

NYIRENDA, ROBERT GWEBE. Born in **Karonga**, Gwebe Nyirenda was educated locally before going to the **Overtoun Institute**, **Khondowe**, where he completed a teacher's course. He worked as a teacher and then for the **Nyasaland** and Tanganyika governments as an interpreter and a clerk. In 1912 Nyirenda was one of the founders of the **North Nyasa Native Association**, the first political and welfare organization to be formed in Nyasaland. Within **Karonga** District, he was regarded as an influential person, a close friend and adviser of **Kyungu Peter Mwakasungula**. Gwebe Nyirenda died at Kasoba, Karonga, in the 1960s. *See also* AFRICAN WELFARE ASSOCIATIONS.

NYIRENDA, SAULOS. Author and historian of the **Tumbuka**-speaking peoples. Nyirenda was born in about 1870 at Mhuju in modern **Rumphi** District. He was nine years old when the Henga-Kamanga rebelled against the **Ngoni** and sought refuge in the **Karonga** lakeshore. He was educated at Karonga and the **Overtoun Institution**, and he was a teacher in Karonga until 1904, when he became a telegrapher for the Africa Trans-Continental Telegraph Company. Nyirenda witnessed the **Arab-Swahili War** of 1887–1995, which he described in his *History of the Tumbuka-Henga People,* translated from ciTumbuka to English by Dr. **Meredith Sanderson** and published posthumously in *Bantu Studies* in 1931. Nyirenda died in 1925. *See also* GONDWE, KANYOLI; MLOZI BIN KAZBADEMA.

NYIRENDA, TOMO. Probably born in the last decade of the 19th century in northern **Malawi**. Nyirenda was a Henga, one of the numerous **Tumbuka**-speaking groups in the area. After attending school at **Khondowe**, he went to **Northern Rhodesia** to seek employment. His first position was in Broken Hill, where he worked as a cook. He then moved to the Jessie Mines in Mkushi. There in February 1925 he met Gabriel Phiri, another **Nyasaland** labor migrant, who converted him to the **Watchtower** Society. Nyirenda turned to preaching the message of the society, and this led to his arrest and imprisonment. Released on a technicality, he resumed preaching in April that year. What was different this time was that in addition to spreading the message, baptizing, and appealing to sorcerers, he widened his mission to detecting them. As he became more famous, he was invited by Chief Shaiwila of the Lala to baptize him, his family, and his subjects, and to identify and kill all the witches in his area. Impressed by his success, Shaiwila and his people began to regard Tomo Nyirenda as a prophet and savior, and they conferred upon him the designation Mwana Lesa—Son of God.

His preaching began to assume a political tone in the sense that he also prophesied the coming of the Americans, who would liberate the Africans from the Europeans, whose property would then be shared by his followers. His message also included the end of **taxation**. In June 1925 he went to Ndola, where he killed six sorcerers before crossing the border into Katanga, Belgian Congo. There he continued with his "witch" finding, killing about 170 suspected sorcerers, which led Belgian officials to seek his arrest. Nyirenda fled back to Northern Rhodesia, and in September he was arrested by the police in Petauke District. In 1926 he and Chief Shaiwila had a two-day trial and were condemned to death.

NYONDO, SAMSON MBOBE. This *mwaulambya* (king of the **Ulambya**) from 1940 to 1975 was a primary school teacher before being installed on the Lambya throne. Known as a progressive ruler, Nyondo encouraged the expansion of Western **education** in his area and helped **Eneah Mulaga** and **Aram Mwenisongole** establish the first full primary school in **Chitipa** District. In 1959 the colonial government deposed the *mwaulambya,* but he was reinstalled three years later. In 1975 the **Hastings Banda** government removed him from office. A few years later, the Lambya kingmakers installed Redson Nyondo as the new *mwaulambya.* Samson Nyondo died in the early 1980s.

NZAMA. Site of the first mission station of the Montfort order of the **Catholic Church** in the **Lake Malawi** area. It is located in the area of **Njobvuyalema**, a subordinate of the **Gomanis**. Under the leadership of Father **Pierre Bourget**, the Montforts arrived at Nzama on July 25, 1901. As their first accommodation, they used a small farmhouse previously owned by a French planter. They began to learn ciMang'anja **(Chewa)**, the local language, and then they translated the Lord's Prayer, the Hail Mary, and the sign of the cross. In February 1902 they started a school, and in December 1904 five nuns belonging to the Congregation of the Daughters of Wisdom arrived at Nzama to help expand the work of the priests. The relations between Njobvuyalema and the Catholic missionaries were generally cordial, except in 1903, when they accused him and his subordinate at Nzama of administering *mwabvi* (poison ordeal). The priests reported the matter to the colonial government, which pronounced the defendants guilty and imprisoned them at **Liwonde** for nine months. On his return from prison in March 1904, Njobvuyalema and the missionaries repaired their relations and proceeded to cooperate.

NZIMA, MUNENE. One of the wives of **Zwangendaba** and mother of **Mhlahlo Jere**, the first M'mbelwa. Zwangendaba's promotion of Munene to *inkosikazi* (great wife) was controversial because the position had long been jointly held by Lompetu and her sister, **Soseya**, both daughters of Zwide. At some stage Lompetu's house was suspected of trying to poison Zwangendaba, leading to the demotion of the sisters and the promotion of Munene; Soseya bore a child, Ntuto, also known as **Mpezeni**. The joint *inkozikazi*s had become necessary because Lompetu was unable to have children and therefore could not produce an heir for Zwangendaba.

NZUNDA, MATEMBO. Former MP for **Chitipa** North and cabinet minister from 1994 to 1999. Nzunda was born in **Ulambya**, Chitipa District. He was educated at Chaminade Secondary School before proceeding to **Chancellor College** and graduating with a law degree. After studying for a master's degree in law at the University of London, he returned to teach at Chancellor College, **University of Malawi**. In the late 1980s he completed studies at Cambridge University and was awarded a Ph.D. degree in commercial law. Nzunda was one of the first activists to advocate for political change in **Malawi**, Consequently, he was subjected to numerous **police** investigations, including a brief detention. In 1992 he was part of the legal team defending **Chakufwa Chihana**, and when the **Alliance for Democracy** (AFORD) party came into being, Nzunda became an adviser to its leadership. In 1994 he took a leave of absence from his university job and successfully contested for the Chitipa North constituency. Later that year he was one of the AFORD members appointed to the **United Democratic Front** (UDF)–led government. When that arrangement ended two years later, Nzunda refused to leave the government. For this he was expelled from AFORD, and in 1999 he unsuccessfully stood as a UDF party–backed independent candidate; that same year he was appointed clerk of the **Lilongwe** City Assembly. Nzunda died on January 10, 2000.

– O –

OBLATES OF THE HOLY FAMILY. Catholic order of Brothers that was the first men's religious community in **Malawi**. Founded in 1928 and based at **Nankhunda** Seminary, the congregation had an unstable beginning because most of the Brothers left the order for different occupations. As time progressed, the Oblates became the foundation of an African clergy in the Catholic Church, especially in southern Malawi.

OPERATION BWEZANI. Operation Bwezani, or "Operation Return Back," refers to the Malawi **army**'s attack on all the major **Malawi**

Young Pioneer (MYP) installations in Malawi on December 4, 1993, in an attempt to disarm and weaken this wing of the **Malawi Congress Party** (MCP). The Young Pioneers' armory stockpile had been a great concern to the army, and in the period leading to the May 1993 referendum and to the **elections** in the following year, opposition groups, through the **National Consultative Council**, had demanded that the powers of the Young Pioneers be greatly diminished.

On December 1, 1993, two soldiers stationed at the **Moyale** barracks in **Mzuzu** were shot by the Pioneers after a heated argument at a tavern. Junior officers and the men at all three army barracks wanted to revenge the deaths of the soldiers, and they were even more incensed by an apparent lack of support from the higher command, which wanted the matter to be settled quietly. On December 3 the middle ranks, junior officers, and men mounted an attack on all principal MYP bases, the heaviest assault being on the Kamuzu Institute of Youth and Youth House, the national headquarters of the organization. Aiming to completely incapacitate the MYP, the soldiers used helicopter gunships and automatic weapons to demolish these buildings. The national headquarters of the MCP in **Lilongwe** was also bombed and razed to the ground, ostensibly because it was suspected of storing some Pioneers' arms. Senior MYP officers were arrested, but some escaped to the bush; their houses were attacked and their property was taken. The government saved the situation by receiving a delegation of soldiers and conceding to their demands, including the immediate retirement of the three most senior officers: General Yohane, commander of the army; General Manyozo, the deputy commanding officer; and General Liabunya, chief of military intelligence. The latter was particularly associated with the MCP, making him a target for many junior officers.

On December 7 President **Hastings Banda**, who had just had brain surgery, broadcast a conciliatory message, requesting the nation to have faith in the government and thanking the soldiers for their willingness to return to their bases. He also announced the appointment of a retired general, Winnifred Mponela, as minister of defense, a position that only Banda himself had held since independence. The situation calmed and the process of disarming the MYP continued in a more orderly manner. In the meantime, an estimated 2,000 Young Pioneers who had fled to **Mozambique** became a concern of the Malawi opposition parties, which feared that they could be used to destabilize the country in the period leading to the first general elections in the country. The **FRELIMO** government of **Mozambique** also worried that this group of Young Pioneers might link with **RENAMO** and cause even bigger problems for the former Portuguese colony. Many of the "rebels" slipped back into Malawi and returned to their homes, where they lived quietly.

OPERATION SUNRISE. In the early morning hours of March 3, 1959, **Nyasaland**'s governor, Sir **Robert Armitage**, decreed that a state of emergency existed in Malawi, allegedly because the **Nyasaland African Congress** (NAC) had entered upon a course of violence and had plotted the murder of all white residents of the colony. Troops were ordered to round up hundreds of active and senior members of the Congress, including Dr. **Hastings Banda, Henry Chipembere**, and **Dunduzu** and **Yatuta Chisiza**. The government sent Banda and his three lieutenants to Gwelo (Gweru) prison in **Southern Rhodesia (Zimbabwe)**. Other senior Congress leaders were sent to Khami prison, Southern Rhodesia, and 1,500 more members were placed in detention, mostly at Kanjedza in **Limbe**. During the emergency, nearly 50 Africans were killed, 21 at **Nkhata Bay** alone; the NAC was banned and its property destroyed. No Europeans died. The official inquiry into this event showed that both the police and the **King's African Rifles** (KAR) had exceeded their authority and had deliberately attacked and mistreated many Congress members. *See also* DEVLIN COMMISSION.

ORGANIZATION OF AFRICAN UNITY (OAU). Formed in 1963 as an association of independent African states. The OAU was the culmination of the Pan-Africanist movement, which had among its long-term aims the establishment of a united African government structure. First on its immediate agenda was to hasten the process of decolonization by giving practical assistance to the nationalist movements, especially those in the white settler states, **Mozambique**, Angola, **Southern Rhodesia**, **South Africa**, and Guinea Bissau. OAU strategies included isolating these states, but President **Hastings Banda** argued that Malawi could not go along with this approach because economic necessity dictated close cooperation with white-ruled Southern Africa. In 1966 the OAU resolved to break diplomatic relations with **Great Britain** over the Unilateral Declaration of Independence of Southern Rhodesia. Malawi abstained in the OAU vote on this matter and did the same when the United Nations (UN) passed resolutions requesting Britain to use force on the rogue regime. Banda viewed OAU boycotts of white-ruled states, as well as political pressure on them, as a waste of time, arguing that such tactics were ineffective and only served to thwart Malawi's development. Although he maintained the Malawi mission at the OAU, he stopped attending

OAU heads of state summits, leaving it to his cabinet ministers to represent him. On the contrary, the **United Democratic Front** (UDF) government has played an active role in OAU affairs, and President **Bakili Muluzi** has personally led Malawi delegations to all important conferences requiring his presence. *See also* FOREIGN POLICY.

ORMSBY-GORE COMMISSION. Established in 1924 to advise on the advantages of a closer association between the British colonies in East Africa and Central Africa, chaired by William Ormsby-Gore, later Lord Harlech. The undersecretary for the colonies at the time, Ormsby-Gore visited all the colonies concerned, and his commission recommended that the infrastructure in the region be improved before the union of the colonies was considered. With regard to **Nyasaland**, the commission took particular interest in the land question, especially the position of Africans on European estates, including those in North Nyasa District, where the **British South Africa Company** (BSAC) held large tracts of land. The Ormsby-Gore Commission expressed concern that such land problems had not been resolved, pointing out, among other things, the importance of promoting African agricultural development, which he viewed as a solution to the matter of labor migration from Nyasaland, itself a consequence of poor economic opportunities in the colony. Convinced that agricultural production would flourish if both Africans and Europeans could be assured of better export facilities, the commission recommended that a rail line be built from northern Lake **Nyasa** to connect with the Central Railway of Tanganyika, whose principal port was at Dar es Salaam. Ormsby-Gore went on to become secretary for colonies (1936–1938) and British high commissioner in **South Africa** (1941–1944).

OSMAN, ALAUDIN. Press officer for President **Bakili Muluzi** since 1994. Alaudin Osman was educated at Chichiri Secondary School, **Limbe**, and worked as an information assistant in **Blantyre** before joining the *Times of Malawi* in the mid-1960s. In the early 1970s, he was appointed editor of the newspaper, becoming the first Malawian to occupy this position. A short while later, he went to Botswana, where he worked for a privately owned paper. In the early 1990s he returned to **Malawi** and in 1992 founded the *Malawi Financial Post*, the first alternative paper to the *Malawi Daily Times* and the *Malawi News*, both of which were linked to the government and the **Malawi Congress Party** (MCP). The *Financial Post* played a leading role as an advocate for political reform in Malawi.

OURY, LIBERT. Belgian-born investor, owner of Portuguese East Africa–based business concerns, including the Mozambique Company and the Beira Works Ltd. Oury was instrumental in the construction of the Trans-Zambesia Railway from **Beira**, to which the **Shire Highland Railway**, completed in 1913, would be linked. Using London contacts such as Sir **Alfred Sharpe**, Oury persuaded the British government to back his railway project, debentures of which were to be guaranteed by the **Nyasaland** government. Economically very weak, the colonial administration in Nyasaland spent much of its meager revenue servicing a venture that had been forced upon it by the imperial authorities. *See also* RAILWAYS.

OVERTOUN INSTITUTION. The leading educational and vocational training center in South Central Africa. It was established in November 1894 at **Khondowe** and named after Lord Overtoun (John Campbell White), one of the Scottish businessmen who supported the **Livingstonia Mission** financially. The institution produced teachers, clergymen, bookkeepers, masons, joiners, medical assistants, and many other skilled personnel, all of whom occupied key positions in many parts of the wider Southern African region. Dr. **Robert Laws** headed the institution from its foundation until 1927, when he retired to Scotland. *See also* EDUCATION; MISSIONS.

– P –

PACHAI, BRIDGLAL. Founding head of the Department of History at the **University of Malawi**. Pachai was born in 1929 in Ladysmith, **South Africa**, where he trained as a teacher and studied by correspondence for his B.A., M.A., and Ph.D. degrees. He became the first person of Indian origin to be awarded a doctorate degree in history by a South African university. He taught at the University of Cape Coast, Ghana, and in 1965 was appointed as senior lecturer and head of Department of History at the University of Malawi, becoming a full professor three years later. In 1971 and 1972 Pachai broadcast a series of talks covering a wide range of topics on the history of **Malawi**. In this way, he helped popularize history in the country, particularly since ciChewa translations were also broadcast on Radio Malawi. The talks were published as *Malawi: History of the Nation* (1973). Pachai published many books on Malawian and South African history, including *The Early History of Malawi* (ed., 1972), *Land and Politics in Malawi* (1975), and *The South African Indian Question* (1971). In 1975 Pachai left Malawi for **Canada**, where he held appointments at Dalhousie University and St. Mary's University, both in Halifax, Nova Scotia. In 1978 he went to the University of Sokoto (now Usman dan Fodio University), where he became dean of the faculty of arts. In the mid-1980s, he returned to Canada and worked for a **nongovernmental organization** (NGO) before retiring.

PAOLUCCI, AUGUSTO. The first Italian to establish a business in the **Lake Malawi** region, with Ippolito Lamagna. Arriving in the **Shire Highlands** in the 1890s, Paolucci and Lamagna, like many Europeans entering the area at the time, became traders and effectively land speculators, buying hundreds of acres of it. Ultimately, Paolucci owned a store in **Blantyre** that stocked a variety of items, including cigars, kitchenware, and alcoholic beverages such as wine, brandy, and whisky. He even tried to import camels to help solve the perennial transport problem in the colony. As more **Indian** traders established their own retail shops, Paolucci was edged out and by 1904 had left the colony.

PASELI BROTHERS. Two brothers, Bali and Smart Paseli, whose popular banjo and acoustic guitar music was regularly featured by the **Central Africa Broadcasting Services** and its successor, the **Federal Broadcasting Corporation**. Born and raised in **Mlumbe**'s area in **Zomba** District, in the 1940s and 1950s, the brothers had worked in **Southern Rhodesia** and, at that stage, their music reflected the life of Malawian immigrant laborers. Typical of such songs are *Nafela moyenda* (I have died in my travels/migrations) and *Kwathu nkutali* (Our home is very far). Easily their most popular composition is *Napolo*, which laments the wrath of the cyclone, **Napolo**, especially the damage it caused in the Zomba area. The music of the Paseli brothers remains popular today and it has influenced a generation of Malawian banjo and guitar players.

PASHANE, MAXWELL KATAYENI. Minister of education (1986–1987) and administrative secretary of the **Malawi Congress Party** (1987–1991). Maxwell Pashane was born in **Mchinji** District, educated at **Zomba** Catholic Secondary School and at **Chancellor College**, **University of Malawi**, where he graduated in 1969 with a B.A. degree in geography. He taught at Bwaila Secondary School in **Lilongwe** and later became headmaster of the institution. He was promoted to the inspectorate division at the Ministry of Education headquarters, rising to the position of chief inspector of schools. In 1986 Pashane was nominated as MP for Mchinji and was appointed minister of education. Within 18 months, he was transferred to the headship of the ruling party's secretariat, an office that carried the cabinet ministerial designation of minister without portfolio. In 1991 he left active politics for health reasons and died shortly thereafter.

PASSFIELD, LORD. Social activist and historian formerly known as Sidney James Webb. He was in the Labour government's cabinet as minister for the colonies from 1929 to 1931, and for a brief period (1929–1930) he also held the portfolio for dominions. In the former capacity Lord Passfield issued his famous Memorandum on Native Policy in East Africa, reaffirming the principle of trusteeship and paramountcy of African interests in that region, as declared by the Duke of Devonshire in 1923. The Passfield Memorandum, published in June 1930, extended the doctrine to **Nyasaland** and **Northern Rhodesia**, a development that upset the European settlers in the two countries, as well as in **Southern Rhodesia**, because their long-term ambition was to establish a closer union of the three British possessions. The memorandum also instructed that equal opportunity be granted to everybody in the acquisition of Crown lands in Nyasaland and Northern Rhodesia. In connection with this, Passfield advised that reasonable credit and lease terms be made more readily available to Africans. He also directed that development must occupy a central position in the policies of the two colonial governments. For Nyasaland, he argued that the future of the country lay in the contributions of the larger and better-established European agricultural firms and the African cultivator rather than the recently arrived small European settler farmer, whom he considered too dependent on government assistance.

PATEL, ROLF. Limbe- and **Thyolo**-based businessman. In the early 1990s Patel was a leading advocate for political reform, becoming a founding member of the **United Democratic Front** (UDF) party. In 1994, he was elected to the National Assembly and was appointed to the cabinet, but within two years he disagreed with his party leadership and founded his own political organization, the People's Democratic Party. Some months before the general **elections** of 1999, Patel returned to the UDF.

PEARCE, FRANCIS BARROW. A captain in the Central African Rifles, renamed **King's African Rifles** (KAR). Pearce was appointed assistant deputy commissioner and vice consul in 1900, and in 1903 and 1911 he served as acting governor of **Nyasaland**. As an officer in the KAR, Pearce took part in campaigns against African communities resisting British rule. In 1902 he commanded a contingent to **Chintheche** District, where the **Tonga**, supported by the Scottish missionaries at **Bandawe**, refused to pay the recently instituted hut tax of six shillings. Promoted to the rank of major, Pearce was acting governor in 1903 when he tried to solve the land problem facing Africans because of the proliferation of European estates. Receiving little support from his superiors, he failed in his attempts. When Sir **Alfred Sharpe** was on leave in 1907, Pearce once more became acting governor. In 1913 he served in a similar capacity and, as in 1903, he attempted to tackle the land issue, this time unsuccessfully initiating legislation aimed at preventing Africans on private estates from being turned into serfs.

PEOPLE'S DEMOCRATIC PARTY. *See* PATEL, ROLF.

PEREGRINO, FRANCIS ZACCHEUS SANTIAGO. Journalist, adventurer, and Pan-Africanist. Peregino was born in Accra in the Gold Coast region of West Africa and was educated there before traveling to the **United States**, where he later became editor of the Buffalo, New York, *Spectator.* In 1900 he left the United States for England, where he attended the first Pan-Africanist Congress before proceeding to **South Africa** in the following year. He settled in Cape Town and within a short period began to edit the *South African Spectator and Coloured Advertiser.* Peregrino came to know many activists on the Southern African political scene, among them **Joseph Booth**. Through the latter he met many Nyasas who went to the Cape and especially those, such as **Eliot Kamwana** and **Peter Nyambo**, who visited Booth's Clifton Bay establishment. The *South African Spectator* also published letters from Nyasas, including **Peter Nyambo**, expressing their anticolonial views.

PETERKINS, E. C. Prominent **Lilongwe**-based European businessman and politician. Peterkins was **United Federal Party** (UFP) and later **Nyasaland Constitutional Party** MP until 1961. Peterkins had many business interests, including a directorship of the *Nyasaland Times* and a shop in Lilongwe in the 1940s and 1950s.

PHAIYA, TADEUS THOMAS. Born at **Kapeni** village in **Mulanje** District in 1946, he attended Mulanje primary schools and **Blantyre** Secondary School. Phaiya obtained a diploma in business studies from the Polytechnic in Blantyre. Prior to being nominated to parliament in 1973, he worked with the Reserve Bank and the **Malawi Development Corporation** (MDC). Subsequently, he served in the Ministries of Trade, Industry, and Tourism; Health; and Local Government. Phaiya was briefly Southern Regional vice secretary of the **Malawi Congress Party** (MCP). In the late 1970s he left active politics.

PHALOMBE. District north of **Mulanje** and southeast of **Zomba**. Inhabited mostly by **Lomwe** and **Yao** peoples, the district was, until the late 1990s, part of **Mulanje** District. Located in the fertile and wet plains, it is one of the most densely populated areas of **Malawi**.

PHELPS STOKES COMMISSION. American charitable foundation. In 1919 the Phelps Stokes Fund appointed a commission to investigate and report on the state of **education** in Africa. Led by Thomas Jesse Jones, a noted specialist on black American education at Hampton Institute, Virginia, the commission included American and British missionaries and Dr. James Kwegyir Aggrey, a leading educationist from the Gold Coast. Although it spent most of the time in South and West Africa, the commission also surveyed the situation in **Nyasaland**. The commission recommended the broadening of African education beyond the evangelistic approach that had been so dominant in the continent. Accepting the fact that Christian **missions** would continue to play the major role in education, the commission recommended that training in **agriculture** should occupy a prominent place on school syllabi. It also strongly urged colonial governments to involve themselves in educational matters, especially in coordinating policy and in providing the needed financial assistance. In 1924 another Phelps Stokes Commission visited Nyasaland, among other countries in East, Central, and Southern Africa. It was partly in response to this commission's proposals and those of the Advisory Committee on African Education in Tropical Africa that the Nyasaland government established the Department of Education in 1926. In pursuit of some of the recommendations of the Phelps Stokes Commission, the Jeanes Fund of the United States funded educational centers that emphasized community work, and among such institutions was the **Jeanes Training Centre** at **Domasi** in **Zomba** District.

PHILLIPS, HENRY ELLIS ISIDORE. The last financial secretary in the colonial government of **Nyasaland** and first minister of finance in the African-dominated government that followed the general **elections** of 1961. Henry Phillips was born in England in 1914, was educated at University College, London, and served in World War II, being held as a prisoner in Japanese camps. In 1946 he joined the Colonial Administrative Service and was posted to **Nyasaland**, where he became first assistant district commissioner (ADC) and **district commissioner** (DC) of **Karonga** District. Two years later, Phillips was transferred to the secretariat in **Zomba** and from 1953 to 1957 was seconded to the Treasury of the **Federation of Rhodesia and Nyasaland** in Salisbury (Harare). On his return to Nyasaland, he became financial secretary and held the position until 1961, when he was appointed minister of finance. Phillips was knighted in 1964, the year he also retired to England. He became managing director of the Development Corporation of the Standard Bank, a position that ensured his continued link with Malawi. Later (1983–1988) he became a member of the board of the National Bank in Malawi, which made him a regular visitor to Malawi. Consequently, he remained in close contact with President **Hastings Banda**.

PHIRI, DESMOND DUDWA. Educator, writer, historian, businessman, and commentator on public affairs. Phiri was born in **Mzimba** District and was educated at **Loudon** and **Livingstonia Mission** schools and at **Blantyre** Secondary School. He completed his education by correspondence, earning a B.A. degree and a postgraduate qualification in economic and social administration from the University of London. He worked in East Africa before joining the administrative division of the Malawi government and served briefly as a diplomat. Upon his retirement, he established the Aggrey Memorial Correspondence School. Phiri is the author of numerous books in his Malawians to Remember series, including *Inkosi Gomani II* (1973), *James Frederick Sangala* (1974), *Charles Chidongo Chinula* (1975), and *John Chilembwe* (1975, revised in 1999). He has also written *From Nguni to Ngoni: A History of the Ngoni Exodus from Zululand to Malawi, Tanzania, and Zambia* (1982).

PHIRI, HANOCK MSOKERA. Religious leader, teacher, uncle, and close friend of former President **Hastings Banda**. Hanock Phiri was born near **Kasungu** around 1884 and was educated at the **Overtoun Institution**, where Dr. **Robert Laws** baptized him into Christianity. Phiri taught at **Livingstonia Mission** schools in Kasungu, including Chilanga, where Hastings Banda was one of his pupils. He was in his mid-twenties when he became Banda's teacher. Early in 1924 he left for **Southern Rhodesia** and worked in Hartley, where he was joined by Banda about two years later. Early in 1917 the two embarked on a journey that took them to Natal, where they briefly worked at a coal mine near Dundee before proceeding to Johannesburg. Phiri and Banda found employment at the Witwatersrand Deep Mine on the periphery of Boksburg. Sometime in 1918, Phiri left for Livingstone, **Northern Rhodesia**, to teach at the Paris Evangelical Mission school in that town. In 1922 Banda asked his uncle to return to **South Africa** to work toward a leadership position in the **African Methodist Episcopal (AME) Church**, which Banda had joined earlier. In late 1923 Phiri was ordained as minister of the AME Church, and in 1924 both attended the AME conference. By the end of that year, Phiri returned to **Nyasaland** to head mission operations of the church near Kasungu. Soon Phiri had established a network of schools subsidized partly by South African church funds.

PHOKA. Name of the indigenous inhabitants of the **Nyika plateau** and the surrounding areas, including the highland region north of the Henga valley, up to and encompassing **Khondowe**. In precolonial times they were widely famous as ironsmiths, their hoes being popular well beyond modern **Malawi**.

PHWEZI EDUCATION FOUNDATION. Based at Phwezi in **Rumphi** District, this establishment was founded in the early 1980s. **Denis Nkwazi** and **Morton Mughogho**, among others, sought means of building an independent School to enable primary school children not selected to the mainstream secondary school system to continue their **education**. With German financial support, they started an educational foundation to fulfill this objective. The foundation bought the buildings at the main camp of the firm that had just constructed the **Chiweta** road, which links **Mzuzu** and the **Karonga** and northern Rumphi lakeshores. Located on the northern banks of the **South Rukuru River** in the southern section of the Henga valley, the camp, consisting of modern accommodations and offices, was turned into the Phwezi Secondary School, having one section for girls and the other for boys, each with a headmaster. Mughogho became the head of the foundation as well as the overall principal of the school. Later the foundation added a technical college to the school.

Many board members of the Phwezi Foundation, as well as its faculty, were former civil servants, politicians, and teachers who at one stage or another had fallen out of favor with the government and the **Malawi Congress Party** (MCP). Some of them had served periods in detention without trial. In 1991 and 1992 Phwezi became one of the centers of the underground movement to institute political reform, and most people associated with the foundation became active in the **Alliance for Democracy** (AFORD). Mughogho became the national chairman, and Nkwazi the national treasurer.

PILANE, ABDUL. Balaka-based businessman and politician had been active in local government affairs in postcolonial **Malawi**. Pilane became active in the political reform movement of the early 1990s and was a founding member of the **United Democratic Front** (UDF) party. He was elected to parliament in 1994 and appointed to the cabinet but had to resign from the government following a corruption-related scandal.

PINTO, SERPA. Portuguese army officer and traveler. In 1889 Major Pinto led an expedition into the **Shire Valley**, ostensibly to undertake a scientific inquiry of the **Lake Malawi** region. Portuguese designs on the region were common knowledge in European diplomatic circles. For some time, they had attempted to involve themselves in inter-African affairs, especially those of the **Kololo**, some of whom were not on particularly good terms with the British, especially those in the **African Lakes Company**. The Portuguese had also already tried to establish working relations with the **Yao** in the Upper Shire. For the British, the Serpa Pinto expedition, which in reality was military in nature, was evidence of the Portuguese determination to proclaim jurisdiction over the **Shire Highlands** and the Shire Valley. The British in the area and most of the Kololo chiefs reconciled their differences and opposed the Portuguese plans. Partly influenced by strong Scottish opinion, the British government under **Lord Salisbury** reacted to the expedition by declaring British protectorate status over the southern Lake Malawi area.

PLAGUE. In 1916, 13 cases of plague were reported at **Karonga**. Although this outbreak was followed by a war on rats, with three million of them eventually being killed, the number of cases increased to 28 in 1917. However, in the following year, there were only five reported cases of the **disease**. Thereafter, cases were reported at **Makanjila** in **Mangochi** District in 1924, at **Neno** in 1939, at **Port Herald** in 1956, at Ngabu in 1963, and in parts of the Southern Region in 1999.

PLAINFIELD INDUSTRIAL MISSION. Original name of the **Malamulo** Mission in **Thyolo**, when it was first established by **Joseph Booth** after his return from the United States in July 1899. During his stay, Booth had become a member of the Plainfield Seventh Day Baptist Church in New Jersey. When the National Baptist Convention appointed him head of a mission it wanted to start in the **Lake Malawi** region, Booth named it after his American congregation. In 1901 Booth seriously considered selling Plainfield to African Americans for purposes of turning it into a settlement of those people of African origins who wanted to return home to Africa. However, in 1902 the mission settlement was sold to the Seventh-Day Adventists, who renamed it Malamulo, turning it into the main center of the Lake Malawi region.

POLICE. From the 1890s to the end of the World War I, there was no real police force in **Nyasaland**. District **collectors**, as the district administrators were called, used uniformed and armed messengers to enforce the law. These messengers were not trained, were undisciplined, and tended to demand favors such as food, chickens, and even women. A response to this situation was a 1909 ordinance that stipulated harsh punishment for unruly policemen. In 1899 the first actual policemen, two in number, were employed by the town of **Blantyre**. Their main duty was to patrol markets and oversee laborers working on roads. Serious proposals for a properly structured police force were made in the prewar period, a step reinforced by the **Chilembwe uprising** of 1915. However, it was only in 1920–1921 that elements of a police department began to appear.

In 1920 Major **Francis Stephens** was appointed chief commissioner of police, and he set about establishing a territory-wide force. In October of the following year, the Nyasaland Police Ordinance was signed by the governor, Sir **George Smith**, marking the official birth of the Nyasaland Police. With headquarters in **Zomba**, the department initially comprised a chief commissioner and his support staff, and four stations in Zomba, Blantyre, **Mulanje**, and **Fort Johnston**. For transportation, this force of less than 100 relied on a fleet of four bicycles. Among their duties were recovery of World War I rifles; registration of bicycles, vehicles, and firearms; supervision of prisons; and criminal investigation. In districts where the department was not present, the earlier system of law enforcement continued. The Criminal Investigation Department was added in 1922, and in the 1930s the force became responsible for immigration duties. Also in the 1930s more outstations were established, and the ranks of assistant inspector and subinspector were created, the former ranks being occupied by **Indians**, the latter by Africans. By the end of the 1930s stations were set up as far north as **Karonga**; except for **Lilongwe**, **district commissioners** acted as officers in charge of the stations in their districts.

At the beginning of World War II, the security branch, the Political Intelligence Bureau, was added to the force, and in the late 1940s radio communications became part of the department's apparatus. Although there was a special prison police during the war, the general police and the **King's African Rifles** (KAR) had to be called in to the central prison in Zomba to quell a prisoner riot in 1949. By 1952 the force had stations and posts in most parts of the Central and Northern Regions, and its total complement was at 705.

The events of the 1950s had a major impact on the reorganization of the police. In 1953 riots concerning land and tax, as well as the imposition of the **Federation**, took place in **Thyolo**, Mulanje, **Ntcheu**, Zomba, and **Port Herald**. More policemen were recruited, and more permanent housing was built for them on most stations. Equally significant was the creation of the antiriot police, consisting mainly of ex-soldiers and older policemen. In the following year, it came to be called the Police Mobile Force (PMF). It had 250 men who were divided into platoons of 36; each platoon was headed by a European officer who had served in the British police or had recently worked in Malaya during the state of emergency in that colony. Some of the European officers were recruited from the British South Africa Police in **Southern Rhodesia**, where racial attitudes toward black peoples were particularly bad, and this tended to influence the officers' dealings with the men under their charge, as well as with the African population in Nyasaland. The PMF was heavily involved in dealing with riots during the 1959 state of emergency, which led to the **Devlin Commission**, and they were noted as particularly harsh in their approach to rioters. In the initial stages of the state of emergency, the governor, Sir **Robert Armitage**, requested and received the assistance of contingents of police from Tanganyika and the two Rhodesias.

Following the state of emergency, the police force expanded further. A two-boat marine division was established on **Lake Malawi**, and a small air wing was also created. More people were recruited into the general police and the PMF so that by 1960 the total complement was 225 officers and 2,604 men. In that year the Police Training College was moved from Zomba to the premises of the Artisan Training School in Kanjedza, **Limbe**. Until the early 1960s, the highest rank an African could expect to occupy was assistant and subinspector; the only exception was Mateyu Numero. In 1958 he became assistant superintendent when he took over headship of the Police Band from an Indian officer. Numero had just completed a course at the British army's Royal Military School of Music. In 1959 **Thomas Gombera** achieved the distinction of being the first Malawian in the Operations Division to attain the rank of inspector of the police force. From the early 1970s, a three months in-service course for noncommissioned officers was instituted at the police school to enable **Africanization** to take place. Among such officers were

Mac Kamwana, who in 1971 became the first Malawian to head the police force.

In the 1970s and 1980s the police continued to Africanize, expand, and modernize. All wings of the force were headed by Malawians, the communications systems were updated, the headquarters were moved to the new capital city, Lilongwe, and a new division was created. Called the Eastern Division, it covered Zomba, **Machinga**, and **Mangochi** Districts. In 1975–1976, hundreds of Malawians suffered indiscriminate and arbitrary political detentions to the extent that even the new prisons at **Mikuyu** and Mpyupyu were filled. It was discovered that Assistant Commissioner **Focus Gwede**, then head of the police intelligence wing, the **Special Branch**, had misused his authority, partly to assist the political ambitions of his friend, **Albert Muwalo-Nqumayo**, at the time minister of state in the Office of the President, a position that included security responsibilities. In 1983 the police were also implicated in the **Mwanza accidents**, in which three cabinet ministers and an MP were killed.

Kamwana, whose post had been redesignated inspector-general, retired in 1986 and was succeeded by his deputy, L. Ngwata, who served for only eight months before being replaced by Elliot Mbedza, previously head of the PMF division. A year later, he retired and was replaced by Milward Namasani, whose main experience was in the Criminal Investigation Division (CID). In 1990 **MacWilliams Lunguzi**, head of the Special Branch, became the new inspector-general, a position he held until 1994, when the **United Democratic Front** (UDF) government recalled former Assistant Commissioner Chikhosa from retirement to lead the Malawi Police. Chikhosa served for over two years and was replaced by Kennedy Chirambo, who in January 2000 retired on health grounds and was succeeded by a new inspector-general.

During the tense period leading to political reforms, the police had to deal with many delicate situations, including an incident in May 1992 when they fired at strikers. Otherwise, the Malawi Police has continued the British tradition of walking the beat unarmed, the baton stick being their main weapon. However, with the rise in violent robberies, occasioned by poverty, disparities in wealth, and a wide circulation of firearms, including the AK47, it has become the practice to arm some of them, especially at night. Increasingly, the PMF are used to deal with violent robbers. For a long time the Malawi Police had a reputation of not being corrupt; however, poor pay and the deteriorating economic situation in the country have rendered many police easily susceptible to bribery. *See also* BANDA, HASTINGS KAMUZU.

POLITICAL DISSIDENTS. During the leadership of Dr. **Hastings Banda**, the term "political dissident" referred generally to people who had fallen out of favor with the **Malawi Congress Party** (MCP) and its government, especially after the **Cabinet Crisis** of 1964. Many dissidents were forced into exile, mainly to **Zambia** and **Tanzania**. Those who were studying abroad during the crisis and openly supported (or were perceived to agree with) the rebelling ministers in Congress also came to be regarded as dissidents. Within **Malawi** there were waves of imprisonments without trial of people reported to be in touch or in sympathy with **exiles** abroad. Government intelligence services infiltrated dissident organizations in exile and are credited with the murder of persons such as **Attati Mpakati** and **Mkwapatila Mhango**.

POLITICAL PARTIES. In the period leading to the first general **elections** in 1961, there were many parties in Malawi (then **Nyasaland**). The **Malawi Congress Party** (MCP), representing the majority of Africans, stood for majority rule; the **United Federal Party** (UFP) fought for the status quo, including the continuation of the **Federation of Rhodesia and Nyasaland**; after the dissolution of the Federation, the UFP in Nyasaland changed to the **Nyasaland Constitutional Party**; the **Congress Liberation Party** was led by **Thamar D. T. Banda**, former president-general of the **National African Congress** (ANC). Other parties were the **Christian Social Democratic Party** of **Chester Katsonga** and the National Liberation Democratic Party led by **Clement Kumbikano**, who had briefly been president of the Nyasaland branch of the Central African Party, which Garfield Todd established after he split from the UFP; its main base was in **Southern Rhodesia (Zimbabwe)**. Sometime after **Pemba Ndovi** was expelled from his position in the MCP, he formed the Convention of African National Union. But the party found little support and was short-lived.

Following the **Cabinet Crisis** of 1964, the MCP national convention adopted one-party status for the Republic of Malawi, which meant that from 1965 on, no other political organization would be allowed in the country. In the meantime, the politicians forced into **exile** formed their own parties. **Henry Chipembere**'s party was called the Pan-African Democratic Party of Malawi, and **Kanyama Chiume** formed the **Congress for the Second Republic**. **Orton Chirwa** established the Malawi Freedom Movement (MAFREMO); **Attati Mpakati** led the Socialist League of Malawi (LESOMA), and after he was assassinated, Grey Kamuyambeni became the leader. Other parties in exile were **Harry**

Bwanausi's United Democratic Movement (UMD) and **Akogo Kanyaya**'s Malawi Democratic Union (UDM).

With the exception of the Pan-African Democratic Party, which virtually ended with the death of its founder in 1975, all the parties previously based outside Malawi took part in the general elections of 1994. They did not do well compared with the **United Democratic Front** (UDF) and the **Alliance for Democracy** (AFORD), the **Malawi Democratic Party** (DP) and the Malawi Congress Party, the first three having been established in 1992. Since then other political parties have been formed: the **United Party** (UP) led by **Bingu wa Mutharika**, the Social Democratic Party (SDP) of Eston Kakhome, and Rev. Daniel K. Mnkhumbwe's Congress for National Unity (CONU). Parties that continue to be active in Malawi's political life are the UDF, MCP, AFORD, MDP, UP, and CONU. In January 2001 **Brown Mpinganjira**, one of the founders of the UDF announced the formation of the National Democratic Alliance which it was expected would evolve into a major political party.

POOLE, WOODSWORTH. Government medical officer at **Zomba** from 1895 to 1897. Poole was born in 1870 and educated at Cambridge University and Guy's Hospital, London. In 1895 he was part of the military expeditions to Chiefs **Kawinga**, **Jalasi**, **Mponda**, and **Makanjila**, and he was the doctor in the final campaign against **Mlozi bin Kazbadema** in December of that year. After government forces captured Mlozi, they took him to Dr. Poole to have his head wounds treated. Shortly after his wounds were treated, the **Swahili-Arab** was executed. Poole, a keen hunter and horseman, founded the **Zomba Gymkhana Club**. After leaving Malawi in 1897, he enlisted in the British war against the Ashanti; Poole died in 1903.

POTTERY. *See* NKOPE BAY; NKUDZI BAY; PREHISTORY.

PRAZOS. These estates were an important means of effecting Portuguese presence and interests in the Zambezi region. The Portuguese monarch would give his subjects titles to land, and as time progressed many *prazos* became powerful, well-armed chiefdoms, headed by people who virtually ignored Portuguese authority. The *prazeros,* as the *prazo* owners were called, were assisted by their **Chikunda** retainers, who often terrorized their African neighbors.

PREFERENTIAL TRADE AREA (PTA). *See* COMMON MARKET FOR EASTERN AND SOUTHERN AFRICA (COMESA).

PREHISTORY. The period of Malawian history for which neither oral traditions nor written sources exist. Archaeology supplies the only dependable evidence, and according to this source, the Early Stone Age peoples inhabiting **Malawi** were hunter-gatherers who lived along the lakeshore and in the river valleys. More environmentally adaptable, Later Stone Age humans moved throughout the country, evidently preferring the uplands. Artifacts such as scrapers, lunates, trapezes, and back blades belonging to these people are found in nearly all of Malawi. In addition to these microliths, some bored stones and polished axes have also been recovered. The men and women who occupied rock shelters and caves in this period were also artists who left geometric and schematic style rock paintings.

Based on the latest archaeological research, carried out seriously and systematically since the 1960s, the Iron Age began in Malawi about 200 A.D. Migrants, perhaps Bantu-speaking, who had knowledge of ironworking, pottery, and agriculture, probably entered the country from an area to the west and settled rapidly by the lakeshore. Although the intruders were culturally superior to the Later Stone Age residents, the two apparently coexisted in the region.

In southern Malawi the pottery style uncovered has been named Nkope ware. The presumably quiet life near **Nkope Bay** allowed these people time to produce large numbers of decoratively rimmed bowls. A related pottery style, called Mwabulambo, after a site in **Karonga** District, is commonly uncovered in northern Malawi. Mwabulambo pots were wide rimmed and undecorated. Sometime in the 10th to 14th centuries, another type of pottery appeared. Called **Kapeni** ware, it is thinner than Nkope and contains grooves and incisions, unlike the earlier pottery.

The migration of the **Maravi** peoples in the 15th to 16th centuries can be substantiated by oral tradition as well as by the recovery of Mawudzu pots made by the Maravi. The pottery is noticeably thinner and more decorative, with chevrons, crosshatching, or herringbones. This ware was produced throughout the period of the Maravi empire into the late 18th century, when new settlers effected additional cultural change. Succeeding in this southern lake region were the **Bisa**, known for their Nkudzi pottery. They interacted with the **Nyanja** inhabitants, but their cultural influence was followed by that of the **Ngoni** and **Yao** immigrants. Thereafter pottery may be termed modern and no longer Iron Age. *See also* NKUDZI BAY.

PRENTICE, GEORGE. Scotsman responsible for numerous advances in **health care.** When Dr. **Robert Laws** went to **Khondowe** to establish the new headquarters of the **Livingstonia Mission** in 1892, Dr. George Prentice arrived at **Bandawe** to take over the headship of the mission station. A keen doctor, Prentice built the first obstetrics and gynecological ward in the country. Upon his transfer to **Kasungu,** where he established the Chilanga Mission in 1900, he became very active in medical work, establishing numerous rural health centers in the district. He is also noted as having been in the forefront in the fight against sleeping sickness, which broke out in the Luangwa-Kasungu, **Nkhotakota,** and south **Mzimba** region after 1910 and continued to be a problem in the 1920s. Prentice baptized **Hastings Banda** at Chilanga, where the latter was a student between 1908 and 1914. In 1917 Prentice volunteered for the war, returning to Kasungu two years later. In 1924 he returned to Scotland.

PRESIDENTIAL COMMITTEE ON DIALOGUE (PCD). A few months after the release of the **Catholic bishops' pastoral letter,** *Living our Faith,* President **Hastings Banda** made some concessions, initiating an exchange of views between members of his cabinet and Malawians at large. This led to the formation of the Presidential Committee on Dialogue, consisting of cabinet ministers and senior **Malawi Congress Party** (MCP) officials. The public was represented by the **Public Affairs Committee** (PAC); together, the two committees came to be known as the **National Consultative Council.**

PRESS HOLDINGS LTD. Largest holding company in **Malawi.** With major ventures in commercial and industrial capital and in agrobusiness, Press has dominated the country's **economy** since the 1970s. In the early 1960s the Press Company, created and owned by Dr. **Hastings Banda,** was primarily concerned with **Malawi Congress Party** (MCP) publications. But after independence in 1964 it expanded its business so much that, by the end of the 1970s, it was in the top 3 percent of investors in Malawi. Its subsidiary, the Peoples Trading Center (PTC), had taken over all the retail shops in **Kandodo** in rural Malawi and built supermarkets in the large urban centers to compete with the latter company's establishments. Press had also entered commercial farming to the extent that it was now the largest producer in Malawi of flue-cured and burley **tobacco.** It controlled 50 percent of Limbe Leaf, the major tobacco processing and exporting firm. Press also had interests in cattle ranches,

rubber and **sugar**, and ethanol production. Besides civil engineering, construction, and property firms, Press's subsidiaries included Press Transport, Press Bakeries, Press Clothing, and Press Produce. In the 1970s Press further bought controlling shares in the National Bank of Malawi and Commercial Bank of Malawi. *See also* BANKING.

Press dominance of Malawi's economy meant that some foreign enterprises, such as the European Development Bank and the **Commonwealth Development Corporation**, invested in projects in which Press was involved. Dr. Banda turned Press into a corporation, and the Malawi government began to guarantee the firm's loans in international markets; in the 1980s the government even paid the firm's debts owed to foreign creditors.

Revenue from Press ventures enriched Dr. Banda and the MCP treasury, financing projects such as the construction and maintenance of houses for leading members of the **League of Malawi Women**. However, after the MCP lost power to the **United Democratic Party** (UDF) party in 1994, the new government challenged the ownership of Press, fearing, among other things, that the firm would continue to place the opposition party in a financially powerful position, thereby turning it into a formidable force. After protracted legal battles, Press was removed from Dr. Banda's control and the MCP, and was assigned a new board of directors.

PRETORIUS, J. LOU. Dutch Reformed Church missionary. Born in **South Africa** in 1903, he went to **Nyasaland** as a missionary at the age of 26 and was stationed at **Nkhoma**. Respected in missionary and government circles, in the late 1950s he served as a member of the federal parliament. Pretorius, also known as a keen historian of Malawi, was an administrator in teacher training colleges in both **Malawi** and **Zambia** and a leading member of the Malawi Censorship Board.

PREZEAU, AUGUSTE. First apostolic prefect of the Shire. Auguste Prezeau was born in France in 1872 and ordained as a priest in 1896. He served in Kingston, Ontario, **Canada**, before becoming one of the three Montfort missionaries to establish stations in the **Lake Malawi** region. The Montfort Marist Fathers, including **Pierre Bourget** (the leader), Prezeau, and **Anton Winnen**, arrived in the **Shire Highlands** in June 1901, and on July 25 they arrived at **Nzama** in chief **Njobvuyalema**'s area, under the ultimate jurisdiction of the Maseko **Ngoni**. At Nzama, they started a school and a **health** clinic and were joined by five nuns belonging to the Daughters of Wisdom at the end of 1904. In the following year, Father Prezeau started a new mission station at **Nguludi** on land that had previously belonged to **Donald Malota**. In the same year, Prezeau was appointed as apostolic prefect on the Shire and assumed the title Monsignor. In 1908 the prefecturate was elevated to an apostolic vicariate, and Monsignor Prezeau became bishop of the Shire. While on leave in France, the new bishop fell ill and died on December 2, 1909, aged 37.

PRICE, THOMAS. Onetime missionary of the Church of Scotland. Price carried out extensive original research into the history and culture of Malawian peoples, especially that of the **Mang'anja**, among whom he worked. Price collaborated with George Shepperson in writing *Independent African: John Chilembwe and the Origins, Setting, and Significance of the Nyasaland Native Rising of 1915* (1958).

PRIVATIZATION. *See* FINANCIAL AND ECONOMIC DEVELOPMENTS; NATIONALIZATION.

PROVIDENCE INDUSTRIAL MISSION. *See* CHILEMBWE, JOHN.

PUBLIC AFFAIRS COMMITTEE (PAC). Dominated by representatives of the churches in Malawi and by members of the **Law Society of Malawi**, the Public Affairs Committee was formed in 1992 to represent the views of the general public in the dialogue with the government and the **Malawi Congress Party** (MCP). Besides acting as a pressure group within Malawi, the PAC actively established contact with church and **human rights** organizations in Europe and North America and successfully sought their assistance in exerting pressure on President **Hastings Banda** and the MCP to institute measures toward political reform. Some early members of the PAC included **Peter Fachi**, **Mordicai Msisha**, **Aaron Longwe**, **Misanjo Kansilanga**, Emanuel Chinkwita, and **Collins Chizumila**. In the post-MCP government era, the PAC has continued to act as a watchdog on behalf of the general public. It writes to the government occasionally and issues public statements on matters such as human rights, public accountability, and the electoral process.

– R –

RAILWAYS. *See* TRANSPORTATION.

RAMAKUKAN. *See* KASISI.

RANGELEY, WILLIAM H. J. Officer in the colonial administrative service in **Nyasaland** and leading student of the history and cultures of the peoples of **Malawi**. William Rangeley was born in 1910 in the **Fort Jameson** District of **Northern Rhodesia (Zambia)**, where his father worked. He attended school in **Southern Rhodesia** (Zimbabwe), and at the Diocesan College, Cape Town, before going to Oxford University, where he joined the colonial service in the mid-1930s. He returned to Oxford to study and obtain a diploma in social anthropology. Rangeley worked in various areas of Nyasaland, including **Nkhotakota** and **Mzimba**, in both of which he was **district commissioner** (DC). A respected scholar, Rangeley found time to carry out original research into the history and culture of the peoples of the **Lake Malawi** region, resulting in a wide range of articles, most of which were published in the Nyasaland Society's **(Society of Malawi)** organ, the *Nyasaland Journal*. His publications formed a strong foundation for future researchers. From 1952 to 1958, when he died in a drowning accident in Cape Town, Rangeley was provincial commissioner of southern Nyasaland. The first stadium in Malawi, located in **Blantyre**, was named after him. The facility's name was later changed to Kamuzu Stadium and after 1994 to the National Stadium.

REFUGEES. *See* HUMAN RIGHTS.

RELIGION. Traditional African religions, Christianity, and Islam are practiced in **Malawi**. Both Protestant and Roman Catholic missionaries introduced their faith during the latter half of the 19th century. Traders associated with the east coast of Africa introduced **Islam** to the area at about the same time. The traditional religious beliefs held by Malawians may be mixed with Christian or Muslim tenets. *See also* MISSIONS; SLAVE TRADE.

RENAMO. *See* MOZAMBIQUE.

RHODES, CECIL JOHN. Mining mogul, politician, and leading player in European imperialism in 19th-century Africa. Cecil Rhodes was born in England in July 1853. Sixteen years later, he joined his brother, **Herbert Rhodes**, in **South Africa**, where they grew **cotton** in the Natal region. In the early 1870s Rhodes joined the hundreds of prospectors who were attracted to the emerging diamond mining industry further west at Kimberley. He became a successful digger and formed his own company, which grew into the De Beers Mining Company in 1890 and, seven years later, the De Beers Consolidated Mines. While doing all this, he returned to England several times to study at Oxford University, among other things. As gold mining was becoming a reality in the Transvaal, Rhodes transferred some of his energies to that area, forming the Gold Fields of South Africa. With so much wealth at his disposal, Rhodes was elected to the Cape parliament, becoming prime minister of the colony in 1890. A year earlier, he had secured a charter to form the **British South Africa Company** (BSAC), through which he planned to execute his ambition of establishing the British empire from the "Cape to Cairo." Although the plan was not fully realized, the BSAC came to control **Southern Rhodesia (Zimbabwe)** and most of **Northern Rhodesia (Zambia)**. Rhodes also became interested in **Nyasaland** (Malawi), buying tracts of land in the new colony and in the early 1890s. He maintained influence in the area through a substantial subvention to **Harry Johnston**'s fledgling administration. In 1896 Rhodes resigned from the office of prime minister because he supported Starr Jameson's failed invasion of the Transvaal. He died in 1902.

RHODES, HERBERT. Cecil Rhodes's eldest brother. Herbert Rhodes farmed **cotton** in Natal before joining the diamond rush in Kimberley, **South Africa**, in the 1870s. More interested in adventure than a settled business life, he sold his **mining** claims and left to travel north of the Zambezi, arriving in the **Lake Malawi** region in the 1880s. He hunted, mostly elephants, along the **Shire River** on the western shores of Lake Malawi, especially in the **Karonga** plains. He built a house in the area between Kambwe lagoon and present-day Karonga *boma,* the first European to do so in that area. Rhodes died when his house at **Chikwawa** burned.

RHODES-LIVINGSTONE INSTITUTE. Famous pioneering Africa-based research center, jointly funded by mining interests in **Northern Rhodesia (Zambia)** and the government in that colony. The Rhodes-Livingstone Institute for Social Research was established in 1938 to carry out independent sociological and anthropological studies that it was hoped would promote race relations on the Copper Belt and along the railway line. Originally based in Livingstone, it moved its headquarters to Lusaka in 1952. Godfrey Wilson, its first director, who had earlier undertaken some research in northern **Nyasaland**, modified the mandate of the institute to include urbanization and socioeconomic change, especially in light of the industrialization taking place in the region. When

Max Gluckman succeeded Wilson in 1942, he broadened the field even more to reflect emerging themes such as African legal systems, and by the 1950s a wide range of topics in the humanities and social sciences were subjects of study. The area covered was also widened to include the two Rhodesias, Nyasaland, and southern Belgian Congo.

Also by the 1950s, the institute was attracting graduate students and postdoctoral students who went on to form the core of Africa specialists in most anthropology departments in England and the **United States**. Many of their papers, some of them pathbreaking, were published in the institute's journal, the *Rhodes-Livingstone's Journal*. Several scholars associated with the Rhodes-Livingstone undertook their research in Malawi. J. Clyde Mitchell (1956) worked on the social systems of the **Yao**; Jaap van Velsen (1959) carried out research among the **Tonga** in **Nkhata Bay**; John Arundel Barnes, David Bettison, Raymond Apthorpe, and others (1958, 1961) worked on the **Mpezeni Ngoni** and urban **Blantyre**, respectively.

When the University of Zambia opened in 1966, the institute became affiliated to it, and five years later it changed its name to the Institute for African Studies of the University of Zambia. Its journal came to be known as *African Social Research*. In 1996 the institute changed its name once again, this time to the Institute for Economic and Social Research of the University of Zambia.

RHODESIA. *See* ZAMBIA; ZIMBABWE.

RHODESIA NATIVE LABOUR BUREAU (RNLB). Formed in Salisbury (Harare) in 1903 to recruit contract labor in northern Zambezia (**Nyasaland, Mozambique**, and **Northern Rhodesia [Zambia]**) for the emerging **mining** and agricultural industries in **Southern Rhodesia (Zimbabwe)**. The recent introduction of **taxes** in Nyasaland and Northern Rhodesia, as well as the rise of forced cash production in Mozambique, made these areas easy targets for the bureau's recruiters, whose methods were initially most ruthless. Ironically, in Nyasaland, the bureau promoted itself as Muthandizi (The Helper) and came to be known by that name; it built recruiting stations in most rural districts, especially in the Northern Region, where poor prospects of employment and problems with cash crops ensured a large pool of prospective labor recruits. Once laborers reached their places of employment in Southern Rhodesia, they encountered very harsh working conditions: extremely low wages, long working hours, poor and unsanitary accommodation, little **health** care, and employers and overseers who had no respect for Africans. For these reasons, one of the first measures taken by the first African-dominated government in Malawi formed in 1961 was to cancel the operations of the Rhodesia Native Labour Bureau.

RICE. A popular grain, rice is grown mainly in the lakeshore areas of **Karonga**, **Nkhotakota**, and **Salima**, and to a lesser extent in **Mangochi**, the Upper and Lower Shire, and in the **Lake Chilwa** area. Although certain types of rice have grown here for a long time, newer varieties such as the fragrant *faya* were introduced in the region by Swahili-Arab traders from the East African coast in the 19th century. The colonial government classified rice as an African economic crop, and during the interwar period it encouraged growers to increase production in order to meet demands for the crop in the growing community and in the neighboring colonies. At the end of the 1930s, plans were made to establish a rice trading concern in Nkhotakota, and in 1945 the **Kota Kota Rice Trading Company** was formed, which played a major role in rice marketing in Malawi. Rice **cooperatives** emerged at the same time, the most successful one being the **Kilupula Rice Growers Co-operative Union** in **Karonga**. For part of the colonial period, Nyasaland was the leading rice producer in South Central Africa, exporting the grain mostly to the Rhodesias (**Zambia** and **Zimbabwe**), **South Africa**, and **Mozambique**.

Although the government disbanded cooperative societies in the 1960s, it stimulated rice production through a bilateral arrangement with the government of Taiwan, which has had a permanent agricultural mission in Malawi since that time, aimed at advising on modern methods of **agriculture**. Rice has been central to this mission, which has emphasized high-yielding varieties and biannual yields. Rice is mainly a smallholder crop, and production fluctuated in the 1990s, marking a 1 percent growth. In tons per thousand the production was 65.3 tons in 1993, 41.1 tons in 1994, 39.1 tons in 1995, 72.6 tons in 1996, and 64.8 tons in 1997.

RICHARDS, EDMUND CHARLES SMITH. Governor of **Nyasaland** from 1942 to 1947. Richards had earlier served in a junior capacity in Tanganyika and Nyasaland, and he had just transferred from Basutoland, where he had been resident commissioner from 1935 to 1942. One of his notable acts in Nyasaland was to establish the **Abrahams Commission** of 1946 with a view to finally solving the land problem.

ROADS. *See* TRANSPORTATION.

ROBERTS, SIR BRYAN. Born and educated in **Great Britain**, Bryan Roberts was solicitor general at independence. After the **Cabinet Crisis** of 1964, he took over from **Orton Chirwa** as attorney general. When **Peter Youens** retired in 1966, Roberts also became secretary to the president and cabinet, and head of the civil service in **Malawi**. He held these positions until 1973, when **George Jafu** took over as head of the civil service and **Richard Banda** became attorney general. Roberts was later knighted (KCMG).

RUBBER. A main export in early colonial Malawi. Rubber (latex) was produced from the local Landolphia vine, which grows naturally in the thick forests of the lakeshore region of **Nkhata Bay** District. In 1903 seeds from Landolphia were nurtured, and within three years, 3 million seedlings were transplanted to a nearby area, which developed into the Vizara Rubber Estates. At about the same time, seedlings of the Para and Castilloa varieties were brought from Ceylon (Sri Lanka) but many did not fare well in the area. By the beginning of World War I, rubber was no longer a significant export of the colony, and although the **African Lakes Company** (ALC) was to maintain the **Vizara** plantation, its production was greatly reduced. The 1980s and 1990s witnessed a revival of interest in rubber, and redevelopment started at Vizara, with the result that the estate expanded beyond its original size.

RUGARUGA. Youthful mercenaries. Sometimes full-time security employees, *rugaruga* guarded prominent traders in 19th-century East Africa. With the help of the fearless *rugaruga*, many such traders, including Mirambo and Msiri, went on to establish powerful polities in their areas. As guns became readily available in the region, *rugaruga* tended to be equipped with guns that they did not hesitate to use. **Mlozi bin Kazbadema** and his commercial associates had their own *rugaruga*, whom Europeans described as ill-tempered and undisciplined. They often accused them of being responsible for violent incidents that led Mlozi and the **Ngonde** into conflicts.

RUMPHI. Name of the *boma* and district that shares borders with all districts of the Northern Region of Malawi. Rumphi is the traditional home of the **Phoka** and other **Tumbuka**-speaking peoples. Agriculturally rich, it is particularly famous as one of the main bean-producing areas of **Malawi**. It is also associated with **coffee**, most of which is grown in the eastern section of the district. Since the 1980s, Rumphi has also become one of the major **tobacco**-growing regions of Malawi. The main features of the district are the Henga valley in the east, the **Nkhamanga** plains in the west, and the rolling **Nyika plateau** in the north. Rumphi has long been linked with Western **education** as the home of the **Livingstonia Mission** and the site of the **Overtoun Institution** and, from the 1980s, as the location of the **Phwezi Education Foundation**. Rumphi *boma* was the seat of the **Northern Co-operative Union** and, in the colonial period, it was a main labor-recruiting district for **mining** and farming establishments in **South Africa** and **Southern Rhodesia (Zimbabwe)**.

RURAL AGRICULTURAL PROJECTS. Integrated rural schemes operating from 1965 to 1975. Sponsored by the **World Bank**, these projects varied in size and scope and focused on **tobacco** and **groundnuts**, as well as a 161,000-acre cattle ranch in the Dzalanyama Forest Reserve. The projects reorganized plot boundaries, built access roads and drainage ditches, and provided credit for seed and fertilizer. Proceeding in several phases, the project expected to serve 100,000 families, or nearly a half million persons in the central plateau area. There were three areas of concentration—**Salima**, Lower Shire, and **Karonga**.

Supported by aid from West Germany, Salima, a central lakeshore project, concentrated on the cash cropping of **cotton**, **rice**, and **maize**, the staple crop for Malawi families. The Lower Shire project had its greatest impact in the vicinity of Ngabu and **Chikwawa**. During phase 1, over 5,000 of the improved farmers were cotton growers; phase 2 expanded from its cotton concentration to include maize and rice. Improved agricultural practices, including ridging, early planting, better seeds, and improved fertilizer, were all targets in this 26,000-family project. The Karonga northern development plan, financed by the World Bank, worked to improve cotton, maize, and **groundnut** yields, as well as resettle farmers in an area that was put into rice production. Attention and service was also given to cattle owners, aiding them with marketing facilities and measures to control livestock diseases.

Additional rural projects included an irrigated rice project near Chikwawa, Hara, and Wovwe, and in the **Dwangwa** River delta, and cotton projects in the Southern Region, particularly in the **Phalombe** Plain and Chikwawa.

RYALL'S HOTEL. A family-owned hotel. Ryall's opened its doors in 1922 and was the premier hospitality facility in **Blantyre** until the late 1960s, when the nearby Mount Soche Hotel was built. During part of the colonial period the hotel, like many similar establishments in Southern

Africa, was closed to Africans. In recent years the hotel, now managed by the Protea Hotels Ltd. for the Blantyre Hotels Ltd., has been greatly expanded and modernized.

– S –

SABBATINI, ALBERTO. One of the most successful **tobacco** farmers in early colonial Malawi. Sabbatini was born in the vicinity of Poggio Mirteto, just north of Rome, Italy, and went to **Nyasaland** in 1904. He bought 17,000 acres of freehold land at Mapanga, about nine miles from **Limbe** on the **Zomba** road, and turned it into a major tobacco-growing farm. He sold tobacco to local exporters and processors and exported some of it directly to European interests. At the end of World War I Sabbatini established sisal estates in the Lower Shire and **Mozambique** and had numerous other business ideas, including an artificial manure–producing factory propelled by power generated from hydroelectricity. When the Great Depression forced him to close most of his operations, including those in the **Blantyre-Limbe** area, he started a transportation company on the Shire and tried a rope- and twine-making factory with the sisal at **Chiromo**; both ventures failed. At the end of the 1930s, he sold his Mapanga estate, which included his striking, castlelike house. Ironically, during World War II, the colonial administration turned the house into a prison for many of the Italians, including Sabbatini himself. After the war, Sabbatini resumed farming and, as in the past, diversified his commercial interests. When he died, his children continued his businesses; the motor repair shop in Blantyre has kept Sabbatini a household name in **Malawi**.

SACRANIE, ABDUL SATTAR. One of the most respected lawyers in **Malawi**. Sacranie was born in **Limbe**, where his father was a prominent businessman. He received a university education in India and qualified as a barrister at one of the Inns of Court in London, England. On his return to Malawi, he practiced law in **Blantyre-Limbe**, establishing a flourishing legal firm, Sacranie & Gow. In the late 1950s Sacranie became leader of the **Asian Convention**, whose sympathies lay with the **National African Congress** (ANC) and its successor, the **Malawi Congress Party** (MCP). He was legal counsel to many African politicians facing trials during the period following the state of emergency of 1959. As leader of the Asian Convention, Sacranie attended the **Lancaster**

House constitutional talks in 1961, and within two years, he became the first non-European mayor of the Municipality of Blantyre-Limbe. After his term in municipal politics, he devoted most of his time to his law practice. His association with Dr. **Hastings Banda** and the MCP continued as he often acted as personal legal adviser to Banda and counsel to the MPC and **Press Holdings Ltd**. Sacranie died in 1984.

SADYALUNDA, FERN NAJERE. First woman cabinet minister in **Malawi.** Born in 1944 in **Lilongwe** District, she trained as a teacher at **Kapeni** College, **Blantyre**, and subsequently obtained a Cambridge School Certificate. In 1974 Sadyalunda was nominated to parliament as a member for Lilongwe, and in October of the following year she was appointed minister of community development and social welfare, the first woman to serve as a cabinet minister in Malawi. In a cabinet reshuffle later she was assigned the ministry of health. Sadyalunda was close to **Albert Muwalo-Nqumayo** and consequently was suspected of being part of the latter's political designs, and she was imprisoned without trial. Upon her release, Sadyalunda retired from politics and became a businesswoman.

SALIM BIN ABDALLA. *See* JUMBE.

SALIMA. Name of the *boma* and district, Salima is located on the southwest lakeshore. Since 1935 it has been the northern terminus of the Malawi rail system. Part of Dowa District until **Malawi** obtained independence from British rule, in the 1970s Salima was linked to the new capital at **Lilongwe** by a **railway**, a project financed by the Canadian government. The district is a major **cotton-** and **rice**-growing area, and it is the site of the German-sponsored Salima lakeshore development project aimed at improving the production of the two crops.

SALISBURY, LORD. Third Marquess of Salisbury and Tory prime minister of Great Britain when the **Lake Malawi** region was declared a British protectorate (1889–1891). Originally reluctant to extend British authority in the area, Lord Salisbury bowed to overwhelming Scottish opinion. Determined to ensure that the work of the **Livingstonia** and **Blantyre Missions** continued without Portuguese-Catholic threat, the missionaries strongly petitioned him to take special interest in this part of northern Zambezia. In 1889 the **Shire Highlands** fell under British rule, and two years later most of what was to become **Nyasaland** followed suit.

SANDERSON, GEORGE MEREDITH. British doctor and student of African **languages** and cultures, Sanderson worked at the various hospitals in **Nyasaland**, including **Karonga** and **Fort Johnston** and **Zomba**, in the period between the World War I and the 1950s. He was medical officer at Karonga during the plague of 1919 and, while in the north, learned two major languages, **Kyangonde** and ciTumbuka, and studied local traditions and customs, publishing results of his researches in the *Journal of the Royal Antropological Institute* and the *Nyasaland Journal*. He also became an authority on **Yao** ethnography and language, on which he published widely, including *A Yao Grammar* (1922), *A Dictionary of the Yao Language* (1954), and with W. B. Brithrey, *An Introduction to Chinyanja* (1953). He also translated and edited Yahanna Abdallah's *Chikala cha Wayao* (1919) as *The Yaos* (1973). On his retirement, Sanderson went to live on Zomba Plateau.

SANGALA, JAMES FREDERICK MATEWERE. Sportsman, gifted organizer, avid reader, and leading intellectual of his time. With **Levi Mumba** and others, he was a founding father of the **Nyasaland African Congress** (NAC). James Sangala was born in December 1900 on the Malosa side of the **Zomba** mountain in Chief **Malemia**'s area. His father, Grant, was a junior chief under Malemia and a mission-trained mason. James Sangala attended Church of Scotland Mission Schools at Malosa (1910–1915) and **Domasi** (1916–1920) before going to the **Henry Henderson Institute** (HHI), **Blantyre** (1920–1923), to complete his education. He trained as a teacher at the HHI (1924–1925) and returned to Zomba, where he taught at **Katsonga** and at the Domasi Central School. In April 1927 he resigned from his teaching job because he refused to follow his headmaster's instructions that he, as an African, should not wear shoes in class. Three years later he joined the civil service as a clerk in the office of the senior provincial commissioner in Blantyre, where his immediate superior was **Ellerton Mposa**. Although happy with his new job, he was to encounter many aspects of racism, such as the insistence that an African should not wear a hat in the presence of a European. Always optimistic, Sangala sought to establish good relations between races. With M. E. Leslie, a European working in the same office, he started the Black and White Club. It was short-lived because after Leslie and his successor, Ion Ramsay, departed, there was no support from the European side.

As a filing clerk, Sangala came across much information on the growing number of **African welfare associations**, and soon he joined the one in **Blantyre** and that in Zomba. It became obvious to him that effective African representation required a vigorous national organization, just as the non-Africans had the **Convention of Associations**. Encouraged by the advice given to him in 1938 by William Henry Mainwairing, a British Labour Party member of the **Bledisloe Commission**, on the power of unity in the fight against colonial rule, Sangala sought to change things. In September 1943 he organized a meeting in Blantyre attended by 21 people, including **Charles Matinga, Charles J. Mlanga**, Andrew Mponda, Frank Kahumbe, **Lewis Bandawe**, Isa Macdonald Lawrence, and Thomas Grant. This and subsequent meetings led to the formation of the Nyasaland African Council. Through the advice of **W. H. Timke**, he contacted Mrs. Margaret Ballinger, the left-leaning member of the South African parliament, and Charles Mzingeli, an activist in **Southern Rhodesia**. The two provided Sangala with material he could use to write a constitution for the new organization. **Levi Mumba** drafted the constitution, which was duly approved in 1944, and the name of the council changed to Nyasaland African Congress. Levi Mumba was elected president-general of the new political party. When he died early in 1945, his deputy, Charles Matinga, became head of the organization.

Although Sangala did not immediately occupy a major office in the NAC, he remained a powerful force in the party. However, in 1950 and in 1953, when Congress's leadership was particularly wanting, Sangala was called on to rescue the organization. Sangala campaigned vigorously against the introduction of the **Federation of Rhodesia and Nyasaland**. At his own expense, he visited most chiefs in the southern province and wrote to all other traditional rulers in the country, dissuading them from accepting the Federation. In 1952 Sangala, **Mtalika Banda,** and Elias Mtepuka toured the Rhodesias to raise money from Malawian workers in the hope of sending a Congress delegation to London to oppose the proposed union. In the following year, Sangala, joined by Anglican Church missionary Rev. **Michael Scott**, visited **Northern Rhodesia** to confer with local African organizations; back home he organized meetings in **Lilongwe** and Blantyre so that people could hear Scott's anti-Federation views. Again, at his own expense, he arranged for as many chiefs as possible to attend such gatherings.

By this time, Sangala had come to embrace peaceful resistance modeled on Gandhi's *satyagraha,* and he always made sure that he had the cooperation of chiefs, especially through the newly formed **Chiefs Union**. To his dismay, peaceful resistance failed, as the 1953 disturbances in **Ntcheu** and four districts in the Southern Region showed. On

September 25 he was arrested and charged with possession of seditious material. But he was acquitted and continued his activism. By the late 1950s Congress was in disarray because, among other things, the leadership had in effect allowed **Wellington Chirwa** and **Clement Kumbikano** to go to the federal parliament. By the end of 1956, Sangala and others had virtually retired from active politics, leaving a younger generation to gradually take over. **Thamar D. T. Banda** became president-general of the NAC.

James Sangala had many interests besides politics, including boxing. He was a keen **football** (soccer) player and organizer—hence his nickname Pyagusi (the slippery feet)—and in 1938 he and his European supervisor founded the **Shire Highlands** Football League, which flourished throughout the 1940s and early 1950s. In 1948 he led a team from Blantyre to play the formidable Grupo Desportivo Rebenta Fongo of **Beira**. Although his team lost, the competition was a rare and cherished experience for Sangala and the Nyasaland players.

After independence, Sangala, now back in his Chief Malemia home, was appointed to the Public Service Commission, which, in addition to his business concerns and interest in church matters, kept him busily occupied.

SANGAYA, JONATHAN DOUGLAS. First Malawian general secretary of the Blantyre Synod of the **Church of Central Africa Presbyterian**. A respected, influential clergymen in postcolonial **Malawi**, Jonathan Sangaya was born of **Ngoni** and **Yao** parentage in **Blantyre** in 1907. He qualified as a teacher, and, except for five years (1940–1945), he taught mostly in local schools until 1948, when he entered theological college at **Mulanje** Mission. After his ordination in 1952, he was posted to Bemvu in **Ntcheu** District. Two years later, he was transferred to **Blantyre Mission**, where he served until 1962, when he became general secretary of the Blantyre Synod, taking over from Rev. **Andrew Doig**. Sangaya died in office in August 1979.

SCHOFFELEERS, JAN MATTHEW. Catholic priest of the Montfort Order, anthropologist, and leading scholar of Malawian culture and history. Matthew Schoffeleers was born in the Netherlands. After his ordination, he became a missionary and went to **Malawi** in 1955. He served in parishes in the Lower Shire and the **Shire Highlands**. In the 1960s he took a sabbatical to study anthropology at Lovenium University, Kinshasha, Congo, and in the mid-1960s he proceeded to Oxford University, England, which in 1968 awarded him a D.Phil degree. His thesis was on the religion of the **Mang'anja**. A year later Father Schoffeleers became the founding director of the Catechetical Training Centre at **Likulezi, Mulanje**. In 1971 he was appointed senior lecturer in anthropology at **Chancellor College, University of Malawi**. In 1976 Schoffeleers returned to the Netherlands to be professor of anthropology at the Free University of Amsterdam and the University of Utrecht. He retired from teaching in the early 1990s but continued to write on Mang'anja history and religion. His numerous publications include *The River of Blood: The Genesis of a Martyr Cult in Southern Malawi, c. AD 1600* (1992); and *Religion and the Dramatisation of Life: Spirit Beliefs and Rituals in Southern and Central Malawi* (1997).

SCOTT, DAVID CLEMENT RUFFELLE. Head of the **Blantyre Mission** from 1881 to 1898. Dr. David Scott was a medical doctor as well as an ordained minister of the Church of Scotland. He took over the mantle of the mission after the scandal that had led to the resignation and dismissal in 1880 of most of the original group of missionaries, including **Duff Macdonald, John Buchanan**, and **George Fenwick**. Convinced that the mission's aims and programs would flourish only with the involvement of local people, Scott promoted programs that strengthened African culture and worked closely with African colleagues. He laid the groundwork for the African church by encouraging his deacons to take charge of mission work in other parts of the **Shire Highlands** and in **Mozambique**.

African students, among them **Joseph Bismarck** and Rondau Kaferanjila from the mission school at **Blantyre**, were sent to **Lovedale** for further education. Others, such as **Mungo Chisuse** and **Nacho Ntimawanzako**, were trained in Scotland. Others still, including **John Gray Kufa**, were trained locally at schools Scott had initiated at the Blantyre Mission: the teacher training, theological, medical assistant, and technical colleges. Scott often spoke against the land and labor situation in the Shire Highlands and in so doing earned the ire of the colonial administration in **Zomba** and the European business and settler community, whose attitude toward indigenous peoples was mostly unfavorable. Without any meaningful experience in construction, Scott and his African workers built an impressive cathedral-like church that was completed in 1892. It is known as St. Michael's and All Angels, Blantyre.

A keen student of **Yao** and **Mang'anja** cultures and languages, Scott wrote *An Encyclopaedic Dictionary of the Mang'anja Language Spoken in British Central Africa* (1892), which is 737 pages long and still highly regarded today. It was revised and edited by **Alexander Hetherwick** under the title *Dictionary of the Nyanja Language* (1929). Another of Scott's numerous contributions was the mission's influential magazine, *Life and Work in British Central Africa*, which published articles covering a variety of subjects. Scott himself used the paper to publicize his views on, among other things, colonial rule. In 1898 Scott retired to Scotland, convinced that he had laid a strong foundation for an African church that was ready to move into the 20th century under a leadership that would be significantly African.

SCOTT, MICHAEL. Liberal Anglican missionary who identified himself with the nationalist aspirations of the peoples of **Nyasaland** and actively supported their opposition to the **Federation of Rhodesia and Nyasalnd**. In 1953 Scott and **James Sangala** addressed meetings of chiefs and other Nyasaland Africans in **Lilongwe** and **Blantyre** to voice opposition to the Federation, and the two visited **Northern Rhodesia** to discuss anti-Federation strategy with local nationalists.

SENA. Language and name of the inhabitants of the area between the Shire-Zambezi confluence and **Chinde** on the east coast. Many Sena migrated north to the **Nsanje** District of **Malawi**, where they intermarried with the **Mang'anja**. Sena is also the name of a town on the Zambezi, just east of the point where the Shire and the Zambezi meet.

SETTLERS' AND RESIDENTS' ASSOCIATION OF NYASALAND (SARAN). SARAN was formed on January 11, 1960, in **Limbe** by **Nyasaland** Europeans, mostly businessmen and farmers, determined to fight the rising tide of African nationalism in the colony. The Europeans therefore sought to establish an organ to present their views to decision makers on the maintenance of the status quo in Nyasaland. The birth of the **Malawi Congress Party** (MCP) at the end of September 1959 had reinvigorated African political activism. **Harold Macmillan** and his colonial secretary, **Iain Macleod**, were set on increasing the pace of decolonization in Malawi; furthermore, Macmillan himself was due to visit the colony in February 1960. The **Monckton Commission** was also about to start an inquiry into the future of the **Federation of Rhodesia and Nyasaland**. And even more worrying for them were indications that Dr. **Hastings Banda** would be released from Gweru prison.

Led by **J. R. Ness**, SARAN was totally against one-man one-vote elections, and it strongly supported the Federation and **Roy Welensky**'s stand on the role of European settlers in the region. It made representations to the **Monckton Commission** and to all levels of colonial and imperial authority, but in the end constitutional changes overtook SARAN, which was virtually dead at the end of 1963. Although some of its leaders left for **South Africa** and **Southern Rhodesia**, most of its membership continued to live in postcolonial Malawi.

SEVENTH DAY MISSIONS. *See* BOOTH, JOSEPH; BAKKER, JAMES; COCKERILL, WALTER; MALAMULO; PLAINFIELD INDUSTRIAL MISSION.

SHARPE, SIR ALFRED. Second commissioner and consul-general (1896–1907), as well as first governor (1907–1910), of **Nyasaland**. Alfred Sharpe was born in Lancaster, England, in 1853. After attending Haileybury College, he trained as a solicitor and then practiced law in Lancaster. He married in 1883 and two years later, he and his family left for Fiji, where he became a sugar planter on Viti Vetu Island; he also worked as a magistrate, covering several islands in the area. As his agricultural venture failed, Sharpe left Fiji for Africa, not to take up the position of district commissioner offered to him in the Gold Coast but to hunt in northern Zambezia. While hunting, he met **Harry Johnston**, who immediately appointed Sharpe as his vice consul. From 1889 to 1890, Sharpe, along with Johnston, negotiated treaties with chiefs in the **Lake Malawi** area, the purpose being to ensure that local rulers did not cede territory to other foreign powers without British approval. In 1891 the Foreign Office declared Malawi a protectorate. Sharpe more than anyone influenced Commissioner Johnston during the early days of the protectorate government, and his legal training and knowledge proved invaluable in framing the judicial and fiscal measures necessary for the new administration. Sharpe was an able replacement when Johnston went on leave, and he was the logical successor to Johnston in 1897.

During his tenure in office, Alfred Sharpe faced problems of **tax**, land, and labor. His attempt to give Africans tax rebates for growing **cotton** failed when European planters provided only their leftover seeds. Although Sharpe realized that continued allocation of land to Europeans had to be restricted, he also wished to encourage settlers of moderate means. The result was that Africans were frequently moved about to accommodate Europeans. Sharpe worked hard to see that Nyasaland was connected to the Mozambican coast via rail, but a large subsidy to build the **Shire Highlands Railway** through suitable cotton-producing territory further increased pressure on already heavily populated land. While objecting to forced labor of Africans for European planters, Sharpe made continued concessions to settlers, who generally ignored government regulations and paid excessively low wages to labor recruits. Malawi laborers preferred to migrate to **Southern Rhodesia (Zimbabwe)** and **South Africa**, where wages were comparatively better, and Sharpe and his successors had to attempt to control the exodus of workers, a phenomenon that grew in subsequent years. Although Sharpe retired in 1910, he returned to Nyasaland on several occasions and wrote many articles on Nyasaland and African affairs. He also published books, including *The Backbone of Africa* (1921). Sharpe died on December 10, 1935.

SHARRER, EUGENE CHARLES. One of the most influential planter-traders in early colonial Malawi. A British national of German extraction, Sharrer arrived in **Nyasaland** in the late 1880s. Within a few years he held title to about 372,500 acres of land in **Blantyre, Thyolo, Zomba,** and **Liwonde.** With his headquarters at Kabula Hill in Blantyre, Sharrer established retail shops, the Kabula Stores, which were rivaled only by the **Mandala** stores operated by the **African Lakes Company** (ALC). In 1895 he formed two companies, the **Shire Highlands Railway Company** (SHR) and the Zambezi Traffic Company, both floated in London, the former with a capital of £100,000 and the latter with a capital of £150,000. Through the two firms, Sharrer was a leading player in the development of **railways** in the Zambezia region. In 1902 he established a holding company, the **British Central Africa Company**, which handled all his land and commercial interests. The SHR concentrated on its proposed line from Blantyre to **Chiromo**; Sharrer also had steamers on the **Shire River** that transported passengers and cargo to and from the Zambezi. A founder of the powerful **Shire Highlands Planters Association**, Sharrer was a major **coffee, tea**, and **tobacco** grower, and he was one of the first people to introduce Egyptian **cotton** to the **Lake Malawi** area.

SHILOH. Center to promote African industry. Established by **Joseph Booth**, Shiloh was located at **Chikunda** in a disused mission station five miles from **Blantyre**. It was named after a place in New Jersey. Shiloh was the center of a self-supporting project, the **African Co-operative Society**, as Booth originally christened it, which was involved in a variety of projects aimed at raising money for its membership. Booth negotiated contracts such as porterage for the **African Lakes Company** (ALC), and only he, as agent/treasurer, controlled the organization's finances and books. The ACS also encouraged religious and general education; it established its own schools and at times supported independent educational schemes such as those of **Morrison Malinki** and **Alexander Makwinja** in Blantyre, **Charles Domingo** in **Mzimba**, and Andrew Mhoni in **Nkhata Bay**. After Booth left Malawi, the Shiloh project was managed by **Walter Cockerill**, who arrived in **Nyasaland** in 1913. However, largely because the government was suspicious of anything relating to Booth and **John Chilembwe**, Shiloh and its associated schemes came to an end after the 1915 uprising.

SHIRE HIGHLANDS. Plateau in southern Malawi. With altitudes ranging from 2,000 to 4,000 feet, the Shire Highlands cover a wide area from the **Zomba** mountain in the west to **Mulanje** in the east. The plateau has been known as the Shire Highlands ever since the first Europeans lived in the area, primarily because of the **Shire River** that forms its western borders and is a major part of the plateau's drainage system. The highlands are also a major agricultural area in Malawi: tea in **Mulanje** and **Thyolo** Districts; **tobacco** in **Zomba, Machinga, Chiradzulu, Blantyre**, and Thyolo; and **coffee** in Mulanje, Thyolo, Zomba, and Chiradzulu Districts. **Maize**, beans, and other staple crops are widely grown in this fertile area. Home to the **Mang'anja**, the indigenous people of the area, it is also inhabited by the **Yao**, the **Lomwe**, and the European settler community. It is the most densely populated section of **Malawi**, and Blantyre, the largest city in the country, is located in the area. *See also* SHIRE VALLEY.

SHIRE HIGHLANDS HOTEL. Popular hotel located on the main street of **Limbe**, not far from the Malawi Railways Headquarters. The Shire Highlands Hotel started operating in the early 20th century. Its distinctive colonial-style architecture makes it one of the landmarks of the city of **Blantyre**. Since the latter part of the 20th century, the hotel has been owned by Blantyre Hotels Ltd. and managed on its behalf by Protea Hotels of **South Africa**.

SHIRE HIGHLANDS PLANTERS' ASSOCIATION. Formed in 1892, the Shire Highland Planters' Association represented a powerful group of European planters led by **Eugene Sharrer**, who was also its first president. A rival organization, the **Nyasaland Planters' Association**, was soon formed and was led by **John Moir**. The two groups fought over **transportation** business, especially **railway** development in the area. Although the two organizations came together to form the **British Central Africa Chamber of Agriculture and Commerce** in 1895, the competition between Moir's **African Lakes Company** (ALC) and Sharrer's companies, such the Kabula Stores, continued.

SHIRE HIGHLANDS RAILWAY COMPANY. Owned by **Eugene Sharrer**, it was formed to promote his railway scheme between **Blantyre** and **Chiromo** in the Lower **Shire Valley**. Established in 1895 and with a capital of £100,000, the company was floated in London and advertised as the most suitable organization to built the rail line. In 1902 it won the bid to construct the line, which was duly completed six years later. In 1915 the company extended the line from Chiromo to Chindio (**Chinde**).

SHIRE RIVER AND VALLEY. The southern extension of the huge rift occupied by **Lake Malawi**. The Shire Valley is extensively covered with floodplains and swamps, the largest of which is Elephant Marsh. The Shire River drains from Lake Malawi and is additionally fed by tributaries in the southern region. As the river tumbles over the escarpment, the current quickens, and rapids and cataracts abound. Nkula Falls hydroelectric site is located along this portion of the Shire River. South of the national border, the river slows substantially before it empties into the Zambezi River and ultimately into the Indian Ocean. The area below the Mpatamanga Gorge in **Chikwawa** District is usually referred to as the Lower Shire Valley, and that above the cataracts as the Upper Shire. Development projects aimed at improving the lives of 63,000 families in the Lower Shire have concentrated on **cotton, rice, sugar, maize**, and fish culture.

SILOMBELA, MEDSON EVANS. Medson Silombela was raised in **Mangochi** District. In 1964 he became one of the lieutenants of **Henry Chipembere** who were determined to overthrow **Hastings Banda**'s government. He and others were accused of killing eight people, including a **police** officer's wife and an official of the **Malawi Congress Party** (MCP). He was finally captured in 1965, tried, sentenced to death, and publicly hanged.

SKINNER REPORT. Report of a commission appointed to examine and recommend on the conditions of the **Nyasaland** civil service as the country approached independence from British rule. Chaired by T. M. Skinner, the commission made its report in May 1964. It recommended, among other things, an increase in the salaries of lower-grade civil servants, a reduction in the salaries of those in the upper grades and status quo for those in the middle grades, and the creation of a pension fund.

Very few of the suggestions were explained to the African civil servants, with the result that deductions in salaries, and especially for the pension fund, were not understood and were deeply resented. When the new prime minister, **Hastings Banda**, supported the Skinner Report, several of his ministers disagreed, stating that their constituents were alarmed. When Banda further announced that he could not hasten **Africanization** of the civil service unless the candidates were qualified, the Skinner Report took on another dimension and became an important factor in the **Cabinet Crisis** of September 1964.

SLAVE TRADE. From the 1850s on, the **Lake Malawi** region became a major part of the East African slave trade and was carried out mainly by the **Swahili-Arabs** and their agents, the **Yao**, some of whom were already Islamized. Even before settling in the southern Lake Malawi area in the 1860s, the Yao had engaged in ivory trade with the peoples of that region. The shift from commerce in ivory and other items to human beings occurred when their Swahili-Arab partners at the coast became deeply involved in the slave trade. Although large areas in the **Shire Highlands** and the Upper **Shire River** became engulfed in the commerce, the main slave trading center in the south was at **Mangochi**, the territory of Yao chief **Mponda**. In the central and northern regions of Malawi, Swahili-Arabs were the principal perpetrators of the slave trade. **Nkhotakota** was a major trading base, handling as many as 10,000 slaves annually in the late 19th century. The Swahili leader, or **Jumbe**, in this central region maintained both economic and political control until 1895, when the newly established British colonial government exiled him to **Zanzibar**. In the extreme north, **Mlozi bin Kazbadema** was accused of carrying on this trade.

Europeans learned of the slave trade as a result of **David Livingstone**'s visits to Malawi. Livingstone observed the trade during journeys made in 1854–1856 and 1858–1859 through south and central Malawi as well as along the western shores of Lake Malawi. When he returned to England, he advocated the promotion of legitimate commerce, Christianity, and Western civilization in this part of Africa, arguing that they would effectively drive out the slave traders. Three missions, the **Universities' Mission to Central Africa** (UMCA), **Livingstonia**, and **Blantyre**, responded immediately to Livingstone's appeals and soon found themselves embroiled in slave disputes, particularly when escaped slaves sought refuge at mission stations.

When the British Foreign Office formally announced the formation of the protectorate in 1891, it instructed the commissioner and consul general, **Harry Johnston**, to stop the slave trade. After persuasion and diplomacy failed, Johnston used troops imported from India to fight any traces of it. In southern Malawi the Yao involved in the slave trade either abandoned it or fled the protectorate. By the end of 1895, Mlozi was captured and executed, and Mwene Heri, the last Jumbe at Nkhotakota, was deposed and sent to Zanzibar.

SMITH, GEORGE. Englishman who joined the British civil service in 1878 as a clerk in the War Office. In the following year, he was transferred to Cyprus, where he served in different capacities: clerk in the chief secretary's office (1879–1883), assistant chief secretary (1883–1891), district commissioner (1891–1893), registrar general (1893–1905), and acting receiver and chief collector of customs (1905–1909). In 1910 he was appointed colonial secretary in Mauritius and three years later was promoted to governor of **Nyasaland**. Sir George Smith (KCMG) is credited with the move toward the establishment of the Nyasaland **police** force in 1921. He retired in 1923 and died in England in 1938.

SOCIETY OF MALAWI. Formerly the Nyasaland Society. This organization, formed in 1946, promotes a better understanding of Malawi's past and present through a healthy discussion of a wide range of subjects, including history, anthropology, **literature**, travel, and the natural sciences. The articles in its main publication, *The Society of Malawi Journal*, reflect the society's aims; it also maintains a reference library for its members and visitors in **Limbe**. In the late 1950s the society was instrumental in encouraging the establishment of the National Museum of Malawi, and in the 1960s it played an equally important role in the creation of the government's **Department of Antiquities**.

SOMANJE, SYDNEY. Businessman, founding member of the **Nyasaland African Congress** (NAC), and treasurer-general of the **Malawi Congress Party** (MCP) from 1964 to 1986. Sydney Somanje belonged to one of the established **Blantyre** families. Educated at **Blantyre Mission**, he became involved in welfare politics in that town and in time became a close associate of **James Sangala**, **Charles Matinga**, **Ellerton Mposa**, and other African leaders in Blantyre and in the Southern Province Native Association. A team player and noted negotiator, Somanje was a key person in the meetings leading to the formation of the Nyasaland African Congress, and he remained an active member of the organization. In 1959 he was part of the group comprising **Orton Chirwa**, **Aleke Banda**, Dina Chechwa Bwanausi, Shadrek Khonje, and others who formed the

Malawi Congress Party, the Central Committee of which he was to be a member. He replaced **Henry Chipembere** as treasurer-general of the MCP and held that position until his death in 1986.

SONGWE RIVER. Marking the northern boundary of **Malawi** with **Tanzania**, the Songwe River rises in southern Tanzania and flows southeast though **Unyiha** and **Ulambya**, cutting between the Misuku hills and **Ndali** hills and into the fertile plains that separate **Ungonde** from **Unyakyusa**, emptying into **Lake Malawi** near Kaporo and becoming one of the main tributaries of the lake.

SORGHUM. Also known as Guinea corn (West Africa) and kaffir corn (Southern Africa), sorghum was the main staple in the **Lake Malawi** region before **maize** (corn) began to replace it in the 19th century. Although it is more resistant to drought than maize, its ripening seeds are a favorite food for birds, making it a labor-intensive crop. A smallholder crop that today is mostly used for beer brewing, sorghum production fluctuated in the 1990s as follows (in thousand tons): 1993, 21.6; 1994, 16.7; 1995, 20.1; 1996, 54.7; and 1997, 46.5.

SOSEYA. Of the village of Emveyeyeni and house of Lompetu, Soseya was the daughter of Zwide and mother of Ntuto, better known as **Mpezeni**, son of **Zwangendaba**. She had become a wife of **Zwangendaba** after her sister, the *inkosikazi* (great wife), had failed to bear a child. However, Mpezeni did not succeed his father as expected because Soseya had been demoted following a suspicion that her house wanted to poison the **Ngoni** leader. Instead, **Munene Nzima** became the *inkosikazi*, and her son, **Mhlahlo**, succeeded his father.

SOUTH AFRICA. South Africa and **Malawi** have close ties dating to the 19th century, when the **Ngoni** migrated into the northern Zambezia region. In the 1880s the first Malawian students from **Blantyre** and **Livingstonia Missions** went to study at **Lovedale**, the Free Church of Scotland educational center in the Eastern Cape of South Africa. Early in the 20th century, **Nyasaland**, like **Mozambique**, became a major labor catchment area for the emergence of **mining** and farming industries in South Africa. Labor agencies recruited thousands of Nyasalanders to South Africa on short-term contracts; many others went to the region on their own, working in a variety of jobs as domestic servants, cooks, and waiters in the hotel industry. Labor recruitment, mainly by the **Witwatersrand Native Labour Association** (WENELA) continued until the 1980s. Another early connection between South Africa and Malawi was tertiary **education**. In the 1950s Malawians such as **Henry Chipembere** and **Orton Chirwa** studied at **Fort Hare University** in the Eastern Cape, an institution that educated many future leaders of Southern Africa. *See also* MIGRANT LABOR.

In 1967 Malawi established diplomatic relations with the South African government, despite the fact that most countries of the world were in the process of imposing economic, political, and cultural sanctions against that country because of its apartheid system. Malawi's action was loudly condemned, but President **Hastings Banda** argued that he had good economic and political reasons for moving closer to South Africa. Banda was interested in obtaining aid for the construction of a new capital at **Lilongwe** and for the completion of the Nacala **railway** line. Other economic motives included the need to expand its export market and develop **tourism** in Malawi. South African business was encouraged to invest in Malawi, and many South African professionals were employed in key positions in industry, especially in the expanding **Press Holdings**.

Banda also pointed out that violence was not the key to changing black and white relations, but promoting a dialogue with South Africa could produce reforms. His dialogue policy, coupled with his anticommunist opinions, were popular in South Africa, which extended an invitation for a state visit to Banda in 1971. During his five-day stay he visited both black and white leaders; shortly after this, the South African government accepted Malawi's ambassador, the first black diplomat to reside in Pretoria. Throughout the Mozambican civil war, Malawi's rail connections to the East Coast were greatly disrupted, resulting in a greater use of Durban for its external trade. **RENAMO**, the resistance movement that fought the **FRELIMO** government and was strongly suspected of receiving assistance from Banda's government, was significantly dependent on South Africa.

When the African National Congress (ANC) won the first universal adult suffrage general elections in South Africa in 1994, the government it formed was not particularly warm toward Malawi because of its history of close relations with the National Party government it had just defeated. Although in the period leading to the elections Banda had given a substantial amount of money to Nelson Mandela on behalf of the ANC, and in spite of the fact that there was a change of government in Malawi at about the same time as in South Africa, the relations remained cool for some time. The situation began to improve as the decade passed; trade and diplomatic relations, which had never been broken, were strengthened. Under a trade agreement, Malawi has an open market with South Africa, meaning that Malawi's goods enter the latter country free as long as they satisfy the 25 percent local content. However, attempts by the **Bakili Muluzi** government to resume contract labor migration to the South African gold mines failed because the high rates of unemployment in South Africa led President Mandela's administration to adopt protectionist measures. A phenomenon following political reforms in South Africa has been the brain drain of highly trained personnel from Malawi, as from other countries north of the Limpopo, to better-paying jobs in South Africa.

SOUTH RUKURU. One of the longest rivers in **Malawi**. A major feeder river into **Lake Malawi**, the South Rukuru rises in southern **Mzimba** District and flows west and then north, entering lake Kazuni in the Mzimba-**Rumphi** border area, where it turns northeast through the gorge at Njakwa, flowing through the Henga valley, passing east of the **Nyika plateau**, and finally dropping into the lake at Mlowe.

SOUTHERN AFRICA. The region marked by **Mozambique**, **Malawi**, **Zambia**, and Angola in the north and **South Africa** in the south to Cape Town. It also includes Botswana, Lesotho, Namibia, and Swaziland. *See also* SOUTHERN AFRICA DEVELOPMENT COMMUNITY.

SOUTHERN AFRICA DEVELOPMENT COMMUNITY (SADC). The Southern Africa Development Community grew out of the Southern Africa Development Coordination Conference (SADCC) formed in 1980 by nine states of **Southern Africa**, including Malawi. The goals of SADCC were to coordinate regional development and to reduce economic dependence on **South Africa**, which at the time was still guided by racial segregationist policies. The other eight SADCC states were **Angola**, Botswana, Lesotho, **Mozambique**, Swaziland, **Tanzania**, **Zambia**,and **Zimbabwe**; in 1990 Namibia also became a member. Together, they represented a population of over 80 million people. Each SADCC member was assigned responsibility for specific sectors of development; for Malawi, it is fisheries, **forestry**, and wildlife. Each member is responsible for initiating project proposals, for seeking financial assistance from donors, and for implementing the projects.

A major priority of the SADCC was to establish transportation outlets independent of South Africa and, more specifically, to rehabilitate three transport corridors: the **Beira** corridor connecting Zimbabwe with the Mozambique coast by rail; the northern corridor linking the region with

Dar es Salaam via the Tazara Railway and the Zambian rail system; and the Malawi corridor to Mozambique's port of Nacala. In Malawi the **transportation** project involved upgrading two transshipment ports and the maintenance of **Chilumba** port on **Lake Malawi** in order to help establish a link between Malawi and Dar es Salaam via the Tazara Railway.

The SADCC has been very effective with its project approach. By the end of the 1980s, the organization had obtained the backing of foreign donors and had completed many of its transport and communication schemes. Ambitious and successful, the SADCC had approved nearly 600 national or regional projects having a net worth of over $7 billion.

In 1994 South Africa joined the SADCC and its aims had to be modified and expanded to reflect this development. The name of this regional organization was changed to Southern Africa Development Community (SADC), and its membership has expanded to include the Democratic Republic of Congo (formerly Zaire), Mauritius, and the Seychelles. In 1997 Malawi hosted the SADC heads of state meeting, and President **Bakili Muluzi** has served a term as chairman of the organization.

SOUTHERN RHODESIA. *See* ZIMBABWE.

SOUTHWORTH COMMISSION. Led by Justice Southworth of **Nyasaland**'s High Court, this commission was appointed by the governor, Sir **Robert Armitage**, to investigate the demonstration that took place on January 26, 1960, at the **Ryall's Hotel**, while **Harold Macmillan**, the British prime minister, was attending a civic luncheon in the hotel. Although a modest demonstration, especially given the state of emergency, its magnitude was much exaggerated in the reports of the press corps accompanying Macmillan. Calls were made locally to inquire into the demonstration, hence the Southworth Commission.

SPECIAL BRANCH. This security division of the **police** dates back to the beginning of World War II, and it expanded greatly with the heightening of African political activities in **Nyasaland**. The Special Branch was to grow even more powerful under Dr. **Hastings Banda**'s leadership when it was used to spy on Malawians, especially those perceived to hold opinions not entirely favorable to the government. The division became an integral part of the abuse of **human rights**, sending many people into long periods of imprisonment without trial, often for unsubstantiated reasons. As a result, it was one of the most feared institutions in **Malawi**. The advent of political reform in the 1990s ushered in a healthier attitude in the Special Branch, which is no longer regarded as acting against the interests of the citizens of Malawi. *See also* GWEDE, FOCUS; MWANZA ACCIDENT AND TRIALS.

STEPHENS, FRANCIS TRANT. Born in England in 1882, Francis Stephens fought in the Anglo-Boer War of 1899–1902, at the end of which he joined the British South African Police in **Southern Rhodesia**. During World War I, he was in the **King's African Rifles** (KAR) and was awarded the Military Cross and the OBE in 1917 and 1919, respectively. In 1920 Stephens was appointed chief commissioner of police in **Nyasaland**, with the specific task of starting a new **police** force that was duly established on October 5, 1921. On his retirement in 1939, Major Stephens was appointed Nyasaland Labour Officer in Salisbury, Southern Rhodesia, where he died in December 1946.

STEWART, JAMES. Long-time head of **Lovedale** College and first chief of the **Livingstonia Mission** of the Free Church of Scotland. Stewart was born in Perthshire, Scotland, in 1832, and he was a scientist on **David Livingstone**'s Zambezi expedition of 1858–1863. In 1867 Dr. James Stewart went to work at Lovedale in the Eastern Cape, **South Africa**. While on leave in Great Britain, he attended Livingstone's funeral at Westminster Abbey. Before returning to Lovedale, Stewart and some of the Free Church leaders advanced a plan for a Christian mission in honor of Livingstone. And having been to the **Lake Malawi** area earlier, he recommended that such a scheme be located in the southern section of the lakeshore area. Stewart himself was to lead the mission, and Lieutenant **Edward Young**, who in 1867 had led an expedition to search for Livingstone, was requested to be the captain of the *Ilala*, the steamboat that took them up the Zambezi and **Shire Rivers** to Lake Malawi.

In 1876 the party arrived at **Cape Maclear**, which was to be the home of the Livingstonia Mission. Stewart, Young, and others circumnavigated Lake Malawi, and after he was sure that the party was beginning to settle in their new environment, Stewart returned to his Lovedale base from where he continued to officially head the mission. Although Dr. **Robert Laws** was the effective field director, Stewart could veto major decisions. By the mid-1880s, headship by proxy was proving to be problematic, and increasingly Laws became the recognized supremo of the Livingstonia Mission. It was because of the connection between Stewart and the Scottish missions in Malawi that, starting from the 1880s, African students from the **Blantyre** and Livingstonia missions went to study at Lovedale. *See also* MISSIONS.

STONE AGE. *See* PREHISTORY.

STRUCTURAL ADJUSTMENT PROGRAMS. *See* FINANCIAL AND ECONOMIC DEVELOPMENTS.

SUGAR. Sugar is an important consumer item in Malawi, and in an attempt to secure its affordability, a sugarcane-producing pilot project, the Alimenda Sugar Scheme, was initiated in the Lower **Shire Valley** in 1949. Abandoned a few years later, it was not until 1963 that **Lonrho** became interested in sugarcane production; two years later, the firm formed a subsidiary, the Sugar Corporation of Malawi (SUCOMA), to manage that agrobusiness. The Malawi government leased SUCOMA nearly 12,000 acres of public land, which now became the **Nchalo** Sugar Estate. When production began in 1966, some 3,500 tons of sugar were produced for local consumption. With the availability of the **United States** and European Union (EU) markets in the 1970s, Lonrho investigated the **Dwangwa** delta in the central lakeshore area for a second production site. Subsequently, the Dwangwa Sugar Corporation (DWASCO) was formed and production began on over 13,000 acres, with another 1,630 acres cultivated by smallholders, also managed by Lonrho. Other investors in SUCOMA were the **Agricultural Development and Marketing Board** (ADMARC) and **Press Holdings**.

Under the 1975 Lomé Convention, 20,000 tons of Malawi sugar were guaranteed a market in the European Union and half of this amount often sold on the world market. **Malawi** also exports sugar to the United States under a quota agreement. Sugar became a major foreign exchange earner until 1982 when the bottom fell out of the sugar market. Overloaded with sugar it could not export, Malawi switched to producing ethanol at **Dwangwa**. This low-octane import substitute is then mixed with regular petroleum. Severe **transportation** problems also forced Malawi sugar producers to reduce output, although in 1990 production went on to exceed 189,000 metric tons. Malawi consumes 70,000 tons and uses 7,000 for ethanol production; the remainder is exported to the European Union, the United States, and Zaire, Burundi, and Rwanda. In 1985 Malawi obtained a contract with the United States for the export of 12,000 metric tons annually at $.08 per pound; in 1987, the United States reduced its import quotas and Malawi dropped from 9,000 to 7,000 tons annually. The government strongly opposed the quota system and sought to abolish it. Sugar exports were valued at $28 million in 1990 and accounted for 10 percent of Malawi's domestic exports. Throughout the 1990s, production of sugar increased; in thousand tons they were as follows: 1993, 123.8; 1994, 196.4;

1995, 224.4; 1996, 217.5; 1997, 218.0. The improvement was partly due to vastly improved international prices. *See also* EXTERNAL TRADE; FOREIGN AID; FOREIGN POLICY.

SUKWA. Indigenous people of the Misuku hills in **Chitipa** District. The Sukwa state, dating to about 1600, was ruled by the Mwenemisuku. Their language, ciSukwa, strongly influenced by **Ndali** immigrants and trading partners, is mutually intelligible with ciLambya. The Misuku hills is one of the **coffee**-producing regions of **Malawi**. From the 1920s to the 1940s Europeans unsuccessfully tried to develop the area into the leading coffee-growing area of the country. In the early 1950s Africans in Misuku formed coffee **cooperatives** out of which developed the Misuku Coffee Growers Co-operative Union. Like most such agricultural organizations, it was disbanded at the government's direction in 1968. Misuku is also associated with oranges, bananas, and potatoes.

SUPREME COUNCIL OF CHIEFS AND CONGRESS. Formed in April 1953 as the organ to coordinate relations between the **Chiefs Union** and the **Nyasaland African Congress** (NAC). The imperial government's determination to impose the **Federation of Rhodesia and Nyasaland** led to the move to establish an organ that could present a united opposition to the new political structure and to other issues that were not in their interest.

SURTEE, ISHMAEL KASSIM. Balaka businessman and politician. Surtee was a prominent leader in the Coloured (mixed race) community. He contested the 1961 **elections** on the higher roll as **Malawi Congress Party** (MCP) candidate for the Central Region. Surtee was Speaker of the Malawi parliament for some years before retiring from politics concentrating on his business interests.

SWAHILI-ARABS. *See* ARAB-SWAHILI WAR; MLOZI bin KAZBADEMA.

– T –

TAMANDA. Located in the **Chewa**-speaking area of the Luangwa valley. In 1908 Tamanda became one of the outstations of the **Livingstonia Mission**. In 1924 Tamanda and **Kasungu** were handed over to the **Dutch Reformed** Mission, a step that **Hastings Banda**, then out of the country, strongly disagreed with.

TANZANIA. A union between Tanganyika and **Zanzibar** formed in 1964. Tanzania shares its southern border with **Malawi**, **Mozambique**, and

Zambia. Many people on the southern side of the **Songwe** speak the same languages as those north of the river. Until the early 1960s, many Malawians worked in Tanzania, and some settled there permanently. The first cabinet of President **Julius Nyerere** included some members of Malawian origin. For most of **Hastings Banda**'s presidency, Malawi-Tanzania relations were lukewarm if not bad. The first problem was that Malawi's **foreign policy**, as articulated at independence in July 1964, was at great variance with that of Tanzania. Banda's increasing closeness to Portuguese Mozambique, **Southern Rhodesia**, and **South Africa** did not please Nyerere, whose government was committed to supporting liberation movements determined to overthrow settler colonialism in **Southern Africa**. In the weeks immediately following July 4, 1964, Nyerere cancelled a state visit to Malawi because of this factor, which was a leading reason for the **Cabinet Crisis** shortly afterward. The relations between the two countries were further strained during the Cabinet Crisis because Nyerere, like **Kenneth Kaunda**, offered political asylum to former members of Banda's cabinet: **Henry Chipembere**, **Kanyama Chiume**, **Orton Chirwa**, **Yatuta Chisiza**, and many others who followed them into exile.

Although President Nyerere assured Malawi that his government would not permit refugees to plot against the Banda government, Dr. Banda made several highly emotional accusations about a planned Tanzanian invasion of his country. The charges proved to be false but were used to justify increased security measures, including arbitrary imprisonments, taken by Banda in Malawi. Relations with Tanzania did not improve in the mid-1960s, when another issue was added, the lake boundary. It has been suggested that the Nyerere government feared that Malawi might permit the Portuguese to operate in the northern **Lake Malawi** region in an effort to pursue **FRELIMO** units, in which case Tanzania needed to assert a claim over the lake. Speeches from Tanzania referred to a median line through Lake Malawi, and remarks from Malawi defied Tanzania's historical claim to the region. In October 1967 tensions were further exacerbated when Tanzania-based Yatuta Chisiza and a small group of supporters entered Malawi with a view to overthrowing the government. Banda felt that the Tanzanian government should have intervened. The following year, President Banda made a rash statement implying that the lands east of the lake belonged to Malawi, not Tanzania. The response from Tanzania was predictable, and both governments engaged in a heated dialogue.

Relations began to thaw in the early 1980s, when the two governments exchanged diplomats at high commission level. In July 1989 Nyerere's successor, Ali Hassan Mwinyi, paid a five-day visit in celebration of Malawi's 25 years of independence. President Banda reciprocated, making an official state visit to Tanzania in October 1991. Talks concentrated on expanding traffic through Dar es Salaam, thus reducing Malawi's need to exit through **South Africa**. Traffic through the northern corridor increased contacts between Malawians and Tanzanians, and dealings at the government level became even better after Banda accepted political reforms that led to the general **elections** of 1994. The new **United Democratic Front** (UDF) government, led by President **Bakili Muluzi**, capitalized on the improved atmosphere to normalize Malawi-Tanganyika relations. *See also* TRANSPORTATION.

TAXES. In 1892 **Harry Johnston** imposed the first taxes in Malawi in the shape of a poll tax, so termed because every person deemed to be an adult had to pay six shillings tax. For purposes of the tax, an adult was defined as a person who was 14 years or older. Initially applied to the area south of **Lake Malawi**, the poll tax was very unpopular. Chiefs, forced to be part of the collecting system, reacted equally unfavorably, especially since those unable to pay it were forced to work for European estates in the **Shire Highlands**. Reverend **David C. Scott** of the **Blantyre Mission** spoke strongly against it. These factors, in addition to the fact that very little revenue was forthcoming, led to changes in 1894. Johnston reduced the tax to three shillings per hut, meaning that the tax would be paid per house rather than per adult.

In 1900 the governor, Sir **Alfred Sharpe**, increased the hut tax to 12 shillings in response to appeals from settler farmers who argued that the fall in **coffee** production that year was attributed to labor shortages and that an upward reevaluation of the tax would force Africans into seeking wage labor on European plantations. Not keen to work under the harsh conditions in the Shire Highlands estates, and afraid of imprisonment if they did not pay the tax, many Africans opted to go into labor migration south of the Zambezi. In 1911 **Governor William Manning** announced the reduction of the African rate, subject to a taxpayer selling prescribed cash crops to European buyers. The generally preferred crops were **cotton** (56 lbs.), **rice** (100 lbs.), and **tobacco** (36 lbs.). Other tax reviews, all containing rebate provisos, were to follow. In 1921 a nonrebate flat rate of six shillings was adopted, and under the 1928 Income Tax Ordinance, non-African males were to pay poll tax at the rate of L2 per adult annually. The income system was revised at regular intervals. *See also* MIGRANT LABOR; SOUTH AFRICA.

In postcolonial Malawi, the basic criterion for taxability is that the work be done, or services rendered, within Malawi. The exceptions to this include salaries from foreign governments or international organizations. There are three types of tax: minimum, graduated, and income tax. The first is paid by all males 18 years or older, regardless of their employment status. Elderly disabled persons are exempt from taxation. Unless employed, **women** do not pay tax. The graduated tax is collected by employers from their employees who earn less than an annual amount of money specified by parliament. Most full-time employees are on pay-as-you-earn income tax, which may be collected weekly or monthly. Taxation on income may take into account marital status, insurance premiums, and educational deductions. The rate of taxation for the first K1,200 is 3 percent. Depending on income, the rate increases to 45 percent. Corporate tax also varies.: Malawi-based companies pay taxes at a fixed rate (38 percent) of chargeable income, and those incorporated externally pay 5 percent additional tax. The government has an array of tax incentives that it uses to encourage local and foreign firms to operate in Malawi. Luxury goods (e.g., cosmetics and alcohol) are subjected to a surtax of 30–35 percent.

In 1999 the Income Tax Department, which for a long time had been responsible for all matters concerning taxation, was replaced by the Malawi Revenue Authority (MRA), one of the **International Monetary Fund** (IMF)–inspired fiscal discipline enhancement measures meant to improve the collection of tax revenue.

TEA. Malawi is Africa's second largest tea producer, and tea is its second major export crop after **tobacco**. It is also the most popular drink in the country, consumed in the majority of households, and the first food item that a host offers a visitor within a few minutes of arrival. Produced mainly in **Mulanje** and **Thyolo**, the first seedlings were brought into the country in 1878 by Jonathan Duncan, a gardener at the **Blantyre Mission**. Unlike **coffee** seedlings, they died. The real beginning of the tea industry in Malawi dates from 1891, when Henry Brown, manager of the recently opened **Lauderdale Estate** at the southern foot of Mulanje mountain, planted the first tea bushes imported from Ceylon (Sri Lanka), where he had worked prior going to the **Shire Highlands**. From Lauderdale Estate, tea spread to other European plantations in the area, and by the early 1900s it had replaced coffee as the colony's leading cash earner. Tea planting attracted individual European farmers as well as some of the Malawi-based companies such as **British & East Africa Ltd.** and the

British Central Africa Company Ltd. It also enticed the larger British-based companies with major tea interests in Asia, among them Brooke Bond and J. Lyons & Company. This highly labor-intensive industry employed thousands of people, including children, at minimum wages; thousands of **Lomwe** immigrants from **Mozambique** also made the tea plantations in Shire Highlands viable, partly explaining why the area is identified with them today.

Tea's preeminence as a cash crop was greatly reduced in the interwar period, especially between 1927 and 1932, primarily because of consecutive excessively rainy seasons and poor prices on the international markets. The tea restrictions that followed the International Tea Agreement of 1933 and World War II further affected the stability of tea production, and by 1952 all individual planters in Malawi had been replaced by companies. The restrictions were lifted at the end of the 1940s, and by the end of the 1950s the Malawi tea industry was healthier than it had been for a long time. In 1957 tea production commenced in **Nkhata Bay** District at the Chombe tea estates, across from the **Vizara rubber** plantation, and remained in operation until the early 1990s, when it was abandoned. After independence, the Malawi government and the **Commonwealth Development Corporation** promoted smallholder production of tea, particularly in the Thyolo-Mulanje region, and today this sector contributes 10 percent of the crop, most of which is exported to the London tea market. Smaller quantities are shipped to **South Africa**, Pakistan, the **United States**, **Zimbabwe**, **Zambia**, and Mozambique. The industry is now modernized, with new processing machines, bed dryers, and fermenting systems.

TEMBO, JOHN ZENAS UNGAPAKE. Teacher, first Malawian minister of finance, first local governor of the **Reserve Bank of Malawi**, and close adviser of President **Hastings Banda**. John Tembo, son of Zenas Tembo, a **Dutch Reformed Church** minister, was born in Dedza District in September 1932. He completed his primary school education at **Mlanda Mission** in 1949, and four years later he obtained his Cambridge School Certificate at **Blantyre** Secondary School. After working for the government Auditor's Department, Tembo received a **Nyasaland** government scholarship to study at Pius College (now the National University of Lesotho), graduating with a B.A. degree in 1958. Early in 1959 he proceeded to the University of Rhodesia and Nyasaland (now the University of Zimbabwe), where in November of that year he was awarded a Certificate in Education.

On his return home, Tembo taught at **Kongwe** Secondary School and at the same time played an active role in the **Malawi Congress Party** (MCP). In 1961 he was elected to the **Legislative Council** (LEGCO) as member for Dedza, and in the following year was appointed parliamentary secretary in the ministry of finance, replacing **Dunduzu Chisiza**, who had died in a car accident. Tembo was reelected to parliament in 1964, and at independence he was appointed minister of finance, the position previously held by **Henry Phillips**, and for a brief time also added the portfolios of Trade and Industry, Development, and Planning. In 1969 he relinquished the Ministry of Finance, moving to Trade and Industry, and in that capacity was responsible for the **Africanization** of Asian business in rural areas. In 1971 he became the first Malawian governor of the Reserve Bank of Malawi, but he retained his growing influence as a member of the Central Executive Committee of the MCP. In the early 1980s President Hastings Banda moved Tembo from the Reserve Bank, and in 1986 he became treasurer-general of the MCP, a post long held by **Sydney Somanje**, who passed away that year. *See also* ASIANS.

Although Tembo held no official government position throughout the 1980s, he became a close adviser of President Banda, acting as an unofficial prime minister and becoming one of the most powerful and feared persons in Malawi. He was chairman of the following, among others: **Press Holdings Ltd.**, Commercial Bank of Malawi, **Air Malawi**, **University of Malawi** Council, and Limbe Leaf Ltd. From 1987 he headed the Malawi delegation to the Joint Security Commission with **Mozambique** and sat on the National Economic Commission created in the late 1980s to deliberate on economic projects, among other functions. These offices, and numerous others, placed him in a dominant position in Malawi's political and economic affairs. In the period leading to political reform, Tembo became minister of state in the President's Office, a particularly influential appointment because its duties included national security matters. He campaigned vigorously against multiparty politics and in 1994 was elected to the National Assembly as MCP member for Dedza, this time sitting on the opposition benches.

In 1995, following the **Mtegha Commission** of 1994, the government charged Tembo, Hastings Banda, and his niece, **Cecilia Kadzamira**, with the death of the four politicians murdered in **Mwanza** District in 1983. They were acquitted later that year. Following Banda's death in 1997, Tembo was elected vice president of the MCP, the presidency going to **Gwanda Chakuamba**. In June 1999 he was returned to parliament, and he has remained active in national politics. *See also* MWANZA ACCIDENT AND TRIALS.

TEMBO, MAWELERA. Mawelera and his elder brother, Makara, sons of Kalengo Tembo, a highly regarded Senga-**Ngoni** traditional doctor, were among the first Christian converts at **Njuyu** mission station. They were baptized in 1890, having been pupils at the school that had opened there in December 1886; Mawelera became one of its teachers. When Rev. Dr. George Steele died in 1895, Mawelera took charge of Njuyu, and in 1900 he had the honor of being one of the four Africans to be appointed to the first Kirk Ngoni session. A very good singer, Tembo is also regarded as the most productive composer of hymns, the majority of which were in ciNgoni. His most famous hymns, "Dumisani u'Yehova lin'zinceku zake" (Oh praise the King of heaven all ye who are his people), has become a classic. Mawelera's career as a teacher and an evangelist continued until he retired in 1934. He died in 1937.

TEMPORARY EMPLOYMENT BUREAU OF AFRICA (TEBA). *See* MIGRANT LABOR; WITWATERSRAND NATIVE LABOUR ASSOCIATION (WNLA).

TENGANI. Area and title of a chief whose ancestors were part of the southward expansion of the **Maravi** in the 16th century. Of the **Phiri** matri-clan and a junior to Lundu, Tengani settled in the vicinity of modern **Nsanje** *boma*. He had overall supervision of the **Khulubvi** shrine, home of **M'bona**. This position, in addition to the key location on the Shire River, ensured that the Tenganis would play a significant role in the political, cultural, and social history of the Lower **Shire Valley**. European travelers, traders, and missionaries entering the **Lake Malawi** area via the **Shire River** had to deal with the Tengani chiefs. Like other rulers of the Shire Valley, they became entangled in economic and political rivalry between the British and the Portuguese at the end of the 19th century.

TENGANI, CHIEF MOLIN. One of the most controversial chiefs in late colonial Malawi, Molin Tengani belonged to the long line of the **Tengani** dynasty of the **Mang'anja** of the Lower **Shire Valley**. Tengani was converted to Christianity in 1902. Although he worked for the **railways** for a time, he became a teacher and taught at several mission schools, including the main one at Chididi. He remained there until 1936, when he was installed Chief Tengani after the death of his uncle, Thenzwa, two years earlier. Against tradition, Molin Tengani refused to observe the obligations of his office to the **Khulubvi** shrine, including repairs to it.

Molin also acquiesced to Christians who refused to undertake their usual Mang'anja duties to the shrine. Furthermore, shrine priests who had hitherto avoided paying government tax were now forced to do so. There was even talk that **M'Bona** had left the area in response to the new chief's attitude toward the shrine, and many people in the area reacted by refusing to observe new agricultural rules, which Molin Tengani tried to enforce on behalf of the government. Rebuilt by its most ardent supporters, the shrine and M'Bona also became the center of opposition to the establishment of the **Federation of Rhodesia and Nyasaland**, which was associated with the new agricultural regulations. This was not helped by the fact that Molin Thengani supported the Federation. Thengani retired in 1963 and died four years later. This marked the end of a feud that has been interpreted by some as competition between traditional religion and Christianity.

TENNENT, A. J. One of the influential European planters in colonial Malawi. Tennent was managing director of the J. Tennent & Company Ltd., a company with many interests, including the Magunda and **Luchenza** estates in **Thyolo** District. Located in an area in which Africans faced the problem of land shortage, there was always an underlying tension between the planters on the one hand and their African neighbors and workers on the other. In August 1953 the Magunda estate was the center of a clash between African workers and Tennent's sons, Basil and Desmond. On August 18 the brothers accused some of their workers of theft, and in the fracas that followed one of the laborers was injured. Rumors spread to the effect that an African had been killed by a planter, and this led to a riot that the **police** had difficulty controlling. Headman **Ngamwane**, the traditional ruler of the area, was arrested and spent a brief time in **Blantyre** prison. Other riots, not directly connected with that at Luchenza, followed in Thyolo, **Mulanje**, and elsewhere in the southern province. *See also THANGATA*; THONDEZA.

THANGATA. CiChewa/ciMang'anja term that means help. In traditional society, it also referred to a system of services exchanged between chiefs and their dependents. In colonial Malawi it referred to labor tenancy practiced mostly on European plantations in the **Shire Highlands**. In this area, African squatters living on a European estate were not required to pay rent, as in most tenant arrangements, but rather were compelled to work a prescribed length of time for the European landlord. The period of time required by the Europeans was frequently increased, and, typically, tenants worked at least one month as "rent" and another month for hut taxes; they were not permitted the privilege of working elsewhere. *Thangata* soon came to be described by African laborers as work that was done without real benefit. Instead, the benefits went to the landlord and to an administration that rarely provided the African with any services in exchange for his taxes. *Thangata* was a major factor in the **Chilembwe uprising**. *See also* TAXES.

When two-thirds of Malawi's male population became involved in World War I, either voluntarily or compulsorily, the *thangata* system was again applied. The men were used as soldiers *(askaris)* and carriers *(tenga tenga)*. They were frequently mistreated, and their experiences generally produced a resentment against colonialism expressed in the postwar era in the rising popularity of dance and **Nyau** societies, in **native associations**, and in **Islam**.

Although Governor **Geoffrey Colby** began to dismantle *thangata* in the early 1950s, notable aspects of it continued to be practiced until the first **Malawi Congress Party** (MCP) government passed legislation abolishing all its vestiges.

THEUNISSEN, BISHOP JEAN-BAPTIST. Bishop of the Archdiocese of **Blantyre** from 1952 to 1968. Theunissen was born in the Netherlands where, just before going to **Malawi** in 1950 as vicar apostolic of Shire, he had been the Dutch provincial for the Montforts. Theunissen had already worked in Africa, having served 12 years as a missionary in **Mozambique** prior to his Dutch posting. In 1952 he became bishop of the Blantyre vicariate. When Pope John XXIII instructed that all vicariates in the colony become dioceses, Blantyre was raised to an archdiocese and Theunissen became archbishop and, consequently, leader of the **Catholic** hierarchy in **Nyasaland**. In October 1960 the archbishop was the subject of a long lead article in the *Malawi News* that attacked him on the suspicion that he was behind a newly formed political organization, the Christian Democratic Party, led by **Chester Katsonga**, a Catholic. Signed by **Aleke Banda**, the newspaper's editor, the article gave the impression that the new party was aimed at forestalling the nationalist ambitions of the **Malawi Congress Party** (MCP). Although the archbishop and the Catholic Church strongly denied the accusation, the relations between Theunissen and the new MCP-led government remained lukewarm. He retired in 1968 and was succeeded by Bishop **James Chiona**.

THOLE, PETER ZIMEMA. From the core **Zansi**, of the M'mbelwa **Ngoni** hierarchy, and a onetime student of Rev. **Walter Angus Elmslie**.

Peter Thole entered the theological course at the **Overtoun Institution** in 1920 and was ordained five years later. In 1927 he was called to Emchisweni Congregation in central **Mzimba** District. In 1926 Thole had been a member of the **Livingstonia** delegation to the **Blantyre** Synod. Although considered a moderate in the numerous disagreements between the African and the European clergy, Thole hosted at his Elangeni home the historic meeting on January 7, 1920, which led to the formation of the Mombera **Native Association**. Well over six feet tall, Thole was (besides **Mawelera Tembo**) one of the most prolific and exciting composers of hymns in the Livingstonia Synod, and almost all his hymns were included in the church hymnal. Thole's father and grandfather had been in the **Zwagendaba**'s original migration group, and many of his compositions were in Zulu. They were incorporated into the Ngoni hymn book, *Izingoma zo Bukristu,* which also benefited from the Zulu one, *Amagama Okuhlabela,* published in Natal. Of Thole, Rev. **Robert Laws** commented, "a remarkable man, a poet and singer. . . . I never heard another native put his soul into singing and bring out the meaning of the words as a message in the way Peter does. . . . I have often seen a large congregation listening with rapt attention to the message of his song" (1934, 8). The commentator, educator, and historian **Desmond D. Phiri** wrote of Thole, "I saw and heard Thole sing . . . in 1947 at the Livingstonia Presbytery. . . . A hymn book in his left hand, an *umshiza* (staff) in the right, his voice towered above our voices just as his height towered over our heights" (1975, 24). Thole died in May 1950.

THONDEZA, CHIEF. *See* GUDU, WILFRID.

THONDWE. Located eight miles from **Zomba** on the Zomba-**Blantyre** road, Thondwe lies in the center of a **tobacco**-growing area. Throughout the colonial period it was associated with large European plantations such as that belonging to **Roy W. Wallace.** This was also an area into which the **Lomwe** migrated and found jobs on tobacco estates. For a long time forms of *thangata* were practiced there. Before the **Africanization** of **Asian** business, Thondwe had a thriving small population of **Indian** retail traders. Thondwe is also famous for its Saturday market, which attracts sellers and buyers from beyond the confines of the area. Declared a rural growth area, Thondwe has a modern **health** clinic, a post office, a **police** station, a school, and an **Agricultural Development and Marketing Corporation** (ADMARC) market. It also is a main center for the **Catholic** Church and the Church of Christ.

THORNE, FRANK OSWALD. Universities' Mission to Central Africa (UMCA). Bishop of **Nyasaland** from 1936 to 1960 and member of the **Legislative Council** (LEGCO) in the 1940s. Frank Thorne was educated at Christ College, Oxford, and at St. Boniface College, Warminster. Ordained in 1922, he joined mission work three years later and was posted to St. Cyprian's Theological College, Tunduru, in the Masasi diocese, southern Tanganyika. In 1936 he replaced Gerald Douglas as bishop of Nyasaland. Thorn was nominated to LEGCO, where often he spoke on African causes.

THORNEYCROFT, GEOFREY. Founder of the Chimpeni estate just south of **Zomba** airport. Thorneycroft was born in England and arrived in **Nyasaland** in 1912 after working in Guyana and the Senna sugar estate in **Mozambique**. In World War I he saw service in **Karonga** and Tanganyika. After losing a leg, he was sent to England for recovery. Thorneycroft returned to Nyasaland in 1919 to grow **tobacco** at the Chimpeni estate, one of the most successful agricultural concerns in **Malawi**. He died in September 1967. His son, and later his grandson, continued to manage Chimpeni.

THYOLO. Name of the district and *boma* located between **Blantyre** and **Mulanje** District, and particularly famous as a major **tea**-producing area in Malawi. Thyolo was also identified with **tung** production from the 1930s to the 1960s. An important center of European agricultural activity, Thyolo was also a major region of **Lomwe** settlement at the beginning of the 20th century. Because of this, land has always been a sensitive matter in the district. *Thangata* was widely practiced here in its purest form, and tension between Africans and Europeans often led to open conflict. In 1966 the Malawi government started a smallholder tea program in Thyolo, based on the Kenya model, and aimed at involving Africans in tea production. Over 1,000 acres are now cultivated by smallholders. To ensure ease of communication between this rich agricultural region and Blantyre-**Limbe**, the road between the two areas has been widened and greatly improved. A major banana-growing district, Thyolo is also the home of the **Malamulo** Mission, the main center of the Seventh-Day Adventist Church in Malawi. *See also* GUDU, WILFRID; TENNENT, A. J.

TIMKE, W. H. Friend of early nationalists in **Malawi**. Timke was born in **South Africa**, went to Malawi after World War I, and was manager of the European planters agricultural cooperative society in **Thyolo** until 1929.

After the cooperative collapsed, he farmed **tobacco** and built stores in Thyolo, which he rented to **Indian** retail traders. He also became active in a European settler organization, the **Convention of Associations**, and for two years sat on the **Legislative Council** (LEGCO). As World War II progressed, Timke grew close to politically minded Africans such as **James Sangala** and encouraged them to better organize themselves so as to realize their nationalist ambitions. Timke advised on the best means of making African opinion known to government officials and European settlers. He encouraged Sangala to contact **Arthur Creech Jones**, then the British Labour Party's shadow colonial secretary, in the hope that questions on the colonial situation in Malawi would be raised in parliament. Timke himself also contacted Creech Jones. Throughout 1944 he urged Sangala and his associates, such as **Charles Matinga**, to demand African representation on all important government bodies, including LEGCO, and to form one organization to represent African opinion. Timke perished when the **MV** *Viphya* sank off the **Chiweta** coast in 1946.

TOBACCO. Malawi's leading export crop for part of the colonial era and throughout the postcolonial period. Commercial tobacco was first grown in the country in 1889 at the Buchanan Brothers estate in **Zomba**. It was slowly taken up by other planters in the **Shire Highlands**, notably **R. S. Hynde**, the **African Lakes Company** (ALC), **Eugene Sharrer**, **Ignaco Conforzi**, **Roy W. Wallace**, and **A. Francis Barron**. Although they grew their own tobacco, they also bought it from African producers. The real expansion of tobacco production took place in the interwar period, when mainly Conforzi, Wallace, and Barron established major estates in central Malawi, mostly in **Lilongwe**, **Mchinji**, Dowa, and **Kasungu**. Here substantial quantities of tobacco was produced by tenant growers who were trained, loaned seeds, and given other assistance by European estate owners, on condition that tobacco was sold to them. By the 1950s tobacco was overtaking **tea** as an export product.

Burley and flue-cured Virginia varieties are grown on estates, whereas oriental (Turkish) fire-cured and sun/air-cured varieties are grown by smallholders; Malawi is second only to the **United States** in the production of dark-fired tobacco. Burley is now Malawi's most important tobacco crop, as there is 50 percent more of it produced than flue-cured tobacco. In the 1970s production expanded as small-scale farmers increased their holding and as market conditions favored Malawi. A major development that decade was the expansion of tobacco growing to northern Malawi, especially **Rumphi**, **Mzimba**, and to a minor extent, **Chitipa**.

Tobacco is marketed through the auction system introduced in 1946, and there are auction floors in Lilongwe, **Limbe**, and **Mzuzu**. Farmers, individual marketing agents who buy leaf from farmers, or larger agencies such as the **Agricultural Development and Marketing Corporation** (ADMARC) and Press Farming present their tobacco at auction floors, where traders from within Malawi and from abroad bid for the tobacco. The auction floors at Lilongwe and Mzuzu process all burley, flue, and sun-cured tobacco from the Northern and Central Regions, and Limbe handles the Southern Region. Until 1987 tobacco smallholders were not permitted to sell on the world market because ADMARC had the monopoly of the rural Malawi produce. The level of tobacco production and export of the late 1980s continued in the early 1990s, going down between 1993 and 1995; bad rains in 1997 led to lower yields, and in the following two years, there was marginal improvement. Throughout the 1990s the tobacco industry had to contend with many problems: the massive devaluation of the **kwacha**, which rendered the cost of fertilizers and agricultural equipment particularly high; increased competition from countries such as **Zimbabwe**; and the campaign against smoking, mostly in the Western hemisphere. *See also* PRESS HOLDINGS LTD.

TOBACCO ASSOCIATION OF MALAWI (TAMA). Organization that oversees the **tobacco** industry in Malawi. TAMA is affiliated with international tobacco bodies, and it seeks to protect and speak for the tobacco industry. In recent years, TAMA has strongly criticized the tenant farmer system that is commonly practiced by many growers, especially on the estates that grow burley tobacco. TAMA blamed the newer African owners for bad management, and at one time it threatened to punish malpractices registered with its office: overcharging for food, late pay, and physical threats. The facilities and conditions on the burley estates tend to be poor, with school enrollment levels well below average.

TONGA. Inhabitants of central and southern **Nkhata Bay** District and northern **Nkhotakota**. The Tonga speak ciTonga, which is an independent language having affinities with ciChewa to the south and ciTumbuka to the north. Mostly patrilocal, descent is generally matrilineal, especially among those linked with traditional rulers such as **Kanyenda**, **Kabunduli**, and Kapunda Banda, who have strong **Chewa-Maravi** connections. Other rulers, including the Mankhambira, are *balowoka*, meaning that they originally came from across **Lake Malawi** and are generally patrilineal. Sections of the Tonga were conquered by the M'mbelwa **Ngoni**, but in the 1870s they successfully rebelled and resisted attempts to resubjugate them. Famous as fishermen, the Tonga hosted Dr. **David Livingstone** when he visited their home in 1859. When the **Livingstonia Mission** set up a base at **Bandawe** in 1882, they were to be the main beneficiaries of Western **education**, producing famous Malawians such as **Eliot Kamwana, Clements Kadalie, Ernest Alexander Muwamba, Orton Chirwa, Wellington M. Chirwa**, and **Aleke Banda**. The Tonga are also strongly associated with labor migration to various parts of Southern Africa.

TOURISM. A government project in postcolonial Malawi. Although a separate governmental department dealing with tourism has existed since the 1960s, **Malawi** has not been very successful in attracting tourists. The Department of Tourism has in the past actively marketed Malawi in European tourism fairs in an effort to penetrate the European and North American sales market. Compared with Kenya, **Zimbabwe**, and **South Africa**, the Malawian tourist industry is not developed, and many prospective visitors would prefer countries with a good infrastructure; also, heavier air traffic makes fares more competitive. Before political changes in Zimbabwe and South Africa, European (white) settlers not welcome in other African countries tended to spend some of their vacation in Malawi. Although they continue to visit Malawi, they now have a wider choice of destinations, including Kenya and **Tanzania**. Furthermore, hotels, local transportation, and fuel in Malawi tend to be very expensive, thereby discouraging prospective tourists. For "backpackers," or "world travelers" as they are sometimes called, Malawi is a popular destination, as they prefer the numerous affordable and more basic facilities along the lake.

Among the attractions drawing visitors to Malawi are **Lake Malawi** and the national parks: **Nyika, Kasungu, Lengwe**, and **Liwonde**. Animals roaming the parks include kudu, elephant, eland, zebra, lion, buffalo, leopard, and antelope. Two hundred species of fish live in Lake Malawi, some of which are not found elsewhere. A variety of wetland birds (tropical and temperate species) and reptiles are also found along the lakeshore. Other popular tourist sites are the mountain areas of **Mulanje, Zomba**, Dedza, and **Viphya**. The **Malawi Development Corporation** (MDC) invested heavily in hotels, modernizing and expanding facilities for tourists. Since the 1990s all the hotels associated with the

MDC, in addition to those of the Blantyre Hotels Ltd., are managed by Protea Hotels of South Africa, and by the Le Meridien group. Private hotels of different standards have mushroomed in the main cities and along the shores of Lake Malawi, among them Kudya Discovery Lodge on the **Shire River** and Kambiri Lodge in **Salima**. Government rest houses and inns, located throughout the country, also provide good accommodation; since the late 1990s they have been part of the government's **privatization** program. Meantime, the government's Hotel Staff Training School in **Blantyre**, in operation since the late 1970s, has continued to train personnel for the hospitality industry.

TOZER, WILLIAM GEORGE. Successor of Bishop **Charles Mackenzie**. William Tozer was educated at St. John's College, Oxford University, and at Wells Theological College. He was vicar of Burgh-cum-Winthorpe, Lincolnshire, when chosen to be the **Universities' Mission to Central Africa** (UMCA) bishop in the **Lake Malawi** area. Soon after his consecration at Westminster Abbey on February 2, 1863, he left for Africa, arriving in the Lower **Shire Valley** in June of the same year. Of a different disposition from his predecessor and with less empathy for the **refugees** and orphans he found at the Chibisa base of the mission, Tozer decided to move the mission to Mount Morambala further south toward the Zambezi-Shire confluence. In 1864 he and other UMCA missionaries left Morambala for **Zanzibar**, where he established a major UMCA presence and founded St. Andrew's College, Kiungani, which was to train hundreds of African clergy, many of whom worked in the Lake Malawi area. In 1873 Tozer resigned his bishopric because of ill health and returned to England, where he died in June 1899.

TRANSPORTATION. The commonest form of travel in **Malawi** is road transportation, and it is also the most practical means of conveying agricultural produce and other trade items from growers and manufacturers to markets. Postindependence Malawi recognized this factor, and in the 1960s it designated 40 percent of development program resources for transportation, the high priority being to integrate the three regions with reliable all-weather roads and to encourage agricultural development by improving access to rural areas. At independence, there were only 242 miles of bituminized roads in all of Malawi; by the 1990s there were over 8,000 miles. In the early 1970s the 168-mile **Zomba-Lilongwe** highway was completed, and by 1982 the 534-mile lakeshore road project from **Mangochi** to **Karonga** was also finished. Not long after this, the Lilongwe-**Mzuzu** road was modernized, as was the Matope road connecting **Blantyre** and the Zomba-Lilongwe road at Nsipe, south of **Ntcheu**. Earlier, the roads from Blantyre to **Chikwawa** in the Lower Shire, and from **Salima** to the **Zambia** border at **Mchinji** via Lilongwe were also upgraded. To enable Malawi's access to the port of Dar es Salaam, **Tanzania**, the British sponsored Karonga-Mbeya road was constructed and improved to all weather standards in 1984. The most recent road scheme, the widening and resurfacing of the Blantyre-**Mulanje** road through the main **tea**-growing area of Malawi, was completed in 1999.

The European Union, the **World Bank**, and the African Development Bank have been particularly involved in financing the realignment and upgrading of roads within Malawi, as well as those linking the country with its neighbors. Secondary and feeder roads have also received the attention of the Malawi government. By the late 1990s many modern and secondary roads and bridges had fallen into a state of disrepair for three principal reasons: there is no control of the weight of haulage transport on Malawi roads; the cost of repairs is high given the massive devaluation of the Malawi **kwacha**; the **International Monetary Fund/World Bank** structural adjustment programs have forced the government to vastly reduce its payroll. Consequently, the Public Works Department, which had always maintained the road system, has retrenched three-quarters of its usual workforce. Instead, the responsibility for road maintenance has been assigned to contractors, many of whom do not have a basic knowledge of road construction.

At independence in 1964, the new Malawi government also recognized the importance of rail transport, especially its ability to secure a cost-effective rail access to the sea. The railway was the core of the Malawi cargo transport system, and roads were used primarily as feeders to bring goods to railheads. Conceived in the 1890s, the railway was slowly extended, starting with the **Blantyre-Nsanje** (Port Herald) rail line, which the **Shire Highlands Railway** Company built between 1902 and 1908. In 1913 the Central Africa Railway Company, like the Shire Highlands Railway associated with **Eugene Sharrer**, extended the line south to **Chinde** (Chindio). Seven years later, the Trans-Zambezi Railway Company constructed the Trans-Zambesia line linking **Beira** with Murraca, opposite Chindio on the banks of the Zambezi River. Until 1935 all goods and passengers were ferried across the river. The construction of the two-and-a-half-mile-long Lower Zambezi bridge commenced in 1931, and the first train crossed it in January 1935. The northern extension from **Blantyre** to **Salima** was also completed by the mid-1930s. The railway system acted as a development agency during the years of the protectorate, determining crop patterns and integrating Malawi laborers into the European settlers' economic schemes. Further extensions of the Malawi rail system did not take place until after independence.

Two years after independence the Malawi government nationalized Malawi Railways, the organization that operated the rail system. In 1970 the government used financial aid from **South Africa** to add a 63-mile-long eastern extension connecting **Liwonde** to the **Mozambique** border at Nayuchi and thence to the Indian Ocean port of Nacala. With a loan from the Canadian International Development Agency (CIDA), in 1974 Malawi began building 70 miles of new track from Salima to Lilongwe. Completed in 1978, this Malawi-Canada project was officially opened in February 1979. **Canada** provided an additional K29 million to link Lilongwe with Mchinji on the Zambian border.

In the early 1990s a French-Portuguese-Canadian consortium rehabilitated the Nacala railway, which had been adversely affected by the civil war in Mozambique. The largest rail project, however, has been the upgrading of the Beira line, the Malawi portion of which, from Nsanje to Dondo, was closed by the **Resistencia Nacional Mozambicana** (RE-NAMO) insurgents. The European Union and the World Bank have been involved in the project. Meanwhile, in 1987 a formal agreement between Malawi and the Tanzania-Zambia railway (TAZARA) opened up the northern corridor, meaning that cargo can now be transported by rail from Dar es Salaam to Mbeya, where it is transferred onto haulage trucks to **Chilumba** on the northern Malawi lakeshore, then via lake transport to Chipoka-Salima, and finally by rail to Lilongwe or **Limbe-Blantyre**. In the late 1990s a third of Malawi's external trade was transported via the northern corridor route, significantly reducing dependence on the more distant South African port of Natal. *See also* MOZAMBIQUE.

In 1999 Malawi Railways was privatized and bought by a Mozambique–North American syndicate, which renamed it the Central East African Railway Company Limited. In March 2000 the new owners announced that they would be investing US$26 million over 15 years, mainly on rolling stock and on the rehabilitation and purchase of new equipment; the restructuring of the rail company will also involve major retrenchments of the workforce. While its passenger service will continue, it planned to concentrate on transporting cargo, such as agricultural produce and fuel, to and from Nampula on the Mozambican coast.

Lake transport is also part of the Malawi Railways corporation. It operates freight and passenger services on MV *Ilala II*, MV *Chauncy Maples*, and MV *Mtendere*. There is a rail/lake interchange station at Chipoka from which there are steamer services to northern ports, including **Likoma** Island and **Chilumba**. **Monkey Bay** is the headquarters of the Lake Services and is the site of **Lake Malawi**'s dry dock.

Also used in Malawi are air and other forms of land transport, including a nationwide daily bus service between Blantyre, Lilongwe, and **Mzuzu**. In the mid-1990s, Stage Coach, the British firm that managed the oldest and largest bus service, sold its fleet to the **Agricultural Development and Marketing Corporation** (ADMARC), primarily because the cost of repairs rose steeply, and because of fierce competition from the numerous local transport companies that had emerged throughout the country.

Air Malawi is the parastatal institution providing air service to Blantyre, Lilongwe, Mzuzu, Karonga, and Mangochi, as well as to several regional destinations, including Lusaka (Zambia), Harare (Zimbabwe), Dar es Salaam (Tanzania), Beira (Mozambique), Nairobi (Kenya), and Johannesburg (South Africa). There are also services to Dubai in the Middle East. The main airport, the Lilongwe International Airport, previously the Kamuzu International Airport (KIA), was inaugurated in 1983 and was constructed to international standards with advanced aeronautical equipment and a capability of handling the latest aircraft. Carriers using the Lilongwe International Airport include British Airways, South African Airways, and the national airlines of Zambia, Tanzania, Kenya, Ethiopia, and Zimbabwe. For most of the 1990s Air Malawi operated at a loss; at the beginning of 2000 it was on the list of parastatal organizations to be privatized.

TRATARIS, NICHOLAS. Greek businessman in **Malawi**. Trataris arrived in the country in the early 1930s and became a successful commercial fisherman. By the early 1950s, the much expanded Trataris family became the dominant bakers in Malawi, supplying bread to all districts in the Southern Region. Their primacy in the baking industry remained unchallenged until the early 1970s, when Press Bakery, a subsidiary of **Press Holdings**, virtually bought them out.

TUMBUKA. Tumbuka, or ciTumbuka, is the dominant language in the Northern Region of **Malawi**. It is the main language of the inhabitants of **Mzimba** and **Rumphi** Districts, and it is widely spoken in **Karonga** District, **Chitipa** South, northern **Nkhata Bay**, and north **Kasungu**.

Tumbuka is also a major language in eastern **Zambia**, especially in Lundazi and Isoka Districts.

TUNG. A bush from which oil is extracted and used in the manufacture of paint and varnish. Tung bushes were first grown in Malawi in 1927 in **Thyolo** and **Mulanje**, and by the beginning of the 1930s it was being produced commercially, attracting some major planters, including **Ignaco Conforzi** and the Naming'omba estates of **Malcolm Barrow**. Its importance increased during World War II, and in the late 1940s the **Colonial Development Corporation** embarked on a very ambitious tung-producing project in the **Viphya Highlands** in northern Malawi. **Mzuzu** was founded as the center of this scheme. Throughout the 1950s thousands of tung trees were planted south and north of the emerging town. **Malawi** became the largest tung-producing country in the British empire and commonwealth. By the late 1960s, the importance of tung to the paint manufacturing industry diminished and prices plummeted, contributing to the virtual demise of the industry in Malawi.

TWEYA, HEZEKEYA MAVUVU. One of the first African church ministers. Of **Tonga-Ngoni** origins, Hezekeya Tweya was educated in **Ungoni** and trained as a teacher. After some years of service, he entered theological college at the **Overtoun Institution**. Following a long probationary period, he, **Yesaya Zerenji Mwasi**, and **Jonathan Chirwa** were ordained on May 14, 1914, the first Africans to become church ministers in the **Livingstonia** Synod of the Free Church of Scotland. He was posted to **Ekwendeni** and in 1917 transferred to **Karonga** to replace Rev. **Duncan R. Mackenzie**, who had temporarily left for war service. In 1923 he was called to Enukweni as a minister, the first African pastor to have such an honor in a congregation in Ngoni-dominated country. A gifted composer, Tweya wrote hymns, some of which were included in the hymnal used in the **Church of Central African Presbyterian** (CCAP) and remain favorites of churchgoers. Tweya was also the founding president of the Mombera **Native Association**. He died in 1930.

– U –

ULAMBYA. Country of the Lambya. The main group lives in **Chitipa** District, where the *mwaulambyas* (rulers) have lived since the Lambya state was founded around 1600. In precolonial times Ulambya covered part of the **Songwe** region of modern southern **Tanzania**, where it bordered with the Safwa, **Nyiha** of Mbozi, and **Ndali**. In the south the Ulambya extended to modern **Zambia**, where their neighbors were the **Namwanga** and **Bisa**. The colonial boundaries established between the British and the Germans divided the Lambya.

UNDALI. Land of the **Ndali**, whose neighbors are the **Sukwa** of the Misuku hills to the south and the **Nyakyusa** to the east.

UNGONDE. Land of the **Ngonde** of the **Karonga** lakeshore, bordering with **Unyakyusa** in the north and with the **Tumbuka**-speaking area of the Mwafulirwa in the south. Ungonde is one of the leading **rice**- and **cotton**-growing areas of **Malawi** and is also known as a cattle area.

UNGONI. Country of the **Ngoni**. Generally understood to mean the area in modern northern Malawi in which the Ngoni, the main **Zwangendaba** group, settled.

UNITED DEMOCRATIC FRONT (UDF). The ruling party of **Malawi** since 1994. the UDF party was formed in September 1992 by people including **Brown Mpingajira**, **Bakili Muluzi**, and **Aleke Banda**, who for some time had been secretly working toward political reform in Malawi. Many in the upper echelons of the UDF, including Bakili Muluzi, Aleke Banda, **Edward Bwanali**, and **Chakakala Chaziya**, held national leadership positions in the MCP and had fallen out favor with Dr. **Hastings Banda** and the ruling party. In the period leading to the referendum of 1993, the UDF and the **Alliance for Democracy** (AFORD) cooperated, thus ensuring a resounding defeat of the **Malawi Congress Party** (MCP) platform of maintaining the status quo.

In the general **elections** of June 1994, Muluzi, the UDF's presidential candidate, won, and the party also became the majority in parliament. The UDF formed the government and, a few months later, included AFORD members in an expanded cabinet; **Chakufwa Chihana**, leader of the AFORD party, was appointed as second vice president. In 1996 this arrangement between the two parties ended, and three years later the UDF campaigned independently and was returned to power. Overwhelmingly, the party's main base is the Southern Region, which is Muluzi's home area and also the most populous part of Malawi. Although it has made inroads into the Central and Northern Regions, it continues to rely heavily on the south for its support.

The economic and social policies of the UDF are not different from those of the AFORD and the MCP. They all believe in free enterprise, but they also advocate government intervention in **health**, **education**, and social services. However, unlike the Malawi Congress Party and its government, Muluzi and the UDF have insisted on respect for the constitution, freedom of association and expression, and general respect for **human rights**. *See also* FOREIGN POLICY.

UNITED FEDERAL PARTY (UFP). *See* NYASALAND CONSITUTIONAL PARTY; POLITICAL PARTIES.

UNITED KINGDOM. *See* GREAT BRITAIN.

UNITED PARTY (UP). Headed by **Bingu wa Mutharika**, the United Party was formed in 1997 and fielded candidates in the June 1999 general **elections**. It failed to win seats in the National Assembly, and its presidential candidate, receiving only 22,073 votes, was defeated. In early 2001 Bingu wa Mutharika disbanded the UP.

UNITED STATES OF AMERICA. Malawi's association with the United States dates to the early 20th century, when **John Chilembwe** studied there and when **John Booth** encouraged American Christian **missions** to set up operations in Malawi. Missions such as the Seventh Day Baptist and the Seventh-Day Adventist played a major role in the life of Malawians. Chilembwe's own **Providence Industrial Mission** (PIM) was greatly assisted by African Americans, including **Landon Cheek** and **Emma DeLany**. Malawi's first president, Dr. **Hastings Banda**, was educated in the United States and was strongly influenced by Americans, especially their anticommunist attitudes. *See also* MALAMULO; PLAINFIELD INDUSTRIAL MISSION.

At independence, relations between the two countries were cordial but suffered a slight setback not long after, when Dr. Banda ejected the Peace Corps from Malawi. The Malawi government was supportive of the American involvement in Vietnam, a policy in line with Dr. Banda's anticommunist leanings. Many Malawians have studied and continue to study at American universities. Dr. Banda visited the United States in 1978, when he was honored at the University of Indiana and the Meharry Medical College, both of which he had attended earlier. In many fields the United States became Malawi's closest ally, and it was a significant aid donor, at times supplanting **Great Britain**. Washington supported projects covering a wide range of areas: **education**, especially through USAID funds targeted at secondary and university scholarships and teacher training programs; **health**; fiscal reform, particularly economic restructuring; and **transportation**, including the rehabilitation of the port of Dar es Salaam. *See also* FOREIGN AID.

Although the post-Banda government has maintained good relations with the United States, the close links between President **Bakili Muluzi**, a Muslim, and Arab countries such as Libya and Sudan have led to fears of Islamic fundamentalist influence in **Malawi**. Muluzi has presented his **foreign policy** as nonaligned, but the United States remains suspicious of it.

UNIVERSITIES' MISSION TO CENTRAL AFRICA (UMCA). The UMCA was formed by the Universities of Cambridge, Oxford, and Durham, and by Trinity College, Dublin, in response to Dr. **David Livingstone**'s address at Cambridge University on December 4, 1856, in which he called on the British to follow up his work in Africa with **missions** and programs aimed at promoting Christianity, commerce, and Western civilization. The first UMCA, High Anglican in nature, led by Bishop **Charles Mackenzie**, left England in October 1860, arriving in the **Shire Valley** in May of the following year and finally establishing a station at **Magomero**, the mission site recommended by Livingstone. This first UMCA mission had problems, and after Mackenzie and other missionaries died, it moved to Chibisa on the Lower Shire. In 1863 Bishop **William Tozer** abandoned the site, moving to Mount Morambala toward the Shire-Zambezi confluence; in 1864 he moved the mission to **Zanzibar**, from which later spread its activities into mainland Tanganyika and back into the **Lake Malawi** region.

UNIVERSITY OF MALAWI. Established in 1964 following recommendations made earlier that year in the Johnston Report, the University of Malawi opened its doors to students in October 1965. Within two years, the university had four constituent institutions: **Chancellor College**, the main campus at Chichiri, **Blantyre**; Soche Hill College, **Limbe**, which had opened in 1963 to train secondary school teachers; the Polytechnic (1965) in Blantyre, the technology and business institute; Bunda College of Agriculture (1967) in **Lilongwe** District; and the Institute of Public Administration, or IPA (Mpemba, Blantyre), which for some time had been primarily a civil service college but expanded to offer degrees in law. In 1974 the IPA and Soche Hill College were absorbed into Chancellor College, which in that year moved to its new location at Chirunga in **Zomba**. The Central University administration offices also moved to a new home in Zomba. Two colleges were added later: in the late 1970s, **Kamuzu College of Nursing** in Lilongwe and Blantyre; in the late 1980s, the College of Medicine in Blantyre. In the mid 1990s the university began to graduate its own medical doctors. Two new institutions that are not directly part of the University of Malawi were established in the early 1980s—the Malawi College of Accountancy, Blantyre, and the Institute of Education, **Domasi**. *See also* EDUCATION; CHANCEL-LOR COLLEGE.

UNYAKYUSA. Country of the **Nyakyusa** north of **Ungonde**, across the **Songwe** in Tanzania. Unyakyusa, whose modern capital is Tukuyu, is one of the major **coffee**- and **rice**-producing areas of Tanzania.

UNYIHA. Land of the **Nyiha**. It is defined as areas north and south of the **Songwe River**, where the Nyiha have always lived. In precolonial times the area north of the Songwe was known as a **cotton**-growing and textile- and ivory-producing region. In colonial times the mountainous parts of the Mbozi sector in southern Tanzania became identified with **coffee** production.

USISYA. Narrow strip of land in northeastern **Nkhata Bay** District. Usisya, the northernmost point that doctor Dr. **David Livingstone** visited during his 1861 expedition, is the home of the **Tumbuka**-speaking people who call themselves waSisya. Their principal food is cassava *nsima* and fish, and their main contacts were their lakeshore neighbors, mostly those in Ruarwe and Mlowe. Until the 1970s the only way to reasonably approach Usisya was by boat. Although the situation has not changed much, there is now a rough, seldom used road that winds down the **Viphya Highlands** to the area.

– V –

VAIL, HAZEN LEROY. Former faculty member of the History Department at **Chancellor College**, **University of Malawi**, and one of the leading historians of Malawi and the neighboring areas. Leroy Vail was born in Boston, Massachusetts. He was educated at Boston College and the University of Wisconsin. From 1968 to 1971, he taught at Chancellor College and carried out pioneering research into ciTumbuka grammar and the precolonial history of the various **Tumbuka**-speaking peoples of northern Malawi, challenging many assumptions that had until then been accepted as given. Vail relocated to the University of Zambia (1973–1978) and, although he extended his interests to **Mozambique** and Zambian history, he continued his study of Malawi history, publishing some of the most important articles on the colonial period. He returned to the **United States** in the late 1970s, holding appointments at several institutions, including the Universities of Virginia and Ohio. In 1984 he joined the History Department at Harvard University and remained there until his death on March 29, 1999. He published widely in linguistics and history, for example, *Colonialism and Capitalism in Mozambique* (with Landeg White); *The Creation of Tribalism in Southern Africa;* and *Power and Praise Poem: Southern African Voices in History* (edited with Landeg White). At the time of his death Vail was working on a dictionary of ciTonga of **Lake Malawi**.

VIPHYA HIGHLANDS. Rising in southern **Mzimba** and stretching northeast toward the lakeshore area of **Rumphi** District. The Viphya Highlands is one of the longest and widest mountain ranges in Malawi. With an elevation of between 4,000 and 7,000 feet, it has a mean annual temperature of 65 degrees Fahrenheit and below, and a rainfall ranging between 59 and 130 inches a year. From the late 1940s the central sections of the Viphya Highlands were designated as a major pine forest and **tung**-development region. Hundreds of acres of trees were planted in the 1950s and 1960s, but by the end of the latter decade the tung project was abandoned. In the 1970s a pulpwood scheme was proposed but eventually discarded and replaced by a low-profile lumber scheme. The city of **Mzuzu** arose out of the original tung project.

VIPHYA PULPWOOD SCHEME. Project to use existing conifer plantations in the **Viphya Highlands** to develop a paper industry in **Malawi**. In the late 1960s, a state corporation, VIPCOR, was created to make this a reality, but by the late 1970s it was becoming clear that the project would be expensive and environmentally disastrous to Malawi. Among other things, manufacturing wastes would have to be deposited in **Lake Malawi**. In the 1980s it was decided that the project would produce plywood and charcoal.

VIPHYA, **MV.** On its third voyage, the MV *Viphya* sank off the **Chiweta** coast of **Lake Malawi** in 1946, constituting Malawi's worst lake accident. Some 194 people died, and only 49 survived. A commission of inquiry into the disaster blamed the structure of the boat, which could not stand the strong eastern *(mwera)* current of the lake; it also attributed blame to the captain.

VIZARA. Located in central **Nkhata Bay**, specifically in the area between the Limpasa *dambo* and the lake, this is the site of the Vizara rubber estate owned by the **African Lakes Corporation**. *See also* RUBBER.

VON WISSMANN, **SS.** German gunship stationed on the eastern (German) side of **Lake Malawi**. Its full name was the SS *Herman Von Wissmann*, after the person responsible for establishing German rule in East Africa. At the beginning of World War I, it was captured by the HMV *Gwendolen* and towed to the British shore of the lake.

VROEMEN, BISHOP EUGENE. First principal of St. Patrick's Secondary School and first bishop of **Chikwawa** diocese. Eugene Vroemen was born in the Netherlands in 1910 and was ordained a Montfort priest in 1937, the year he was also posted to **Nyasaland**. After working mainly in the **Blantyre** vicariate, including founding (in 1951) St. Patrick's Secondary School near **Limbe**, in 1965 Vroemen was appointed bishop of the new diocese of Chikwawa, which he headed until 1979, when he retired to the Netherlands. He died there in 1992.

– W –

WALLACE, ROY W. One of the major **tobacco** planters in colonial Malawi. With **A. Francis Barron** and **Ignaco Conforzi**, he pioneered the system of tenant tobacco farming. Until the interwar period, Wallace had concentrated on his estates in **Thondwe**, but in the 1920s he extended his operations to **Lilongwe**, **Mchinji**, and Dowa Districts, where he depended largely on African tenant farmers.

WALLER, HORACE. Lay missionary with the **Universities' Mission to Central Africa** (UMCA) party led by Bishop **Charles Mackenzie**. Only 27 years old when he left England for Africa, Waller was unwaveringly devoted to the ideals of Dr. **David Livingstone** and therefore to the aims of the project. A very hardworking person, he fought to keep the mission in the **Lake Malawi** area. When he lost, he left the services of the UMCA. Waller was known for his commitment to the orphans and freed slaves at **Magomero** Mission. Determined not to abandon them, he took some of the orphans to Cape Town and left them there. After a short time, he proceeded to England. He was ordained and became rector of Twywell, Northamptonshire, where he died in February 1896.

After returning from Africa, Waller maintained his keen interest in the continent. He gave speeches on Africa, he encouraged Christian **mission** projects to Africa, and he was such a fervent supporter of the **Livingstonia Mission** that the mission's first party, led by Lieutenant **Edward D. Young**, named a mountain on the shores of Lake Malawi after him. He published extensively on the Lake Malawi region, including *Livingstone's Last Journals* (editor, 1874); and the *Title Deeds to Nyasa-land* (1887).

WANDERERS FOOTBALL CLUB. One of Malawi's premier **football** (soccer) clubs. Wanderers have dominated the country's sports scene for nearly 40 years. With their clubhouse on Makata road a few yards from the National stadium, Wanderers have won many national cups and have taken part in numerous regional and continent-wide soccer competitions, including the Africa Cup of Clubs and the CAF Cup Winner. The club's name has changed from time to time, depending on the sponsorship; for most of the 1980s, it was called Limbe Leaf Wanderers because it was endorsed by Limbe Leaf Tobacco Company, and for part of the 1990s it was known as Telecom Wanderers to reflect the financial backers. Many prominent Malawian businessmen, professionals, and politicians are members of Wanderers Club, and the clubhouse is a popular social venue for most of them.

WAUCHOPE, GEORGE WILLIAMS. Teacher, preacher, and the last of the African missionaries from **Lovedale** recruited to work among the M'mbelwa **Ngoni**. George Wauchope, sometimes known as George Williams, came from Bedford, Cape Province, and commenced his services with the **Livingstonia Mission** in December 1883. He was to work at Kaning'ina, at Chinyera, and mostly at **Njuyu**. After **William Koyi** died in 1886, Wauchope became the mission's principal emissary to the Ngoni ruling hierarchy. Wauchope and his supervisor, Dr. **Walter Elmslie**, did not get along well, primarily because of the ease with which the South African mixed with the Ngoni, contrary to Elmslie's insistence that there should be some distance between them. Viewing his work in a wider context, Wauchope did not hesitate to join the Ngoni in their celebrations, including those marking the coming of age. His work among the Ngoni, like that of Koyi and Scottish missionary Charles Stuart, was partly supported by contributions from the Highbury Congregational Church, London, England. Fondly called *matandani* (the loved one) by the Ngoni, Wauchope returned to **South Africa** in 1888 after the mission refused to renew his contract.

WATCHTOWER MOVEMENT. Deriving its inspiration from the Watchtower Bible and Tract Society, also known as the **Jehovah's Witnesses**, the Watchtower Movement, or Kitawala, in **Nyasaland** and the Rhodesias tended to emphasize African aspects of Christianity. It increasingly assumed political characteristics, stressing the

Second Coming of Christ, which would free African peoples from ill-nesses, poverty, death, and European authority. Among the prominent leaders of the movement were **Eliot Kamwana Chirwa** and **Tomo Nyirenda**. Most members of Kitawala became active in the main-stream Jehovah's Witnesses.

WATERSTON, JANE. In 1879 Jane Waterston became one of the first three women to qualify as medical doctors in Great Britain. She then pro-ceeded to join the **Blantyre Mission**, where, besides doing medical work, she became very involved in the social welfare of the new urban Africans, especially the **women**. Waterston also worked at **Cape Maclear**. In the 1930s she went to Cape Town, **South Africa**.

WEBB, SIDNEY. *See* PASSFIELD.

WELENSKY, SIR ROY (ROLAND). Prime minister of the **Federation of Rhodesia and Nyasaland** from 1956 to 1963. Roy Welensky was born in 1907 in Salisbury (Harare), **Southern Rhodesia (Zimbabwe)**, where his Lithuanian father and Afrikaner mother kept a boarding house after emigrating from **South Africa**. At the age of 14, Welensky started working, first as a storekeeper and then as a railway fireman. He also dis-tinguished himself as a boxer, and from 1926 to 1928 he was Rhodesia's champion. He became a locomotive driver and relocated to Broken Hill, **Northern Rhodesia (Zambia)**, where he became a trade union activist and rose to the leadership of the Railway Workers Union. In 1938 he was elected to the Northern Rhodesia Legislative Council, and four years later he and six other council members founded the Labour Party.

Increasingly, Welensky was identified with the amalgamation of the Rhodesias. Later he worked hand in hand with Sir **Godfrey Huggins** to campaign for the reality of the Federation of Rhodesia and Nyasaland and founded the Federal Party, which in 1958 became the **United Fed-eral Party**. Welensky was knighted in 1953, the year Huggins appointed him minister of transport, communications, and posts in the federal gov-ernment. Two years later, he was promoted to the deputy prime minister, and in 1956 he became prime minister of the Federation; he also held the portfolios of External Affairs and Defense. Welensky strongly resisted any attempts to dissolve the Federation, and in the days before the state of emergency in 1959, Welensky assured Sir **Robert Armitage** of his support through the provision of extraterritorial security services, which duly arrived in the following weeks. His commitment to the Federation made him one of Dr. **Hastings Banda**'s bitterest political opponents from the time they met in London in 1945 to the time the Federation was dissolved in 1963. Welensky spent his last 12 years in retirement in England, where he died in 1991.

WHITE FATHERS. Formerly known as Society of Our Lady of Africa. The White Fathers were founded by a Frenchman, Cardinal Charles Lavigerie, in 1867, as a missionary order to work in Africa. Their main training base was in Algiers, Algeria, and from there they were sent to work in different parts of the continent. At the advice of Bishop **Joseph Dupont**, White Fathers opened their first mission station in the **Lake Nyasa** region at **Mponda** in 1889 but soon left for **Bemba** country in **Northern Rhodesia (Zambia)**. They returned to the Malawi area in 1902 and worked mostly in the Central and Northern regions. *See also* MISSIONS.

WIESE, KARL. German adventurer and trader, and one of the creators of the **North Charterland Exploration Company**. Karl Wiese appeared on the **Mozambique** section of Luangwa valley in the 1880s. Married to a Tete slave trader, he, like many Portuguese of the time, had many **Chikunda,** who formed his retinue of security men and commercial assistants. In 1885 he settled in **Mpezeni**'s area, and within five years he was falsely claiming to have signed treaties with Mpezeni, who was known to oppose such agreements. When **Harry Johnston, Alfred Sharpe,** and the British government refused to believe him, he began to publicize the existence of large gold deposits in the region. This attracted the attention of some London businessmen and **Cecil Rhodes**'s **British South Africa Company** (BSAC). Together they formed the North Charterland Exploration Company in 1895 to manage Wiese's claims of concessions from Mpezeni, amounting to 10,000 square miles of Mpezeni's total domain. When he came to realize what had transpired, Mpezeni was disturbed but called for calm. However, his son, **Nsingu**, took action and in 1897 killed two Europeans. The rest, including Wiese, appealed for assistance, which duly came from the **Blantyre**-based Central African Rifles. Nsingu was captured and killed.

WIGAN, WILLIAM. British doctor. Trained at St. Bart's Hospital, University of London, Dr. Wigan arrived at the **Universities' Mission to Central Africa**'s (UMCA) hospital, **Likoma** Island, in 1914 and is credited with improving **health** care services in many parts of rural **Malawi** and **Mozambique**. In 1917 he joined the **King's African Rifles**; upon demobilization two years later his area of medical coverage extended to southern Tanganyika, a region formerly under German authority. Wigan established rural health centers, including those at Linti, **Malindi**, and Milo, Malosa, **Mponda**, and Matope. He retired in 1947 at the age of 70.

WILDLIFE. *See* TOURISM.

WINNEN, ANTON. One of the first Montfort missionaries to arrive in Malawi in 1901. Father Winnen was born in the Netherlands in 1874. Ordained in 1898, he was a professor at Schimmer Seminary in that country before opting to serve in Africa. Considered an intellectual, Winnen was adept at learning new **languages**, an ability that was particularly useful at **Nzama**, his first station in the **Lake Malawi** area. He also excelled at masonry and joinery, skills that proved invaluable in his missionary work. In less than two years, Winnen had mastered enough ci-Chewa to write a collection of New Testament stories for use in local congregations, and in 1906 the books arrived from printers in Salzburg, Austria. In 1907, three years after serving as head of the Nzama mission station, Father Winnen returned to teach at the Sainte Marie seminary in the Netherlands.

WITWATERSRAND NATIVE LABOUR ASSOCIATION (WNLA). Popularly known as WENELA. This organization was formed in 1900 by the South African Chamber of Mines to act as its labor recruiting agency, mainly in the area north of the Limpopo: **Mozambique**, **Southern Rhodesia**, **Northern Rhodesia**, and **Nyasaland** (Malawi). It negotiated with the governments in those colonies on matters concerning **migrant labor** in the South African mines. In time it had a major presence in Malawi with an office in **Lilongwe** and suboffices in main labor catchment districts such as **Chitipa**, **Karonga**, **Mzimba**, **Rumphi**, Dedza, and **Blantyre**. The Chitipa and Karonga stations also drew labor from Tanganyika. In the early 1980s the WNLA changed its name to Temporary Employment Bureau of Africa (TEBA). *See also* MIGRANT LABOR.

WOMEN. Ninety-three percent of Malawi's women live in rural areas outside the four major urban centers—**Blantyre**, **Lilongwe**, **Mzuzu**, and **Zomba**. Rural-based women are more involved in farming than men, and most crops and fieldwork are in the hands of women. On average, women spend as many hours doing farmwork as they do tending to domestic responsibilities such as meal preparation and child care. With the exception of the fishermen in the **Lake Chilwa** area, men in general seem to have more leisure time. Men in polygamous areas certainly have more leisure time vis-à-vis women than men in monogamous regions. It is usually noted that women work largely on subsistence crops and only work with cash crops at harvest time. In fact, nearly 40 percent of the **to-bacco** nursery and planting work is done by women, and the relatively skilled technique of **cotton** spraying is more frequently undertaken by women. As men leave their farms in search of employment in the estate sector and elsewhere, there is an increase in women's responsibility for smallholder farms. As many as 30 percent of the heads of households in rural Malawi are women.

Throughout the postcolonial era, there has been a notable gap between government's acknowledging female farmers on the one hand, and including and absorbing their talents into society on the other. Prevocational, vocational, and technical training programs are promoted essentially for men. Since appointing women as agricultural officers would be an unpopular policy when unemployment exists for men, it is discouraged. The publications of the **Malawi Congress Party** (MCP) government acknowledged the leading role that Malawi women play in **agriculture**, including those whom the government honored as *achikumbi*, or progressive farmers. Extension services were not usually available to women unless either they or their husbands were associated with the MCP. Other government services desired most by women are literacy courses, and whenever and wherever these are offered, women dominate the student ranks. Women want to learn to read for several reasons: to be able to attend home craft classes held throughout the country, to more easily follow agricultural processes, and to write and read letters. In President **Hastings Banda**'s time, basic literacy was a significant route toward position and privilege in the **League of Malawi Women**.

Women earn money usually by selling their own produce, often **maize**, but also beer, beans, chickens, and goats. They spend their meager incomes on items such as salt, paraffin, soap, clothes, school fees, and government **taxes**. In the village and urban markets more vendors are women than men. At these markets women sell foodstuffs, clothes, pottery, fruits, and vegetables.

To help women get involved in family planning, in the early 1980s the Malawi government, at the behest of and with the help of the **World Bank**, introduced the **Child Spacing** Program, which was free to all mothers. The **United Democratic Front** government has created a Ministry of Women, led by a woman, and one of its major responsibilities is the implementation of the National Gender Policy. The latter dictates the methods of executing women's **health** programs, including family planning. The policy also deals with nutrition, general gender issues, economic empowerment, and women's rights under the law. In post-Banda Malawi, there are also many **nongovernmental organizations** with agendas aimed at promoting the empowerment of women. *See also* WOMEN AND EDUCATION.

WOMEN AND EDUCATION. Throughout the colonial period, Western **education** for women lagged far behind that of their male counterparts, largely because parents preferred to spend their resources on boys rather than on girls, since they thought girls should get married when they came of age. In addition, opportunities for young girls and women were limited by the churches, which managed nearly all schools. At the **Overtoun Institute** of the **Livingstonia Mission** only a small percentage of those examined were female: 22 percent in 1898, 14 percent in 1900, and 5 percent in 1935. From 1903 to 1917, academic subjects were dropped for girls and replaced with skills for a subordinate or domestic role: dusting, sweeping, cooking, laundry, sewing, and nursing. African women were rarely among the women teachers recruited by the mission; in 1939 only 12 women were employed out of a total of 1,334 teachers. As a result of Rev. **Donald Fraser**'s influence, women were able to act as congregational advisers, but as late as 1935 they were not admitted to full membership and they were never invited to participate at Presbytery. Although public comments were made about the lack of training facilities for women, there was no interest in effecting a change that would correct this lack of opportunity. Similar situations obtained at the **Henry Henderson Institute** of the **Blantyre Mission** and at other Protestant institutions.

Opportunities for Malawi women were not much better in the **Catholic** sphere, with the exception of the formation of a religious order in the 1920s. Two women, Elizabeth Nyambala and Martha Phiri, were permitted to begin the Little Servants of the Blessed Virgin Mary Order, which was patterned after the Daughters of Wisdom. Novices were initially taught only to read, write, and sew, but in the 1930s they were given an education allowing them to become teachers. As more convents manned by African and foreign nuns opened schools, more girls received basic education; however, things did not improve significantly.

The **Hastings Banda** government campaigned to improve girls' enrollment in schools and opened opportunities to enable them to proceed to secondary and tertiary education. Although the attitude of some parents changed slowly, others responded favorably, especially as it became clear that job opportunities increased. However, in spite of the government encouragement, female participation in the educational system has remained considerably below that of the male. Less than 33 percent of girls reach the primary leaving certificate level, and less than 30 percent of those continue into the secondary school system. The proportion of children, regardless of sex, who attend school is always higher in the urban areas and definitely higher when the mothers are better educated. Although nursing schools have a predominantly female student population, most tertiary institutions reflect the rest of the country in the dominant gender of students. With the exception of the **Kamuzu College of Nursing**, male students outnumber females by more than two to one.

WORLD BANK. *See* FINANCIAL AND ECONOMIC DEVELOPMENTS; FOREIGN AID.

WORLD WARS. *See* ARMY.

– Y –

YANU YANU BUS COMPANY. *See* MAKHUMULA, JAMES LEANARD.

YAO. Inhabitants of **Balaka**, **Mangochi**, **Machinga,** and most of the **Shire Highlands** and parts of the **Salima** lakeshore. The Yao settled in the **Lake Malawi** region between the 1860s and 1880s, their original home being northern **Mozambique**. Their contact with their new home long predated the 19th century in that they had been active in the ivory trade between the Indian Ocean and the Luangwa valley, where their main trading partners were the **Bisa**. They remained interested in the ivory trade even as they moved into southern Malawi permanently, but by that time they had also become interested in the **slave trade**. In the Lake Malawi area, they settled mostly among the **Mang'anja/Nyanja**, many of whom they conquered, establishing numerous polities, including those of **Chikumbu**, **Kapeni**, **Mlumbe**, Mataka, **Jalasi**, **Makanjila**, **Makandanji**, **Mponda**, **Kawinga**, **Kuluunda**, and **Zarafi**. From 1891 to 1895, the Yao and the British colonial administration, led by **Harry Johnston**, were in perpetual conflict, partly because the Yao resisted British rule and partly because the Europeans did not like the Yao involvement in the ivory and slave trade. The **African Lakes Company** (ALC) felt their prospects of dominating the commerce in ivory were impeded by the Yao interest in it; Christian missionaries and the government were greatly disturbed by the Yao slave traders. Some Yao were Muslims, and **Islam** was to become the main religion for many of them. This did not endear them to some Europeans, especially those who wanted to see Christianity prevail in the region.

YIANNAKIS, NICHOLAS. Tobacco grower and commercial fisherman. Nicholas Yiannakis arrived in Malawi in the early 1930s, becoming one of the first Greek citizens to set up business in the British colony. Born on the island of Limnos, Greece, Yiannakis, accompanied by his brothers, Christos and Stavros, first went to Namwera, **Mangochi** (Fort Johnston) District, where they became tobacco growers. They engaged in the **transportation** business briefly before becoming the first large-scale European fishermen. From their base in the area between Mangochi *boma* and **Monkey Bay**, they dominated the fish industry in Malawi, which hitherto had been largely the preserve of Africans. Using sophisticated equipment, they caught between 50 and 770 short tons per year, and they used their own trucks to transport fish to major centers in Malawi as well as to **Southern Rhodesia** (Zimbabwe). In 1950 Nicholas bought out his brothers and continued to be a dominant force in commercial **fishing** until the 1960s.

YOUENS, PETER WILLIAM. Secretary to the prime minister and cabinet and head of the Malawi civil service from 1964 to 1966. Youens joined the Colonial Administrative Service 1939 and served in World War II from 1939 to 1940. From 1942 to 1948 he was in the Sierra Leone District Administration, first as assistant district commissioner (ADC) and later as **district commissioner** (DC). For a brief period he was commissioner and a member of the colony's **Legislative Council** (LEGCO). In 1951 he was transferred to **Nyasaland**, where, starting as assistant secretary, he rose to deputy chief secretary two years later, a position he held until he received another promotion in 1963. Between 1953 and 1961 he was a member of the Nyasaland LEGCO. Youens was secretary of the cabinet during the **Cabinet Crisis** of 1964. He was targeted by Malawian civil servants, who were most unhappy with the recommendations of the **Skinner Report**, itself an issue of major concern to the rebel cabinet ministers. Peter

Youens retired from the civil service in 1966 and returned to England, where he joined the world of business.

YOUNG, EDWARD DANIEL. Commander of the 1867 search expedition that went to the Zambezi-**Lake Malawi** region to look for Dr. **David Livingstone** after reports reached Great Britain that the missionary and traveler had died. Lieutenant Edward Young was also commander of the first **Livingstonia Mission** party in 1875. Young, an Englishman from Lydd, Kent, was divisional officer in the Coast Guard Service at nearby Dungeness when the sponsors of the Livingstonia Mission requested him to lead it. The Lords of Admiralty granted him leave of absence, and he took command of the party, including the *Ilala I*, which he navigated from the mouth of the Zambezi, up the **Shire River**, and finally to Lake Malawi. Young's mission party left London on May 21, 1875, reached Cape Town on June 21, and on October 11 arrived at Chief **Mponda**'s headquarters near the point where the Shire flows out of the lake. A day later they entered the lake and proceeded to **Cape Maclear**, which was to be the first seat of the mission. After a few weeks Young, **Robert Laws**, **Henry Henderson**, and others sailed around the lake, visiting some of the places where Young had stopped in 1867. On November 2, 1876, Young left Cape Maclear for England, leaving charge of the mission to Dr. **James Stewart** and his deputy, Laws. In 1868 Young had published *The Search after Livingstone*; when he returned from Cape Maclear, he published articles in the *Royal Geographical Society Magazine* on his second journey to the Lake Malawi region. He also published *Nyassa: A Journal of Adventure* (1877).

YOUNG, HUBERT WINTHROP. Governor of **Nyasaland** from 1932 to 1934. During his brief tenure as governor, Hubert Young presided over the introduction of the **Native Authority Ordinance of 1933**, which greatly revised the **indirect rule** system in Nyasaland. He also tried to grapple with the question of Africans on private estates, which was partially resolved by his successor through the institution of the **African Trust Land**. From 1934 to 1938 Young was governor of **Northern Rhodesia** (Zambia), and from 1938 to 1942 of Jamaica.

YOUNG, SIR EDWARD HILTON. *See* HILTON YOUNG COMMISSION.

YOUNG, THOMAS CULLEN. Livingstonia missionary, anthropologist, linguist, and historian of Malawi. Cullen Young was born in Glasgow, Scotland, in October 1880. In 1902 he qualified as a chartered accountant and in 1904 was admitted to the membership of the Institute of Accountants and Actuaries. He proceeded to study theology first in Glasgow and after a year at New College, Edinburgh. His father, John Young, was a friend of **Robert Laws** of **Livingstonia Mission** that Thomas Cullen joined in 1904. Young served at the **Overtoun Institution**, **Karonga**, and **Loudon**. He was ordained just before World War I, and on returning to **Nyasaland** he was posted to **Tamanda**. He soon joined the war service as an intelligence agent attached to the Rhodesian forces fighting in Tanganyika. From 1916 to 1919 he was at **Kasungu**, where he met **Hastings Banda**; from 1920 to 1925 at the Overtoun Institution again; and from 1927 to 1931, when he left the services of the Livingstonia Mission, Young was stationed at Loudon for the second time. Upon his arrival in Great Britain in 1931, he joined the Religious Tract Society as deputy secretary and home superintendent. From 1940 to 1946 he was general secretary of the United Society for Christian Literature. Cullen Young died on June 14, 1955.

Young is known for promoting studies in the **languages**, cultures, and history of the Lake Malawi peoples, and he published many articles and books in these fields. Just before he died, the University of Edinburgh awarded him an honorary M.A. degree in recognition of his contributions to African research. His numerous publications include *Notes on the Speech and History of the Tumbuka-Henga Peoples* (1923); *Notes on the Customs and Folklore of the Tumbuka-Kamanga Peoples* (1931); *Notes on the History of the Tumbuka-Kamanga Peoples* (1932); *African Ways and Wisdom* (1937); and *Contemporary Ancestor* (1940). In the late 1930s Cullen Young met Hastings Banda, his former student at Kasungu and now a medical doctor in Great Britain. They became friends and together edited *Our African Ways of Life* (1946). Young also encouraged and helped Malawian writers to publish their manuscripts. He translated **Ntara**'s *Man of Africa* from ciChewa into English (1933) and later assisted in the publication of *The Headman's Enterprise* (1949), also by Ntara. He also edited and oversaw the publication of **Yesaya Chibambo**, *My Ngoni of Nyasaland* (1942).

YOUNG, REV. WILLIAM PAULIN. Teacher, missionary, and principal of the **Overtoun Institution** from 1927 to 1937. William Paulin Young, brother of **Thomas Cullen Young**, joined the **Livingstonia Mission** in 1910, was stationed at **Loudon**, and saw service in Europe during World War I. Upon his return to **Nyasaland** in 1922, he became headmaster of the Overtoun Institution's school. Strongly influenced by the ideas of

Donald Fraser, under whom he had worked at Loudon, Young did not agree with the mission educational policy that Dr. **Robert Laws** had championed at Livingstonia and satellite stations. Laws believed in training Africans in technical skills such as motor mechanics, masonry, and carpentry, but he was also determined to produce an African student who was intellectually developed. To this end, he fought hard, unsuccessfully, to build a college patterned on his own at Aberdeen University, Scotland. Young and Fraser strongly agreed with the recommendations of the **Phelps Stokes Commission**, which emphasized agricultural education and crafts rather than European-based **education**. When Laws was forced to retire in 1927, Young took over headship of the Livingstonia Mission and became principal of the Overtoun Institution. He immediately set out to implement his ideas on education, but by the time he retired in 1937, his policies, compared with those of his predecessor, had made little headway.

YOUTH. Malawi youth have played an exceptionally active role in their nation's development. During Dr. **Hastings Banda**'s rule, the League of Malawi Youth was a major vehicle though which they participated in the political economy of the country. The Youth League was formed in 1958 as a wing of the **Nyasaland African Congress** (NAC) and later the **Malawi Congress Party** (MCP). The party's leadership used the Youth League to recruit new members, to raise funds through membership cards, and to mobilize support for the party. They were the marshals at party rallies and acted as body guards for senior party officials. Even though the league stressed discipline in the organization, the members' youthful enthusiasm often overcame them, leading to overzealousness and unwarranted conduct in their dealings with the public.

In 1963 the **Malawi Young Pioneers** (MYP) evolved out of the Youth League, and its structure was based on models in Ghana and Israel, countries that trained the first group of Malawian instructors. Later the Ministry of Youth and Culture was established to oversee, among other departments, the MYP. This ministry continued to depend on Israeli experts to train Young Pioneers at advanced levels. MYP bases were established in all districts of Malawi. Students not selected to secondary schools went through a 10-month training in leadership, agricultural development, citizenship, and self-help skills. Sessions covered physical education, close order drill, agricultural and community development techniques, the role of the MCP, **health**, and carpentry. Coursework also stressed the party's cornerstones: unity, loyalty, obedience, and discipline.

About one-third of the trainees were **women**. Upon completing their training, some of the graduates, regardless of gender, returned to their villages and helped effect agricultural change. Most joined agricultural settlement schemes or taught in trade schools; others worked with the **police** in teams patrolling neighborhoods. During Youth Week, observed annually throughout the country, both youth and adults completed various self-help development projects such as building houses for teachers, school rooms, bus shelters, and bridges.

An Enterprises Division of the MYP was established for the purpose of bringing revenue to the organization. These commercial activities, called Spearhead Enterprises, soon acquired a cattle ranch in **Ntcheu**, a dairy at Mapanga, a poultry unit at **Nasawa**, a garment factory in **Blantyre**, and 14 farms growing **tobacco**, **maize**, **coffee**, **cotton**, and vegetables throughout the country. Spearhead was financed by a Treasury guarantee, itself fully supported by President Hastings Banda. In 1978 its operations were questioned, and its flimsy finances were exposed; by 1980, it ended in receivership.

A legislative edict of 1965 converted the MYP into an integral part of the Malawi security forces. The police could not arrest a Pioneer without his or her district commander's consultation. The MYP established its own security services, including a division that dealt with foreign countries, especially those hosting Malawian **exiles**. The movement also maintained powerful arms and ammunition independently of the police and the Malawi **army**, making it a force to reckon with. The authority of the movement was reduced in 1980 when **Gwanda Chakuamba**, commander of the MYP for part of the 1960s and throughout the 1970s, lost power and was imprisoned. From that time on, the Pioneers' paramilitary role waned as the command of the Malawi army objected to this elite corps having the same facilities and equipment as theirs. The tensions between the army and the MYP culminated in **Operation Bwezani** of December 1993, which marked the beginning of the end of this wing of the MCP. After the elections of 1994, the MYP organization was disbanded.

– Z –

ZAMBEZI INDUSTRIAL MISSION (ZIM). Joseph Booth's first Christian mission. It was established in 1892 from his **Mitsidi** base just outside the emerging town of **Blantyre**. Its name refers to Booth's vision of the Zambezi area as the center from which his Christian message would spread to the rest of the world. It would be a self-sustaining Baptist mission in which Africans would play a full role. Africans would be trained in **agriculture** and other skills to enable them to be economically independent. Booth's view was that Africans, like all other peoples, had the God-given ability to manage their own affairs, depending on opportunity, and he sought to show this at his mission stations. Within a year, about a million **coffee** bushes were planted at Mitsidi and the nearby **Nyasa Industrial Mission**, also founded by Booth. From Mitsidi, ZIM activities spread to parts of Blantyre and the **Shire Highlands**, including **Thyolo**, where he established the Bible Training College. The mission also extended north through **Zomba** into **Gomani**'s jurisdiction in **Ntcheu**/Dedza, which later constituted one of its most successful areas of operations. The success of the ZIM became a concern to other missionaries, mostly those at **Blantyre Mission** who complained about Booth's form of Christianity, his taking their converts, and his labor policies. Some European employers also criticized ZIM's methods of labor recruitment, which made it a difficult competitor. Booth severed relations with ZIM, but by that time it had established roots in **Nyasaland** and produced leaders such as **John Chilembwe**.

ZAMBIA. Before gaining independence from **Great Britain** in October 1964, Zambia was called **Northern Rhodesia** because in the late 19th and early 20th centuries, a significant part of it fell under the jurisdiction of the **British South Africa Company** owned by **Cecil Rhodes**. Zambia borders with **Tanzania** and Zaire in the north, Angola in the west, Namibia, **Zimbabwe**, and **Mozambique** in the south, and **Malawi** in the east. Zambia and Malawi share ethnic and language groups all along their border: Lambya and **Tumbuka**, and **Chewa**/Nyanja-speaking peoples. Like Malawi, it is landlocked and depends on road and rail to export its goods, mainly refined copper, zinc, and tobacco. It exports mostly to Japan, China, the European Union, and **South Africa**, the last two dominating the country's import trade. Active in inter-African affairs, Zambia has been a major player in the **Organization of African Unity** (OAU), the British Commonwealth, the **Common Market for Eastern and Southern Africa** (COMESA), and the **Southern Africa Development Community** (SADC). From the 1960s to the early 1990s, Zambia was the home in exile for many liberation movements, including the Zimbabwe People's Party (ZAPU), the Southwest Peoples Party (SWAPO) of Namibia, and the African National Congress (ANC) of

South Africa. This generosity exposed Zambia to military attacks from south of the Zambezi. Its inability to use the Mozambican port of **Beira** via Rhodesia (Zimbabwe) greatly contributed to the declining economy of the country in the 1970s.

Zambia was part of the **Federation of Rhodesia and Nyasaland**, and although Dr. **Hastings Banda** is credited with leading the fight against the union, **Kenneth Kaunda** and **Harry Nkumbula** of Zambia also played a decisive role in its dissolution. Kaunda, Zambia's first president (1964–1991), never endorsed Banda's dialogue with South Africa, even though he would concede that Malawi had been an effective mediator in negotiations with the apartheid regime. Although relations between Malawi and Zambia have been strained at times, generally they have been and continue to be warm.

In 1991 Kaunda's United National Independent Party (UNIP) lost to the Movement for Multi-Party Democracy (MMD), a new political organization led by trade unionist Frederick Chiluba, who went on to win for the second time four years later.

ZANSI. The original followers of **Zwangendaba**. They had joined the party in the southeast, in the vicinity of today's Kwazulu-Natal. As Zwangendaba assimilated people during his party's trek, this initial **Ngoni**-speaking group became close advisers of the chief, enjoyed special privileges, and guarded their status with pride.

ZANZIBAR. In 1964 this island off the Tanganyika coast joined with Tanganyika to form **Tanzania**. Zanzibar has a long connection with the **Lake Malawi** area in that many of the **Swahili-Arab** traders, including the **Jumbe** of **Nkhotakota** and **Mlozi bin Kazbadema**, who operated in the latter area claimed strong links with Zanzibar. Most of the ivory and **slaves** from the Lake Malawi area went to the main markets at Zanzibar, and some of the people who live there today trace their history to **Malawi**.

ZARAFI. *See* JALASI.

ZARAKUTI, FRED. One of the freed slaves who constituted the community at the **Universities' Mission to Central Africa** (UMCA) station at **Magomero**. Zarakuti, a **Mang'anja**, was also among those whom Lovell Procter and **Horace Waller** took to Cape Town when **Bishop Tozer** moved the mission out of the **Shire Valley**. In 1876 Zarakuti joined Lieutenant **Edward Young**'s first **Livingstonia Mission** party and with **Albert Namalambe** acted as interpreter and assistant at **Cape Maclear** and

Bandawe. Zarakuti was dismissed from mission service in 1879 for, among other reasons, excessive social life, especially affairs with women. He returned to Cape Town, but two years later he was back in the **Shire Highlands** as an employee of the **African Lakes Company** (ALC).

ZEIL, WILLIAM ROBERT. Originally from Natal, **South Africa**. Zeil was an employee of the **North Charterland Exploration Company** administered from Chief **Mpezeni**'s area in the Luangwa valley. In January 1899 he and five armed assistants, including two members of the company's police force, went to the **Ngoni** country under the M'mbelwa to buy cattle. The Ngoni, already suspicious of a European who came from the recently conquered Mpezeni, their close relative, were unimpressed by Zeil's conduct. They accused him and his employees of deceit, physical violence, and raping their women, and they chased him out of their area. As they departed with many stolen cattle, Zeil's party shot at people, killing two men and wounding an elderly woman. Government police and warriors from Inkosi **Mzukuzuku** tried to pursue the offenders who escaped back into the company's territory.

Upon **Alfred Sharpe**'s appeal to the company's administrator, Zeil was repatriated to **Ekwendeni**, where his case was heard under the judgment of Captain **Francis Pearce** of the **Nyasaland** administration, assisted by two European assessors, Andrew Forbes, a **Bandawe**-based businessman, and **William Murray**, a **Livingstonia** missionary. Charged with nine offenses, Zeil was found guilty of eight, sentenced to imprisonment for six months or a fine of £50, and had to pay £9.10s. to the aggrieved; he was also ordered to return the cattle. When Zeil repeated the crime, he was deported from the area. An immediate result of the Zeil incident was the "Purchase of Cattle from Natives Ordinance," which Sharpe instituted in February 1899 to discourage a repetition of the case. The ordinance determined that cattle buyers had to obtain business permits from a **collector** and had to declare the quantity to be bought, the lowest price to be paid, and the names of traditional rulers from whose areas the business was to be conducted. Finally, cattle traders had to show the collector of the area the cattle and proof of purchase.

ZIMBABWE. With a population of just over 11,000,000 people, Zimbabwe borders with **Zambia** in the north, Botswana in the west and southwest, **South Africa** in the south, and **Mozambique** in the west. From the end of the 19th century to 1965, when the settler government declared unilateral independence from the British, it was called **Southern Rhodesia**. It was named Rhodesia from 1965 to 1980, when the African majority took control and changed the name to Zimbabwe, after the precolonial state. Malawi has had strong links with Zimbabwe dating back to the beginning of the 20th century, when, as Southern Rhodesia, it was a major destination of Malawian labor. Some people went there on their own, others through the **Rhodesia Native Labour Bureau**, also known as Mthandizi. Today, over a million people of Malawian origins live in Zimbabwe. Strong economic relations between the two countries have existed since the early 20th century, and such ties were greatly strengthened during the years of the **Federation of Rhodesia and Nyasaland**, when 39 percent of Malawi's imports came from its neighbor to the west.

When the Ian Smith regime announced its unilateral declaration of independence (UDI) in 1965, the British imposed both diplomatic and economic sanctions. The **Organization of African Unity** (OAU), the British Commonwealth, and the United Nations imposed mandatory sanctions on Rhodesia. Although Malawi complied with most of the 1966 sanctions, it refused to implement the additional list of 1968. While agreeing to reduce Malawi's economic ties with Rhodesia, President **Hastings Banda** pointed out that Malawi would suffer more than the rebellious country from the severance of economic ties. From Banda's point of view, Malawi's economy was too fragile not to maintain a "friendly relationship" with Rhodesia. The Malawi government further argued that sanctions harmed the 95 percent black majority in Rhodesia and encouraged additional hostility in the white ruling minority.

In 1980 Rhodesia became Zimbabwe, with Robert Mugabe of the Zimbabwe African National Union (ZANU) as prime minister; a few years later, his status changed to executive president. Initially relations were strained, but as ZANU took into consideration the assistance Banda gave it during the fight for constitutional changes, relations greatly improved and have remained good. Zimbabwe continues to be one of Malawi's major commercial partners, and the two have a free trade agreement that specifies the terms allowing for exchange of goods without tariffs through the **Common Market for Eastern and Southern Africa** (COMESA). Both countries, being landlocked, have always relied heavily on the **Mozambique** port of **Beira**; both countries were badly affected by the civil war in Mozambique and had to channel their trade through **South Africa**, their other significant trading partner. A founding member of the **Southern Africa Development Community**

(SADC), Zimbabwe is a major player in African affairs; Mugabe has served as chairman of the OAU, and more recently he has been actively involved in attempts to solve the dispute between the government of the Democratic Republic of the Congo and the rebels backed by Rwanda and Uganda.

Since 1980 one of the major problems facing President Mugabe's government has been the shortage of land. Most of the fertile land is owned by white commercial farmers, regarded as essential to the economy of Zimbabwe. Although African small-scale producers constitute the majority of the population of Zimbabwe, there is not sufficient land to distribute to everyone. The problem caused great tension in the period leading to the 2000 elections. Threatened by the rising popularity of Morgan Tsvangirai's labor-connected Movement for Democratic Change, Mugabe announced that he would order that land owned by white farmers be appropriated and given to rural black Zimbabweans. He did not discourage the veterans of the guerrilla war against settler colonialism from organizing takeovers of white-owned farms. Eventually, it was agreed that a more orderly means of redistributing land would be discussed by the various interested parties. Mugabe's Zimbabwe National Union, Patriotic Front (ZANU PF), won the controversial elections, albeit with a reduced majority.

ZOMBA. Capital of **Malawi** from 1891 to 1975. Zomba is also the name of the district of which Zomba is the headquarters. Zomba town (about 55,000 people) is 42 miles north of **Blantyre**, located on the slopes of the mountain of the same name in the **Shire Highlands**. This very fertile region was originally inhabited by the **Mang'anja**, but between 1860 and 1875 it was conquered by the **Yao,** who proceeded to rule it under Chiefs **Mlumbe**, **Malemia**, **Kuntumanji**, and Chikowi. When the first **Blantyre Mission** party of **Henry Henderson** and **Tom Bokwito** stopped in Zomba, very near the spot of the future capital, their host was **Kalimbuka**, a junior of Malemia. Within three years, Zomba became the first major substation of the Blantyre Mission, Kalimbuka and Malemia having granted permission for the missionary presence in the area. **John Buchanan**, one of the mission's agriculturalists, was posted to Zomba. Upon his dismissal in 1880, he remained there and began to grow **coffee** and **sugar** cane along the Mlungusi and Kalimbuka streams, which flow into **Lake Chilwa**.

From 1885 to 1891, Buchanan acted as British vice consul, When Captain A. G. S. Hawes became consul in 1885, he chose Zomba as the site of the colonial administrative center, partly because Buchanan was already there, partly because neither he nor Buchanan had particularly warm relations with the European community in Blantyre, and partly because it placed him in a good position to keep an eye on the **slave trade** routes in the area immediately south of **Lake Malawi**. Soon the Residency, as the official accommodation of the consul was called, was built on the banks of Mlungusi, just upstream from the mission station. Now called the Government Hostel, the Residence lost its position in 1904, when the Government House was built. In 1964 the name of the Government House changed to State House, becoming one of the numerous official residences of President **Hastings Banda**.

Zomba remained the seat of government for Malawi until 1975, when **Lilongwe** became the national capital. Parliament continued to meet in Zomba until after the 1994 general **elections**, when it was decided to turn part of the new State House in Lilongwe into the venue for the National Assembly. Since 1973 Zomba has been a university town, home to **Chancellor College** and the central administrative offices of the **University of Malawi**. The Malawi National Examination Board is also located there, as are the Forestry Research Institute and the **National Archives of Malawi**.

ZOMBA GYMKHANA CLUB. Located in the center of **Zomba** close to the State House, formerly the official Residence of the colonial governors. The Zomba Gymkhana Club was, throughout the colonial period, the center of social and sports life for European residents of the capital. With tennis courts, a billiard room, a nine-hole golf course, a **football** (soccer) field that also served as a cricket ground, a badminton court, a hall that could be turned into a theater, two bars, a lounge, and dining facilities, the club was also the venue for sports competitions between the various European clubs in the colony, mainly those in **Blantyre**, **Limbe**, **Thyolo**, **Mulanje**, **Lilongwe**, and **Mzuzu**. Until Sir **Glyn Jones** became governor in 1960, the membership of the Gymkhana Club was closed to Africans. Jones, however, refused to be its patron, a position always held by governors, as long as race was a factor in its membership. From that time on, Africans were allowed to join, and by the late 1970s they were in a majority.

ZULU GAMA. After the **Ngoni** leader **Zwangendaba** died, one of his councillors *(nduna),* Zulu Gama, led a splinter group to the Songeya region of Southern **Tanzania**, where they later clashed with the Maseko **Ngoni**.

ZWANGENDABA. Leader of one of the most remarkable migrations in modern history. Zwangendaba was a son of Hlatshwayo, a famous general of the House of Elangeni, and founded numerous **Ngoni** states north of the Zambezi. Zwangendaba, head of the semiautonomous Ncwangeni Jele who lived in the vicinity of St. Lucia in northern Kwazulu Natal, became an important *nduna* (headman, councillor) and general of Zwide, the leader of the Ndwandwe Confederacy. After Zwide lost to Shaka, the Zulu chief, at the battle of Mhlathuse in 1818, Zwangendaba and his followers fled the wrath of Shaka and embarked on a 2,000-mile trek that lasted 30 years, conquering, raiding, and assimilating various ethnic groups they encountered. The party first headed to the Delagoa Bay area of **Mozambique** and then turned northwest into modern **Zimbabwe**, where they destroyed the weakening Rozwi state. In 1835 they crossed the Zambezi near Zumbo into the Luangwa valley toward the Senga country, entering modern south **Mzimba**, where, at Mawiri, **Mhlahlo M'mbelwa Jere** was born around 1840. At this point the party struck north toward Ufipa in modern Tanzania; according to Ngoni traditions, scouts had established the existence of a very good stock of red cattle there. Zwangendaba died around 1848, just short of his destination.

Since all of Zwangendaba's prospective heirs were minors, a major succession dispute broke out. **Ntabeni**, Zwangendaba's brother and adviser, assumed the regency of the Jere family. But soon he died too, and his followers, including his son Ngodoyi, left north toward Lake Victoria and were not heard of again. When Mgayi, the second regent, died, a more serious split occurred. Zulu Gama and his followers moved east and settled in the Songea, the border region between the modern states of **Tanzania** and **Mozambique**; **Mpezeni** moved southwest to the **Bemba** country and then southeast to the Luangwa valley, where he settled in the modern **Chipata** region. His brother, **Mpherembe**, who originally joined him, returned to the main group, which, led by the third regent, Nduna **Gwaza Jere**, had reentered the northern Malawi area. There, under the new *inkosi* (king), **M'mbelwa**, they established a major polity covering present-day day **Mzimba** District.

Bibliography

When democracy returned to Malawi in the early 1990s, restrictions on publications, vigorously enforced through the Censorship Act of 1968, were greatly relaxed, which has led to a proliferation of literature on the country. Some of the recent publications cover new fields, others are revisionist, others still try to explain the very period of limitations on freedom of expression.

The main depository of primary sources for Malawi history remains the National Archives in Zomba. For the colonial period, it is essential to further consult the appropriate files in the Public Records Office, London. Depending on the nature of the research project, the Church of Scotland documents in the National Library of Scotland in Edinburgh are likely to prove useful. Other foreign mission headquarters in Europe and North America, including the Vatican Archives in Rome, also hold documents of direct importance to Malawi. The Rhodes House in Oxford, England, and the Society of Malawi offices and library in Limbe contain a variety of sources relevant to Malawi's history. Furthermore, the Malawi Collection in the library of Chancellor College, University of Malawi, Zomba, is a major source of material on Malawi.

A number of major bibliographical collections pertaining to Malawi have been published in the last forty years. The first significant one was *A Bibliography of Malawi* compiled by Edward E. Brown, Carol A. Fisher, and John B. Webster (1965); four years later, John Webster and Paulos Mahome updated it, producing *A Supplement to a Bibliography of Malawi*. The 3,300 unannotated entries in the original publication and those in the 1969 edition are listed according to twenty-four subject classifications, including agriculture, anthropology, education, Christian missions, travel, and zoology. The book reflects the extent of the literature on Malawi in the early 1960s. Although it continues to be useful to researchers today, it has been greatly superseded by more recent, specialized bibliographies, including Ray Jackson, *An Annotated Bibliography of Education in Malawi* (1976), Stan Made et al., *One Hundred Years of ChiChewa Writing, 1875–1975: A Selected Bibliography* (1976); S. Mwiyeriwa, *Vernacular literature of Malawi, 1854–1975* (1976); John W. East, *Reference Works for Malawian Studies: A Select and Annotated List* (1982); and E. J. Mwendera, *A Short History and Annotated Bibliography on Soil and Water Conservation in Malawi* (1989).

Two bibliographical studies are highly recommended. "Malawi: Twenty-Five Years of Independence," by J. Kalley et al. (*Southern Africa Update* 5, no. 1: 1990), is a survey with 745 items listed under twenty-three subject categories, and it is very extensive in its coverage of the literature. More valuable and definitely most comprehensive of them all is Samuel Decalo, comp., *Malawi: Second Edition* (1995).

The book starts with a useful introduction to the history of Malawi, followed by a list of dissertations on subjects directly relevant to Malawi. It has 508 annotated and numbered entries, besides many other items that are added to the main descriptions.

Many books and journal articles, mostly memoirs or travel accounts of missionaries and adventurers, describe Malawi in the nineteenth century. Among them are David Livingstone, *Narrative of an Expedition to the Zambezi and Its Tributaries, 1858–64* (1865); Duff MacDonald, *Africana or the Heart of Heathen Africa*, vols. 1–2 (1882). However, the first notable attempt to present an overview of the Lake Malawi region is Harry Johnston, *British Central Africa* (1897). Relying heavily on the author's own observations and the works of others, the book deals with numerous topics including fauna and flora, ethnic groups and their cultures, and the establishment of British authority in the 1880s and 1890s. A more analytical study of the extension of British rule to this area will be found in, among others, Roland Oliver, *Sir Harry Johnston and the Scramble for Africa* (1958); and A. J. Hannah, *The Beginnings of Nyasaland and North-Eastern Rhodesia* (1959). Both books are based primarily on missionary and official British sources and do not evaluate the African reaction to the foreign intrusion. Readers interested in Malawi, especially in the African response to colonialism, should start with George Shepperson and Thomas Price, *Independent African: John Chilembwe and the Origins, Setting and Significance of the Nyasaland Native Rising of 1915* (1958). Generally considered a classic, the book also delves into relations between Western Christian missionaries and Africans, between the various missionary societies themselves, and between the missionaries and the colonial government. With an abundance of primary sources and the thoroughness of skilled writers, Shepperson and Price explore the background to the events of January and February 1915.

The 1960s marked the beginning of a new approach to writing about Malawi, one that was careful to encompass African perspectives. This necessitated the use of oral evidence and the need to revisit the hitherto ignored literature by local writers. The result was a number of theses, books, and articles, including Robert Rotberg, *The Rise of Nationalism in Malawi and Zambia, 1873–1964* (1964) and the doctoral theses of, among others, B. S. Krishnamurthy (1964), McCracken (1967), Andrew Ross (1968), Roderick Macdonald (1969), Roger Tangri (1970), and Emily Maliwa (1970). The enthusiasm and hope for newly independent African nations tended to influence the new writing in the sense that often authors became less critical in assessing actions of Africans during the colonial period. The 1960s also witnessed the beginnings of serious academic interest in precolonial history which, as the bibliography in John G. Pike's *Malawi: A Political and Economic History* (1969) shows, had hitherto been left to amateur historians. From the 1970s on, doctoral theses, books, and articles, all with useful bibliographies, became part of the increasing literature on Malawi. Typical of them are E. A. Alpers (1975), L. Vail (1972), H. W. Langworthy (1973), K. M. Phiri (1975), M. A. Vaughan (1981), O. J. M. Chipeta (1982), O. J. M. Kalinga (1985), and E. C. Mandala (1991), as well as the numerous publications of Matthew Schoffeleers.

The Early History of Malawi (1972), edited by Bridglal Pachai, contains the work of twenty-four authors and covers events from prehistoric times to the early twentieth century, another example of the emerging historiography of the 1960s. Articles such as those by M. Channock and R. Palmer, however, demonstrate the more balanced approach that was to be a major aspect of historical analysis of Malawi from the 1970s on.

The first notable overview of the political history of Malawi is T. David Williams, *Malawi: Politics of Despair* (1978), which nevertheless reflects the gaps that result from restricted access to the National Archives of Malawi and restraints on oral interviews. It is to be hoped that the gaps will be filled now that freedom of expression has returned to Malawi. Other books in the field of politics were published in the 1970s: Philip Short, *Banda* (1974), which has important sources, some of them not attributed; Carolyn McMaster, *Malawi Foreign Policy and Development* (1974); Kanyama Chiume, *Kwacha: An Autobiography* (1975). In 1992 Guy Mhone edited *Malawi at the Crossroads: The Post-colonial Political Economy,* representing the first major review of Malawi under President Banda. More recently, biographies such as those by Colin A. Baker have added more to the bibliography of the political and administrative history of the Lake Malawi area.

Also in the 1960s and 1970s, studies reevaluating Christian missionary activities, going beyond the earlier works by Roland Oliver (1951) and George Shepperson (1958), were undertaken and, in many cases, published. They include Ian and Jane Linden, *Catholics, Peasants, and Chewa Resistance in Nyasaland, 1889–1939* (1974); and John McCracken, *Politics and Christianity in Malawi, 1875–1940: The Impact of the Livingstonia Mission in the Northern Province* (1977). Howard B. Bicker's "A Missionary Strategy for Evangelism in Central Africa: An Examination of People-Movement Strategy in the Historical Cultural Context of Malawi" (Ph.D. diss., Southwestern Baptist Theological Seminary, 1977); and C. M. Pauw, "Mission and Church in Malawi: The History of the Nkoma Synod of the Church of Central Africa Presbyterian, 1889–1962" (D.Th. diss., University of Stellenbosch, 1980). As the main part of this bibliography demonstrates, many dissertations on Christianity were written in the 1980s and 1990s.

In social sciences, Mary Tew's *Peoples of the Lake Nyasa Region* (1950) constituted a pioneering anthropological and sociological study and was accompanied by a useful bibliography. It was followed by J. C. Mitchell, *The Yao Village* (1956); Margaret Read, *The Ngoni of Nyasaland* (1956); and Jaap van Velsen, *The Politics of Kinship: A Study of Social Manipulation among the Lakeside Tonga of Nyasaland* (1964). Since the 1960s, further advances have been made in this general area, and useful bibliographical sources are found in the works of scholars such as Matthew Schoffeleers, Laurel Birch de Aguilar, Hari Englund, and Deborah Kaspin. Many social scientists have joined health specialists in assessing the effects of AIDS on Malawian societies, and there is a growing body of literature on this virus. Paul Kishindo (1995), Ezekiel Kalipeni (1997), and Wiseman Chirwa (1995, 1997, 1999) provide good starting points. In the economic field, the following organizations regularly issue invaluable reports: the Malawi National Statistical Office, the Reserve Bank of Malawi, the various commercial banks in Malawi, the International Monetary Fund, the World Bank, the United Nations Economic Commission for Africa, the African Development Bank, the Southern Africa Development Community, the Common Market of Eastern and Southern Africa, and various nongovernmental agencies. The *Africa Research Bulletin*, published in Exeter, England, on a monthly basis, is another important source on economic and political issues.

As Steve Chimombo's *A Bibliography of Oral Literature in Malawi, 1860–1986* (1987) shows, progress has equally been made in the literary field, both in vernacular and in English, adding to the earlier works of Aubrey Kachingwe (1966), Legson Kayira (1965, 1967, 1969), Stevenson Kumakanga (1944), Samuel Ntara (1934,

1944), David Rubadiri (1965), and others. In English, the Writers Workshop at Chancellor College has been central to the emergence of a generation of writers that includes Frank Chipasula, Jack Mapanje, Dede Kamkondo, Paul Zeleza, Anthony Nazombe, and James Ngombe, all of whose works have been published by Heinemann and Longman in their African Writers Series, and by the Limbe-based Popular Publications in their Malawian Writers Series. The latter also publishes in ciChewa.

For scientists, Clemence Namponya, *Annotated Bibliography of Agriculture in Malawi, 1930–1980* (1985); and J. H. A. Maida, *National Inventory of Scientific Publications* (1991) are good starting points. As local research institutions and universities attract well-trained scientists, the literature in this field will continue to increase. Books such as Brian Morris's *The Power of Animals: An Ethnography* (1998) contain useful bibliographies that identify some of the areas in which research is being undertaken and published.

Since the reintroduction of freedom of expression, many more books about Malawi have been published dealing with different aspects of the postcolonial era. Serious attempts by authors such as John Lwanda (1994, 1996) and Peter Forster (1994) have been made to reassess Kamuzu Banda as a national leader. However, one of the most exciting developments is the emergence in Malawi of the Kachere Series, under the general editorship of Professors Joseph C. Chakanza and K. R. Ross of the Theology and Religious Studies Department at Chancellor College, University of Malawi. Most of the Kachere Series books deal with religion and politics, and they are a prime example of a successful multidisciplinary approach to studying and understanding societies in nation building. J. C. Chakanza and K. R. Ross, eds., *Religion in Malawi: An Annotated Bibliography* (1998) is a good introduction to the subject.

The following bibliography on Malawi is extensive but not exhaustive. In order to make it easier to find specific subjects, the bibliography has been divided into the following categories:

1. General
   a. General Information and Guides
   b. Demographic Facts and Figures
   c. Travel and Description
   d. General Bibliographies
2. Culture
   a. Arts
   b. Linguistics
   c. Literature
3. Economics
   a. Agriculture
   b. Commerce, Industry, and Labor
   c. Development and Monetary Issues
   d. Transportation and Communications
4. Gender
5. History
   a. Archaeology
   b. Precolonial Period

    c. Colonial Period
    d. Postcolonial Period
    e. Biographies and Memoirs
  6. Politics
    a. Administration, Government, Elections
    b. Constitution, Law, Justice, and Human Rights
  7. Society
    a. Anthropology and Sociology
       i. General
      ii. Rural
      iii. Urban
    b. Education
    c. Religion and Missions
  8. Science
    a. Earth Sciences
    b. Geography, Environment, and Conservation
    c. Health and Medicine
    d. Natural Sciences
  9. Select List of Malawi Periodicals

GENERAL

General Information and Guides

Agnew, S., and M. Stubbs, eds. *Malawi in Maps*. London: University Press, 1972.

Bailey, Bernadine. *Malawi*. New York: Sterling, 1973.

Briggs, Philip. *Guide to Malawi*. Chalfont St. Peter, U.K.: Brandt, 1996.

Carter, Judy. *Malawi: Wildlife, Parks, and Reserves*. London: Macmillan, 1987.

Catholic Secretariat of Malawi. *Catholic Directory of Malawi, 1983–1986*. Lilongwe: Catholic Secretariat of Malawi, 1985.

Crowther, Geoff. *Africa on a Shoestring*. Berkeley: Lonely Planet, 1989.

Cundy, H. M., and K. E. Cundy. *Zomba Mountains: A Walker's Guide*. Blantyre: Malawi Correspondence College, 1975.

Eastwood, F. *Guide to the Mulanje Massif*. Johannesburg: Lorton, 1979.

Garland, Vera, and F. Johnston. *Malawi: Lake of Stars*. Blantyre: Central Africana, 1993.

Harold, Nelson D. *Area Handbook for Malawi*. Washington, D.C.: U.S. Government Printing Office, 1975.

Hertslet, E. *Map of Africa by Treaty*. London: Her Majesty's Stationery Office, 1894.

Howey, Linda S. *A Study of Indigenous and International Non-Governmental Organizations Working in Malawi*. Lilongwe: USAID, 1989.

Hulsbomer, A. *Malawi*. Chalfont St. Peter, U.K.: Brandt, 1991.

Kandoole, B. F., and K. M. Kings. *Twenty-Five Years of Independence in Malawi, 1964–1989*. Blantyre: Dzuka, 1989.

Knight, Ian E. *Malawi: An Outline Guide for Expatriate Contract Employees*. London: Royal Commonwealth Society, 1983.

Lane, Martha S. B. *Malawi*. Chicago: Children's, 1990.

Legum, Colin, ed. *African Contemporary Record: Annual Survey and Documents*. New York: Africana, 1969–1989.

Malawi Development Corporation. *Investing in Malawi*. Blantyre: Malawi Development Corporation, 1989.

Malawi Export Promotion Council. *Malawi Buyer's Guide*. Blantyre: Malawi Export Promotion Council. Published annually.

Malawi Government. *The Malawi Government Directory 1990*. Zomba: Government Printer, 1990.

Malawi Government. Department of Surveys. *The National Atlas of Malawi*. Blantyre: Department of Surveys, 1985.

Malawi Ministry of Information. *Malawi: An Official Handbook*. Blantyre: Ministry of Information. Published annually.

——. *Malawi Yearbook*. Blantyre: Ministry of Information. Published annually.

Martin, Colin. *Maps and Surveys of Malawi*. Cape Town: Balkeme, 1980.

Martine, Maurel. *Visitor's Guide to Malawi*. Edison, N.J.: Hunter, 1990.

Mitchell, J. C. *Map and Gazetteer of Tribes in the Federation*. Salisbury: University College, n.d.

Murray, Stephen. *A Handbook of Nyasaland*. London: Crown Agents, 1922.

National Statistics Office. *Malawi Statistical Yearbook*. Zomba: Government Printer. Published annually.

Niesen, Karen L. and Christine Y. Onanga, *The Republic of Malawi 2000. A Country Guide Series*. AACRAO-AID Project, 1996.

Nyasaland Advisory Committee on Publicity. *Nyasaland Calling: A Travel Guide to the Nyasaland Protectorate*. Salisbury: Rhodesian Printing and Publishing, 1935.

O'Toole, Thomas. *Malawi in Pictures*. Minneapolis: Lerner, 1988.

Rake, Alan. *Traveler's Guide to Central and Southern Africa*. London: IC Publications, 1990.

Randall, Peter. *Guide to Malawi*. Johannesburg: Winchester, 1971.

Read, Frank. *Malawi, Land of Promise: A Comprehensive Survey*. Blantyre: Ramsay Parker Publications, 1967.

Roy, D. B. *The Malawi Collection*. Blantyre: Malawi Institute of Architects, 1984.

Stuart-Mogg, David. *A Guide to Malawi*. Blantyre: Central Africana, 1996.

Tattersall, David. *The Land of the Lake: A Guide to Malawi*. Blantyre: Blantyre Periodicals, 1982.

USAID. *Malawi Entrepreneur's Handbook*. Lilongwe: USAID, 1990.

William Collins & Sons. *Atlas for Malawi*. Limbe: Government Printer, 1968.

Demographic Facts and Figures

Atkins, Guy. "The Nyanja-Speaking Population of Nyasaland and Northern Rhodesia: A Statistical Estimate." *African Studies*, March 9, 1950.

Chinguwo, Rodwell. *Components Variations in Rural-Urban Fertility in Malawi in Studies in African and Asian Demography*. Cairo, 1987.

Chipande, Graham. "The Impact of Demographic Changes on Rural Development in Malawi." In *Population, Food, and Rural Development in Malawi*. Edited by Ronald Lee et al. Oxford: Clarendon, 1988.

Christiansen, Robert. "The Pattern of Internal Migration in Response to Structural Change in the Economy of Malawi, 1966–1977." *Development and Change* 15, no. 1 (1984).

Coleman, Gilroy. "The African population census of Malawi: census 1901–1966." *Society of Malawi Journal* 27, pt. 1 (1974); pt. 2, 2(1974).

Fetter, Bruce. "Colonial Microenvironments and the Mortality of Educated Young Men in Northern Malawi, 1897–1927." *Canadian Journal of African Studies* 23, no. 3 (1989).

———. "Malawi: Everybody's Hinterland." *African Studies Review* 25 (1982).

House, William J., and G. Zimalirana. "Rapid Population Growth and Poverty Generation in Malawi." *Journal of Modern African Studies* 30, no. 1 (1992).

Malawi Government. Department of Surveys. *The National Atlas of Malawi*. Blantyre: Department of Surveys, 1985.

Mlia, Justice, and R. N. Mlia. "Demographic Data Resource for Colonial Malawi." In *Demography from Scanty Evidence: Central Africa in the Colonial Era*. Edited by Bruce Fetter. Boulder: Lynne Rienner, 1990.

National Statistics Office. *Malawi: Population Census 1966: Final Report*. Zomba: Government Printer, 1971.

———. *Malawi Population Census 1977*. Zomba: Government Printer, 1984.

———. *Malawi Family Formation Survey 1984*. Zomba: Government Printer, 1987.

———. *Population and Housing Census 1987: Preliminary Report*. Zomba: Government Printer, 1987.

———. *Malawi Population and Housing Census 1987*. Zomba: Government Printer, 1987.

———. *Malawi Population and Housing Census 1987*. 3 vols. Zomba: Government Printer, 1993.

———. *Malawi Population and Housing Census 1997: A Preliminary Report*. Zomba: Government Printer, 1997.

Segal, Edwin S. "Projections of Internal Migration in Malawi: Implications for Development." *Journal of Modern African Studies* 33, no. 2 (1985).

Travel and Description

Corbett, G. *Report on Tour through the Union of South Africa South Rhodesia and Nyasaland Protectorate*. Port Louis, 1925.

Cotterill, H., ed. *Travels and Researches among the Lakes and Mountains of Eastern and Central Africa*. London: J. Murray, 1878.

Debenham, Frank. *Nyasaland: Land of the Lake*. London: HMSO, 1955.

Drummond, Henry. *Tropical Africa*, London: Hodder & Stoughton, 1988.

———. *Nyasaland: Travel Sketches in Our New Protectorate*. London: Hodder & Stoughton, 1890.

Foskett, Reginald, ed. *The Zambezi Journal and Letter of Dr. John Kirk*. Edinburgh: Oliver & Boyd, 1965.

Gibbons, Alfred. *Exploration and Hunting in Central Africa, 1895–96*. London: Methuen, 1898.

Johnson, William P. *Nyasa: the Great Water*. London: Oxford University Press, 1922.

Lacerda, E. A., and J. Francisco. *The Lands of Cazembe: Lacerda's Journey to Cazembe in 1798*. London: John Murray, 1873.

Livingstone, D. and C. *Narrative of an Expedition to the Zambesi and Its Tributaries*. London: Murray, 1865.

Lyell, Denis. *Nyasaland for the Hunter and Settler*. London: Horace Cox, 1912.

Martelli, George. *Livingstone's River: The Story of the Zambezi Expedition*. London: Chatto & Windus, 1970.

Moir, Jane. *A Lady's Letters from Central Africa*. Glasgow: J. Maclehose, 1891.

Rankin, D. *The Zambesi Basin and Nyasaland*. Edinburgh: Blackwood, 1893.

Shepperson, George. "The Literature of British Central Africa." *Rhodes Livingstone Institute Journal* 22 (1958).

Tabler, E. C., ed. *The Zambezi Papers of Richard Thornton*. London: Chatto & Windus, 1963.

Thompson, J. *To the Central African Lakes and Back*. London: Sampson Low, 1881.

Universities Mission to Central Africa. *Atlas*. London, 1903.

Wallis, J. P., ed. *The Zambezi Expedition of David Livingstone*. London: Chatto & Windus, 1956.

——, ed. *The Zambezi Journals of James Stewart*. London: Chatto & Windus, 1952.

Young, Edward. Nyassa: *A Journal of Adventure Whilst Exploring Nyassa Central Africa*. London: Murray, 1877.

General Bibliographies

Aradoom, Fassil. *University of Malawi Publications: A Guide*. Washington, D.C.: Library of Congress, 1979.

Blackhurst, Hector. *African Bibliography*. Manchester: Manchester University Press, 1985.

Brown, Edward, et al. *A Bibliography of Malawi*. Syracuse: Syracuse University Press, 1965.

Bullwinkle, Davis. *Women in Eastern and Southern Africa: A Bibliography, 1976–1985*. Westport, Conn.: Greenwood, 1989.

Casada, James. *Dr. David Livingstone and Henry Morton Stanley: A Bibliography*. New York: Garland, 1977.

Chakanza, J. C. *An Annotated List of Independent Churches in Malawi, 1900–1981*. Zomba: University of Malawi Department of Religious Studies, 1983.

——. "Provisional Annotated Chronological List of Witch-Finding Movements in Malawi, 1850–1980." *Journal of Religion in Africa* 15, no. 3 (1985).

——. "New Religious Movements in Malawi: A Bibliographical Review." In *Exploring New Religious Movements: Essays in Honour of Harold W. Turner*. Edited by A. F. Walls and W. R. Shenk. Elkhart: Mission Focus Publications, 1990.

Chancellor College Library. *Research in Progress in Malawi and about Malawi*. Zomba: Chancellor College, 1976.

——. *Working List of Publications, 1973–1976*. Zomba: Chancellor College, 1976.

Chimombo, Steve. *A Bibliography of Oral Literature in Malawi, 1860–1896*. Zomba: University of Malawi, 1987.

————. "Creative Writing in Malawi: A Bibliography." *Researches in African Literatures* 18, no. 3 (1987).

Daube, J. M. *Education in Malawi: A Bibliography*. Limbe: University of Malawi, 1970.

Decalo, Samuel. *Malawi*. 2d ed. Oxford: Clio, 1995.

Dickie, J., and A. Rake. *Who's Who in Africa*. London: African Buyer and Trader, 1973.

East, John W. "Reference Works for Malawian Studies: A Select and Annotated List." *MALA Review* 3, no. 1 (1982).

Jackson, Raymond. *An Annotated Bibliography of Education in Malawi*. Zomba: Chancellor College, 1976.

Likagwa, K. K. *Malawian Theses*. Zomba: University of Malawi Library, 1983.

Made, Stanley, et al. *One Hundred Years of Chichewa in Writings, 1875–1975: A Select Bibliography*. Zomba: University of Malawi, 1976.

Maida, J. H. A. *National Inventory of Research Projects and Priority Areas of Research*. Blantyre: Office of the President, Department of Research and Environmental Affairs, 1991.

————. *National Inventory of Scientific Publications*. Blantyre: Office of the President, Department of Research and Environmental Affairs, 1991.

Malawi Department of Information. *Republic of Malawi Parliament Bibliographies*. Blantyre: Department of Information, 1986.

Mgomezulu, Gadi G. Y. "A Comprehensive Author and Subject Index to the Society of Malawi Journal 1948–1978." *Society of Malawi Journal* 32, no. 2 (1981).

Msiska, A. W. C. *Africana Periodicals: A Select Bibliography*. Zomba: Chancellor College. 1975.

————. *An Annotated Bibliography of Theses and Dissertations Held by Chancellor College Library*. Zomba: Chancellor College Library, 1988.

————. *A Bibliography of Plans, Reports, and Surveys of Malawi Held by the University Library*. Zomba: University of Malawi Library, 1973.

Namponya, C. R. *Contributions from Bunda: A List of Papers and Publications from Bunda College of Agriculture*. Lilongwe: Bunda College of Agriculture, 1978.

National Archives of Malawi. *Malawi National Bibliography*. Zomba: National Archives of Malawi, 1968.

National Archives of Rhodesia and Nyasaland. *A Select Bibliography of Recent Publications*. Salisbury: Government Printer, 1960.

National Library Service. *Books about Malawi*. Blantyre: National Library, 1969.

National Research Council. *National Register of Research Publications, 1965–1975*. Lilongwe: National Research Council, 1975.

Nsomba, Vote D. *Refugee Problem in Malawi: Annotated Bibliography on Refugees in Malawi from National Newspapers, October 1986–March 1989*. Zomba: Chancellor College Library, 1989.

Pollak, O., and K. Pollak. *Theses and Dissertations on Southern Africa: An International Bibliography*. Boston: African Studies Center, 1976.

Ross, Kenneth R., ed. *Christianity in Malawi: A Source Book*. Gweru: Mambo, 1996.

Rousseau, Marguerite. *A Bibliography on African Education in the Federation of Rhodesia and Nyasaland*. Salisbury: Cassell, 1958.

Segal, Ronald, ed. *Political Africa: A Who's Who of Personalities and Parties.* New York: Praeger, 1961.

Taylor, Sidney, ed. *The New Africans: A Guide to the Contemporary History of Emergent Africa and Its Leaders.* London: Paul Hamlyn, 1967.

University of Malawi. *An Interim Bibliography of Development in Malawi.* Limbe: Government Printer, 1971.

Walker, Audrey A. *The Rhodesias and Nyasaland: A Guide to Official Publications.* Washington, D.C.: Library of Congress, 1965.

Webster, J., and P. Mohome. *A Supplement to a Bibliography on Malawi.* Syracuse: Syracuse University Press, 1969.

CULTURE

Arts

Blackmum, Barbara, and Matthew Schoffeleers. "Masks of Malawi." *African Arts* 5, no. 4 (1972).

Brandel, Rose. *The Music of Central Africa.* The Hague: Martin, 1961.

Chilivumbo, Alifeyo. "Malawi's Lively Art Form." *Africa Report* 16, no. 7 (1971).

——. "Vimbuza and Mashawe: A Mystic Therapy." *African Music Society Journal* 5 (1972).

Conner, Michael, Michael Wayne. "The Art of the Jere and Maseko Ngoni of Malawi, 1818–1964." Ph.D. diss., Indiana University, 1991.

Faulkner, Laura Birch. "Basketry and Masks of the Chewa." *African Arts* 21, no. 3 (1988).

Friedson, Steven Michael. "The Dancing Prophets of Malawi: Music and Healing among the Tumbuka." Ph.D. diss., University of Washington, 1991.

——. *Dancing Prophets: Musical Experience in Tumbuka Healing.* Chicago: University of Chicago Press, 1996.

Kamlongera, Christopher. "An Example of Syncretic Drama from Malawi's Malipenga." *Research in African Literatures* 17, no. 2 (1986).

——. *Theater for Development in Africa with Case Studies from Malawi and Zambia.* Bonn: Education Science and Documentation Centre, 1989.

——. "Theatre for Development: The Case of Malawi." *Theatre Research International* 8, no. 3 (1982).

Kerr, David. *African Popular Theatre.* London: James Currey, 1995.

——. "The Best of Both Worlds? Colonial Film Policy and Practice in Northern Rhodesia and Nyasaland." *Critical Arts* 7, no. 1 (1993).

——. "Community Theatre and Public Health in Malawi." *Journal of Southern African Studies* 15, no. 3 (1989).

——. "An Experiment in Popular Theatre: the Travelling Theater Tour to Mbalachanda." *Society of Malawi Journal* 35, no. 1 (1982).

——. "Ideology, Resistance, and the Transformation of Performance Traditions in Malawi." *Marang* 10 (1993).

——. "Theatre and Social Issues in Malawi: Performance, Audiences, Aesthetics." *New Theatre Quarterly* 4, no. 4 (1988).

———. "Unmasking the Spirits: Theatre in Malawi." *Drama Review* 31, no. 2 (1987).

Kerr, David, and Mike Nambote. "The Malipenga Mime of Likoma Island." *Critical Arts* 3, no. 1 (1983).

Koma-Koma, W. P. *M'ganda Kapena Malipenga.* Limbe: African Literature Bureau, 1965.

Kubik, Gerhard. "Donald Kachamba's Kwela Music." *Society of Malawi Journal* 32, no. 11 (1979).

———. "Ethnomusicological Research in Southern Parts of Malawi." *Society of Malawi Journal* 21, no. 1 (1968).

———. *The Kachamba Brothers' Band: A Study of Neo-Traditional Music in Malawi.* Institute of African Studies Paper, no. 9. Lusaka: University of Zambia, 1975.

———. *Malawian Music: A Framework for Analysis.* Zomba: University of Malawi Centre for Social Research, 1987.

———. "The Southern Africa Periphery: Banjo Traditions in Zambia and Malawi." Die Welt der Musik: The World of Music 31, no. 1 (1989).

Kumpukwe, Joyce. "S. L. Mbewe: Creator and Producer of Malawi Radio Plays." *Baraza* 1 (1983).

Lindgren, N., and Matthew Schoffeleers. *Rock Art and Nyau Symbolism in Malawi.* Department of Antiquities Publication no. 18. Lilongwe: Malawi Government Department of Antiquities, 1978.

Msosa, James. "How Poetic Are Nyau Songs?" *Kalulu* 2 (1977).

Nurse, George. "Popular Songs and Natural Identity in Malawi." *African Music* 3, no. 3 (1964).

Timpunza-Mvula, Enoch. "Chewa Women's Songs: A Verbal Strategy of Manipulating Social Tensions." *Women's international Forum* 9, no. 3 (1986).

Smyth, Rosaleen. "The Central African Film Unit's Images of Empire, 1948–1963." *Historical Journal of Film, Radio, and Television* 3, no. 2 (1983).

Yoshida, K. "Masks and Secrecy among the Chewa." *African Arts* 26 (1993).

Zanten, Wim van. "Malawian Pago Music from the Viewpoint of Information Theory." *African Music* 6, no. 3 (1983).

Linguistics

Abdallah, Yohanna B. *Chikala cha Wayao,* trans. and edited by G. M. Sanderson as *The Yaos.* London: Cass, 1973.

Atkins, Guy. "The Parts of Speech in Nyanja." *Nyasaland Journal* 3 (January 1950).

———. "Suggestions for an Amended Spelling and Word Division in Nyanja." *Africa* 20 (1950).

Barnes, Bertram Herbert. *Nyanja-English Vocabulary.* London: Society for the Promotion of Christian Knowledge, 1913.

Bresnan, J., and Sam Mchombo. "Topic Pronoun and Agreement in Chichewa." *Language* 63, no. 4 (1987).

ChiChewa Board. *Chichewa Orthography Rules.* Zomba: ChiChewa Board, 1980.

Elmslie, Walter A. *Introductory Grammar of the Tumbuka Language.* Livingstonia: Mission Press, 1923.

——. *Introductory to the Ngoni (Nguni) Language as Spoken in Mombera's Country*. Aberdeen: Fraser, 1891.

——. *Notes on Tumbuka Language, as Spoken in Mombera's Country*. Aberdeen: Fraser, 1891.

——. *Table of Concords and Paradigm of Verbs of the Ngoni Language*. Aberdeen: Fraser, 1891.

Gray, Ernest. "Some Proverbs of the Nyanja People." *African Studies* 3, September 1944.

Henry, George. *A Grammar of Chinyanja Language Spoken in British Central Africa on and the near Shores of Lake Nyasa*. Aberdeen: Fraser, 1891.

Hetherwick, Alexander. *A Dictionary of the Nyanja Language*. London, 1929.

——. *A Handbook of the Yao Language*. London: Society for the Promotion of Christian Knowledge, 1902.

——. *A Practical Manual for the Nyaja Language*. London: Society for the Promotion of Christian Knowledge, 1916.

Hynde, R. S. *Yao Primer and First Reader.* 1890.

——. *Yao-English Primer*. London: Society for the Promotion of Christian Knowledge, 1994.

Kayambazinthu, Edrine. "Patterns of language Uses in Malawi: A Socio-Linguistic Investigation in Domasi and Malindi Areas of Malawi." *Journal of Contemporary African Studies* 8–9, no. 1–2 (1989–1990).

Kishindo, Pascal J. "An Historical Survey of Spontaneous and Planned Development of Chichewa." In *Language Reform: History and Future*. Vol. 5. Edited by I. Fodor and C. Hagege. Hamburg: Helmut Buske, 1990.

——. "The Impact of National Language on Minority Languages: The Case of Malawi." *Journal of Contemporary African Studies* 12, no. 2 (1994).

——. "The Politics of Language in Contemporary Malawi." In *Democratization in Malawi: A Stocktaking*. Edited by Kings M. Phiri and Kenneth R. Ross. Blantyre, Malawi: CLAIM, 1998.

Laws, Robert. *The Table of Concords and Paradigm of Verbs of the Chinyanja Language as Spoken at Lake Nyasa*. Edinburgh: J. Thin, 1885.

Moto, Francis. "Aspects of Tonal Assignment in Chewa." *Journal of Contemporary African Studies* 3, no. 1–2 (1983–1984).

Mtenje, Alfred. "Tone Shift Principles in the Chichewa Verb." *Lingua* 72, no. 2–3 (1987).

Price, Thomas. "Nyanja Linguistic Problems." *Africa* 13, no. 2 (1940).

——. *A Short English-Nyanja Dictionary*. Lusaka: Publication Bureau, 1957.

——. "The Written Representation of Intervocative Glides in Nyanja." *African Studies* 3 (June 1944).

Riddell, Alexander. *A Grammar of Chinyanja Language as Spoken at Lake Nyassa*. Edinburgh: McLaren, 1980.

Russel, Michael. *Nyanja Notebook*. London: Longmans & Northern Rhodesia and Nyasaland Joint Publication Bureau, 1952.

Sanderson, G. Meredith. *A Dictionary of the Yao Language*. Zomba: Government Printer, 1954.

——. "Tumbuka Proverbs." *Nyasaland Journal* 5, no. 1 (1952).

——. *A Yao Grammar*. London: Society for the Promotion of Christian Knowledge, 1922.

Sanderson, G. Meredith, and W. B. Brithrey. *An Introduction to Chinyanja*. Edinburgh: Oliver & Boyd, 1953.

Scott, David Clement Ruffelle. *Cyclopaedic Dictionary of the Mang'anja Language Spoken in British Central Africa*. Edinburgh: Foreign Mission Committee of the Church of Scotland, 1892.

Turner, William Y. *Tumbuka-Tonga English Dictionary*. Blantyre: Hetherwick, 1952.

Vail, Leroy. "Noun Classes in Tumbuka." *African Studies* 30, no. 1 (1971).

Watkins, Mark Hanna, "A Grammar of Chichewa." *Language* 24 supplement, April–June 1937.

Whiteley, W. H. *A Study of Yao Sentences*. London: Oxford University Press, 1966.

Young, Thomas Cullen. *Notes on the Speech of the Tumbuka-Kamanga People of Nyasaland*. Livingstonia: Mission Press, 1923.

Literature

Banda, Tito. *A Bitter Disapproval*. Limbe: Montfort, 1987.

———. *Sekani's Solution*. Limbe: Montfort, 1979.

Chafulumira, E. W. *Kazitape*. 1960.

———. *Kantini*. London: Macmillan, 1961.

———. *Mfumu Watsopano*. Lusaka: Educational Company of Zambia, 1962.

———. *Mkazi Wabwino*. Lusaka: Publications Bureau, 1952.

Chimombo, Steve. *The Basket Girl*. Limbe: Popular Publications, 1991.

———. *A Bibliography of Oral literature in Malawi, 1860–1986*. Zomba: University of Malawi, 1987.

———. "Contemporary Malawian novels." Ed.D. diss., Columbia University, 1980.

———. *Malawian Oral Literature: Aesthetics of Indigenous Arts*. Zomba: University of Malawi Centre for Social Research, 1988.

———. *Napolo Poems*. Zomba: Manchinchi Publishers, 1987.

———. "Oral Literature Research in Malawi: A Survey and Bibliography." *Research in African Literatures* 14, no. 4 (1987).

———. *Python! Python!* Zomba: Wasi Publications, 1992.

———. *The Rainmaker*. Limbe: Popular Publications, 1978.

———. *A Referendum of the Forest Creatures*. Zomba: Wasi Publications, 1993.

Chipasula, Frank M. *O Earth, Wait for Me*. Johannesburg: Ravan, 1987.

Dothi, Janet. *Mawu Otsutsana*. Limbe: Popular Publications, 1988.

Gibbs, James. *Nine Malawian Plays*. Limbe: Montfort, 1976.

———. "Singing in the dark rain: poets, novelists and censorship in Malawi." *Index on Censorship* 17, 2 (1988).

Gondwe, Walije, *Love's Dilemma*. London: Macmillan, 1985.

Gray, Ernest. "Some Proverbs of the Nyanja People." *African Studies* 3 (September 1944).

———. "Some Riddles of the Nyanja People." *Bantu Studies* 13 (1939).

Gumbi, Eunice. *Tili Tonse*. Limbe: Popular Publications.

Holland, M. *Folklore of the Banyanja*. Glasgow: Glasgow University Press, 1950.

Johnson, William Percival. *Chinyanja Proverbs*. Cardiff: Grangetown Printing Works, 1924,

Kachingwe, Aubrey. *No Easy Task*. African Writers Series. London: Heinemann, 1966.

Kalitera, Aubrey. *Daughter, Why Daughter?* Blantyre: Pen Books, 1983.

————. *Mother, Why My Mother?* Blanytre: Pen Books, 1983.

Kamkondo Dede. *The Children of the Lake: Silvo and the Cruel Chief*. Limbe: Popular Publications, 1987.

————. *Silvo and the Cruel Chief*. Limbe Popular Publications, 1989.

Kapuzah, W. *Ungoni Uzimba ndi Miyambi*. Ncheu: Zambezi Mission Press, 1941.

Kayira, Legson. *The Detainee*. London: Heinemann, 1974.

————. *Jingala*. London: Longman, 1969.

————. *The Looming Shadow*. London: Longman, 1968.

Khomani, Peter J. "Substance and Form in Seven Sena Folk Tales." *Kalulu* 1, no. 1 (1976).

Kittermaster, Michael. *District Officer*. London: Constable, 1957.

Kumakanga, Stevenson L. *Nzeru Zakale za ku Nyasaland*. Zomba: Nyasaland Education Department, 1944.

Lipenga, Ken. *Waiting for a Turn*. Limbe: Montfort, 1981.

Loga, John. *Malipilo a Dodolido*. Limbe: Popular Publications, 1979.

Mapanje, Jack. "Censoring the African poem: Personal Reflections." Edited by Kirsten H. Petersson and Per Wastberg. *Criticism and Ideology: Second Annual African Writers Conference*. Uppsala: Scandinavian Institute of African Studies, 1988.

————. *Of Chameleons and Gods*. London: Henemann, 1981.

————. *The Chattering Wagtails of Mikuyu Prison*. London: Heinemann, 1993.

Moto, Francic. *Nzeru Umati Nzako Nzokuuza*, Limbe: Popular Publications, 1987.

Mphande, Lupenga. "Dr Hastings Kamuzu Banda and the Malawian Writers Group: the (un)making of a cultural tradition." *Researches in African Literatures* 27 (1996).

Nazombe, Anthony, J. M. *The Haunting Wind: A New Poetry from Malawi*. Limbe: Dzuka, 1990.

————. "Malawian Poetry of the Transition: Steve Chimombo's 'A Referendum of the Forest Creatures' and Jack Mapanje's 'The Chattering Wagtails of Mikuyu Prison.'" In *Church, Law, and Political Transition in Malawi, 1992–94*. Edited by Matembo S. Nzunda and Kenneth R. Ross. Blantyre: CLAIM, 1995.

Ng'ombe, James L. *King's Pillow and Other Plays*. London: Evans, 1986.

————. *Sugarcane with Salt*. Longman. 1989.

Ntaba, Jolly Max. *Mwana wa Mzako*. Limbe: Popular Publications, 1982.

Ntara, Samuel Y. *Man of Africa*. London: Religious Tract Society, 1934.

Paliani, Richard. *Kuthamagira Kalata*. Limbe: Popular Publications, 1987.

Rattray, Robert S. *Folklore Stories and Songs in Chinyanja*. London: Society for the Promotion of Christian Knowledge, 1907.

Read, Margaret. "Songs of the Ngoni People." *Bantu Studies* 11 (March 1957).

Rubadiri, David. *No Bride Price*. Nairobi: East Africa Publishing House, 1967.

Roscoe, Adrian, and Mpalive-Hangson Msiska. *The Quiet Chameleon: Modern Poetry from Central Africa*. New York: Hans Zell, 1992

Singano, E., and Roscoe Singano. *Tales of Old Malawi*. Limbe: Montfort, 1974.

Werner, Alice. "A 'Hare' Story in African Folklore." *Journal of African Society* 4 (October 1904).

Young, T. Cullen. *African New Writing: Short Stories by Africans*, London, 1947.
———. "Ngoni Stories." *Nada* 5 (1957).
———. "Some Proverbs of the Tumbuka-Kamanga Peoples of the Northern Province of Nyasaland." *Africa* 4 (July 1931).
Zeleza, Paul. *Night of Darkness and other Stories*. Limbe: Montfort, 1976.
Zeleza, Tiyambe. *Smouldering Charcoal*. London: Heinemann, 1992.
Zingani, Willie. *Ndaziona Ine*. Limbe: Popular Publications, 1981.

ECONOMICS

Agriculture

Baker, Colin. "The Development of Agricultural Administration in Malawi." *Quarterly Journal of Administration*, April 1974.
Barber, W. *The Economy of British Central Africa*. Stanford: Stanford University Press, 1961.
Brown, Peter, and Arthur Young. *The Physical Environment of Central Malawi with Special Reference to Soils and Agriculture*. Zomba: Government Printer, 1965.
Carvalho, D., et al. *Mid-term Evaluation of the Agricultural Assistance Programme (ASAP)*. Lilongwe: USAID/Malawi, 1993.
Casson, Joseph. *Agricultural Labor Conditions in Nyasaland*. Etampes, n.d.
Catt, David. *Progress in African Agriculture: An Economic Study in Malawi*. Aberdeen: School of Agriculture, 1969.
Channock, Martin L. "Agricultural Change and Continuity in Malawi." In *The Roots of Rural Poverty in Central and Southern Africa*. Edited by Robin Palmer and N. Parsons. London: Heinemann, 1977.
———. "Notes for an Agriculture History of Malawi." *Rural Africana* 20 (1973).
———. "The Political Economy of Independent Agriculture in Colonial Malawi: The Great War to the Depression." *Journal of Social Science* 1 (1972). Also appeared in *Malawi Journal of Social Science* 1 (1972).
Chipeta, W. "Land Tenure and Problems in Malawi." *Society of Malawi Journal* 24, no. 1 (1971).
Chirwa, W. C. "Fishing Rights, Ecology, and Conservation along Southern Lake Malawi, 1920–1964." *African Affairs* 95 (1996).
Clements, J. *Land Use in Nyasaland*. Oxford: Imperial Forestry Institute, 1937.
Davies, William. *Fifty Years of Progress: An Account of the African Organization of the Imperial Tobacco Company, 1907–1957*. Bristol: Imperial Tobacco Company, 1958.
Dean, Edwin. *The Supply Responses of African Farmer: Theory and Measurement in Malawi*. Amsterdam: North Holland, 1966.
Dequin, Horst. *Agricultural Development in Malawi*. Munich: Weltforum-Verlag, 1969.
Farrington, J. *Farm Surveys in Malawi*. Reading, U.K.: University of Reading Agricultural Department, 1975.
Hadfield, J. *Vegetable Gardening in Central Africa*. Cape Town: Parnell, 1960.
Hadlow, G. G. S. J. "The History of Tea in Nyasaland." *Nyasaland Journal* 15, no. 2 (1962).

Hirschmann, David, and Megan Vaughan. *Women Farmers of Malawi*. Berkeley: University of California Press, 1984.

Kalinga, Owen J. M. "Early Attempts at Aquaculture in Malawi and Implications for Future Projects." *Journal of Asian and African Studies* 27, no. 3–4 (1993).

———. "The Master Farmers' Scheme in Nyasaland, 1950–1962: A Study of a Failed Attempt to Create a 'Yeoman' Class." *African Affairs* 92 (1992).

———. "Rice Production and Marketing in Colonial Malawi in the Inter-War Period." *TransAfrican Journal of History* 19 (1990).

Kauffman, I. H. *A Study of Agricultural Co-operative Societies in Nyasaland*. Washington, D.C.: Agency for International Development, 1963.

Kettlewell, Richard Wildman. *Agricultural Change in Nyasaland*. Stanford University Food Research Institute Paper, 1965.

———. *An Outline of Agrarian Problems and Land Policy in Nyasaland*. Zomba: Government Printer, 1955.

Kydd, Jonathan. "Maize Research in Malawi: Lessons from Failure." *Journal of International Development* 1, no. 1 (1989).

Lavrijsen, J. *Food Supply of Lilongwe, Malawi*. Utrecht: Geographical Institute, 1976.

Lele, Uma. *Structural Adjustment, Agricultural Development, and the Poor: Lessons from the Malawian Experience*. Washington, D.C.: World Bank, 1989.

Liebenow, J. Gus. "Food Self-Sufficiency in Malawi: Are Successes Transferable?" In *Drought and Hunger in Africa: Denying Famine Future*. Edited by Michael H. Glantz. Cambridge: Cambridge University Press, 1987.

Livingstone, I. "Agricultural Development Boards in Malawi." In *Tropical Boards in Tropical Africa*. London: Kegan Paul, 1985.

McCracken, John. "Fishing and the Colonial Economy: The Case of Colonial Malawi." *Journal of African History* 28, no. 3 (1987).

———. "Peasants, Planters, and the Colonial State: The Case of Malawi, 1905–1950." *Journal of East African Research and Development* 12 (1982).

———. "Planters, Peasants, and the Colonial State: The Impact of the Native Tobacco Board in the Central Province of Malawi." *Journal of Southern African Studies* 2, no. 2 (1983).

Malawi National Statistical Office. *A Sample Survey of Agricultural Small Holdings in Southern Region Malawi*. September–November, 1965. Zomba: Government Printer, 1965.

———. *A Small Survey of Agricultural Small Holdings in the Central Region of Malawi*. March–May 1966. Zomba: Government Printer, 1966.

———. *A Small Survey of Agricultural Small Holdings in the Chikwawa District Malawi*. September–November 1965. Zomba: Government Printer, 1966.

Mandala, Elias C. "Commodity Production, Subsistence, and the State in Africa: Peasant Cotton Agriculture in the Lower Tchiri (Shire) Valley of Malawi, 1907–1951." In *Geographic Perspectives in History*. Edited by Eugene D. Genovese and L. Hochberg. London: Basil Blackwell, 1989.

———. "Peasant Cotton Agriculture, Gender, and Intergenerational Relationships: The Lower Tchire (Shire) Valley in Malawi, 1906–1940." *African Studies Review* 25, no. 2–3 (1982).

———. "'We Toiled for the White Man in Our Own Gardens': The Conflict between Cotton and Food in Colonial Malawi." In *Cotton, Colonialism, and Social*

History in Sub-Saharan Africa. Edited by A. Isaacman and R. Roberts. Portsmouth, N.H.: Heinemann, 1995.

———. *Work and Control in a Peasant Economy: A History of the Lower Tchiri Valley in Malawi, 1890–1960.* Madison: University of Wisconsin Press, 1990.

Mann, H. *Report on Tea Cultivation and Its Development in Nyasaland.* London: Crown Agents, 1933.

Maxwell, W. A. "The Shire Valley Project." *Nyasaland Journal* 7, no. 2 (1954).

Mhone, Guy C. Z. "Agriculture and Food Policy in Malawi: A Review." In *The State of Agriculture in Africa.* Edited by Thandika Mkandawire and Nnaceur Bourename. London: CODESRIA, 1987.

———, ed. *Malawi at the Crossroads: The Post-Colonial Political Economy.* Harare: SAPES Books, 1992.

Ministry of Agriculture. *Malawi: Rural Energy Survey.* Lilongwe: Government of Malawi, 1981.

Ministry of Agriculture and Livestock Development. *The Agricultural and Livestock Strategy and Action Plan.* Lilongwe: Government of Malawi, 1995.

Mkandawire, R. M. "Markets, Peasants, and Agrarian Change in Post-Independence Malawi." *Journal of Contemporary African Studies* 4, no. 1–2 (1984–1985).

Morgan, W. B. "The Lower Shire Valley in Nyasaland: A Changing System of African Agriculture." *Geographical Journal* 119 (1953).

Nankumba, J. Sinoya. *A Case Study of Tenancy Arrangements on Private Burley Tobacco Estates in Malawi.* Morrilton, Ark.: Winrock International Institute for Agricultural Development, 1989.

Ng'ong'ola, Clement. "Malawi's Agricultural Economy and the Evolution of Legislation on the Production and Marketing of Peasant Economic Crops." *Journal of Southern African Studies* 12, no. 2 (1986).

Ng'ong'ola, D. H., et al. *The Maize Market in Malawi.* Lilongwe: Agricultural Policy Unit, Bunda College, University of Malawi, 1997.

Ngwira, Naomi Aretha. "The Role of Dimba Land and Small-Scale Irrigation in Smallholder Farmers' Food Security in Malawi: An Application of Safety First Chance–Constrained Target Motad Mathematical Programming." Ph.D. diss., Michigan State University, 1994.

Palmer, Robin. "The Nyasaland Tea Industry in the Era of International Tea Restrictions, 1933–1950." *Journal of African History* 26, no. 2–3 (1985).

———. "White Farmers in Malawi before and after the Depression." *African Affairs* 84, no. 335 (1988).

Payr, Gerhard. *Forderung Traditioneller Kleinbauern in Salima, Malawi.* Munich: Weltforum-Verlag, 1977.

Rangeley, W. H. J. "A Brief History of the Tobacco Industry in Nyasaland, Parts 1–2." *Nyasaland Journal* 10, no. 1–2 (1957).

Sahn, D. E., and J. Aruplpragasam. "Land Tenure, Dualism, and Poverty in Malawi." In *Including the Poor.* Edited by M. Lipton and J. van der Gaag. Washington, D.C.: World Bank, 1993.

Sampson, H. *Existing Conditions of Cotton Cultivation in Nyasaland and Suggestions for Their Improvement.* London, 1922.

Sarborough, Venessa. *Domestic Food Marketing Liberalisation in Malawi: A Preliminary Assessment.* Ashford, U.K.: Wye College Department of Agricultural Economics, 1990.

Scmick, H. *Malawi Tobacco: Annual Report.* MI7001. Washington, D.C.: USDA, 1997.

Spring, Anita. *Using Male Research and Extension Personnel to Women Farmers.* East Lansing: Michigan State University, 1987.

Terry, P. T. "African Agriculture in Nyasaland, 1858–1864." *Nyasaland Journal* 14, no. 2 (1961).

———. "The Rise of the African Cotton Industry in Nyasaland." *Nyasaland Journal* 15, no. 1 (1962).

Tobacco Association of Malawi. "Tobacco Crops Are Not Responsible for Deforestation." News release, 4 March 1996.

Tobin, Richard J., and W. Knausnberger. "Dilemmas of Development: Burley Tobacco, the Environment, and Economic Growth in Malawi." *Journal of Southern African Studies* 24, no. 2 (1998).

UNCTAD. *Economic Role of Tobacco Production and Exports in Countries Depending on Tobacco as a Major Source of Income.* UNCTAD/COM/63, GE.95-51627. Geneva: UNCTAD, 1995.

Urquhart, D. *Report on the Possibilities of Growing Cocoa in the Protectorate of Nyasaland.* Bourneville, 1958.

USAID/Malawi. *Malawi Agricultural Sector Assistance Programme (ASAP) 612–0239, PAAD Amendment.* Lilongwe: USAID/Malawi, 1994.

USAID/Malawi and Ministry of Agriculture and Livestock (MOALD). "Evaluation of the 1991–1992 Smallholder Burley Programme." Lilongwe: MOALD, 1993.

———. *USAID/Malawi Results Review and Request, FY 96.* Lilongwe: USAID/Malawi, 1997.

Vail, Leroy. "Peasants, Migrants, and Plantations: A Study of the Growth of Malawi's Economy." *Journal of Social Science* 11, no. 1 (1984).

———. "The State and the Creation of Malawi's Agricultural Economy." In *Imperialism, Colonialism and Hunger: East and Central Africa.* Edited by R. I. Rotberg. Lexington: D.C. Heath, 1983.

Vaughan, Megan. *The Story of an African Famine: Gender and Famine in Twentieth Century Malawi.* Cambridge: Cambridge University Press, 1987.

Von Rumker, A. *Die Organisation Bauerlicher Betriebe in der Zentralregion Malawis.* Frankfurt, 1972.

Weiss, Eric. "Intranational variations in Key Determinants of Food Security." Ph.D. diss., University of Arizona, 1998.

Wilson, Godfrey. *Land Rights of Individuals among the Nyakyusa.* Lusaka: Rhodes-Livingstone Institute, 1938.

World Bank. *Malawi Agricultural Sector Memorandum: Strategy Options in the 1990s.* Washington, D.C.: World Bank, 1995.

———. "Memorandum to the Executive Directors: Policy on Tobacco." R91-225. Washington, D.C.: World Bank, 1991.

Young, A. *Preliminary Soil Map of Nyasaland.* Zomba: Government Printer, 1960.

Commerce, Industry, and Labor

Baker, Colin. "Depression and Development in Nyasaland, 1929–1939." *Society of Malawi Journal* 6, no. 3 (1972).

Banda, Hastings K. *The Challenge Met.* Zomba: Government Printer, 1976.

Bettison, David. *Cash Wage and Occupational Structure in Blantyre-Limbe.* Lusaka: Rhodes-Livingstone Institute, 1958.

——. *Patterns of Income and Expenditure in Blantyre-Limbe.* Lusaka: Rhodes-Livingstone Institute, 1961.

——. *Poverty in Central Africa.* Lusaka: Rhodes-Livingstone Institute, 1959.

Boeder, Robert Benson. "Malawians Abroad: A History of Labor Migration from Malawi to Its Neighbors, 1890 to the Present." Ph.D. diss., Michigan State University, 1974.

Bolnick, B. R. "Moneylenders and Informal Financial Markets in Malawi." *World Development* 2 (1992).

Broad, Daniel. *Southern and Northern Rhodesia and Nyasaland Economic and Commercial Conditions.* London: His Majesty's Stationery Office, 1950.

Buchanan, John. "Industrial Development in Nyasaland." *Geographical Journal* 3 (1983).

Chilivumbo Alifeyo. "On Labour and Alomwe Immigration." *Rural Africana* 24 (1974).

Chipeta, C., and M. L. C. Mkandawire. "The Informal Financial Sector in Malawi." *African Review of Finance of and Banking* 2 (1992)

Chipeta, M. O. J. "Labour in Colonial Malawi: A Study of the Malawian Working Class, c. 1891–1961." Ph.D. diss., Dalhousie University, Halifax, Nova Scotia, Canada, 1986.

Chirwa, W. C. "Alomwe and Mozambique Immigrant Labor in Colonial Malawi." *International Journal of African Historical Studies* 27 (1994)

——. "Child and Youth Labour on the Nyasaland Plantations, 1890–1953." *Journal of Southern African Studies* 19, no. 4 (1993).

——. "The Malawi Government and the South African Labour Recruiters, 1974–1992." *Journal of Modern African Studies* 34, no. 4 (1996).

——. "'Theba Is Power': Rural Labour, Migrancy, and Fishing in Malawi, 1890s–1985." Ph.D. diss., Queen's University, Kingston, Ontario, Canada, 1992.

Christiansen, Robert, and L. A. Stackhouse. "The Privatization of Agricultural Trading in Malawi." *World Development* 17, no. 5 (1989).

Commercial Data International. *Country Review: Malawi, 1998/1999.* Houston: Commercial Data International, 1998.

Cotterill, Henry. "The Nyassa—with Notes on the Slave Trade and the Prospects of Commerce and Colonization of That Region." *Journal of the Royal Society of Arts* 3 (1878).

Coutts, R. R. The Distribution of Artisinal Fishing Crafts in Lake Malawi and Malombe." *Journal of Social Science* 7 (1978).

Dorien, Ray. *Venturing to the Rhodesia and Nyasaland.* London: Johnson, 1962.

Hooker, James. *The Businessman's Position: Observations on Expatriate Commerce in Malawi.* Hanover American Universities Field Staff, 1971.

Igboagye, A. A. *Informal Sector in Lilongwe: A Survey of Informal Activities in Garages, Metal Fabricating, Tinsmithing, and Woodworking.* Addis Ababa: Jobs and Skills Programme for Africa.

International Institute of Labor Studies [IILS]. *Labor Problems in the Economic and Social Development of Malawi.* Geneva: International Institute of Labor Studies, 1967.

Johnston, H. H. "Commercial Development in Central Africa and Its Beneficial Results on the Slave Traffic." *Journal of the Tyneside Geographical Society O.S.* 3 (1894).

Kydd, J., and R. Christiansen. *Structural Change and Trends in Equity in the Malawian Economy, 1964–1980.* Zomba: Government Printer, 1981.

Lindskog, Per A. "Some Observations on the Market-Place Exchange System of Malawi." *Society of Malawi* 34, no. 1 (1981).

McCracken, John. "Labour in Nyasaland: An Assessment of the 1960 Railway Workers Strike." *Journal of Southern African Studies* 14, no. 2 (1988).

McGarry, Brian. *The Market for Dried Fruits and Vegetables in Malawi, Tanzania, and Zambia.* Harare: McGarry, 1988.

Mhone, Guy C. Z., ed. *Malawi at the Crossroads: The Post-Colonial Economy.* Harare: SAPES Books, 1990.

Mkandawire, C. "Nyasaland Unions in a Turmoil." *Free Labor World*, April 1961.

Munger, Edwin. *Trading with the Devil.* Hanover: American Universities Field Staff, 1969.

Page, Melvin, ed. *Land and Labor in Rural Malawi.* East Lansing: Michigan State University, 1973.

Palmer, Robin. "Working Conditions and Worker Responses on Nyasaland Tea Estates." *Journal of African History* 27, no. 1 (1986).

Perekezani, Doze, and C. Thindwa. *Supply Survey of Rural-Based Products.* Blantyre: Blantyre Malawi Export Promotion Council, 1993.

Power, Joey. "'Individualism Is the Antithesis of Indirect Rule': Co-Operative Development and Indirect Rule in Colonial Malawi." *Journal of Southern African Studies* 18, no. 2 (1992).

Sanderson, F. E. "The Development of Labour Migration from Nyasaland, 1891–1914." *Journal of African History* 2 (1961).

Seltzer, George. "High-Level Manpower in Nyasaland's Development." In *Manpower and Education: Country Studies in Economic Development.* Edited by F. H. Harbison and Charles A. Myers. New York: MacGraw-Hill, 1965.

Sharpe, A. "Trade and Colonization in British Central Africa." *Scottish Geographical Magazine* 17 (1901).

Tyson, John. "The Development of African Capitalism in Malawi: A Working Paper." Chancellor College History Department Seminar Paper no. 10, 1987.

Woods, Tony. "'Bread with Freedom and Peace': Rail Workers in Nyasaland, 1954–1975." *Journal of Southern African Studies* 17, no. 4 (1992).

Wright, F. C. *African Consumers in Nyasaland and Tanganyika.* London: H. M. Stationery Office, 1955.

Development and Monetary Issues

Adam, Christopher, et al. "Malawi." In *Adjusting Privatization: Case Studies from Developing Countries.* London: J. Currey, 1992.

Amer, J. *A Key to Development in Southern Malawi.* Blantyre, 1966.

Barber, William. *The Economy of British Central Africa: A Case Study of Economic Development in a Dualistic Society.* London: Oxford University Press, 1961.

Blake, Wilfred. *Central African Survey: Facts and Figures of Rhodesia and Nyasaland*. London: A. Redman, 1961.

Center of African Studies. *Malawi: an Alternative Pattern of Development*. Edinburgh: University Press, 1984.

Chikhula, Prany L. "The Implementation of Basic Human Needs as a Toool of Economic Development: Some Evidence from Malawi's Sectoral Growth." Ph.D. diss., Howard University, 1983.

Commercial Data International. *Country Review: Malawi, 1998/1999*. Houston, Tex.: Commercial Data International, 1998.

Department of Economic Planning and Development. *Statement of Development Policies, 1987–1996*. Zomba: Government Printer, 1987.

Hardy, Ronald. *The Iron Snake*. London: Collins, 1965.

Harrigan, J. R. "Programme and Aid Conditionality: The Case of the World Bank's Structural Adjustment Loans to Malawi." Ph.D. diss., Manchester University, 1995.

Humphrey, David. *Malawi since 1964*. Zomba: University of Malawi Economics Department, 1974.

International Monetary Fund. *Policy Framework papers-Malawi* "Malawi—Enhanced Structural Adjustment Facility Policy Framework Paper, 1998/99–2000/01." <www.imf/external/np/pfp/Malawi/tables.htm>.

Irvine, A. G. *The Balance of Payments of Rhodesia and Nyasaland, 1945–1954*. London: Oxford University Press, 1959.

Kaluwa, Ben. *The Structural Adjustment Programme in Malawi: A Case of Successful Adjustment?* Harare: SAPES Books, 1992.

Kydd, Jonathan, and A. Hewitt. "Limits to Recovery: Malawi after Six Years of Adjustment." *Development and Change* 17, no. 3 (1986)

———. "Malawi: Making Use of Effective Aid." *IDS Bulletin* 17, no. 2 (1986).

Lee, Margaret. *SADCC: The Political Economy of Development in Southern Africa*. Nashville, Tenn.: Winston-Derek, 1989.

Lele, Uma. "Structural Adjustment, Agricultural Development, and the Poor: Some Lessons from the Malawian Experience." *World Development* 18, no. 9 (1990).

Mhone, Guy C. Z., ed. *Malawi at the Crossroads: The Post-Colonial Economy*. Harare: SAPES Books, 1992

Mlia, J. R. N. "Subnational Planning in Transition: The Case of Malawi." In *Subnational Planning in Southern and Eastern Africa*. Edited by A. H. J. Helmsing and K. H. Wekwete. Aldershot, U.K.: Avebury, 1990.

Morton, Kathryn. *Aid and Dependence: British Aid to Malawi*. London: Croom Helm, 1975.

Mukhoti, Bela. *The IMF and Malawi: A Case Study*. Washington, D.C.: U.S. Department of Agriculture, 1986.

Mwanza, A. M., ed. *Structural Adjustment Programmes in SADC: Experience and Lessons from Malawi, Tanzania, Zambia, and Zimbabwe*. Harare: SAPES Books, 1992.

Pryor, Frederic L. *The Political Economy of Poverty, Equity, and Growth: Malawi and Madagascar*. Washington, D.C.: World Bank, 1990.

Sahn, David, and Jahan van Fausum. "Adjustment without Structural Change: The Case of Malawi." In *Adjusting to Policy Failure in African Economies*. Edited by David Sahn. Ithaca, N.Y.: Cornell University Press, 1990.

Smit, P. *Current Trends of Development in Malawi*. Pretoria: Africa Institute of South Africa, 1968.

Thomas, Simon. "Economic Developments in Malawi since Independence." *Journal of Southern African Studies* 2, no. 1 (1975).

Thompson, C., and H. Woodruff. *Economic Development in Rhodesia and Nyasaland*. London: Dobson, 1954.

Williams, Shirley. *Central Africa: the Economics of Inequity*. London: Fabian Bureau, 1960.

Woodruff, H., and C. Thompson. *Economic Development in Rhodesia and Nyasaland*. London: Dobson, 1954.

World Bank. *Malawi Human Resources and Poverty: Profiles and Priorities for Action*. World Bank Report no. 15437-MAI. Washington, D.C.: World Bank, 1996.

Transportation and Communications

Baker, C. A. "Administration of Posts and Telecommunications, 1891–1874." *Society of Malawi Journal* 29, no. 2 (1976).

——. "Malawi's Early Road System." *Society of Malawi* 24, no. 1 (1971).

——. "The Postal Services in Malawi before 1900." *Society of Malawi Journal* 24, no. 1 (1971)

Crosby, Cynthia A. "A History of the Nyasaland Railways, 1895–1935: A Study in Colonial Economic Development." Ph.D. diss., Syracuse University, 1974.

Capeny, S. H. F. "Railway Schemes in Relation to British Central Africa." *Scottish Geographical Magazine* 17 (1901).

Dann, H. C. *The Romance of the Posts of Rhodesia British Central Africa and Nyasaland: Descriptions of the Early Postal Services*. London: F. Godden, 1940.

Day, John. *Railways of Southern Africa*. London: Black, 1963.

Hammond, Gerald. *Report on the Nyasaland Railways and Proposed Zambesi Bridge*. London: His Majesty's Stationery Office, 1927.

Hill, Mervyn. *Permanent Way*. 2d ed. Nairobi: East Africa Railways and Harbours, 1949.

McKinnon, Murlene. "Commerce, Christianity, and the Gunboats: An Historical Study of Malawi Lake and River Transport." Ph.D. diss., Michigan State University, 1977.

Mhone, Guy C. Z., ed. *Malawi at the Crossroads: The Post-Colonial Economy*. Harare: SAPES Books, 1992.

Nock, Oswald. *Railways of Southern Africa*. London: Black, 1971.

Perry, John. "The Growth of the Transport Network of Malawi." *Society of Malawi Journal* 22, no. 2 (1969).

Rees, J. D. *Nyasaland and the Shire Highlands Railway*. London: British Central Africa Co., 1908.

Talbolt, W. D. Some Notes on the Dhows of Fort Johnston District." *Nyasaland Journal* 15, no. 2 (1962).

Vail, Leroy. "Railway Development and Colonial Underdevelopment: The Nysaland Case." In *The Roots of Rural Poverty in Central and Southern Africa*. Berkeley: University of California Press, 1977.

Williams, S. G. B. "Some Old Steam Ships of Nyasaland." *Nyasaland Journal* 11, no. 1 (1958).

GENDER

Apthorpe, Raymond. "Rhodesia and Nyasaland." In *Women's Role in the Development of Tropical and Subtropical Countries*. Brussels: International Institute of Differing Civilizations, 1959.

Butler, Lorna M. "Bases of Women's Influence in the Rural Malawian Domestic Group." Ph.D. diss., Washington State University, 1976.

Chipande, G. *The Position of Women in Malawi*. Lilongwe: University of Malawi, 1985.

Chipande, G. H. R., and M. M. Mkwezalamba. "Income-Generating Activities and Rural Women in Malawi: A Search for a Viable Strategy." *Journal of Social Sciences* 13 (1986).

Chipande, G. H. R. "Innovation Adoption among Female-Headed Households: The Case of Malawi." *Development and Change* 18, no. 2 (1987).

Clark, Barbara. "The Work Done by Rural Women in Malawi." *Eastern Africa Journal of Rural Development* 8, no. 1–2 (1975).

Davidson, Jean. "Tenacious Women: Clinging to Banja Household Production in the Face of Changing Gender Relations in Malawi." *Journal of Southern African Studies* 19, no. 3 (1993).

Davison, Jean. *Agriculture, Women, and Land*. Boulder: Westview, 1988.

———. "Changing Relations of Production in Southern Malawi's Households: Implications for Involving Women in Development." *Journal of Contemporary African Studies* 11, no. 1 (1992).

Hirschmann, David. *Bureaucracy and Rural Women: Illustrations from Malawi*. East Lansing: Michigan State University, 1984.

———. *Women, Planning, and Policy in Malawi*. New York: Commission for Africa, 1985.

———. *Women's Participation in Malawi's Local Councils and District Development Committees*. East Lansing: Michigan State University, 1985.

Hirschmann, David, and Megan Vaughan. "Food Production and Income Generation in a Matrilineal Society: Rural Women in Zomba, Malawi." *Journal of Southern African Studies* 10, no. 1 (1983).

———. *Women Farmers of Malawi: Food Production in the Zomba District*. Berkeley: University of California Institute of International Studies, 1984.

Ingberg, Lila, et al. "A Comparison of Rural Women's Time-Use and Nutritional Consequences in Two Villages in Malawi." In *Gender Issues in Farming Systems Research and Extension*. Edited by Susan V. Poats. Boulder: Westview, 1988.

International Monetary Fund. "Malawi—Enhanced Structural Adjustment Facility Policy Framework Paper, 1998/99–2000/01." *Policy Framework papers-Malawi* <www.imf/external/np/pfp/Malawi/tables.htm>.

Kaunda, Jonathan Mayuyuka. "Agricultural Credit Policy, Bureaucratic Decision Making, and Subordination of Rural Women in the Development Process: Some

Observations on the Kawinga Project, Malawi." *Journal of Southern African Studies* 16, no. 3 (1990).

Laws, Robert. *Women's Work at Livingstonia*. Paisley, Scotland, 1886.

Mandala, Elias C. "Peasant Cotton Agriculture, Gender, and Interregional Relationships: The Lower Tchire (Shire) Valley of Malawi, 1906–1940." *African Studies Review* 25, no. 2–3 (1982).

———. "Capitalism, Kinship, and Gender in the Lower Tchire (Shire) Valley of Malawi, 1860–1960: An Alternative Theoretical Framework." *African Economic History* 13 (1984).

Mkandawire, R. M, J. J. Asiedu, and B. Mtimuni. *Women and Food Processing in Malawi*. Lilongwe: Bunda College of Agriculture, 1987.

Msukwa, Louis A. H. *A Feasibility Study on Income-Generating Activities for Women in Karonga, Kasungu, and Mangochi Districts: A Final Report*. Zomba: University of Malawi Center for Social Research, 1989.

Ntara, Samuel Y. *Nchowa: Life Story of a Chewa Woman*. London: Longmans, 1949.

Phiri, I. A. "African Women in Religion and Culture: Chewa Women in the Nkhoma Synod of the Church of Central Africa Presbyterian: A Critical Study from Women's Perspective." Ph.D. diss., University of Cape Town, 1992.

———. "The Initiation of Chewa Women of Malawi: A Presbyterian Women's Perspective." *Religion in Malawi* 5 (1995).

———. "Women in Theological Education in Malawi." *Religion in Malawi* 1 (1991).

———. *Women, Presbyterianism, and Patriarchy: Religious Experience of Chewa Women in Central Malawi*. Blantyre: CLAIM, 1997.

Phiri, K. M. "Role of the Christian Community in Development: A Historical Background to the Present Situation in Malawi." *Journal of Social Science* 11, no. 1 (1984).

Spring, Anita. *Agricultural Development in Malawi: A Project for Women in Development*. Boulder: Westview, 1989.

———. "Men and Women Smallholder Participation in Stall-Feeder Livestock Program in Malawi." *Human Organization* 45, no. 2 (1986).

———. "Putting Women in the Development Agenda: Agricultural Development in Malawi." In *Anthropology of Development and Change in East Africa*. Edited by D. W. Bronkesha and P. D. Little. Boulder: Westview, 1988.

———. "Using Male and Extension Research to Target Women Farmers." In *Gender Issues in Farming System Research and Extension*. Edited by Susan V. Poats et al. Boulder: Westview, 1988.

Timpunza Mvula, Enoch. "Chewa women's songs: a verbal strategy of manipulating social tensions." *Women's Studies International Forum* 9, 3 (1986).

———. "The Pounding Song as a Vehicle of Social Consciousness." *Outlook* 1 (1982).

———. "Tumbuka Pounding Songs in the Management of Familial Conflict." In *Cross Rhythms*. Edited by Daniel Avorgbedor and Kwesi Yankah. Bloomington, Ind.: Trickster, 1987.

UNICEF and Government of Malawi. *The Situation of Children and Women in Malawi*. Lilongwe: UNICEF, 1987.

Vaughan, Megan. "Household Units and Historical Process in Southern Malawi." *Review of African Political Economy* 34 (1985).

———. "Which Family? Problems in Reconstruction of the History of the Family as an Economic and Cultural Unit." *Journal of African History* 24, no. 2 (1983).

———. *Women in the Estate Sector of Malawi: The Tea and Tobacco Industries.* Geneva: International Labour Organization, 1986.

World Bank. *Women and Development in Malawi.* Washington, D.C.: World Bank, 1991.

HISTORY

Archaeology

Clark, J. Desmond. "Archaeological Investigations of a Painted Rock Shelter in Central Malawi." *Society of Malawi Journal* 26, no. 1 (1973).

———. "Archaeology in Malawi." *Society of Malawi Journal* 19, no. 2 (1966).

———. "Prehistory in Nyasaland." *Nyasaland Journal* 9, no. 1 (1956).

Clark, J. Desmond, and C. V. Haynes. "An Elephant Butchery Site at Mwanganda's Village, Karonga, Malawi, and Its Relevance for Paleolithic Archaeology." *World Archaeology* 1 (1969).

Cole-King, P. A. *Mwalawolemba on Mikolongwe Hill.* Zomba: Government Printer, 1968.

———. *Kukumba Mbiri Mu Malawi: A Summary of Archaeological Research to 1973.* Zomba: Government Printer, 1973.

Crader, Diana C. *Hunters in Iron Age Malawi: The Zooarchaeology of Chencherere Rockshelter.* Lilongwe: Malawi Ministry of Education and Culture, 1984.

Davidson, S., and P. N. Mosley. "Iron Age in the Upper North Rukuru Basin of Northern Malawi." *Azania* 23 (1988).

Juwayeyi, Yusuf Medadly. "The Later Prehistory of Southern Malawi: A Contribution to the Study of Technology and Economy during the Later Stone Age and Iron Age Periods." Ph.D. diss., University of California, 1981.

Kaufulu, Zefe M., and Nicola Stern. "The First Stone Artifacts to Be Found *in Situ* within the Plio-Pleistocene Chiwondo Beds in Northern Malawi." *Journal of Human Evolution* 16, no. 7–8 (1887).

Mawby, J. E. "Fossil Vertebrates from Northern Malawi." *Quarternaria* 13 (1970).

Meadows, M. E. "Late Quaternary Vegetation History of the Nyika Plateau, Malawi." *Journal of Biogeography* 11, no. 3 (1984).

Mgemezulu, Gadi G. Y. "Archaeology Revisited." *Society of Malawi Journal* 32, no. 2 (1979).

———. "The Origins and Development of Agriculture in Southern Africa: The Place of Malawi." *Journal of Social Science* 8 (1980–1881).

Robinson, K. R. *Iron Age Occupation North and East of the Mulanje Plateau, Malawi.* Lilongwe: Ministry of Education, 1977.

———. *The Iron Age of the Southern Lake Area of the Malawi.* Zomba: Government Printer, 1970.

———. *Iron Age of the Upper and Lower Shire.* Zomba: Government Printer, 1973.

———. "A Preliminary Report on the Archaeology of Ngonde." *Journal of African History* 7, no. 2 (1966).

Sandelowsky, B., and K. Robinson. *Fingira.* Zomba: Government Printer, 1968.

Summers, Rodger, et al. *Prehistoric Rock Art of the Federation of Rhodesia and Nyasaland.* Salisbury: National Publications Trust, 1959.

Werner, W. B., and J. van der Merwe. "Mining for the Lowest Grade Ore: Traditional Iron Production in Northern Malawi." *Geoarchaeology* 2, no. 3 (1987).

Wood, Rodney. "Stone Age Cultures in Nyasaland." *Nyasaland Journal* 4, no. 1 (1951).

Yamane, K., et al. "Lacustrine Environment during Lower Beaufort (Upper Permian) Karoo Deposition in Northern Malawi." *Palaeogeography, Palaeoclimatology, and Palaeogeology* 70, no. 1–3 (1989).

Precolonial Period

Abdallah, Y. B. *The Yaos*. Blantyre: Publishing Bureau, 1952.

Alpers, Edward. *The East African Slave Trade*. Nairobi: East African Publishing House, 1967.

———. *Ivory and Slaves*. Berkeley: University of California Press, 1975.

———. "The Yao in Malawi: The Importance of Research." In *The Early History of Malawi*. Edited by B. Pachai. London: Longman, 1972.

Barnes, Bertram H. *Johnson of Nyasaland*. Westminster, U.K.: UMCA, 1933.

Barnes, John. *Politics in a Changing Society*. Cape Town: Oxford University Press, 1954.

Brown, R. *The Story of Africa and Its Explorers*. 4 vols. London: Cassell, 1892–1895.

Buchanan, John. *The Shire Highlands as Colony and Mission*. London: Blackwood, 1885.

Cairns, H. Alan. *Prelude to Imperialism: British Reactions to Central African Society, 1840–1890*. London: Routledge Kegan Paul, 1965.

Carr, Barbara. *Not for Me the Wilds*. London: Bailey Brothers, 1963.

Chadwick, Owen. *MacKenzie's Grave*. London: Hodder & Stoughton, 1959.

Chafulumira, E. *Mbiri ya Amang'anja*. Zomba: Education Department, 1949.

Chamberlin, D., ed. *Some Letters from Livingstone, 1840–1872*. London: Oxford University Press, 1940.

Chibambo, Y. *My Ngoni of Nyasaland*. London: United Society for Christian Literature, 1942.

Cole-King, P. A. *Cape Maclear*. Zomba: Government Printer, 1968.

———. *The Livingstone Search Expedition, 1867*. Zomba: Government Printer, 1968.

———. *Occasional Papers*. Zomba: Government Printer, 1969.

———. "Transport and Communication in Malawi to 1891, with a Summary to 1918." In *The Early History of Malawi*. Edited by B. Pachai. London: Longman, 1972.

Coupland, Reginald. *Kirk on the Zambesi*. Oxford: Clarendon, 1928.

———. *Livingstone's Last Journey*. London: Collins, 1945.

Fleming, C. J. W. "The Zwangendaba Succession." *Society of Malawi Journal* 25, no. 2 (1972).

Forster, Peter G. "Cullen Young, Yesaya Chibambo, and the Ngoni." *Society of Malawi Journal* 44, no. 1 (1991).

Fotheringham, L. M. *Adventures in Nyasaland: A Two-Year Struggle with the Arab Slave Dealers in Central Africa*. London: Sampson Low, 1891.

Hamilton, R. A. "The Route of Gaspar Bocarro from Tete to Kilwa in 1616." *Nyasaland Journal* 7, no. 2 (1954)

Hetherwick, Alexander. *The Romance of Blantyre*. London: Jones Clark, 1931.

Jhala, Violet, L. "The Yao in the Shire Highlands, 1861–1915: Political Dominance and Reaction to Colonialism." *Journal of Social Science* 9 (1982).

Johnston, Alex. *The Life and Letters of Sir Harry Johnston*. New York: Jonathan Cape & Harrison Smith, 1929.

Johnston, H. H. *British Central Africa: An Attempt to Give Some Account of a Portion of Territories under British Influence North of the Zambezi*. London: Methuen, 1897.

Kalinga, Owen J. M. "The Establishment and Expansion of the Lambya Kingdom of Malawi." *African Studies Review* 21, no. 2 (1978).

———. "Trade, the Kyungus, and the Emergence of the Ngonde Kingdom of Malawi." *International Journal of African Historical Studies* 12, no. 1 (1979).

———. "The Karonga War: Commercial Rivalry and Politics of Survival." *Journal of African History* 21 (1980).

———. "Towards a Better Understanding of Socio-Economic Change in Eighteenth and Nineteenth Century Ungonde." *Cahiers d'Etudes Africaines* 24, no. 1 (1984).

———. "The Balowoka and the Establishment of States West of Lake Malawi." In *State Formation in Eastern Africa*. Edited by A. I. Salim. Nairobi: Heinemann, 1984.

———. *A History of the Ngonde Kingdom of Malawi*. Berlin: Mouton, 1985.

Kirk, John. *Zambesi Journal and Letters, 1858–63*. Edinburgh: Oliver & Boyd, 1965.

Langworthy, Harry, W. "Chewa or Malawi Political Organization in the Precolonial Era." In *The Early History of Malawi*. Edited by B. Pachai. London: Longman, 1972.

———. "Swahili Influence in the Area between Lake Malawi and the Luangwa Valley." *African Historical Studies* 4, no. 3 (1971).

Linden, Ian. "The Maseko Ngoni Ngoni at Domwe, 1870–1904." In *The Early History of Malawi*. Edited by B. Pachai. London: Longman, 1972.

Linden, Ian, and Jane Linden. *Mwali and Luba Origins of the Chewa: Some Tentative Suggestions*. Berkeley: University of California Press, 1974.

Livingstone, W. P. *Laws of Livingstonia*. London: Hodder & Stoughton, 1921.

Lugard, F. *The Rise of Our East African Empire*. Edinburgh: Blackwood, 1893.

McCracken, John. "Religion and Politics in Northern Ngoniland, 1881–1904." In *The Early History of Malawi*. Edited by B. Pachai. London: Longman, 1972.

Macmillan, Hugh W. "The Origins and Development of the African Lakes Company, 1878–1908." Ph.D. diss., University of Edinburgh, 1970.

Mandala, E. C. "The Nature and Substance of Mang'anja and Kololo Traditions: A Preliminary Survey." *Society of Malawi Journal* 31, no. 1 (1978).

Marwick, M. G. "History and Tradition in East Central Africa through the Eyes of the Northern Rhodesia Chewa." *Journal of African History* 4, no. 3 (1963).

Michie, W. D. *Lands and People of Central Africa*. London: Longman, 1981.

Nkonjera, Andrew. "History of the Kamanga Tribe of Lake Nyasa: A Native Account." *Journal of African Society* 10 (1911); 11 (1912).

Ntara, Samuel. *Headman's Enterprise: An Unexpected Page in Central African History*. London: Lutterworth, 1949.

———. *History of the Chewa*. Wiesbaden: Steiner, 1973.

——. *Man of Africa.* London: Religious Tract Society, 1934.

Nurse, George T. *Height and History in Malawi.* Zomba: Government Printer, 1969.

——. "The name 'Akafula.'" *Society of Malawi Journal* 20, no. 2 (1967).

——. "The Ntumbe." *Society of Malawi Journal* 30, no. 2 (1977).

——. "The People of Bororo: A Lexicostatistical Enquiry." In *The Early History of Malawi.* Edited by B. Pachai. London: Longman, 1972.

Nyirenda, Saulos. "History of the Tumbuka Henga People." *Bantu Studies* 5 (1931).

Pachai, B. *The Early History of Malawi.* London: Longman, 1972.

Phiri, Kings M. "Chewa History in Central Malawi and the Use of Oral Tradition." Ph.D. diss., University of Wisconsin, 1975.

——. "Political Change and the Chewa and Yao of the Lake Malawi Region, c. 1750–1900." In *State Formation in Eastern Africa.* Edited by A. I. Salim. Nairobi: Heinemann Educational Books, 1984.

——. "The Pre-Colonial History of Southern Malawi: An Interpretive History." *Journal of Social Science* 8 (1980–1981).

——. "Pre-Colonial States of Central Malawi: Towards a Reconstruction of Their History." *Society of Malawi Journal* 41, no. 1 (1988).

——. "Some Changes in the Matrilineal Family System among the Chewa of Malawi since the Nineteenth Century." *Journal of African History* 24 (1983).

——. "Traditions of Power and Politics in Early Malawi: A Case Study of Kasungu District from about 1750 to 1933." *Society of Malawi Journal* 35, no. 1 (1982).

——. "Yao Intrusion into Southern Malawi, Nyanja Resistance, and Colonial Conquest." *TransAfrican Journal of History* 13 (1984).

Phiri, Kings M., O. J. M. Kalinga, and H. H. K. Bhila. "The Northern Zambezia–Lake Malawi Region." In *General History of Africa.* Vol. 4. Edited by B. A. Ogot. Berkeley: University of California Press, 1992.

Pike, John G. "A Pre-Colonial History of Malawi." *Nyasaland Journal* 35, no. 1 (1965).

Rangeley, W. H. J. "Some Old Chewa Fortresses in Kota Kota." *Nyasaland Journal* 4, no. 1 (1951).

——. "Mtwalo." *Nyasaland Journal* 5, no. 1 (1952).

——. "Mbona: The Rainmaker." *Nyasaland* 4 (1953).

——. "Ancient Iron Workings on the Nyika Plateau." *Nyasaland Journal* 13, no. 1 (1960).

——. "The Amachinga Yao." *Nyasaland Journal* 15, no. 2 (1962).

——. "The Yao." *Nyasaland Journal* 16, no. 1 (1963).

——. "The Earliest Inhabitants of Nyasaland." *Nyasaland Journal* 16, no. 2 (1963).

Rankin, Daniel. *Zambesi Basin and Nyasaland.* Edinburgh: Blackwood, 1893.

Schoffeleers, Matthew. "Father Mariana's 1624 Description of Lake Malawi and the Identity of the Malawi Emperor Muzura." *Society of Malawi Journal* 45, no. 1 (1992).

——. "The Meaning and Use of the Name *Malawi* in Oral Traditions and Pre-colonial Documents." In *The Early History of Malawi.* Edited by B. Pachai. London: Longman, 1972.

——. "Myth and History: A Reply to Christopher Wrigley." *Journal of African History* 29, no. 3 (1988).

——. *River of Blood: The Genesis of a Martyr Cult in Southern Malawi, c. A.D. 1600.* Madison: University of Wisconsin Press, 1992.

——. "Trade Welfare and Social Inequalities in the Lower Shire Valley 1590–1622." *Society of Malawi Journal* 33, no. 2 (1980).

——. "The Zimba and the Lundu State in the Late Sixteenth Century and Early Seventeenth Centuries." *Journal of African History* 28, no. 3 (1987).

Shepperson, George, ed. *David Livingstone and the Rovuma.* Edinburgh: Edinburgh University Press, 1964.

Simmons, Jack. *Livingstone and Africa.* London: English Universities Press, 1955.

Spear, Thomas T. *Zwangendaba's Ngoni, 1821–1890: A Political and Social History of a Migration.* Occasional Paper no. 4. Madison: University of Wisconsin African Studies Program, 1972.

Swann, Alfred. *Fighting the Slave Hunters in Central Africa.* 2d ed. London: Cass, 1969.

Taylor, Don. *Rainbow on the Zambesi.* London: Museum Press, 1952.

Thompson, T. Jack. "The Origins, Migration, and Settlement of the Northern Ngoni." *Society of Malawi Journal* 34, no. 1 (1981).

Vail, Leroy. "The Making of the 'Dead North': A Study of the Ngoni Rule in Northern Malawi, c. 1855–1907." In *Before and after Shaka: Papers in Nguni History.* Edited by J. B. Peires. Grahamstown: Institute of Social and Economic Research, 1981.

——. "Suggestions towards a Reinterpreted Tumbuka History." In *The Early History of Malawi.* Edited by B. Pachai. London: Longman, 1972.

Velsen, Jaap van. "Notes on the History of the Lakeside Tonga of Nyasaland." *African Studies* 8, no. 3 (1959).

Wand, Karl. "The Race to Discover Lake Malawi." *Society of Malawi Journal* 35, no. 1 (1984).

Webster, J. B. "Drought, Migration, and Chronology in the Lake Malawi Littoral." *Transafrican Journal of History* 9, no. 1 (1980).

White, Landeg. *Magomero: A Portrait of an African Village.* Cambridge: Cambridge University Press, 1987.

Wiese, Carl. *Expedition into East-Central Africa, 1888–91.* Norman: University of Oklahoma Press, 1983.

Wilson, Godfrey, *The Constitution of the Ngonde.* Rhodes-Livingstone Paper, 1939.

Wilson, Monica. *Peoples of the Nyasa-Tanganyika Corridor.* Communications from the School of African Studies, University of Cape Town, 1958.

——. "Reflections on the Early History of North Malawi." In *The Early History of Malawi.* Edited by B. Pachai. London: Longman, 1972.

Winterbottom, J. M. *History of the Ngoni and Chewa-Nsenga.* Lusaka: Rhodes-Livingstone Institute, 1936.

Wright, Marcia, and P. Larry. "Swahili Settlements in Northern Zambia and Malawi." *African Historical Studies* 4, no. 3 (1971).

Wrigley, Christopher. "The River-God and Historians: Myth in the Shire Valley and Elsewhere." *Journal of African History* 29, no. 3 (1988).

Young, Edward. *Nyassa: A Journal of Adventures.* London: Murray, 1877.

Young, T. Cullen. "Intertribal-Mixture in North Nyasaland." *Royal Anthropological Institute* 63 (1933).

Young, T. Cullen, ed. *Notes on the History of the Tumbuka-Kamanga Peoples.* Livingstonia: Mission Press, 1932.

Colonial Period

Armitage, Robert. "Nyasaland." In *Rhodesia and East Africa.* Edited by F. S. Joelson. London: East Africa and Rhodesia, 1958.

Arnold, C. W. B. "Slave-Boy to Priest." *Nyasaland Journal* 2, no. 1 (1949).

Axelson, E. "Portugal's Attitude to Nyasaland during the Period of the Partition of Africa." In *The Early History of Malawi.* Edited by B. Pachai. London: Longman, 1972.

Baker, C. A. "Dr Banda's Arrest and Release from Detention, 1959–1960." *Society of Malawi Journal* 49, no. 3 (1996).

———. *Johnston's Administration, 1891–1897.* Zomba: Government Press, 1971.

———. *Seeds of Trouble: Government Policy and Land Rights in Nyasaland, 1946–1964.* London: British Academic Press, 1993.

———. *State of Emergency: Crisis in Central Africa, Nyasaland 1959–1960.* London: I. B. Tauris, 1997.

Banda, H. K., and H. Nkumbula. *Federation in Central Africa.* London, 1951.

Boeder, Robert. *Silent Majority: A History of the Lomwe in Malawi.* Pretoria: African Institute of South Africa, 1984.

Brelsford, W. V., ed. *Handbook to the Federation of Rhodesia and Nyasaland.* London: Cassell, 1960.

Chanock, Martin. "Ambiguities of Malawian Political Tradition." *African Affairs* 74 (1974).

———. *Law, Custom, and Social Order: The Colonial Experience in Malawi and Zambia.* Cambridge: Cambridge University Press, 1985.

Chiume, M. K. *Kwacha: An Autobiography.* Nairobi: East Africa Publishing House, 1975.

———. *Nyasaland Demands Secession and Independence.* Cairo: Middle East Publications, 1959.

———. *Nyasaland Speaks: An Appeal to the British People.* London: Union of Democratic Control Publications, 1960.

Clegg, Edward. *Race and Politics: Partnership in the Federation of Rhodesia and Nyasaland.* London: Oxford University Press, 1960.

Clutton-Brock, Guy. *Dawn in Nyasaland.* London: Hodder & Stoughton, 1959.

Colby, Geoffrey F. T. "Recent Developments in Nyasaland." *African Affairs* 55, no. 22 (1956).

Cole-King, P. A. *Lilongwe: A Historical Study.* Zomba: Government Printer, 1971.

Creech-Jones, Arthur. *African Challenge: The Fallacy of Federation.* London: Africa Bureau, 1952.

Creighton, Thomas R. *Southern Rhodesia and the Central African Federation.* New York: Praeger, 1960.

Dachs, Anthony J. "Politics of Collaboration: Imperialism in Practice." In *The Early History of Malawi.* Edited by B. Pachai. London: Longman, 1972.

Debenham, Frank. *Nyasaland: The Land of the Lake.* London: Her Majesty's Stationery Office, 1956.

Duff, Hector. *Nyasaland under the Foreign Office.* London: Bell, 1903.

Dunn, Cyril. *Central African Witness: Observations of a Correspondent, 1954–58.* London: Gollancz, 1959.

Fabian Colonial Bureau. *Four Colonial Questions: How Should Britain Act?* London: Fabian, 1944.

Duff, H. *Nyasaland under the Foreign Office*. London: George Bell, 1903.

Dunn, Cyril. *Central African Witness*. London: Gollancz, 1959.

Ferris, N. S. *Know Your Rhodesia and Know Your Nyasaland: 300 Selections from the Rhodesian Herald*. Vol. 1. Salisbury: Rhodesia Printing and Publishing Company, 1956.

Franck, Thomas. *Race and Nationalism: The Struggle for Power in Rhodesia-Nyasaland*. New York: Fordham University Press, 1960.

Franklin, H. *Unholy Wedlock: The Failure of the Central African Federation*. London: Allen & Unwin, 1963.

Fraser, Donald. *The Future of Africa*. London: Young People's Missionary Movement, 1911.

Gale, William. *Deserve to be Great: The Story of Rhodesia and Nyasaland*. Bulawayo: Stuart Manning, 1960.

Gann, Lewis. *The Birth of a Plural Society*. Manchester: Manchester University Press, 1958.

Gann, Lewis, and M. Gelfand. *Huggins of Rhodesia: The Man and His Country*. London: London University Press, 1964.

Garland, Vera, ed. *Lady of the Lake: The Story of Lake Malawi's M.V. Chauncy Maples*. Blantyre: Central Africana, 1991. This is a reprint of A. E. M. Anderson-Morshead, *The Building of the Chauncy Maples* (1903). In this volume Garland completes the story of the *Chauncy Maples* from 1902 to 1990.

Gibbs, Peter. *Avalanche in Central Africa*. London: Muller, 1961.

Gray, Allen. *Rhodesia and Nyasaland Today*. London: South Africa, 1962.

Gray, Richard. *The Two Nations: Aspects of the Development of Race Relations in the Rhodesias and Nyasaland*. London: Oxford University Press, 1960.

Griswold, Robert. *The British Policy of Partnership in the Federation of Rhodesia and Nyasaland*. Ann Arbor: University of Michigan Microfilms, 1959.

Hanna, Alexander. *The Beginnings of Nyasaland and North-Eastern Rhodesia, 1859–1895*. Oxford: Clarendon, 1956.

———. *The Story of the Rhodesias and Nyasaland*. London: Faber & Faber, 1960.

Hazlewood, Arthur, and P. Henderson. *Nyasaland: The Economics of Federation*. Oxford: Basil Blackwell, 1960.

Irons, Evelyn. *The Federation of Rhodesia and Nyasaland*. New York: Doubleday, 1960.

Joelson, F. S. *Eastern Africa Today*. London: East Africa, 1928.

———. *Eastern Africa Today and Tomorrow*. London: East Africa, 1934.

Johnston, A. *The Life and Letters of Sir Harry Johnston*. London: Jonathan Cape, 1929.

Jones, Griffith. *Britain and Nyasaland: Study of the Political Development of Nyasaland under British Control*. London: Allen & Unwin, 1964.

Kalinga, Owen J. M. "The British and the Kyungus: A Study of the Changing Status of the Ngonde Rulers during the Period 1891–1933." *African Studies* 38, no. 2 (1979).

———. "Resistance, Politics of Protest, and Mass Nationalism in Colonial Malawi, 1950–1960: A Reconsideration." *Cahiers d'Etudes Africaines* 143, no. 36 (1996).

Keatley, Patrick. *The Politics of Partnership: The Federation of Rhodesia and Nyasaland*. Harmondsworth, U.K.: Penguin, 1963.

Krishnamurthy, B. S. "Economic Policy: Land and Labour in Nyasaland, 1890–1914." In *The Early History of Malawi*. Edited by B. Pachai. London: Longman, 1972.

———. "Land and Labour in Nysaland, 1891–14." Ph.D. diss., University of London, 1964.

Lamba, Isaac C. "Missionaries and Ethnography in Malawi: A Study of the Maravi and Yao to 1920." *Society of Malawi* 38, no. 1 (1985).

———. "Moulding the Ideal Colonial Subject: The Scouting Movement in Colonial Malawi up to 1961." *TransAfrican Journal of History* 14 (1985).

———. "The Scramble for Malawi: A Case Study in Humanitarian Imperialism." *Malawi Journal of Social Science* 6 (1977).

Leys, Colin, and R. C. Pratt, eds. *A New Deal in Central Africa*. London: Heinemann, 1960.

Liebenow, J. Gus, and R. I. Rotberg. "Federalism in Rhodesia and Nyasaland." In *Federalism in the Commonwealth: A Bibliographical Commentary*. Edited by W. S. Livingstone. London: Cassell, 1963.

Linden, Ian. "The Maseko Ngoni Ngoni at Domwe, 1870–1904." In *The Early History of Malawi*. Edited by B. Pachai. London: Longman, 1972.

Lloyd-Jones, W. K. A. R.; *Being an Unofficial Account of the Origin and Activities of the King's African Rifles*. London, 1926.

McCracken, John. "British Central Africa." In *Cambridge History of Africa*. Vol. 7. Edited by A. D. Roberts. Cambridge: Cambridge University Press, 1986.

———. "Democracy and Nationalism in Historical Perspective: The Case of Malawi." *African Affairs* 97, no. 387 (1998).

———. "Economics an Ethnicity: the Italian Community in Malawi." *Journal of African History* 32, no. 2 (1991).

———. "'Marginal Men': The Colonial Experience in Malawi." *Journal of Southern African Studies* 15, no. 4 (1989).

———. *Politics and Christianity in Malawi, 1875–1940: The Impact of the Livingstonia Mission in the Northern Province*. Cambridge: Cambridge University Press, 1977.

———. "Religion and Politics in Northern Ngoniland, 1881–1904." In *The Early History of Malawi*. Edited by B. Pachai. London: Longman, 1972.

———. "Underdevelopment in Malawi: The Missionary Contribution." *African Affairs* 76, no. 303 (1977).

Macmillan, Hugh W. "The Origins and Development of the African Lakes Company: 1878–1908." Ph.D. diss., University of Edinburgh, 1970.

Mair, Lucy. *The Nyasaland Elections of 1961*. London: Institute of Commonwealth Studies, 1962.

Mandala, Elias C. "Capitalism, Kinship, and Gender in the Lower Tchire (Shire) Valley in Malawi, 1860–1960: An Alternative Theoretical Framework." *African Economic History* 13 (1984).

———. *Work and Control in a Peasant Economy: A History of the Lower Tchiri Valley in Malawi, 1890–1960*. Madison: University of Wisconsin Press, 1990.

Marlow, Cyril. *History of Malawi Police Force*. Zomba: Government Printer, 1971.

Mason, Philip. *The Birth of a Dilemma*. London: Oxford University Press, 1958.

———. *Year of Decision: Rhodesia and Nyasaland in 1960*. London: Oxford University Press, 1960.

Maugham, R. C. *Nyasaland in the Nineties*. London: L. Williams, 1935.

———. *Zambezia*. London: J. Murray, 1910.

Maynard, E. *The Federation of Rhodesia and Nyasaland: The Multi-Racial State*. Salisbury: Rhodesia National Affairs Association, 1960.

Mell, A. H. *History of the Old Residency and Government House*. Zomba, 1960.

Merensky, A. *Deutsche Arbeit am Nyasa*. Berlin, 1894.

Morris, Martin. *A Brief History of Nyasaland*. London: Longmans, Green.

Morrow, Sean. "'War Came from the Boma': Military and Police Disturbances in Blantyre, 1902." *Society of Malawi Journal* 41, no. 2 (1988).

Mtewa, Mekki. "Problems of Oedipal Historicism: The Saga of John Chilembwe, the Malawian." *Journal of Black Studies* 8, no. 2 (1977).

Mufuka, Nyamayaro. *Mission and Politics in Malawi*. Kingston, Ontario: Limestone, 1977.

Murray, A. C. *Nyasaland*. Amsterdam: Crown Agents, 1897.

Mwase, Gideon S. *Strike a Blow and Die: A Narrative of Race Relations in Colonial Africa*. Cambridge: Harvard University Press, 1967.

Nyasaland African Congress. *Why We Oppose Federation*. Lilongwe, 1952.

Oliver, Roland. *Sir Harry Johnston and the Scramble for Africa*. New York: St. Martin's, 1957.

Pachai, Bridglal. *Land and Politics in Malawi, 1875–1975*. Kingston, Ontario: Limestone, 1978.

———. *Malawi: The History of the Nation*. London: Longman, 1973.

Page, Melvin E. *The Chiwaya War: Malawians in World War I*. Boulder: Westview, 1992.

———. "The Great War and Chewa society in Malawi." *Journal of Southern African Studies* 6, no. 2 (1980).

———. "The War of Thangata: Nyasaland and the East African Campaign, 1916–18." *Journal of African History* 19, no. 1 (1978).

Palmer, Robin H. "Johnson and Jameson: A Comparative Study in the Imposition Of Colonial Rule." In *The Early History of Malawi*. Edited by B. Pachai. London: Longman, 1972.

Pearson, D., and W. Taylor. *Break-up: Some Economic Consequences for the Rhodesias and Nyasaland*. Salisbury: Phoenix Group, 1963.

Phillips, C. E. *The Vision Splendid: The Future of the Central African Federation*. London: Heinemann, 1960.

Pollock, Norman. *Nyasaland and Northern Rhodesia: Corridor to the North*. Pittsburgh: Duquesne University Press, 1971.

Power, Joey. "Individual Enterprise and Enterprising Individuals: African Entrepreneurship in Blantyre and Limbe, 1907–1953." Ph.D. diss., Dalhousie University, Halifax, Nova Scotia, Canada, 1990.

———. "Individualism Is the Antithesis of Indirect Rule: Cooperative Development and Indirect Rule in Colonial Malawi." *Journal of Southern African Studies* 18, no. 2 (1992).

Rotberg, Robert I. "The Federation Movement in British East and Central Africa." *Journal of Commonwealth Political Studies* 2 (1964).

———. "The Rise of African Nationalism: The Case of East and Central Africa." *World Politics* 15 (1962).

———. *The Rise of Nationalism in Central Africa*. London: Oxford University Press, 1966.

Sanger, Clyde. *Central African Emergency*. London: Heinemann, 1960.

Schmidt, Werner. *Federation von Rhodesian and Nyassaland*. Bonn: Kurt Schroeder, 1959.

Scott, Michael. *African Episode*. London: Africa Bureau, 1953.

Sharpe, Alfred. "Recent Developments in Nyasaland." *Journal of African Society* 9, no. 36 (1910).

Shepperson, George. "External Factors in the Development of African Nationalism, with Particular Reference to British Central Africa." *Phylon* 22, no. 3 (1961).

———. "The Place of John Chilembwe in Malawi Historiography." In *The Early History of Malawi*. Edited by B. Pachai. London: Longman, 1972.

Shepperson, George, and Thomas Price. *The Independent African*. Edinburgh: Edinburgh University Press, 1958.

Stuart, Richard G. "Christianity and the Chewa: The Anglican Case, 1885–1950." Ph.D. diss., University of London, 1974.

Tangri, Roger K. "Colonial Settler Pressures and the African Move to the Politics of Representation and Union in Nyasaland." *Journal of African History* 13, no. 2 (1972).

———. "The Development of Modern African Politics and the Emergence of a Nationalist Movement in Colonial Malawi, 1871–1958." Ph.D. diss., University of Edinburgh, 1970.

———. "Inter-War 'Native Associations' and the Formation of the Nyasaland African Congress." *TransAfrican Journal of History* 1, no. 1 (1971).

———. "The Rise of Nationalism in Colonial Africa: The Case of Colonial Malawi." *Comparative Studies in Society and History,* 1968.

Tanser, George. *A History of Nyasaland*. Cape Town: Juta, 1960.

Thomson, John. *Conceived in Fraud: The Face of Central African Federation*. London: Liberal Publications, 1960.

Vail, Leroy. "The Making of an Imperial Slum: Nyasaland and Its Railways, 1895–1935." *Journal of African History* 16, no. 1 (1975).

———. "The Political Economy of East-Central Africa." In *History of Central Africa*. Vol. 2. Edited by D. Birmingham and P. M. Martin. Harlow: Longman, 1983.

Vail, Leroy, and L. White. " Tribalism and the Political History of Malawi." In *The Creation of Tribalism in South and Central Africa*. Edited by L. Vail. London: James Currey, 1989.

Vaughan, Megan. "Famine Analysis and Family Relations: 1949 in Nyasaland." *Past and Present* 108 (1985).

———. *The Story of an African Famine: Gender and Famine in Twentieth Century Malawi*. Cambridge: Cambridge University Press, 1987.

Velsen, Jaap van. "The Establishment of the Administration in Tongaland." *Historians in Tropical Africa*. Salisbury, 1962.

———. "Some Early Pressure Groups in Malawi." In *The Zambezian Past: Studies in Central African History*. Edited by Eric Stokes and R. Brown. Manchester: Manchester University Press, 1966.

Venter, Denis. "From Interest Groups to Party Formation in Colonial Malawi." *Journal of Contemporary African Studies* 14, no. 1–2 (October 1984–April 1985).

Waller, Horace. *Nyasaland: Great Britain's Case against Portugal*. London: E. Stanford, 1890.

White, Landeg. *Magomero: Portrait of a Village*. Cambridge: Cambridge University Press, 1987.

——. "Tribes and the Aftermath of John Chilembwe and the New Jerusalem." *African Affairs* 83, no. 333 (1984).

Williams, Shirley. *Central Africa: The Economics of Inequality*. London: Fabian Bureau, 1960.

Williams, T. David. *Malawi: Politics of Despair.* Ithaca, N.Y.: Cornell University Press, 1978.

Wood, J. R. T. *The Wellensky Papers: A History of the Rhodesia and Nyasaland.* Durban: Graham, 1983.

Woods, Anthony Edward, Jr. "Accumulation and Order: The State and Society in Colonial Malawi, 1891–1929." Ph.D. diss., Michigan State University, 1991.

——. "Mass Nationalism and Traditional Troubles in Colonial Malawi." *TransAfrican Journal of History* 22 (1993).

——. "The Myth of the Capitalist Class: Unofficial Sources and Political Economy in Colonial Malawi, 1895–1924." *History in Africa* 16 (1989).

Postcolonial Period

Ammann, Beat. "Poverty Discipline and Dignity in Malawi." *Swiss Review of World Affairs* 39, no. 10 (1990).

Brieztse, Paul. "The Chilobwe Murders Trial." *African Studies Review* 17, no. 2 (1974).

Chakanza, J. C. "The Pro-Democracy Movement in Malawi: The Catholic Church's Contribution, 1960–1992." *Religion in Malawi* 4 (1994).

Che-Mponda, Alek Humphrey. "The Malawi-Tanzania Border and Territorial Dispute 1968: A Case Study of Boundary and Territory in the New Africa." Ph.D. diss., Howard University, 1972.

Chimwene Wanga, "The Littlest Revolution." *Africa Today* 12 (April 1965).

Chipembere, H. B. M. "Malawi in Crisis, 1964." *Ufahamu* 1, no. 2 (1970).

——. "Malawi's Growing Links with South Africa: A Necessity or a Virtue." *Africa Today* 18, no. 2 (1971).

Chirwa, C. W. "The Politics of Ethnicity and Regionalism in Contemporary Malawi." *African Rural and Urban Studies* 1–2 (1994).

——. "Regionalism, Ethnicity, and the National Question in Malawi." *Southern Africa Political and Economic Monthly [SAPEM]* 8, no. 3–4 (1994–1995).

Chisiza, D. K. *Africa: What Lies Ahead*. New Delhi: Indian Council for Africa, 1961.

——. *Realities of African Independence*. London: Africa Publications Trust, 1961.

Chiume, M. W. Kanyama. *Kwacha: An Autobiography.* Nairobi: East Africa Publishing House, 1975.

Cullen, Trevor. *Malawi: A Turning Point*. Edinburgh: Pentland, 1994.

Decalo, Samuel. *The Stable Minority: Civilian Rule in Africa*. Gainesville, Fla.: FAB Books, 1998.

Donge, Jan Kees van. "Kamuzu's Legacy: The Democratization of Malawi." *African Affairs* 94 (1995).

——. "The Mwanza Trial as a Search for a Usable Malawian Political Past." *African Affairs* 97, no. 386 (1998).

Englund, Harri. "Between God and Kamuzu: The Transition to Multiparty Politics in Central Malawi." In *Postcolonial Identities in Africa*. Edited by R. Werbner and T. Ranger. London: Zed, 1996.

———. "Brother against Brother: The Moral Economy of War and Displacement in the Malawi-Mozambique Borderland." Ph.D. thesis, Manchester University, 1995.

Forster, Peter G. "Culture, Nationalism and the Invention of Tradition in Malawi." *Journal of Modern African Studies* 32 (1994).

Hedges, David. "Notes on Malawi-Mozambique Relations, 1961–1987." *Journal of Southern African Studies* 15, no. 4 (1989).

Henderson, R. D'A. "Relations of Neighbourliness: Malawi and Portugal, 1964–1974." *Journal of Modern African Studies* 15, no. 3 (1977).

Hodder-Williams, Richard. "Malawi's Decade under Dr. Banda: The Revival of Politics." *Round Table* 252 (October 1973).

———. "'Support' in Eastern Africa: Some Observations from Malawi." In *The Politics of Africa: Dependence and Development*. Edited by T. M. Shaw and K. A. Heard. London: Longman, 1979.

Ihonvbere, Julius O. "From Despotism to Democracy: The Rise of Multiparty Politics in Malawi." *International Studies* 34, no. 2 (1997).

Kalinga, Owen J. M. "The Production of History in Malawi in the 1960s: The Legacy of Sir Harry Johnston, the Influence of the Society of Malawi and the Role of Dr. Kamuzu Banda and His Malawi Congress Party." *African Affairs* 97, no. 389 (1998).

Kaspin, Deborah. "The Politics of Ethnicity in Malawi's Democratic Transition." *Journal of Modern African Studies* 33 (1995).

Lwanda, John L. *Kamuzu Banda of Malawi: A Study in Promise, Power, and Paralysis*. Bothwell, Scotland: Dudu Nsomba, 1992.

———. *Promises, Power Politics, and Poverty: Democratic Transition in Malawi, 1961 to 1996*. Bothwell, Scotland: Dudu Nsomba Publications, 1996

McMaster, Carolyn. *Malawi Foreign Policy and Development*. London: Julian Friedman, 1974.

Malawi Congress Party. *The Malawi Congress Party and Rules and Regulations Governing the Discipline of the Malawi Congress Party*. Limbe: Malawi Congress Party.

Matthews, Ronald. *African Powder Keg: Revolt and Dissent in Six Emergent Nations*. London: The Bodley Head, 1966.

Mayall, James. "The Malawi-Tanzania Boundary Dispute." *Journal of Modern African Studies* 11, no. 4 (1973).

Mhone, Guy, C. Z., ed. *Malawi at the Crossroads: The Post-Colonial Political Economy*. Harare: SAPES Books, 1992.

Mpakati, Attati. "Malawi: The Birth of a Neocolonial State." *African Review* 3, no. 1 (1973).

———. "Malawi Neocolonial Profile." *World Marxist Review* 22, no. 6 (1979).

Newell, J. "An African Army under Pressure: The Politicisation of the Malawi Army and 'Operation Bwezani': 1992–1993." *Small Wars and Insurgencies* 6, no. 2 (1995).

———. "'A Moment of Truth'? The Church and Political Change in Malawi, 1992." *Journal of Modern African Studies* 33, no. 2 (1995).

Nzunda, Matembo, and K. R. Ross, eds. *Church, Law, and Political Transition in Malawi, 1992–94.* Gweru: Mambo, 1995.

Ott, Martin, et al., eds. *Malawi's Second Democratic Elections: Process, Problems, and Prospects.* Blantyre: CLAIM, 2000.

Phiri, Kings M., and K. R. Ross, eds. *Democratizaton in Malawi: A Stocktaking.* Blantyre: CLAIM, 1998.

Power, Joey. "Remembering Du: An Episode in the Development of Malawian Political Culture." *African Affairs* 97, no. 388 (1998).

Ross, Kenneth R. "The Renewal of the State by the Church: The Case of the Public Affairs Committee in Malawi." *Religion in Malawi* 4 (1995).

Ross, Kenneth R., ed. *God, People, and Power in Malawi: Democratization in Theological Perspectives.* Blantyre: CLAIM, 1996.

Schoffeleers, Matthew. *In Search of Truth and Justice: Confrontations between Church and State in Malawi, 1960–1994.* Blantyre: CLAIM, 1999.

Searle, Chris. "Struggling against the 'Bandastan': An Interview with Attati Mpakati." *Race and Class* 21 (Spring 1980).

Vail, Leroy. "Ethnicity, Language, and National Unity: The Case of Malawi." In *Working Papers in Southern African Studies.* Edited by P. L. Bonner. Johannesburg: Ravan, 1988.

Vail, Leroy, and L. White. "Tribalism in the Political History of Malawi." In *The Creation of Tribalism in Southern Africa.* Edited by Leroy Vail. London: James Currey, 1989.

Venter, Denis. "Malawi: The Transition to Multiparty Politics." In *Democracy and Political Change in Sub-Saharan Africa.* Edited by John Wiseman. London: Routledge, 1995.

Biographies and Memoirs

Allen, Herbert. *Shadows on the Wall.* Lilongwe: Herbert Allen, 1988.

Allighan, G. *The Welensky Story.* Cape Town: Purnell, 1962.

Alport, Cuthbert. *The Sudden Assignment.* London: Hodder & Stoughton, 1965.

Ambali, Augustine. *Thirty Years in Nyasaland.* London: UMCA, 1931.

Arnold, W. B. "Slave Boy to Priest." *Nyasaland Journal* 2, no. 1 (1949).

Badawe, Lewis Mataka. *Memoirs of a Malawian.* Blantyre: CLAIM, 1971

Baker, Colin. *Development Governor: A Biography of Sir Geoffrey Colby.* London: British Academic Press, 1994.

———. *Retreat from Empire: Sir Robert Armitage in Africa and Cyprus.* London: I. B. Tauris, 1998.

———. *Sir Glynn Jones: A Proconsul in Africa.* London: Palgrave, 2000.

Ballantyne, M. M. S., and R. H. W. Shepherd. *Forerunners of Modern Malawi: The Early Missionary Adventures of Dr James Henderson, 1895–1898.* Lovedale: Lovedale Press, 1968.

Barnes, B. H. *Johnson of Nyasaland: A Study of the Life and Work of William Percival Johnson, D.D.* London: UMCA, 1933.

Bismark, Joseph. *A Brief History of Joseph Bismark.* Occasional Papers of the Department of Antiquities. Zomba: Government Printer, 1969.

Boeder, Robert. *Alfred Sharpe of Nyasaland: Builder of an Empire.* Blantyre: Chancellor College, 1981.

Bradley, Kenneth. *Diary of a District Officer*. London: Harrap, 1966.

Campbell, George H. *Lonely Warrior*. Blantyre: CLAIM, 1975.

Chiume, M. W. Kanyama. *Kwacha: An Autobiography*. Nairobi: East Africa Publishing House, 1975.

Christie, Iain. *Samora Machel: A Biography*. London: Zed, 1989.

Crawford, Daniel. *Thinking Back: Twenty-two Years without a Break in the Long Grass of Central Africa*. New York: George Doran, 1913.

Doig, Andrew B. *It's People Who Count*. Edinburgh: Pentland, 1997.

Dubbey, John. *Warm Hearts, White Hopes*. Pretoria: Penrose Books Printers, 1994.

Elmslie, Walter Angus. *Among the Wild Ngoni*. Edinburgh: Oliphant & Ferrier, 1889.

Fotheringhan, L. M. *Adventures in Nyasaland: A Two Year Struggle with the Arab Slave Dealers in Central Africa*. London: Low, Marston, 1891.

Frank, Cedrick N. *Petro's Progress: From Slavery to Priesthood: An African Tale*. London: UMCA, 1957.

Fraser, Agnes R. *Donald Fraser of Livingstonia*. London: Hodder & Stoughton, 1934.

Fraser, Donald. *African Idylls*. London: Seeley Service, 1923.

——. *The Autobiography of an African (Daniel Mtusu)*. Westport: Negro University Press, 1970.

——. *Winning a Primitive People*. London: Seeley Service, 1914.

Garland, Vera. *Missionary in Malawi, 1936–1974*. Edited by Francis Bell. Malosa, 1976.

Goodall, J. *Goodbye to Empire: A Doctor Remembers*. Edinburgh: Pentland, 1987.

Goodwin, Harvey. *Memoir of Bishop Mackenzie*. Cambridge: Deighton, Bell, 1864.

Gray, Ernst. *Fun in the Bush*. Nottingham: United Reformed Church, 1989.

Grogan, E., and A. Sharpe. *From the Cape to Cairo*. London: Hurst & Blackett, 1920.

Hetherwick, Alexander. *The Romance of Blantyre*. London: James Clark, 1932.

Hetherwick, Alexander, ed. *Robert Hellier Napier in Nyasaland*. Edinburgh: Blackwood, 1925.

Hine, John. *Days Gone By: Being Some Account of Past Years Chiefly in Central Africa*. London: Murray, 1924.

Hofmeyr, J. W. L. *Attie Hofmeyr van Nyasaland*. Sellenbosch: Administrative Bureau, 1921.

Jackson, Bill. *Send Us Friends*. Belfast: Author, 1996.

Johnson, William P. "Seven Years' Travel in the Region East of Lake Nyasa." *Proceedings of the Royal Geographical Society* 6 (1884).

——. *The Mission Steamers*. London: UMCA, 1910.

——. *My African Reminiscences, 1875–1896*. London: Butler & Tanner, 1924.

Johnston, Harry H. *The Story of My Life*. Indianapolis: Bobbs-Merrill, 1923.

Kadalie, Clements. *My Life and the ICU*. New York: Humanities Press, 1970.

Kilekwa, Petro. *Slave Boy to Priest: The Autobiography of Padre Petro Kilekwa*. London: UMCA, 1937.

Langworthy, Emily Booth. *This Africa Was Mine*. Stirling, 1952.

Langworthy, Harry. *"Africa for the African": The Life of Joseph Booth*. Blantyre: CLAIM, 1996.

Laws, Robert. *Reminiscences of Livingstonia*. London: Oliver & Boyd, 1934.

Livingstone, David. *Last Journals*. London: Dent, 1874.
——. *Missionary Travels and Researches in South Africa*. New York: Harper Brothers, 1858.
Livingstone, D., and C. Livingstone. *Narrative of an Expedition to the Zambezi and Its Tributaries, 1858–64*. London: Murray, 1865.
Livingstone, William P. *Laws of Livingstonia*. London: Hodder & Stoughton, 1923.
——. *A Prince of Missionaries: Alexander Hetherwick*. London: James Clarke, 1931.
Lugard, Frederick. *The Rise of Our East African Empire: Early Efforts in Nyasaland and Uganda*. 2 vols. London: Blackwood, 1893.
McIntosh, Hamish. *Robert Laws: Servant of Africa*. Edinburgh: Handsel, 1993.
MacDonald, Duff. *Africana, or the Heart of Heathen Africa*. 2 vols. London: Simpkin & Marshall, 1882.
Macpherson, Fergus. *North of the Zambezi: A Modern Missionary Memoir*. Edinburgh: Handsel, 1998.
Malinki, K. Morrison. *The History of Pastor K.M. Malinki*. N.p., n.d.
Maugham, R. C. *Africa as I Have Known It*. London: Murray, 1929.
——. *Nyasaland in the Nineties*. London: L. Williams, 1935.
Mkandawire, Austin C. *Living My Destiny: A Medical and Historical Narrative*. Limbe: Popular Publications, 1998.
Moir, Frederick. *After Livingstone: An African Trade Romance*. London: Hodder & Stoughton, 1924.
Moir, Jane F. *A Lady's Letters from Central Africa: A Journey from Mandala, Shire Highlands, to Ujiji, Lake Tanganyika, and Back in 1890*. Blantyre: Central Africana, 1991.
Morris, Colin. *The Hour after Midnight*. London: Longmans, 1961.
M'Passou, Denis B. *Josiah Mtekateka: From Priest's Dog-Boy to a Bishop*. Chilema, Zomba: self-published, 1979.
Munger, Edwin S. *President Kamuzu Banda of Malawi*. Hanover, N.H.: American Universities Field Staff, 1969.
Oliver, Roland. *Sir Harry Johnston and the Scramble for Africa*. London: Chatto & Windus, 1957.
Pachai, Bridglal, ed. *The Memoirs of Lewis Mataka Bandawe*. Blantyre: CLAIM, 1971.
——. "Samuel Josia Ntara: Writer and Historian." *Society of Malawi Journal* 21, no. 2 (1968).
Perham, Margery. *Lugard: The Years of Adventure*. London: Collins, 1956.
Phiri, Desmond Dudwa. *Charles Chidongo Chinula*. Lilongwe: Longman, 1975.
——. *Inkosi Gomani II: Maseko-Ngoni Paramount Chief*. Blantyre: Government Printer, 1973.
——. *John Chilembwe*. Lilongwe: Longman, 1974.
Proctor, Lovell J. *The Central African Journal of Lovell J. Proctor, 1860–1964*. Edited by Norman R. Bennet and M. Ylvisakar. Boston: African Studies Center, Boston University, 1971.
Ransford, Oliver. *Livingstone's Lake: The Drama of Nyasa*. New York: Crowell, 1966.
Rowley, H. *The Story of the Universities' Mission to Central Africa from Its Commencement under Bishop Mackenzie to Its Withdrawal from the Zambezi*. London: Saunders, Otley, 1867.

———. *Twenty Years in Central Africa: Being the Story of the Universities' Mission to Central Africa.* London: Wells Carder, 1967.

Randolf, B. W. *Arthur Douglas, Missionary on Lake Nyasa: The Story of His Life.* London: UMCA, 1920.

Retief, M. W. *William Murray of Nyasaland.* Lovedale: Lovedale Press, 1958.

Robertson, Wilfrid. *Mandala Trail: A Tale of Early Days in Nyasaland.* London: Oxford University Press, 1956.

Seaver, George. *David Livingstone: His Life and Letters.* London: Lutterworth, 1957.

Shepperson, George, and Thomas Price. *The Independent African.* Edinburgh: Edinburgh University Press, 1958.

Short, Philip. *Banda.* London: Routledge & Kegan Paul, 1974.

Smith, E. H. *John Cuthbert Smith: Thirty-Six Years in Nyasaland.* London: Priory, n.d.

Stewart, James. *From Nyassa to Tanganyika: The Journal of James Stewart CE in Central Africa, 1876–79.* Edited by T. Jack Thompson. Blantyre: Central Africana, 1989.

Tengatenga, James. "The Good Being the Enemy of the Best: The Politics of Bishop Frank Oswald Thorne in Nyasaland and the Federation, 1936–1961." *Religion in Malawi* 6 (1996).

Thompson, T. Jack. *Christianity in Northern Malawi: Donald Fraser's Missionary Methods and Ngoni Culture.* Leiden: Brill, 1995.

Vlok, T. C. B. *Elf Jaren in Midden Africa.* 2d ed. Neerbosch, 1901.

Ward, G. *The Life of Charles Alan Smythies.* London: UMCA, 1989.

Welensky, Roy. *Welensky's 4,000 Days: The Life and Death of the Federation of Rhodesia and Nyasaland.* London: Roy Publishers, 1964.

Weller, John C. *The Priest from the Lakeside: The Story of Leonard Kamungu of Malawi and Zambia, 1877–1913.* Blantyre: CLAIM, 1971.

White, P. J. *Dienares van God.* Stellenbosch: CVS, 1947.

Winspear, F. C. "Some Reminiscences of Nyasaland." *Nyasaland Journal* 13, no. 2 (1960).

Wood, J. K. *The Welensky Papers.* Durham, N.C.: Graham, 1983.

POLITICS

Administration, Government, Elections

Baker, C. A. "The Development of Administration to 1897." In *The Early History of Malawi.* Edited by B. Pachai. London: Longman, 1972.

Baker, Colin. "Administrative Reform in Nyasaland." *Quarterly Journal of Administration* 6, no. 3 (1972).

———. "The Administrative Service of Malawi: A Case Study of Africanization." *Journal of Modern African Studies* 10, no. 2 (1972).

———. "Civil Response to War: The Nyasaland Civil Service, 1914–1918." *Journal of African Studies* 11, no. 1 (1984).

———. "Civil Response to War: The Nyasaland Civil Service, 1939–1945." *Society of Malawi Journal* 38, no. 1 (1985).

——. "The Development of the Civil Service in Malawi, 1891–1972." Ph.D. diss., University of London, 1981.

——. *Development Governor: A Biography of Sir Geoffrey Colby*. London: British Academic Press, 1994.

——. *The Evolution of Local Government in Malawi*. Ile-Ife: University of Ife Press, 1975.

——. "The Genesis of the Nyasaland Civil Service." *Society of Malawi Journal* 41, no. 1 (1988).

——. "Incremental but Not Disjointed: The Evolution of the Civil Service in Colonial Nyasaland." *International Journal of African Historical Studies* 31, no. 2 (1998).

——. *Retreat from Empire: Sir Robert Armitage in Africa*. London: I. B. Tauris, 1998.

——. *Sir Glyn Jones: A Proconsul in Africa and Cyprus*. London: Palgrave, 2000.

——. "Staff Continuity in Nyasaland." *African Affairs* 75, no. 302 (1976).

Barnekov, Timothy. *An Inquiry into the Development of Native Administration in Nyasaland, 1888–1939*. Syracuse: Syracuse University Press, 1968.

Benion, M. J. "Training for Localisation of the Public Service." *Journal of Local Administration Overseas* 5, no. 1 (1966).

Bottomani, Isaac B. "The Relationship between Politics and Administration: A Political Neutrality Dilemma for Bureaucrats in Malawi." *Saipa* 21, no. 1 (1986).

Bowman, E. *The Training of Native Authorities in Community Work: A Nyasaland Experiment*. Blantyre: Jeanes Conference, 1936.

Chimombo, Moira, ed. *Lessons in Hope: Education for Democracy in Malawi: Past, Present, Future*. National Initiative for Civic Education (NICE), Series 1. Zomba: Chancellor College, 1999.

Chipeta, Chinyamata. "Towards More Effective Control of Public Expenditure in Malawi." *Journal of Social Science* 11, no. 1 (1984).

Clayton, Anthony, and D. Killingray. *Khaki and Blue: Military and Police in British Colonial Africa*. Athens: Ohio University Center for International Studies, 1989.

Dzimbiri, L. B. "The Malawi Referendum of June 1993." *Electoral Studies* 13, no. 3 (1994).

Graham-Jolly, H. G. "The Progress of Local Government in Nyasaland." *Journal of African Administration* 7 (1955).

Hailey, Lord. *An African Survey*. London: Oxford University Press, 1938.

——. *Native Administration in British African Territories*. Pt. 2, *Central Africa: Zanzibar, Nyasaland, Northern Rhodesia*. Nyasaland. London: HMSO, 1950.

Hirschmann, David. *Women's Participation in Malawi's Local Councils and District Development Committees*. East Lansing: Michigan State University, 1985.

Hooker, James. *Tradition and the Traditional Courts: Malawi's Experiment in Law*. Hanover, N.H.: American Universities Field Staff, 1971.

Kadzamira, Zimani D. "Local Politics and Administration of Development in Malawi." Ph.D. diss., University of Manchester, 1974.

——. "Local Politics and Administration during the Colonial Period in Malawi." *Journal of Social Science* 3 (1974).

Kandoole, B. F., and K. M. Phiri. *Twenty-Five Years of Independence in Malawi, 1964–1989*. Blantyre: Dzuka, 1989.

Khofi, L. M. *Malawi Parliament: Practice and Procedure*. Zomba: Government Printer, 1974.

Konovalov, Eugenii. *Malawi*. Moscow: Mysl, 1966.

Mackay, Peter. *A Portrait of Malawi*. Zomba: Government Printer, 1964.

Miller, R. A. "District Development Committees in Malawi: A Case Study of Administration." *Journal of Development Overseas* 9 (1970).

Jere, Ndinda S., and D. Z. Mkandawire. *An Outline of Our Government*. Blantyre: CLAIM, 1987.

Moyse-Bartlett, Hubert. *King's African Rifles: A Study in the Military History of East and Central Africa, 1890–1945*. Aldershot, U.K.: Gale & Polden, 1956.

Mtewa, Mekki. *Malawi Democratic Theory and Public Policy*. Cambridge, Mass.: Schenckmann, 1986.

Munger, Edwin. *President Kamuzu Banda of Malawi*. Hanover, N.H.: American Universities Field Staff, 1969.

Njoloma, James. *The Malawi Army*. Lilongwe: James Njoloma, 1991.

Richardson, Henry J., III. "Administration in the Malawi Government and Its Relation to Social Change." In *The Administration of Change in Africa: Essays in the Theory and Practice of Development Administration in Africa*. Edited by E. Philip Morgan. New York: Dunellen, 1974.

Report of the Commission to Examine the Salary Scales and Conditions of Services of Local Officers. Zomba: Nyasaland Government, May 1964.

Schimmelfenning, Else. *Malawi*. Bonn: K. Schroeder, 1965.

Shepperson, George. "The Military History of British Central." *Rhodes-Livingstone Institute Journal* 26 (1959).

Short, Philip. *Banda*. London: Routledge & Kegan Paul, 1974.

Simukonda, Henry. "Rural Transformation and Smallholder Agriculture in Malawi: A Case Study of the Karonga Rural Development Project." Ph.D. diss., University of Wales, 1983.

Speck, S. W. "African Local Government in Malawi: Its Development and Politics under British Rule." Ph.D. diss., Harvard University, 1969.

Thomson, T. D. "Soil Conservation: Some Implications." *Journal of African Administration* 2, no. 2 (1953).

Williams, T. David. *Malawi: The Politics of Despair*. Ithaca, N.Y.: Cornell University Press, 1978.

Constitution, Law, Justice, and Human Rights

Africa Watch. *Where Silence Rules: The Suppression of Dissent in Malawi*. New York: Human Rights Watch, 1990.

Amnesty International. *Malawi: Human Rights Violations Twenty-Five Years after Independence*. London: Amnesty International, 1989.

———. *Malawi: Preserving the One-Party State: Human Rights Violations and the Referendum*. London: Amnesty International, 1993.

———. *Malawi Prison Conditions, Cruel Punishment, and Detention without Trial*. London: Amnesty International, 1992.

Brietzke, Paul. "The Chilobwe Murder Trials." *African Studies Review* 17, no. 2 (1974).

——. "Murder and Manslaughter in Malawi's Traditional Courts." *African Journal of Law* 18 (1974).

——. "Witchcraft and Law in Malawi." *East African Law Journal* 8, no. 1 (1973).

Broke-Taylor, J. D. A. *Land Law in Malawi*. Zomba: University of Malawi, 1977.

Catholic Bishops of Malawi. *Living Our Faith: Pastoral Letter from the Catholic Bishops, 1992*. Lilongwe: Episcopal Conference of Malawi, 1992. Also published by the CIIR as "The Truth Will Set You Free," *Church in the World* 28 (1992).

Catholic Institute for International Relations. *Malawi: A Moment of Truth*. London: CIIR, 1993.

Chanock, Martin. *Law, Custom, and Social Order: The Colonial Experience in Malawi*. Cambridge: Cambridge University Press, 1985.

——. "Neo-Traditionalism and Customary Law in Malawi." *African Law Studies* 16 (1978).

Chimango, L. J. "Traditional Criminal law in Malawi." *Society of Malawi Journal* 28, no. 1 (1975).

Duly, A. W. R. "The Lower Shire District: Notes on Land Tenure and Individual Rights." *Nyasaland Journal* 1, no. 2 (1948).

Fleming, C. J. M. "Crime and Punishment in Northern Malawi." *Society of Malawi Journal* 30, no. 1 (1977).

——. "The Law of Obligation in Northern Malawi." *Society of Malawi Journal* 27, no. 1 (1974); 1–2 (1975).

Hooker, J. "Tradition and 'Traditional Courts.' Malawi Experiment in Law." *American University Fieldstaff Reports* 5, no. 3 (1971).

Ibik, J. O. Malawi. *The Law of Land, Succession, Movable Property, Agreements, and Civil Wrongs*. London: Sweet & Maxwell, 1971.

——. *The Law of Marriage and Divorce: Re-assessment of Africa*. London: Sweet & Maxwell, 1970.

International Centre Against Censorship. *The Referendum in Malawi: Free Expression Denied*. Article 19, Issue 22. London: International Centre Against Censorship, 1993.

——. *Malawi Past: the Right to Truth*. Article 19, Issue 29. London: International Centre Against Censorship, 1993.

Johns, Vince. *An Introduction to the Law of Business Organizations*. Zomba: University of Malawi, 1982.

Khofi, L. M. *Malawi Parliament: Practice and Procedure*. Zomba: Government Printer, 1974.

Leys, Colin. "An Election in Nyasaland." *Political Studies* 5 (1957).

Mair, Lucy. *The Nyasaland Elections of 1961*. London: Athlone, 1962.

Malawi Government. *Republic of Malawi Constitution*. Zomba: Government Printer, 1994.

Maliwa, Emily Nyamazao. "Customary Law and the Administration of Justice, 1890–1933." M.Phil. thesis, University of London, 1967.

——. "The Legal Status of Women in Malawi from the Colonial Period to Independence." Ph.D. diss., University of London, 1970.

Maluwa, Tiyanjana. "The Legal Regime for the Protection of Refugees in Malawi." In *Malawi at the Crossroads: The Post-Colonial Economy*. Edited by Guy C. Z. Mhone. Harare: SAPES Books, 1992.

Mapanje, J. "Letter from Malawi: Bittersweet Tears." *Index on Censorship* 2 (1995).

Moggeridge, L. T. "The Nyasaland Tribes, Their Customs, and Their Poison Ordeal." *Journal of the Royal Anthropological Institute* 32 (1902).

Mutharika, A. Peter. *Malawi: Reflections on the Democratization Process, the Constitution, and the Rule of Law.* St. Louis, Mo.: A. Peter Mutharika, 1994.

Newman, David. *Criminal Procedure and Evidence in Malawi.* Zomba: University of Malawi, Department of Law, 1982.

Ng'ong'ola, Clement. "Controlling Theft in the Public Service: Penal Law and Judicial Responses in Malawi." *Journal of African Law* 32, no. 1 (1988).

———. "The Design and Implementation of Customary Land Reforms in Central Malawi." *Journal of African Law* 26, no. 2 (1982).

———. "Land Law and Economic Development in Malawi." Ph.D. diss., University of London, 1983.

———. "Managing the Transition to Political Pluralism in Malawi: Legal and Constitutional Arrangements." *Journal of Commonwealth and Comparative Politics* 34, no. 2 (1996).

———. "The State, Settlers, and Indigenes in the Evolution of Land Law and Policy in Colonial Malawi." *International Journal of African Historical Studies* 23, no. 1 (1990).

Nzunda, Matembo. "New Company Law for Malawi." *Journal of African Law* 33, no. 1 (1989).

Rangeley, W. H. J. "Notes on Chewa Tribal Law." *Nyasaland Journal* 1, no. 3 (1948).

Roberts, Arthur Simon. "The Constitution of Malawi." *Journal of African Law* 8, no. 3 (1964).

———. "The Growth of an Integrated Legal System in Malawi: A Study in Racial Distinctions in the Law." Ph.D. diss., University of London, 1967.

———. "Matrilineal Family Law and Custom in Malawi." *Journal of African Law* 4 (1960).

Roland, H. R. "Nyasaland General Elections, 1964." *Journal of Local Government Overseas* 3 (1964).

Wanda, Bocye. "Colonialism, Nationalism, and Tradition: The Evolution and Development of the Legal System of Malawi." Ph.D. diss., University London, 1979.

———. "Customary Family Law in Malawi: Adherence to Tradition and Adaptability to Change." *Journal of Legal Pluralism* 27 (1988).

———. "Legal Aid Services in Malawi." *African Law Studies* 11 (1974).

Whitaker, E. J. *Rhodesia and Nyasaland Law Reports, 1961.* Salisbury: Byland, 1961.

SOCIETY

Anthropology and Sociology

General

Apthorpe, R. *Present Interrelations in Central African Rural and Urban Life.* Lusaka: Rhodes-Livingstone Institute, 1961.

——. *Social Relations in Central African Industry*. Lusaka: Rhodes-Livingstone Institute, 1958.

Apthorpe, R., and J. C. Mitchell. *The Traditional and Modern Roles and Statuses of Bantu Women in the Two Rhodesias and Nyasaland*. Brussels: INCIDI Conference, 1958.

Banda, H. K., and T. C. Young. *Our African Way of Life*. London: Lutterworth, 1946.

Barnes, John. *Politics in a Changing Society: A Political History of the Fort Jameson Ngoni*. London: Oxford University Press, 1954.

Bettison, David. *The Social and Economic Structure of Seventeen Villages, Blantyre-Limbe Nyasaland*. Lusaka: Rhodes-Livingstone Institute, 1958.

Birch de Aguilar, Laurel. "Masks in Social Roles." *Society of Malawi Journal* 47, no. 2 (1994).

——. "Masks: Outsiders and Socio-Historical Experience." *Society of Malawi Journal* 47, no. 2 (1994).

——. *Inscribing the Mask: Interpretation on Nyau Masks and Ritual Performance among the Chewa of Central Malawi*. Frisbourg: University Press, 1996.

Black, Colin. *The Lands and Peoples of Rhodesia and Nyasaland*. London: Macmillan, 1961.

Boeder, Robert B. "Malawi Burial Societies and Social Change in Zimbabwe." *Journal of Contemporary African Studies* 1, no. 2 (1982).

Coleman, Gilroy. *Economic Development and Population Change in Malawi*. Norwich, U.K.: School of East Anglia Development Studies, 1983.

Coudenhove, H. *My African Neighbors: Man, Bird, and Beast in Nyasaland*. Boston: Little, Brown, 1925.

Dotson, Floyd, and Lillian Dotson. *The Indian Minority of Zambia, Rhodesia, and Malawi*. New Haven: Yale University Press, 1968.

Engberg, Lila E., et al. "Production Activities, Food Supply, and Nutritional Status in Malawi." *Journal of Modern African Studies* 25, no. 1 (1987).

Englund, Harri. "The Self in Self-Interest: Land, Labour, and Temporalities in Malawi's Agrarian Change." *Africa* 69, no. 1 (1999).

——. "Witchcraft, Modernity, and the Person: The Morality Of Accumulation in Central Malawi." *Critique of Anthropology* 16 (1996).

Ettema, W., and L. Msukwa. *Food Production and Malnutrition in Malawi*. Zomba: University of Malawi Centre for Social Research, 1985.

Flemming, C. J. W. "The Matripostestal Family in Northern Malawi." *Society of Malawi Journal* 24, no. 1 (1971).

Fraser, Donald. *African Idylls: Portraits and Impressions of Life on a Central African Mission Station*. London: Seeley Service, 1923.

——. *Winning a Primitive People*. London: Seeley Service, 1914.

Gwengwe, J., and A. Risdon. *Educating Away Your Fears of Witchcraft*. Limbe: Literature Bureau, 1965.

Heckel, Benno. *The Yao Tribe, Their Culture and Education*. London: University of London, 1935.

Hooker, James. *Population Review, 1970: Malawi*. Hanover, N.H.: American Universities Field Staff, 1971.

Kamwambe, G. *Malawi Population Census, 1966: A Methodological Report*. Zomba: Government Printer 1971.

Kandawire, J. A. K. "Local Leadership and Socio-Economic Changes in Chingale Area of Zomba District in Malawi." Ph.D. diss., University of Edinburgh, 1972.
———. *Thangatha: Forced Labour or Reciprocal Assistance.* Zomba: University of Malawi, 1979.
———. "Village Segmentation and Class Formation in Southern Malawi." *Africa* 50, no. 2 (1980).

Kampuzah, W. *Ungoni Uzimba ndi Miyambi.* Ncheu: Zambezi Mission Press, 1941.

Kaspin, Deborah D. "Chewa Visions and Revisions of Power: Transformations of the Nyau Dance in Central Malawi." *Modernity and Its Malcontents: Ritual and Power in Postcolonial Africa.* Edited by Jean Comaroff and John Comaroff. Chicago: University of Chicago Press, 1993.
———. "Elephants and Ancestors: The Legacy of Kingship in Rural Malawi." Ph.D. diss., University of Chicago, 1990.

Kubik, Gerhard. *Nyau: Maskenbunde in Sudlichen Malawi.* Vienna: Verlag der Osterreichischen Akademie der Wissenschaften, 1987.

Lane-Pool, E. *The Native Tribes of the Eastern Province of North Rhodesia.* Lusaka, 1938.

Langworthy, Emily Booth. *This Africa Was Mine.* Stirling: Stirling Tract Enterprise, 1952.

Laws, Robert. *Reminiscences of Livingstone.* Edinburgh: Oliver & Boyd, 1934.

Lawson, Audrey, ed. *Makolo Athu.* Zomba: Education Department, n.d.

Lindskog, Per L. *Why Poor Children Stay Sick: The Human Ecology of Child Health and Welfare in Rural Malawi.* Uppsala: Scandinavian Institute of African Studies. 1989.

Mackenzie, Duncan. *The Spirit-ridden Konde.* London: Seeley, 1925.

Marwick, M. G. "Another Modern Anti-Witchcraft Movement in East Central Africa." *Africa* 20, no. 2 (1950).
———. "History and Tradition in East Central Africa through the Eyes of the Northern Rhodesia Chewa." *Journal of African History* 4 (1963).
———. *Sorcery in Social Setting: a Study of the Northern Rhodesia Chewa.* Manchester: Manchester University Press, 1965.

Metcalfe, M. "Some Nyasaland Folk-Lore Tales." *Nyasaland Journal* 7, no. 2 (1954).

Mitchell, James. *Education as a Factor in African Mate Selection.* Salisbury: Rhodes-Livingstone Institute, 1956.
———. *Factors in Urban Growth in Bantu Africa with Special Reference to the Federation of the Rhodesias and Nyasaland.* Salisbury: University College, 1958.
———. "The Yao of Southern Nyasaland." In *Seven Tribes of British Central Africa.* Edited by Elizabeth Colson and Max Gluckman. Manchester: Manchester University Press, 1951.
———. *The Yao Village: A Study in the Social Structure of a Malawian Tribe.* Manchester: University Press, 1956.

Mitchell, James, ed. *An Outline of the Sociological Background of African Labor.* Salisbury: Ensign, 1961.
———. *Social Networks in Urban Situations: Analyses of Personal Relationships in Central African Towns.* Manchester: Manchester University Press, 1969.

Mtika, Mike Mathambo. "Social and Cultural Relations in Economic Action: Peasant Food Security in the Context of the Acquired Immune Deficiency Syndrome (AIDS) Epidemic in Malawi." Ph.D. diss., Washington State University, 1998.

Ntara, Samuel Y. *Man of Africa*. Translated and edited by T. Cullen Young. London: Religious Tract Society, 1934.

——. *Headman's Enterprise*. Translated and edited by T. Cullen Young. London: Lutterworth, 1949.

Nurse, George. *Clanship in Central Malawi*. Vienna: Stiglmayr, 1978.

——. *Peoples of Southern Africa*. Oxford: Clarendon, 1985.

Peltzer, Karl. *Some Contributions of Traditional Healing Practices towards Psychosocial Health Care in Malawi*. Frankfurt: Psychologie, 1987.

Peters, P. E. "Against Odds: Matrilineality, Land, and Gender in the Shire Highlands of Malawi." *Critique of Social Anthropology* 17 (1997).

Philip, D. K. *Onani Angoni*. London: Macmillan, 1963.

Phipps, B. A. "Evaluating Settlement Schemes: Problems and Implications: A Malawi Case Study." *Provisional Council for the Social Sciences in East Africa* 5 (1970): 488–509.

Read, Margaret. *The Ngoni of Nyasaland*. London: Oxford University Press, 1956.

——. *Growing Up among the Ngoni of Nyasaland*. London: Methuen, 1959.

Redmayne, Alison. "Chikanga: An African Diviner with an International Reputation." In *Witchcraft Confessions and Accusations*. Edited by Mary Douglas. London: Tavistock, 1970.

Schoffeleers, J. M., ed. *Guardian of the Land*. Gwelo: Mambo, 1978.

——. *Religion and the Dramatization of Life*. Blantyre: CLAIM 1997.

——. *In Search of Truth and Justice: Confrontation between Church and State in Malawi, 1960–1994*. Blantyre: CLAIM, 1999.

Steel, George. *Native Diseases and Practice among the Ngoni*. London: Occasional Papers from Nyasaland, 1894.

Stubbs, Michael. *Spatial Demographic Social and Economic Characteristics of the Population of Malawi*. Blantyre: Chancellor College, 1970.

Tew, Mary. *The People of the Lake Nyasa Region*. London: Oxford University Press, 1950.

Thompson, T. *Notes of African Customs in Nyasaland*. Zomba: Government Printer, 1957.

Van Der Post, Laurens. *Venture to the Interior*. New York: Morrow, 1951.

Velsen, J. van. "Labour migration as a positive facor in the continuity of Tonga tribal society." Edited by Aidan Southal. *Social Change in Modern Africa*. Oxford: Oxford University Press. 1961.

——. *The Politics of Kinship: A Study in Social Manipulation among the Lakeside Tonga of Nyasaland*. Manchester: Manchester University Press, 1964.

Walker, P. A. "Report on the Socio-Economic Survey." In *Environmental Monitoring Pregramme (MEMP 1), Phase One (1993–1995): Final Report*. Annex 3. Lilongwe: University of Arizona/Clark University, 1996.

Wendroff, Arnold P. "Trouble-Shooters and Trouble-Makers: Witchfinding and Traditional Malawian Medicine." Ph.D. diss., City University of New York, 1985.

Werner, Alice. *The Natives of British Central Africa*. London: Constable, 1905.

Wilson, G., and M. Wilson. *The Analysis of Social Change Based on Observation in Central Africa*. Cambridge: Cambridge University Press, 1945.

Wilson, Godfrey. *The Constitution of Ngonde*. Lusaka: Rhodes-Livingstone Institute, 1939.

Wilson, Monica. *For Men and Elders: Change in the Relations of Generations of Men and Women among the Nyakyusa-Ngonde People, 1875–1971.* New York: Africana, 1977.

———. *Good Company: A Study of Nyakyusa Age–Villages.* London: Oxford University Press,1951.

———. *The Peoples of the Nyasa-Tanganyika Corridor.* Cape Town: University of Cape Town, 1958.

———. *Rituals of Kinship among the Nyakyusa.* London: Oxford University Press, 1957.

Winterbottom, J. M. *History of the Ngoni and Chewa-Nsenga.* Lusaka: Rhodes-Livingstone Institute, 1936.

Young, T. Cullen. *African Ways and Wisdom.* London: United Society for Christian Literature, 1937.

———. *Notes on the Customs and Folklore of the Timbuka-Kamanga Peoples.* Livingstonia: Mission Press, 1931.

Rural

Centre of African Studies. *Malawi: An Alternative Pattern of Development.* Edinburgh: University of Edinburgh Centre of African Studies, 1984.

Chipande, Graham. "The Impact of Demographic Changes on Rural Development in Malawi." In *Population, Food, and Rural Development.* Edited by Ronald Lee et al. Oxford: Clarendon, 1988.

Chilimampunga, Charles D. "Rural-Urban Migration and Economic Development in Malawi." Ph.D. diss., University of Waterloo, 1992.

Davidson, Jean. "Tenacious Women: Clinging to Banja Household Production in the Face of Changing Gender Relations in Malawi." *Journal of Southern African Studies* 19, no. 3 (1993).

Ghambi, R. T. "Rural Growth Centres: The Malawi Example." Edited by H. D. Kammeier and P. J. Swan. *Equity with Growth? Planning Perspectives for Small Towns in Developing Countries.* Bangkok: Asian Institute of Technology, 1984.

Kaunda, Jonathan B. M. "Malawi: Development Policy and the Centralized State: A Study of Liwonde Agricultural Development Division." Ph.D. diss., University of East Anglia, 1988.

Livingstone, Ian. "Minimum Wage Policy, Rural Development, and Poverty Alleviation in Malawi." *Development and Change* 26 (1995).

Mkandawire, R. M. "Agrarian Change and Food Security among Smallholder Farmers in Malawi." In *Food Policy and Agriculture in Southern Africa.* Edited by Richard Mkandawire and Khabele Matlosa. Harare: SAPES Books, 1993.

———. "Customary Land, the State, and Agricultural Change in Malawi: The Case of the Chewa Peasantry in the Lilongwe Rural Development Project." *Journal of Contemporary African Studies* 3, no. 1–2 (1983–1984).

Moyo, C. M. "Local Participation in Rural Development Projects: The Case of Malawi." Ph.D. diss., University of Edinburgh, 1984.

Msukwa, Louis A. H. *A Feasibility Study on Income-Generating Activities for Women in Karonga, Kasungu, and Mangochi Districts: A Final Report.* Zomba: University of Malawi Center for Social Research, 1989.

———. *Oxfam Malawi Country Review*. Zomba: University of Malawi Center for Social Research, 1986.

Simukonda, Henry. "Rural Transformation and Smallholder Agriculture in Malawi: A Case Study of the Karonga Rural Development Project." Ph.D. diss., University College of Swanzie, 1983.

Thim, Heinz-Ulrich, et al. *Establishing Rural Service and Growth Centres: With Seven Case Studies from Malawi*. Hamburg: Verlag Weitarchiv, 1986.

Vaughan, Megan. "Kinship and Class: Stratification in the Zomba-Chilwa Area of Southern Malawi." Chancellor College History Department Staff Seminar Paper, 1978.

———. "Social and Economic Change in Southern Malawi: A Study of Rural Communities in the Shire Highlands and Upper Shire Valley from the Mid-Nineteenth Century to 1915." Ph.D. diss., University of London, 1981.

Urban

Bettison, David G. *Cash Wages and Occupational Structure, Blantyre-Limbe, Nyasaland*. Communication no. 9. Lusaka: Rhodes Livingstone, 1958.

———. *Demographic Structure of Seventeen Villages, Blantyre-Limbe*. Communication no. 11. Lusaka: Rhodes-Livingstone, 1958.

———. "The Private Domestic Servant of Blantyre-Limbe." *Nyasaland Journal* 12, no. 1 (1959).

Bettison, David G., and R. J. Apthorpe. "Authority and Residence in a Peri-Urban Social Structure, Ndirande, Nyasaland." *Nyasaland Journal* 14, no. 1 (1961).

Blinkhorn, T. A. "Lilongwe: A Quiet Revolution." *Finance and Development*, June 1971.

Chilivumbo, Alifeyo B. "The Ecology of Social Types in Blantyre." In *Town and Country in Central and Eastern Africa*. Edited by David Parkin. Oxford: Oxford University Press. 1975.

Kaluwa, B. M. "Performance of New Capitals as Regional Policy Measures: A Case Study of Lilongwe in Malawi." *Journal of Social Science* 9 (1982).

Kerlen, H. "Malawi District Centres Study: Aspects of Implementation and Institutional Framework." In *Equity and Growth? Planning Perspectives or Small Towns in Developing Countries*. Edited by H. D. Kammeier and P. J. Swan. Bangkok: Asian Institute of Technology, 1984.

Lamport-Stokes, John. "Blantyre's Early Buildings." *Society of Malawi Journal* 36, no. 2 (1983).

Lavrijsen, J., and J. J. Stekenburg. *The Food Supply of Lilongwe, Malawi*. Utrecht: Geografish Instituut Rijksuniversiteit, 1976.

Makuwila, Kamia. "African Entrepreneurship around Blantyre District from the 1890s to the 1950s." Chancellor College History Department Seminar Paper no. 10, 1981–1982.

Mhango, Geoffrey L. Du. "The Economics and Success of "People's Participation in the Production and Management of Low Income Urban Housing in Developing Countries." Ph.D. diss., University of California, 1990.

———. "The Informal Mechanisms for the Financing and Construction of Housing in Cities and Services Schemes of Malawi: A Case Study of Blantyre City." *Journal of Social Science* 12 (1985).

Mitchell, J. C. "Types of Urban Social Relationships." In *Present Interrelations in Central African Rural and Urban Life.* Edited by R. J. Apthorpe. Lusaka: Rhodes-Livingstone Institute, 1958.

Mlia, J. R. N. "Subnational Planning in Transition: The Case of Malawi." In *Subnational Planning in Southern and Eastern Africa.* Edited by A. H. J. Helmsing and K. H. Wekwete. Aldershot, U.K.: Avebury, 1990.

———. "Urbanization and Rural Development in Malawi." *Journal of Social Science* 7 (1978–1977).

Myburgh, D. W., and J. A. van Zyl. "Size Relationships in Urban System of Malawi." *African Insight* 22, no. 2 (1992).

National Statistical Office. *Blantyre-Limbe Income-Expenditure Survey (BLIS), August 1965.* Zomba: Government Printer, 1987.

———. *Urban Household Expenditure, 1979/80.* Zomba: Government Printer, 1983.

———. *Urban Housing Survey 1987: Blantyre and Lilongwe Cities.* Zomba Government Printer, 1989.

Pachai, B. "The Story of Malawi's Capitals: Old and New, 1891–1961." *Society of Malawi Journal* 24, no. 1 (1971).

Pennant, Thomas G. E. "The Growth of Small-Scale Renting in Low-Income Urban Housing in Malawi." In *Housing Africa's Poor.* Edited by Philip Amis and Peter Lloyd. Manchester: Manchester University Press, 1990.

———. "Housing the Urban Labour Force in Malawi: An Historical Overview, 1930–1980." *African Urban Studies* 16 (1983).

———. "Towards a History of Urban Housing in Malawi." *Journal of Social Science* 12 (1985).

Potts, Deborah. "Capital Relocation in Africa: The Case of Lilongwe District in Malawi." *Geographical Journal* 151, no. 2 (1985).

Power, Joey. "Individual Enterprise and Enterprising Individuals: African Entrepreneurship in Blantyre and Limbe, 1907–1953." Ph.D. diss., Dalhousie University, 1990.

Rangeley, W. H. J. "Early Blantyre." *Nyasaland Journal* 7, no. 1 (1954).

Richards, Geraint. *From Vision to Reality: The Story of Malawi's Capital.* Johannesburg: Lorton, 1974.

Williams, S. G. B. "The Beginnings of Mzuzu with Some Biographical Notes of Some Viphya Tung Project Managers." *Society of Malawi Journal* 22, no. 1 (1969).

Education

American Council on Education. *Survey Team on Education in Malawi.* Washington, D.C.: Agency for International Development, 1964.

Banda, Kelvin N. *A Brief History of Education in Malawi.* Blantyre: Dzuka.

Blood, A. *The Fortunate Few: Education in East and Central Africa.* London: Universities' Mission to Central Africa, 1954.

Charlton, E. E. *Education Planning in Malawi.* Paris: UNESCO, 1973.

Chimwenje, Dennis Danny. "Curriculum Planning and Decision Making Process in Secondary Schools in Malawi." Ed.D. diss., University of Massachusetts, 1990.

Donnelly, W., et al. *Education Project*. Zomba: Government Printer, 1965.

Fletcher, Basil. *The Background of Educational Development in the Federation*. Salisbury: University College of Rhodesia, 1959.

Hanson, J. *Secondary-Level Teachers: Supply and Demand in Malawi*. East Lansing: Michigan State University, 1969.

Harawa, Bernard A. "The Union of Malawi: Its Emergence, Development, and Activities from 1943 to 1973." Ed.D. diss., Columbia University Teachers College, 1974.

Hunter, G., and L. Hunter. *Adult Education in the Federation of Rhodesia and Nyasaland and Kenya*. Nairobi, 1959.

Hyde, K. *Gender Streaming as a Strategy for Improving Girls' Academic Performance: Evidence from Malawi*. Zomba: University of Malawi Centre for Social Research, 1993.

——. *Instructional and Institutional Barriers to Girls' Achievements in Secondary Schools in Malawi: Preliminary Survey Results*. Zomba: University of Malawi Centre for Social Research, 1993.

Hyneman, Stephen. *The Evaluation of Human Capital in Malawi*. Washington, D.C.: World Bank, 1980.

——. "The Formal as a Traditional Institution in an Underdeveloped Society: The Case of Northern Malawi." *Paedagogica Historica* 12, no. 2 (1972).

Jee-Peng, Tan, et al. *User Charges for Education: The Ability and Willingness to Pay in Malawi*. Washington, D.C.: World Bank, 1984.

Jones, Thomas J. *Education in East Central and South Africa*. New York: Phelps-Stokes Fund, 1925.

Kandawire, J. "Education and Rural Development in Colonial Nyasaland." *Journal of East Africam Research and Development* 4, no. 2 (1974).

Kanyuka, Martin Cecil. "Moral Regulation of Young Offenders in Malawi: A Study of the Chilwa Approved School." Ph.D. diss., University of Toronto, 1990.

Kishindo, Paul. "The Case of Non-Formal Vocational Education for Out Of School Youths in Rural Malawi." *Development Southern Africa* 10, no. 3 (1993).

Klees, Steven J. "The Need for a Political Economy of Educational Finance: A Response to Thobani." *Comparative Education Review* 28, no. 3 (1984).

Lamba, Isaac C. "The Cape Dutch Reformed Church Mission in Malawi: A Preliminary Historical Examination of Its Educational Philosophy And Application, 1899–1931." *TransAfrican Journal of History* 12 (1983).

——. "The History of Post-War Education in Colonial Malawi, 1945–1961," Ph.D. diss., University of Edinburgh, 1984.

——. "Moulding the Ideal Colonial Subject: The Scouting Movement in Colonial Malawi up to 1961." *TransAfrican Journal of History* 14 (1985).

Lawless, C. J. "An Investigation into the Use of Programmed Learning Materials in Malawi Secondary Schools." Ph.D. diss., University of Reading, 1973.

Laws, Robert. "Native Education in Nyasaland." *Journal of African Society* 28 (1929).

Lola, Edrinne E. "Piaget's Theory of Formal Operational Thinking and the Teaching of History in Malawi Secondary Schools." *Journal of Social Science* 8 (1980–1981).

McCracken, John. "The University of Livingstonia." *Society of Malawi Journal* 27, no. 2 (1974).

Macdonald, Roderick J. "A History of African Education in Nyasaland, 1875–1945." Ph.D. diss., University of Edinburgh, 1969.

——. "The Socio-Economic Significance of Educational Initiatives in Malawi, 1899–1939." *TransAfrican Journal of History* 2, no. 2 (1972).

Malawi Ministry of Education and Culture. *Secondary School Teacher Needs: 1981–88.* Lilongwe: Malawi Ministry of Education, 1982.

Nsaliwa, Christina Doris. "Decentralization of Educational Decision-Making in Malawi." Ph.D. diss., University of Alberta, 1996.

Nyirenda, D. M. C. "An Evaluation of the Implementation of National Curriculum Changes in Science and Mathematics in Malawi: With Reference to Parallel Changes in England and Wales." Ph.D. diss., University of Nottingham, 1994.

Pachai, Bridglal. "A History of Colonial Education for Africans." In *Independence without Freedom: The Political Economy of Colonial Education in Southern Africa.* Edited by A. T. Mugomba and M. Nyaggah. Oxford: ABC-Clio. 1980.

Pretorius, J. L. "The Story of African Education in Malawi, 1875–1941." In *Malawi Past and Present.* Edited by B. Pachai et al. Blantyre: CLAIM, 1971.

Steytler, J. G. *Education Adaptation with Reference to African Village Schools.* London: Sheldon, 1939.

Thobani, Mateen. "Changing User Fees for Social Services: Education in Malawi." *Comparative Education Review* 28, no. 3 (1984).

Van Breugel, J. W. M. "The Religious Function of the Nyao among the Chewa of Malawi." *Cultures et Development* 17, no. 3 (1985).

Wilkinson, Michael. Recent Development in Legal Education in Malawi." *Indian Socio-legal Journal* 5, no. 1–2 (1979).

Woods, A. W. "Training Malawi's Youth: The Young Pioneers." *Community Development Journal* 5, no. 3 (1970).

Religion and Missions

Amanze, James. "The Bimbi Shrine in the Upper Shire and Its Relationship with Yao Chiefs, 1830–1925." *Journal of Social Science* 9 (1982)

Anderson-Moreshead, A. E. *The History of the Universities Mission to Central Africa.* Vol. 1. London: UMCA, 1955.

Ballantyne, M., and R. Shepard. *Forerunners of Modern Malawi: The Early Missionary Adventures of Dr. James Henderson, 1895–98.* Alice, South Africa: Lovedale, 1968.

Barnes, Bertram. *Johnson of Nyasaland.* Westminster: UMCA, 1933.

Blaikie, William. *The Life of David Livingstone.* New York: Negro University Press, 1969.

Blood, A. G. *The History of the Universities' Mission to Central Africa.* Vol. 2, *1907–1932.* London: UMCA, 1957.

——. *The History of the Universities' Mission to Central Africa.* Vol. 3, *1933–1957.* London: UMCA, 1962.

Bone, David S. "Christian Missionary Response to the Development of Islam in Malawi, 1879–1986." *Bulletin on Islam and Christian-Muslim Relations in Africa* 2, no. 3 (1984).

——. "Islam in Malawi." *Journal of Religion in Africa* 13, no. 2 (1982).

——. "Muslim Minority in Malawi and Western Education." *Journal of the Institute of Muslim Minority* 6, no. 2 (1985).

——. *Religion in Malawi: Current Research.* Zomba: University of Malawi Department of Religious of Studies, 1983.

Catholic Bishops of Malawi. *The Truth Will Set You Free.* London: CIIR, 1992. Originally "Living Our Faith," the pastoral letter of the Catholic bishops of Malawi read in all Catholic churches on March 8, 1992.

Chadwick, Owen. *MacKenzie's Grave.* London: Hodder & Stoughton, 1959.

Chakanza, Joseph Chaphadzika. *An Annotated List of Independent Churches in Malawi.* Zomba: University of Malawi, 1980.

——. "The Independency Alternative: A Historical Survey." *Religion in Malawi* 4 (1994).

——. "The Pro-Democracy Movement in Malawi: The Catholic Church's Contribution." *Religion in Malawi* 4 (1994).

——. "Religious Independency in Malawi: The Catholic Church, a Negative Case." *AFER* 24 (1982).

——. "Religious Independency in Southern Malawi." In *Ministry of Mission to African Independent Churches.* Edited by D. A. Shenk. Elkhart, Ind.: Mennonite Board of Missions, 1987.

——. "Religious Revitalization in Malawi: The African Ancestors' Religion." *Journal of Humanities* 3 (1989).

——. "Sectarianism in Joseph Booth's Mission Foundations, 1925–1975: The Death of Creative Factors." *Religion in Malawi* 2, no. 1 (1988).

——. "Towards an Interpretation of Independent Churches in Malawi." *Africa Theological Journal* 11, no. 2 (1982).

——. "Unfinished Agenda: Puberty Rites and the Response of the Roman Catholic Church in Southern Malawi, 1901–1994." *Religion in Malawi* 5 (1995).

——. *Voices of Preachers in Protest, the Ministries of Two Prophets: Eliot Kamwana and Wilfred Gudu.* Blantyre: CLAIM, 1998.

Chakanza, Joseph Chaphadzika, ed. *Islam Week in Malawi.* Blantyre: CLAIM, 2000.

Chamberlin, D. *Some Letters from Livingstone, 1840–1892.* London, 1940.

Chingota, F. "A Historical Account of the Attitude of the Blantyre Synod of the Church of the Central Africa Presbyterian towards Initiation Rites." *Religion in Malawi* 2, no. 1 (1988).

Chiphangwi, S. D. "Why People Join the Christian Church: Trends in Church Growth in the Blantyre Synod of the Church of Central Africa Presbyterian, 1960–1975." Ph.D. diss., University of Aberdeen, 1978.

Chirnside, Andrew. *The Blantyre Missionaries: Discreditable Disclosures.* London: Ridgeway, 1880.

Chirwa, Wiseman C. "Musokwa Elliot Kenan Kmwana Chirwa: His Religious and Political Activities, and Impact in Nkata Bay, 1908–1956." *Journal of Social Science* 12 (1985).

Colvin, Tom, ed. *Blantyre Mission with Prayer and Praise.* Blantyre: Hetherwick, 1976.

——. *A Record of Father and Founders of Blatyre Synod.* Blantyre: CCAP Synod of Blantyre, 1976.

Coupland, Reginald. *Livingstone's Last Journey*. London: Collins, 1945.

Debenham, Frank. *The Way to Ilala: David Livingstone's Pilgrimage*. London: Bell, 1955.

Dijk, R. "Fundamentalism and Its Moral Geography in Malawi: The Representation of the Diasporic and Diabolical." *Critique of Anthropolgy* 15, no. 2 (1995).

Domingo, Charles. *Letters of Charles Domingo*. Edited by Harry Langworthy. Sources for the Study of Religion in Malawi no. 9. Zomba: Sources for the Study of Religion in Malawi, 1963.

DuPlessis, J. *The Evangelization of Pagan Africa: A History of Christian Missions to the Pagan Tribes of Central Africa (Yao, Ngoni, Tonga)*. Cape Town: Juta, 1930.

Elmslie, Walter. *Among the Wild Ngoni: History of Livingstonia Mission*. London: Oliphant & Ferrier, 1899.

Emtage, J. E. R. "The First Mission Settlement in Nyasaland." *Nyasaland Journal* 8, no. 1 (1955).

Ferrari, Lisa Louise. "The Influence of Moral Authority in International Relations: A Case Study of the Catholic Church under John Paul II." Ph.D. diss., Georgetown University, 1998.

Ferrari, Lisa Louise, and Godfrey Banda. "The Last Church of God and His Christ." *Journal of Religion in Africa* 29, no. 4 (1999).

Fielder, Klaus. "At the Receiving End: The Jehovah's Witnesses' Experience in One-Party Malawi." In *God, People, and Power in Malawi: Democratization in Theological Perspective*. Edited by Kenneth Ross. Blantyre: CLAIM, 1996.

———. "Joseph Booth and the Writings of Malawian History: An Attempt at Interpretation." *Religion in Malawi* 6 (1996).

Fields, Karen E. *Revival and Rebellion in Colonial Central Africa*. Princeton: Princeton University Press, 1985.

Forster, Peter G. "Missionaries and Anthropology: The Case of the Scots of Northern Malawi." *Journal of Religion in Africa* 16, no. 2 (1986).

———. *T. Cullen Young: Missionary and Anthropologist*. Hull, U.K.: Hull University Press, 1989.

Fraser, Agnes R. *Donald Fraser of Livingstonia*. London: Hodder & Stoughton. 1934.

Fraser, Donald. *The Future of Africa*. London: Church Missionary Society, 1911.

———. *Winning a Primitive People*. London: Seeley Service, 1914.

Goodwin, Harvey. *Memoir of Bishop Mackenzie*. Cambridge: Deighton Bell, 1864.

Gray, Ernst. "The Early History of the Churches of Christ: Missionary Work in Nyasaland, Central Africa, 1907–1930." Churches of Christ Occasional Paper no. 1. Cambridge, 1981.

Greenstein, Robert C. "The Nyasaland Government Policy toward African Muslims, 1900–25." In *From Nyasaland to Malawi: Studies in Colonial History*. Edited by R. J. Macdonald. Nairobi: East African Publishing House, 1975.

Henderson, James. *Forerunners of Modern Malawi*. Alice, South Africa: Lovedale, 1968.

Hetherwick, Alexander. *The Building of the Blantyre Church, Nyasaland, 1888–1891*. Blantyre: Church of Central Africa Presbyterian, 1940.

———. *The Gospel and the African*. Edinburgh: T.& T. Clark, 1932.

———. "Islam and Christianity in Nyasaland." *Muslim World* 17, no. 2 (1927).

———. *The Romance of Blantyre*. London: James Clark, [1931].

Hicks, T. H. *Hornbill Hill: A Mission in Nyasaland*. London: Central Africa House Press, 1953.

Hinchcliff, Peter. "The Blantyre Scandal: Scottish Missionaries and Colonialism." *Journal of Theology for Southern Africa* 46 (March 1984).

Hofmeyr, A. L. "Islam in Nyasaland." *Moslem World* 2 (1912).

Hooker, James R. "Witnesses and Watchtower in the Rhodesias and Nyasaland." *Journal of African History* 6, no. 1 (1965).

Inwood, Charles. *An African Pentecost: The Record of a Missionary Tour in Central Africa*. London, 1911.

Jack, J. *Daybreak in Livingstonia*. New York: Young People's Missionary Movement, 1900.

Jeal, Tim. *Livingstone*. New York: Dell, 1973.

Jenkins, P. "Mission Accomplished." *Society of Malawi Journal* 39, no. 1 (1996).

Johnson, W. P. *My African Reminiscences, 1875–1895*. London: Butler & Tanner, 1924.

Kalilombe, Patrick A. "The African Local Churches and the World-Wide Roman Catholic Communion: Modification Of Relationships, as Exemplified by Lilongwe Diocese." In *Christianity in Independent Africa*. Edited by E. Fashole-Luke et al. London: Rex Colins, 1978.

———. *Doing Theology at the Grassroots: Theological Essays from Malawi*. Gweru: Mambo, 1999.

———. "From Outstations to 'Small Christian Communities': A Comparison between Two Pastoral Methods in Lilongwe Diocese." Ph.D. diss., University of California, 1983.

———. "From Outstations to Small Christian Communities." *Spearhead* 82 (1984).

———. "Outline of Chewa Traditional Religion." *Africa Theological Journal* 9, no. 2 (1980).

Kalinga, Owen J. M. "Jordan Msumba, Ben Ngemela, and the Last Church of God and His Christ, 1924–1935." *Journal of Religion in Africa* 13, no. 3 (1982).

Kamnkhwani, H. A. "An Evaluation of the Historiography of Nkhoma Synod, Church of Central Africa Presbyterian." Ph.D. diss., University of Stellenbosch, 1990.

Kaspin, Deborah, "Chewa Visions and Revisions of Power: Transformation of the Nyau Dance in Central Malawi." In *Modernity and Its Discontents*. Edited by Jean Comaroff and John Comaroff. Chicago: University of Chicago Press, 1993.

Keable, R. *Darkness or Light: Studies in the History of UMCA* London: UMCA, 1914.

Kishindo, J. H. A. *Mbiri ya Ecclesia Anglicana ku Nyasaland, 1860–1960*. Cape Town: Oxford University Press, 1960.

Langworthy, Emily Booth. *This Africa Was Mine*. Stirling: Stirling Tract Society, 1952.

Langworthy, Harry W. *Africa for Africans: The Life of Joseph Booth*. Blantyre: CLAIM, 1996.

———. "Charles Domingo, Seventh-Day Baptist and Independency." *Journal of Religion in Africa* 15, no. 2 (1985).

———. "Joseph Booth, Prophet of Radical Change in Central and Southern Africa, 1891–1915." *Journal of Religion in Africa* 16 (1986).

Laws, Robert. *Reminiscences of Livingstone*. Edinburgh: Oliver & Boyd, 1934.

———. *Women's Work at Livingstonia*. Paisley, 1886.

Linden, Ian. "Chewa Initiation Rites and Nyau Soceities: The Use of Religious Institutions in Local Politics at Mua." In *Themes in the Christian History of Central Africa*. Edited by T. O. Ranger and J. Weller. London: Heinemann, 1974.

———. *The Mponda Mission Diary, 1889–1891*. Lilongwe: White Fathers, 1989.

Linden, Ian, with Jane Linden. *Catholics, Peasants, and Chewa Resistance in Nyasaland, 1889–1939*. London: Heinemann, 1974.

———. "John Chilembwe and the 'New Jerusalem.'" *Journal of African History* 12, no. 4 (1971).

Livingstone, W. P. *Laws of Livingstonia*. London: Hodder & Stoughton, 1921.

Lohrentz, Kenneth P. "Joseph Booth, Charles Domingo, and Seventh-Day Baptists in Northern Nyasaland, 1910–12." *Journal of African History* 12, no. 3 (1971).

Long, Norman. "Bandawe Mission Station and Local Politics, 1878–1886." *Rhodes-Livingstone Journal* 32 (1962).

McCracken, John. "Church and State in Malawi: The Role of the Scottish Presbyterian Missions." In *The Role of Christianity in Development and Reconstruction*. Edited by I. Phiri et al. Nairobi: All Africa Council of Churches, 1996.

———. "Livingstone and the Aftermath: The Origins and Development of Livingstonia." In *Livingstone: Man of Africa*. Edited by B. Pachai. London: Longmans, 1973.

———. "Livingstonia in the Development of Malawi: A Reassessment." *Bulletin of the Scottish Institute of Missionary Studies* 10 (1994).

———. "Livingstonia Mission and the Evolution of Malawi, 1873–1939." Ph.D. diss., Cambridge University, 1967.

———. "New Perspectives on the History of Christianity in Malawi." *Journal of Religion in Africa* 29, no. 4 (1999).

———. *Politics and Christianity in Malawi, 1875–1940: The Impact of the Livingstonia Mission in the Northern Province*. Cambridge: Cambridge University Press, 1977.

———. "The Underdevelopment in Malawi: The Missionary Contribution." *African Affairs* 76, no. 303 (1977).

McCulloch, Mary. *A Time to Remember: The Story of the Diocese of Nyasaland*. London: UMCA, 1959.

McDonald, L. J. "Mackenzie's Grave." *Nyasaland Journal* 14, no. 1 (1960).

McIntosh, Hamish. "Contracts of Employment and the Influence of Class in the First Thirty Years of the Livingstonia Mission." *Scottish Church History Society* 23, no. 1 (1987).

———. "The Effects of the War of 1914–18 on the Livingstonia Mission." *Bulletin of the Scottish Institute of Missionary Studies* 4–5 (1988–89).

———. *Robert Laws: Servant of Africa*. Carberry, Scotland: Handsel, 1993.

———. "Robert Laws as a Preacher." *Bulletin of the Scottish Institute of Missionary Studies* 3–4 (1985–1987).

Macdonald, Roderick J. "Religious Independency as a Means of Social Advance in Northern Nyasaland in the 1930s." *Journal of Religion in Africa* 3, no. 2 (1970).

———. "The Rev. Dr. Daniel Sharpe Malikembu and the Reopening of Providence Industrial Mission, 1926–39: An Appreciation." In *From Nyasaland to Malawi: Studies in Colonial History*. Edited by R. J. Macdonald. Nairobi: East African Publishing House, 1975.

————. "Reverend Hanock Msokera Phiri and the Establishment in Nyasaland of the African Methodist Episcopal Church." *African Historical Studies* 3, no. 1 (1970).

Macpherson, Fergus. "The Ncherenje Memorial Stone." *Nyasaland Journal* 13, no. 1 (1960).

————. *North of the Zambezi: A Modern Missionary Memoir.* Edinburgh: Handsel, 1998.

————. "Sumu za Chifipa: Christian Songs in Malawi." *Bulletin of the Scottish Institute of Missionary Studies* 6–7 (1990–1991).

————. "The 1959 Emergency at Livingstonia." *Bulletin of the Scottish Missionary Studies* 10 (1994).

Maples, Ellen. *Journals and Papers of Chauncy Maples.* London: Longmans Green, 1899.

Martelli, George. *Livingstone's River.* London: Chatto & Windus, 1970.

Mgawi, K. J. *CCAP Nkhoma Synod: Mbiri ya Mpingo ndi Mudzi wa Nkhoma 1896 mpaka 1996.* Nkhoma: Nkhoma Synod, n.d.

Mijoga, Hilary B. P. "Hermeneutics in African-Instituted Churches in Malawi." *Missionalia* 24, no. 3 (1996)

Morris, L., and M. *Livingstone. Trail Blazer for God.* Mountain View, CA: Mountain View Press, 1959.

Morrison, James Horne. *Streams of the Desert: A Picture of Life in Livingstonia.* London: Hodder & Stoughton, 1919.

Moyo, Fulata L. "Church and Society and Government: A Survey and Evaluation of the Prophetic Ministry of the Livingstonia Synod of the CCAP, 1964–1992." M.A. thesis, University of Zimbabwe, 1993.

Msiska, Mpalive Hangson, "Notes on Identity Formation at a Mission School." *Bulletin of the Scottish Institute of Missionary Studies* 10 (1994).

Mufuka, Kenneth. *Mission and Politics in Malawi.* Kingston, Ontario: Limestone, 1976.

Murray, Andrew C. *Nyasaland en mijjne Ondervindingen Aldaar.* Amsterdam, 1897.

————. *Ons Nyasa Akker.* Stellenbosch, 1931.

Murray, William H. *Mbiri ya Misyoni ya DRC M'dziko la Nyasa.* Nkhoma: Nkhoma Mission Press, 1948.

————. *Op Pad.* Cape Town, 1940.

Musopole, Augustine C. "The Chewa Concept of God and Its Implications for the Christian Faith." M.A. thesis, University of Malawi, 1984.

————. "Towards a theological method in Malawi." *Journal of the Theology for Southern Africa* 82 (1993).

Muyebe, Stanslaus O. P., and A. Muyebe, S. J. *The Religious Factor within the Body of Poltical Symbolism in Malawi, 1964–1994: A Bibliographical Essay.* Universal Publishers/www.upublish.com, 1999.

Mwakanandi, D. S. "The Role of African Traditional Religion in the Promotion of Christian Faith in Malawi." D.Th. diss., University of Stellenbosch, 1990.

Mwasi, Yesaya Zerenje. *Essential and Paramount Reasons for Working Independently.* Limbe: CLAIM, 1998.

Nankwenya, I. A. J. "Christian Influence on Education in Malawi up to Independence with Special Reference to the Role of the Catholic Missionaries." D.Ed. Diss., University of South Africa, 1977.

Ncozana, S. S. "Mvano and Evangelism in the Synod of Blantyre." *Africa Theological Journal* 15, no. 3 (1966).

——. *Sangaya: A Leader in the Synod of Blantyre Church of Central Africa Presbyterian*. Blantyre: CLAIM, 1996.

——. "Spirit Possession and Tumbuka Christians." Ph.D. diss., University of Aberdeen, 1985.

Nzunda, M. N., and K. R. Ross, eds. *Church, Law, and Political Transition in Malawi, 1992–94*. Gweru: Mambo, 1995.

Ott, Martin. *African Theology in Images*. Blantyre: CLAIM, 2000.

——. "The Church and Culture on Display: The Opening of the Chamare Museum in Mua." *Religion in Malawi* 8 (1998).

Pachai, B., ed. *Livingstone: Man of Africa*. London: Longman, 1973.

Patel, Nandini. "The Hindus in Malawi." *Religion in Malawi* 6 (1996).

Parratt, John. "African Independent Churches in Malawi." *Journal of Social Science* 9 (1982).

——. "The Mbombwe Case." *Exploring the New Religious Movements: Essays in Honour of Harold Turner*. Edited by A. F. Walls and W. R. Shenk. Elkhart: Mission Focus, 1990.

——. "Religious Independency in Nyasaland: A Typology of Origins." *African Studies* 38, no. 2 (1979).

——. "Y. Z. Mwasi and the Origins of the Blackman's Church." *Journal of Religion in Africa* 9, no. 3 (1978).

Pauw, C. M. "African Independent Churches in Malawi: Background and Historical Development." In *African Churches Today: Kaleidoscope of Afro-Christianity*. Edited by M. C. Kitshoff. Lewiston, N.Y.: Edwin Mellen, 1996.

——. "Independency and Religious Change in Malawi: A New Challenge for the Church." *Missionalia* 21, no. 3 (1993).

——. "Mission and Church in Malawi: The History of Nkhoma Synod of the Church of Central Africa Presbyterian, 1889–1962." D.Th. diss., University of Stellenbosch, 1980.

Phiri, I. A. "African Women in Religion and Culture: Chewa Women in the Nkhoma Synod of the Church of Central Africa Presbyterian: A Critical Study from Women's Perspective." Ph.D. diss., University of Cape Town, 1992.

——. "The Initiation of Chewa Women of Malawi: A Presbyterian Women's Perspective." *Religion in Malawi* 5 (1995).

——. *Women, Presbyterianism, and Patriarchy: Religious Experience of Chewa Women in Central Malawi*. Blantyre: CLAIM, 1997.

——. "Women in Theological Education in Malawi." *Religion in Malawi* 1 (1991).

Phiri, K. M. "Role of the Christian community in Development: A Historical Background to the Present Situation in Malawi." *Journal of Social Science* 11, no. 1 (1984).

Pretorious, J. L. "An Introduction to the History of the Dutch Reformed Church Mission in Malawi, 1889–1914." In *The Early History of Malawi*. Edited by B. Pachai. London: Longman, 1972.

——. "The Story of the Dutch Reformed Church Mission in Nyasaland." *Nyasaland Journal* 10, no. 1 (1957).

Pretorius, Pauline. "An Attempt at Christian Initiation in Nyasaland." *International Review of Missions* 34 (1950).

Price, E., ed. "Gdidi Mission Sation, Nyasaland." *South African Pioneer* 26, no. 1 (1913).

Quinn, Anne-Lise. "Holding on to Mission Christianity: Case Studies from a Presbyterian Church in Malawi." *Journal of Religion in Africa* 20, no. 4 (1995).

———. "Working on the Protestant Ethic: Life in a Presbyterian Community in Malawi." Ph.D. diss., Cambridge University, 1993.

Randolf, B. *Arthur Douglas: Missionary on Lake Nyasa*. London: UMCA, 1912.

Rangeley, W. H. "Mbona the Rainmaker." *Nyasaland Journal* 6, no. 2 (1952).

———. "Nyasaland Rain Shrines." *Nyasaland Journal* 5, no. 2 (1952).

———. "Nyau in Kota Kota District." *Nyasaland Journal* 2, no. 2 (1949); 3, no. 2 (1950).

Ranger, T., and J. Weller, eds. *Themes in the Christian History of Central Africa*. London: Heinemann, 1975.

Reijnaerts, H., A. Neilsen, and M. Schoffeleers. *Montfortians in Malawi: Their Spirituality and Pastoral Approach*. Blantyre: CLAIM, 1997.

Retief, M. W. *William Murray of Nyasaland*. Alice, South Africa: Lovedale, 1958.

Riddel, Alexander. *A Reply to 'the Blantyre Missionaries: Discreditable Disclosure' by Andrew Chirnside*. Edinburgh: Blackwood. 1880.

Robertson, William. *The Martyrs of Blantyre*. London: James Nisbet, 1903.

Roome, W. J. *A Great Emancipation: A Missionary Survey of Nyasaland Central Africa*. London: World Dominion Press, 1926.

Ross, Andrew C. "The African: 'A Child or a Man'? The Quarrel between the Blantyre Mission of the Church of Scotland and the British Central African Administration." In *The Zambezian Past: Studies in Central African History*. Edited by Eric Stokes and Richard Brown. Manchester: Manchester University Press, 1966.

———. *Blantyre Mission and the Making of Modern Malawi*. Blantyre: CLAIM, 1996.

———. "The Blantyre Mission and the Problems of Land and Labour, 1891–1915." In *From Nyasaland to Malawi: Studies in Colonial History*. Edited by Roderick J. Macdonald. Nairobi: East African Publishing House, 1975.

———. "Forty-Five Years of Turmoil: Malawi Christian Churches, 1949–1994." *International Bulletin of Missionary Research* 18, 2 (1994).

———. "Livingstone and the Aftermath: The Origins and Development of the Blantyre Mission," Edited by B. Pachai. *Livingstone: Man of Africa*. London: Longman, 1973.

———. "Wokondedwa Wathu: The Mzungu Who Mattered." *Religion in Malawi* 8 (April 1998).

Ross, Kenneth R. "Current Ecclesiological Trends in Northern Malawi." *Journal of Religion in Africa* 29, no. 4 (1999).

———. *God, People, and Power in Malawi: Democratization in Theological Perspective*. Blantyre: CLAIM, 1996.

———. *Gospel Ferment in Malawi: Theological Essays*. Gweru: Mambo, 1995.

———. *Here Comes Your King! Christ, Church, and Nation in Malawi*. Blantyre: CLAIM, 1998.

———. "Preaching in Mainstream Christian Churches in Malawi: A Survey and Analysis." *Journal of Religion in Africa* 25 (1995).

———. "The Renewal of the State by the Church: The Case of the Public Affairs Committee in Malawi." *Religion in Malawi* 5 (1995).

Ross, Kenneth R., ed. *Christianity in Malawi: A Source Book*. Gweru: Mambo, 1996.

——. *Church, University, and Theological Education in Malawi*. Zomba: University of Malawi Department of Theological and Religious Studies, 1995.

Schoffeleers, Matthew M. "The AIDS Pandemic, 'The Prophet' Billy Chisumpe, and the Democratization Process in Malawi." *Journal of Religion in Africa* 29, no. 4 (1999).

——. *Evil Spirits and the Rites of Exorcism in the Lower Shire Valley of Malawi*. Limbe: Montfort, 1967.

——. "The History and Political Role of the Mbona Cult among the Mang'anja." *Historical Study of African Religions*. Edited by T. O. Ranger and I. N. Kimambo. London: Heinemann, 1972.

——. *In Search of Truth and Justice: Confrontation between Church and State in Malawi, 1860–1994*. Blantyre: CLAIM, 1999.

——. "The Nyau Societies: Our Present Understanding." *Society of Malawi Journal* 29, no. 1 (1978).

——. *Pentecostalism and Neo-Traditionalism: The Religious Polarization of a Rural District in Southern Malawi*. Amterdam: Free University Press, 1985.

——. *Religion and the Dramatization of Life: Spirit Beliefs and Rituals in Southern Malawi and Central Malawi*. Blantyre: CLAIM, 1996.

——. *River of Blood: The Genesis of a Martyr Cult in Southern Malawi, c. A.D. 1600*. Madison: University of Wisconsin Press, 1992.

Schoffeleers, Matthew M., ed. *Guardians of the Land: Essays in Central African Territorial Cults*. Gwelo: Mambo, 1978.

Seaver, George. *David Livingstone: His Life and Letters*. London: Lutterworth, 1957.

Selfridge, John. *The Church's First Thirty Years in Nyasaland (now Malawi), 1861–1891*. Nkhoma: Nkhoma Press, (1976).

Shepperson, G. "Church and Sect in Central Africa." *Rhodes-Livingstone Journal* 33 (1963).

——. "Ethiopianism and African Nationalism." *Phylon* 14 (1953).

——. "The Jumbe of Kota Kota and Some Aspects of the History of Islam in Malawi." In *Islam in Tropical Africa*. Edited by I. M. Lewis. London: Hutchinson, 1969.

——. "Nyasaland and the Millennium." In *Millenial Dreams in Action*. Edited by Sylvia L. Thrupp. The Hague: Mouton, 1962.

——. "The Politics of Church Separatist Movements in British Central Africa, 1892–1916." *Africa* 24, no. 3 (1954).

Shepperson, G., and Thomas Price. *Independent Africa: John Chilembwe and the Origins, Setting, and Significance of the Nyasaland Native Rising of 1915*. Edinburgh: Edinburgh University Press, 1958.

Sindima, Harvey Jeffrey. *The Legacy of the Scottish Missionaries in Malawi*. Lewiston, N.Y.: Edwin Mellen Press, 1992.

——. "Malawian Churches and the Struggle for Life and Personhood: Crisis and Rapture of Malawian Thought and Society." Ph.D. diss., Princeton Theological Seminary, 1987.

Stone, W. Vernon. "The Livingstonia Mission and the Bemba." *Bulletin of the Society for African Church History* 2 (1968).

Stuart, Richard. "Anglican Missionaries and a Chewa *Dini* Conversion and Rejection in Central Malawi." *Journal of Religion in Africa* 10, no. 1 (1979).
———. "Christianity and Chewa: The Anglican Case, 1885–1950." Ph.D. diss., University of London, 1974.
Taylor, Helen M. *Tunes from Nyasaland*. Livingstonia: Livingtonia Mission, 1959.
Thompson, T. Jack. "African Leadership in the Livingstonia Mission, 1875–1900." *Journal of Social Science* 2 (1973).
———. *The Blantyre Centenary, 1876–1976*. Blantyre: CLAIM, 1976.
———. *Christianity in Northern Malawi: Donald Fraser's Missionary Methods and Ngoni Culture*. Leiden: Brill, 1995.
———. "An Independent Church Which Never Was: The Case of Jonathan Chirwa." *Exploring New Religious Movements: Essays in Honour of Harold W. Turner*. Edited by A. F. Walls and W. R. Shenk. Elkhart: Mission Focus Publications, 1990.
———. "The Legacy of Donald Fraser." *International Bulletin of Missionary Research* 18, no. 1 (1994).
———. *Livingstonia, 1875–1975*. Blantyre: CLAIM, 1975.
———. "Speaking for Ourselves: The African Writers of Livingstonia." *Bulletin of the Scottish Missionary Studies* 10 (1994).
———. "True Love and Roots: A Centenary Re-Assessment of the Work of William Koyi among the Ngoni." *Society of Malawi Journal* 39, no. 2 (1986).
———. "Xhosa Missionaries in Late Nineteenth-Century Malawi: Strangers or Fellow Countrymen?" *Religion in Malawi* 8 (April 1998).
Thompson, Van D. "Preparations for Urban Evangelism in Capital City Baptist Church, Lilongwe, Malawi." D.Min. diss., Southern Baptist Theological Seminary, 1990.
Thorold, Alan. "Metamorphoses of the Yao Muslims." In *Muslim Identity and Social Change in SubSaharan Africa*. Edited by Louis Brenner. Bloomington: Indiana University Press, 1993.
———. "Yao Conversion to Islam." *Cambridge Anthropology* 12, no. 2 (1987).
Vail, Leroy. "Religion, Language, and Tribal Myth: The Tumbuka and Chewa of Malawi." *Guardians of the Land: Essays on Central African Territorial Cults*. Edited by J. M. Schoffeleers. Gwelo: Mambo, 1978.
Van Dijk, Rick A. "Young Malawian Puritans: Young Preachers in a Present-Day Urban African Environment." Ph.D. diss., University of Utrecht, 1992.
———. "Young Preachers in Post-Independence Malawi: The Significance of an Extraneous Identity." In *New Dimensions in African Christianity*. Edited by P. Gifford. Nairobi: AACC, 1992.
———. "Young Puritan Preachers in Post-Independence Malawi." *Africa* 62, no. 2 (1992).
Van Velsen, Jaap. "The Missionary Factor among the Lakeside Tonga on Nyasaland." *Rhodes Livingstone Journal* 26 (1959).
Vezeeua, Roland. *The Apostolic Vicariate of Nyasa: Origins and First Developments, 1889–1935*. Rome: Historical Department, Missionari d'Africa, 1989.
Von Rumker, A. *Die Organisation Bauerlicher Betriebe in der Zentralregion Malawis*. Frankfurt, 1972.
Waldman, Marilyn. "The Church of Scotland Mission at Blantyre, Nyasaland: Its Political Implications." *Bulletin of the Society of African Church History* 2, no. 4 (1968).

Warren, N., ed. "Assemblies of God in Malawi, 1947–1972." Assemblies of God, n.d.

Weller, John C. *Mainstream Christianity to 1980 in Malawi, Zambia, and Zimbabwe*. Gwelo: Mambo, 1984.

Wilson, George H. *The History of the Universities' Mission to Central Africa*. London: UMCA, 1936.

Winspear, F. C. "A Short History of the Universities' Mission." *Nyasaland Journal* 13, no. 2 (1960).

Wishlade, R. L. *Sectarianism in Southern Nyasaland*. London: Oxford University Press, 1965.

White, Landeg. *Magomero: Portrait of an African Village*. Cambridge: Cambridge University Press, 1987.

Young, T. Cullen. "The Idea of God in Northern Nyasaland." In *African Idea of God*. Edited by Edwin Smith. Edinburgh: Edinburgh University Press, 1950.

SCIENCE

Earth Sciences

Baker, Colin A. "Geomorphology and the Mlanje Mountain." *Society of Malawi Journal* 19, no. 1 (1966).

Bloomfield, K., and A. Young. "The Geology and Geomorphology of Zomba Mountain." *Nyasaland Journal* 14, no. 2 (1961).

Bloomfield, Keith. "The Petrology of the Basement Complex in Part of Southern Nyasaland with Particular Reference to Infracrustal Rocks." Ph.D. diss., Leeds University.

Chatupa, J. C. "Mineral Exploration in Malawi." *Malawi Geographer* 19 (1979).

Crow, M. J. "Malawi Meteorites, 1899–1981." *Society of Malawi Geographers* 36, no. 1 (1983).

Crossely, R. "Controls of Sedimentation in the Rift Valley." *Sedimentary Geology* 40 (1984).

Crossley, R., and J. M. Crow. "The Malawi Rift." In *Geodynamic Evolution of the Afro-Arabian Rift Valley System*. Rome: Accademia Nazionale dei Lincie, 1980.

Dixey, F. "The Mlanje Mountains of Nyasaland." *Geographical Review* 17 (1927).

———. "The Nyasaland Section of the Great Rift Valley." *Geographical Journal* 63 (1926).

Neuland, H. "Abnormal High Water Levels of Lake Malawi? An Attempt to Assess the Future Behaviour of the Lake Water Level." *GeoJournal* 9, no. 4 (1984).

Ottley, D. "Mineral Resources Potential in Malawi." *Mining Magazine,* February 1989.

Pike, John G. "The Hydrology of Lake Nyasa." *Journal of the Institute of Water Engineers* 19, no. 7 (1964).

———. "The Movement of Water in Lake Nyasa." *Nyasaland Journal* 10, no. 2 (1957).

———. "The Sunspot/Lake Level Relationship and the Control of Lake Malawi." *Society of Malawi* 21, no. 2 (1968).

Piper, D. P., et al. "A Stratigraphic and Structural Reappraisal of Central Malawi: Results of a Deotraverse." *Journal of African Earth Sciences* 8, no. 1 (1989).
Thatcher, E. C., and K. E. Wilderspin. *The Geology of the Upper Mchinji-Upper Bua Area.* Zomba: Government Printer, 1968.

Geography, Environment, and Conservation

Agnew, Swanzie. "Environment and History." In *The Early History of Malawi.* Edited by B. Pachai. London: Longman, 1972.
———. *The Waters of Malawi: Developments since Independence.* Zomba: Chancellor College Geography/Earth Sciences Department, 1976.
Agnew, Swanzie, and Michael Stubbs. *Malawi in Maps.* London: University of London Press, 1972.
Brown, Peter, and Anthony Young. *The Physical Environment of Central Malawi.* Zomba: Government Printer, 1965.
French, D. "Confronting an Unsolvable Problem: Deforestation in Malawi." *World Development* 4 (1986).
Government of Malawi. *DREA: Environmental Monitoring Programme for Malawi.* Lilongwe: DREA, 1993.
Halcrow, W. *The Valley Project.* 3 vols. London: Halcrow & Partners, 1954.
Hornby, Arthur. *Climate of Central Nyasaland.* Salisbury, 1933.
Jere, G. Z. *Energy and Mineral Resources Development and the Environment.* MOREA, NEAP Task Force no. 3, 1996.
Kalipeni, Ezekiel. "Internal Migration and Development in Malawi: A Geographic Perspective." Ph.D. diss., University of North Carolina, 1986.
———. "Population Growth and Environmental Degradation in Malawi." *Africa Insight* 22, no. 4 (1992).
Kalipeni, Ezekiel, ed. *Population Growth and Environmental Degradation in Southern Africa.* Boulder: Lynne Rienner, 1994.
Lane-Poole, E. *The Human Geography of the Fort Jameson District.* Lusaka: Government Records, 1932.
Lovemore, J. D., et al. *Common Use Indigenous Trees and Forest Products in Malawi: The Case of Four Villages Close to Chimaliro Forest Reserve.* FRIM Report no. 93008. 2d ed. Zomba: Forest Research Institute, 1995.
McCracken, John. "Colonialism, Capitalism, and Ecological Crisis in Malawi: A Reassessment." In *Conservation in Africa.* Edited by D. Anderson and R. Grove. Cambridge: Cambridge University Press, 1987.
Martin, Colin, G. C. *Maps and Surveys of Malawi: A History of Cartography and the Land Survey Profession.* Cape Town: Balkema, 1980.
Ministry of Research and Environmental Affairs [MOREA]. *Malawi Environmental Monitoring Programme: First Environmental Monitoring Report.* Lilongwe: MOREA, 1996.
Moodie, S. "Environmental Indicators and Change: Results of a Quantitative Survey of Smallholders in Four Catchments." In *The Malawi Environmental Monitoring Programme,* Annex 1, University of Arizona, 1996.
Mponda, F. "Malawi: Disappearing Forests Go Up in Smoke." *Africa Information Afrique,* 1986, available at http://csf.colorado.edu/ipe/aia.html.

Mwendera, E. J. *A Short History and Annotated Bibliography on Soil and Water Conservation in Malawi*. Maseru: SADDC, 1989.

Pike, J., and G. Rimmington. *Malawi: A Geographical Study*. London: Oxford University Press, 1965.

Rankin, Daniel. *The Zambesi Basin and Nyasaland*. Edinburgh: Blackwood, 1893.

Strong, C., and D. Gibb. *A Geography of Rhodesia Zambia and Malawi*. Salisbury: Longmans of Rhodesia, 1964.

Thomas, Michael, and G. Whittington, eds. *Environment and Land Use in Africa*. London: Methuen, 1969.

Tobin, Richard J., and W. I. Knausenberger. "Dilemmas of Development: Burley Tobacco, the Environment, and Economic Growth in Malawi." *Journal of Southern African Studies* 24, no. 2 (1998).

Topham, Paul. *The Physiography of Nyasaland and Its Effect on the Forest Flora of the County*. Oxford: Oxford University Press, 1933.

U.S. Department of State. Bureau of Intelligence and Research. *International Boundary Study: Malawi-Mozambique*. Washington, D.C., 1971.

Varady, Robert G. *Draft Environmental Profile of Malawi*. Washington, D.C.: Department of State, 1982.

Willis, Bailey. *East African Plateaus and Rift Valley*. Washington, D.C.: Carnegie Institute, 1936.

Worthington, E. B. *The Wild Resources of East and Central Africa*. London: H.M. Stationery Office, 1961.

Young, Anthony. *A Geography of Malawi*. London: Dent, 1964.

Health and Medicine

AIDS Secretariat. *Malawi AIDS Control Programme: Medium-Term Plan II, 1994–1998*. Lilongwe: AIDS Secretariat, 1994.

Baker, Colin A. "The Government Medical Service in Malawi, 1891–1974." *Medical History* 20, vol. 3 (1976)

Bullough, C. H. W. "Traditional Birth Attendance in Malawi." M.D. diss., University of Glasgow, 1980.

Chimwanza, B. M. "Food and Nutrition in Malawi." Ph.D. diss., University of London, 1982.

Chirwa, I. "AIDS Epidemic in Malawi: Shaking Cultural Foundations: Network." *Network* 13 (1993).

Chirwa, Wiseman C. "Alien AIDS in Southern Africa: The Malawi–South African Debate." *African Affairs* 97, no. 386 (1997).

———. "Malawi Migrancy, Labour, and the Politics of HIV/AIDS, 1985 to 1993." In *Crossing Boundaries: Mine Migrancy in a Democratic South Africa*. Edited by J. Crush and W. James. Ottawa: International Development Research Council, 1995.

———. "Migrancy, Sexual Networking, and Multi-Partnered Sexuality in Malawi." *Health Transition Review* 7, suppl. 3 (1997).

———. "Sexually Transmitted Diseases in Colonial Malawi." In *Histories of Sexually Transmitted Diseases and HIV/AIDS in Sub-Saharan Africa*. Edited by P. W. Setel, M. Lewis, and M. Lyons. Westport, Conn.: Greenwood, 1999.

Engberg, Lila E., et al. "Production Activities, Food Supply, and Nutritional Status in Malawi." *Journal of Modern African Studies* 25, no. 1 (1987).

Ettema, Wim, and Louis Msukwa. *Food Production and Malnutrition in Malawi.* Zomba: University of Malawi Centre for Social Research, 1985.

Garland, Peter. "Hope over Experience." *Society of Malawi Journal* 38, no. 1 (1986).

Gelfand, Michael. *Medicine and Custom.* Edinburgh: Livingstone, 1964.

Gelfand, Michael, ed. *Doctor on Lake Nyasa: Being the Journal and Letters of Dr. Wordsworth Poole, 1895–1897.* Salisbury: Mambo, 1961.

———. *Lakeside Pioneers: Socio-Medical Study of Nyasaland, 1875–1970.* Oxford: Basil Blackwell, 1966.

Hancock, John D. "Assessing the Impact of AIDS on the Growth Path of the Malawian Economy." *Journal of Development Economics* 43 (1993).

Howard, R. *Report to the Medical Board of the Universities' Mission on the Health of European Missionaries in Likoma Diocese.* London, 1904.

Kalipeni, E. "Determinants of Infant Mortality in Malawi: A Spatial Perspective." *Social Science and Medicine* 37, no. 2 (1993).

Kalipeni, E., and Philip Thiuri, eds. *Issues and Perspectives on Health Care in Contemporary Sub-Saharan Africa.* Lewiston, N.Y.: Edwin Mellen, 1997.

King, Michael, and Elspeth King. *The Story of Medicine and Disease in Malawi: The 130 Years since Livingstone.* Limbe: Montfort, 1991.

Kishindo, Paul A. K. "High-Risk Behaviour in the Face of the AIDS Epidemic: The Case of Bar Girls in the Municipality of Zomba, Malawi." *Eastern Africa Social Science Review* 11 (1995).

———. "Sexual Behaviour in the Face of Risk: The Case Of Bar Girls in Malawi's Major Cities." *Health Transition Review* 5 (1995).

Lindskog, Per, and Jan Lundevist. *Why Poor Children Stay Sick: The Human Ecology of Child Health and Welfare in Rural Malawi.* Uppsalla: Scandinavian Institute of African Studies, 1988.

Mkandawire, Selina C. Mhango. "An Investigation of Protein-Energy Malnutrition in Malawi with Reference to Children in the Age-Group Infancy to Five Years." Ed.D. diss., Columbia Teachers College, 1991.

Molesworth, B. David. "Malawi Leprosy Project." *Society of Malawi Journal* 21, no. 1 (1968).

Morris, Brian. "Herbalism and Divination in Southern Malawi." *Social Science and Medicine* 23, no. 4 (1986).

———. "Mushrooms: For Medicine, Magic, and Munching." *Nyala* 16, no. 16 (1992).

Morris, Brian, and Jerome D. Msonthi. *Chewa Medical Botany: A Study of Herbalism in Southern Malawi.* London: International African Institute, 1996.

Msonthi, Jerome D. "The Herbalist Association of Malawi as a Profession." *Society of Malawi Journal* 37, no. 2 (1984).

———. "Traditional Birth Attendants in Malawi: Their Role in Primary Health Care and Development." *Society of Malawi Journal* 36, no. 1 (1983).

Peltzer, Karl. *Ethnomedicine in Four Different Villages in Malawi.* Staff Seminar Paper no. 30. Zomba: University of Malawi, Department of Psychology.

———. *Some Contributions of Traditional Healing Practices towards Psychosocial Health Care in Malawi.* Frankfurt: Fachbuchhandlung für Psychologie, 1987.

Phoya, Ann M. M. "An Exploration of the Factors That Influence Early Prenatal Care Enrollment and Compliance Behaviour among Rural Malawian Pregnant Women." D.N.Sc. diss., Catholic University of America, 1993.

Ponninghaus, J. M., et al. "Epidemiological Study of Leprosy in Northern Malawi." *Leprosy Review* 58, no. 4 (1987).

Ponnighaus, J. M., and P. E. M. Fine. "Leprosy in Malawi." *Transactions of the Royal Society of Tropical Medicine and Hygiene* 82, no. 6 (1988).

Pretorius, Pauline. "Medical Work of the Dutch Reformed Church Mission in Nyasaland." *Central African Journal of Medicine* 2, no. 6 (1956).

Probst, Peter. "Mchape 95, or, the Sudden Fame of Billy Goodson Chisupe: Healing, Social Memory and the Enigma of the Public Sphere in Post-Banda Malawi." *Africa* 69, no. 1 (1999).

Schoffeleers, Matthew. "The AIDS Pandemic, the Prophet Billy Chisupe, and the Democratization Process in Malawi." *Journal of Religion in Africa* 29, no. 4 (1999).

Vaughan, Megan. *Curing their Ills: Colonial Power and African Illness.* Cambridge: Polity, 1991.

———. "Syphilis, AIDS, and the Representation of Sexuality: The Historical Legacy." In *Action on AIDS in Southern Africa: The Maputo Conference on Health in Transition in Southern Africa, April 1990.* Edited by Zena Stein and Anthony Zwi. New York: Committee for Health in Southern Africa/HIV Center for Clinical and Behavioral Studies, Columbia University, 1991.

———. "Syphilis in Colonial East and Central Africa: The Social Construction of an Epidemic." In *Epidemics and Ideas: Essays on the Historical Perception of Pestilence.* Edited by T. Ranger and P. Sack. Cambridge: Cambridge University Press, 1992.

Watt, J., and M. Brayer-Brand Wijk. *Medicinal and Poisonous Plants of Southern and Eastern Africa.* 2d ed. Edinburgh: F. Livingstone, 1962.

Wendroff, Arnold P. "Trouble-Shooters and Trouble-Makers: Witchfinding and Traditional Malawian Medicine." Ph.D. diss., City University of New York, 1985.

William, Thomas C. B. *Before the Winds of Change.* Suffolk, U.K.: Halesworth, 1984.

Winter, Eric R. de. *Health Services in a District in Malawi.* Assen, Netherlands: Van Gorcum, 1972.

Natural Sciences

Belcher, C. *The Birds of Nyasaland.* London: C. Lockwood and Son, 1930.

Benson, C. *A Checklist of the Birds of Nyasaland.* Blantyre: Nyasaland Society, 1953.

Bertram, C., et al. *Report on the Fish and Fisheries of Lake Nyasa.* London: Crown Agents, 1942.

Brenan, J. P. *Plants Collected by the Vernay Expedition.* Bronx: Botanical Gardens, 1954.

Chapman, John. *The Evergreen Forests of Malawi.* Oxford: Commonwealth Forestry Institute, 1970.

Chapman, John. *The Vegetation of the Mulanje Mountains, Nyasaland.* Zomba: Government Printer, 1962.

Hayes, G. D. "Nyala and the Lengwe Game Reserve." *Society of Malawi Journal* 20, no. 2 (1967).

Huxley, Julian. *Conservation of Wild Life and Natural Habitats in Central and East Africa*. Paris: UNESCO, 1961.

Lemon, Paul. *Natural Communities of the Malawi National Park*. Zomba: Government Press, 1964.

Lyell, D. *Wild Life in Central Africa*. London: Field & Queen, 1913.

McCracken, John. "Experts and Expertise in Colonial Malawi." *African Affairs* 81, no. 322 (1982).

Morris, Brian. *Common Mushrooms of Malawi*. Oslo: Fungi Flora, 1987.

———. *The Power of Animals: an Ethnography*. Oxford: Berg, 1998.

———. *A Short History of Wildlife Conservation in Malawi*. Occasional Paper no. 64. Edinburgh: University of Edinburgh Centre of African Studies, 1964.

———. "Wildlife Depredations in Malawi: The Historical Dimension." *Nyala* 18 (1995).

Palgrave-Coates, Olive. *Trees of Central Africa*. Salisbury: National Publications Trust, 1957.

Stewart, Margaret. *Amphibians of Malawi*. Albany: SUNY Press, 1967.

Topham, P., and R. Townsend. *Forestry and Soil Conservation in Nyasaland*. Oxford: Oxford University Press, 1937.

Wieke, P. *The Plant Diseases of Nyasaland*. Kew, U.K.: Commonwealth Mycological Institute, 1953.

Willan, R., and D. McQueen. *Exotic Forest Trees in Nyasaland*. Sydney: Commonwealth Forestry Conference, 1957.

Williamson, Jessie. *Useful Plants of Malawi*. Zomba: Government Printer, 1960.

SELECT LIST OF MALAWI PERIODICALS

Articles on Malawi appear in a variety of sources published locally and internationally. The reader need only check the indexes of these journals to obtain any article and its date of publication. Reviewing back issues can be richly rewarding, particularly in such periodicals as the *Malawi News*, the *Daily Times* (Malawi), the *Nation*, the *Chronicle*, the *UDF News*, and the *Guardian* (Malawi). Among the academic journals in which articles relating to Malawi appear are: *Religion in Malawi*, *Society of Malawi Journal, New African, African Business, Africa Confidential, Rhodes-Livingstone Institute Bulletin, Journal of African History, African Studies Review, Africa Today, African Affairs, Journal of Southern African Studies, Southern Africa Political and Economic Monthly, Journal of Contemporary African Studies, Ufahamu, Journal of African History, Journal of Imperial and Commonwealth History, International Journal of African Historical Studies, TransAfrica Journal of History*, and *World Development*.

Select list of other periodicals published in Malawi at various times:

The African. White Fathers Publication. Lilongwe. Bimonthly. In English, Nyanja, Tumbuka.

Agricultural Development and Marketing Corporation. Limbe. Annual reports.

Agricultural Research Council of Malawi. Ntondwe. Annual reports.

Agrinform. Zomba. Weekly.

Air Malawi. Blantyre. Annual reports.

Amalgamated Packaging Industries (Malawi) Ltd. Director's report and statement of accounts. Blantyre. Annual.

Arima Newsletter. Association of Religious Institutes of Malawi. Lilongwe. Monthly.

Association for the Teaching of English in Malawi Journal. Blantyre. Monthly.

Backgrounder. Blantyre. Department of Information. Bimonthly.

Bible Society in Malawi. Blantyre. Annual reports.

Blantyre/Limbe Co-operative Society. Blantyre. Annual.

Boma Lathu. Chickewa. Monthly.

Building Construction Civil Engineering and Allied Workers Union. Limbe. Annual.

Bunda College of Agriculture. Lilongwe. Research bulletins.

Catholic Church Newsletter. Limbe. Bimonthly.

Central African Railways Company Report of the Directors. Limbe. Annual.

Central Region Extension Newsletter. Lilongwe. Monthly.

Chambo Magazine. Mpwepwe. Monthly.

Chameleon: The Magazine of the Science Centre. Domasi. Irregular.

Commercial Bank of Malawi Annual Report.

Christian Service Committee for the Churches in Malawi. Report. Blantyre. Annual.

Council of Women (Malawi). Limbe. Annual reports.

Dziko. Chancellor College Geographical Society. Limbe. Annual.

Ecclesia. Newsletter of Church of the Province of Central Africa. Likwenu. Monthly.

Economica Africana. Economics Society. Limbe. Irregular.

Electricity Supply Commission of Malawi. Annual report and statement of accounts for the year. Lilongwe.

Enterprise. Blantyre Printing and Publishing Company. Monthly.

Field Newsletter. Department of Agriculture. Mzuzu. Monthly.

Focus on Malawi. English. Quarterly.

Gongwe la Mlinda. Watch Tower Bible & Tracts Society. Blantyre. Monthly.

Here's an Idea. Peace Corps. Blantyre. Irregular.

History in Malawi. Chancellor College, Department of History. Limbe. Annual.

International Council for Bird Preservation. Newsletter. Chileka. Irregular.

Jacaranda. Limbe. Annual.

Journal of Social Science. Limbe. Annual.

Kachebere Major Seminary. Mchinji. Annual.

Kalata wa ma mission ena. Seventh-Day Adventist Church. Blantyre. Quarterly.

Kalata wa uthenga wa sukulu za Kwacha. Dept. of Community Development. Zomba. Monthly.

Kalulu: Bulletin of Malawi Oral Literature. University of Malawi. Zomba.

Kotale wa sabata sukulu. Seventh-Day Adventist Church. Malamulo. Quarterly.

Kuanika (Light). Presbyterian Church of Central Africa. Mkhoma. Monthly.

Lilongwe Land Development Project. Lilongwe. Annual.

Mala. Bulletin. Library Association of Malawi. Lilongwe.

Malawi. Agriculture Department. Lilongwe. Regular bulletins.

Malawi. Antiquities Department. Lilongwe. Irregular.

Malawi. Development and Planning Ministry. Compendium of statistics. Zomba. Annual.

Malawi. Economic Report. Zomba. Annual.
Malawi. Government Gazette. Lilongwe. Weekly.
Malawi. Information Ministry. Blantyre. Daily digest.
Malawi. Monthly bulletin of key economic indicators. Lilongwe.
Malawi. *Sash: Survey of Agricultural Small Holdings.* Lilongwe. Quarterly.
Malawi. Meteorological Office. Totals of monthly and annual rainfall. Blantyre.
   Annual.
Malawi. Statistical Office. Annual statement of external trade. Lilongwe.
Malawi. Ministry of Transport and Communications. Lilongwe. Monthly summary.
Malawi: An Official Handbook. Department of Information. Blantyre. Annual.
Malawi Broadcasting Corporation. Blantyre. Annual reports.
Malawi Calling: MBC Official Programme Guide. Blantyre. Bimonthly.
Malawi Council of Social Service. General directory. Blantyre. Annual.
Malawi Development Corporation. Blantyre. Annual reports.
Malawi Features. Department of Information. Blantyre. Monthly.
Malawi Housing Corporation. Blantyre. Annual report.
Malawi Labor News. Malawi Congress of Labor. Blantyre. Weekly.
Malawi Mizinthunzi. Department of Information. Blantyre. Monthly.
Malawi Mwezi Uno. Dept. of Information. Blantyre. Monthly.
Malawi National Bibliography. National Archives. Zomba. Annual.
Malawi National Library Service. Blantyre. Annual report.
Malawi Railways Ltd. Directors' report and accounts. Limbe. Annual.
Malawi Red Cross Society. Blantyre. Annual reports.
Malawi Smallholder Tea Authority. Thyolo. Annual reports.
The Malawi Sportsman. Blantyre. Quarterly.
Malawi This Week. Blantyre. Weekly.
Malawi Tung Board. Blantyre. Annual reports.
The Malawian Geographer. Blantyre. Annual.
Mathmag: Magazine of the Mathematical Association of Malawi. Limbe. Quarterly.
Moni. Limbe. Monthly. In English and Nyanja.
Montfort College. Annual report of special course for teachers of the blind. Limbe.
   Annual.
Moyo. Health Extension Service. Blantyre. Bimonthly.
Mulanje Mountain Club. Circular. Blantyre. Irregular.
National Bank of Malawi. Annual reports.
National Trading Co. Blantyre. Annual reports.
Nyasaland Journal; *see Society of Malawi Journal.*
Odi. Writers Group, University of Malawi. Limbe. Quarterly.
Odini Chichewa/English. Bimonthly.
Patent and Trade Marks Journal. Zomba. Monthly.
Poly-view. The Polytechnic, University of Malawi. Blantyre.
   Annual.
Society of Malawi Journal. Blantyre. Biannual.
Sunde Sukulu Quarterly. Limbe. Quarterly.
Tea Research Foundation of Central Africa. Mulanje. Quarterly.
This Is Malawi. English. Monthly.
The Times. Blantyre. Twice weekly.

Ulimi m Malawi (Farming in Malawi). Zomba. Monthly.
University of Malawi. Chronicle. Limbe. Irregular.
University of Malawi Bulletin. Blantyre. Monthly.
University Students Magazine. Limbe. Irregular.
Vanguard. Limbe. Irregular.
Vision of Malawi. Department of Information. Blantyre. Quarterly.
WASI: Magazine for Writers. Domasi, Zomba.

About the Authors

Owen J. M. Kalinga is a graduate of the Universities of Malawi (B.A.), Birmingham (M.A.), and London (Ph.D.). He has taught at the Universities of Malawi, Dalhousie (Canada), Jos (Nigeria), Lesotho, and the Western Cape (South Africa); currently he is professor of history at North Carolina State University. He has published widely on the Lake Malawi region and is presently working on a biography of "General" Flax Katoba Musopole.

Cynthia Crosby's research interests lie in the social and economic developments in Eastern Africa and Malawi in particular; her publications include a bibliography on Kenya and a chapter on the railways in *From Nyasaland to Malawi*. She received a Ph.D. from the Maxwell Graduate School at Syracuse University and a B.A. from the University of Rochester. A high school teacher and administrator for many years, Dr. Crosby has recently directed her administrative efforts to adult literacy education.